MEMOIRS

OF

ALLEGHENY COUNTY

PENNSYLVANIA

PERSONAL AND GENEALOGICAL

WITH PORTRAITS

VOLUME II

MADISON, WIS.
NORTHWESTERN HISTORICAL ASSOCIATION
1904

INDEX, VOLUME I

A

	PAGE.
Abbott, August	325
Abernathey, Samuel	213
Ackerman, Nick	311
Albrecht, Nicholas	262
Alderson, William	548
Allebrand, Charles W	553
Allman, John G	242
Anderson, Charles A	206
Anderson, Charles F	108
Armstrong, Elmer	156
Armstrong, John H	76
Armstrong, William B	442
Arnold, William A	474
Aston, Walter	417

B

Bailey, Samuel G	462
Bair, David F	559
Baird, George H	546
Baker, Millard F	419
Barker, Olin G. A	127
Barnett, James E	502
Barr, Francis X	77
Battles, John	430
Beale, George W	483
Beck, Robert	347
Bedell, Milton	253
Behen, Dennis Æ	502
Beinhauser, Louis	424
Bekavac, Bosiljko	220
Bellingham, Uriah	84
Benham, William M	112
Benner, Thomas M	146
Berkenbush, John	558
Bernhard, Charles P	430
Best, William E	505
Bickerton, James	286
Black, Alexander	82
Black, Howard L	515
Black, Walter R	121
Bleichner, John A	64
Boden, Daniel	494
Boden, George W	538
Bohlander, John P	539
Bollman, Edward W	421
Bolster, Peter	228
Boothe, Willis A	465

	PAGE.
Borgmann, William	542
Bost, Frank	385
Bost, William	277
Botkin, Lester H	320
Bowes, S. Cameron	383
Boyd, Samuel F	245
Bradley, John	82
Brady, Nicholas H	89
Brierley, Robert	264
Brinker, Addison J	215
Brown, J. A. A	54
Brown, J. O	412
Brown, John L	219
Brown, John T	327
Brown, John W	113
Brown, Michael J	233
Browne, William R	436
Buckley, Jeremiah D	95
Buente, Henry H	310
Bullion, John J	160
Burgoon, J. A	373
Burkert, Philip C	392
Burns, Simon	30
Burroughs, Hamilton S	57
Byrne, Patrick C	90

C

Cahen, Alfred	138
Cahill, John	451
Caldwell, John	32
Callery, James D	438
Calvert, George H	415
Campbell, Joseph	343
Campbell, W. J	345
Campbell, William W	130
Carnahan, Thomas D	36
Carney, Jeremiah	111
Carney, John	103
Carter, Charles G	116
Chalmers, George B	94
Chaplin, James C	370
Chaplin, J. Crossan	364
Chaplin, John H	359
Chaplin, John M	366
Chaplin, William C	360
Clark, James A	55
Clark, Robert W	525
Cluley, Robert E	458

INDEX

Name	Page
Cochrane, Robert K	226
Cole, Orange S	185
Collingwood, David F	78
Conlin, Milo G	271
Connor, James R	422
Cook, Lawrence B	511
Cooper, Charles A	176
Corlett, Edward S	110
Coulter, Samuel	459
Cox, John F	497
Craig, Hugh S	509
Craig, Isaac	357
Craig, Robert C	326
Crump, Stephen S	552
Cunningham, Finley R	485
Cunningham, Robert J	130

D

Dabbs, Benjamin L. H	75
Daggette, Alvin St. C	179
Daube, Henry	548
Davidson, Henry M	205
Davis, Carroll P	489
Davis, Charles	37
Davis, David L	163
Davis, Frank B	470
Davis, Lewis E	524
Davis, Ralph C	491
Davis, Thomas G	92
Demmel, Philip	432
Deverts, Charles O	421
Dickson, A. B	199
Dickson, James	199
Dickson, James W	150
Dierstein, Frederick	282
Dilworth, Linford L	461
Dodds, William	92
Dolan, Patrick	111
Dorrington, John K	109
Dorsey, William J	295
Downey, John	76
Doyle, Joseph A	288
Doyle, Paul B	190
Dublin, David B	316
Duff, Davidson	398
Duff, John M	251
Duff, Josiah S	235
Duffner, John B	221
Dunn, J. C	528
Duvall, Samuel M	91

E

Eckbreth, William C	272
Edgar, Thomas	463
Edlis, Adolph	53
Edwards, Frederick W	53
Eickemeyer, W. E	530
Elicker, Jacob	512
Elphinstone, James A	52
Englehart, William F	175
Erskine, W. H	535
Evans, William	519
Evert, Henry C	441
Ewing, Robert M	136
Eynon, Henry	71

F

Name	Page
Faidley, Elijah P	296
Fair, D. O	382
Fairfield, John	402
Fairman, John A	214
Fawcett, William G	337
Fife, Jared B	535
Fife, Joseph P	486
Filcer, William J	312
Fisher, John A	287
Fisher, Mary	128
Fisher, William	128
Fite, John	204
Flood, Edward H	133
Flowers, George W	134
Ford, Cornelius F	108
Ford, William A	217
Fording, Thomas	42
Forrester, William G	299
Forsyth, Andrew W	115
Forsythe, George B	334
Foster, George M	437
Francies, William H	450
Frauenheim, Edward J	80
Frederick, Frank H	232
Fullerton, James M	86

G

Name	Page
Gabler, Thomas C	518
Gailey, Oliver A	249
Gaub, Otto C	258
Gerdts, Fred	507
Geyer, William	257
Gilchrist, Joseph J	248
Glenn, William J	448
Glojnaric, Francis	224
Goldstrohm, Charles F	304
Gosser, George W	97
Gottfried, Julius	371
Grabe, George A	418
Graebing, John, Jr.	225
Graham, Thomas	508
Granger, Thomas S	280
Gray, Alexander	210
Gray, James W	208
Gray, William	559
Gregg, Edward R	527
Green, James H	395
Grelle, Henry	59
Grenet, Samuel J	244
Grierson, Malcolm	98
Griscom, William A	492

	PAGE.
Groetzinger, John	423
Guffey, James M	46
Guffey, Wesley S	20
Guiler, William G	513

H

Hamilton, Amelia	393
Hamilton, Charles A	557
Hamilton, Charles W	151
Hamilton, James B	33
Hanlon, Matthew A	88
Harkins, Frank B	220
Harper, James G	425
Harvey, George H	397
Harvey, Thomas W	227
Harvey, William H	493
Haslett, Edwin C	375
Hauser, Henry	218
Hays, George L	261
Hays, Joseph	123
Heath, Robert H	317
Heisel, William	536
Henderson, John H	35
Henderson, Robert L	352
Henry, John	159
Henry, John C	456
Hepline, George W	148
Hering, Frederick	387
Hershberger, Thomas P	90
Hill, Lucius L	125
Hill, William	478
Hilldorfer, Joseph P	411
Hock, John	229
Hogg, George	529
Holliday, George L	18
Holozsnyay, Alex	281
Holtzman, Louis F	301
Hope, William A	504
House, George L	451
House, Jesse M	501
Hunter, John M	118

I

Imbrie, Addison M	495
Irwin, James H., Sr	260

J

Jastrzembski, Stanley	196
Jenkins, Edwin B	212
Johns, Harry E	292
Johnson, George A	140
Johnston, Edward P	349
Johnston, George C	526
Johnston, John A	402
Jones, Evan	518
Jones, Jenkin	48
Jordan, William	184

K

	PAGE.
Kambach, George J	125
Kane, James F	138
Kappeler, Herman	237
Kaufman, William	114
Keane, John H	230
Kelly, A. J., Jr	489
Kelly, James L	418
Kennedy, Joseph	305
Kennedy, Robert	487
Kennedy, Robert B	376
Keyes, John A	344
Kimberlin, John C	289
Kimberlin, William E	234
Kimmey, Edson	107
King, Henry L	472
King, William D	439
Kintner, Joseph J	498
Kirkbride, George T	541
Kirschler, Charles F	70
Kistler, Jonas M	313
Klaus, Nicholas G	425
Klumpp, Frank J	173
Knoderer, Charles F	557
Kraus, Jacob W	491
Kuhn, Arthur J	499
Kuhn, John E	198

L

Lambie, John S	24
Lang, William	424
Lantz, Jesse S	303
Latimore, Willmer A	259
Latshaw, Henry B	389
Lawrence, E. A	412
Lawry, James	276
Lawson, Lindley S	279
Lawson, Oscar P	323
Layton, Robert D	444
Lea, William H. H	183
Leadbeater, John	283
Leader, William J	521
Leslie, A. H	34
Leslie, Millard F	79
Leuschner, Albert F	543
Levy, Isaac A	428
Lewis, Charles A	513
Lightenheld, Gustavus J	333
Lighthill, Charles W	211
Lindsay, Robert H	433
Lindsey, William T	69
Linsley, William H	466
Livingston, Charles L	457
Lobingier, Chauncey	509
Locke, Charles A	124
Logan, William H	155
Lohrey, Henry	427
Lowe, Harry W	87
Lowry, John K	510
Lutz, Anton	39
Lynch, Humphrey	434

INDEX

M

Name	Page
MacBroom, William	314
MacCloskey, Thomas D.	149
MacMath, Joseph	381
Magee, Christopher, Jr.	106
Malarkey, Andrew J.	341
Malone, Robert J. H.	101
Manning, William G.	223
Marks, Ulysses G.	151
Marshall, William T.	433
Martin, Charles E.	470
Martin, John A.	436
Martin, J. B.	336
Martin, Robert S.	478
Mattern, Robert G.	141
Maurer, George	346
Maxey, William S.	144
McAlinney, John J.	102
McCabe, Francis J.	222
McCabe, James H.	182
McCabe, Joseph E.	481
McCall, Elliot	238
McCandless, J. Guy	38
McCann, Alonzo N.	469
McCarthy, Daniel J.	121
McClarin, John A.	473
McClelland, Robert W.	522
McClure, Thomas G.	63
McCormick, Richard	231
McCurdy, Steward LeRoy	164
McDermott, Thomas	480
McElhinney, Samuel	315
McFail, Charles B.	100
McGarey, David J.	41
McGeary, Jesse M.	56
McGovern, Charles C.	85
McGrogan, John	378
McGunnegle, Daniel K.	51
McIlvain, Edward J.	208
McKee, Joseph H.	321
McKelvy, William H.	537
McKenna, Charles F.	64
McKinley, William C.	58
McLain, Theodore R.	109
McMasters, James V.	443
McNally, John	234
McPartland, Frank J.	302
Mead, Morris W.	47
Means, William A.	74
Mercer, J. Carson	55
Merriman, Thomas	560
Metcalf, George H.	298
Meyer, Albert P.	115
Meyer, Edward	462
Miller, Andrew S.	120
Miller, Harold A.	522
Miller, Harry W.	249
Miller, Henry A.	520
Miller, Jacob Jay	374
Mitchell, David E.	116
Mitchell, Joseph, Jr.	429
Molney, Coursin I.	239
Molamphy, John M.	263
Monahan, Lawrence P.	145
Montgomery, John	269
Montgomery, Nathaniel	162
Moore, G. Wash.	43
Moore, John W.	391
Moreland, Thomas B.	81
Morris, Walter	147
Morrow, James E.	401
Morrow, John	338
Morton, Edward	545
Muehlbronner, Charles A.	44
Mueller, F. W.	73
Mueller, Gustave A.	256
Mueller, Michael F.	307
Murphy, James P.	431
Murphy, Marion H.	126
Murray, William W.	436
Mustin, William I.	40

N

Naylor, Henry B.	531
Negley, Henry H.	447
Nesbit, John W.	68
Neu, Emil W.	306
Neville, John	355
Newlin, William E.	139
Noble, William V.	335

O

Ober, John P.	73
Obey, Gustavus B.	468
Obushkevich, Theofan A.	202
O'Donnell, Simon	240
O'Leary, Timothy	50
Omslaer, John	340
Orbin, Frank	442
Orris, John M.	284
Orzechowski, M. J.	550
Ostermaier, Robert	49
Oyer, Christian F.	119

P

Pagan, Robert B.	388
Painter, Josiah	353
Palen, Gilbert	270
Palmer, Robert	496
Parker, George B.	122
Parker, William J.	413
Patterson, Fred W.	201
Patterson, Isaac N.	455
Pearson, Frank C.	434
Pedder, Charles J.	85
Peebles, George E.	497
Perrine, J. K. M.	166
Perry, Thomas	45
Petty, John M.	500
Philips, James F.	186
Phillips, John	384

INDEX

	PAGE
Phillips, Mrs. Robert	384
Phillis, Clarence L	104
Phipps, Henry	17
Pierce, John	103
Pirl, Frederick W	308
Pitcairn, Andrew J	458
Pitcock, D. M	412
Pitts, Arthur B	319
Prestley, John L	137
Prosser, Thomas	532
Pruett, Abner B	246

Q

Quaill, George H	476
Queck, Harry P. H	297

R

Radcliffe, John N	482
Ralston, Benedict S	268
Ralston, Samuel H	266
Ramage, R. H	471
Randolph, E. N	437
Reed, James H	423
Reel, Charles C	324
Reel, David, Jr	403
Renshaw, Thomas	464
Reukauf, Christian	379
Richards, George W	551
Ridgway, Frank	60
Riehl, Leonard	547
Rinehart, A. Walter	99
Rinehart, C. C	255
Ritter, Horace S	181
Roberts, George L	116
Robinson, William	440
Rodgers, Arthur D	117
Rook, Charles A	21
Ross, Mansfield A	169
Ross, William S	250
Rott, Louis	273
Rowe, William R	46
Rowley, Thomas A	83
Ruhlandt, Charles J	440
Ruoff, Frederick	454
Russell, James A	291
Russell, John M	480

S

Sachs, Charles H	97
Samson, Hudson	27
Sarver, William H	453
Saupp, Frank D	96
Scandrett, Thomas B	197
Schell, John E	394
Schellman, Frank J	254
Schleich, Simon	243
Schmitt, Charles	267
Schoults, James M	540
Schreiner, Edward	508

	PAGE
Schroedel, Justus	416
Schroeder, Adolph H	503
Schulz, Charles A	278
Schulz, Rudolph	281
Schulz, Victor H	318
Scott, William	490
Scott, William M	158
Seibel, Harry J	165
Seifried, Frank J	157
Shaffer, Theodore J	31
Shaw, William C	177
Sheasley, Jesse H	241
Sherran, James	59
Sherrard, R. M	533
Shields, James W	330
Shoemaker, James K P	293
Shroyer, William F	332
Siebert, Peter W	26
Simon, Charles W	420
Sloan, John	556
Smail, Edward J	152
Smalley, Robert E	545
Smith, Albert Y	78
Smith, William U	188
Snaman, George W	348
Sneathen, Frank F	467
Snee, Sylvester J	473
Soffel, Jacob	93
Sparr, Emil	520
Spicer, Charles A	247
Staab, Anthony	486
Staley, John A	493
Steel, Christian D	172
Steen, William J	57
Steffy, Walter E	285
Stengel, George H	96
Stevenson, William M	460
Stewart, Joseph	339
Stewart, William A	524
Stone, Stephen P	75
Stork, Adam	212
Stottler, Sylvester	328
Stouffer, Benjamin W	67
Stowe, Edwin H	19
St. Peter, Paul	51
Strang, John Y	332
Subasic, Joseph	309
Suter, James A	171
Sutkaitis, John	209
Sutter, George L	196
Szabo, John	193

T

Thein, George	400
Theis, George W	88
Theobald, Charles E	133
Thompson, James H	153
Thompson, William E	29
Thomson, Henry D	555
Tonnele, Theo	414
Toole, Stephen J	119

INDEX

	PAGE.
Torrance, Francis J	445
Torrence, David R	25
Trautman, Jacob	506
Treacy, James R	479
Tredway, William T	167
Tressel, Jacob	380
Tschume, Frederick	399
Tunstall, William	350

V

Vernon, Joseph A	550
Vierheller, Edward C	77
Voegtly, Jacob J	443
Voegtly, Nicholas H	443
Vogt, Aug. A	198
Vogt, William	534
Vokolek, William	516
Vondera, Charles H	517
Vondera, Christian F	377
Von Moss, Charles	294

W

Wachter, John	396
Waite, Thomas C	252
Walker, Huston Q	135
Walker, James D	71
Walker, John J	452
Wallace, Clarence E	142
Wallace, John I	426
Walsh, William F	100
Walter, Labanna H	174
Walton, William L	52
Watson, Robert L	544

	PAGE.
Watson, William M	475
Weber, Joseph A	322
Weir, Albert	549
Weis, Joseph	236
Weller, John S	123
Wiggins, Hubert P	274
Wilcox, Fred F	195
Will, Silas A	488
Williams, Edward J	390
Willock, Curtis M	143
Wills, Lafayette	224
Wilson, George W	435
Wilson, John A	484
Wilson, John M	154
Wilson, Lewis W	526
Wilson, Thomas J	132
Winters, Anna T	554
Wolfe, William W	191
Wright, Jesse H	463
Wylie, Daniel W	189

Y

Young, Annie L	351
Young, Hugh	66
Young, Robert C	351
Young, Robert O	511

Z

Zahniser, William J	67
Zimmerman, George H	386
Zinsser, Louis	162
Zoeller, William F	205

INDEX, VOLUME II

A

	PAGE
Abbott, Edward	410
Abbott, Walter S	444
Aber, Robert E	341
Adams, Thomas B	267
Addenbrook, Thomas	107
Alperman, Frederick	38
Alter, W. B.	300
Alter, William S	177
Ambrose, Parks A	490
Anderson, John T	220
Arthurs, Charles	60
Atkins, George T	374
Atwater, Harry	276
Auld, David W	476
Auld, V. Arthur	30
Austen, John T	498
Ayers, J. Bucher	468

B

	PAGE
Baehr, George	280
Bailey, Charles M	23
Baird, Thomas W	307
Baldwin, Edward I	241
Bame, Jacob E	355
Bard, Edward	471
Barker, Thomas W	315
Barndollar, William L	230
Barnhart, Charles K	198
Barr, L. O	440
Bash, Elmer J	425
Baxter, R. H	321
Beattie, Jeremiah A	458
Beatty, Robert	335
Beck, Calvin	385
Beck, John J	487
Bedell, J. J	72
Beedle, Evan	298
Belsmeyer, August	497
Bennett, William	108
Berg, Henry	194
Bert, Peter	174
Bestwick, Jacob	21
Bew, William	327
Bickel, Christ L	504
Biehl, Charles	213
Bishoff, Lowery H	471
Black, Abram H. S	495
Black, Francis B	429
Black, R. L	443
Blackburn, James P	79
Blackley, Hamilton MacI	130
Blayney, John S	287
Blind, Henry L	357
Blose, Daniel P	38
Blumenthal, Maximilian	211
Boax, Charles F	472
Bock, John N	450
Bollje, Theodore	57
Boots, E. W	464
Boss, Gustav A	524
Bowman, Daniel	394
Boyd, David S	219
Boyle, Andrew J	206
Boyle, John C	266
Bradshaw, William P	283
Brandt, Herman P	522
Brassert, Herman A	485
Braun, Jacob J	134
Brennan, John	272
Briney, S. A	363
Brinker, William M	400
Brinton, Samuel McG	251
Brockman, Thomas W	193
Brooks, Lawrence A	488
Brown, James, Jr	40
Brown, J. Wilbert	35
Bruner, Harry E	333
Brush, F. S	463
Bryce, Charles K	119
Burkman, John	197
Burtner, George	423
Butler, Robert	264

C

	PAGE
Calhoun, David K	135
Calhoun, John F	61
Cameron, Lewis O	365
Camp, Oliver C	413
Campbell, Anson B	65
Campbell, James	88
Campbell, Joseph L	112
Campbell, William O	390
Campbell, William V	95
Carnegie Free Library, The	244
Carney, David K	337

	PAGE.
Carothers, Joseph C	494
Carothers, Robert T	41
Carson, James	233
Carter, John	37
Chambers, M. W	493
Clark, Samuel D	427
Clay, Rachel A	243
Clay, William H	316
Clifford, John M	273
Clifford, Joseph B	90
Clinton, William J	450
Coe, John S	414
Cole, George H	282
Coleman, Andrew	501
Conkle, Robert F	525
Conner, Alfred D	212
Conway, David M	406
Conwell, Stephen C	158
Conwell, William	418
Cook, Robert H	391
Coursin, B. L	469
Coursin, Frederick H	82
Craft, William A	489
Crawford, E. R	24
Crawford, Harry B	39
Crawford, John Jay	216
Cribbs, Fielding D	116
Cribbs, Hyatt M	115
Cribbs, Oliver L	181
Croft, J. A	439
Crosby, George A	469
Cross, John C	254
Crossland, William	277
Crouch, William H	319
Crusan, William A	526
Crytzer, George W	416
Cunningham, David H	361
Cunningham, Joseph	361
Cunningham, William H	386
Cunningham, William P	352
Curry, William L	464
Czepananis, Stephen J	147

D

Dahlstrom, Charles F	26
Datt, Charles T	351
Daum, Adam	330
Day, Joseph R	172
Dean, E. W	465
Debolt, George S. T	138
De Long, Charles F	63
Denny, John	152
Dersam, John N	62
Dexter, Emery E	54
Dick, George A	526
Dick, John A	432
Dick, William	434
Dieterich, Jacob	245
Dinsmore, Samuel W. S	200
Dithrich, W. J	202
Dittmer, Emil F. A	204

	PAGE.
Donaghy, Joseph F	195
Donnell, John H	192
Dougan, Howard G	501
Dougherty, Oscar R	100
Douglass, Wm. L	289
Duerr, George H	228
Duncan, Archibald	42
Duncan, George	57
Duncan, James W	86
Dunlap, David D	261
Dunn, Joseph C	437
Duster, John	164
Duwell, Charles	514

E

Eckert, Ferdinand C	523
Edmundson, George L	20
Edwards, Elmer M	236
Einsporn, Albert	342
Ellerman, Christian	269
Ellison, Ellwood W	389
Elwarner, Charles C	380
Elwell, John D	409
Elwood, Robert D	238
Emmert, Peter F	104
Engelhardt, J. A	150
Erhard, Ernest L	505
Etheridge, Harry	447
Enwer, Joseph E	252
Evans, Oliver	506
Evans, William	74
Everett, Frank M	443

F

Falkenstein, George J. F	442
Faulk, Philip	364
Fawcett, Christopher C	92
Fawcett, John W	97
Fawcett, Thomas R	321
Fawcett, William D	84
Fawcett, William L	464
Fell, Charles	479
Ferguson, John A	160
Ferguson, Thomas	339
Ferree, Harry W	529
Fidler, Joseph	32
Fiedler, Charles P	459
Fink, Frederick	509
Finney, Edward C	507
Fisher, John W	58
Fisher, Julius K	467
Firestone, Henry	66
Forsythe, George W	274
Forsythe, Lewis	271
Foss, John M	504
Foster, David A	77
Friedman, Henry	29
Fryer, Amos	301
Fulton, Joseph K., Sr	186

G

Gardner, Samuel L	157
Gardner, Thomas D	199
Geeting, John A	73
German, William J	55
Gibson, Robert M	346
Giles, John	41
Gillen, John H	133
Gillespie, Andrew	170
Givins, Albert J	483
Glover, Anthony W	479
Goeddel, Charles	123
Goldsmith, Louis J	137
Goodwin, Herman W	176
Gordon, Ezekiel, Jr	485
Gordon, Robert W., Jr	94
Gorzynski, John S	98
Graham, Norman R	490
Granger, William L	513
Gray, G. E. Frank	231
Gray, H. W	448
Greene, Bennett P	332
Greer, D. Newton	109
Griffin, Hezekiah C	460
Griffith, Joseph	248
Griffith, Joshua N	155
Griffith, McKinstry	34
Gross, Michael	63
Gross, Otto J	178
Gundy, Thomas S	161
Guttridge, Charles B	115

H

Haber, Louis	481
Hallam, F. F	440
Hamilton, James B	329
Hamilton, Samuel	371
Hammer, Michael	214
Hammitt, J. Lewis	458
Hanna, John W	234
Hardt, Henry	349
Hardt, John	438
Hardwick, Walter	478
Hardy, Daniel M	50
Hardy, William	442
Harper, Cassius M. C	253
Harrison, George	121
Harrison, Richey C	120
Harrison, William R	388
Hart, George B	210
Hartig, Anton	234
Hauer, George I	247
Hayes, John	128
Hazlett, James E	345
Heath, William H	370
Heckert, William H	348
Heidenkamp, Joseph	397
Heile, Peter	328
Held, Fred	90
Hemphill, John W	404
Henderson, Harry E	285
Herwick, George B	456
Herwig, William K	457
Hezlep, William W	238
Hickey, John	313
Hieber, Charles J	375
Hill, Jabez J	61
Hinkel, Fred C	377
Hitchens, George E	55
Hodgson, Jesse	144
Hoffman, Philip L., Jr	78
Hoffmeyer, Charles K	508
Holinger, Emil F	462
Holland, Paul R	217
Holtzheimer, Joseph G	218
Horner, Samuel J	398
Howat, William	106
Huey, Daniel	385
Huggins, Raleigh R	314
Hughes, Benjamin W	431
Hughes, John A	438
Hultz, John	405
Humphrey, Walter N	242
Hundhausen, Herman	138
Hunter, Orlando M	50
Hunter, William L	432
Hunter, William L	484
Hutchison, Henry F	179
Hutchison, Peter	208
Huth, Conrad	311
Hynes, Bernard J	506

I

Irvin, James A	91
Irvine, J. Q. A	210
Irwin, Benjamin C	196
Ivory, Peter	362

J

Jackel, John, Sr	71
Jackman, Andrew	353
Jackman, William	354
Jacobs, George	127
Janda, Valerian J	142
Jaquay, Gideon H	258
Johnstin, U. Grant	503
Johnston, George R	451
Johnston, James L	383
Johnston, William E	278
Jones, John B	229
Jones, John O	140
Jones, Richard L	168
Jones, Thomas C	52

K

Kapteina, John	326
Karns, James E	259
Karns, James E	302
Katchmar, Anton J	225
Kazinczy, Albert	477

INDEX

Name	PAGE
Kelly, Henry E.	499
Kelly, Matthew F.	89
Kemp, James F.	99
Keppel, John N.	455
Kerr, Henry M.	492
Kerr, John	215
Kerruish, John R.	513
Kidd, Walter S.	167
King, William	303
Kirkpatrick, Allen	474
Kirkpatrick, Joseph O.	263
Kline, Alpha K.	473
Klingensmith, Barkley J.	399
Knorr, Victor C.	118
Knox, William J.	105
Koch, Peter	22
Koehler, Charles D.	447
Koehler, George A.	256
Kola, Frank	481
Kooser, Henry C.	515
Kovats, Kalman	85
Krauth, Frederick	122
Krigbaum, Conard G.	446
Krogmann, Clement	500
Kunkel, Frank C.	148
Kuntz, Peter P.	263

L

Name	PAGE
Lamb, George H.	470
Lane, Dilla A.	495
Lang, Adam	498
Langsdorf, Peter S.	28
Larimer, Thomas McM.	487
Lashell, George A.	250
Lauck, John E.	33
Laughner, Perry O.	209
Lawson, Chalmers M.	54
Lee, Caleb, Jr.	395
Lee, Henry E.	436
Lenhart, David G.	507
Lewis, John F.	466
Lewis, Thomas J.	52
Lippert, Ernest T.	151
Little, David B.	478
Little, John C.	322
Loeb, Milton	389
Loeffert, John	270
Logan, George W.	507
Lohman, Henry J.	22
Lonabaugh, Albert	236
Long, James N.	36
Loucks, William L.	408
Lourey, William P.	165
Love, Thomas J.	491
Lowers, John F.	125
Luckert, John	466
Lynch, David H.	452
Lynch, Madison B.	271
Lyon, Florence M.	291
Lyon, William R.	291

M

Name	PAGE
McAlpin, William	417
McBride, Herman J.	133
McCaffrey, Samuel P.	511
McCarthy, Maurice	320
McCarty, R. Lee	25
McCaw, William J.	103
McClinton, William	401
McClure, Andrew F.	516
McClure, Daniel R.	141
McClure, John C.	493
McClure, Matthew L.	126
McCormick, S. C.	222
McCullough, William	435
McCune, D. P.	453
McCune, W. C.	47
McDermott, Congal A.	441
McDowell, James A.	304
McElroy, Archibald D.	76
McFarland, George I.	258
McFetridge, George H.	166
McFetridge, William	171
McGeary, George H.	480
McGinley, John S.	392
McGinley, Neil	476
McGinniss, Thomas A.	433
McLaughlin, H. A.	136
McMahon, Joseph M.	415
McMullen, P. S.	260
McPherson, J. Clyde	336
McWilliams, George A.	418
MacDougall, Duncan	98
Madden, Francis J.	524
Marshall, Henry L.	338
Marshall, William S.	356
Martin, Harry R.	412
Martin, John	480
Martin, J. Will	279
Martin, Taylor McI.	262
Masters, Frank R.	229
Maurhoff, Emil E.	188
Meckel, Gustave A.	156
Medvetzky, Julius	475
Meeds, Harrison P.	163
Melhorn, John K.	295
Mellon, James A.	412
Metcalf, Orlando	402
Mettler, J. W.	284
Metzler, J. H.	310
Meyers, Charles A.	454
Meyer, William C.	139
Miller, J. Clyde	189
Miller, Samuel D.	275
Millheim, John H.	334
Milligan, J. Knox	474
Milliken, Samuel	402
Mills, Isaac	243
Mills, James K.	468
Mills, Stephen D.	467
Miner, F. B.	377
Monnier, Henry	350
Montgomery, John R.	257

INDEX

Name	PAGE
Montgomery, Samuel P.	232
Moore, Charles	423
Moore, George H	143
Morgan, John T	191
Morgan, Lewis N	124
Moore, Thomas	68
Morressey, P. J	59
Morrison, James	445
Mullet, Samuel	344
Murphey, Harry O.	96
Murphy, Patrick J	101
Murray, John H.	528
Muth, Frederick L	226
Myers, Samuel M	488
Myers, W. Harvey	430

N

Name	PAGE
Naudler, John S	44
Needling, August J	504
Nicholas, William	182
Nicol, John F.	457
Nimmo, Alexander A	45
Norman, Thomas, Jr	153

O

Name	PAGE
O'Brien, J. E.	446
O'Brien, Leo F	53
O'Donovan, Michael C	185
Oeffner, Peter J	207
Oertel, Frank L	120
Oncken, John P.	325
O'Shea, Cornelius	396
Overy, Joseph	162
Owens, George T	411

P

Name	PAGE
Painter, John W	36
Pancoast, George W	290
Parker, Charles	105
Parry, Thomas L	117
Pastre, George F.	93
Patterson, James H	247
Patterson, Peter	48
Patterson, Peter C	453
Patterson, William H	222
Peairs, Andrew F	502
Penney, James L	460
Petty, A. Lewis, Jr	24
Pfaub, George N	482
Pfeifer, Edward J	486
Pfordt, Charles C.	419
Phillips, Charles A.	486
Philips, O. H	113
Poundstone, John A	146
Power, John H	367
Powers, Edward W	201
Pratt, Frank W	461
Price, B. Frank	149
Pugh, E. J	378

Q

Name	PAGE
Quaill, David R	358
Quaill, Elizabeth (Reel)	358
Quaill Family, The	358
Quaill, George	358

R

Name	PAGE
Rankin, Charles A	80
Rankin, John I	494
Rankin, John W	502
Rea, Thomas R	456
Reed, William A	227
Reel, Wiley G	368
Reel, William H	373
Reese, William S	434
Reinhart, Joseph	499
Rickenbaugh, John R.	197
Rhoades, Peter F	286
Rhoades, Sylvester E	522
Riblet, Harry L	369
Richards, Arthur J	56
Richards, Wm. Henry	59
Riethmiller, George W	491
Riggs, Robert L	17
Rinard, John	111
Robb, John D	312
Roche, Joseph T	94
Romine, John R	75
Roose, Arthur E.	129
Roseborough, William J	475
Rosenberg, David	49
Rosensteel, Thomas W.	221
Roth, Jacob	31
Roth, Joseph	30
Rotharmel, John P.	103
Rotzsch, Louis E	67
Rowley, Daniel G	318
Rudert, Paul	420
Russell, W. F.	305
Ryan, John M	529

S

Name	PAGE
Sargeant, W. A	183
Schmidt, Aristide J	316
Schmitt, John	512
Schopp, Lawrence	517
Schrandt, Frederick W	265
Schuetz, Elmer A	299
Schwarz, George	422
Schwitter, Fred	366
Scott, Alexander M	114
Scott, David	340
Scott, George H	175
Scott, Harry C	317
Scott, John	403
Sefton, Frank	343
Seifert, Edward O	78
Serena, John E	20
Shaffer, J. O	424
Shale, Jacob B	43

	PAGE
Shaner, James	497
Shanks, John I	376
Sheets, William L	28
Shields, John	312
Shields, Robert J	503
Shultz, Herman	496
Sieber, William	70
Simons, Hugh	387
Sinn, Charles J	409
Skelly, John K	86
Smith, Albert G	281
Smith, Duane P	77
Smith, Samuel B	324
Snyder, Daniel A	246
Snyder, George W	124
Sober, Craig M	429
Soles, Anderson	81
Soles, Clarence E	68
Soles, Wesley C	75
Spence, David	159
Spencer, Daniel B	448
Sproat, H. H	463
Stahl, James W	470
Staley, William J	154
Stamm, Henry	455
Stanton, William M	255
Stark, Christ	427
Starke, Emil C	268
Starke, Richard H	118
Stebick, Edward J	102
Stein, John	518
Stephens, Louis M	240
Stevens, Joseph D	400
Stewart, John W	180
Stewart, Samuel E	145
Stitt, Meredith C	324
Stone, George R	27
Stone, William A	40
Street, George T	472
Sullivan, J. Bailey	386
Sullivan, N. K	407
Sutter, Charles	173

T

	PAGE
Taylor, Dos	205
Taylor, Francis A	514
Taylor, Samuel	520
Thompson, George W	267
Thompson, Harvey	331
Thompson, Lloyd F	393
Thompson, Matthew J	265
Tibby, William C	269
Tinstman, Abraham O	239
Todd, L. Lewis	473
Trich, Edward M	45

U

	PAGE
Uhlinger, Charles	180

V

	PAGE
Van Kirk, Herbert S	446
Van Sciver, William K	131
Verner, Thomas H	80
Vogel, Adam	436
Vogeley, Jacob G	308
Vogt, John J	187
Volkay, Eugene	392

W

	PAGE
Walker, Clarence A	46
Walker, James	379
Walsh, Charles H	96
Wampler, James N	461
Warner, Herbert L	422
Warren, George B	51
Weaver, George P	226
Weigle, Charles R	382
Weigle, Philip	382
Weigle, William	297
Wellinger, John G	213
Wernke, F. W	67
Wertz, J. George	232
Westwood, Howard H	483
Wheatley, John C	518
Wheeler, Hiram J	249
White, D. M	72
White, Thomas W	47
White, William B	190
Wiggins, Samuel L	64
Wilkins, John	379
Williams, Ulysses G	237
Wilson, William F	388
Wise, John	527
Wise, William E	510
Wittman, John M	235
Wittman, Joseph J	203
Wolf, David	426
Wolf, Melchior, Sr	519
Wolfe, Frank	451
Wolferd, William	428
Wolff, Frank	223
Wolff, John A	132
Woodside, Samuel P	309
Woodward, James F	42

Y

	PAGE
Yates, William E	383
Yochum, A. M	381
Yost Bros	449
Young, Clyde F	444
Young, John F	169

Z

	PAGE
Zenn, Philip	26
Zimmermann, Henry	421

MEMOIRS

OF

ALLEGHENY COUNTY, PENNSYLVANIA

VOLUME II

ROBERT L. RIGGS, one of the foremost citizens of McKeesport, is descended from an ancestry which can be traced for over three centuries. Edward Riggs, the first of that name in America, was born in Lincolnshire, England, in 1590. He came to Boston with his wife, two sons and four daughters in 1633, and settled at Roxbury, Mass., and in 1634 was granted the privilege of citizenship. He had a son, Edward, born in England in 1614, who came to America with his parents, and on April 5, 1635, married a Miss Roosa. The second Edward and his wife moved later to a place afterwards known as Riggs Hill, near Milford, Conn., where they resided for a number of years, and then, in 1665, moved and settled with a colony at Derby, N. J. They were the parents of three sons and one daughter, viz.: Edward, Samuel, Joseph and Mary. The father died in 1668. Edward Riggs, the third of that name, was born in Roxbury, about 1636, was married in 1660, and reared a family of ten children. The third born was named Edward. He was born in Newark, N. J., about 1668, and about 1692 married Alphia Stoughton. They lived most of their lives near the village of Milbourn, N. J., and had six boys and one girl: Edward, Daniel, Samuel, Thomas, Joseph, Mary and David. David Riggs, son of Edward and Alphia (Stoughton) Riggs, was born at Basking Ridge, N. J., in 1709. He married Elizabeth Cox and resided in Middlesex county, N. J. Mr. and Mrs. David Riggs had six children, of whom the second was named Joseph. He was born at Baskingridge, N. J., April 24, 1740, and, when about twenty-one years old was married to Miss Leah Cosad, of true Dutch stock. They were the parents of eight children. Of these, the second, Edward, was born near Hightstown, N. J., July 21, 1764. When twenty years old he moved west and located on the waters of Short creek, near Wheeling, W. Va., and the following year went to Pittsburg, Pa., where, in May, 1785, he was married to Mary Higbee. In 1786 he located on a 400-acre tract some ten miles southwest of Pittsburg, on Peters creek, where he spent the rest of his days as a farmer. He was in religious belief a Baptist, and when he died, Oct. 4, 1843, he was buried in the Peters creek burying ground of the Baptist church. Edward and Mary (Higbee) Riggs had six children, as follows: Nancy, born June 20, 1787, and on April 30, 1807, married to Elijah Townsend; Eleanor, born Nov. 10, 1791; Joseph, born Nov. 18, 1794; John, born March 6, 1800; Edward, born July 2, 1802, and Mary, born May 11, 1810. John Riggs, father of the subject of this sketch, was born on the old homestead near Library, Pa., and, in January, 1821, was married to Mary Philips, granddaughter of Rev. David Philips, a pioneer Baptist minister, who came to Pennsylvania from South Wales and founded the Peters Creek Baptist church. He left a numerous family. His daughter, Mary, was born April 13, 1800, and died Jan. 25, 1882. Her husband died Feb. 22, 1848. Mr. and Mrs. John Riggs were the parents of the following children: David, born May 3, 1822; Sarah, born July 31, 1824; Edward, born Sept. 28, 1826; Josiah, born Jan. 17, 1829; Lewis, born Aug. 14, 1831; Joseph B., born Feb. 10, 1834; John P., born March 2, 1836; Robert L., born Aug. 26, 1838; William J., born Dec. 21, 1840; Obadiah H., born July 6, 1843, and Isaac W., born May 1, 1846. All of the children lived to mature age. Robert L. Riggs, the subject of this sketch, was born and reared on the old Riggs farm, near what is now Library, in Snowden township, Allegheny Co., Pa. When a boy, he attended the district school and then completed his education at Bethel academy. Being thrown onto his own resources by the death of his father, he supported himself for several years by teaching school, and for two years, 1864-1866, acted as principal of the McKeesport schools. He next embarked successfully in the drug business, with Jesse Sill as a partner, the partnership continuing until the death of Mr. Sill, in 1878. While in the drug business, Mr. Riggs improved his spare moments by studying telegraphy, the P. & A. telegraph office being located in his private office until the company was combined with the Western Union telegraph company. After the combination, he had charge of the Western Union office and transmitted many messages. After the death of his partner, Mr. Riggs conducted the drug business for about two years alone, and then, in 1880, engaged in the planing mill and lumber business with James R. Gemmill and John A. Lucas, under the firm name of Gemmill, Riggs & Co., the concern owning the property now occupied by the National lumber company. In 1885 Mr. Riggs sold out his interest in this concern, and in 1889 again embarked in the same business in company with Bert Hubbell, the second partnership lasting about three years. Since that time he has not been actively engaged in business, his attention being required altogether in looking after his extensive real estate holdings. On April 19, 1864, Mr. Riggs married Miss Cordelia C. B. Whigham, daughter of John and Margaret (Cunningham) Whigham. Mr. and Mrs. Riggs at once began housekeeping in McKeesport, and have resided there ever since. Seven children were born to them, as follows: Effa W., born Jan. 21, 1865; Jessie J., born Jan. 26, 1868, and died Sept. 21, 1891; Thomas Alvin, born March 2, 1871; William W., born Feb. 3, 1874, and died Sept. 7, 1874; Viola M., born Dec. 16, 1875; Clifford R., born Dec. 14, 1878; Walter Lee, born Nov. 24, 1882. Mr. Riggs has long been one of the leading citizens of McKeesport, and has been actively interested in all movements tending toward the betterment of the city. He was treasurer of McKeesport in 1878 and 1879, and was for fifteen years a member of the board of education, being most of the time either secretary or president of that body. He was one of the prime movers in the establishment of the McKeesport hospital, and has been on the board of trustees almost continuously since its organization. He was also one of the organizers of the bank of McKeesport, and for many years one of the directors of that institution. Mr. Riggs has long been one of the most respected members of the Baptist church, having been a deacon in the church for thirty-four years, or since February, 1869. He was also, from 1865 to 1894, with the exception of two years, superintendent of the Baptist Sunday-school. In politics he is a republican.

JOHN ELMER SERENA, coal dealer and member of the select council of McKeesport, was born in that city, in 1864, son of John and M. J. Serena. He was reared in McKeesport and educated in the public schools, and at seventeen went into the shipping department of the National tube works, where he remained as clerk eleven years. In 1892 he went into the coal business, on Water street, in company with his father, and has been successfully engaged in that business ever since. In 1901 he was elected to the select council of McKeesport, and has since been an influential member of that body, where he has served on numerous important committees. He is in politics a republican, and takes great interest in local party questions. In religious belief he is a Presbyterian. Mr. Serena is a member of the American Mechanics. He was married, June 6, 1893, to Eva Porter, daughter of John and Eliza Porter, and has one son, John R.

GEORGE L. EDMUNDSON, of the firm of Hunter & Edmundson, funeral directors, 600 Market St., McKeesport, was born in Lincoln township, Allegheny Co., Pa., on Nov. 14, 1871, on the same farm on which his father, Havilla G. Edmundson, only son of Levi Edmundson, was born June 16, 1842, and died June 7, 1879. His mother, Sarah C. Edmundson, oldest daughter of Joseph Peairs, of Elizabeth township, Allegheny county, remained on the farm until 1890, when her present home was built at Rhodes Station, now a part of Glassport. In 1891 Mr. Edmundson entered the employ of the Diamond lumber company, remained with this concern two years, and then began a successful career as an undertaker with the firm of W. W. Hunter & Son. In 1899 he was made a member of the firm, which was then called W. W. Hunter, Son & Co., and two years later, upon the retirement of Mr. W. W. Hunter, the name was again changed and has been known since then as Hunter & Edmundson. Mr. Edmundson married Mary R. Harrison, daughter of John and Mary Harrison, of McKeesport, and has one daughter, Helen R. The family reside in the second ward, McKeesport. Mr. Edmundson is in political belief a republican. He is a member of the First Presbyterian church of McKeesport.

JACOB BESTWICK, merchant, of McKeesport, was born in New Brighton, Beaver Co., Pa., July 25, 1846, and is a son of Henry and Mary Bestwick. He was educated in the public schools, and was apprenticed to a tinsmith at Warren, Ohio. In 1863, while only sixteen years old, he ran away and joined Company K, 86th Ohio volunteer infantry. After a year's service he was discharged, but after two months at home he again enlisted and served three months in a Pennsylvania regiment. He then joined an organization known as the Independent Scouts, under Captain J. K. Weaver, and served until the close of the war. Returning to New Brighton, he went to work with his brother as a tinsmith, married Miss Katherine Burkel, of Chambersburg, in 1866, and forming a partnership with his brother Isaac, engaged in business for two years in New Brighton. He went west and worked nine months, and after that was for two years employed as foreman for W. W. Bradshaw, in Pittsburg. Coming to McKeesport, he worked two years for Stewart & Bowman, and then bought out the business, which he has continued to run since that time. To-day there is no man in business in McKeesport who was in business when Mr. Bestwick started, over thirty years ago. Mr. Bestwick is a prominent and enthusiastic member of the Masonic fraternity, in which he has held various honorary positions. He is P. M. of Lodge No. 375; P. H. P. of Pittsburg commandery, No. 1, Knights Templars; and a member of Duquesne chapter, No. 193, Syria temple, and the Mystic Shrine. He also belongs to several other societies, being a member of Lodge No. 207, Knights of Pythias; Robinson lodge, No. 455, of New Brighton, I. O. O. F.; McKeesport lodge, No. 136, B. P. O. Elks, and is past commander of Post No. 59, G. A. R. Mr. Bestwick is a member of the Methodist Episcopal church. He and his wife have one son, John, who married Miss Mollie Peterson, of McKeesport.

HENRY J. LOHMAN, architect, of McKeesport, was born in New Baltimore, Somerset Co., Pa., in 1862, son of Francis J. and Elizabeth Lohman. He was educated in the public and normal schools of his native State until he reached the age of sixteen, when he learned the carpenter's trade, and was a carpenter and builder for a number of years. He came to McKeesport in 1887, and in 1890 opened an office in the National bank of McKeesport building, as an architect, and has been located there ever since. In the practice of his profession he has been very successful, and has planned many of the finest and best residence and business blocks in McKeesport, and other cities and towns throughout the country. Mr. Lohman, with his wife, and their son, Hunter, reside at 427 Olive St., in the second ward. Mrs. Lohman was formerly Miss Emma Hunter, of McKeesport. In politics Mr. Lohman is a democrat.

PETER KOCH, a successful McKeesport real estate and insurance man, was born in Germany in 1854. He was educated in the public and night schools, and at an early age learned the blacksmith trade, with his father, and continued to work at this trade until he reached his majority. He then worked for several years in railroad work. After this he spent some years as a plumber and manufacturer of beer pumps. In 1881 he decided to try his fortunes in America, and after a residence of about a month in Pittsburg, he came to McKeesport, and spent fifteen months in the employ of the National tube company, after which he engaged in the liquor and hotel business, and worked for Anton Heidger. One year later Mr. Heidger died, and afterwards Mr. Koch bought out the widow's interest, and ran the business alone until October, 1892, his place being known as the Hotel Columbia. After this he was engaged, until 1896, as bookkeeper, and then went to Cleveland, Ohio, where he bought a restaurant. He sold this property in 1898, and in 1899 returned to McKeesport, where he built some houses. In 1900 he started in the regular real estate and insurance business, at which he has since continued. Mr. Koch was married, in 1883, to Miss Frances Ness, daughter of Adam and Mary Ness, of Indiana county, and has one daughter, Anna. The family reside in McKeesport, in the third ward. They are members of St. Peter's Roman Catholic church.

CHARLES M. BAILEY, retired steamboat captain and pilot, of McKeesport, was a riverman for fifty years, prior to his retirement in 1899. Since then he has lived a quiet life, in the old home at 1601 Fifth Ave. Captain Bailey was born in McKeesport in 1835, son of Joseph M. and Nancy Bailey, and attended the public schools until he reached the age of fourteen. In 1849 he went onto the river, and took his first trip to Cincinnati. His father died in 1850. In the same year Captain Bailey became sub-pilot, and was employed thus for two years on the steamers Shriver and Jensee, which carried freight and passengers from West Newton to Pittsburg. After this he was engaged until 1854 on a tow-boat carrying coal to Cincinnati, and was after that, until 1860, mate on the steamer Hercules. He was then made pilot on the river from Pittsburg to Louisville, and in 1864 became captain and pilot. He was in Nashville when the news came of the death of Abraham Lincoln. He was in the government service all during the war, carrying coal from Smithland to Nashville. After the war he returned to Pittsburg, and was employed as captain and pilot on various boats up to the time of his retirement. Captain Bailey was married, Oct. 4, 1860, to Miss Elizabeth Coleman, daughter of Thomas Coleman, of McKeesport, and has one son, William McClelland, who has been for four years clerk of the common council of McKeesport. The captain is a charter member of Aliquippa lodge, No. 375, F. and A. M., and has been a member of Pittsburg harbor, No. 25, American Brotherhood of Steamboat Masters and Pilots, since 1892. In national politics he is a democrat.

A. LEWIS PETTY, JR., editor and manager of the McKeesport Herald and the Braddock Herald, was born in Sewickley, Allegheny Co., Pa., in 1875. In 1879 he moved with his parents to Duncan Falls, Ohio, attended the district schools there, and then studied at Beaver college, at Beaver, Ohio. After this he spent two years with his father, then taught a year at Rush university, Holly Springs, Miss., and, in 1898, came to Pittsburg, and began his career as a journalist as sub-reporter on the Pittsburg News. Here his ability was soon recognized, and he became editorial writer and edited a humorous column. In 1902 he came to McKeesport, where he assumed the position of editor of the Herald, and now has complete charge of the paper. Mr Petty married, in 1902, Miss Grace Peters, daughter of John R. and Susan Peters, of Georgetown, Pa. In politics Mr. Petty is a republican. He is a member of the First Methodist Episcopal church of McKeesport, and is one of its board of stewards. He and his wife reside in McKeesport, in the second ward.

E. R. CRAWFORD, president of the McKeesport tin plate company, was born in Mifflin township, Allegheny Co., Pa., in 1870, and is a son of the late James C. and Matilda Crawford. The family moved to California, Washington county, in 1876, and there E. R. Crawford attended the normal school until his twelfth year, when he returned with his parents to Mifflin township. He stayed with his father on a farm until his fifteenth year, and then entered the employ of the United States iron and tin plate company at Demmler, Pa., as office boy. Here, his abilities being at once appreciated, he rose to be time-keeper, paymaster, shipping clerk, and, in 1896, was made secretary of the company. He continued in this capacity until the concern was sold out to the American tin plate company, in 1898, when he was made manager of the plant. In 1899 he became assistant auditor;

held that position until Dec. 1, 1901, when he left the company to become president of the McKeesport tin plate company, which has recently completed a well-equipped plant at Port Vue, Pa. The plant was started in operation March 16, 1903. In politics Mr. Crawford is a republican. He is a prominent and enthusiastic member of the Masonic fraternity, being a member of McCandless lodge, No. 390; a life member of McKeesport chapter; a member of Pittsburg commandery, No. 1, Knights Templars, of Western Pennsylvania consistory, and Syria temple.

R. LEE McCARTY, manager of the Evans estate, and a well-known McKeesport real estate man, was born in Frederick county, Va., in 1865, son of the late Andrew and Joanna McCarty. The McCarty home was on the bank of the Opequan creek, and Sheridan passed it in his famous ride from Winchester. The subject of this sketch was educated in the schools of his native county, and, when sixteen years old, came to McKeesport, and was for several years clerk in a grocery. He then, in partnership with Mr. G. B. Warren, started a grocery at 411 Market St., the firm moving afterwards to 413 Market St., where they ran the store for two years. In 1896 Mr. McCarty took up the management of the Evans estate, and has been occupied with that business since then. He is one of the influential citizens of McKeesport, and takes a great interest in all movements in its behalf. He was one of a committee which was appointed to arrange for getting the new $10,000,000 tube works to come to McKeesport, and had charge of the options, which amounted, in value, to nearly $1,000,000. In 1897 Mr. McCarty married Miss Ida M. Tilbrook, daughter of Thomas Tilbrook, the first mayor of McKeesport. Two children have been born of this union, Lilian and R. L., Jr. The family reside in McKeesport, in the sixth ward. Mr. McCarty is an influential member of the Central Presbyterian church, an elder, and clerk of the session. He is a member of Royal Arcanum, No. 238, and Protected Home Circle, No 141, being an accountant of the last-named lodge. In political belief he is a republican.

CHARLES F. DAHLSTROM, a well-known McKeesport real estate man and formerly for three years councilman from the eleventh ward, was born in Sweden in 1865. He was educated in Sweden, and at the age of twenty came to McKeesport. Here he attended a business college about two years, and then worked in the bending department of the National tube works about fifteen months. After this Mr. Dahlstrom spent two years as clerk in a grocery on Walnut street, in the eleventh ward, then bought out the store and ran it seven years. In 1897 he started in the real estate business in company with C. J. Erickson, and has continued at that business up to the present time. He is a hustling, wide-awake business man, and has met with deserved success. He married Miss Selma Peterson, of McKeesport, and has three children, Walter C., Albert F. and Dora C. Mr. Dahlstrom is in politics a republican.

PHILIP ZENN, general manager of the Riverton yards, for the Monongahela Consolidated coal and coke company, was born in McKeesport in 1848, a son of George and Catherine Zenn, and was educated in the public schools. Upon leaving school, he worked a year for the James Stevenson machine company, whose plant was then located where the White opera house now stands. After this he engaged for a time in building flat boats on the Youghiogheny river, and then in running coal on the rivers. Some sixteen years ago he became a partner in the John Shouh company, in the sawmill and boat-building business, in which he has been successfully engaged ever since. In 1899 the concern was consolidated with the Monongahela Consolidated coal and coke company, and Mr. Zenn has since acted as general manager of the Riverton yards. The yards have a capacity of ten coal boats per week. Mr. Zenn has other extensive business interests, being a director of the McKeesport manufacturing company, manufacturers of tin plate, with mills and offices in Port Vue borough; of the Citizens' National bank of McKeesport; of the McKeesport title and trust company; of the Youghiogheny ice company, of McKeesport, and the Bluestone land and lumber company, of West Virginia; of the Elk Lick lumber company, of Hamilton, W. Va., and a member of the Crossman Bartlett lumber company, of Clearfield, Pa. Mr. Zenn was married, in 1880, to Miss Sarah A. Watson, daughter of Gervis Watson, of McKeesport. They have had six children, of whom one, George H., is now deceased. The others are: Bessie M., Sarah Anna, John W., Philip H., Jr. and Harry L. Mr. Zenn is an influential member of the Coursin street Methodist church, in which he has held all the offices to which a layman is eligible. He is a member of the Masonic fraternity, belonging to Lodge No. 395, of McKeesport.

GEORGE R. STONE, an employe of the National tube company, McKeesport, and member of the firm of Trich & Stone, insurance agents, was born in Stoneboro, Pa., March 11, 1868, son of Joseph A. and Josephine Stone, and came to McKeesport with his parents when three years old. He received his early education in the public schools, and then attended the Penn military college at Chester, Pa. He then went to St. Joseph, Mo , where he spent a year as assistant engineer for the Missouri river improvement company, and then, returning to McKeesport in 1888, was for three years employed by the Deweese-Wood company. After that, he was for three years bill clerk for the Pittsburg, McKeesport & Lake Erie railroad company, and has since then been employed in various important capacities by the National tube company. He is also a member of the firm of Trich & Stone, which does an extensive business in fire, life and accident insurance. Mr. Stone is a member of the National Union and the Independent Order of Heptasophs. He married Miss Rachel E Blose, stepdaughter of the late S. E. Carothers, of McKeesport, and has two children, Josephine Louise and Rachel E. In politics Mr. Stone is a republican, and in religious belief a Presbyterian, and is a member of the select council, representing the sixth ward.

WILLIAM L. SHEETS, real estate dealer, McKeesport, was born in Brownsville, Pa., Feb. 5, 1860, son of John and Irene Sheets. He was educated in the schools of his native city and at Washington and Jefferson college, and came to McKeesport, in 1884, and engaged in mercantile pursuits for five years. After this he was general manager of the Farmers' and Mechanics' S. F. and L. A., of Pittsburg, for eight years. After this he was for four years general manager of the Monongahela valley saving fund, J. Painter being president of the company, and was during that time, for three years, also general manager of the Monyough land company of Glassport. Since then he has been engaged in the real estate business, and has been successful in handling many large property transactions. Mr. Sheets was married, in 1880, to Miss Sarah E. Ruppert, of Westmoreland county, and has six children, W. Harry, Elizabeth A., James E., Margaret S., Irene and Welda. Mr. Sheets is in politics a democrat. He is a member of McKeesport lodge, No. 136, B. P. O. Elks. Mr. Sheets and family reside in McKeesport, in the seventh ward.

PETER S. LANGSDORF, alderman from the sixth ward, McKeesport, was born in that city, Aug. 11, 1867, and was educated in the public and German Lutheran schools. Leaving school at fourteen, he spent two years in the employ of the Chambers glass company, of McKeesport. He was then for several years engaged as shearman for the Deweese-Wood company, and after that spent two years in a similar capacity with the United States tin plate company. In 1887 he went into the insurance business, representing the Metropolitan insurance company; continued at this a year, and then engaged, at 723 Fifth Ave., in the fruit and confectionery business. Mr. Langsdorf was elected, in 1900, to a seat in the common council of McKeesport, for a two-year term. In the following year he was elected for a five-year term as alderman, receiving at that time the largest majority ever obtained by a candidate in a ward contest in the history of McKeesport. Mayor Falkenstein has appointed him his chief deputy mayor of the city. Mr. Langsdorf is a member of the German Lutheran church and of the B. P. O. Elks, No. 136. He was married, July 3, 1889, to Miss Maggie Wolf, daughter of John L. Wolf, of McKeesport. The family reside in the sixth ward.

HENRY FRIEDMAN, junior partner of the firm of Joseph Roth & Sons, foreign bankers, was born in Hungary in 1870, son of Bernard Friedman. He attended school in his native country until he reached the age of eighteen, and then came to America. He spent four years in New York, and attended an evening school, where he obtained knowledge of the English language. After acquiring knowledge of the latter, and with the help of five foreign languages he had mastered, he succeeded in getting a position with M. Rosett, foreign banker, New York. Having been with this firm for some time, Mr. Friedman accepted a position with M. Rosenbaum, foreign banker, in Philadelphia, Pa. After being with the latter for seven years, he came to McKeesport in 1900, and, on January 16th of that year, married Miss Anna Roth, daughter of Joseph Roth, and became a member of the firm of Joseph Roth & Sons, foreign bankers, doing business at 422 Locust St., McKeesport, Pa. In politics Mr. Friedman is a republican. He resides in the fourth ward, McKeesport, Pa. He is a member of the A. H. congregation, "Gemulas Chesad," and several other lodges. Mr. Friedman, although comparatively young, has had considerable experience in the banking business, and helped a great deal to build up the firm of which he is at present a member. Besides being a member of the firm of Joseph Roth & Sons, he is a member of Roth, Schnitzer & Co., of Pittsburg; Loeb, Roth & Co., of Monessen, Pa.; a director of the First National bank of Sutersville, Pa.; a shareholder of the Westmoreland brewing company, of the same place, and is interested in several other enterprises.

V. ARTHUR AULD, of the firm of Foster & Auld, McKeesport, is a son of J. P. Auld, and was born in Effingham, Ill., April 1, 1875. He came to McKeesport with his parents in 1876, attended the public schools there, and graduated from the high school. He then completed his education at Washington and Jefferson college, graduating from that institution in 1898, and spent several years as instructor in languages in the McKeesport high school. He then gave up teaching to go into the furniture business in company with D. A. Foster, the firm buying out the Long furniture company, at 523-525 Walnut St. Mr. Auld belongs to McKeesport lodge, No. 583, F. and A. M.; Pittsburg commandery, No. 1, Knights Templars; McKeesport chapter, No. 282, Syria temple, and Penn consistory. In political belief he is a republican. He resides in Versailles township.

JOSEPH ROTH, founder of the widely-known and successful banking firm of Joseph Roth & Sons, McKeesport, Pa., is a native of Austria-Hungary, where he was born in 1845, and where he obtained his early education. When a young man, he decided to cast his fortunes in America, and bidding adieu to home and friends, he sailed for the United States. The first year after his arrival was spent at various points in endeavoring to find a suitable location. Finally, he drifted to Pittsburg, and having mastered the shoemaker's trade prior to leaving his native land and nothing more inviting offering itself, he decided to open a shop and earn sufficient money to send for his wife, whom he had left to follow as soon as he had established himself in some permanent location. Therefore, after almost another year of hard toil, he was joined by his wife, who energetically set about to assist her husband by keeping boarders. Thus, at the end of three years, through their combined efforts, they had saved quite a snug little sum of money, and really laid the foundation for Mr. Roth's future success. About this time he decided to engage in mercantile pursuits in McKeesport, and opened a grocery store on Peach street, which he conducted for some time with success. His last business venture before engaging in banking was the opening of a shoe store on Fourth street. And it was while conducting this store that he conceived the idea of establishing himself in his present extensive banking interests. Mr. Roth perceived that there was no one to handle the affairs of the large foreign element of the city, who not only desired to patronize a local bank in their interest, but also desired a bank through which they could transact business with their relatives and friends in the Fatherland. So, grasping the situation, he at once established the business at the corner of Locust and Jerome streets. This was in 1888, and after two years, in which the business grew rapidly and in which he had been ably assisted by his son, Jacob Roth, they removed to their present location, No. 422 Locust St., in 1890. Mr. Roth has been eminently successful in all of his undertakings, and through honesty, perseverance and industry, he has accumulated quite a fortune. He has liberally rewarded each of his children as they grew up, and has financed each with a financial start in life, treating his daughters in this matter the same as his sons. As stated in the beginning of this sketch, he was married prior to leaving Austria-Hungary, his marriage occurring in 1865, to Miss Katherine Burger. Mr. and Mrs. Roth have five children, two sons and three daughters. They are: Jacob, Isadore, Esther (the wife of H. Firestone), Lottie (the wife of S. Firestone) and Anna (the wife of H. Friedman). In politics Mr. Roth is a republican and an influential citizen of the third ward.

JACOB ROTH, one of the leading financiers of McKeesport and the Pittsburg district, and treasurer of the banking firm of Joseph Roth & Sons, was born in Austria. He was only six years of age when he arrived with his parents in this country, and therefore received his education in the public schools of Pittsburg. He was of an industrious turn when a boy, and for several years he sold newspapers and assisted his father about the store. When still a youth he entered the employ of the First National bank of McKeesport, and for several years had charge of the foreign department of the bank. This training admirably fitted him for the partnership with Joseph Roth & Sons, which firm was organized in 1888. He was one of the founders of the Westmoreland brewing company, having financed it with $200,000, and is at present treasurer of the company. He is president of the First National bank of Sutersville, and is a member of the firm of Loeb, Roth & Co., Monessen. He financed a large tin plate establishment at Allegheny city, known as the Star enameling company. He is ably assisted by Mr. Friedman, his partner, in all of his various enterprises, and as he speaks seven different languages, he is a favorite among the large foreign element of McKeesport, who entrust their business to him. As a result, the firm of Joseph Roth & Sons do the largest banking business in McKeesport. The firm has banking connections in all foreign countries, as well as in the United States. Mr. Roth and wife, who was Miss Claudia Loeb, reside in the second ward. They were married in Sunbury, Pa., and have one child, Madeline.

JOSEPH FIDLER, of McKeesport, Pa., a leading real estate dealer and alderman of the city, was born in England, in 1844, being a son of the late Benjamin and Elizabeth Fidler. Mr. Fidler was educated in the schools of his native land, began at an early age to learn the boot and shoe business, later worked at the machinist trade, and was also engaged in brick-laying. He went into the steel mills, worked in all departments, and mastered the details of that calling. In 1868 he came to the United States, located at Pittsburg, and became a puddler in the steel mills of Lewis, Bailey, Dalzell & Co. After severing his connection with this company, he was for the next five years in the employ of Lewis, Oliver & Philips, of Pittsburg. In 1874 he removed to McKeesport, where for six years he was a welder for the National tube company; then to Pittsburg as manager for the Soho tube mills; one year later became manager for the Frankstown rolling mill; next went with the Continental tube works as welder, and remained with that concern for five years. Mr. Fidler was next connected with the Metropolitan life insurance company for two years, in Pittsburg, and in 1895 returned to McKeesport, where he engaged in his present business of buying and selling real estate. In 1895 he was elected an alderman of the city, has been honored by his constituents with re-election every time since, and is now a leading member of that body. During the term of

Mayor André, Mr. Fidler was often called upon to act as mayor of the city, and managed the affairs of the chief executive office with rare skill and ability. Mr. Fidler was married the first time to Sina Jones, and to them were born three children, one of whom is living, Mrs. Emma L. Stanier, of Tarentum. He was married again to Eliza, daughter of Hamilton and Nancy Stewart, and they have one daughter, Martha Scott. Mr. Fidler is a republican and a member of the First Methodist church.

JOHN E. LAUCK, superintendent and general manager of the McKeesport tin plate company, of McKeesport, Pa., has had a long, varied and successful career. He was born in Lexington, Ky., in 1862, received a college education, and then entered the employ of the Adams express company, in Lexington, Ky. After that he spent two years with the dry goods firm of Appleton, Lancaster & Duff, and four years with the Chesapeake & Ohio railroad company, being advanced during that time to chief clerk and cashier of the Lexington office. In 1887 he left Kentucky and became teller of the Bank of Wichita, Kan. The bank, which was run by Kentucky people, William Carlisle being its president, was afterwards reorganized as the Fourth National bank, Mr. Lauck acting as its cashier until 1890. Returning, then, to Kentucky, he organized the First National bank of Middlesborough and the Bank of Cumberland Gap, Tenn., and became interested in the Middlesborough town and land company and the American association, concerns with a capital of $22,000,000. In 1892 he returned to his old home, Lexington, Ky., where he engaged in the brokerage business, and invested in gas property and real estate in Anderson and Alexandria, Ind. At the same time he became interested in the tin plate business at Middleton, Ind., and, upon leaving there, came to Pittsburg, where he undertook the management of the Star tin plate works. In 1896 he gave up this position and became general manager of the United States iron and tin manufacturing company, at McKeesport, doubled the capacity of the plant, and had charge until Jan. 1, 1902. He then became connected with the McKeesport tin plate company, which built a plant at McKeesport, and has been director in the concern and general manager of the plant since then. The works are among the finest and most complete in America, and under the able management of Mr. Lauck the affairs of the company are prospering. Mr. Lauck is a member of the Knights of Pythias, B. P. O. Elks and F. and A. M He was married, in 1886, to Miss Katherine Clohesey, of Lexington, Ky., and has two children, Katherine and Mary E.

McKINSTRY GRIFFITH, of Tarentum, Pa., the county tax clerk in the prothonotary's office, was born at McKee's Rocks, Allegheny Co., Pa., June 16, 1847, son of Joseph and Eliza (Wilkinson) Griffith, both natives of Ireland, who came to Halifax, Nova Scotia, where they were married. In 1836 they located at Sharpsburg, Allegheny county, and two years later removed to McKee's Rocks, where they remained for nine years, then coming to Deer Creek, in West Deer township, and locating on a farm now owned by the subject of this sketch. This farm consists of sixty-seven acres, and is located at Rural Ridge. Joseph Griffith was a leading republican, and held many township offices. He and his wife were members of the Methodist church. Of eleven children who were born to them, six survive. His maternal grandparents were John and Alice (McKinstry) Wilkinson, the former an officer of the British army. The Griffiths are of Welsh descent, while his paternal grandparents resided in Ireland. McKinstry Griffith was reared in West Deer township, attended the common schools and the public schools of Allegheny city, and was graduated from the Iron City college in 1867. For one year he followed the occupation of a drover, then settled on the farm in West Deer township, where his father had located, and engaged in farming until 1891, when he removed to Tarentum, and for nine years prospered in the grocery business. He has served as tax clerk in the prothonotary's office for the last six years, and in 1894 held a position in the office of the clerk of the courts. He has always been an ardent republican, an active worker for that party, and while residing in West Deer township was a school director. He has valuable property in Tarentum, and owns the farm on which he resided in West Deer township. He has been a member of the Methodist church since 1864, has been a steward for twenty-nine years, and was superintendent of the Sunday-school while living in West Deer township. Mr. Griffith was married, on Oct. 8, 1868, to Eliza Herron, a native of Ireland, who immigrated to Pennsylvania with her parents, John and Sarah Herron, who spent their declining years in Pittsburg. Mr. and Mrs. Griffith are the parents of nine children: Marietta, William A. (deceased), James H., John M. (deceased), John M., Sarah E., Edna B., Ida C., and May (deceased). Mr. Griffith has given all of his children liberal educations, they having attended the schools of Tarentum. John M. is a graduate of Allegheny college, and is prominently identified with the real estate and insurance business in Tarentum. Mr. Griffith has taken a leading part in the affairs of the community in which he lives, and is one of the substantial citizens of Tarentum.

J. WILBERT BROWN, division superintendent of the Pittsburg, McKeesport & Connelsville street railway, was born in Armstrong county, Pa., in 1872, and is a son of J. S. Brown. He attended a local academy when a boy, studied two years at the Western university in Pittsburg, and completed his education at the School of Electricity in Washington, from which he was graduated in 1898. Upon graduation, Mr. Brown became night car inspector for the McKeesport, Wilmerding & Duquesne street railway company, was employed for a time as electrician for the United traction company, and after that returned to the service of the McKeesport, Wilmerding & Duquesne company, as foreman of the company's shops at East McKeesport. He remained with this company until 1900, was then appointed master mechanic for the Pittsburg, McKeesport & Connellsville company, and in the spring of 1901 was promoted to his present responsible position as division superintendent, in which office he has charge of the McKeesport division, embracing twenty-five miles of road. Mr. Brown is an influential Presbyterian, being a member of the board of deacons of the First Presbyterian church of McKeesport. In politics he is a republican. He resides in McKeesport, in the eighth ward.

JAMES N. LONG, manager at McKeesport for the Pittsburg brewing company, is an energetic young business man who has, in a short time, risen by his own merits to a responsible position. He was born in Allegheny, Pa., in 1875, son of Leon J. and Angenette Long, attended the Allegheny schools, and took a business course at Duff's college, in Pittsburg. His first employment was with E. H. Merrill, architect, of Pittsburg, where he worked a year. After that he was employed for seven months by D. J. Kennedy, dealer in builders' supplies, and later was connected with the Pennsylvania title and trust company until 1897. In that year he entered the employ of the McKeesport brewing company, now incorporated with the Pittsburg brewing company, and has, since May, 1901, had charge of the management of the company's interests at McKeesport, in the capacity of superintendent. On Nov. 16, 1897, Mr. Long married Lottie M. Reno. In politics he is a republican, while his religious affiliations are with the United Presbyterian church.

JOHN W. PAINTER, banker, senior member of the firm of Joseph Finch & Co., distillers, and a well-known resident of McKeesport, was born in Westmoreland county, Pa., in 1839, being a son of John Painter. He received his preliminary education in the public schools, attended Beaver college, and finished his schooling at the Presbyterian college at Haysville. Upon leaving school, he embarked in business at Guffey Station, and for two years kept a general store there in company with Joseph Finch. He also engaged in the same business for a year in McKeesport, in 1865, in partnership with Theodore Woods, then sold out and went to Pittsburg, where he went into the distillery business in company with his former partner, Mr. Finch. The business was first carried on at the corner of First street and Cherry alley, and in 1869 was moved to McKane and Second streets, on the

South Side. Mr. Finch died in 1884, and in 1885 Mr. Painter took into partnership Mr. James D. Ponticrat, the firm name continuing, however, as Joseph Finch & Co. Mr. Painter occupies a prominent place in the public life of McKeesport, being a member of the board of trustees of the McKeesport hospital. He was at one time for four years postmaster at Boston, Pa., under President Cleveland. He was married, in 1867, to Miss Isabel Cornell, of Mount Washington, and has one son, Robert C., who married Miss Laura Henderson. Mr. Painter is a member of Lodge No. 375, F. and A. M., and also of the Royal Arcanum. He resides in McKeesport, in the fifth ward.

JOHN CARTER, of McKeesport, Pa., a well-known citizen, was born in Somersetshire, England, July 14, 1848, being a son of James and Maria Carter. He was educated in the parochial schools of his native country, and on leaving his studies engaged in farming for five years. For the next three years he was coal-mining, then worked in a wholesale grocery store as shipping clerk, and, in 1872, came to the United States. He settled in Pittsburg, mined coal in the twenty-second ward of that city for twelve years, and then engaged in the same business at Alfsville, Pa., for three years. Later he came to McKeesport, secured employment with the National tube mills, and for the past seven years has held his present position of gas reverser in the coupling-forge department. Mr. Carter was married, in 1869, to Annie Young, of England, and they have nine children: Charles J., Constance E., Jennie E., Sarah Y., James, Annie, John, Minnie and Harry. He is prominently identified with the republican party; has served as member of the common council of McKeesport since 1897, his present term expiring in 1904. Mr. Carter takes great interest in politics, believing it to be the duty of all good citizens to personally charge themselves with the duty of seeing that only good and true men should occupy positions of honor and trust, and thus he wields a potent influence for purity in politics. Mr. Carter's family are members of the United Brethren, and he is identified with the Foresters and the Sons of St. George.

DANIEL P. BLOSE, M D., of McKeesport, Pa., prominent as a physician, was born in McKeesport, Jan. 7, 1878, a son of Rhody and Sarah M. Blose. Dr. Blose attended the public schools, graduated from the high school in 1896, and matriculated at the medical department of the University of Pennsylvania. He was graduated from that noted school in 1900, and for one year was resident physician in a hospital at McKeesport. Later he went abroad to prosecute his medical studies, taking a special course at the University of Vienna; then to the hospitals of Prague, Bohemia; later to Germany and Dublin, and, in 1902, returned to McKeesport and commenced the active practice of his profession. Dr. Blose maintains offices at No. 530 Fifth Ave., and enjoys a splendid patronage. He is a member of several college societies and the First Presbyterian church. He is highly regarded in the city where he has passed almost his entire career, and possesses the esteem and friendship of a large number of the leading people of McKeesport.

FREDERICK ALPERMANN, contractor, was born in Brunswick, Germany, Oct. 22, 1841. His father, also named Frederick, died when Mr. Alpermann was a boy. The subject of this sketch learned the cabinet-maker's trade in Germany, and, in 1868, came to America to try his fortunes in a new country. For a short time he worked at his trade in New York, and then came to Pittsburg, where he remained several years. In 1877 he came to Etna, where he has since resided. He entered the employ of the Isabel furnace company, where he continued two years, and then worked as a pattern-maker for another concern. In 1890 Mr. Alpermann started in business for himself as a contractor, and is still successfully engaged in this line. In 1897 he was elected councilman of Etna borough, his first political office, entering politics, not from a desire for political preferment, but because he felt it his duty to serve his borough, proving himself to be an able and conscientious councilman. Mr. Alpermann was married, in 1871, to Amelia Miller, daughter of Frederick Miller, a native of Baden, Germany. Mr. and Mrs. Alpermann have nine children, seven boys and two girls. Mr. Alpermann taught all his sons the carpenters' trade, and provided for their entertainment a club house in the rear of his dwelling. The children of Mr. and Mrs. Alpermann are: Herman F. C., born July, 1872, a carpenter by trade, living at home; August, born April 4, 1874; William G., born Dec. 3, 1875; Lena, born Sept. 30, 1877, living at home; Charles F., born Nov. 10, 1879, a carpenter and baseball player, living at home; Minnie B., born Aug. 28, 1882, at home; Frederick, Jr., born July 10, 1884, a carpenter, living at home; Albert, born July 4, 1886, also a carpenter, at home; Edward, born Nov. 24, 1891, in school. Mr. Alpermann is a member of the I. O. O. F.; the German library, of Pittsburg; Sharpsburg business men's club, and Etna fishing club. He is a republican in politics.

HARRY B. CRAWFORD, foreman of the pattern department, Monongahela furnace, National tube company, of McKeesport, was born in Brownsville, Pa., in 1866. When two years old, he moved with his parents, Samuel S. and Esther Crawford, to Port Perry, where he received his education in the public school. Leaving school at seventeen, he went into the Edgar Thompson steel works, in Braddock, to learn the patternmaker's trade, spent six years with this company, three years in the Homestead steel works, and, in 1893, entered the employ of the National tube company at McKeesport. Here he has since held the responsible position of foreman of the pattern department of the Monongahela furnace. In political belief Mr. Crawford is a republican, and has taken a lively interest in local party affairs. He is a member of Youghiogheny lodge, No. 583, F. and A. M., and belongs to the First Methodist Episcopal church of Port Perry, Pa. Mr. Crawford was married, in 1897, to Miss Lillian G. Frederick, daughter of J. M. and Anna Frederick, of Braddock. Mr. and Mrs. Crawford live in the sixth ward, McKeesport.

JAMES BROWN, JR., city clerk of McKeesport, was elected to this position for a two-year term on April 6, 1903. For several years a prominent republican of the eighth ward, he was, prior to obtaining his present office, chosen to fill an unexpired term as clerk of the common council and ex-officio clerk of the water department, his services there showing him to be a man well qualified for the office of city clerk. Mr. Brown is a native of Scotland, born in 1871, and came to America in 1887 with his parents. The subject of this sketch, having attended the common schools in Scotland, supplemented his education by taking a commercial course at a college in McKeesport, and then was employed for six months in the United States tin plate works. Entering, then, the service of the National tube company, he was employed by this concern twelve years, acting for the last five years as foreman of the bundling department. Mr. Brown is a member of McKeesport lodge, No. 136, B. P. O. Elks, and of Titus lodge, No. 207, Knights of Pythias. He belongs to the Presbyterian church.

WILLIAM A. STONE, agent at Glassport for the Pittsburg & Lake Erie railroad company, was born in Dravosburg, Pa., in 1865. When six years old he moved with his parents, Joseph A. and Josephine Stone, to McKeesport, where he attended the public schools, completing his education later at the Penn military college, at Chester, Pa., from which he was graduated in 1885. He returned to McKeesport, where he obtained a position as bill clerk for the Pittsburg & Lake Erie railroad company; was later, for eleven years, employed in the capacity of cashier, and, in 1902, was made agent at Glassport. Mr. Stone is a prominent and influential member of the Masonic fraternity, being a member of Youghiogheny lodge, No. 583, F. and A. M.; McKeesport chapter, No. 282, R. A. M.; Ascalon commandery, No. 59, Knights Templars; Pennsylvania consistory, of Pittsburg, and Syria temple, A. A. O. N. M. S., of Pittsburg. He is also a member of Lodge No. 81, Independent Order of Heptasophs, and Lodge No. 512, National Union. He belongs to the First Methodist Episcopal church. Mr. Stone was married, in 1890, to Miss Louella Penney, of McKeesport. They have three children, Helen I., Joseph A., Jr., and Jessie P.

ROBERT T. CAROTHERS, a well-known real estate man and formerly mayor of McKeesport, was born in Westmoreland county, Pa., in 1848, and resided there until 1865, when he moved with his parents to Uniontown, Fayette county. He attended the public schools, and was also for a year a student at Millersville normal school. Mr. Carothers came to McKeesport in 1882 and started a livery business, which he ran until 1900. He was also, from 1884 to 1890, proprietor of the National hotel at McKeesport. Mr. Carothers was appointed mayor of McKeesport in 1896, and was, in 1897, elected to that office for a three-year term. He is now successfully engaged in the real estate business. Mr. Carothers was married, in 1893, to Miss Carrie F. Onions.

JOHN GILES, city assessor of McKeesport, was born at Walls End, England, April 26, 1838, and came to McKeesport with his parents in 1853. He was for many years a coal miner, was successful in that work, and for ten years acted as mine boss for the Westmoreland company. He came to McKeesport some seventeen years ago, was for a time employed by the National tube works, and was then for some years janitor of one of the city schools. He was elected to his present responsible position of city assessor in February, 1903, receiving at that time the indorsement of both parties. Mr. Giles married Miss Rebecca Painter, and they have had ten children, of whom six are living. In politics he is a republican. Mr. Giles is a member of the I. O. O. F., Knights of Pythias, and the Ancient Order of United Workmen.

ARCHIBALD DUNCAN, select councilman from the fourth ward, McKeesport, was born in Glasgow, Scotland, May 2, 1868. Coming to McKeesport with his parents in 1872, Mr. Duncan attended the public schools there until he reached the age of sixteen, when he began his long service with the National tube company. In the employ of this company he has been advanced from place to place, until now he is superintendent of the Lapwell mill. Mr. Duncan has served one five-year term in the select council of McKeesport, and at the last election received the indorsement of all parties, a circumstance which speaks well for his work as a member of that body. Mr. Duncan was married, in 1896, to Miss Katherine Williamson Murray. Mrs. Duncan is a great-granddaughter of Collen Williamson, who was a thirty-third degree Mason, a prominent man in his time, and who was invited by President Washington to come from his home in Glasgow to be present at the laying of the corner-stone of the national capitol at Washington, Sept. 18, 1793.

JAMES F. WOODWARD, superintendent of the McKeesport city hospital, was born in New Brighton, Pa., Feb. 19, 1868. In 1872 he moved, with his parents, Mr. and Mrs. John H. Woodward, to Pittsburg, where he went to school until he reached the age of eighteen, attending first the public schools and then the Western university. Upon leaving school, he spent a year as a bookkeeper, and was then for two years employed in the office of the county commissioners. After this he became clerk in the Western Pennsylvania hospital, was soon afterwards promoted to assistant superintendent, and held this position six years. He came to McKeesport to become superintendent of the city hospital in January, 1895, and has held this position ever since, having proved himself competent and faithful in fulfilling the duties of the office. Mr. Woodward was married, March 10, 1892, to Miss

Belle Mawhinney, daughter of John Mawhinney, of Oakland, Pa., and has one daughter, Helen. He is a member of McKeesport lodge, No. 136, B. P. O. Elks, and is an enthusiastic Mason, being a thirty-second degree Mason, a Knight Templar and Shriner. He is a member of the Young Men's Tariff club of Pittsburg, and is prominent in local party affairs, being vice-chairman of the republican city committee. In religious belief he is a Presbyterian.

JACOB B. SHALE was born near Ligonier, Westmoreland Co., Pa., in 1855, was educated in the common and private schools, came to Allegheny county in 1877, located in McKeesport, where he embarked in the grocery business, and later in the dry goods and notion business. In company with Mr. W. J. Sharples, Mr. Shale erected a planing mill, and engaged in the lumber business and general contracting. He also, with a number of associates, organized the McKeesport building and loan association with a capital of $1,000,000, of which Mr. Shale was elected its president, serving in that capacity for four years, and declining re-election. Later, in connection with some business associates, he organized the McKeesport construction company, of which he was president and manager during its successful existence. In 1884 he was appointed postmaster of the city, which position he filled for four years and eight months, establishing the free delivery system and improving the mail service in general. At the expiration of his term, he purchased one-half interest in the Daily News, and afterwards a controlling interest, which he still retains. The News is the leading daily in western Pennsylvania outside of Pittsburg. When the United press association, of which the News was a member, failed, in 1897, the Publishers' press association was established, and Mr. Shale was elected president and general manager, with headquarters in New York city. This position he has filled up to the present time. The association has had a phenomenal growth, and is now recognized as the only rival of the Associated press. Mr. Shale has recently organized the Cripple river hydraulic mining company, with a capital of $1,000,000, chartered under the laws of the State of New York, and has been elected president and general manager. The company owns some very valuable property near Nome, Alaska. While all his commercial enterprises have met with good success, Mr. Shale's time has not been given up wholly to business, for he has taken a prominent part in social and church work. He may well be classed as one of Allegheny county's most prominent citizens.

JOHN S. NAULDER, of McKeesport, Pa., a successful dentist, was born in Westmoreland county, Pa., on Dec. 25, 1848, a son of James and Barbara A. Naulder. Dr. Naulder attended the district school until his sixteenth year, and then went to Millersburg academy. Later he began the study of dentistry, and after perfecting himself in that profession, commenced its practice in Fayette county, Pa., in 1871. Later he removed to Elizabeth and maintained branch offices in McKeesport. In 1877 Dr. Naulder gave up his office at Elizabeth, and has since devoted his entire attention to his McKeesport practice, which has grown to large proportions and demands his whole time. Dr. Naulder is the inventor and owner of the patent for making the Naulder gauze dental plate, which is getting to be so commonly used by the advanced members of the dental profession. This plate is regarded as a notable improvement in prosthetic dentistry, and the long-sought substitute for the ordinary rubber plate. This plate is made of one or two pieces of pure aluminum gauze swaged in a screw press and moulded to the proper shape, strengthened and reinforced by non-oxidizing wire bands, all soldered together into one piece by forcing hot rubber into the interstices. Dr. Naulder was married, on Oct. 24, 1878, to Tirza Johnson, of Pittsburg, Pa., and to them were born three children, Clarence, Ethel and Mary. He is a member of the United Presbyterian church, the republican party, and is prominent in the social circles of McKeesport.

EDWARD M. TRICH, alderman from the fifth ward, McKeesport, was born in that city, March 7, 1850, and attended the public schools there until he reached the age of seventeen, when he went to an academy at Smithfield, Pa., and there completed his education by three years of study. Mr. Trich then became a painter, and was for twenty years a contractor in that line in McKeesport. He has long been prominent in public life, and has a most excellent record in the city service. Mr. Trich was elected school director in 1888, and served on the school board of McKeesport ten years, being its president in 1896. After this he was sergeant of police for five years, and then resigned. In 1896 he was elected alderman in the fifth ward, and has represented that ward in the council ever since. Mr. Trich married Miss Sarah McCully, daughter of the late Major John W. McCully, of McKeesport. Mr. and Mrs. Trich have three daughters: Margaret Louisa, now Mrs. R. E. Erwin; Anna V., wife of R. E. Taylor, and Nellie J., who married Dr. Nathan Phillips.

ALEXANDER A. NIMMO, a well-known McKeesport manufacturer, was born in Scotland, Aug. 10, 1855, son of Alexander and Margaret (Arbuckle) Nimmo. He was educated in Scotland, worked there three years as a bookkeeper, and then, in 1877, came to the United States, and was for two years a bookkeeper in Philadelphia. In 1879 he came to McKeesport, where he worked sixteen months for T. M. Jenkins, and then formed a partnership with M. R. Smith, the firm running a general store in McKeesport until 1890. In that year they went into the coal business in Westmoreland county, and six years later bought a coal mine in Fayette county. This mine was managed under the name of Smith & Co. until 1899, when it was sold to the trust, and Mr. Nimmo and his partner started an ornamental iron works at No. 719 Jerome St., McKeesport, where they have since engaged in manufacturing. Mr. Nimmo is a prominent republican, has served as councilman, and was for three years member of the school board. He is a member of the Presbyterian church. On July 5, 1883, he married Miss Anna M. Smith, daughter of Samuel I. and Mary J. Smith, of Cumberland county, Pa., and has two children, Lloyd A. and Smith R. Mr. Nimmo and family reside in the second ward.

CLARENCE A. WALKER, of McKeesport, Pa., health officer of that city, was born in Westmoreland county, Pa., in 1853, and is a son of Jeremiah and Olive Walker. He accompanied his parents to Buena Vista, Allegheny county, when quite young, and there attended the public schools until sixteen years of age, when he commenced to learn the painters' trade. He worked at that business for two years at Boston, Pa.; then went to Blairville, and there served out his apprenticeship. Subsequently he removed to Pittsburg, where he worked at his trade for one year, and returning to Buena Vista, went into business on his own account. In 1878 Mr. Walker located at McKeesport, and there continued his business of painting, with some slight interruptions, until 1902, when he was elected to his present position of health officer, and turned over his painting establishment to his son, C. E. Walker. Mr. Walker is a prominent republican, and has occupied several positions of importance in connection with the municipal government. He was appointed a school director to fill the unexpired term of Florian Smith, and at the expiration of that term was elected to the same position from the first ward. Subsequently he removed to the third ward, and was the first water commissioner of McKeesport, serving three years in that important capacity, and being re-elected for another three-year term. Mr. Walker was married, in 1875, to Nancy J. Boyd, of Boyd's Hollow, Pa., to whom were born four children, Collomore E., Jennie, Olive and Eliza, the last two named deceased. Mr. Walker is a member of the Masons, the Junior Order of American Mechanics; also member of the Woodmen of the World, and the Cumberland Presbyterian church.

W. C. McCUNE, president of the Dravosburg dock company, located at Dravosburg, Pa., was born in Elizabeth, Pa., in 1861, being a son of Thomas and Sarah McCune, now deceased. He was educated in the public schools, and spent ten years on the river as a carpenter and calker. Thus prepared by experience for more responsible work, he became superintendent at West Elizabeth for O'Neil & Co., boat builders and repairers, remaining with this firm twelve years, until 1903, when he accepted his present position. In 1882 Mr. McCune married Sarah B. Powers, daughter of Calvin and Gertrude Powers, of Elizabeth, and has three children, Bessie, Hattie and William C. In religious belief the family is Methodist. Mr. McCune is a prominent Mason, a member of the Elizabeth lodge, and took the thirty-second degree in Masonry at Pittsburg. In politics he is a republican. While in West Elizabeth he took an active interest in municipal affairs, and served on the council and school board. At present he is president of Dravosburg borough council.

THOMAS W. WHITE, borough engineer for Glassport and Monessen, and city engineer of McKeesport, was born in McKeesport, Pa., in 1876, and is a son of ex-Select Councilman Patrick White. He was educated at St. Peter's parochial school, and then entered the employ of Taylor, Romine & Scott, where he remained seven years, and thoroughly learned civil engineering. After leaving the firm of Taylor & Romine, he took a trip around the world with John T. Butler, working their way on a cattle ship. For a time he was water boy on the street improvements in McKeesport, working for Patrick Ridge. Mr. White formed a partnership with L. L. Robbins, under the firm name of Robbins & White, with offices in the Lysle & Van Kirk building. A year later Mr. White bought out his partner's interest, and has since been in business for himself. Although young in years, Mr. White has proved himself careful, able and conscientious, and has been successful in his chosen profession. He was elected city engineer of McKeesport by the city council on April 12, 1903. He is an earnest worker in St. Peter's church, and has been for two years president of the Young Men's institute of that church. He is a member of the Fraternal Order of Eagles and of Branch No. 26, C. M. B. A. In politics he is a republican. Mr. White resides in the first ward, McKeesport.

PETER PATTERSON, of McKeesport, Pa., consulting engineer of the National tube company, was born in Jedburgh, Scotland, May 12, 1842, a son of the late Peter Patterson, a blacksmith and engineer and a descendant of a long line of Scottish ancestors, and of his wife, Isabella (Burns) Patterson. Mr. Patterson attended the public schools of his native town, and then became an apprentice in his father's shop. On completing his apprenticeship, he went to Edinburgh, Scotland, where he worked in several engineering establishments, and later went to Glasgow and became connected with some of the marine engine works. During these various services he secured a thoroughly practical training, which has been of vast assistance to him in his subsequent career. In 1866 Mr. Patterson came to America, and, after working a short time in Connecticut, went to New York city, where for four years he was employed as a machinist. In 1871 he secured a position as machinist at the National tube works, of Boston, Mass., and six months later was sent to McKeesport, Pa., to erect machinery in the mill then being built. Subsequently he was made foreman-machinist and held that position for a number of years. He was an important assistant in the erection of the National rolling mills department of the National tube company, and later became superintendent of the National tube works. He satisfactorily filled that position until 1897, when he became consulting engineer of the National tube works company, and manager of the United seamless tube works, the latter works having been designed and constructed by him. Mr. Patterson continued to fill these positions until the spring of 1902, when he became consulting engineer of the National tube company. He has invented a number of very valuable improvements, as well as much machinery and a number of processes used in pipe and tube manufacturing, and is a man thoroughly equipped for the arduous duties of his profession. He was married, in 1868, to Mary Rae, of Aberdeen, Scotland, and to them were born six children: Peter C., mechanical engineer of the National tube works and a mechanic of prominence and ability; Isabella; John R., assistant cashier for the McKeesport title and trust company; Mary E.; Thomas, draftsman for the National tube company; Jean E. Mr. Patterson is a member of the engineers' society of western Pennsylvania, with which he has been connected for the past twenty years. He is a member of the First United Presbyterian church, and has served as a trustee for a number of years.

DAVID ROSENBERG, a well-known McKeesport merchant, and an influential member of the select council of that city, was born in Austria, in 1866, son of Henry and Louisa Rosenberg. He attended the schools of his native country until he reached the age of thirteen, and then, emigrating to America, located at McKeesport, where he has since resided. On coming to McKeesport, Mr. Rosenberg spent nine years in the National tube works, and then, in company with B. Firestone, embarked in the grocery and meat business on Fourth street. Four years later he bought his partner's interest, and has successfully conducted the business alone since then. Mr. Rosenberg was elected to the select council of McKeesport in 1900, and still holds that position. He has served on numerous important committees, and is now chairman of the police committee. Mr. Rosenberg was married, about eleven years ago, to Miss Esther Leborgich, a native of Austria, and has six children. Mr. Rosenberg has, since coming to America, become conversant with eight languages, an accomplishment which is of great use to him in dealing with the varied foreign population of McKeesport. He and his family reside in the first ward. He is a member of Lodge No. 581, F. and A. M.; Lodge No. 561, I. O. O. F., and Zion lodge, No. 59, K. of P.

DANIEL M. HARDY, hotel keeper, McKeesport, was born in that city in 1872, being a son of David and Jane Hardy. He was educated in the public schools and at Gresly business college, and then began his business career in the employ of the McKeesport ice company. He remained with this company eleven years, a part of that time having complete charge of all its business. He left this responsible position to go into business for himself, in 1899, and has kept a hotel at 1017 Fifth Ave. since then. Mr. Hardy is a prominent member of the McKeesport lodge, No. 136, B. P. O. Elks, and has filled all the chairs in the lodge except that of exalted ruler. In politics he is an influential republican, and is a member of the republican city committee. He is a member of the Methodist church. Mr. Hardy is an expert marksman, being a member of the McKeesport gun club, in which he holds the championship. Mr. Hardy was married, Aug. 27, 1900, to Miss Anna Hale, daughter of Thomas and Anna Hale, of Wilkinsburg, and has one son, Hale D. He and his family reside at No. 1017 Fifth Ave., in the sixth ward.

ORLANDO M. HUNTER, vice-president and manager of the W. W. Hunter company, and partner in the firm of Hunter & Edmundson, was born at Library, Allegheny Co., Pa., in 1862. His parents were W. W. Hunter, still living, and Sarah A. Hunter, now deceased. Mr. Hunter came to McKeesport with his parents when four years old, attended the public schools, and then took a commercial course at Duff's business college, in Pittsburg. He then entered the employ of his father, who was an undertaker, and, in 1885, was taken into the firm, which then became W. W. Hunter & Son. This continued until 1899, when Mr. George L. Edmundson was taken into partnership, and the firm name was changed to W. W. Hunter, Son & Co. On July 1, 1902, W. W. Hunter sold his interest to his son, and retired from the business, which has since that time been run under the name of Hunter & Edmundson. The livery business is conducted in the name of the W. W. Hunter company, a corporation. Mr. Hunter was married, in 1883, to Miss Bella Caughery, daughter of the late W. Y. Caughery, of Lincoln township, Allegheny county, and has two children, Frank C. and Isabella A. He is an enthusiastic Mason, having attained the thirty-second degree in that order; is a Shriner and a Knight Templar. He is a member and past master of the McKeesport lodge, No. 583. He is also a member of Jr. O. U. A. M., No. 109, and B. P. O. Elks, No. 136. Mr. Hunter is one of the best-known business men in McKeesport, where he has several other interests besides his livery and undertaking business. He is director of the People's bank of McKeesport and the McKeesport title and trust company. In politics he is a republican, and in religion a Presbyterian. Mr. Hunter's home is in the seventh ward, McKeesport.

GEORGE B. WARREN, son of C. B. and Susan Warren, was born in Elizabeth township, Allegheny Co., Pa., in 1852. He has been engaged, since 1897, in the wholesale grocery business at 513 Sinclair St., McKeesport, under the firm name of Patterson, Warren & Co. Mr. Warren was educated in the district schools of Elizabeth township, and after that worked seven years on his father's farm. Coming then to McKeesport, he engaged for ten years in the grocery and produce business at 418 Market St., and then was for five years a wholesale commission merchant, located in the Odd Fellows building. He has engaged in the wholesale grocery business since then, and has been successful. Mr. Warren was married, in November, 1879, to Miss Sarah B. Symington, of Allegheny city. They have five children, Susan M., Robert L., Bingham S., Lloyd and Gene Isabella. The family reside in the fifth ward. Mr. Warren is one of the progressive and prosperous McKeesport business men, is vice-president of the McKeesport title and trust company, and was formerly one of the founders and president of the Citizens' National bank. In politics he is a republican. He is a member of the Royal Arcanum, and belongs to the First United Presbyterian church.

THOMAS C. JONES, attorney, formerly city attorney of McKeesport, was born in Pittsburg, Pa., in 1860. He is a son of David and Elizabeth Jones. He attended the public schools, McKeesport academy and Waynesburg college, and received his legal education at the University of Michigan law school, at Ann Arbor, Mich., from which he graduated in 1884. He was admitted to the bar of Allegheny county in 1885, and has successfully engaged in the practice of his profession since that time, having an office at 426 Diamond St., Pittsburg, and one in McKeesport, at 521 Walnut St. Mr. Jones takes an active interest in the welfare of his city, is one of the directors and the treasurer of the Carnegie free library, was formerly city attorney of McKeesport, and, prior to that, for three years a member of the council. He is a member of the Masonic fraternity, belonging to the lodges of Pittsburg and McKeesport. In 1889 Mr. Jones married Miss Minnie E. Muse, daughter of John J. Muse, of Versailles township, and has three children, Harry M., Thomas C., Jr., and Eleanor Z. In political belief Mr. Jones is a republican. He and his family reside in McKeesport, in the fifth ward.

THOMAS J. LEWIS, paymaster for the W. Deweese-Wood company (American sheet steel company), was born in Wales, in 1871, being a son of Thomas E. and Rachel Lewis. The Lewis family moved to America when the subject of this sketch was less than three years old, settling first at Johnstown, later at Irwin Station, and finally at McKeesport. Thomas J. Lewis attended school at Irwin Station and McKeesport, where he was a newsboy while attending school, and at thirteen left his books to become messenger boy for the Baltimore & Ohio railroad company. Shortly afterwards he left this company to enter the employ of the Deweese-Wood company, now the American sheet steel company, as office boy. In the employ of this concern he was promoted to clerk, then assistant paymaster, and, in 1903, succeeded George Falkenstein as paymaster, a position for which his long and faithful service had amply qualified him. Mr. Lewis is a member of the Knights of Malta, the Royal Arcanum, the Youghiogheny lodge of Masons, and of McKeesport lodge, No. 136, B. P. O. Elks. He belongs to the Presbyterian church. In politics he is a republican. Mr. Lewis' home is in McKeesport, in the sixth ward.

LEO F. O'BRIEN, of McKeesport, Pa., a successful merchant tailor, was born in Newcastle, Pa., in 1870, and is a son of the late Col. Edward O'Brien and of his wife, Theresa. Mr. O'Brien attended the parochial school of his native town, and completed his education by a course in the local high school. On leaving school, he began to carry newspapers for a stationery and news store, and eighteen months later began with a wholesale grocery establishment. One year afterwards he went to Bradford, and there began to learn tailoring, spending nine and one-half years there at that trade. He returned to Newcastle for one year, and then came to McKeesport, where for three years he was manager of a tailoring establishment. When that concern went out of business, Mr. O'Brien engaged in merchant tailoring at the corner of Smithfield and Sixth streets, Pittsburg, and there prospered for two years. In March, 1900, he opened his present merchant tailoring establishment at No. 219 Fifth Ave., McKeesport, and is now one of the most prosperous business men in his line in the city. Mr. O'Brien is a prominent member of the great American fraternity, the Benevolent and Protective Order of Elks; is a trustee of the local lodge, and active in the interests of this society. He is also a member of C. M. B. A., of A. O. H., and of St. Peter's Roman Catholic church of McKeesport. Mr. O'Brien's father was a member of the Pennsylvania infantry during the Mexican war, and later was distinguished as colonel of the 134th Pennsylvania volunteers in the great struggle between the States. Mr. O'Brien is an honorary member of the regiment commanded by his father.

CHALMERS M. LAWSON, of McKeesport, Pa., was born in Clarion county, Pa., July 28, 1862, educated in the public schools, and was engaged in the oil business throughout western Pennsylvania until 1887, when he opened a pool and billiard room at Carnegie, Pa. He removed to McKeesport eleven years ago, since which time he has been interested in a number of other enterprises, being at present manager of the Hileman-James company, 404 Frick building, Pittsburg, Pa.; also director in the Farmers' manufacturing company; also a member of the firm of Lawson & Sowden, dealers in automobiles and bicycles, and the Pittsburg casket company, No. 1024 Fifth Ave., Pittsburg, Pa.

EMERY E. DEXTER, photographer, has been successfully engaged in that business in McKeesport since 1895. In that year he purchased the photograph gallery of J. W. Fennell, on Fifth avenue, carried on the business there until April 1, 1903, when he moved his studio to its present well-equipped quarters at No. 517 Walnut St. He has met with marked success as a photographer, and some fifteen beautiful and costly prizes won in national and State conventions give evidence of his skill in this art. Mr. Dexter was born at Bower Hill, Washington Co., Pa., in 1870, moved to Carnegie at an early age, with his parents, Lyman and Martha, and was educated there in the public schools. As a boy, he served some time in a glass factory, then came to McKeesport, and was employed from 1884 to 1895 in the Buttwell department of the National tube company's works. In politics Mr. Dexter is a republican. He is a prominent and enthusiastic Mason, being a member of Lodge No. 583, Chapter No. 282, Commandery No. 59, and Syria temple, of Pittsburg. He also belongs to the Knights of Malta and Knights of the Mystic Chain. He is married and, with his wife and two sons, lives in the seventh ward. Mrs. Dexter was formerly Miss Mary L. Harmer, of Wellsville, Ohio.

GEORGE E. HITCHENS, of McKeesport, Pa., a well-known steel blower, was born at La Salle, Ill., in 1874, and is the son of the late Thomas A. Hitchens and his wife, Julia. Young Hitchens attended the public schools of his native State and completed his educational training in the high schools of La Salle. In 1890 he removed to McKeesport and secured employment as a measurer of tubing with the National tube company. Two years later he became shipping clerk for the same concern, and, in 1894, went with the Pittsburg steel works as foreman of the metal yards, and gradually worked his way up to his present position of blower. He was married, in 1895, to Grace Tate, of McKeesport, Pa., and they have three children, Olive, Walter and George. Mr. Hitchens is an ardent member of the prohibition party, and has done much to advance the cause of temperance by his able and persistent efforts against the liquor traffic. He is prominently identified with the Methodist church, and is a member of the Woodmen of the World. Mr. Hitchens is a man of integrity and probity of character, and commands the respect of all who know him.

WILLIAM JAMES GERMAN, a prominent real estate broker of McKeesport, was born in Versailles township, Allegheny Co., Pa., June 4, 1870, son of William S. and Katherine German. He was educated at first in the public and parochial schools of McKeesport, and then took a business course in Holy Ghost college, Pittsburg. He began his business career as clerk in the purchasing department of the National tube works company, at McKeesport, and was advanced to positions in the order and receiving departments. In 1890 Mr. German was appointed chief of the registration and money order department of the McKeesport postoffice under Postmaster Elmer M. Soles, and held this position four years and four months. In 1895 he went into the real estate business with the firm of Gilbert F. Myer & Co., remained with this concern two years, and then, in 1897, started a new business, under the firm name of Blair & German, with offices in the People's bank building. This partnership lasted until July 1, 1901, when Mr. Blair withdrew, and Mr. German has successfully managed the business alone since that time. Mr. German was married, in 1899, to Miss Elizabeth Ruth Haley, of Philadelphia, and has one son, William F. Mr. German is a member of McKeesport lodge, No. 136, B. P. O. Elks, and of the Americus club, of Pittsburg. In politics he is a republican. He and his family reside in the seventh ward, McKeesport.

ARTHUR J. RICHARDS, of McKeesport, Pa., secretary of the city board of health, was born in Pittsburg, Pa., in 1864, being a son of David and Lydia Richards. He accompanied his family to McKeesport when only six years of age, there attended school, and when eleven years old secured employment in the tube department of the iron mills of the National tube company. Later he went with Barnes Bros.' laundry, and was in charge of their McKeesport branch for nearly twelve years. In 1901 Mr. Richards was appointed meat and milk inspector of McKeesport, and after serving six months he resigned to engage in the wholesale milk and cream business in Pittsburg. In 1903 he was elected to his present position of secretary of the board of health of McKeesport. He is a republican in politics, and, in 1897, was elected to the select council for a term of four years, the third year of which he served as president of that body. In 1902 he was appointed a member of the board of health, and resigned that office to accept his present position. Mr. Richards is prominently connected with a number of fraternal orders, holding membership in the Masons, the Junior Order of American Mechanics, the Knights of the Maccabees, the Woodmen of the World, and others. He is also a member of the Cumberland Presbyterian church. He was married to Alberta Dougherty, of McKeesport, and they have had three children, Walter G., Hazel L. (deceased) and Annie E. Mr. Richards is widely known in McKeesport, and his popularity is attested by the number of positions of importance which his constituents have given him.

GEORGE DUNCAN, master mechanic, was born in Scotland in 1864, being a son of George and Mary Duncan. He began his education in Scotland, came to McKeesport with his parents in his eighth year, and finished his schooling there. Leaving school at twelve, he spent three years in the Buttwell mill of the National tube works company, a similar time in the Lapwell mill department, and then began to learn the machinists' trade. After serving his time, he worked as journeyman for a number of years, and was given charge of the machine shops in March, 1890, and held this position until 1893, when he was promoted to superintendent of the Buttwell mill. Here he remained until May, 1901, when he was made master mechanic. Mr. Duncan was married, in 1888, to Miss Anna M. Held, daughter of Louis and Catherine Bangart Held, of McKeesport, and has one daughter, Anne Sinclair. In politics he is a republican. He is a member of Lodge No. 375, F. and A. M.; Titus lodge, No. 207, Knights of Pythias, and belongs to the Cumberland Presbyterian church. His home is in the second ward, McKeesport.

THEODORE BOLLJE, of McKeesport, Pa., street commissioner, was born in Baldwin township, Allegheny Co., Pa., June 16, 1853, being a son of Herman B. and Elizabeth Bollje, both deceased. His mother was the first president of the ladies' aid society of the Evangelical German Lutheran church, and was a woman known for her many deeds of charity and benevolence. He was educated in the schools conducted by the German Lutheran church, and on leaving his studies, secured employment with the W. Deweese-Wood company, starting in their mill and continuing with them for eighteen years, filling all stations from the lowest to the highest, that of a roller. Then he engaged in the confectionery business in the Hartman block, on Fifth avenue, for a short time, and later went to the National tube company as a shearer. He remained in that position until he was elected to his present office of street commissioner, and is making a fine record in that important place. He is a republican in politics, and has his residence in the first ward, where his family have resided since 1858. Mr. Bollje is a Mason of prominence, holding membership in the Commandery and the Shrine, and is also a member of the Benevolent and Protective Order of Elks.

JOHN W. FISHER, of McKeesport, Pa., manager of the Atlantic refining company, of McKeesport, Pa., was born in Cumberland, Md., in 1851, and is the son of John W. and Matilda Fisher. Mr. Fisher attended the schools of his native town until 1867, when he accompanied his parents to Pittsburg, and there resumed his studies in the eleventh ward school. He went into a foundry, learned that business, and later went to work with his father, who had charge of a machine shop at Mt. Savage, for the Cumberland & Pennsylvania railroad. He lived on a farm near Cumberland for three years, later returned to Pittsburg, continued his schooling, and worked in a machine shop during his vacations. After attaining his majority, he was with the Westinghouse air brake company and the Mackintosh-Hemphill company for twelve years, and from 1875 to 1879 was deputy sheriff of Baltimore county, Md. For one year he was a traveling salesman from Pittsburg for E. T. Burroughs, in the wire screen business, then went with the Standard oil company at Pittsburg as a salesman for the Pittsburg district, and later spent twelve months in the office of that company. In 1891 Mr. Fisher was placed in charge of the Atlantic refining company at McKeesport, and has since ably filled that important position. He was married, in 1872, to Elanora Walters, of Baltimore, and they have three children, John W., Jr., Robert E. and C. R. Mr. Fisher is a member of the republican party and the Methodist church, and is one of the leading men of the city where he makes his home.

P. J. MORRESSEY, chief of police at McKeesport, was born in Trenton, N. J., in 1862, and attended the public schools until he reached the age of fourteen, when he gave up his studies to go to work as water boy in a rolling mill. At seventeen he had become a rougher, and he then went into the heating department. His first work was at Bethlehem, and in 1879 he came to McKeesport, where he worked in the National rolling mills until the strike of 1882. He then took an extended western trip, stopping at Pueblo, Col., and at other places, and in 1887 returned to McKeesport and resumed his work in the mills. He became a member of the McKeesport police force in 1897, starting as a patrolman, and in 1899 was made chief, in which position he has since served, and shown himself an efficient man for the place. Chief Morressey is a member of St. Peter's Roman Catholic church. He was married, in 1887, to Miss Kate Murry, of Bethlehem, Pa., and has two children, Josephine and Peter.

WM. HENRY RICHARDS, superintendent of the works of the United States tin plate company at Demmler, has risen to his present responsible place by long and faithful service in other positions. Mr. Richards was born in England in 1858, son of William and Sarah Richards; lived there until his fourteenth year, attending school, and then came with his parents to Leechburg, Pa., where he finished his education. Going into the tin and sheet iron mills at Leechburg, he worked on the cold rolls four years; then came to Demmler, where he was a roller until 1882, when he went to Apollo, Pa., and worked a short time as a sheet roller there. His next position was at Canonsburg, where he had charge of the cold rolls three years, and later went to sheet rolling in a larger mill. Being promoted to assistant superintendent, he held that position four years, and then accepted a position to superintend the erection of a new tin plate mill at New Kensington, Pa. He built a mill there, got it into shape, and was superintendent eight years, resigning at the end of that time, in December, 1902, to accept his present position at Demmler. Mr. Richards was married, in 1870, to Miss Anna Lewis, daughter of Mark and Sarah Lewis, of Demmler. Mr. and Mrs. Richards have four children, William, Mark J., Roy W. and Bertha M. In politics Mr. Richards is a republican, and has served in the city council of New Kensington. In religious belief he is a Methodist. He is a member of F. and A. M., Royal Arcanum, B. P. O. Elks, and Maccabees.

CHARLES ARTHURS, heater for the National tube company, at McKeesport, was born in England in 1861, and came to America in 1868 with his parents, Joseph and Ann Arthurs. The family settled near Huntingdon, in the Broad Top mountains, and moved about two years later to Irwin, Westmoreland county. Charles Arthurs attended the public schools, then engaged in coal mining for a time, and in 1878 started on a two-year tour through the west. Returning to Pennsylvania, he worked as a coal miner at Carnegie until 1883, and then went to McKeesport to begin his long service with the National tube company, as second helper. He was promoted two years later to first helper, was for eight years extra heater, and has been heater since then. Ever since he became of age, Mr. Arthurs has taken an active interest in politics. He was for a number of years a member of the republican county committee, different times represented the sixth ward as a delegate to the county convention, and in 1891, when McKeesport was incorporated into a city, he was elected as a member of the common council from the sixth ward for a two-year term. He was elected to the school board in 1898, and in 1903 was honored by a re-election. He is a member of Lodge No. 571, I. O. O. F.; Sons of St. George, No. 50, and Independent Order of Heptasophs, No. 81. He is a member of the Coursin Street Methodist church. Mr. Arthurs was married, in 1880, to Mary M. Willard, daughter of Henry Willard, of Carnegie. They have had seven children: Joseph H., Charles, Jr. (deceased), Thomas W., Alfred, Sarah E., Violet W. and Robert J. B. (deceased).

JABEZ J. HILL, son of Hiram Hill, of McKeesport, and probably the best-known barber of that city, was born in England in 1874. He came to America with his parents in 1880, the family locating at McKeesport, and was educated in the public schools there. Upon leaving school, he spent six months in a saw-mill, and was then employed in various capacities in the National tube works for four years. In 1890 he learned the barber trade, and in 1893 started in the business for himself at No. 1215 Fifth Ave., where he has since been located, and keeps a popular shop. In political belief he is a republican, and takes an active interest in the local affairs of his party. In the last election he was a candidate for councilman in the sixth ward, and was elected, receiving 509 votes. Mr. Hill is a member of the Sons of St. George, No. 152, and of Lodge No. 136, B. P. O. Elks.

JOHN FRANCIS CALHOUN, attorney and solicitor for East McKeesport, was born in Lincoln township, Allegheny Co., Pa., in 1862, son of Alexander and Sarah Lincoln. He attended first the district schools, then McKeesport academy, and Curry university, of Pittsburg, and finally studied law at the Ann Arbor law school, in Michigan. Graduating from that institution in 1890, Mr. Calhoun came to McKeesport, where for two years he practiced alone, and then formed a partnership with Mr. G. A. Johnson, which has continued to date. He also has an office in McKeesport. In political belief he is a republican, and has served on the McKeesport school board, representing the tenth ward, for the past nine years. In the practice of his profession, Mr. Calhoun has met with unusual success. He was for seven years solicitor for Reynoldton, until that borough was made a part of McKeesport, was solicitor for Port Vue nine years, and is at present solicitor for East McKeesport. He is a member of Royal Arcanum, No. 105, and Junior O. U. A. M., Hero council, No. 666. He belongs to the

Methodist church. Mr. Calhoun was married, in 1884, to Miss Sarah M. Dias, daughter of Alfred Dias, of Elizabeth township, Allegheny county, and has one son, Noel A. Mr. Calhoun is an excellent marksman, devoted to the sport, and has for six years held all records for trap shooting for the western half of Allegheny county.

JOHN N. DERSAM, a prominent McKeesport merchant, and chairman of the select council of that city, was born at Coal Valley, Allegheny Co., Pa., Nov. 17, 1866, and attended the district schools there until his ninth year. Moving then with his parents to Dravosburg, Allegheny county, he attended school there two years, and then, the family having moved to McKeesport, he worked for a year and a half on the ferryboat "Nora." Mr. Dersam was then employed by the National tube company, and after this in the heating department of the National rolling mills, and then, in company with his father, he made a four-year tour of the western and southwestern part of the United States. He returned to McKeesport in 1885, and on March 19, 1886, began his business career as a hatter and men's furnisher at No. 131 Fifth Ave. He has successfully engaged in this business since then, being located, since 1887, at No. 145 Fifth Ave. Mr. Dersam's political career has been a brilliant one. In 1891 he was elected to represent the second ward in the common council, held this position two years, and then moved into the fifth ward. Here he was elected to the common council, in 1894, and served four years. Then, in 1897, he was elected to the select council, being the youngest man ever chosen to that office in the history of McKeesport. His services in this body have won him two re-elections, and he was chosen chairman of the select council without opposition. His present term expires in 1905. Mr. Dersam was married, Jan. 5, 1886, to Miss Kate Nagel, daughter of Louis Nagel, of McKeesport. Mr. Dersam is a member of the following lodges: Knights of Pythias, Odd Fellows, the Masonic order, and the Jr. O. U. A. M. and is a member of the German Lutheran church.

CHARLES F. DeLONG, son of James L. and Mary E. DeLong, and a prominent insurance man of Pittsburg and McKeesport, was born in McKeesport in 1874. He attended the public schools, then the Cheltenham military school, in Philadelphia, and finished his education at the University of Pennsylvania. He studied medicine while attending the university, but, owing to an accident, was compelled to change his plans, and, in 1894, he engaged in the insurance business. He opened an office at first at 508 Walnut St., and in April, 1902, moved to his present commodious quarters at 509 Market St. He has also, since March, 1902, had an office at 341 Fourth Ave., Pittsburg. Mr. DeLong is a member of McKeesport lodge, No. 136, B. P. O. E.; Lodge No. 238, R. A., and Lodge No. 364, I. O. O. F. He is also a prominent clubman, being a member of the Houston club, Philadelphia; the Americus club, Automobile club and Keystone club, Pittsburg, and the Quaker club, McKeesport. Politically, he is a republican, and in religion a Methodist. Mr. DeLong was married, Oct. 21, 1896, to Miss Bertha F. Allebrand, daughter of John A. and Rachel Allebrand, and has two children, Eleanor V. and John A. The family reside in McKeesport, in the second ward.

MICHAEL GROSS, a well-known McKeesport merchant, and councilman from the tenth ward, was born in Mifflin township, Allegheny Co., Pa., in August, 1849, son of Peter and Margaret Gross. He received a common-school education in the district schools, after which for a number of years he was interested in the coal business, and in steamboating on the Ohio river. Mr. Gross is prominent in local political affairs. During the first administration of President Cleveland he was appointed postmaster of what was then known as Reynoldton, now tenth ward, McKeesport. He kept a grocery in Reynoldton nine years, and then moved to his present location, 317-319 Atlantic Ave., McKeesport, where he does a large business in general merchandise. In Reynoldton Mr. Gross was one of the foremost citizens and was burgess at the time it became the tenth ward. He has since then represented the ward for five years in the select council of McKeesport. Mr. Gross was married, in 1872, to Miss Margaret Elizabeth Elster, of Mifflin township, and has had by this marriage six children, Minnie, Frederick W., Elizabeth, George, Henry and Grover. Mrs. Gross and the eldest daughter, Minnie, are now deceased. Mr. Gross is president of one of the largest breweries in Allegheny county. It is at present undergoing completion, and will be called the Tube City brewing company.

SAMUEL L. WIGGINS, M. D., of McKeesport, Pa., a prominent general practitioner of medicine, was born in Indiana county, Pa., in 1849, a son of James and Eliza Wiggins. He first attended the district schools and completed his classical training at the Elderton academy, of Armstrong county. He read medicine at home, later attended Jefferson medical college, of Philadelphia, and was graduated from that famous school of medicine in 1873, with the degree of doctor of medicine. Dr. Wiggins began his professional career at Livermore, and two years later removed to Black Lick, where he practiced with much success for ten years. He spent one year at Philadelphia, taking postgraduate courses, and in 1886 came to McKeesport, where he has since practiced. Dr. Wiggins maintains offices at No. 224 Sixth Ave., and has a splendid clientele. He is quite prominent in Masonic circles, having taken the Knight Templar and thirty-second degrees and being a member of the Mystic Shrine. He is a member of the First Presbyterian church, and a member of the board of sessions of that institution. His political affiliations are with the democrats, and he is an ardent supporter of the doctrines of that great party. Dr. Wiggins stands high among the physicians of McKeesport, and is held in high esteem by his entire acquaintanceship.

ANSON B. CAMPBELL, insurance agent at McKeesport, was born in New Lisbon, Ohio, Oct. 23, 1837. He attended the public schools there until 1845, when the family moved to Elizabeth township, Allegheny Co., Pa. Here he attended the public schools, and afterwards studied two years at the Monongahela academy. Mr. Campbell then studied medicine for a year and a half, and, in 1861, gave up his books to join the Union army, as a member of Company M, 100th regiment, Pennsylvania volunteer infantry. This regiment was called by its commander, Col. Daniel Leisure, the "Roundhead regiment," after Cromwell's famous soldiers of that name. Mr. Campbell's war-record is a most creditable one. A short time after his enlistment he was elected second lieutenant, and afterwards became captain of his company. He was with his regiment at the taking of Hilton Head and Bay Point; moved thence to Beaufort, S. C., where he remained until May, 1862, and took part in the capture of a fort on the mainland, which was accomplished after a serious brush with the rebels. He then returned to Hilton Head, and from there went to James island, remaining on the island from June 1st to July 4th, and then came back to Hilton Head. From Hilton Head the regiment was sent by transport to Newport News, Va., and from there went to Aquia creek, and thence to Fredericksburg, stopping about four weeks at the latter place. The Roundheads then went to reinforce Pope in the Slaughter mountains, but arrived too late to be of service, and, on Aug. 16th, retreated to Kelley's Ford and crossed the river with the confederates close behind. Mr. Campbell fought two days at second Bull Run; then fell back with his regiment to Centerville, where they made a stand and remained over Sunday, and on Monday helped defeat the rebels at Chantilly. The regiment then marched to Washington, in August, 1862, stayed there one day, and then went into Maryland and took part in the battle of South mountain, on Sept. 14, 1862. Thence they participated in the battle of Antietam, and pursued the rebels to Shepherd's Ford, and then, having lost the trail, camped at Pleasant Valley until October 26th. From there they went to Fredericksburg and took part in the battle of that name, on December 13th. At South mountain, Mr. Campbell was wounded twice, and, early in 1863, resigned to attend the bedside of his mother, who died in March. His war service over, he remained at home until March, 1864, when, with a number of friends, he left for Idaho, the party making the journey by ox-team from Nebraska City until they reached their destination. He reached Virginia City in August, remained there until October, and then, with a party of sixty-five, started for the headwaters of the Yellowstone. Here they built thirteen boats, sawing the lumber with whip-saws, and started on a journey which no man had ever made before—a journey fraught with unknown perils and countless hardships. They went, first, 1,000 miles to the Missouri river, then down the Missouri to Sioux City, Ia., being attacked twice on the way by Indians. Mr. Campbell was married in October, 1866, and took a trip of a month to the East at that time. In the same year he began his long and successful career as an insurance agent. In politics Mr. Campbell is a republican. He was elected to the State legislature in 1879 and re-elected in 1881, and has served his borough fifteen years as a member of the school board, being secretary of the board thirteen years. In religion he is a Baptist, has been a deacon thirty years and fifteen years Sunday-school superintendent. He is a member of the G. A. R.

HENRY FIRESTONE, a well-known McKeesport merchant, was born in Austria-Hungary in 1864, was educated in his native country and learned the butchers' trade there. In 1881 he came to America, locating at McKeesport, where he worked four years for the National tube company. July 2, 1885, he started for himself in the meat business at Nos. 340, 342 and 344 Fourth Ave., McKeesport. In 1886 he formed a partnership with a brother, S. Firestone, and the firm conducted a general merchandise business until 1898, since which time the subject of this sketch has been in business alone. Mr. Firestone is recognized as one of McKeesport's most able and energetic business men, and his career thus far has been most successful. Mr. Firestone was married, May 29, 1889, to Miss Ester Roth, daughter of Joseph Roth, mentioned elsewhere in this book, and has seven children, Bertha, Edith, Annie, Rosa, Lillian, Henry and Ruth. The family reside in McKeesport, in the fifth ward.

LOUIS E. ROTZSCH, member of the select council of McKeesport from the eighth ward, is a native of McKeesport, born in 1873. He is a son of William and Earnestine Rotzsch, of Germany. Mr. Rotzsch was educated in the public schools, leaving school at fifteen to become a tube worker in the National tube works. He remained at this employment seven years, then spent three years as a crucible steel worker in the Fort Sterling works, and in 1899 started in the liquor business, in which he has since been engaged. In politics Mr. Rotzsch is a republican, active in local party campaigns, and in 1903 was elected to represent the eighth ward in the select council, receiving at that time almost the entire vote of the ward, but later resigned to become chief of police. Mr. Rotzsch is a member of the McKeesport Turners' society and of Lodge No. 136, B. P. O. Elks, of McKeesport.

F. W. WERNKE, of McKeesport, Pa., the proprietor of the Wernke carriage and wagon works, was born in Pittsburg, Pa., in 1855. He is the son of John F. and Elizabeth Wernke, and was educated in the public schools of Pittsburg and in Iron City college. After leaving school, he was engaged with his father, who was at that time in the carriage and wagon business, known as the firm of S. W. Saward & Co., of Pittsburg, Pa. By strict attention to business, he acquired a thorough knowledge of the carriage and wagon trade. He came to McKeesport, Pa., and with his brother, C. H. Wernke, started the business which he now conducts. In 1894 Mr. Wernke became the sole owner of the carriage and wagon plant, located at the corner of Jerome and Sheridan streets, which is the leading institution of its kind in the city. He is a member of the republican party, a Knight Templar Mason and also a member of the English Lutheran church. He is prominently identified with the commercial and social life of McKeesport.

CLARENCE E. SOLES, comptroller of McKeesport, Pa., was born in that city Jan. 26, 1869, and attended the public schools there until 1884. He then entered the Maryland agricultural college and graduated from that institution. Returning, then, to McKeesport, he was, until April, 1894, assistant postmaster. In that year he was elected by the select council of McKeesport to the office of city clerk, a position which he filled most creditably for nine years. In the spring election of 1903 he was elected to his present position of city comptroller. In politics Mr. Soles is a republican, and in religion a Methodist. He is a member of Ben-Hur lodge, No. 3, and Lodge No. 375, F. and A. M.; also of McKeesport lodge, No. 136, B. P. O. E. Mr. Soles was married, in 1893, to Miss Jeanette A. Lewis, of McKeesport, and has one son.

THOMAS MOORE, deceased, for half a century a most prominent citizen of McKeesport and other places in Allegheny county, also for half a century a Freemason, was born in Mt. Joy, Lancaster Co., Pa., in 1818, and died in McKeesport, May 10, 1898, after an illness of ten days, of inflammation of the bowels, the disorder being no doubt aggravated by the burden of nearly eighty years. Mr. Moore began his business career in a distillery at the age of eight years, and continued therein until he was seventeen years old, when he learned the coopers' trade. In 1838 he married Miss Mary Jane Wilson, of Westmoreland county, and shortly afterward engaged in coal mining, and in 1842, after selling out his interest in this industry, bought a flouring mill in Possum Hollow, Allegheny county, from his father-in-law, and had just fully repaired the structure when it was destroyed. Mr. Moore then built a distillery on the same ground and, until 1860, produced the famous Possum Hollow brand of whiskey. In 1859 he had erected a distillery on First avenue, Pittsburg, which he operated two or three years, then turning it over to his son-in-law; but in a short time this distillery was converted into a pickle factory, known as the Heinz pickle factory, the plant now being used for the manufacture of copper tacks. In the meantime, Mr. Moore again turned his attention to coal mining, buying the Wilson and Scott Haven mines, and controlling the output for a radius of twenty-five miles around his headquarters. In 1864 he organized the Youghiogheny Hollow coal company, the capital stock of which was fixed at $500,000, and of this company Thomas Moore was elected president and William Moore secretary and treasurer. The company, which was at that time one of the largest in the country, purchased 1,000 acres of land at a place known as Shaner Station, and the mines there sunk produced on an average 100,000 tons of coal annually, valued at the place of shipment at $600,000. In 1866 Mr. Moore bought back the Possum Hollow distillery, operated it until 1871, then tore it down and built a new one at Scott Haven, which he completed in 1872. About 1877 reverses occurred in the coal trade, and Mr. Moore suffered with the rest of the operators. In 1878 he located in McKeesport, purchased land and erected a distillery, which is still in operation, with a capacity of from forty to fifty barrels per day. Connected with it is a warehouse in which may be stored from 40,000 to 50,000 barrels, this distillery being now operated by the heirs to the estate. In 1886 Mr. Moore re-entered the coal trade, bought a large tract of coal land at Manor Station, on the Pennsylvania railroad, but shortly afterward, meeting with a favorable opportunity, sold out. At one time Mr. Moore owned several vessels, which he utilized for distributing his output of coal among the ports of Lake Erie, but, always alive to business speculation, he disposed of these vessels for a distillery at Buffalo, N. Y.; after realizing from it a fortune in five years, reverses came, and he was forced to the wall, temporarily, as mentioned above. In politics Mr. Moore was a democrat, and twice served his party in the State legislature. His religious views coincided with the doctrines of the Protestant Episcopal church, and at his demise he was a member of St. Stephen's congregation at McKeesport. To the marriage of Mr. Moore with Miss Jane Wilson there were born six children, viz.: William, deceased; Robert J., deceased; Morrison R.; Odessa, now Mrs. Fred Crabtree, of McKeesport; Mrs. Martha Ament, of Shaner Station, and Mrs. Elizabeth Finch, deceased. The honored mother of this family, after a married life of fifty years, passed away April 22, 1889, deeply mourned by the surviving members. April 18, 1893, Mr.

Moore again married, choosing for his second helpmate Miss Elizabeth Heath. Hon. Thomas Moore was one of the most sagacious and enterprising of the native-born business men of the Keystone State. He was a man who was very fond of his home, and was at the same time charitable and public-spirited. He hewed his way to fortune, and died one of the wealthiest men of McKeesport. He won for himself an imperishable name as a promoter of the coal industries of the State, and as a distiller gained a reputation that extends through the length and breadth of the land. His mortal remains now rest in peace in Versailles cemetery, and his unspotted name has been left as a precious heritage to the surviving members of his family.

WILLIAM SIEBER, of McKeesport, Pa., a well-known insurance and real estate agent, was born in Germany in 1848, son of Frederick and Mary Sieber, both natives and life-residents of Germany. Mr. Sieber was educated in the splendid schools of the Fatherland, and, on leaving school, learned the glaziers' trade. Four years later he enlisted in the German army, saw two years of active service, five years as a reserve and five years subject to call. During the period of his active service he participated in the Franco-Prussian war, and at the expiration of his term returned home and resumed the glaziers' trade. In 1881 he came to America, settling at McKeesport and securing a position with the National tube company. He continued in the mill until 1887, when he went into the insurance business, and later added real estate. In 1892 Mr. Sieber returned to Germany on a visit to his father, and on his return to America resumed the real estate and insurance business, with his office at No. 312 Ringgold street, where he has a splendid patronage. He was married, in 1873, to Christina Schilling, who was also a native of the same part of Germany, and to them have been born seven children: Aggie, Alvin, Charles, Henry, William, Jr., Francis and Helen. Mr. Sieber is a member of the Heptasophs, the German Beneficial Union and the democratic party. Mr. Sieber has been a member of the German Protestant church of McKeesport for fifteen years, and is also a member of the local Turners.

JOHN JACKEL, SR., wholesale liquor dealer, of McKeesport, was born in Germany in 1855; attended the public schools until his seventeenth year, and then came to America, arriving at McKeesport in August, 1871. He worked for several years as a butcher at McKeesport, and in 1876 opened a meat market on Fifth avenue, near Market street. In the following year he sold out and returned to Germany, was gone six months, and during that time met and married Miss Agatha Nicholas, and brought his wife back with him to McKeesport. He bought out his old business and ran it for several years, and then, in 1882, moved to the corner of Tubeworks alley and Fifth avenue, where he had erected a new brick building. Here he remained in business several years, then moved to a new location on Sixth street, and had a shop there four years, when, his health failing, he was compelled to give up business for a time. His final venture was in the wholesale liquor business. He started in partnership with William Denney, but at the end of a year, in 1894, Mr. Jackel bought out his partner's interest, and has since then run the business alone, his location being No. 411 Blackberry alley. Mr. Jackel and wife have seven children, all living: William T., John, Jr., Anna, Katherine, George, Fred and Albert. Of these, William T., the eldest, is in business with his father; John, Jr., has been with Edmundson & Hamilton in the dry-goods business for seven years; Katherine graduated from the high school in 1902, and is at home; George is in the grocery business, and Fred and Albert are in school. Mr. Jackel is an influential member of the German Protestant church, and has been president of the church for six years. He is a member of the I. O. O. F., the Heptasophs, A. O. U. W., German Benefit Union, and the Turners. In politics he is a republican. His home is in the fourth ward. Mr. Jackel, although loyal to his adopted country, retains an affection for his native land, made it a visit in 1903, leaving here on the twenty-fifth anniversary of his marriage, and after a most enjoyable visit with his mother, whom he had not seen for twenty-five years, and whom he found in excellent health, he returned home on October 1st.

J. J. BEDELL, haberdasher and men's furnisher, of McKeesport, and alderman from the sixth ward, was born in Finleyville, Washington Co., Pa., in 1871, son of Andrew and Elizabeth Bedell, both now deceased. Mr. Bedell came to McKeesport with his parents in 1872, and was reared there and educated in the public schools. He left school at an early age to go to work in the National rolling mill, and then, at eighteen, started a men's furnishing business on Fifth avenue, McKeesport. He is now located at No. 215 Fifth Ave., where he has an extensive patronage and carries a full line of goods. In 1897 he was elected to the common council of McKeesport, and so pleased his constituents in performing the duties of the office that they re-elected him for three terms. He served two years as president of the council. Mr. Bedell is a republican in politics, and is a leader in local party affairs. In religious belief he is a Presbyterian. Mr. Bedell and family reside in the sixth ward. Mrs. Bedell was formerly Miss Sarah Cherrington, of McKeesport. Mr. and Mrs. Bedell have three children, Corineen A., Georgia A. and Themala E.

D. M. WHITE, of McKeesport, Pa., a prominent contractor and real estate dealer, was born in Brookville, Jefferson Co., Pa., Oct. 27, 1860, son of Thomas and Margaret White. When only four years of age, he accompanied his parents to Elizabeth, Pa., where he attended the public schools, and later began clerking in a grocery store. He went with his father into the carpenters' trade, and was so engaged until his twenty-third year. In 1875 the family removed to McKeesport, where he worked at carpentering until his twenty-sixth year, at that time taking up contracting also and continuing in that line until 1900. He embarked in the real estate business, buying, building and selling, and he has made a decided success of that vocation, being among the most prominent handlers of real estate of McKeesport. Mr. White was married, on Sept. 12, 1882, to Marion Nesbitt, of McKeesport, Pa., and they have the following five children: John A., D. Wallace, James Edward, Charles and Adelaide. Mr. White is an ardent member of the democratic party, and has served three terms as a member of the common council of McKeesport, despite the fact that the city is overwhelmingly republican. He was first elected to the common council in 1898 for a two-year term; re-elected in 1900, and during that term served as president of that body; again elected in 1902, and his present term will expire in 1904. Mr. White's continued elections are great tributes to his political strength and personal popularity, as democratic majorities are almost unknown quantities in that city. Mr. White is a Presbyterian in his religious faith and affiliates with the local church of that denomination.

JOHN A. GEETING, son of the late Isaac Geeting, was born in Cincinnati, Ohio, in 1846. He has had a long and varied career, being at different times a school teacher, lawyer, editor and public officer, and finally a real estate dealer. Mr. Geeting was educated in the public schools and at Farmers' college, College Hill, Ohio, after which he taught school for five years in Ohio and Indiana. In 1868 he went into the newspaper business, and was also admitted to the bar, practicing in Washington, Daviess Co., Ind. Mr. Geeting resided in Washington some twenty years, and, while there, took a prominent part in local political issues, and held the positions of justice of the peace, councilman, school director, city commissioner and deputy county clerk, filling the last-named office four and a half years. In 1888 he came to McKeesport, where for four years and a half he was editor of the McKeesport Times, and during that time wrote the editorials for every issue of the paper. He was burgess of Reynoldton in 1891, and clerk and water superintendent from 1892 to 1895. He then moved to Duquesne, where he purchased the Observer, and ran that paper two years. He was borough clerk of Duquesne one year. Selling out his business interests in Duquesne, Mr. Geeting spent three years in eastern Maryland, and then returned to McKeesport, where he has since been engaged in the real estate business. He was at first associated with Gilbert F. Myer. Mr.

Myer sold his interest in the business to Mr. T. D. Gardner. Mr. Geeting was married, in 1865, to Miss Elizabeth Bacon, of Hamilton, Ohio, and has seven children, four of whom are now married. In politics Mr. Geeting is a republican. His home is in the second ward, McKeesport.

WILLIAM EVANS, of McKeesport, Pa., a prominent citizen, was born in Pittsburg, Pa., in 1852, and is the son of the late John Evans and his wife, Jane. Mr. Evans was educated in the public schools of his native city, and during the Civil war sold papers to support his widowed mother, his father having died in 1862. At the age of eleven years, Mr. Evans began work in the Woods mill at Saw Mill Run, and four years later went with the J. Painter & Sons mill, in the thirty-fourth ward, Pittsburg. He remained with that concern until 1889, when he came to McKeesport and went with the National rolling mill company, and since has been engaged with that concern, with the exception of one year spent at Homestead. For the past twenty-five years Mr. Evans has occupied the responsible position of a roller and is highly regarded by his employers. He was married, in 1875, to Mary Swearer, of Brownsville, Pa., who died on Jan. 20, 1903, leaving two children, John H. and Effie. Mr. Evans is a leading member of the republican party, and was a member of the school board of the thirty-sixth ward of Pittsburg, serving two terms. In 1899 he was appointed a member of the water commission of McKeesport, and in 1903 was elected, receiving the unanimous vote of the city council, and after election, was chosen president of that board for a three-year term. Mr. Evans is prominently identified with a number of the leading fraternal orders, being a Knight Templar Mason and Shriner, a member of the B. P. O. Elks and the Heptasophs, and is a contributing member of the Methodist church. Mr. Evans is a man of genuine worth, who has succeeded in the world by his own efforts, and is a striking example of what ability and energy may accomplish under a republican form of government.

JOHN R. ROMINE, civil engineer, son of Charles and Clarisa Romine, was born in New Jersey in 1849. He was educated in the public schools and at Stockton academy, and then learned civil engineering, at which he has since continued. He went to Missouri in 1870, worked there a while, and then was employed in various places until 1885. In that year he came to McKeesport and formed a partnership with E. J. Taylor, under the name of Taylor & Romine. The partnership was dissolved in 1898, but the name continues. Mr. Romine has been successful in his profession and has had charge of various important engineering works. He and his wife reside in the third ward, McKeesport. They have one daughter, Louise. Mrs. Romine was formerly Miss Mary J. Balliett, and was a daughter of the late John Balliett. Mr. Romine is a member of the McKeesport lodge, No. 136, B. P. O. Elks, the Heptasophs and Ben-Hur. He is a member of the board of directors of the McKeesport and Versailles cemetery association. Mr. Romine was borough engineer of McKeesport from 1887 to 1889. In political belief he is a republican.

WESLEY C. SOLES, real estate dealer, now, with an interesting family, occupying a cozy and comfortable home at the corner of Penn avenue and Locust street, was born in McKeesport, Pa., in 1848, son of Lewis and Catherine Soles, who settled in McKeesport in 1830. W. C. Soles, whose name heads this article, was educated in the common schools; at the age of twenty he was attacked with the western gold fever, and made the trip by going in a small boat from St. Louis, up the Missouri river to the headwaters, or Fort Benton. After spending two years dodging the Indians and panning out gold-dust near where Butte City is now located, he returned to his native city and went into carpentering and contracting work until the spring of 1883, when he embarked in the real estate business, in which he has been very successful. His office is located at No. 507 Locust St., and is always busy. He is a republican, and was appointed in 1900 to take the census for the eighth legislative district. He is a member of the Masonic fraternity, a chapter member, a Knight Templar and a Mystic Shriner. He was married, in 1881, to Miss Emma Smith, daughter of Thomas Smith, of Wilkinsburg, Pa., and has seven children, namely: T. Frank, Eva L., Scott A., Charles W., Robert S., Louis C. and Cynthia Catherine. He is now and has been engaged in many of the business enterprises in the city.

ARCHIBALD D. McELROY, M. D., of McKeesport, Pa., a prominent physician, was born in Westmoreland county, Pa., in 1862, a son of Samuel and Elizabeth McElroy. Dr. McElroy was educated in the district schools, which he attended until his fourteenth year, and then accompanied his parents to Cleveland, Ohio, where he went into the converting department of the Cleveland rolling mill. Four years later he returned to Pennsylvania, attended the Ligonier academy for a term, and taught school for a session. Then he went to Ada, Ohio, and there attended the university during the summer, taught in the winter, and was graduated in a scientific course in 1887. Returning to Cleveland, he secured employment in the mill for one year, and then went to Braddock, Pa., as assistant ticket agent for the Pennsylvania railroad, for sixteen months. Later he was a train messenger for the Adams express company for a year. Returning to Cleveland, he was employed in the mill for a short time, then took the civil service examination and worked in the Cleveland postoffice for six months. He attended the Cleveland homœopathic medical college, was graduated in 1893, and for a short time practiced in Cleveland. Subsequently, Dr. McElroy removed to Apollo, Pa., where he remained for three years, and, in 1897, came to McKeesport, where he holds high rank as a general practitioner of medicine. He was happily married, in 1897, to Mary E. Jackson, of Apollo, Pa., to whom were born two children, Howard and Charles. Dr. McElroy is a member of the Royal Arcanum, the Junior Order of American Mechanics, Knights of Pythias, and the republican party.

DUANE P. SMITH, a prominent manufacturer of McKeesport, and for eight years member of the school board, was born in McKeesport, Pa., Dec. 12, 1869. He attended the grade schools, then the high school, and after graduating, took a supplementary course in a business college. Thus prepared, he began his successful business career, and since 1888 has been connected with the McKeesport machine company. In 1895 he was elected to the school board, and has served as school director continuously since that time, being for four years secretary of the board. He has also served on the republican city committee, and is prominent in local affairs. Mr. Smith was married, in 1894, to Miss Allie Reed, daughter of Samuel H. Reed, of Knoxville, Pa. He is a member of Lodge No. 109, Jr. Order of American Mechanics, and McKeesport lodge, No. 238, Royal Arcanum. Mr. Smith is a member of the Baptist church.

DAVID A. FOSTER, of the firm of Foster & Auld, furniture dealers, of McKeesport, was born in that city in 1874, being a son of A. D. and Amanda L. Foster. He attended the McKeesport public schools, and then took a commercial course at the Iron City business college in Pittsburg. After this he was employed by the Howard plate glass company, of Duquesne, for about six months, and then, coming to McKeesport, was engaged for several years by R. E. Stone, a prominent furniture dealer, and learned the business thoroughly, and then, in December, 1901, formed a partnership with V. A. Auld and opened a store at Nos. 523 and 525 Walnut St., where the firm is now in business, and doing well. In politics Mr. Foster is a republican, and at the last election was a candidate for school controller of the sixth ward. He was defeated by a majority of seventy-six votes. Mr. Foster attends the First Baptist church. He is a member of the American Mechanics, the Knights of Malta, and McKeesport lodge, No. 583, F. and A. M.

PHILLIP L. HOFFMAN, JR., was born at Dravosburg, Allegheny Co., Pa., Dec. 14, 1858, being a son of Phillip and Caroline Hoffman. He attended the public schools, studied for a short time at Duff's business college, and then worked for his father, who was a blacksmith by trade. Coming to McKeesport in 1875, he entered the employ of the National tube company as assistant time-keeper, was later promoted to time-keeper, and has served in this capacity ever since. On Sept. 1, 1891, Mr. Hoffman married Miss Hannah L. Nill, daughter of D. and Hannah Nill, and has eight children, Anna, Emma, Johanna, Phillip, William, John, Elizabeth and Frederick. He is a member of Lodge No. 44, F. and A. M., of McKeesport; Lodge No. 552, I. O. O. F., and Titus lodge, No. 207, Knights of Pythias. He is a member of the German Lutheran church. In politics Mr. Hoffman is a republican. His home is in the seventh ward, McKeesport.

EDWARD O. SEIFERT, of McKeesport, Pa., a leading dentist, was born in Jefferson county, Pa., in 1878, a son of Edward and Josephine Seifert. Dr. Seifert received his earliest instruction in his native county, and when quite young accompanied his parents to McKeesport, where he attended the graded and high schools. In 1897 he matriculated at the dental department of the University of Pennsylvania, and was graduated from that famous school in 1900. He returned to McKeesport, began practicing with Dr. A. C. Cope, and continued with him until July 5, 1902, when he opened an independent office in the Keystone building, on Locust street. Dr. Seifert now has a high standing among the dentists of western Pennsylvania, and has a splendid practice among the best people of that section. He is prominently identified with the Masons, being a member of Commandery No. 1, K. T., of Pittsburg, and Penn consistory, Valley of Pittsburg, S. P. R. S., thirty-second degree, and of the Mystic Shrine. Dr.

Seifert is also a member of the Theta Nu Epsilon and the Xi Psi Phi Greek letter fraternities, the Darby dental association, the First Methodist church, and the republican party. Dr. Seifert is a young man of sterling qualities, is making a decided success of his professional career, and stands high in the esteem of all who know him.

JAMES P. BLACKBURN, M. D., of McKeesport, Pa., a well-known physician, was born in Fayette county, Pa., in 1863, a son of the late John Blackburn and his wife, Margaret Irwin Blackburn. Dr. Blackburn attended the public schools, later the State normal school at California, Pa., and then the Jefferson academy, of Canonsburg, Pa., where he prepared himself for college, subsequently attending Washington and Jefferson college. He read medicine under Dr. Louis Sutton, of West Newton, Pa.; later matriculated at the medical department of the University of Pennsylvania, and was graduated from that famous school in 1891; to this he added a post-graduate course in the London hospitals. For one year he was located at the Allegheny county hospital at Woodville, Pa.; was appointed physician to the Western Pennsylvania penitentiary at Riverside, Allegheny county, and six months later became physician to the Pittsburg city hospital at Homestead, Pa. In 1893 Dr. Blackburn resigned that position to take up private practice, located at McKeesport, and has since enjoyed a large practice in that city. He has his residence and office at No. 313 Penn Ave., and ranks high among the leading physicians of McKeesport. He was married, on Sept. 24, 1896, to Emma C. Menke, of Homestead, Pa., and they have one child, Bernice. Dr. Blackburn is a republican, and served as school controller in 1898. He has been surgeon to the local hospitals, and also for the Pittsburg & Lake Erie railroad since 1894, and has rendered splendid service in those positions. He is closely identified with the higher branches of Masonry, having taken the Chapter and Knight Templar degrees, and is a member and trustee of the First Presbyterian church.

THOMAS H. VERNER, superintendent of the water department, McKeesport, was born in Westmoreland county in 1864. He came to McKeesport when a boy, attended school there, and afterwards completed his education at the Iron City business college, which he attended until he reached the age of twenty-one. Mr. Verner was for many years successfully engaged as a contractor in McKeesport, at first alone, and afterwards for ten years in company with his brother, S. S. Verner, and then, in 1898, was elected to the position which he has since ably filled. In politics he is a republican. He is a member of McKeesport lodge, No. 136, B. P. O. Elks, and is an enthusiastic member of the Masonic fraternity, in which he has attained the thirty-second degree, and is a Knight Templar and Shriner. Mr. Verner was married, in 1900, to Miss Minnie Hamilton, of Duquesne, Pa., and has one son, Thomas H., Jr. The family reside in McKeesport, in the fifth ward.

CHARLES AUSTIN RANKIN, M.D., was born in Mifflin township, Allegheny Co., Pa., Nov. 25, 1873, and has been a practicing physician in McKeesport since 1896, his office being at No. 1020 Walnut St. He is a son of William and Mary A. Rankin. William Rankin, for several years retired from active life, resides at No. 1016 Walnut St. He was born in Mifflin township in 1836, received in the district schools of the time such education as they afforded, and was a farmer until he reached the age of forty-eight, since which time he has resided in McKeesport. He was married, in 1859, to Miss Mary A. McClure, of Mifflin township, and has, besides the subject of this sketch, two older children, Howard M. and Mary E. Dr. C. A. Rankin attended the McKeesport public schools, graduating from the high school in 1892, and prepared for professional life at the Western Pennsylvania medical college, graduating from that institution in March, 1896. Coming to

McKeesport, he began a successful practice, at which he has since been engaged. On April 12, 1899, he married Miss Bell Allen, daughter of Mrs. Helen Allen, of Coal Valley, Allegheny county. Dr. Rankin is a member of the alumni association of his university, belongs to the Allegheny county medical society, and is a member of the staff of the McKeesport hospital. He is also a member of the Home Guards of America, the Order of Americus, the Knights of the Maccabees, Foresters of America, and Aliquippa lodge, No. 375, Free and Accepted Masons. The doctor belongs to the Methodist Episcopal church.

ANDERSON SOLES, of McKeesport, Pa., has passed his entire life in the city of which he is now an honored citizen. He was born in 1861 on a farm located in what is now the eighth ward, and is the son of Alexander and Catherine (Dunn) Soles. His father died in 1886, but his mother, who is a native of Scotland, is still living. Anderson obtained his education in the common schools of his native town, and worked on the farm with his father until the latter's death, when he succeeded to the estate. In 1887 he opened stone quarries on the old homestead, in a small way at first, but his business gradually increased until at the present time his operations are on an extensive scale. Besides operating the quarries, he is a contractor of stone work of all kinds and employs a number of men in the various branches of his business. He was married, in 1884, to Miss Molly Catherine Livingstone, of Johnstown, Pa., and three children have been born to them, viz.: David L., born in 1887; Herbert A., born in 1888, and Walter D., born in 1890. In politics Mr. Soles is a republican, and he stands high in the councils of his party. He has served two terms as a member of the common council from the eighth ward, after which he was elected to the select council. He was re-elected to this body at the special election in May, 1903. Both his business and his political career have been characterized by a strict attention to the matter in hand. Concerning his rules of conduct, it might be truthfully said that he is guided by the Biblical injunction, "Whatsoever thy hands find to do, that do with thy might."

FREDERICK H. COURSIN, a prominent real estate dealer, of McKeesport, is a descendant of one of the pioneer families of that city. His ancestors came originally from New Jersey. His grandfather, Peter Coursin, a carpenter by trade, located in Elizabeth in the latter part of the eighteenth century. His family consisted of three daughters and two sons: the oldest daughter married a Belum Grimes, of West Elizabeth; Catherine, afterwards Mrs. Hamilton, died at the age of ninety-nine years, two months and twelve days; Nancy, afterwards the wife of George Cunningham; Isaac, who was drowned in early manhood, and Benjamin, the youngest of the family. Peter Coursin lived to the extreme old age of 101 years. Benjamin Coursin began his business career in the boat yards of Samuel Walker, at Elizabeth, where he rose to be foreman and held that position for several years. He then formed a partnership with James Irwin and Richard Stephens as contractors and builders of steam vessels. The firm conducted a successful business until 1849, when the partnership was dissolved. Mr. Coursin then went to McKeesport and located on the Reynoldton side of the Youghiogheny river, in what is now the tenth ward of the city of McKeesport. There he erected a sawmill, and soon afterwards began the boat-building business on his own account. He prospered in his undertaking, and also became interested in a number of steamboat lines operating on the different rivers of the country. After the Civil war he was succeeded by the firm of Hommit, Milliken & Chrissinger. This gave Mr. Coursin an opportunity to devote his time and attention to the different transportation companies in which he was interested, the principal ones being the Northern Line packet company, which ran twelve large steamers, the finest on the Western waters, between St. Louis and St. Paul; the Pittsburg, Brownsville & Geneva packet company, and the Elizabeth & Pittsburg line. In each of these companies he was a director, and he was the president of the last-named for several years. At one time the Northern Line paid dividends amounting to fifty per cent. of the capital invested. The others also paid large dividends. Besides his shares in these lines, Mr. Coursin held an interest in several large steamers plying between Pittsburg and New Orleans, Cincinnati, St. Louis and other points. At that time Elizabeth township included all the territory at present embraced in the townships of Elizabeth, Forward and Lincoln, and on election days some of the voters would have to go several miles to reach the voting place at Elizabeth. On such occasions Benjamin Coursin, who was an ardent republican, would furnish one of his steamers to transport the voters of his party living along the river to the polls and return them to their homes after they had cast their votes. He died at his home in Reynoldton, in his eighty-eighth year. His wife was Christina Rhoads, the daughter of Frederick and Elizabeth Rhoads, who lived in a palatial stone mansion overlooking the Monongahela river, opposite the mouth of Peters creek. Benjamin and Christina Coursin were the parents of seven children—six sons and one daughter. They were: Isaac, Benjamin B., Frederick H., John McD., David, James P. and Mary E. Isaac, the eldest son, was engaged in several enterprises, first among them being the boat-building industry, in which he was associated with his uncle, George Cunningham. Later he was interested with his father-in-law, Mr. Wilson, in the milling business, at Bloomington, Ill. During the Civil war, and for some years afterwards, he was in the internal revenue service. Benjamin B., the second son, was at one time extensively interested in the coal mining industry, operating the Aliquippa mines in Mifflin township, now owned by what is known as the "River Combine." He was also the owner of the McKeesport Times, then a weekly paper, but now the Daily Times. At the present time he is the owner and manager of the Clementine bath house at Mt. Clemens, Mich., the famous health resort. He is also the owner of the Eastman hotel, the finest at Mt. Clemens. John McD., the fourth son, enlisted in early manhood in Company I, 9th Pennsylvania reserve corps, but died about 1864 from lung trouble, brought on by a severe cold. David died in his infancy, and James P., the youngest son, is now the proprietor of the popular Ringgold hotel in McKeesport. The daughter is now Mrs. B. D. Downey, of New Philadelphia, Ohio, and is interested with her brother in real estate transactions. Frederick H. Coursin, the third son of the family, began business as a coal operator in the sixties. In this business he met with success and abandoned it only to go into the banking business with his father. They opened the first bank in McKeesport, which, after a number of years, was sold to the Commercial banking company, of Pittsburg, and operated as a branch of that institution. After a few years it was reorganized as the First National bank of McKeesport, and it is one of the strongest financial institutions in western Pennsylvania. Mr. Coursin is at present engaged in buying and selling real estate. He is one of the large property owners of the city, and his office, at No. 519 Market St., is one of the leading real estate marts of McKeesport. Mr. Coursin married Miss Louise, the daughter of Robert and Augusta (Von Sabach) Forsythe. Mrs. Coursin's mother is a native of Saxe-Coburg-Gotha, Germany. To this marriage there were born ten children, viz.: Harry, Frederick and Edna, deceased; William, now in charge of an engineering corps on the Wabash railroad, and stationed at Bridgeville; George, who is in the real estate business at Glassport; Augusta, now the wife of William Larmer, the representative of the Westinghouse company at Manchester, England; Sarah F., at home, a teacher in the McKeesport schools; Ruth D., now attending art school in Pittsburg; John B., a graduate of Staunton military academy and preparing himself for a surveyor, and Martha J., attending school and living at home with her parents. Mr. Coursin is a member of the Methodist Episcopal church of McKeesport, and all his transactions have been characterized by his uprightness and fair dealing.

WILLIAM DEWEESE FAWCETT, of McKeesport, Pa., a leading dentist, was born in the city where he now resides on Feb. 8, 1870, a son of Thomas R. and Katherine B. Fawcett. Dr. Fawcett accompanied his parents to Pittsburg when only one year of age, and was educated in the elementary branches at the Birmingham school, on the South Side. Then for one year he clerked in a shoe store, later went with the Oliver wire company to learn the machinist trade, and received his certificate as a machinist on May 8, 1890. Dr. Fawcett remained with that concern for seven years, and became foreman of the steam-fitting department. While occupying that position he attended the Iron City college in the evenings, and on Oct. 4, 1897, matriculated at the dental department of the Western University of Pennsylvania. He prosecuted his studies there with great vigor, achieved high standing in his classes, and during his vacations worked at his trade to secure funds for the needs of the succeeding year. He was graduated on April 4, 1899, and a short time afterwards was licensed to practice by the

State board of examiners. Dr. Fawcett also holds a certificate from the State of Ohio, and is a graduate of the Pittsburg school of anatomy. He has practiced his profession with much success since Oct. 15, 1899, maintains splendidly-equipped offices in the Dittmer block, on Fifth avenue, McKeesport, and has a large and lucrative practice. Dr. Fawcett was married, on Oct. 2, 1902, to Eliza Ann, daughter of J. William and Sarah E. Mitchell, of Elizabeth, Pa., and their wedded life has been one of ideal felicity. Dr. Fawcett is a member of the Psi Omega fraternity, the Odontological society of western Pennsylvania, the alumni association of the Western University of Pennsylvania, the Masons, the First Methodist church, and the republican party. Dr. Fawcett and his wife are very popular, and are prominent in the social circles of McKeesport.

REV. KALMAN KOVATS, pastor of St. Stephen's (Magyar) Roman Catholic church, McKeesport, was born in Hungary in 1863. He received a liberal education in the schools of his native country, was a professor there two years, for six years a minister, and for three years editor of a political newspaper. Coming to America in 1899, he took charge of St. Stephen's parish, and has had charge since then. He has also been instrumental in organizing many churches in various parts of the country. Besides his ministerial duties, Rev. Kalman Kovats is editor and manager of the Magyarok Csillaga, a paper that has a wide circulation among the Magyars throughout America. The paper is now four years old. Father Kovats' church has a membership of about 1,500, and the house of worship, which was dedicated in August, 1901, cost approximately $50,000, which bespeaks the greatest liberality on the part of the congregation. Andrew Carnegie, who is interested in the Magyars, recently offered to donate $1,500 toward a church organ, if the congregation would duplicate the amount. Father Kovats, with characteristic energy, started out immediately in search of contributions, and in a comparatively short time raised enough money so that the congregation might fulfill its part of the contract.

JAMES W. DUNCAN, superintendent of the butt-weld department of the National tube company at McKeesport, is a young man who has, in a comparatively short time, risen by his own efforts to a position in which he has charge of 900 men. Mr. Duncan was born in McKeesport in 1874, son of George and Mary Duncan, was educated in the McKeesport public schools, and went to work in the piping department of the National tube company. Later he became millwright, and after that was promoted to his present responsible position. His home is in the fourth ward, McKeesport. He is a member of Titus lodge, No. 207, Knights of Pythias.

JOHN K. SKELLEY, indisputably the leading merchant of McKeesport, and well it can be said of the Monongahela valley, has had a varied and deeply interesting career. With untiring energy, perseverance and stable honesty, he has won for himself an enviable position in the healthy business world. Bright, entertaining and withal cheerful, even under the weight of a decidedly strenuous business career, Mr. Skelley is continually adding to his wide circle of admirers. Prominent and influential, his remarkable and most successful career is the guiding star for many a younger merchant whose ambition points to the pinnacle upon which McKeesport's merchant prince sits. Mr. Skelley is decidedly a self-made man. In tender years the bright-faced messenger boy, weary of a treasury, sought a more arduous duty. In the lad's mind's eye he believed he saw in the station of a printers' "devil" the first rung in a ladder that would lead to fame, but fortune's kindly hand led the boy from the printing office of John W. Pritchard, an able and conscientious editor, to the duty of a paper carrier at a salary of two dollars per week. During the boy's career as messenger for the Western Union telegraph company, he gained a valuable knowledge of the town and its people, and it served him well as a carrier of newspapers. He carried newspapers for a number of years and attended the parochial school. When about seventeen years of age, or in 1878, he left school and purchased a newspaper route, which he conducted with energy and profit for nine years, having at that time probably 3,000 customers. In 1878 young Mr. Skelley established a cigar store and took into partnership his brother, H. C. Skelley. The capital was small, but by commendable industry, patient perseverance and strict integrity, he carved for himself a way to a greater business career —great then, but exceedingly small as the mind of the merchant of to-day recurs to the struggling times of his boyhood days. In the course of ten years the young merchant saved sufficient money from the two enterprises to enter the dry-goods business, and, in July, 1889, he disposed of his interests to purchase the dry-goods establishment of Ferdinand Riber. His brother was at the beginning associated with him in the business, but upon his death, Aug. 29, 1889, Mr. Skelley bought the interest, and has since individually conducted the business. In 1895 Mr. Skelley moved to his present location, and has now the largest and by far the best equipped mercantile establishment in McKeesport. In addition, Mr. Skelley owns dry-goods stores in Monessen and Turtle Creek, and is president of the Skelley dry-goods company, which operates stores in Homestead and Braddock. He has a controlling interest in the firm of Skelley & Haney, McKeesport, and Haney & Co., No. 710 Penn Ave., Pittsburg. A new venture in which he has lately become interested is the Skelley & Haney furniture company, McKeesport, of which he is president. Mr. Skelley is a director of the First National bank of McKeesport, and is the youngest member of the board of that substantial institution. Besides, he is a director in the Union National bank of Braddock, and is prominently identified with banking institutions at Turtle Creek, Monessen and Homestead, and in other financial concerns. He is a member of the McKeesport lodge of Heptasophs, the National Union, Ben-Hur and other secret and beneficial organizations. He carries a very heavy life insurance. John K. Skelley was born at Latrobe, Westmoreland Co., Pa., in 1862. He is a son of Michael and Ann Skelley. He attended the parochial school at Latrobe for a brief period, and in 1871 went to McKeesport, where he has since resided. Mr. Skelley's mother and one sister are living. He was twice married. His first wife was Miss Elizabeth Kane, of Fort Wayne, Ind. By that union seven children were born, four of whom are living. In the fall of 1902 he married Miss

Anna Harvey, a daughter of Mr. and Mrs. Charles K. Harvey, of McKeesport, formerly of Greensburg, Pa. Mr. Skelley is now in the full prime of matured manhood, enjoying good health, possessing all the desired comforts of life, and surrounded by a happy family and a host of warm and admiring friends, who are justly proud of his success and his high standing in the town and who fully appreciate his great moral worth as a man and a citizen.

JAMES CAMPBELL, general inspector of the National tube works, is a native of Prince Edward Island, where he was born in the year 1838. At the age of fourteen he left the parish school and went to sea on a merchantman, but while on a voyage to the United States he left his ship, soon afterward engaging as a sailor on an American vessel. From that time until about the year 1870 he followed the sea, the last few years being passed as master of a ship. During the Civil war he served in the United States navy, and was for three and a half years with Farragut. He was present at the famous naval engagement in Mobile bay, was with the fleet at Galveston when Harriet Law was taken, and participated in the blowing up of Westfield. Part of the time during his service he was a petty officer, and was honorably discharged from the navy in 1864. Upon giving up a seafaring life, he entered the employ of the tube works, first at Boston, and later at McKeesport. Altogether he has been with the company for thirty-three years; twenty-two years of that time were spent in the finishing department, and for the last four years he has held the position of general inspector. He came to McKeesport while it was still a borough, and for eleven years was a member of the common and select council. Four years of that time he was chairman of the select council, and was a member of that body when the city government was organized in 1891. In politics he is a republican, and it was as a representative of that party that he was elected to the council, though while serving in that capacity he never allowed his partisanship to stand in the way of the public good. He is a member of the Grand Army of the Republic, Aliquippa lodge of Masons, the Heptasophs, and the Protected Home Circle. He is the son of Roderick and Isabella (Stewart) Campbell. His father was a native of Prince Edward Island, though both his grandfathers were full-blooded Scotchmen. After coming to McKeesport, he married Mary J., daughter of Richard A. Hitchens, of that city. They have six sons and two daughters, viz.: Roderick, aged twenty-four years; Hector, twenty-one; Edmund, sixteen; Lilly, fourteen; James, ten; Horace, eight; Laura, seven, and George, six. Roderick, Hector and Edmund are employed in the tube works, and the younger children are still in school. The long residence of Mr. Campbell in McKeesport, his efficient services in the select council, and his interest in all questions relating to the general welfare, combine to render him one of the best-known men in the city. His home is at No. 530 Olive St.

MATTHEW F. KELLY, assistant superintendent of the seamless tube mill, National tube company, at McKeesport, was born in Mifflin township, Allegheny county, Dec. 19, 1856, son of Thomas and Katherine Kelly, and was educated in the public schools. At an early age he began to work on his father's farm, after which he was employed for a time about the neighboring coal mines. For two years he worked as clerk in a general store, and at seventeen began to learn the machinists' trade in the Pittsburg & McKeesport car and locomotive works. He remained at this for about three years, and in July, 1877, entered the employ of the National tube company, at McKeesport, as an employe in the tool department. He was made assistant foreman of this department in 1879; seven years later, foreman of the axle department; in 1891, general foreman over the galvanizing thread department, dipping department and C. J. department; in 1896, superintendent of the lapwell department, and in 1897 was given his present responsible position. He has risen rapidly by dint of industry and attention to duty. Mr. Kelly is a member of Lodge No. 207, Knights of Pythias, and Royal Arcanum, No. 367. He is a member of the First Methodist Episcopal church of McKeesport. In politics he is a republican. In 1879 he married Anabelle Waltower, of McKeesport, and to them have been born seven children, Lillie J., Clifton L., Blanche, Calvin E., Enoch B., Anabelle and Maud C. Mr. Kelly and family reside in McKeesport, in the second ward.

FRED HELD, a well-known McKeesport barber, was born in Pittsburg, Pa., in 1863, and is a son of Louis and Katherine Held. In the same year the family moved to McKeesport, where Mr. Held was educated in the public schools and at the Normal academy. His father being a barber, Fred Held learned that trade, and, upon his father's retiring in 1886, succeeded to the business, in which he has been successfully engaged ever since at No. 420 Market St. On Feb. 12, 1888, Mr. Held married Miss Anna Dietrich, daughter of Alex. and Lena Dietrich. They have four children, Fred J., Louis A., Amelia K. and Anna H. The family reside in the first ward, McKeesport. In politics Mr. Held is a republican, and in religious affiliation a member of the German Lutheran church. He belongs to the Woodmen of the World.

JOSEPH B. CLIFFORD, M. D., of McKeesport, Pa., a prominent physician, was born in Westmoreland county, Pa., in 1864, and is the son of the late C. M. Clifford. He was educated in the district schools of his native county and at the Ligonier academy. On leaving school, he taught in his home county for two years, and then for six years was engaged in commercial pursuits. In 1891 he matriculated at the Homœopathic college, and the same year went to the medical department of Wooster university, the following year attended the Cleveland university of medicine, and was graduated from that institution in 1893. On graduating, Dr. Clifford came to McKeesport, and has since successfully practiced his profession in that city. In 1903 he, in company with two other gentlemen, purchased the Dunshee block at Nos. 512 and 514 Fifth Ave., and are remodeling that structure for the McKeesport natatorium and medical institute, which concern has a capital of $150,000 and of which he is president. He was married to Lillias J. Greenawalt, of Scottdale, Pa., and to them have been born four sons: Charles, a student at Western Pennsylvania medical college; Elmer, a cadet at the Kentucky military institute; Carl and Joseph. Dr. Clifford is a member of the board of health, and has served as president of that body. He is a leading republican of McKeesport and an active worker for the success of his party. Dr. Clifford is one of the most prominent Masons of that city, having taken all degrees to and including the consistory, and is closely identified with that ancient fraternity. He is also a member of the Elks, the Royal Arcanum, the Heptasophs, the Woodmen of the World and the Independent Order of Foresters.

JAMES A. IRVIN, a knobbler at the rolling mills of the National tube works, was born in Mifflin township, Allegheny Co., Pa., in 1865. While still in his boyhood, he came to McKeesport, where he attended the public school in the first ward, which was then called Oakdale, working meantime in the Wood's mill, where he was employed for nine years. For the last sixteen years he has been in the employ of the National tube works, in the rolling mill department. He is now serving his second term as a member of the select council, representing the ninth ward. In the council he has been for six years chairman of the property committee, and is a member of the sewer, ordinance and fire committees. In politics he is a republican, and was elected to the council on that ticket. His paternal ancestors were old settlers of western Pennsylvania. His grandfather was born at Davis Island Dam, and his father, John A. Irvin, was born in Mifflin township, where he followed the occupation of coal miner for many years, and from which place he enlisted as a volunteer in the Civil war. He died there in 1889. His mother, Amelia C., was born at Peoria, Ill., in 1847, and is living in Chicago. James A. Irvin was married, May 10, 1888, to Annie, daughter of Conrad Dittmer, a prominent merchant tailor of McKeesport. Four children have come to bless the union: Elmer R., fourteen years old; Nellie, twelve; Annie, ten, and James A., four. Believing in the old adage that "a rolling stone gathers no moss," the subject of this sketch has always lived near his birth-place, where he has been honored by his neighbors and trusted by his employers. He is a member of the A. O. U. M. and the Heptasophs, in both of which orders he is a respected member.

CHRISTOPHER COLUMBUS FAWCETT, of McKeesport, Pa., a prominent citizen, was born in the borough of Birmingham, now Pittsburg, Pa., in 1837, a son of the late William Fawcett and his wife, Margaret. Mr. Fawcett attended the schools of his native borough until his fifteenth year, when he accompanied his parents to McKeesport, and there attended the public schools. He took a course of instruction at Meadville, and later attended a special course of study at Beaver college. In 1861, when twenty-three years of age, he enlisted in the United States army for service in the war between the States, and served with great distinction in that sanguinary contest. He was wounded at the battle of the Wilderness, and in front of Petersburg was so severely injured that he was incapacitated for active work for a year. He saw nearly every phase of the hardships incident to a military career, participated in many of the leading battles, and made a splendid record in that terrible struggle. After the war, he returned to his home at McKeesport, and shortly afterwards entered the china and glass business at Pittsburg. Subsequently he removed to Braddock, Pa., but continued his business at Pittsburg until 1901, when he disposed of his commercial interests and retired from active participation in business affairs. In 1896 Colonel Fawcett returned to his old homestead at White Oak Level, and there now resides. He was married, on Nov. 28, 1865, to Sarah E. Milliken, of McKeesport, and to them were born six children: William L.; Lula Belle, wife of George A. Kutcker; Annie R., wife of J. J. Boax; Mary Edna; Frank M., and Unwena M. Colonel Fawcett has been a member of the Masons since 1867, was charter member of the Braddock Fields lodge, No. 510, of which he was treasurer for fourteen years, and served as their representative in the Grand Lodge. He is a member of the Union Veterans' league and the Grand Army of the Republic, and active in his affiliations with those orders. He is a republican in politics, and is closely identified with that party. While residing at Braddock, Pa., he was one of the incorporators of the city, served as its treasurer for three years, a member of the council for two years, and for twenty-two years was a member of the school board, serving as president of that body for two years, and the rest of his service occupied the position of secretary. He is a member of the Coursin Street M. E. church, and has been superintendent of the Sunday-school in Braddock for twenty-eight years. Colonel Fawcett possesses a relic of the Civil war that he prizes most highly. It is a star from the original battle-flag of the 63d Pennsylvania regiment, which was organized in August, 1861, and mustered out in September, 1864. Immediately after the cessation of hostilities, Colonel Fawcett delivered to Governor Curtis the old flag, the staff of which had been shot away on several occasions, and the flag itself had been riddled by shot and shell, and as the governor prepared to receive this sacred emblem, a star fell from its tattered folds and alighted on Colonel Fawcett's shoulder. This was taken as a good omen, the star was carefully treasured, and is to-day among his most valued possessions.

GEORGE F. PASTRE, justice of the peace at Glassport, was born in Allegheny, Pa., in 1866, being a son of the late George and Mary Pastre. The father, a barber by trade, died in 1889, and for two years after that the subject of this sketch ran his shop. Afterward he went to Chicago, remaining there three years; then to Port Arthur, Texas, in the employ of the Guardian trust company. In the terrible Galveston flood he lost all he had, and returned to Pittsburg. A few months later he located in Glassport, where for a time he kept a barber shop, acting also as correspondent for the McKeesport Times, and in July, 1902, became justice of the peace. In 1903 he was elected to this position for a five-year term. Mr. Pastre was married, in 1887, to Miss Mary Bingle, of Pittsburg, and is the father of five children, viz.: Howard O., Anna May, George, Clara and Fred. He resides with his family in the borough of Glassport. In politics he is an ardent republican, while his religious affiliations are with the German Lutheran church. He is a member of Lodge No. 101, Royal Arcanum, and Lodge No. 367, Knights of the Maccabees. Mr. Pastre was educated in the public schools of the sixth ward, Pittsburg, and prior to his father's death, was for nine years shipping clerk for William K. Gillespie, a wholesale grocer.

ROBERT W. GORDON, JR., son of R. W. and Martha A. Gordon, is one of McKeesport's enterprising and progressive merchants. He was born in McKeesport in 1878, where he attended the public schools, graduating from the high school in 1895. He then completed his education at Washington and Jefferson college, and, returning to McKeesport, was employed in various capacities in the First National bank for five years. In 1902 he bought from H. O. Murphy the stationery business on Fifth avenue which he now owns. Mr. Gordon is a young man well qualified by education and experience for a business career. He is also prominent in politics, especially in local affairs, and is one of the leading republicans in the eighth ward. He is an enthusiastic member of the Masonic fraternity, in which he has attained the thirty-second degree, and is a member of the McKeesport lodge of that order. Mr. Gordon attends the First Methodist Episcopal church of McKeesport.

JOSEPH T. ROCHE, the well-known and popular painter and paper-hanger, was born in Clearfield county, Pa., in 1875, and is a son of Michael and Annie (McGinty) Roche. His mother died in 1899. Up to the age of fifteen he attended the public schools of Mt. Pleasant, Pa., where he received the greater part of his education. At the age of fifteen he went to work for Daniel Stratton, at the painters' trade. He remained with Mr. Stratton for eleven years, learning the painting and decorating trades in all the different branches. In 1899 he went into business for himself, forming a partnership with John P. Rotharmel, under the firm name of Rotharmel & Roche. The new firm established itself at the corner of Sixth avenue and Locust street, in the city of McKeesport, where a general business in house and sign-painting, paper-hanging, decorating, etc., is conducted. Joseph T. Roche is a fine example of a self-made man. Compelled by circumstances to forge his own way through the world, he accepted the situation, and by taking advantage of every opportunity that offered, he has kept pace with the march of events, and is one of the progressive men of his generation. In his spare time he has improved his mind by reading, and he has kept himself fully informed with regard to current events. He takes an active interest in affairs relating to the welfare of the city, and in February, 1903, he was elected to represent the fourth ward in the common council. He is now serving his first term in that body, and has already demonstrated by his ready grasp of public questions that the people of the ward made no mistake in electing him. He is unmarried, and the only fraternal order to which he belongs is that of the Eagles, being a member of Lodge No. 285, of McKeesport.

WILLIAM V. CAMPBELL, a prominent young McKeesport insurance man, son of A. B. and Eliza Campbell, is a native of that city, and was educated in the public schools, graduating from the high school in 1890. He then went into the National bank of McKeesport, starting as messenger, and was advanced from one position to another until, at the end of five years, he was teller. He then left the bank, and, in 1895, went into the insurance and loan business with his father, and has continued in that line up to date. He still, however, works part of each year in a bank during the busy season, his experience gained in the National bank making him a valuable man in an emergency. Mr. Campbell was appointed postmaster of the city of McKeesport March 2, 1903, took charge of the office March 19, 1903, and on July 1st the office was advanced from a second to a first-class postoffice. Mr. Campbell is a member of the McKeesport lodge, No. 375, F. and A. M., and the Knights of Malta. In politics he is a republican, active in local party affairs, and a man of great influence in the community. He is a member of the Fifth Avenue Baptist church and secretary of its board of trustees. Mr. Campbell was married, in 1895, to Anna J. Longabaugh, of McKeesport, daughter of George W. Longabaugh. Mr. and Mrs. Campbell reside in the fourth ward.

HARRY O. MURPHEY, manager of the Glassport coal company, of Glassport, Pa., is a rising young business man, who has already proved himself to be a man of sound judgment and business ability. He was born in McKeesport in 1874, was educated in the public schools and at the Park institute in Pittsburg, and then went to work in the First National bank, in which he filled several important positions. After seven years in the bank, he became manager of the Glassport coal company, and also of the Lynne coal company, located at Milesville, Pa., and has held that position ever since. He was also for a time manager of the McKeesport stationery company, but has sold out his interest in that concern. Mr. Murphey and wife reside in the second ward, McKeesport. Mrs. Murphey was formerly Miss Lynne Roberts. In politics Mr. Murphey is a republican. He is a member of the First Methodist Episcopal church of McKeesport.

CHARLES H. WALSH, assistant postmaster of McKeesport, was born in New Brighton, Beaver Co., Pa., in 1868, son of William E. Walsh; attended the school of his native town, and, in 1884, came to McKeesport, where he took a commercial course at Wood's business college. He then entered the employ of the Singer sewing machine company, being located first at McKeesport, and then at Pittsburg, where he remained in the service of the company twelve years. After this he worked for a number of years for the National tube company, at McKeesport, as timekeeper, keeper of the pay-rolls, and in various other important capacities. On March 24, 1903, he was appointed to his present position as assistant to Postmaster W. V. Campbell. Mr. Walsh is a prominent Mason, and has risen high in that order. He is a member of Aliquippa lodge, No. 375, F. and A. M.; secretary of McKeesport chapter, No. 282, R. A. M.; Mt. Moriah council, No. 1, R. and S. M.; member of Pittsburg commandery, No. 1, K. T.;

of Pennsylvania consistory, of Pittsburg, and Syria temple, A. A. O. M. S., of Pittsburg. Besides this, he is connected with various other organizations, being a member of the Knights of Malta, Woodmen of the World, is secretary of Tube City council, No. 378, Jr. O. U. A. M., and treasurer of Planet circle, No. 65, Brotherhood of the Union. In politics he is a republican, while his religious affiliations are with the First Presbyterian church. His home is in the seventh ward. Mr. Walsh was married, in 1897, to Miss Ida Gumbert, daughter of Capt. John Gumbert, of Belleview, Pa.

JOHN W. FAWCETT, M. D., of McKeesport, Pa., for many years a leading druggist, was born in McKeesport in 1854, being a son of William and Margaret Fawcett. Dr. Fawcett was educated in the primary studies in the district schools, and later completed his literary training in the Mt. Union college, in Stark county, Ohio. He then matriculated at the Jefferson medical college, of Philadelphia, Pa., and was graduated from that noted seat of learning in 1877. He practiced his profession with much success at Pine Run, Pa., for four years, and then was compelled to take a vacation for two years on account of his impaired physical condition. In 1882 he opened a drug store at No. 901 Fifth Ave., McKeesport, and prospered in that business until 1903, when he disposed of his stock of drugs to Miles Richards, now devoting his attention to his private interests. Dr. Fawcett was married, in 1880, to Mary P., daughter of Capt. John Gince, of McKeesport, and their wedded life has been a happy one. Dr. Fawcett is a prominent member of the republican party, and served on the McKeesport school board for eight years, two years of which time he was president of that body. He is a member of the Masons, the Junior Order of American Mechanics and the Knights of Pythias. He is also a member of the Coursin Street Methodist church and a trustee of same. Dr. Fawcett is well known in the financial world, and is a director of the McKeesport title and trust company, and also in the McKeesport tin plate company.

JOHN S. GORZYNSKI, pastor of St. Mary's Polish Roman Catholic church, McKeesport, was born in Koronowo, Province of Posen, Poland, April 25, 1869. He received a part of his education in the schools of his native country, and then coming to Pennsylvania, attended St. Vincent's college from 1886 until 1887. He then spent a year at Cyrill and Methodins Polish seminary, Detroit, Mich., but returned to St. Vincent's in 1888 and finished his course there. He was ordained on April 23, 1893, and did his first ministerial work at Connellsville with Father Daniel O'Connel. Father Gorzynski remained there one and a half years, then spent two and a half years as pastor of St. Ladislas' church at Natrona, leaving the latter position to accept his present charge. During his pastorate at McKeesport, Father Gorzynski has remodeled the church at a cost of $12,000, and built a convent and parish house, and has endeared himself in the hearts of all his people.

DUNCAN MacDOUGALL, superintendent for the Pittsburg steel foundry company at Glassport, is of Scotch birth, but has lived in America since he was six years old. He was born in 1870, and came to Pennsylvania with his parents, the family locating at Chester, where Mr. MacDougall was educated in the public schools, and later went to work for the Standard steel casting company. He remained with this company eight years, and during that time was advanced from office boy to assistant superintendent. He spent a year with the Franklin steel casting company, a year and a half as assistant manager of the casting department of the Otis steel company, and a year in the employ of Shickle, Harrison & Howard, of St. Louis. His first position with the Pittsburg steel foundry company was that of eastern sales agent. Five months later he was made superintendent of the Glassport works, which are the largest steel casting works in the United States, employing

400 men. In 1893 Mr. MacDougall married Miss Elizabeth McClure, of Chester, Pa., and has two daughters, May and Elizabeth. In religious belief Mr. MacDougall is a Presbyterian, and in politics a republican. He is a member of the Masonic lodge of Cleveland, and I. O. O. F. and Knights of the Golden Eagle of Chester.

JAMES F. KEMP, of McKeesport, Pa., a successful business man and a prominent citizen, was born in Pittsburg, Pa., in 1866, son of the late Andrew Jackson Kemp and of his wife, Lucetta. Mr. Kemp was educated in the fifth and sixth ward schools of his native city, and on leaving school he became a clerk for D. P. Black. Two years later he went with Smith Bros. in the tin and hardware business, where he learned the trade in which he is now engaged, and remained with that firm for ten years. In 1889 Mr. Kemp came to McKeesport, opened a tin-roofing establishment, later added slate roofing, and now enjoys about the largest patronage of any institution of that kind in the city. His home and works are located in the tenth ward, at No. 405 Ann St. Mr. Kemp was happily married, in 1889, to Missouri Lemon, and they have had five children: Cordelia, Charles, Lucetta, Otto H. (deceased) and Missouri. Mr. Kemp is closely identified with the republican party and an active worker for its interests. In 1890 he was elected to the office of school director for a term of three years, then re-elected for a similar term, and served as secretary of the board during his entire service of six years. The next two years he was a member of the city republican committee, in 1901 was elected to the common council, and, in 1903, re-elected for another term of two years. He is a member of the Junior Order of American Mechanics, the Odd Fellows, the Knights of Pythias, the Woodmen of the World and the Masons. He is prominently connected with the Methodist Episcopal church, has served as a steward for fourteen years, and takes great interest in all works of the church. In 1898 Mr. Kemp admitted his younger brother, Andrew, as a partner in the business, and the firm of James F. Kemp & Bro. has prospered since its inception.

JOSEPH D. STEVENS, of McKeesport, Pa., dispatcher for the Pittsburg railroad company at that point, was born in Waterbury, Conn., in 1865, and is the son of John D. and Katherine Stevens. The family removed to Irwin, Pa., and it was in the parochial school of that town that young Stevens was educated in the primary branches, and later attended St. Vincent college at Latrobe, Pa. On leaving school, he secured employment with the Carnegie company at Scotia, and later was with the same company at Beaver Falls for four years. Mr. Stevens went to Allegheny city as motorman on the car lines, and in 1901 was appointed dispatcher for the Pittsburg railroad company in that city. He continued in that capacity at Allegheny city until 1902, when he was transferred to McKeesport, and since has acted as dispatcher for the Pittsburg railroad in that city. Mr. Stevens was married, in 1891, to Katherine Nagel, of East Liverpool, Ohio. Mr. Stevens is a member of St. Peter's Catholic church of McKeesport, and also of the republican party. Mr. Stevens is well known in the city where he now resides, and has a large circle of warm and faithful friends.

OSCAR R. DOUGHERTY, of McKeesport, Pa., a prominent brick manufacturer, was born in that city on March 2, 1860, being a son of Jamieson and Rachael Dougherty. Young Dougherty was educated in the public and district schools, and, on leaving his books, began to learn his present business. He was with Peter Sworner for five years, working with other concerns in the brick business until 1898, when he began his present business of brick manufacturing in the eleventh ward of McKeesport, and since has prospered at that location. Mr. Dougherty has been a member of the common council for the past five years, his last term having expired in April, 1903. He was married, in 1885, to Johanna Speelman, also a native of McKeesport, and to them five children have been born, viz.: Lila, Daisy O., Oscar, Jr., Charles and George J. Politically, Mr. Dougherty is an independent democrat, and is a member of the city and county committees of his party. His family attend the Methodist church, and are prominent in the religious and social circles of McKeesport.

PATRICK J. MURPHY, the well-known hotel keeper, of McKeesport, Pa., is a native of Mifflin township, Allegheny Co., Pa., where he was born in the year 1859. All the schooling he ever received was during the three years when he was from six to nine years of age. When he was nine years old he went to work for I. D. Risher, in what is known as the old Montooth mines, and between that time and his twenty-fifth birthday he filled every position about the mines, both below and above ground. During these years Mr. Murphy lived the strenuous life, being several times arrested for taking the part of his fellow workmen in the mines, which finally forced him to give up the business and seek a more congenial occupation. His mother died in 1874, while the family were living at Fort Pitt, Pa., and his father was killed in the fatal Camp Hill cut in 1875. This left him at the age of sixteen without the sympathy and advice of his parents, and since that time he has fought the battle of life in his own way unassisted. When he was barely twenty-one he was elected to the office of constable, and was re-elected annually for fifteen years. Three years after his first election to this office he opened a private detective agency in the city of Pittsburg, which he conducted successfully until 1895. In 1893 he started a restaurant and liquor store in McKeesport, which he managed until 1898, when he opened his present place of entertainment at Nos. 212 and 214 Smithfield St. Mr. Murphy is a republican in politics, and his party fealty is of the kind that never wavers. He was elected in 1901 to the McKeesport common council from the fourth ward, and was re-elected in February, 1903. He was married, in 1878, to Miss Gertrude K. Meyers, of Coultersville, Pa., and they have had seven children. Five of their children—Elizabeth, Mary, Emma Katherine, Gertrude and John E.—are still living, and two daughters—Annie and Sarah—are deceased. Mr. Murphy is a member of McKeesport lodge, No. 136, B. P. O. Elks, and of Pittsburg Aerie, No. 76,

Fraternal Order of Eagles. Whatever degree of success he may have obtained is due to his energy and inherent force of character. Thrown upon the world at an early age, with a limited education, he has met and overcome obstacles as they presented themselves with a courage that is highly commendable. In business, in political circles and in his fraternal organizations, he has made friends by his good nature, which is almost proverbial, and by a steadfast adherence to correct principles.

EDWARD J. STEBICK, attorney, at No. 422 Fifth Ave., Pittsburg, with a night office at No. 721 Braddock Ave., Braddock, was born at Lock Haven, Pa., Jan. 6, 1866. His father, John Stebick, was born near Regensburg, Bavaria, Oct. 11, 1841, son of Adam John and Margaret (Fisher) Stebick. Adam J. Stebick served as bodyguard for King Ludwig while in Bavaria, and in 1844 moved to America and located at St. Mary's. Here his son, John Stebick, learned the carriage and wagon-makers' trade, and was engaged at this occupation in St. Mary's fifteen years before moving to Braddock, twenty-six years ago. In Braddock, John Stebick kept a wagon shop at No. 735 Braddock Ave. for many years, until the property became too valuable to be used in that way, and a business block was erected in place of the shop. Mr. Stebick has since retired from active business. Sarah (Cook) Stebick, the mother of our subject, was the daughter of John Cook, an old resident of Lock Haven. Edward J. Stebick, the subject of this sketch, was educated in the Braddock schools, and later attended the State normal school at California, Pa. He completed his education in the law department of the University of Michigan, in 1891, and spent the following year as principal of the Wilmerding schools. He began to practice law Dec. 12, 1892. On Sept. 7, 1897, Mr. Stebick married Bessie, daughter of George and Helen (Barber) Strauss, of Williamsport. Mr. and Mrs. Stebick have one daughter, Helen, born July 30, 1898. Mr. Stebick is a member of Golden Rule lodge, No. 30, F. and A. M., of Ann Arbor, Mich.; of the Royal Arcanum and Maccabees of Braddock. He also belongs to the American Insurance Union of Cincinnati, Ohio. In political belief he is a republican.

WILLIAM J. McCAW, for sixteen years in the harness business in McKeesport, was born in County Antrim, Ireland, in 1865, son of William and Annie Jane McCaw. He attended the schools of his native country until he reached the age of sixteen, and then, coming to America, located in what is now Carnegie, Pa., where he made his home with an uncle, and soon thereafter began learning the harness trade in McKeesport. He then worked four months for the W. Deweese-Wood company, and then, returning to harness-making, spent three years in the employ of S. O. Lowry. He then bought out his employer, and has successfully run the business ever since. His establishment is located at No. 232 Fifth Ave. Mr. McCaw was married, in 1888, to Miss Agnes Cherry, daughter of Thomas and Jeanette Cherry, of North Versailles township, Allegheny county, and has two sons, William W. and Homer W. The family reside in a comfortable home in the fifth ward, McKeesport. Mr. McCaw is a republican, and his religious affiliations are with the Presbyterian church.

JOHN P. ROTHARMEL, the senior partner of the firm of Rotharmel & Roche, painters and decorators, whose place of business is at the corner of Sixth avenue and Locust street, is a native of Fayette county, Pa., where he was born in 1868. His father was Peter A. Rotharmel, born in 1838, and his mother was Susan (Pool) Rotharmel, born in 1835. During his early boyhood, John attended the public schools of West Newton, Pa. He then went to the Westmoreland county schools for a while, and in 1885 started in to learn the painters' trade with Frank Markle, of McKeesport. He worked at his trade as a journeyman painter until 1892, when he started in business for himself. In 1897 he was married to Miss Margaret Kelley, of McKeesport, and has two children, Bertrude E., born in 1898, and Margaretta, born in 1900. In 1899 he formed a partnership with Joseph T. Roche in a general house and sign-painting, decorating, paper-hanging and kalsomining business. In politics Mr. Rotharmel is a democrat, and he takes a lively interest in all questions affecting the public welfare. He is a member of Camp No. 23, Woodmen of the World, of McKeesport, which is the only fraternal order to claim his membership.

PETER F. EMMERT, senior member of the firm of Emmert & Connelly, plumbers, at 504 Braddock Ave., Braddock, was born in Birmingham, South Side, Pittsburg, March 1, 1849. His parents, Philip and Christiana (Grintz) Emmert, having died when Mr. Emmert was a small boy, he was brought up at the W. A. Passavant orphan home in Butler county, learning the machinists' trade. When a little under sixteen years old, he enlisted in Company D., 77th Pennsylvania volunteers, where he served until the close of the Civil war. In the seventies Mr. Emmert engaged in drilling wells, and continued in this business for many years. He was married March 2, 1886, and has since that time resided in Braddock, where he owns a fine home at 212 Camp Ave., near the place where Camp Copeland was located during the Civil war. From the business of drilling wells, Mr. Emmert turned to plumbing, and has for many years been engaged in this trade. The firm of Emmert & Connelly, of which Mr. Emmert has been senior partner since 1900, does an extensive business in gas, steam and water fitting, and carries a complete line of plumbers' supplies. In February, 1897, Mr. Emmert was elected for a three-year term as mayor of Braddock, and during his administration made many friends, by his faithful and efficient management. In politics he is a republican. He is a member of Braddock Field lodge, No. 510, F. and A. M.; Shiloh chapter No. 357, R. A. M.; Tancred commandery, No. 48, Knights Templars, and Syria temple, A. A. O. of M. S. His wife, Alice Catharine Emmert, is the daughter of Henry and Maria (Pound) Carson. Her father was, for many years prior to his death, in 1896, in the harness business at 615 Braddock Ave., the business now being carried on by his sons, Clarence and Murill. Mr. and Mrs. Emmert have two daughters, Camilla Magdaline, a senior in Braddock high school, and Irene Eveline, also in high school.

CHARLES PARKER, head blacksmith for the W. Deweese-Wood company, now the American sheet steel company, is serving his third term as councilman in McKeesport. He has served two terms in the common council, and is now a member of the select council. Mr. Parker was born in England in 1867, educated there, and in his seventeenth year came to McKeesport with his parents, Edwin and Charlotte Parker, both now deceased. Here he worked ten years as a blacksmith for the National tube company, being employed after that for seven years by the Westinghouse company, and then came to his present position with the W. Deweese-Wood company as head blacksmith. In politics he is a republican, actively interested in local party issues, and fills a large place in the public life of McKeesport. His religious affiliations are with the Episcopal church. In 1888 Mr. Parker married Sarah Briggs, of McKeesport. They have five children, Herbert, William, Charles, Maude and Blanche. Mr. Parker is a member of the Foresters, Sons of St. George, and the Fraternal Order of Eagles. He belongs to the Amalgamated Association of Engineers.

WILLIAM J. KNOX, assistant superintendent of the National galvanizing works at Versailles, is a native of McKeesport, son of W. F. and Elizabeth Knox, and was born in 1861. When a boy, he attended the public schools, and completed his education at Allegheny college, Meadville, Pa. Upon leaving school he worked some three years in McKeesport in the drug business, and then became assistant foreman of the National galvanizing works at McKeesport. He was afterwards promoted to foreman, and when the new mills were built at Versailles, was made assistant superintendent, which responsible position he has since held. On Dec. 16, 1902, Mr. Knox married Miss Margaret Knox. He and his wife reside in Versailles borough. Mr. Knox is a prominent member of the First Presbyterian church of McKeesport, in which he holds the position of deacon. In political belief he is a republican. He is an enthusiastic member of the Masonic fraternity, being a member of Aliquippa lodge, No. 375, of McKeesport; McKeesport chapter, No. 282; Mount Marie council, No. 2; Pittsburg commandery, No. 1, Knights Templars, and Pennsylvania consistory, Valley of Pittsburg. He belongs to the Masonic country club, of Pittsburg.

WILLIAM HOWAT, superintendent of public works in Braddock, was born in Scotland, Oct. 20, 1841, son of William and Jane (Hamilton) Howat. He received his early education in Scotland and studied surveying there. In 1864 he came to America on a prospecting tour, but returned to Scotland the same year and married Margaret, daughter of John Brown, of Ayrshire, and, in 1867, came back to America, which has since been his home. Of the six children of Mr. and Mrs. Howat, three died in infancy and William, Jr., was killed at a railroad crossing in Braddock in 1891. Of the two remaining children, Elizabeth is the wife of Thomas Carr, superintendent of mason work at the National steel works at Youngstown, Ohio, and John, who married Miss Ida Boyle, of Braddock, is general manager of the Sharon tin plate mill. On coming to America for the second time, Mr. Howat became a surveyor for Bennett's branch of the Allegheny Valley railroad. From 1872 to 1877 he worked as assistant engineer in Pittsburg, and then was for some time employed in railroad survey work in southwestern Virginia. From 1889 to 1892 he engineered the Braddock sewer system and then went to Baltimore, where he superintended the building of the great tunnel which passes under the city for a distance of a mile and a half. Since 1897 he has been employed in Braddock, where he has superintended the building of several important engineering works and had charge of the grading and paving of the principal streets. He also planned the water-works reservoir, which was built in 1898. Mr. Howat, although not an ardent politician, favors the principles of the republican party. In religion he and his wife are Presbyterians.

THOMAS ADDENBROOK, superintendent of construction of the Carnegie steel company, of Braddock, was born in Birmingham, England, Nov. 24, 1847, son of Joseph and Harriet (Hughes) Addenbrook, and grandson of John and Elizabeth (Underhill) Addenbrook. Thomas Addenbrook was a dissenter, and suffered persecution on account of his faith. He was by profession a builder and contractor, and taught the trade to his son. Thomas Addenbrook came to America in 1870, going first to Detroit, where he remained four months, and then went to Pittsburg to construct the Lucy blast furnace. He afterwards had charge of the building of the Soho blast furnaces, and, in 1873, came to Braddock and commenced the construction of the Edgar Thompson steel works, now the Carnegie plant, and has been engaged with that company ever since. The plant has eleven blast furnaces, which produce more than 1,000,000 tons of pig iron yearly, and employs between 4,000 and 5,000 men. It is in the superintendence of the building of new brick and stone structures for this immense plant that Mr. Addenbrook's time is employed. Mr. Addenbrook was married in England, March 1, 1870, to Rebecca, daughter of James and Sarah (Powell) Tomlins. From this union were born: Thomas W. D., graduate of Oberlin college, class of 1900, now assistant to his father for the Edgar Thompson steel works and blast furnaces; Sarah Louise Edith, a graduate of Braddock high school, now teaching in the borough schools, and two children who died in infancy. Mrs. Addenbrook died in June, 1880, and three years later Mr. Addenbrook married Eliza, daughter of Matthew and Martha (Ross) Henning, whose ancestors were early settlers on Turtle creek. The children of this second marriage are: Rebecca, attending Braddock high school, class of 1905, and Gertrude and Clara Helen, also in school. Mr. Addenbrook is president of Braddock circle, No. 83, P. A. C., and is a member of Braddock Ben-Hur, and the Foresters of America. He is president of the Braddock board of health and the Braddock board of education, and has been a member of the latter body for the past thirteen years. In political belief he is a republican. He and his family are Congregationalists. Mr. Addenbrook has recently erected and occupied a beautiful home in Wilkinsburg.

WILLIAM BENNETT, chief of Braddock police, is a son of Elisha C. and Letetia (McFarland) Bennett, the former an Englishman, who married Miss McFarland in Ireland and came to America in the early forties. Elisha Bennett served in the Mexican war, and on the advent of the Civil war enlisted in the 19th regulars. Five of his sons also fought in the war. William Bennett, the subject of this article, was born in Allegheny City, Pa., Oct. 13, 1845. He attended the public schools, and in early youth commenced working in the Pittsburg glass factory, where he remained about two years, and also in other places until the outbreak of the Civil war. On Sept. 24, 1861, he enlisted in Company E, 54th Pennsylvania volunteers, where he served three years, and then re-enlisted and served until the close of the war. During this time he fought in the battles of New Market, on the Shenandoah, Piedmont, Lexington, Lynchburg, Winchester, Fisher's Hill, Cedar creek, Fort Gregg, in front of Petersburg, and at High Bridge, Va. At High Bridge, April 9, 1865, he was taken prisoner with his command, but on the fall of Appomattox and Lee's surrender three days afterwards, he was released. Returning to civil life, Mr. Bennett was married, July 3, 1865, to Sarah Ann, daughter of Jesse and Elizabeth (Hamel) Critchlow, both parents being descended from pioneer families of that section. After marriage he was employed at the Cambria iron works at Johnstown, Pa., until 1873, and worked in the Michigan forests until September, 1876. Returning to Braddock, he accepted a position in the Edgar Thompson steel works, where he remained until the strike of 1888. March 1, 1890, he became a patrolman on the Braddock police force, and on April 15, 1894, was promoted to the position of chief, in which position he has materially improved the moral tone and working qualities of the force by his executive ability and unassuming Christian conduct. To Chief Bennett and wife have been born thirteen children. Earl was drowned when eighteen months old, and Sadie died of scarlet fever at about the same age. Stephen M. and Daniel were both killed at the blast furnace in early manhood. Of the boys, William J. has been for nine years constable in the third ward; Joseph is roller in a wire mill; Albert is a mechanic in the steel works, and Herbert a machinist in the car barns of the Pittsburg electric railway. Of the girls, Lizzie is the wife of Thomas Hunter, a machinist of Braddock; Anna is the wife of William Rothrauff, a Braddock policeman; Jessie is married to John Lowers, assistant postmaster of the city, and Pearl and May are at home. In national politics Mr. Bennett is a republican. He is a member of Camp No. 1, Union Veteran Legion, of Pittsburg, and Major Harper post No. 181, G. A. R. He and his wife and three daughters are members of the First Baptist church of Braddock.

D. NEWTON GREER, principal of the Greer business college, which occupies the third story of the building at 837 Braddock Ave., was born in Mechanicsburg, Indiana Co., Pa., Dec. 26, 1859. He attended public schools in his native village, and the Lumber City academy, a classic school of high order, of which his father was principal. After graduating and teaching two terms in the public schools of Clearfield county, he removed to Westmoreland county and engaged in public school work, teaching two winter terms under Superintendent J. R. Spiegel, and employing the summer months in pursuing a special course of study at the Greensburg normal school. When twenty years old he graduated from Iron City college of Pittsburg, Pa., and was then for the next three years engaged in dry goods business at Scottdale. In October, 1886, Mr. Greer, in company with M. E. Bennett, organized a commercial and art school at Johnstown, Pa. The next year the homestead of the late Hon. D. J. Morrell was leased, the school was called the Morrell institute, and soon had an attendance of over 300 pupils, and became of more than local repute. After the sweep of the Johnstown flood (1889) little remained of the institute, but Mr. Greer, with remarkable energy, went to work again to build up the school, nor did he relax his efforts until the enrollment crept up to the former number. In 1895 he disposed of his interests, and in 1898 opened the Greer business college in Braddock, Pa., which is now thoroughly established and enjoys a reputation for thorough work, holding sessions every day and evening, except in the month of August. Mr. Greer was married, Dec. 20, 1893, to Miss Jean Harris, and has one child, David Newton, Jr., born Sept. 29, 1898. His first child, Collins Harris, died when four years old. Mr. and Mrs. Greer are members of the United Presbyterian church of Braddock, and Mr. Greer is an elder of that church. Mr. Greer and wife are both descended from old and well-known families. Mr. Greer's father, Rev. Joseph C. Greer, served as captain of Company H, 206th Pennsylvania volunteers, during the Civil war. On the fall of Richmond this regiment was one of the first to enter, and Rev. Greer delivered the first sermon preached in Richmond by a northern divine after the fall of the confederacy. James A. Greer, a full cousin of Rev. Joseph Greer, was recently retired from the United States navy with the rank of rear-admiral. Joseph C. Greer was the son of William and Abigail (Collins) Greer. Abigail (Collins) Greer was the daughter of Joseph and Abigail (Byram) Collins, and a descendant of Nicholas Byram, who was born in England, about 1610, and came to America in 1633, settling in Massachusetts. A descendant of Nicholas Byram, Ebenezer, Jr., born in 1716, married Abigail, daughter of Ebenezer Alden, and great-granddaughter of John and Priscilla (Mullens) Alden, made famous by Longfellow's "Courtship of Miles Standish." Sidney J. (Shryock) Greer, mother of D. Newton Greer, was the daughter of David Shryock, and sister of D. W., John T. and L. B. W. Shryock, prominent in business and educational circles. David A. Harris, the father of Mrs. Greer, has been for twenty years connected with the Cambria iron company, Johnstown, Pa. He is the son of William Harris, of Vinco, Cambria Co., Pa. His wife, Margaret (Cooper) Harris, is the daughter of the late Colonel James and Elizabeth (Boyd) Cooper, for whom Coopersdale, now twenty-third ward, Johnstown, was named. Mr. Greer has been before the public as an institute instructor and is frequently called upon to adjust difficulties in account-keeping. His pleasing address and gentlemanly manners have made for him many friends, and in the fields of past labors he still holds their respect and good wishes—for he is true to his friends and has a long memory for kindnesses shown him, being anxious to redeem all favors.

JOHN RINARD, a prominent insurance agent and real estate dealer of Braddock, was born March 4, 1840, son of George and Mary M. (Cogan) Rinard. George Rinard was a son of John Rinard, Sr., whose maternal grandfather was a pioneer settler at Bloody Run, now Everett, Bedford Co., Pa. The Rinards were early settlers at Long Meadows, near Philadelphia. John Rinard, the subject of this sketch, was reared at Johnstown, and was married there, May 19, 1864, to Lucinda, daughter of Matthew and Matilda (Row) Spigelmire, who were of German descent. The following children were born from this union: George, who died in infancy; James M., foreman in the steel department of the Edgar Thompson works; William E., who died when twenty-six years old, and Charles E., a graduate of the Bellevue hospital medical college, of New York, now practicing medicine in Homestead. Mrs. Lucinda Rinard died Nov. 24, 1890, and Mr. Rinard was married, Dec. 1, 1901, to Mrs. E. Euginia (Boyd) Flickinger, of Clarion county, daughter of Samuel and Mary (Thompson) Boyd, whose ancestors lived in Scotland. Mrs. E. Euginia Rinard's children are: Lillian, a graduate of Braddock high school, now in millinery work; Emma, also a graduate of the high school, at home; Quindara D., a seamstress, at home. Mr. Rinard was superintendent of the steel department of the Edgar Thompson works from 1875 to 1889, and for many years vice-president of the First National bank. He served for four years as school director, but has declined further political preferment. Since 1890 he has been in the real estate business with Samuel E. Stewart as partner, and occupies offices in the Dean building, on Library street, where he has built up an extensive and profitable business. Mr. Rinard is a member of Cambria lodge, No. 278, F. and A. M., of Johnstown, and also of the chapter of Royal Arch Masons there. He belongs to Court Pride of the Union of Braddock Foresters. In political belief he is a republican. He and his family live in a fine home at No. 400 Camp Ave. They are members of the Calvary Presbyterian church.

JOSEPH LOUIS CAMPBELL is the son of John and Rachel Campbell and a grandson of William Campbell, whose father, Thomas Campbell, came to this country from Scotland and during the Revolutionary war was, according to history, a messenger for Washington. William Campbell, son of Thomas and grandfather of Joseph L., was a veteran of the war of 1812, and his sons, with one exception, were all soldiers in the war of the Rebellion. John and Rachel Campbell, the parents of the subject of this article, celebrated their golden wedding, Jan. 10, 1897, at McKeesport, Pa., where John Campbell has charge of the bridge that spans the Youghiogheny river. Joseph L. Campbell was born in Jacktown, Westmoreland Co., Pa., May 16, 1858. He attended school only until he was twelve years old, and afterward worked in mines and mills until he reached the age of twenty-five. He then became solicitor for a daily newspaper and subsequently one of the proprietors of the Braddock Evening Times, his partner being the late Will H. Large. After Mr. Large's death, Mr. Campbell sold out his interest in the Evening Times and became a reporter and solicitor for the Braddock Daily News, assisting in placing before its readers the first issue of that paper. In 1893 he was elected justice of the peace for North Braddock by a majority of thirty-two over the combined votes of three other candidates, and was re-elected in 1898 and 1903 by votes over his opponents of four to one. He is now serving his third term in this office, having discharged his duties with marked ability and fidelity. He also does a considerable business in writing deeds, bonds and mortgages, in the management of property, insurance, and in the collection of rents. In politics Mr. Campbell has always been a republican, prominent in local party affairs, and has been for a number of years a member of the Allegheny county republican executive committee. He is a member of the Junior O. U. A. M., Knights of Malta, and Maccabees, is a past officer of the first-named organization, and during the administration of Stephen D. Collins, as State councillor, was deputy State councillor for the Braddock and Turtle creek valley district.

REV. O. H. PHILIPS, pastor of the First Christian church of Braddock, was born near Library, Allegheny Co., March 17, 1849. His parents, Richard and Sarah (Higbee) Philips, lived on a farm in that vicinity. His ancestors on the paternal side came to America from Wales about five generations back, while the Higbees were settlers of Connecticut as early as 1640. Mr. Philips was educated at the Millersville State normal school, and later took the non-resident course of the Wesleyan university of Bloomington, Ill., and holds the pedagogic degree of M. E. D. and honorary degree of A. M. He was superintendent of the Tarentum schools from 1873 to 1875, principal at Sewickly 1875–85, and headmaster of the Sewickly academy from 1885 to 1890. While still connected with the last-named institution, in 1889, he commenced the Christian ministry at Carnegie, where he founded a church of which he was pastor four years and a half previous to his call to Braddock, in October, 1893. The church of which he is minister now occupies a commodious meeting-house on Braddock avenue, at the foot of Fifth street, valued, with grounds, at $35,000, and has a membership of over 300. Since coming to Braddock, Mr. Philips has led a very active life, and has been the means of greatly reviving his church and the denominational interests of this section. He is first vice-president of the Western Pennsylvania Christian Missionary society, life director in the American Christian Missionary society of the Christian church, member of the board of directors of the Children's Home society, and an active worker in the Anti-saloon league. He also recognizes that there is good in the fraternal organizations, and is serving as chaplain of Braddock Field lodge, No. 510, F. and A. M., besides being a member of the Royal Arcanum and Braddock Home Guards. Rev. O. H. Philips was married, Dec. 27, 1877, to Minnie M., daughter of Felix Negley and Mary (Wilhelm) Humes, of Tarentum. The children of Mr. and Mrs. Philips are: Mabel, born Jan. 26, 1879, now teaching music; Eugene Negley, born Dec. 11, 1884, now in his senior year at Bethany college, and Dorothy M., born April 17, 1887, now attending the Braddock schools.

ALEXANDER M. SCOTT was born in Mifflin township, Allegheny Co., Pa., Jan. 18, 1851. His father, Thomas Scott, was the son of James and Nancy (Jamison) Scott, who were married in Ireland and came to America in 1836, and, after ten years' residence in Butler county, moved to Allegheny county. There James Scott died, July 3, 1862, at the age of eighty-three. His wife, Nancy (Jamison) Scott, died, April 30, 1883, at the remarkable age of ninety-six. The parents of James Scott were Thomas and Mary (Wilson) Scott, natives of Scotland, who moved to the north of Ireland early in the nineteenth century. Lucinda (Snodgrass) Scott, the mother of our subject, was the daughter of John and Sarah (Becket) Snodgrass. Mr. and Mrs. Snodgrass had five children, besides Lucinda: John S., Alexander M., William, Sarah and Elizabeth. After the death of his first wife, Thomas Scott married Maggie, daughter of David Moore. The children of this union are Lucinda, Samuel, Mary, Howard, Annie, Blair and Maggie. After fifty-six years at his home in Mifflin township, Thomas Scott died in 1902, in the ninety-first year of his age. Alexander M. Scott, the subject of this article, commenced clerking when thirteen years old, in a general merchandise store at Camden, Allegheny county, and in 1872 became managing partner in the Lysle Bailey company of that place. In 1889 he became managing partner in the firm of Allen Kirkpatrick & Co., wholesale grocers at No. 903 Liberty Ave., Pittsburg. The business, which was established in 1852, has met with unqualified success under Mr. Scott's efficient management, and has an extensive trade in a radius of 300 miles from Pittsburg. Mr. Scott is director and stockholder in a number of Allegheny county banks, is president of the board of control for the North Braddock schools, and an active member and worker in the United Presbyterian church. He was married, in March, 1885, to Margaret Bell, daughter of Allen and Rebecca (Bell) Kirkpatrick. The children of Mr. and Mrs. Scott are: Margaret C., born June 16, 1895, and Rebecca Kirkpatrick, born Feb. 26, 1901.

CHARLES B. GUTTRIDGE, a prominent tobacco merchant and member of the council of Rankin, was born in Akron, Ohio, Oct. 29, 1873. When only nine years old he began working in the mines, but, by strict economy and business ability, he was enabled to make a start in the world for himself, and now has an extensive and profitable tobacco business. In politics he is a member of the republican party, and was elected a member of the council of Rankin in 1896. He has held this position continuously since that time, and has proved himself a man of good judgment and sound ability. Mr. Guttridge was married, March 16, 1897, to Miss Emma Offenhauser, of Cleveland, Ohio. His wife died some time ago. Mr. Guttridge is a member of the F. and A. M., Knights of Malta, Woodmen of the World, and K. G. E.

HYATT M. CRIBBS, a prominent politician, merchant and real estate man, of Verona, was born in Armstrong county, Pa., June 12, 1865. His parents, John R. and Elizabeth A. (Mays) Cribbs, were both natives of Clarion county, Pa., the father born Feb. 18, 1830, and the mother April 5, 1832. They came to Allegheny county in 1870 and located at Logan's Eddy, where Mr. Cribbs engaged for three years in the hotel business, and later, moving to Verona, started a general store there. He remained in business in Verona until his death, which occurred March 5, 1897, the store being run for the last ten years under the firm name of John R. Cribbs & Son. In political belief he was a republican, was for several years a member of the Verona council, and also served as a member of the school board. Although not a church member, he was a liberal contributor to Christian work. John R. Cribbs and wife had five sons and five daughters, of whom four sons and four daughters are living. Mr. Cribbs was a grandson of John R. Cribbs, a native of Indiana county, and a blacksmith by trade, while his wife was a daughter of Thomas Mays, a farmer by vocation, and a veteran of the war of 1812. Hyatt M. Cribbs, the subject of this sketch, began his successful business career when only sixteen years old, and has ever since been engaged in business, with the exception of one year spent on a railroad. He attended the Verona schools in his youth, then took a course in Duff's business college. Mr. Cribbs' first business venture was in a store at Graver's coal works. He is now a member of the well-known firm of John R. Cribbs & Son, the business being in lumber, hardware and builders' supplies. He is also interested in real estate, being a partner in the firm of Cribbs & Allison, and has built thirty-three houses in Verona. Mr. Cribbs is an influential member of the republican party, was postmaster at Verona under President Harrison, and is at present serving his sixth year as councilman. He is secretary of the Verona board of trustees of the Methodist Episcopal church, and vice-president of the Verona bureau of trade. Mr. Cribbs was married, on Nov. 12, 1892, to Miss Ida M. Whitmore, of Wilkinsburg, Pa., and has three children, John R., Hyatt M. and Merrill W. He is a member of Verona lodge, No. 548, F. and A. M., Tancred commandery, Zerubbabel chapter, Pittsburg consistory, and Syria temple, Nobles of Mystic Shrine, and is also a member of Jr. O. U. A. M.

FIELDING D. CRIBBS, general merchant at Verona, was born in Armstrong county, Pa., Dec. 12, 1862; is a son of John R. Cribbs, but was reared in Verona, and educated in the Ceronia public schools. He was employed for a time in a steel works, and also worked a short time as a carpenter, but has spent most of his life in mercantile pursuits. His business has been, for the past three years, located in the store he now occupies, a well-equipped building twenty-four by sixty feet in size, of one-story and a basement, containing two large warerooms. Besides this, Mr. Cribbs has other extensive business interests. He is a stockholder in the Pittsburg wholesale grocery company, the Verona ferry company, and is also interested in the Vista Hermosa, a Mexican sugar company, the main office of which is in Chicago. He is an ardent republican, although never an aspirant for office. He is a member of the Royal Arcanum, Modern Woodmen of

America, Jr. O. U. A. M., and the Iroquois, of Verona. Mr. Cribbs was married, in 1888, to Miss Eliza Wilson, of Penn township, Allegheny county, and has had two children, Margaret (deceased) and Charles F. Mr. and Mrs. Cribbs are members of the Verona United Presbyterian church.

THOMAS LEWIS PARRY, a retired mill roller of Homestead, was born in South Wales, Feb. 6, 1837, son of John and Mary (Lewis) Parry, both natives of Wales. His father was for many years agent for a company for collecting rents, and also served some time on the police force. Thomas L. Parry was reared in Wales, and received a limited education in the common schools. When sixteen years old, he went to work as assistant at the blacksmith trade. Four years later, in 1857, he came to America, locating first at Tamagua, Pa., where he remained a year, and then at Danville, Pa., where he was employed for two years as a blacksmith. From Danville he went to Columbia, Lancaster county, where he worked for a short time at his trade, and then was engaged for six years as a roller. The next sixteen years were spent as a roller at Harrisburg, with the exception of two years, when he was employed at the same trade in St. Louis. He also spent one year in Ohio as a roller. In 1880 Mr. Parry came to Allegheny county, locating the next year at Homestead, where he has since resided. Until the strike of 1882, he was employed as a superintendent and roller, and retiring from the mill, was engaged for two years as a wholesale liquor dealer in Homestead. Mr. Parry was twice married. His first wife was Margaret, daughter of William and Elizabeth Williams, of Danville, who bore him three children: Mary, now Mrs. William Colgan; William John, and Elizabeth, now Mrs. David Evans. His second wife was formerly Mrs. Miriam (Evans) Morgan, daughter of Reese and Elizabeth (Jeffries) Evans, of Danville, and a native of Wales. Three children of this second union are living: Sarah, George and Miriam. Miriam is now the wife of Herbert Wiggins. Mr. Parry is a prominent citizen of Homestead, a member of Germania lodge, No. 509, South Side, Pittsburg, and a director and stockholder of the First National bank of Homestead. In politics he is a republican.

VICTOR C. KNORR, son of William F. Knorr, was born in Germany, Sept. 17, 1844. He came to America in 1850 and received his education in this country. He learned the druggist trade and followed this line of business for forty years, starting in Pittsburg in 1872, but retired in 1901. Mr. Knorr joined the 2nd New York volunteers in 1863, and fought in the Civil war until discharged, June 21, 1865. His record during the war was an honorable one, and he came out with the rank of sergeant. Mr. Knorr was married, in 1873, to Mary R. Stifel, of Cincinnati, Ohio. Mr. and Mrs. Knorr have four children: Rosa A., William A., Victor J. and May A. Mr. Knorr has been for many years a prominent republican of Braddock. He was for six years president of the school board, and has been secretary of that body one year. He is also sergeant of police and assistant secretary of the health department of Braddock. Mr. Knorr is a member of the Major A. M. Harper post, No. 181, department of Pennsylvania, G. A. R.; Royal Arcanum and Knights of Malta. In religion he is a Presbyterian.

RICHARD H. STARKE, harness manufacturer, was born in Saxonburg, Butler Co., Pa., Jan. 1, 1868, son of Frederick and Minnie (Helmbold) Starke, natives of Germany, who came to Saxonburg in 1838. The father died in 1886, at the age of fifty-six, but the mother is still living, at the age of seventy years. They had ten children, of whom eight are living. The paternal grandparents of the subject of this sketch, Ferdinand and Johanna Starke, came to Butler county in 1828, and spent their last days there. His maternal grandparents, Mr. and Mrs. John G. Helmbold, also came to America from Germany in 1838, and died in Butler county. Frederick Starke, although by trade a cabinetmaker, followed painting for a livelihood for many years. In political belief he was a republican. With his wife, he belonged to the German Evangelical Protestant church. Richard H. Starke, whose name heads this article, was reared and educated in Butler county, and at fifteen began to learn the harness-makers' trade. He spent five years at his trade in Tarentum, then engaged in the harness business in Saxonburg two years, and in 1891 returned to Tarentum and formed a partnership with his brother, E. C. Starke. This partnership being dissolved in 1895, Mr. Starke has since engaged in the business for himself, and has been most successful, his success being due solely to his own ability and perseverance. In politics he is a republican, and has served in the council three years. He is a member of Pollock lodge, No. 502, F. and A. M.; Lodge No. 240, Knights of Pythias, and of Tarentum lodge, No. 587, I. O. O. F. Mr. Starke married, on Sept. 21, 1892, Miss Ida C. Pfeil, of Pittsburg, and has had one son, Wilbur A., deceased. Mr. and Mrs. Starke are members of the Cumberland Presbyterian church.

CHARLES K. BRYCE, superintendent of the Homestead glass works, and one of the best-known and most popular citizens of Homestead, was born in Pittsburg, Pa., Jan. 21, 1852. After a common-school education, he became an apprentice at the glass trade, and after serving his time as apprentice, was employed as mould-maker and designer in the same trade with the firm of Bryce, Walker & Co., and worked for this concern several years. In 1879 Mr. Bryce established the Homestead glass works, there being associated in the enterprise with him his father, who was the pioneer glass-maker of Pittsburg, J. B. Higbee and J. A. Doyle, Sr. Mr. Bryce has been superintendent of the company since its start, and has made the Homestead glass works famous all over the country, while he has won for himself an enviable reputation as a glass-maker. In 1880 Mr. Bryce organized in Homestead an independent fire company, of which he has ever since been chief. The fire department is his particular hobby, and he has made it an organization unsurpassed by that of any city in Pennsylvania. Although a man over fifty years old, Mr. Bryce has lived temperately, and is one of the best-preserved and most active men in the vicinity.

FRANK L. OERTEL was born in Butler county, Pa., Jan. 19, 1872. His parents, Henry and Matilda Oertel, came to America from Germany. Mr. and Mrs. Henry Oertel moved to Pittsburg when their son was only a year old, and there Frank L. Oertel received his education in the schools of the sixteenth ward. In 1890 he commenced the painting and paper hanging business, and in 1894 engaged in contract work, in which he has met with encouraging success. He secured his present location at 149 Penn Ave., Turtle Creek, in 1901, and a few months later entered partnership with J. Herman Benner. Mr. Oertel was married, April 27, 1896, to Miss Myra Blanche King. Mrs. Oertel's father, Nicholas King, was the son of John and Mary Ann King, while her mother, Miriam (Jones) King, was the daughter of David and Margaret Jones. Mr. and Mrs. Oertel have three children: David Henry, born May 15, 1897; Myra Alice, born April 21, 1899, and Frank Nicholas, born Nov. 28, 1902. Mr. Oertel is tyler of Turtle Creek lodge, No. 613, F. and A. M.

RICHEY CALVIN HARRISON was born in Pennsylvania township, Allegheny Co., Pa., Aug. 24, 1864. His parents were George and Rachel (Bond) Harrison, mentioned elsewhere in this book. Mr. Harrison received a common school education in the schools of his native county, and for seven years followed the vocation of a stock dealer. Subsequently he was engaged in agricultural pursuits for four years with his father, and in 1892 began farming for himself. Mr. Harrison is a prominent man in his community, where he has served in several public positions, and is now president of Wilkins township. After serving one year on appointment as tax collector, he was elected to that office for a three-year term. He has also served a term as school director and one as township auditor. Besides the sixty-acre tract on which he resides, Mr. Harrison owns two houses and lots in Newtown, a suburb of Turtle Creek. He is a member of Valley lodge, No. 613, F. and A. M. Mr. Harrison was married, Dec. 16, 1891, to Annie M., daughter of Joseph and Sarah E. (Lenhart) Johnston, and granddaughter of John and Martha (Saam) Johnston. Mrs. Harrison's mother, Sarah E. (Lenhart) Johnston, was the daughter of Christopher Lenhart, whose father's family were pioneer settlers of Allegheny county. The children born to Mr. and Mrs. Harrison are: Adella M., born May 19, 1894; George Richey, born Jan. 5, 1897; James G., born May 14, 1900, and Mildred McIntosh, born Dec. 12, 1901.

GEORGE HARRISON, a prominent farmer of Wilkins township, was born near McKeesport, Pa., June 25, 1829, son of William and Elizabeth Harrison. William Harrison was of Scotch descent, son of John Harrison, but was reared in Pennsylvania, while his wife was a descendant of the pioneer Germans of eastern Pennsylvania. George Harrison received his education in Wilkinsburg, and was, for many years, employed on the river, where he learned the ship carpenter's trade. When about thirty years old, he turned his attention to farming, and has followed this vocation successfully for over forty years. He has served a term as supervisor of Wilkins township, and was for six years school director. For the past forty years he has been a member of Hailman lodge, No. 321, F. and A. M., of East End, Pittsburg. Mr. Harrison married, June 25, 1851, Rachel, daughter of Benjamin and Huldah (Key) Bond, of Philadelphia. Of the children of this union, William is employed in the Westinghouse plant in Wilkinsburg; George died at the age of forty-one; Benjamin is a rail straightener at the Edgar Thompson steel plant, Braddock; John W. is a machinist in Wilmerding; Huldah is the wife of Norman McIntosh, railroad clerk at Turtle Creek; Richey Calvin is a farmer of Wilkins township; Kate J. is married to George Elkins, of Braddock, and Oliver D. is employed at the Edgar Thompson steel works in Braddock. Mrs. Harrison died in 1890, and in June, 1892, Mr. Harrison was wedded to Mrs. Sarah J. Christy, daughter of John and Esther Dodds, of Youngstown, Westmoreland Co., Pa., and widow of J. W. Christy, of Wilkins township. Of the children of Mr. and Mrs. J. W. Christy, James William is a farmer residing near Wilkinsburg; Sarah Elizabeth is a seamstress at home; Mary Ellen lives in Wilkinsburg; Carrie A. died at the age of eighteen; Annie B. is the wife of W. Hodgson, of Turtle Creek; Laura May is at home; Susan Alice is a music teacher, and George Alvin is employed in the Westinghouse plant. Mr. Harrison and family are members of the Beulah Presbyterian church of Wilkins township.

FREDERICK KRAUTH, a retired butcher residing in Tarentum, was born in Germany, Sept. 28, 1826, son of Jacob and Ursula (Maisenbacher) Krauth, both natives of Germany, where the father died. Mr. Krauth and his mother came in 1847 to America, where two other members of the family had preceded them, one emigrating in 1836 and the other in 1843. The mother died in Natrona, Allegheny county, in 1860. Mr. Krauth was educated in Germany. On coming to America, he worked for a time in Louisville, Ky., as a cabinet-maker, and then learned the trade of a butcher, which he followed from 1849 until 1890. He was a butcher in Tarentum for over fifty years, and is by far the oldest butcher in that part of the country. He was successful in his business and amassed a considerable fortune. He was one of the fifteen who built the rolling mill at Canton, Ohio, and has been interested in many other business ventures. He was treasurer of the Glasgow oil company from the time it was organized until it went out of business, and was, in 1860, engaged in the oil business at Smith's Ferry, Pa. He was also, during the seventies, director of the First National bank of Tarentum. Mr. Krauth is now stockholder in the J. H. Baker manufacturing company, the Fidelity glass company and the National bank of Tarentum. He is also interested in the Building and Loan association of Tarentum. In politics he is a republican, and has served as councilman and cemetery trustee. Mr. Krauth was married, April 17, 1852, to Miss Catherine Faas, a native of Germany who came to America with her parents when about eight years old. Mr. and Mrs. Krauth have had nine children, of whom three—Charles, Matilda and Margaret—are living. The others were: Katie, Mary, William, Frederick, George and

Benjamin F. Charles has now succeeded to his father's butcher business. Mr. and Mrs. Krauth are members of the German Evangelical Protestant church, of which Mr. Krauth has been an elder ever since he came to Tarentum. They celebrated their golden wedding anniversary April 17, 1902.

CHARLES GOEDDEL, a prominent plumber and gas-fitter of Homestead, was born in Birmingham, now South Side, Pittsburg, Pa., Jan. 22, 1856, son of Philip and Elizabeth (Drum) Goeddel, both natives of Germany. Philip Goeddel came to America in 1844, and after a short residence in Pittsburg and Tennessee, returned to Germany and was married. In 1844 he brought his wife to America, and settled in Birmingham, where he was engaged for a short time in the saloon business, then became a gardener, following this vocation until 1874, when he retired and located at Castle Shannon, Baldwin township, Allegheny county, where he now resides, at the age of eighty. His family consisted of six children, four of whom grew to maturity. Of these, Caroline, afterwards Mrs. Fred Sanders, is dead, and three are living: Charles, Matilda (now Mrs. Gottlieb Kinley) and Henry. Charles Goeddel, the subject of this sketch, was reared and educated in Allegheny county, and has always resided in that county. He was married, March 6, 1879, to Kate E., daughter of Christian and Helena (Schmeltz) Abbott, natives of Germany, who settled in Allegheny county. Mr. and Mrs. Goeddel have had four children, of whom three—Gustave, Christian and Matilda—are living. In early life Mr. Goeddel served an apprenticeship as a plumber, but followed farming as a livelihood for three years after marriage. He located in Homestead in 1884, and spent the next eight years of his life in the employ of the Carnegie steel company. In 1892 he embarked in the plumbing and gas-fitting business, in which his ability and honest methods have won him a large and lucrative patronage. Mr. and Mrs. Goeddel are members of the First Presbyterian church of Homestead. Mr. Goeddel has served his city as a member of the board of education, and was for three years secretary of that body. In 1902 he was appointed councilman from his ward to fill a vacancy. Politically, he is a republican.

LEWIS N. MORGAN, city assessor of McKeesport, was born in Pittsburg, Pa., in 1864, but came to McKeesport in 1875, and has resided in the first ward of that city almost continuously since. He received a common-school education and was then for several years employed in the National tube works. In 1883 he went into the grocery business with his brother, Charles Morgan, and was engaged in this business for five years, then, from 1889 to 1897, he managed the Morgan hotel in McKeesport. He then spent two years in a trip throughout the western and northwestern part of the United States, and, on returning to McKeesport, was elected, in 1900, to the position of city assessor, an office which he has filled most creditably. Besides this, Mr. Morgan has served his city eight years as a member of the school board and was for one year president of that body. He was married, in 1887, to Miss Margaret Williams, daughter of Edward Williams, of McKeesport, and to them were born two children, a boy and a girl, of whom the boy is living. Mr. Morgan is a member of the Royal Arcanum and of Lodge No. 375, F. and A. M., and of the Heptasophs.

GEORGE W. SNYDER, a prominent grocer of Turtle Creek, was born in Patton township, Allegheny Co., Pa., March 2, 1858. His father, John Snyder, kept a general store at Export, Westmoreland county, for many years, while his mother, Elizabeth (Weaver) Snyder, was the daughter of Adam and Elizabeth Weaver, who came to this country from Germany. George W. Snyder was educated in the Pittsburg schools, and then devoted several years to agricultural pursuits. In 1891 he started in business in company with R. T. Henderson. He later purchased the store of R. S. Craig, on Penn avenue, and established the business in the C. H. Snyder building. As his business was constantly increasing, Mr. Snyder erected, in 1898, the two-story brick building at 143 Penn Ave., Turtle Creek, which he now occupies, and where he has built up an excellent trade. Mr. Snyder was married in February, 1882, to Eva, daughter of John and Mary (Glenn) Oyler, of Westmoreland county. John Oyler was a son of Jeremiah Oyler, an early settler of Franklin township, Westmoreland county, while his wife came from Armstrong county. Of the children of Mr. and Mrs. George W. Snyder, Elizabeth, born July 21, 1883, is now taking a course in music at Bethany college, in West Virginia; Ida, born Sept. 25, 1885, is also attending Bethany college; John died when seven years old; Harry, Homer, Frank and George W., Jr., are younger children at home. Mr. Snyder and family are members of the Turtle Creek Reformed church. Mr. Snyder was elected school director in 1901. He lives in a handsome residence on Show avenue, which he purchased in 1890.

JOHN F. LOWERS, assistant postmaster of Braddock, was born in Braddock, April 23, 1873, son of Samuel and Annie (Hunter) Lowers. Samuel Lowers, who was a son of Robert and Nancy Lowers, was born in Blairsville, Pa., Aug. 4, 1842, and was a painter in Braddock for many years, almost up to the time of his death in 1896. His brothers, James, Moses and Smith, were soldiers in the Civil war, as were also John and George Hunter, maternal uncles of our subject. His wife, Annie Lowers, is a daughter of George and Euphemia (McDougal) Hunter, both of which families came to America from Scotland about the middle of the past century. Of the children of Samuel and Annie (Hunter) Lowers, besides John F., the subject of this sketch, Nancy is the wife of Levi Goughenour, a merchant of North Braddock; Samuel B. clerks at Alexander Brothers' laundry; Euphemia is the wife of I. W. Duncan, a Braddock milk dealer; Mary died in infancy; Carrie is a bookkeeper; George is special delivery clerk in the postoffice, and Roy is at home. Mrs. Lowers lives at No. 228 Rebecca St., Braddock. Her mother, Mrs. Euphemia Hunter, resides with her. John F. Lowers was married, in 1895, to Jessie O., daughter of William Bennett, chief of police in Braddock. Mr. and Mrs. Lowers have one child, Ione, born in September, 1900. Mr. Lowers received a grammar school education, and, at the age of sixteen, began working in the steel mills, where he was a stationary engineer seven years, and for three years inspector of rails. He was appointed to his present position of assistant postmaster in July, 1892, and has proved himself a capable official. Mr. Lowers is a member of Monongahela council, No. 122, Jr. O. U. A. M., and is chairman of the board of directors of that organization; financial secretary of the Knights of the Ancient Essenic order; member of the Edgar Thompson council of the Royal Arcanum. He is president of the North Braddock volunteer fire department, chairman of the auditors of North Braddock, and treasurer of the John Dalzell republican club of that city.

MATTHEW L. McCLURE, a prominent architect of Homestead, is a brother of Daniel R. McClure, and a son of Abdiel and Anne (Risher) McClure. The genealogy of the McClure family is given in another place in this book, in connection with the life of Daniel R. McClure. Matthew L. McClure was born on the site where Homestead now stands, Dec. 24, 1841, and was reared and educated in Mifflin township. At the age of sixteen he began as apprentice at the carpenter trade under his father, and continued at this vocation until Sept. 28, 1862, when he became a soldier in the Civil war, enlisting as a private in Company H, 14th Pennsylvania cavalry, where he served until the close of the war, being honorably discharged May 30, 1865. During the war he fought with distinction in the battles of Rocky Gap, Droop mountain, Winchester, Martinsburg, Strausburg, Lynchburg and others. He was present at the burning of Chambersburg, and was among those who pursued and punished those who were responsible for the burning of that city. After his return home, Mr. McClure was for three years engaged in the manufacture of boxes in Pittsburg, returning to his vocation as a carpenter, which he followed for several years in Erie county. About 1878 he became a contractor and builder, and was successfully engaged in this work in Homestead until 1888. Since then he has given all his attention to his profession as an architect, and has met with flattering success. Mr. McClure designed the First National bank building, the McClure building and many of the finest residences in Homestead, and his field takes in all territory along the Monongahela river as far as Monongahela

City. Mr. McClure, in 1866, married Hannah S., daughter of Rev. James F. and Mary Reed, of Union City, Pa., and has two children, Abdiel Reed, associated in business with his father, and Florence L., now Mrs. Amos E. Gillespie. He also has two grandchildren, Helen McClure Gillespie and James Reed Gillespie. Mr. McClure and family are members of the Presbyterian church, of which Mr. McClure has been for several years an elder. He is a member of Alexander Hayes post, No. 3, G. A. R., of Pittsburg, and Encampment No. 1, Union Veteran legion, of Pittsburg. In politics he is a republican.

GEORGE JACOBS, real estate and insurance agent at Homestead, was born in Franklin county, Pa., Aug. 10, 1850. His parents, Adam and Charlotte Jacobs, were natives of Germany who came to America and located in Franklin county in 1844, where Adam Jacobs followed his vocation as a shoemaker until 1850, and then moved with his family to White county, Ill., where he was a farmer up to the time of his death, in 1852. He left a widow and six children: Adam, Nicholas (deceased), Charlotte (deceased), Catherine (Mrs. William Briggs), George and Barbara (deceased). After the father's death, the family returned to Franklin county, removing later to Homestead, where Mrs. Jacobs, then the widow of Jacob Kohler, died in 1886. After a common-school education in the public schools, George Jacobs became an apprentice at the bakers' trade, at which he served with one firm for three years, and then worked as an employe of the same firm for four years more. Embarking in business for himself, in 1874, on the South Side, Pittsburg, he conducted a bakery there for eight years, and, in 1882, started a similar business at Homestead, which he maintained for twelve years. From 1894 to 1902 Mr. Jacobs kept one of the largest groceries in Homestead. He has recently given his attention to real estate and insurance, and is a member of the firm of Jacobs & Blackley. In 1871 Mr. Jacobs married Emma C., daughter of John Greemroth. Of five children born of this union, two are living, Ella C. and Florence F. Mr. and Mrs. Jacobs are members of the Lutheran church. Mr. Jacobs is a member of Homestead lodge, No. 582, F. and A. M.; Homestead lodge,

No. 355, A. O. U. W.; Boaz council, No. 814, R. A., and Amity conclave, No. 96, Heptasophs. He has been a member of the Homestead school board for the past nine years, and secretary of that organization for the past two years. He is president of the Homestead business men's association, and of the borough council of Homestead, in which he is serving his first term. In politics he is an ardent republican.

JOHN HAYES, station agent of the P. C. & Y. railroad, at Carnegie, was born in Belmont county, Ohio, April 14, 1861. His parents were Dennis and Catherine (Kelley) Hayes, natives of Ireland, who came to Ohio in the latter forties, and were married at Steubenville, Ohio, in 1853. After a short residence in Steubenville, they moved to West Wheeling, Ohio, and in 1868 to Beaver, Pa. At both places Mr. Hayes was employed as section boss for the Cleveland & Pittsburg railway, being employed in the same capacity for the same railroad over forty years. He died, March 1, 1902, when seventy-five years old, and his wife, Dec. 30, 1895, at the age of sixty-six. Both were prominent and well-known people, and active members of the Roman Catholic church. Eight children were born to Mr. and Mrs. Dennis Hayes. Of these, William died when twenty-three years old, and Dennis in infancy. Of the surviving children, besides John, the subject of this sketch, Catherine is now the wife of James Mahoney, a member of the police force at Allegheny; James, a resident of Wellsville, Ohio, is supervisor in the employ of the C. & P. R. R. Co.; Mary is now Mrs. James O'Grady, of Wellsville, Ohio.; Johanna is now Mrs. Cornelius Cain, of Beaver, Pa., and Dennis (the second of that name) is foreman in a Pittsburg mill. John Hayes attended school when a boy in Beaver county, Pa., and after school days worked on the section with his father for three years. He became station agent at Beaver, Pa., where he remained one year, and in 1884 came as station agent to Mansfield, now Carnegie. This position he has held in Carnegie nineteen years, and his faithful attention to duty and uniform courtesy have won him the confidence of his employers and the good-will and esteem of the community. On June 10, 1886,

Mr. Hayes was married to Miss Mary Sullivan, youngest daughter of Michael and Julia Sullivan, natives of Ireland, both deceased. One sister of Mrs. Hayes, Catherine, afterwards Mrs. Daniel Carey, is now deceased, but a brother, Timothy, who lives at Delta, Col., and one sister, Julia, now Mrs. Andrew Miller, of Douglas, Ariz., are living. Mr. and Mrs. John Hayes are the parents of ten children, all living: Catherine, William E., John L., Mary, Nellie, Margaret, Joseph, Elsie, Sullivan and Geraldine. All but the three youngest, Joseph, Elsie and Geraldine, are in school. Mr. and Mrs. Hayes are members of St. Luke's Roman Catholic church. Mr. Hayes is a prominent member of the Catholic Mutual Benefit association, of which he has been president, secretary and financial secretary. He is also a member of the Knights of Columbus.

ARTHUR E. ROOSE, a prominent physician of East Pittsburg, was born in Westmoreland county, Pa., Nov. 1, 1869, son of Henry Noah and Malinda (Trump) Roose. Henry N. was the son of Henry and Sarah (Haines) Roose, German pioneers who settled first in Ohio and later moved to Westmoreland county. His wife was the daughter of John and Hettie (Zuck) Trump, who came from Germany to Westmoreland county in the early part of the last century. Dr. Roose graduated from the Greensburg seminary in 1892, and received his diploma from the Jefferson medical college of Philadelphia in 1895. Soon after graduation he located in East Pittsburg, then a hamlet of about 300 inhabitants. The population has now grown to 4,500, and the doctor's practice has kept pace with the growth of the city. In August, 1891, he commenced the erection of his beautiful brick residence and office building, which is centrally located on Linden avenue. Dr. Roose was married, March 17, 1895, to Lena, daughter of John C. and Hannah (Kintigh) Fox, both of Mt. Pleasant, Westmoreland county. The children born of this union are: Robert Lisle, born Sept. 17, 1896, and Arthur Eugene, born July 3, 1901. Dr. Roose and his wife are members of the First United Brethren in Christ church. The congregation of this church is now erecting a neat $15,000 building in which to worship. The doctor is a member of St. John's lodge,

No. 487, I. O. O. F.; Court Busy Bee, No. 174, Foresters of America, and of the Turtle Creek lodge, Knights of Maccabees. Dr. Roose has been too busy with his profession to give much time to politics, but was prevailed upon to serve as councilman, and elected, in March, 1902, for a three-year term, is proving himself an able legislator, being president of the council.

HAMILTON MacILVANE BLACKLEY, of the firm of Jacobs & Blackley, real estate, insurance and mortgage brokers, was born in Pitt township, now thirteenth ward, Pittsburg, Nov. 10, 1862, son of Joseph and Isabella (Cokain) Blackley. His paternal grandfather was James Blackley, a native of Scotland, who spent most of his life in Ireland as a stone-cutter, and was killed while building a jail at Belfast. He married a Miss MacIlvane. Thomas Cokain, the maternal grandfather of the subject of this sketch, was born in Scotland, came to America in the early forties, settled in Pitt township, and was for many years engaged in the manufacture of coke. He married Isabel Parks, a native of Ireland. Joseph Blackley, son of James Blackley, came to America from Ireland in 1846, and located in Lawrenceville, Pa., where he was engaged in the dairy business up to 1861, when he moved to Pitt township and became a partner with his father-in-law, Thomas Cokain, the firm being the first to engage in the manufacture of coke in Allegheny county. He continued in this business up to 1890, and was also interested in coal and coke in other parts of Pennsylvania. He has, since 1893, retired from active life, and lives on his farm in Deemston borough, Washington county. He had two children who grew to maturity, Hamilton MacIlvane, the subject of this sketch, and Ida B., who is now the wife of John P. Magill, of Youngstown, Ohio. Hamilton M. Blackley was reared and educated in Allegheny county, where he attended the Pittsburg public schools, graduated in 1879 from the twenty-sixth ward school, and in the same year graduated from the Iron City business college. He began his business career as a bookkeeper for his father at the coke works, and owned a share in the business from 1885 to 1890. In 1892 and 1893 he was employed as clerk with the Carnegie steel company at Homestead, and has been, since 1893 up to the present time, a clerk in the office of the recorder of Allegheny county. In 1899 he became a member of the firm of E. H. Morton & Co., in the real estate and insurance business at Homestead. The firm of Jacobs & Blackley, of which he is now a partner, was formed Nov. 1, 1902, and is doing a rapidly increasing business. He was treasurer of Mifflin township, Allegheny county, for five years, being legislated out of office when the township classification act went into effect in 1900. Sept. 14, 1882, Mr. Blackley married Miss Anna M. Carney, daughter of William and Mary (Ward) Carney, of Homestead, and has three children, Bryce E., Joseph H. and Mabel H. Mr. and Mrs. Blackley are members of the Episcopal church at Homestead. Mr. Blackley is a past master of Homestead lodge, No. 582, F. and A. M.; a member of Duquesne chapter, No. 193, R. A. M., of Pittsburg; Pittsburg commandery, No. 1, K. T., and Boaz council, No. 814, R. A. M. In politics he is a stanch republican. Mr. Blackley is an ex-member of the old "Duquesne Grays," of Pittsburg. He was, in 1897, president of the Western Pennsylvania farmers' association, and has been, since 1895, a member of the Pennsylvania State Association of Volunteer Firemen.

WILLIAM KAGBY VAN SCIVER, a prominent painting and paper-hanging contractor of Homestead, was born in Washington, D. C., April 7, 1867, son of Levi and Susan (Beatley) Van Sciver. Levi Van Sciver, a fisherman by occupation, was a son of Velonvi Van Sciver, also a fisherman, who was born in Philadelphia, of Dutch ancestry. On his mother's side, William K. Van Sciver is a grandson of Kagby Beatley, a native of Virginia, who spent most of his life as a fisherman, and was captain of a boat which plied up and down the Potomac river. Mr. Van Sciver, the subject of this sketch, is the only survivor of a family of seven children. He was reared in Washington, and attended the public schools until he reached the age of sixteen, when he began his apprenticeship as a painter and paper-hanger. Coming to Homestead in 1884, he worked as a journeyman for several years, and also spent a short time at his trade in Youngstown, Ohio. Since 1896 he has been a contractor in Homestead, and now owns the largest paint and wall-paper store in the city, where he carries a very complete stock and does a flourishing business. On April 30, 1888, Mr. Van Sciver married Miss Margaret Mahoney, daughter of Thomas and Margaret (Hartey) Mahoney, of Hubbard, Ohio, and has four children living, Pearl, Edward, Beatrice and Eliza J. Mr. Van Sciver is in religious belief a Presbyterian, and in politics a democrat. He is a member of the senior and junior orders of A. O. U. W. and the Heptasophs.

JOHN ANDREW WOLFF, a well-known contractor and builder of Homestead, and vice-president of the Kilgore & Atkinson sporting goods company, was born in Washington township, Armstrong Co., Pa., Jan. 5, 1858. His paternal grandfather was a pioneer farmer of Armstrong county, and was married to Margaret Sandle. Valentine Wolff, father of the subject of this sketch, was born in Armstrong county in 1828, and still resides there, where he has been for many years a successful farmer. He married Catherine Croyle, daughter of Joseph and Nancy (Mainer) Croyle. Joseph Croyle was a potter by trade. Mr. and Mrs. Valentine Wolff reared a family of eleven children, eight sons and three daughters, as follows: John A., Rose C. (Mrs. Ernest Pattrell), Samuel H., David, Christian (deceased), Elizabeth (Mrs. Dwight Wolff), Wilbur, Joseph, Nannie, George and James. John A. Wolff, the subject of this sketch, was reared on a farm in his native county and educated in the common schools. In 1881 he located in Pittsburg, began to work at the carpenters' trade, then as a journeyman, up to 1889. In 1890 he embarked for himself as a carpenter and builder, and has been successfully occupied in this work continuously since. On Sept. 10, 1885, Mr. Wolff married Miss Jennie E. Barnhart, daughter of Henry and Margaret Barnhart, of Braddock, and has three children, Annie B., Louretta Jean and Frederick William. Mr. and Mrs. Wolff are members of the First Presbyterian church of Homestead. Mr. Wolff is a member of Homestead lodge, No. 1049, I. O. O. F.; No. 288, Carpenters and Joiners of America, and No. 21, Order of Americus. In politics he is a republican.

HERMAN J. McBRIDE, a popular and successful druggist of Etna, Pa., was born in Paxton, Ill., in 1873, and is a son of M. B. McBride, who was a prominent attorney in Butler, Pa., up to the time of his death, in March, 1900. Mr. McBride's mother is still living in Butler, where she was reared, although born in Pittsburg. She is the daughter of Herman J. Berg, who was an oil producer in Pennsylvania in the early sixties. She has three sons, Herman J., Frank and Eugene. Herman J. McBride learned the drug business, and, in 1899, started a drug store at Etna, where he enjoys the confidence of his many customers. He was married, Oct. 24, 1900, to Miss Mary Ganster, daughter of George and Philomina (Ackerman) Ganster, of Etna. Mr. and Mrs. McBride have one child, George Herman, born Jan. 16, 1902.

JOHN H. GILLEN, the oldest established funeral director at Homestead, was born near Delmont, Westmoreland Co., Pa., Nov. 9, 1854, son of Allen and Julia A. (Hill) Gillen, both natives of Pennsylvania. His paternal grandfather, Allen Gillen, a native of Ireland, of Scotch-Irish parentage, was one of the pioneer settlers of Allegheny county, while his maternal grandfather, James Hill, who was of German descent, was a farmer in Westmoreland county. Allen Gillen, father of the subject of this sketch, was reared in Allegheny county, and when a young man ran a stage-coach between Pittsburg, Philadelphia and Baltimore. Later he located in Westmoreland county, where he spent the rest of his life as a farmer. He was twice married, first to a Miss Bair, and had one son by this marriage, William S. He married as his second wife Julia Ann Hill, and had by this marriage three sons, Jacob, John H. and Allen. John H. Gillen, the subject of this sketch, was reared in Westmoreland county, educated in the public schools and at Delmont seminary, graduating from the seminary in 1874. For several years Mr. Gillen was a farmer, and, in April,

1882, located at Elizabeth, Allegheny county, where he was engaged for two years in the livery business. Coming to Homestead in 1884, he embarked in the undertaking business, at which he has been successfully engaged for over eighteen years. Mr. Gillen was married, March 20, 1877, to Sarah S., daughter of James and Harriet (Dewalt) Irwin, of Westmoreland county, and has two children, Anna M., wife of Oliver H. Blakely, and Laura. Mr. Gillen and family are members of the First Presbyterian church of Homestead. Mr. Gillen is a member of Homestead lodge, No. 582, F. and A. M.; Boaz council, No. 814, R. A.; Magdala lodge, No. 650, B. P. O. E.; No. 1 commandery, K. T.; Mystic Shrine, and Zerubbabel chapter, No. 162, R. A. M. In politics he is a republican.

JACOB J. BRAUN, of Sharpsburg, Pa., a well-known merchant, was born on the Sharp farm near the present town of Sharpsburg, Allegheny county, Dec. 12, 1856, and was educated in the common schools of his native county. His educational training was limited to a few years, on account of the death of his mother and the prolonged sickness of his father, and when ten years of age he secured employment in an oil refinery. He remained with this concern for five years, and then engaged as a clerk for P. Kiel, Jr., in the grocery business, continuing in that capacity for six years. Mr. Braun has had a diversified business career, having been a butcher, drover, rougher in the Lewis, Bailey, Dalzell & Co.'s mills, heater in steel works, and then worked in the rolling mill of Morhead Brothers & Co., until the strike in 1891, when he began his present business at No. 111 Eighteenth St. Mr. Braun has made a success of his mercantile venture, and his business has prospered from its inception. He was married to Elizabeth Neyoma, daughter of William K. and Artliza (Miller) Mulholland. To them were born four children: Robert J., a machinist in the Carbon steel company, of Pittsburg; Charles A., clerk for Heinz & Co., of Allegheny city; Albert H., an employe of the West Pennsylvania railroad company, and Leona May, wife of Albert Krotzer, a leading grocer of Kittanning, Pa. Mr. Braun is prominently identified with the leading secret orders, holding membership in Sharpsburg lodge, No. 752, of the Odd Fellows, and representing that lodge in the grand lodge on five different occasions; in the Masonic fraternity; in the George Washington lodge, No. 423, of the Junior Order of American Mechanics, and representative to the State council for eight terms. He is a member of Grace Methodist church, and in politics is a republican. Mr. Braun has resided in Sharpsburg during his business career, and is a substantial citizen of that city.

DAVID KING CALHOUN, a prominent farmer of West Homestead, was born in Mifflin township, Allegheny Co., Pa., April 3, 1831. He lives on the farm patented by his maternal grandfather, Robert Hays, in 1803. Robert Hays was a native of Ireland, but spent a great part of his life in Mifflin township, where he died. His wife was Nancy Reid. Mr. Calhoun is descended, on his father's side, from James Calhoun, who was born in County Donegal, Ireland, in 1723, and came to America in 1733. He died in Allegheny county, Feb. 4, 1799. James Calhoun's son, David Calhoun, the grandfather of the subject of this sketch, married Eleanor King. David Calhoun was among the first settlers of Mifflin township, where he located in 1784. He was born in Lancaster county, Pa., in 1757. He served in the Revolutionary war, and took part in many of the battles of that war. He fought at Brandywine; at Camden, under General Gates; at Guilford courthouse, under General Green, and saw General Cornwallis deliver up his sword at Yorktown. His patent for 320 acres of land in Mifflin township was granted in 1803. At the beginning of the War of 1812, David Calhoun, then fifty-four years old, shouldered his musket and marched to General Harrison's headquarters, but, on account of his age, was ordered back to guard Fort Pitt, where he remained during the rest of the war. During this period he held the rank of captain. He died Aug. 18, 1834, and his wife, Eleanor (King) Calhoun, died April 12, 1831, both being buried in the Mifflin church cemetery. The parents of David King Calhoun, the subject of this sketch, were John K. and Mary (Hays) Calhoun. They were married Dec. 30, 1824. John K. Calhoun followed farming all his life. He was born Oct. 17, 1796, and died Dec. 13, 1869, and his wife, Aug. 2, 1873. David King Calhoun, the subject of this article, has always followed farming as a vocation. His wife was formerly Miss Alice P. Hays, daughter of Thomas and Sarah (Stewart) Hays, and granddaughter, on her father's side, of Jacob Hays. Jacob Hays, born in 1778, was married, in 1799, to Jane Hardin, then a girl of twenty, who was a daughter of Thomas Hardin, an officer in the Revolution. Jacob Hays was a son of Abraham Hays, who came from Maryland and settled in Mifflin township, opposite Braddock, in 1769. Abraham Hays married Miss Fannie Pitter, daughter of a distinguished French officer who fought in the Revolutionary war. Mrs. Calhoun's maternal grandfather was Lazarus Stewart, the first sheriff of Allegheny county, who officiated at the first and only public hanging in Allegheny county. David K. Calhoun and wife are the parents of seven children: Mary H., John K. (deceased), Sarah J., Flora H., Alice E., David R. and Charles S. (deceased). Mr. Calhoun is an attendant and supporter of the United Presbyterian church. In politics he is a republican.

H. A. McLAUGHLIN, of Aspinwall, Pa., superintendent of the water and light departments of that city, was born on Aug. 6, 1842, in Fairview township, Butler Co., Pa., son of John and Katharine (Green) McLaughlin, and the grandson of Patrick McLaughlin, one of the first settlers of Butler county. Mr. McLaughlin was reared on his father's farm and was educated in the schools of Fairview township. When eighteen years of age he became assistant to his father in conducting the farm, and at the death of his father, took charge of it, successfully combining farming with the oil business until 1894, when he removed to Aspinwall, Pa. There he became connected with the Aspinwall land company as assistant superintendent of the water plant, and, in 1898, when the borough bought the water and light plant, he still held the position of assistant superintendent. In June, 1902, he was promoted to the superintendency of the water and light plants, and also was given charge of the sewer and highway departments, filling both positions very ably. Mr. McLaughlin was married, on Oct. 11, 1877, to Katharine, daughter of William and Rosanna (Ferry) McCarthy, of Brady's Bend, Armstrong county, and to them were born the following children: Clarence, who conducts a barber shop in Aspinwall; Harry, a machinist, of Pittsburg; John C., a teacher of the piano in Sharpsburg and Aspinwall; Rose Emma, a stenographer, of Pittsburg; Richard F., a stenographer for the Pennsylvania railroad company at Pittsburg; Katharine Agatha and Joseph Emmett, attending school. Mr. McLaughlin served one term as constable in Butler county, two terms as assessor, and was tax collector during the oil excitement in that vicinity, collecting $15,000 in taxes in one year, this being the greatest amount ever secured in that township. He has also invented a folding bed of merit. He is a member of the Catholic church and the republican party, and is an honored citizen of Aspinwall.

LOUIS J. GOLDSMITH, a prominent merchant in Braddock, was born in New York city, in October, 1852. His parents, Josiah and Bertha (Wenneck) Goldsmith, came to this country from Amsterdam, Holland, before the middle of the past century. Louis J. Goldsmith attended school until he was fourteen years old, and then began clerking, and has since devoted his life to mercantile pursuits. In 1881, in company with his brother-in-law, Leo A. Katz, he started a small clothing store on Main street. After five years the Baldridge building was secured and the business greatly enlarged. In 1895 it had outgrown these quarters and the first section of its present quarters was secured, at Nos. 803, 805, 807 and 809 Braddock Ave. The business now occupies the two adjoining stores, also, and has grown into a department store of which any city might well be proud. Mr. Goldsmith was married, Aug. 27, 1882, to Hannah, daughter of Abraham and Julia (Hecht) Katz, and has four children. Edna is a graduate of Darlington seminary, of Westchester, Pa., class of 1901; Josiah will graduate from Shady Side, Pittsburg, class of 1905; Malcom is attending Braddock high school, and Herbert is also in school. Mr. Goldsmith is a member of the Heptasophs, Woodmen of the World, Jr. O. U. A. M., of Braddock, past grand of Angerona lodge, I. O. O. F., of Pittsburg, and of the Concordia club, of Pittsburg. He and his family are members of Rodef Sholem temple, Reformed Hebrew congregation of Pittsburg.

GEORGE S. T. DEBOLT, the oldest established wholesale and retail dealer in grain, hay and feed of all kinds in Homestead, was born in Monongahela township, Greene Co., Pa., July 3, 1863. His parents, Teegarden S. and Catherine (Tanner) Debolt, were both born in Greene county, and of German descent. Teegarden S. Debolt, a distiller by trade, was for many years in the employ of William Gray & Sons. George S. T. Debolt was reared in his native township and educated in the public schools. In 1888 he came to Homestead, where he entered the employ of W. S. B. Hays, as a farmer. Later he was employed in the mills of the Carnegie steel company, and in 1895 embarked in his present business, in which he has met with marked success, and is the leading merchant in his line in Homestead. He is also interested in real estate. On Oct. 14, 1891, Mr. Debolt was married to Sarah J., daughter of George and Sarah (Renn) Pollin, of Pittsburg, and has three children, Mino T., George E. and Mary Ethel Renn.

HERMAN HUNDHAUSEN, of Cheswick, Pa., superintendent of the Standard leather company, was born at Berlin, Germany, June 15, 1861, and is a son of Charles and Augusta (Damman) Hundhausen, the former the proprietor of a leather factory in Germany. Mr. Hundhausen was educated in Berlin and at the college at Crefeld, which latter institution he attended for eight years. In 1878 he left school and engaged in the manufacture of patent leather with his father, remaining in this business in Germany until 1891, when he came to America and located in Newark, N. J. He assisted in the formation of a company to conduct a patent leather works, and was successfully engaged in that business until 1898. He removed to Cheswick, Pa., and organized the Standard leather works, of which concern he is superintendent, director and stockholder. He is also superintendent of the branch of this company which is located at Allegheny city. They make patent leather and enamel for the shoe, furniture and carriage trade, with a capital of $400,000, and do a large and profitable business. He was married, in 1894, to Augusta Behnke, of Newark, N. J., but a native of Germany, and they have two children, Herman and Theodore. Mr. Hundhausen is a member of the Lutheran church, is a republican and is one of the leading citizens of Cheswick.

WILLIAM C. MEYER, of Sharpsburg, Pa., the oldest merchant and chief of the fire department, was born in Allegheny city, Pa., March 28, 1844, son of William Meyer, a native of Prussia, who came to Allegheny county in the early part of its history, and for many years was a well-known grocery man of Allegheny city. W. C. Meyer attended the fourth ward school of Allegheny city for two years, and when only twelve years of age, faced the world to earn a living, securing employment first in the Banner cotton factory, of Allegheny city. Three years later he went with the Hope cotton factory, in the batting room, and after one year transferred the scene of his employment to McCaulay's glass house, of Pittsburg, where he remained about four months. He was with McClintock, of Pittsburg, in the keg factory; for one year with the Shoenberge steel mill as pull-up boy, and with Knapp & Woods, of Pittsburg, in the nut and bolt factory. In 1861 he learned carpentering, and worked at that trade until the day that Lincoln was killed, when he quit that business to clerk in the dry-goods store of his brother, H. H. Meyer, in Allegheny city. He remained in that capacity for two years, and in 1867 came to Sharpsburg, where he started a dry-goods store with $2,200 of borrowed money. The first year his sales amounted to $25,000 and assured the success of his venture. He now has the finest dry-goods and department store in Sharpsburg, occupies a large three-story building and enjoys a splendid patronage. He helped organize the Columbian fire company of Allegheny city in 1859 and organized the first company in Sharpsburg in 1871. He was elected first chief by the council, and has served as chief ever since, bearing the reputation of being one of the best fire fighters in the county. He was the organizer of the Western Pennsylvania State firemen's association, and has taken an active interest in its workings. Mr. Meyer was married, in 1867, to Sophia, daughter of Herman and Sophia (Beckfield) Milter, and to them have been born seven children: W. H. J., cashier of the Turtle Creek National bank; Charles H., with the right of way department of the C. D. & P. telephone company; Edward J., manager of the Sharpsburg supply company; Albert P., an attorney of Pittsburg; Herbert H. and Howard, in their father's store, and Lilian, a student of the public schools. He is a member of the First German Lutheran church, and is an ardent member and active worker for the republican party. He was one of the organizers of the Concord orphans' home, in 1882, which is supported by the Lutheran church synod, and this magnificent institution is a monument to his benevolence and humanity. Mr. Meyer is known to almost every one in that section of the county, and possesses their confidence and esteem. His career has been one of probity and honor, and no man stands higher than he in his community.

JOHN O. JONES, clerk of North Braddock, was born at Irwin, Pa., Jan. 20, 1875, but has lived in Braddock since he was two years old. His parents, David D. and Mary (Reese) Jones, came originally from Wales, and his maternal grandmother, Mrs. Reese, was one of the many who lost their lives in the Johnstown flood in 1889. The children of David D. and Mary Jones are: Mary, wife of Dr. Bartilson, of Braddock; John, the subject of this sketch; Margaret, at home; Anna, now teaching at Shady Park, and Harry, attending the North Braddock grammar school. David D. Jones followed his trade as a stone-cutter until he was severely injured, in 1887, and has since been employed as watchman at the steel works. John O. Jones was educated in the North Braddock schools, and also took a course at Curry university, of Pittsburg. He was for some time employed at the Bessemer mills, and was then for several years connected with the Union switch and signal company, of Swissvale. In January, 1900, he was appointed to the responsible position which he now holds, and has made an enviable record for himself by conscientious performance of the duties of his office. The borough of North Braddock elected its first officers in May, 1897, and the census of 1900 gave it a population of over 6,300. Mr. Jones is a member of Braddock Field lodge, No. 510, F. and A. M.; is a thirty-second degree Mason; Tancred commandery, No. 48, Knights Templars, and Syria temple, A. A. O. of the M. S., of Pittsburg.

DANIEL RISHER McCLURE is a member of one of Pennsylvania's old and prominent families. He is descended from John McClure, who came to America from the north of Ireland about 1705. He married Janet McKnight, and settled in what is now Cumberland county, taking up a large tract of land, on part of which the city of Carlisle was afterwards built. He died in 1757, leaving, among others, a son, John McClure, who was, at the time of his father's death, coroner of Cumberland county. Two years later Mr. McClure disposed of his property at Carlisle and removed to Pittsburg, or Fort Pitt, as it was then called, immediately after its capture by the English. Here he engaged in the Indian trade and became very wealthy. He married Martha Denny, daughter of William Denny, and aunt of Major Ebenezer Denny, the first mayor of Pittsburg. In 1786 John McClure purchased 329½ acres of land where Homestead now stands, a part of this property still being in the possession of the McClure family. John McClure's second son, also John, married Agnes Toppins, of Westmoreland county, and farmed the large plantation on the banks of the Monongahela river which was left to him by his father. Mr. and Mrs. McClure raised a family of ten children, among whom was Abdiel, father of our subject, born July 18, 1816. Abdiel McClure was a man of unusual prominence in religious and business affairs, and was universally loved and respected. Politically he was a republican, and held the office of recorder for Allegheny county from 1863 to 1866. After this he farmed "the Homestead," and also became interested in wholesale business in Pittsburg. When he sold 113 acres of the farm to the Homestead bank and life insurance company, of which he was a member, he wisely set apart building lots for schools and churches. He was also a contractor and builder; conducted a planing mill at Homestead; was for several terms justice of the peace, and often chosen to settle estates. He was an earnest Christian, a ruling elder in the Presbyterian church, and during the latter part of his life actively interested in temperance reform. Mr. McClure married Anne W. Risher, born in Allegheny county Dec. 14, 1818. She was the daughter of Daniel C. and Sarah (Cready) Risher, and a direct descendant of Daniel Risher, who served in Braddock's army in 1755. Daniel R. McClure, the subject of this article, was born in Homestead, Oct. 17, 1846; attended the public schools and Penn institute, and later graduated from Duff's business college. He served for two years as deputy county recorder, and then became bookkeeper in the old Fort Pitt bank, and is now a director in the First National bank and president of the Homestead building and loan association. He was for four years a councilman, and has always been prominent in public life. When a young man, he worked for his father in the Homestead planing mill, and was for some time engaged in the grocery trade. For several years past, however, his time has been mainly occupied in the care of the family estates. He is a prominent member of the Masonic fraternity and a member of the Presbyterian church. Mr. McClure was married, Feb. 2, 1876, to Miss Mary E. Gleasdall, daughter of Joseph and Mary E. (McCaslin) Gleasdall, of Pittsburg. Mr. and Mrs. McClure have three children, Daniel R., Mary G. and Robert M.

VALERIAN J. JANDA, pastor of St. Michael's Archangel Slovak Catholic church, Homestead, was born in Pilsen, Bohemia, Oct. 26, 1874. His parents, John and Anna (Title) Janda, came to America in 1880, and located in Chicago, where Father Janda was raised and educated. After attending St. Procopius' parochial school and St. Ignatius' college, of that city, he completed his education at St. Paul's seminary, a school attended by theological and philosophical students, graduating from that institution in 1895. In September, 1897, he was ordained to the priesthood by Bishop Phelan, and assigned to St. Michael's church, which, under his supervision, has increased in membership from 60 to 250 families, and now has an aggregate of about 1,200 members. In connection with the church is a parochial school, in charge of the Sisters of St. Joseph, with an enrollment of 190 pupils. During the five years of Father Janda's pastorate, he has secured for his church the three adjoining properties, which are used as a convent and parochial residence, and has maintained his parish in a flourishing condition. On Sunday, Sept. 28, 1902, Father Janda celebrated the fifth anniversary of his connection with the parish, and was on this occasion presented with a handsome silver service by the trustees of the congregation, as a mark of appreciation for his faithful services. Father Janda is a member of the First Catholic Slovak union of America, and numerous other Catholic societies.

GEORGE H. MOORE, SR., postmaster at Verona and a leading citizen of that place, was born in Johnstown, Pa., Sept. 23, 1845, and is a son of George H. and Mary M. (Mercer) Moore, the father a native of England, who came to America when twelve years old. He was a boatman on the old canal between Johnstown and Pittsburg, and acted as agent for Leach & Co. He died in Cincinnati in 1854, at the age of thirty-eight, and his wife, in 1859. They had five children, of whom four, two sons and two daughters, are living. The subject of this sketch received but a limited education when a boy, and, in 1859, started out to make his own living. He located in Iowa, and remained there until 1862, when he enlisted in Company G, 21st regiment, Iowa volunteer infantry. He served with this regiment all during the war, as musician, and, having been mustered out in July, 1865, returned to Iowa, and a short time afterwards came to Pittsburg. Mr. Moore resided in Pittsburg until 1876, and has since then made Verona his home, filling a large place in local activities. He was engaged in the oil business for some ten years, and spent several years as an oil refiner. For the past ten years he has been local agent and foreman for the Philadelphia gas company, and has been superintendent of the Verona water-works for ten years. In political belief Mr. Moore is a republican. He has served his borough two terms as burgess, four terms as alderman, and was for nine years justice of the peace. He resigned the latter position in 1897, to become postmaster. He is a member of the Royal Arcanum. Mr. Moore was married, in 1866, to Miss Mary Porter. She died in 1867, and, in 1879, he married Miss E. A. Cribbs, daughter of

J. R. Cribbs. Mr. and Mrs. Moore have had eight children, of whom all but Walter, the third born, are living. They are: George H., Bess D., Walter, Florence, R. Hyatt, J. R., Mary M. and Helen.

JESSE HODGSON, a prominent dealer in drugs at Verona, was born in Washington county, Pa., May 11, 1863, and is a son of John and Margaret (Harden) Hodgson. John Hodgson, born in England, July 15, 1812, came to America when eighteen years old, in company with his parents, Thomas and Mary (Seikield) Hodgson, who settled in 1832 in Birmingham, Allegheny county, then moved in 1842 to Collier township, where Thomas died, in 1844, and his wife, at the age of eighty-four, in 1868. The maternal grandparents of the subject of this sketch were James and Sarah (Hays) Harden, natives of America, though of French and Irish descent. James Harden's father, also named James, was a soldier in the Revolution. Sarah (Hays) Harden was a daughter of Abraham Hays, who married Miss Fannie Pettee, a French lady, and, in 1767, settled with his wife in Allegheny county, a mile above Homestead, on property still held by their descendants. Abraham Hays was an earnest Presbyterian, an honest and upright man. He was a son of William Hays, a native of Scotland, who settled in Ireland and died there. John Hodgson, father of the subject of this sketch, spent most of his life in the coal business and in farming. He and his wife were members of the Twentieth Street Presbyterian church, South Side, Pittsburg. He died in 1891, but his widow is still living, and well and strong at eighty-three. He and his wife had seven children, of whom three are living, William, Jesse, and Mrs. Mary Goff, who lives on the South Side, Pittsburg. Jesse Hodgson, the subject of this sketch, was reared in Pittsburg and educated in the public schools. He worked in Pittsburg for some time as a nailer, and then spent fifteen years as traveling salesman for Healy & Bigelow, of New Haven, Conn. He came to Verona in 1891 and, in 1900, engaged in the drug trade, in which he has been most successful. Mr. Hodgson is a republican, but has never aspired to hold office. He is a member of Iona lodge, Knights of Pythias, and the B. P. O. E. of Greenville, Pa. Mr. Hodgson was married, in 1888, to Miss Sarah Wray, of Indiana county, Pa. They have one adopted child, Grant Hodgson. They are members of the United Presbyterian church at Verona. A brother of Jesse Hodgson, William B. Hodgson, is foreman for the tin and copper shop of the Pennsylvania railroad company, at Verona. He was born in Cannonsburg, Washington Co., Pa., Aug. 29, 1857, and was educated in the Pittsburg public schools. He then learned the tinsmith trade, worked at it for a time in Pittsburg, and for two years in the west, and in 1882 came to Verona, where he has since been employed, and risen to the responsible position which he has held for the past two years. He is a republican in politics, was for three terms justice of the peace, and eleven years school director. He is a member of Verona lodge, No. 548, F. and A. M., and General McClellan lodge, No. 150, Jr. O. U. A. M. Mr. Hodgson was married, in 1884, to Miss Anna B. Gray, of Verona, and has three children, Bessie, Margaret and Lois. He and his wife are members of the St. John's Episcopal church of Oakmont.

SAMUEL E. STEWART, a prominent real estate and insurance man of Braddock, was born in Clarion county, Pa., Nov. 30, 1861. His father, Robert Stewart, was the son of Robert, Sr., and Sarah (McCall) Stewart, both old settlers of Clarion county, and his mother, Catharine (Peters) Stewart, was the daughter of Jacob Peters, of Armstrong county, who married a Miss Bristel, of Westmoreland county. Samuel E. Stewart attended the public schools, took the Clarion county State normal course, and taught for three years in his native county. He later conducted a meat market in Rimersburg for two years, and in 1895 located in Braddock, where for a year he devoted himself to mercantile pursuits. He went into the real estate and insurance business with John Rinard, and the firm now carries on an extensive business, with offices in the Dean building on Library street, under the name of Rinard & Stewart. Mr. Stewart was married, Aug. 25, 1892, to Luella K., daughter of Samuel and Mary (Thompson) Boyd. Mr. and Mrs. Stewart have one son, Robert L., born Nov. 7, 1893, now attending the Braddock schools. Mr. Stewart is a member of Valetta commandery, No. 129, Knights of Malta, and of the Woodmen of the World. He and his wife are members of the Calvary Presbyterian church of Braddock.

JOHN ALVIN POUNDSTONE, a popular grocer of Tarentum, was born in Masontown, Fayette Co., Pa., Dec. 17, 1855. He is a great-grandson of John Poundstone, a native of Germany, who came to America about 1750 with two brothers, and located in Fayette county, where he spent the rest of his life, and a grandson of John Poundstone, who was born in Fayette county, and died there in 1902, at the advanced age of ninety-nine. The grandfather was for three-quarters of a century an honored member of the Lutheran church, was by trade a cabinet-maker, but also, when a young man, ran keel boats on the Monongahela river, and was for some years a farmer. In politics he was a life-long democrat, and held various township offices, being for many years a school director. His wife, Susan (Rider) Poundstone, a native of Fayette county, died there in 1869. They were the parents of ten children, of whom four are living. The father of the subject of this sketch, William H. Poundstone, also a native of Fayette county, is living, at the age of seventy-six. In political belief he is a democrat, and has held various township offices. He is a member of the Cumberland Presbyterian church, of which his wife, Mary J. (Debolt) Poundstone, was also a member, and who died in 1868. She was a daughter of Reason and Anna (Long) Debolt, the father an early settler of Fayette county, and the mother a native of Greene county. John A. Poundstone, whose name begins this article, lived in Masontown till he reached the age of twelve, was educated in the country schools of Fayette county, and, when a boy, began to learn the blacksmith trade, at which he worked from 1871 to 1893. After that he was employed in the revenue service until April, 1900, and in October of that year came to Tarentum, where he has since engaged successfully in the grocery business. In politics he is an ardent democrat, actively interested in the welfare of his party. He is a member of Tounaleuka lodge, No. 365, I. O. O. F., and Jr. O. U. A. M., and was a charter member of the Heptasophs at Uniontown, of which place he was for twenty-five years a resident. In 1878 Mr. Poundstone married Miss Alice White, of Uniontown, daughter of Joseph White, a marble dealer of that place. Mrs. Poundstone died in 1897, and, in December, 1899, he married Miss Irene Miller, of Allegheny county, by whom he has one child, Mary L. Several of Mr. Poundstone's relatives took an active part in the Civil war, and his grandfather, John Poundstone, was a member of the State militia. His father, William H. Poundstone, served three years and three months as a member of Company K, heavy artillery, in which he enlisted in 1861, and Mr. Poundstone's uncle, R. L. Debolt, served as musician throughout the war. Another uncle, Jesse Poundstone, was for three years, during the Civil war, fife major, while a brother of Jesse Poundstone, John W. Poundstone, also fought three years in the Civil war.

STEPHEN JOSEPH CZEPANANIS, pastor of St. Peter and St. Paul's Lithuanian Roman Catholic church, Homestead, was born in Mikiciai, Lithuania, Dec. 26, 1869, son of Martin and Rose (Zelionis) Czepananis. After attending the public schools of Lithuania, he attended the Suvalkai gymnasium, and then spent a year at the Seinai seminary, and was, from 1892 to 1895, a soldier in the Russian army. After completing his service in the army, he came to America, landing at Philadelphia May 16, 1895. After five months in Luzerne county, Pa., Father Czepananis spent several years at Detroit in preparation for the ministry, attending the schools of St. Ciril and Methodius, and on July 1, 1900, was ordained to priesthood by Bishop Foley, of Detroit. On August 1st of the same year he was assigned to his present charge by Bishop Phelan, of Pittsburg. This church was established in 1894, the same year as that in which St. Joseph's Lithuanian beneficial society was organized. In March, 1899, a subscription for funds for a church building was started, and later a location was secured on Fourth avenue. The church was completed in 1901 and dedicated on the 9th day of June of that year. The church now has a membership of 140 families, and an aggregate enrollment of over 900, a considerable proportion of its members being residents of Duquesne and Braddock. Since Father Czepananis has been pastor there has been an increase in membership of over 200. Father Czepananis is a member of the Lithuanian Roman Catholic alliance of America, Concord of Lithuanian Catholics of America, and the Lithuanian Catholic educational society.

FRANK C. KUNKEL, of Homestead, a well-known real estate broker, was born in Irwin, Pa., June 14, 1879, and is a son of Jacob R. and Anna M. (Bickerstaff) Kunkel. He is of Dutch extraction, his grandfather twice removed coming from Holland early in the eighteenth century, was a scout in General Bouquet's army on its march to Fort Pitt. Another grandparent was a colonel under General Forbes. In 1818 his great-grandfather settled in Westmoreland county and built the stone house which still stands there and is of such historic interest. On his mother's side, his ancestors are from New York State, and are likewise famous for their martial prowess, his mother's father falling in the battle of the Wilderness in the Civil war. Jacob R. Kunkel, father of Frank C., was one of the most prominent and best-known business men of western Pennsylvania up to the time of his death, in 1884. Of the four children of Jacob R. and Anna M. Kunkel, three are living: Frank C., Howard and Rufus. Frank C. Kunkel obtained his early educational training in the public schools of Homestead, where his family had removed when he was quite young, and graduated from the high school of that place. He attended the Grove City college, and later the Pennsylvania State college. He studied law at the University of California until the outbreak of the Spanish-American war. At this time his military and patriotic nature called him to enlist in the 10th Pennsylvania infantry, later known as the "fighting 10th," in which he served in the Philippines until the cessation of hostilities. He returned to his home in Pennsylvania, and shortly afterward accepted an assignment as special correspondent for the Pittsburg Dispatch, the Pittsburg Post and the Philadelphia Press, and accompanied the congressional party that was sent to investigate the conditions in the Philippine islands. This trip took him around the world. Returning in 1902, he embarked in the real estate business at Homestead, and later became manager of the Coraopolis realty company, severing his connection with them to take charge of the mortgage department of the Land, Title and Trust company, of Pittsburg. Mr. Kunkel's success has been phenomenal for a man of his age, and he has met with much encouragement in the financial world. He is a republican, takes an active part in politics, but has constantly eschewed public office, though strongly urged to accept the position of tax collector of Homestead. He is a member of the Masons, the Royal Arcanum, and is a stockholder of the Fidelity realty company, of Homestead, the Coraopolis savings and trust company, and the Munhall land company, of Munhall, Pa. Mr. Kunkel contemplates finishing his law course at Harvard in the near future.

DR. B. FRANK PRICE was born in Meigs county, Ohio, Nov. 1, 1845. He is the son of Charles and Sarah (Sisson) Price, being the fifth of a family of twelve children. Both his parents were born near Charleston, W. Va., in 1811. Dr. Price received his early education in the public schools and at Nelson's college in Cincinnati, and at the age of sixteen, he enlisted with the 7th Ohio light artillery, where he served three years. During the war he fought in the battles of Pittsburg Landing, Corinth, Iuka and in many other minor engagements. On being mustered out in 1865, he was married to Mary F., daughter of P. K. and Mary Kerrigan, of Noblesville, Ind. To this union were born three children: John S., who died at the age of twenty-one; Jerome B., born June 5, 1872, who graduated from Duff's mercantile college of Pittsburg in 1891, and is now working his father's farm near Portland, Ohio; and Ruth, born April 6, 1891, now attending the Braddock public schools. In 1866 our subject commenced the study of medicine, under the preceptorship of the late Dr. Hayworth, of Ravenswood, W. Va., and in 1869 entered the Cincinnati college of medicine and surgery, from which he was graduated in 1872. He located, after graduation, at Wadesville, W. Va., practiced there successfully for ten years, and then moved to Braddock, where he has since resided. The doctor has been an extensive reader, and a writer of more than ordinary ability, his contributions to local journals securing always the marked attention of thoughtful readers. He has been too much occupied with his profession to give much attention to politics, but has served a term as president of the Braddock board of health, and represents the second ward in council. In political belief he is a republican. Dr. Price is a member of Pomeroy lodge, No. 164, F. and A. M.; Wilkinsburg lodge of Elks; Knights of Malta; Patriotic Order Sons of America, and the Esthenic order. He has been for ten years surgeon of Major Harper post, No. 181, G. A. R., and is a comrade of Encampment No. 1, Union Veteran legion, of Pittsburg. He is a member of the Allegheny county and American medical associations, and takes an active interest in the profession to which he has been for thirty years devoted. The doctor and his wife are members of the First Methodist church of Braddock.

JOHN A. ENGELHARDT, of Millvale, Pa., a retired shoe dealer, was born in Bavaria, Germany, May 7, 1825, son of John and Rebecca (Ehrlinger) Engelhardt. His father was a shoemaker in Germany and was a member of the victorious army of the Fatherland in the Franco-Prussian war, but was taken as a prisoner of war and died shortly after his release. John A. Engelhardt was educated in the public schools of his native country, and when fourteen years of age began to learn shoemaking, and there worked at that trade until 1853, when he came to the United States and located in Pittsburg. There he was connected with a Pittsburg shoe firm for seven years, and then opened a place of his own, selling and making shoes. He prospered in this venture at Pittsburg until 1873, when he came to Millvale and worked at his trade until his retirement from active business in 1893. He was married, in 1853, to Margaret Popp, of Germany, and they had eight children, the living ones of whom are: Albert, mail carrier, of Pittsburg; Andrew, in butcher business in Pittsburg; John, foreman for a prominent butcher in Pittsburg; Louis, butcher in Allegheny city; Augustus, a traveling salesman for a wholesale meat packer; Elizabeth, wife of Fred J. Qualman, of Millvale. Two died, Marie, wife of F. F. Walther, and Matthew, a mechanic. Mr. Engelhardt is a member of the German Lutheran church, and is a highly esteemed citizen of the town in which he has passed the last thirty years of his life.

ERNEST THEODORE LIPPERT, of Millvale, Pa., a prominent saw manufacturer, was born in Prussia, Sept. 21, 1841, son of Karl and Christina (Brockman) Lippert, both natives and life residents of Prussia. They had a family of six children, five of whom are now living. His father was a glass manufacturer in the old country, as was also his paternal grandfather. Mr. Lippert was educated in the splendid and thorough schools of the Fatherland, and there learned the trade of glass-blowing. He came to America in 1867, located at Pittsburg and worked at his trade for several months. Then he made a tour of the United States, returned to Pittsburg, and went to work for the firm of Lippincott, Bakewell & Co., manufacturers of saws. He continued with that concern until 1880, when he engaged in the manufacture of saws on his own account, the industry being established under the name of the Penn saw works, and located at No. 626 Grant St., Pittsburg. In 1889 Mr. Lippert purchased the trade, name and good-will of the Pittsburg saw works from Hubbard & Co., and consolidated the same with his former business, maintaining, however, the two plants under their distinctive names. In 1896 he built and equipped a large plant at Millvale under the name of the Penn saw works, in the borough of Millvale, where he has resided since 1874. The Millvale plant consists of a large four-story brick factory building, with commodious two-story tempering plants, yards and other accessories, together covering an entire block. The works are fully equipped with steam power, steam hammer saw-making machinery, and all mechanical requisites for making superior products. Their output, which is a valuable one, embraces saws and general mill supplies of all descriptions. Mr. Lippert is a thoroughly practical saw maker, of thirty-five years' experience, and employs from seventy-five to 100 men, a large percentage of whom are experts in their respective lines. It has always been a carefully observed rule of action with Mr. Lippert to strive for the best products and to be satisfied with nothing short of as perfect an article as human ingenuity can devise. He has been twice married—first, to Annie Morton, of Pittsburg, in 1869, who bore him two children and died in 1881; the second time, to Mrs. Wilhelmina Pfischner, a widow and the mother of seven children by a previous marriage, and they have had five children. He and his wife are members of the German Lutheran church of Millvale, and he has been a trustee of that body for the past twenty-five years. He is a republican in his political affiliations, and has been a member of the borough council for the last ten years, having two years more to serve on his present term. Mr. Lippert is a man of many sterling qualities, and possesses the respect and esteem of the entire community.

JOHN DENNY, a trusted employe at the Tarentum paper mill, was born in Armstrong county, Pa., Jan. 29, 1844, and was a son of Ecard and Christina (Shafer) Denny, natives of Germany. The father fought with distinction in the famous battles of Waterloo and Moscow. Later he married and came to America, settling first in Buffalo, N. Y., and moving after some years to East Deer township, Allegheny county, where he spent his last days on a farm. He died, Aug. 19, 1869, when seventy-seven years old, and his wife in 1890, at the age of eighty-two. They were the parents of eight children, five of whom are living—three sons and two daughters. Ecard Denny was a farmer in Germany, and spent the last years of his life at that vocation, but was also for some years, after coming to America, engaged in various business pursuits. In politics he was a republican. He and his wife were members of the German Evangelical Protestant church. Mr. Denny helped build the church of that denomination in Tarentum, and afterwards served as trustee. John Denny, whose name begins this article, was reared and educated in East Deer township, and was for many years a farmer by vocation. Afterwards he worked fourteen years for the Pittsburg plate glass company. In politics a republican, he takes a keen interest in the welfare of his party. He has served a term in the council, has also held the office of constable, and has acted as election inspector. During the Civil war he served nine months as a member of Company F, 123d regiment, Pennsylvania volunteer infantry, taking part in the battles of second Bull Run and Antietam, and being wounded in the latter engagement by a bursting shell. A brother, Hudson Denny, was captain of a company that was organized in Oil City.

He also fought at Antietam and second Bull Run, and helped bury the dead after the latter battle. He, too, was wounded by a shell. Captain Denny now lives in Wildwood, Pa. John Denny was married, in 1867, to Miss Rosina Sentrick, of Butler county, and had three children, viz.: Lillie M. (deceased), Frank E. and Annie P. Mrs. Denny died Feb. 17, 1900. Mr. Denny is identified in religious belief with the Methodist church, as was his wife.

THOMAS NORMAN, JR., a popular druggist of Hites, has been successfully engaged in that business since 1885. He has been justice of the peace for the past twenty-one years, and was re-elected not long ago for another five-year term. He is also interested in the German National building and loan association of Pittsburg. Mr. Norman was born in England, Nov. 28, 1845, and came to Allegheny county with his parents in 1855. His father, Thomas Norman, Sr., was for many years a boot and shoe manufacturer in Pittsburg, and spent his last years in Normantown. In politics he was a democrat, and, with his wife, Louisa (Dean) Norman, belonged to the Episcopal church. Mrs. Norman died in 1881, at sixty-seven, while Mr. Norman died on Feb. 17, 1901, at the advanced age of eighty-four. They were the parents of fifteen children, of whom only three are living. Thomas Norman, Jr., was educated in England and Pittsburg, and before going into the drug business spent about twenty years in the coal mines, and worked for a time on canal boats. In politics he is a republican, loyal to his party, and actively interested in its welfare. He is a member of Tarentum lodge, No. 587, I. O. O. F., and of the Orangemen of Hites. He is married and, with his family, belongs to the Methodist Episcopal church. His wife, whom he married Dec. 13, 1871, was formerly Miss Mary M. Weisenstein, a native of Butler county, Pa., born March 15, 1845. Her father, Jacob Weisenstein, was born in Germany, and died in Butler county at the age of fifty-six, while her mother, Mary (St. Clair) Weisenstein, a native of Butler county and a member of a pioneer family, lived to be seventy-seven years old. To Mr. and Mrs. Norman have been born five children: Mary S., Thomas D., Gottlieb F., Louise J. and Robert K.

WILLIAM JOHN STALEY, superintendent of the water-works at Tarentum, and one of the more prosperous and well-to-do men of that city, was born in East Deer township, Allegheny Co., Pa., Dec. 17, 1842. He is the son of James M. and Julia (McNeal) Staley, and grandson of William Staley, a native of Pennsylvania and pioneer settler of Allegheny county, where he died at the age of sixty-five. His wife also died in Allegheny county. James M. Staley lived, when a young man, in Bakerstown, but afterwards married and moved to Freeport, going later to Tarentum, where he died in 1875, and his wife in 1899. They were the parents of seven children—three sons and four daughters—four of whom are living. James Staley was, in early life, a farmer, afterwards superintendent of a salt works, and later superintendent in the oil fields, but retired from active life several years before his death. In politics he was a republican. He and his wife were members of the Methodist Episcopal church, in which he held the honorary position of steward. The maternal grandfather of the subject of this sketch was John McNeal, a native of Pennsylvania, who died at an advanced age in Allegheny county. He married a Miss Diller, who was born at Squirrel Hill, Allegheny county, and died at Ward's Run, in the same county. William J. Staley, whose name begins this sketch, was reared and educated in Tarentum and at Bailey's Run, and at an early age began to work in the oil fields. He was thus employed from 1858 to 1868, and farmed seven years, acting at the same time as superintendent of an oil refinery. In 1875 he came to Tarentum, where he engaged for four years in mercantile pursuits, and put up the first opera house in the town. He managed the opera house five years and rented it two years, after which it burned down. Besides the opera house, he built a skating rink which for two years enjoyed a liberal patronage. For several years past he has served as superintendent of the water-works system at Tarentum, and has proved an able and conscientious official. In political belief a republican, Mr. Staley has served two terms in the Tarentum council. He is a member of K. O. T. M., and, with his wife, belongs to the Methodist Episcopal church. In 1867 he married Mary Hopple, a native of Germany, who came to America in 1848, when three years old. Mrs.

Staley's father, John Hopple, died while on his way to America, but her mother, Elizabeth (Burke) Hopple, is living, at the age of eighty-eight years. Mr. and Mrs. Staley are the parents of seven children, viz.: William W., Dorothy J., John M., Marie E., Jemima E., Elmer and Mabelle C. Mr. Staley has, by thrift and industry, acquired considerable means, and is the owner of much valuable property. He has a farm in Beaver county, four store rooms in Tarentum, on Fifth avenue, and a beautiful residence, built on part of the old homestead land on East Tenth avenue, where he has resided with his family for the past thirteen years.

JOSHUA N. GRIFFITH, an old and respected citizen of Braddock, was born in Somerset county, Pa., Oct. 13, 1843. His parents were Eli and Elizabeth Griffith, prominent and respected citizens of Somerset county. Mr. Griffith received his education in the public schools of his native county, and in 1858 moved with his parents to Johnstown, Cambria county, where he worked on a farm for a while, and later in the mills. He was employed in the mills when the Civil war broke out, and during the war enlisted in the 192d Pennsylvania volunteers for one year, and was honorably discharged eight months later at the close of the war, returning to the mills. Mr. Griffith was married, Jan. 25, 1866, to Emma L., daughter of Edward and Rebecca Thomas. Mrs. Griffith was born Aug. 25, 1859, and was educated in the public schools of Johnstown. Seven children have been born of this union, as follows: Sadie, wife of P. L. Brisbane, of Braddock; Effie, wife of A. S. Gearing, Jr.; Forest, in business in North Braddock; Elmer, in the shoe business; William T., also in the shoe business; May, wife of Harry Wright, of Braddock, and Maudie, who died in infancy. Mr. J. N. Griffith came to Braddock in 1876, and accepted a position in the Edgar Thompson steel works, where he remained until 1887. He was then elected assessor, and later held the position of tax collector for ten years. Since 1898 he has been engaged in the insurance business, and has been very successful. He was first connected with the American relief association, and later resigned to accept a position with the Pittsburg sick and accident insurance company. He is now connected by charter with the National beneficial association of Pennsylvania, with an office at No. 708 Pennsylvania Ave., Pittsburg. Mr. Griffith is a member of Braddock Field lodge, No. 529, I. O. O. F.; Major A. M. Harper post, No. 181, G. A. R., and the Knights of Malta. His home is at No. 804 Talbot Ave. Mr. Griffith is imbued with the inherent thrift and industry of the people of his race, has always been energetic in the promotion of civil, social and personal prosperity, and is one of Braddock's honored citizens.

GUSTAVE A. MECKEL, for twenty-seven years superintendent for William B. Scarfe & Sons company, of Oakmont, Pa., was born in Allegheny city, Pa., Dec. 11, 1846, and is a son of Frank W. and Anna M. (Aschenbach) Meckel, both natives of Saxony, who came in an early day to Allegheny county, and died there. His maternal grandparents were John B. and Anna (Young) Aschenbach, also natives of Saxony, and early settlers of Allegheny. Frank Wm. Meckel, father of the subject of this sketch, was a sheet and plate iron worker, being in the employ of W. B. Scarfe & Sons for forty years, and was for many years foreman in the plant. He was politically a republican. He and his wife were members of the reformed church. Frank Wm. Meckel and wife had twelve children, of whom six are now living. The father died in 1876, and the mother is now living at the age of seventy-seven. Gustave A. Meckel, whose name stands at the head of this sketch, was educated in the public schools; at the age of sixteen, he began work for W. B. Scarfe & Sons company, and has been in their employ ever since, rising from a low position to the responsible place of superintendent. The firm is a large and flourishing one, and does an extensive business in the manufacture of structural steel works, range boilers, tanks, stacks, ice cans, corrugated iron high-pressure cylinders, water filters, water purifying plants, etc. Mr. Meckel is a prominent republican and influential in local party politics. He is a member of Hope lodge, No. 243, Knights of Pythias; Lodge No. 548, F. and A. M.; Knights of Khorassan; Allegheny lodge, National Union, No. 288, and League of American Wheelmen. He was married, in 1875, to Miss Anna M. Worthington, of Allegheny city, and has two children, Alice M. and

Frank W. Alice is the wife of Allen Rohrback, of Frederick, Md., and has three children, Martin N., Gustave A. and Alice. Frank spent nine months in the Spanish-American war with the 18th Pennsylvania volunteers. He is now employed as a foreman in government work. Mr. Meckel is at the present time burgess of Oakmont borough.

SAMUEL LAWRENCE GARDNER, of McKee's Rocks, borough engineer, was born in Washington county, Pa., in the township then known as Plumsick, May 17, 1849, son of Samuel and Jane (Noah) Gardner, of Scotch-Irish and Dutch extraction. The Noah family came to America on the "Mayflower," and have since been prominent in the affairs of the country. Nine children were born to Samuel and Jane Gardner, seven of whom, besides the subject of this sketch, are now living, viz.: John; Peter N.; Rebecca, wife of Edward Gardner; Belinda Jane, wife of John Snyder; Margaret Anne, now Mrs. Francis Adams; Nancy, wife of Ridgely Caldwell, and Martha. Elizabeth, wife of William Durlan, died some years since. The elder Gardner was a prosperous blacksmith, a stanch democrat and for many years an elder in the Presbyterian church. Samuel L. Gardner was educated in the district schools and at the State normal school, of West Liberty, Ohio Co., W. Va. In 1870 he left school to engage in the railroad business, serving as yard clerk and passenger brakeman until 1875, when he became a street-car conductor and worked in the cities of Pittsburg and Chicago. In 1878 he began to learn the profession of civil engineering under R. L. McCully, of Pittsburg, Pa., and was with him for two years. He became railroad surveyor for the Santa Fé, Prescott & Phœnix railroad, where he remained until 1892, when he went to California for a year. Later he returned to Pittsburg, resumed his former position with R. L. McCully, and two years afterwards was elected to his present position of borough engineer of McKee's Rocks. Mr. Gardner has made a fine record in that position, and stands high in the esteem of the people of that city. Mr. Gardner has been married three times: First, to Mary O'Brien, by whom he had one son, Walter E., now a farmer of Washington county; the second time, to Mary Boland, of New

Brighton, Pa., by whom he had a son, James G. Blaine, of Coraopolis; then, to Mrs. Christina Watson, widow of Harry Watson, of Allegheny city, and they have a young daughter, Rebecca Jane. Mr. Gardner is a republican, attends the United Presbyterian church, and is a member of the Order of Americus.

STEPHEN C. CONWELL, of the firm of Maurhoff & Conwell, Brackenridge, was born in Allegheny city, Pa., April 13, 1851, and is a son of Stephen C. and Caroline (Hesker) Conwell, the former a native of Allegheny county, and the latter of Germany. The father was a son of Stephen Conwell, a Scotchman, and Mary (Dyer) Conwell, pioneers of Allegheny county, who afterwards moved to Macon city, Mo., and died there. The grandparents of the subject of this sketch were Charles and Caroline Hesker, both of whom died in Pittsburg. Charles Hesker was a native of Germany. Stephen C. Conwell, father of the subject of this article, was a chairmaker by trade, and worked at this business in Pittsburg for many years. He also followed for a time the vocation of a coal boat pilot, at one time kept a hotel in Pittsburg, and was, in 1845, captain of the Niagara volunteer fire company. In politics he was a democrat. He served with distinction in the Civil war, enlisting in 1861 and serving continuously from then until 1865, except for a time in 1863, when he was incapacitated by sickness. He died in July, 1885, and his wife on Dec. 6, 1894. They had a family of seven children, all but one of whom are living. Stephen C. Conwell, whose name begins this sketch, was reared in Pittsburg, was educated there, and for some years engaged in the manufacture of cigars in Pittsburg. He also spent about two years in the hotel business there, and, in November, 1885, came to Harrison township, where for two years he kept a hotel. After this he engaged again for a time in the manufacture of cigars, and then embarked in his present business, in company with E. E. Maurhoff. The firm of Maurhoff & Conwell has been most successful, and does a constantly increasing business in sanitary sewering, and the selling of salt-glazed sewer pipe and building blocks. In politics Mr. Conwell is an ardent republican, influential in local party affairs, and was elected in 1902 for a three-year term as councilman in Brackenridge. He is a prominent property owner in Brackenridge, where he has a store building, two dwelling-houses and several building lots, and is a stockholder in the People's National bank of Tarentum. His religious views are liberal, and he gives generously to churches of all denominations, as well as to other worthy charities. In 1874 Mr. Conwell married Christina Nagle, of Allegheny county, by whom he has had eight children, viz.: Charles A., Amanda, Blanche (deceased), Gertrude, Caroline, Raymond, Howard and Stephen C., Jr.

DAVID SPENCE, of McKee's Rocks, Pa., a retired mill worker and a prominent citizen, was born in Manchester, England, in 1832, came to America in 1865, and the following year settled in Allegheny county. His paternal grandfather was a dry-goods merchant, of Belfast, Ireland, lived to the ripe old age of ninety-seven years, and, in later life, was an excise inspector for the British government. His paternal great-grandfather left a large estate, which is still in the courts of chancery. In 1868 Mr. Spence brought his parents to Pittsburg, where they resided the rest of their lives, his father dying in 1870 at the age of seventy-five years, and his mother dying the following year at the age of seventy-eight years. His father was a bricklayer by trade, and in his younger days was a sailor, having been connected with the American merchant marine and having made a landing at New York city, prior to coming to the country to reside in 1868. They had three children: Mary, widow of a Mr. Blumley, of England; David, and Ann, widow of Samuel Wilson, of Ireland. The two daughters now reside in South Africa, where they possess large means, Mrs. Wilson recently selling several coal mines to Cecil Rhodes. David Spence was first married in England, in 1853, to Emma Rowan, and they had two children, Thomas R. and Henry D. She died in 1865, at the age of twenty-nine years. His second marriage was, in 1867, with Ann J. Heslip, who died in 1875, after bearing the following children: William D., Charles W., George K. and Blanche (deceased). He was again married, in 1879, to Prudence Heslip, a sister of his second wife, and they have had four children, Annie B., Clarence G., Edgar T. and Olive P. Mr. Spence followed steel rolling for nearly fifty years, was in the employ of the Pittsburg steel works for the greater part of that time, and, in 1900, retired from active business. He rolled the wire for the cables for the Brooklyn bridge, and was a master of his trade. He has accumulated a fine property and is now taking life quietly, free from the cares that too often beset old age.

JOHN ALBERT FERGUSON, of Coraopolis, Pa., a prominent financier and banker, was born in Independence township, Beaver Co., Pa., March 12, 1840, and is the only child of John Ferguson. He is of Scotch-Irish descent, and his father was by profession a tanner, who began with nothing and by thrift and energy acquired a competency. John A. Ferguson attended the public schools of Allegheny county until he was sixteen years of age, and then commenced work with his father in the tannery. He remained there until he was twenty-three years old, when he engaged in farming and stock-raising, following these occupations until 1890. In 1889, at the death of his father, he became the possessor of a large estate, which he has handled very successfully and increased its finances greatly. In 1890 Mr. Ferguson came to live at Coraopolis, since which time he has taken a prominent place in the financial world. He was a prime mover and one of the chief financiers in the organization of the Coraopolis & Neville Island street railway company. In 1897 he organized the Coraopolis National bank, being elected president, which position he still holds. He was largely instrumental in establishing the Ohio Valley trust company, in 1901, and was elected president of that institution. He is connected with a number of other institutions, being treasurer of the West Pittsburg oil refinery and president of the Coraopolis cemetery company. He has been an extensive owner and operator in various oil fields, being the owner of several large tracts of oil lands in Allegheny and Beaver counties. In 1862 Mr. Ferguson was married to Maria Jane Holmes, of Independence township, Beaver Co., Pa., their children being: Samuel S., of Independence township; Martha L., wife of Scott A. Connell, of Coraopolis; Lula B., wife of Rev. James H. McCormick, of Conneaut Lake, Pa.; Francis Ferguson, at home; Charles B. Ferguson, secretary and treasurer of the Ohio Valley trust company, and Ollie J., wife of Nevin Ferree, of Coraopolis, Pa. Mr. Ferguson has been a stanch democrat during his entire life, casting his first vote for Stephen A. Douglas. He is connected with, and a supporter of, the Presbyterian denomination. Quiet and reserved in all his habits of life, he is public-spirited in a high degree, and is one of Allegheny county's most substantial citizens.

THOMAS SCOTT GUNDY, for many years conductor on the Allegheny Valley railroad, was born in Beaver county, Pa., May 12, 1844. His father was James Gundy, an Englishman, who came to the United States in 1840, and died in Beaver county in 1848. His mother, Mary Gundy, died in 1889. James and Mary Gundy were the parents of six children, five sons and one daughter. After the death of her first husband, Mrs. Gundy married Robert Kay, a native of England, who settled in Washington county. James Gundy, father of the subject of this sketch, was a superintendent of mines, and on coming to America became a farmer, and also a teamster, his route being between Pittsburg and Frankford, Pa. The man whose name heads this sketch received a limited education, which he has supplemented by a wide general knowledge gained in his long and eventful career. At the age of fourteen he learned the blacksmith trade, working at it four years. On Dec. 24, 1864, he began his career as a railroad man, on the Pennsylvania railroad, and six years later entered the employ of the Allegheny Valley railroad company. He began as a brakeman, but has been for thirty-five years a conductor, twenty-one years on a passenger train. He is now the oldest conductor on his division. Mr. Gundy was married, May 14, 1868, to Miss Mary Buck, a native of Germany, who came with her parents to America when five years old. Mr. and Mrs. Gundy are the parents of four sons and one daughter, viz.: William K., daylight foreman for the Westinghouse company, at Turtle Creek; John L., bookkeeper for the Standard oil company, at Pittsburg; Harry S., fireman and engineer on the Allegheny Valley railroad; Simon M., timekeeper and draftsman at the Verona tool works, and Mollie E., wife of Ernest Stone, daylight foreman for the Westinghouse company, at Turtle Creek. Mr. Gundy has lived in Oakmont twenty-one years, and is among the most respected and influential citizens of that place. He and his family are members of the First Presbyterian church of Oakmont. He is a member of Verona lodge, No. 548, F. and A. M., and the Society of Railway Conductors. Mr. Gundy is a democrat, but has never aspired to political preferment.

JOSEPH OVERY, of Cleveland, Ohio, a prominent oil producer, was born in London, England, Feb. 5, 1843. He is a son of Samuel and Eliza (Reeves) Overy, the father being a shoe merchant in London, where he spent his entire life. Joseph Overy received his educational training in the schools of his native city, and at the age of thirteen, abandoned his studies to accept a position in the stationery house of Richards & Co., in St. Martin's lane. He remained in this business for four years, and then accompanied his mother to America, going direct to Cleveland, Ohio, where he worked on his uncle's farm for two years, and afterward for the Austin powder company for one year. During his stay in Cleveland, Mr. Overy attended the Erie Street Baptist church and Sunday-school, of which J. D. Rockefeller was assistant superintendent and William Rockefeller teacher of his class. In the winter of 1863–64 he went into the oil regions of Pennsylvania and engaged in drilling wells at Pioneer, seven months after which he began contracting for the Densmore oil company, near Petroleum Centre, of which the father of A. J. Cassett, of the Pennsylvania railroad, was president. After two years he took interests in the oil wells at Bennehoop Run, took leases of John Bennehoop, and was at his house shortly after the great robbery. In 1870, in company with Wesley Chambers and others, Mr. Overy purchased the first farm south of Bear Creek that was sold for oil purposes, operating it himself, and using the first large casing for drilling which was taken into the Parker oil field. He has the distinction of having the first well that flowed in that region without first being torpedoed or tubed. Mr. Overy operated successfully a number of farms from Parker to Carbon Center, and was president of the Keystone pipe line which was laid from St. Joe to Freeport. In 1890 he came to Pittsburg, continuing in the oil-producing business in the Wildwood, Coraopolis and Moon oil fields. Mr. Overy is a republican in his politics, and is very prominently identified with the Masonic fraternity, holding membership in the Trinity commandery, of Bradford, and the Pennsylvania consistory and Syria temple, of Pittsburg. Mr. Overy is universally regarded as a man of the highest integrity and probity of character, and the possessor of excellent business qualifications.

HARRISON PAGE MEEDS, of the firm of Meeds Bros. & Co. (limited), was born in Pittsburg, Pa., April 4, 1869. The other members of this firm are J. B. Meeds, Alice A. Meeds, Mrs. B. E. Reed, of Verona, and Mrs. Mary Robinson, of Madison, Ind. The firm was originally known as Euwer Bros. & Co. (limited), but the name was changed to Meeds Bros. & Co. in 1896. J. B. D. Meeds, grandfather of the man whose name heads this article, was born in England, came to Philadelphia when two years old, and to Pittsburg as early as 1834. He was a prominent educator of that city for many years, and was connected with the Dollar savings bank as early as 1865. H. P. Meeds, Sr., the father of our subject, married Augusta Barker, daughter of Sylvester Barker, who came to Pittsburg from Vermont in an early day and engaged in the planing mill business. Mr. and Mrs. Meeds had five children, all of whom are living. Mrs. Meeds died in April, 1872. H. P. Meeds, the subject of this sketch, was educated in Pittsburg, graduating from the central high school in 1889. He began his mercantile career at an early age, and has been most successful. The firm of Meeds Bros. & Co. (limited), deals in furniture, carpets and clothing, and occupies two stores, one 60 by 125 feet in size, the other 35 feet wide by 117 feet long. Although never an aspirant for public office, in politics Mr. Meeds is a republican. He is influentially connected with various societies, being a member of Verona lodge, No. 987, I. O. O. F.; Iona lodge, No. 141, Knights of Pythias; General McClellan lodge, No. 150, Jr. O. U. A. M.; Edgewater council, No. 484, Royal Arcanum, and Alice Cary lodge, No. 120, Daughters of Rebecca, of Pittsburg. In 1896 he married Miss Millie F. Calhoun, of Verona, and has one child, Nellie Augusta. Mr. and Mrs. Meeds are members of the

First Presbyterian church of Oakmont. J. B. Meeds, brother of H. P. Meeds, and a member of the same company, was born Oct. 22, 1860, and was reared and educated in Pittsburg, where, after the usual preliminary schooling, he attended the Western university. After leaving school, he was employed for several years by the Allegheny & Pittsburg railroad companies, but has been connected with Meeds Bros. & Co. since 1888. He now has charge of the furniture department. Mr. Meeds is a member of Iona lodge, No. 141, Knights of Pythias; Washington camp, No. 675, P. O. L. of A., Royal Arcanum, and Woodmen of the World. In politics he is a republican, but, like his brother, has never sought political preferment. He is a member of the Methodist Episcopal church of Oakmont, where he resides.

JOHN DUSTER, contractor, of Tarentum, was born in Germany in 1862, and came to America in 1876, with his parents, Peter and Mary Catharine (Frey) Duster, both now deceased. The family located first in Louisville, Ky., from whence Mr. and Mrs. Duster moved first to Alabama, and then to St. Louis, where Mr. Duster died in 1891. His wife died at Butler, Pa., in 1902. They had fourteen children, of whom seven are now living, all in America. John Duster, the subject of this sketch, was educated in Germany, and on coming to America remained with his parents until 1882, when he went to Jeffersonville, Ind., to work in a carshop. From Jeffersonville he went to St. Joseph, Mo., where he engaged for a short time in lead mining, going from there to South St. Louis. Shortly afterwards he returned to Jeffersonville, to work in a plate glass factory, his father having been a plate glass worker before him. He next moved to Tarentum, where he has since resided. From 1883 to Oct. 1, 1887, he was employed as a glass worker by Captain Ford, after which he bought the ferry at Tarentum and ran it for four and a half years. In 1892 he engaged in the wholesale produce business in Pittsburg, still retaining his residence in Tarentum, and then went into the business of moving houses, in which he has since been successfully occupied. In 1902 he organized the Duster contracting company, which is engaged in the same business. Mr. Duster is a stockholder in the People's

National bank of Tarentum. He is a member of the Heptasophs of Tarentum, and B. P. O. E., and was one of the committee which organized the local lodge of that order, established in 1901. In politics he is a prominent republican, and has served his borough three years as councilman. Mr. Duster was married, in 1885, to Miss Ida M. Harris, of Tarentum, and has four children, Gertrude E., Effie D., Helen E. and Raymond S.

WILLIAM P. LOUREY, of Aspinwall, a well-known justice of the peace and borough assessor, was born at Brattonville, Armstrong Co., Pa., July 21, 1842. He is a son of Alexandria and Nancy (Armstrong) Lourey, descended from very old families who were distinguished on account of their connection with the patriot army that wrested independence from the mother country. Mr. Lourey was educated at the Dayton academy, his last year's work being interrupted by his enlisting in the 14th Pennsylvania volunteers, on April 28, 1861. On August 14th he was discharged, but re-enlisted on the same day in Company C, 105th Pennsylvania volunteers. After serving two years, the regiment re-enlisted as veteran volunteers until the close of the war. He entered the service as a private, rose to be color-bearer, and finally received the commission of second lieutenant, serving in that capacity until the cessation of hostilities. He saw distinguished service in the army of the Potomac from the time McClellan took command until May 5, 1864, when he was so severely wounded that he retired from active service. Prior to this he was wounded at the battle of Fair Oaks, May 28, 1862; shot through the leg at the battle of Fredericksburg, Dec. 13, 1862; and wounded in the right side at the battle of the Wilderness in 1864. He was married, on Oct. 23, 1867, to Rebecca J., daughter of John and Anna Hartman, and to this union were born two children: James A., foreman carpenter for Charles A. Hastings, and Bessie A. His first wife died on July 13, 1872, and he was married on Oct. 13, 1875, to Lizzie A., daughter of Thomas and Elizabeth Kay, and to them were born three children: Jennie, wife of C. L. Dauber, foreman of an elevator shop; Francis T., an architect with H. D. Gilchrist, Frick building, Pittsburg; and Walter G., who died

May 17, 1898. Mr. Lourey is a member of Sharpsburg lodge, No. 328, of the Heptasophs; Manorville lodge, No. 932, of the Odd Fellows; Aspinwall lodge, No. 238, of the Junior Order of American Mechanics; Tarentum lodge, No. 320, of the Ancient Order of United Workmen, and of the Union Veteran legion, No. 1, of Pittsburg. He is a leading member of the Evangelical Lutheran church, and has occupied many prominent official positions in connection with it. He was elected county commissioner of Armstrong county on the republican ticket in 1872, and served four years. He served two terms as justice of the peace in Armstrong county, and on his removal to Tarentum in 1884, he followed the vocation of a carpenter. In 1892 he came to Aspinwall, worked at his trade until 1894, when he was elected justice of the peace, which office he has since held, having been again elected in 1903. He is also borough assessor, and is generally regarded as one of the leading men of his community. His ancestors served in the Revolutionary war; his father was a soldier in the Civil war; he also participated in that great struggle, and his son took part in the Spanish-American war, serving in the artillery branch of the service in Porto Rico. His family have served their country on all occasions when it was threatened with danger from within or without, and have been ever ready to respond to the nation's call.

GEORGE H. McFETRIDGE, a leading citizen of Hites, and associated in the brick and coal business with his brother, William McFetridge, whose sketch appears elsewhere in this work, was born in Derry county, Ireland, May 14, 1855, came to Allegheny county in infancy, and was educated here in the public schools. He is now a partner in all the concerns in which his brother is interested, except in the mercantile business, from which he retired in 1902. He is also interested in real estate with Charles Uhlinger, the firm being known as Charles Uhlinger & Co. Like his brother, Mr. McFetridge began life a poor boy, and has by ability and perseverance won for himself a competence. He has for a number of years resided in Hites, Pa., and is recognized as one of the most influential citizens of that place. He is vice-president and director of the People's National bank of Tarentum, one of the leading stockholders in the First National bank of Natrona, and also owns stock in the Fidelity glass company and Baker manufacturing company, both of Tarentum. In politics he is an ardent republican, although not an aspirant for office. He is a prominent and enthusiastic Mason, being a member of Pollock lodge, No. 502, F. and A. M., of Tarentum; Shiloh chapter, No. 257, R. A. M.; Tancred commandery, No. 48, K. T., and Syria temple, A. A. O. N. M. S. He is also a member of B. P. O. Elks. On Jan. 20, 1886, Mr. McFetridge married Miss Adelaide Kluenspise, of Philadelphia, Pa. Mr. and Mrs. McFetridge have one son, George L. McFetridge.

WALTER S. KIDD, of McKee's Rocks, Pa., member of the firm of Kidd Bros. & Burgher steel wire company, was born in Yorkshire, England, March 1, 1847, son of William and Elizabeth (Hall) Kidd. His ancestors were strictly English in their origin, and a great-uncle of his mother was with the duke of Marlborough at the battle of Blenheim, and fell mortally wounded in that sanguinary conflict. His father was a wire manufacturer in Cawthorne, England, for many years, and died nearly half a century since. Walter S. Kidd obtained his early educational training in the splendidly equipped schools of his native shire, and when fourteen years of age entered the wire manufacturing plant of his father, who had previously died, and the business was then being conducted by the family. He remained with that plant until he was twenty-two years of age, when he came to America and secured employment with the firm of Washburn & Moen, of Worcester, Mass., the largest manufacturers of steel wire in the United States. He was with that concern for five years, and then attended a literary course of three years at Butler university, of Indianapolis, Ind. Mr. Kidd then became general superintendent of the wire factory of R. H. Wolff & Co., of Peekskill, N. Y., where he remained for two years. In 1895 the present firm of Kidd Bros. & Burgher steel wire company was formed. Their factory was located at McKee's Rocks, now at Aliquippa, where they have a finely equipped plant and employ half a hundred skilled workmen. Mr. Kidd is also financially interested in the Vulcan crucible steel company, which operates a large plant at Aliquippa, Pa. He was married, in 1876, to Vina E., daughter of Isaac Barnes, of Barnesville, Ohio, and they have four children. Mr. Kidd is a republican, an elder in the Christian church, and a man of unusual integrity and probity of character. He has an appreciative regard for the rights of his fellow-man, and enjoys the respect and esteem of all with whom he meets.

RICHARD L. JONES, deceased, was born in England in 1813; moved to Dublin, Ireland, when a boy; was educated, and afterwards engaged in business there. Mr. Jones came to America in 1848 with three brothers. Of these, Samuel was, for many years, a professor at Jefferson college; Benjamin a teacher in the Pittsburg schools, in the twenty-eighth ward, and William also a prominent educator. A fourth brother, James, was a prominent physician in London, and a talented musician and composer of music. Richard L. Jones, on coming to America, settled at Verona, and bought a farm there, which he managed for a number of years before retiring from active life. He was fond of gardening and a great lover of trees and flowers, a prominent man in his day, and a man universally admired and respected. He was always faithful to the republican party, but never aspired to office. He was a member of the Episcopal church. Mr. Jones was married, Aug. 16, 1859, to Miss Susan Hawk, who survives him, and lives a retired life on the old farm. Mrs. Jones is a daughter of Joseph and Elizabeth (Steen) Hawk, who came from Greensburg, Westmoreland county. Mr. Hawk lived to the advanced age of eighty-seven, and his wife to the age of eighty-three. They had fourteen children, of whom all grew to maturity, and four are still living. Mr. Hawk's father was Daniel Hawk, a veteran of the War of 1812, who died at the age of ninety-five, while his mother, Mary (Bricker) Hawk, lived to be ninety. Mr. and Mrs. Richard L. Jones had two children, Emma and Ida A. Emma is now the wife of John S. Kennedy, and has had two children, of whom one, Marion, Jr., died in infancy, and one, Margaret F., is living. Ida married Samuel Eakin Stewart, who died in 1895, leaving three children, John Clark, Ida A. and Samuel E. J. Mr. Stewart was a prominent young lawyer and politician of Pittsburg. He was born in Allegheny city, Pa., June 30, 1856. He was a graduate of Washington and Jefferson college, and studied law with his uncle, R. E. Stewart, of Braddock. Mr. Stewart was a young man, for whom a bright future might have been expected. He represented his district in the State legislature for eight years. He was, with his wife, a member of the United Presbyterian church.

JOHN F. YOUNG, of McKee's Rocks, Pa., a successful paper-hanger and decorator, was born in Robinson township, Allegheny county, Aug. 14, 1868, and is the son of Richard B. and Mary (Ferree) Young. His parents had three children, two of whom are now living, the other one being Adda L., wife of Charles Smith, of St. Louis, Mo. His father is now sixty-seven years of age, and is the agent at St. Louis for several manufacturing concerns. Mr. Young is descended from an old family, his great-grandfather having been John Young, Sr., the son of James and Mary (Scott) Young, and was born in Lancaster county, Pa., and, when a mere child, removed with his mother's family to what is now Robinson township, Allegheny county. His son was John Young, Jr., born on July 16, 1803, and was married on Dec. 30, 1824, to Hanna, daughter of John and Esther P. (Scott) Phillips. John Young, the second of that name and the grandfather of our subject, was a captain of the Pennsylvania militia, at one time clerk of the orphans' court of Allegheny county, and died in Robinson township, April 17, 1873. Hanna P. Scott was born on Oct. 14, 1801, at Miller's Run, Washington Co., Pa., and was the mother of Richard B. Young, who was born on June 24, 1836. Richard Young served in the Civil war as a captain in Colonel Gallup's regiment of Pennsylvania volunteer heavy artillery, and was married, on Jan. 1, 1863, to Mary Olivia, daughter of Powel Ferree, a French Huguenot, who immigrated to America at an early date. John F. Young attended the public schools of Robinson township until he was sixteen years of age, then engaged in farming for the next twelve years, and when twenty-eight years of age, went to McKee's Rocks, where he has since prospered as a paper-hanger and decorator. He was married to Jennie Linton, of Robinson township, and they have had three children: Raymond R. L., born Oct. 19, 1897, and died July 1, 1899; Marion A., a daughter, born March 1, 1901, and died Dec. 14, 1901, and La Verne A., born May 9, 1903. Mr. Young is a Master Mason, a member of the republican party, and attends the United Presbyterian church.

ANDREW GILLESPIE, retired, of Tarentum, was born in Ireland, May 27, 1834. His parents, Samuel and Jane (Blair) Gillespie, both natives of Ireland, came to Allegheny county in 1839, and spent their last days here. Samuel Gillespie was a farmer. In politics he was a republican. He died March 29, 1864, and his wife Feb. 16, 1858. The subject of this sketch is one of eleven children, six sons and five daughters, of whom two sons and two daughters are living. Mr. Gillespie was reared on a farm and educated in the country schools. He was for many years a chairmaker and also a coal dealer. He formerly lived in Dubois, Clearfield county, and in Brookville, Jefferson county, but since 1890 has resided in Tarentum, where he owns a comfortable home. He also owns stock in the People's National bank of Tarentum, and has money invested in other securities. Since coming to Tarentum he has been retired from active business. Mr. Gillespie was married, April 5, 1855, to Miss Alice J. Thompson, of Allegheny county, and has four children living, all married: Margaret is now Mrs. W. Kearney, of Tecumseh, Kan., and has three children, James, Andrew and Winnie; Linnie married Robert McFarland, of Ridgway, Pa., and has six children, Andrew Gillespie, R. Clifford, Ella Ophelia, Edith May, Robert Eugene and Eva Clair (deceased); May is now Mrs. DeLancy, of East End, Pittsburg, and Jennie is the wife of George B. Bennett, and has two children, Ada M. and Olive. Mr. Gillespie took as his second wife Emma Dawson, of Tarentum. Mr. Gillespie is a veteran of the Civil war, and a member of the G. A. R. of Tarentum. He enlisted first in Company F, 123d Pennsylvania volunteer infantry, in which he served nine months, and then, in 1864, enlisted in Company M, 15th Pennsylvania cavalry, where he served until the close of the war. He was on duty all during his term of service, fought at Fredericksburg and in many minor engagements. In politics Mr.

Gillespie is a republican. He is a member of the Methodist Episcopal church, as are three of his daughters, the other being a Baptist.

WILLIAM McFETRIDGE, one of the foremost business men of Hites and a prominent resident of that city since 1871, began his business career in 1879. In that year, in company with his brother, George H., he embarked in the general merchandise business, under the name of McFetridge Bros. George H. McFetridge retired from the mercantile business in 1902. In 1891 Peter Bert was admitted to partnership, and the firm has since been known as McFetridge, Bert & Co. William McFetridge engaged in the manufacture of brick, in company with his brother, George H., in 1884, and has been most successful. Two years later they added coal mining to their other interests, were successful in this, and have for several years been interested also in oil wells, which are bringing good returns. William McFetridge has long filled an important place in the business and political life of Hites. In politics he is an ardent republican, and has been for many years an influential member of the school board. He is a member of Pollock lodge, No. 502, F. and A. M., of Tarentum, and belongs to the Methodist Episcopal church. In 1875 he married Miss Ella V. Denney, of Hites, and is the father of five children. Mr. McFetridge was born in Derry county, Ireland, May 7, 1850, and came to America in May, 1856, with his parents, George and Sarah (Long) McFetridge. He was reared in Allegheny county, educated in the public schools, and worked in the coal mines before going into business in 1879. His parents were both natives of Derry county, the father being born in 1818 and the mother in 1826. Mr. McFetridge, Sr., spent his active years in this country working in the salt wells, but has for several years lived a retired life. In politics he is a republican, while his religious affiliations are with the United Presbyterian church. Mrs. McFetridge died July 12, 1890. George McFetridge and wife were the parents of nine children, seven of whom grew to manhood and womanhood, viz.: William, Nancy J. (deceased), George H., Robert, Hannah C., Lovina and Joseph.

JOSEPH RODGERS DAY, a prominent liveryman of Homestead, was born near Steubenville, Jefferson Co., Ohio, Dec. 2, 1837, son of George and Sarah (Gamble) Day, natives, respectively, of Maryland and Pennsylvania. His paternal grandfather, also named George Day, a soldier in the Revolution, came to Washington county before 1800, and conducted the first tannery in Washington county. George Day, the father of the subject of this article, was a tanner and farmer of Jefferson county. He died in 1848. George Day married Sarah Rodgers as his first wife and had by this marriage eleven children, as follows: Kate, who married John Robinson; Nancy, who married John Stone; Rachel, afterwards Mrs. John McDonald; Sally, who married Otis Shaw; Fanny, who became the wife of Joseph McCoy; Jane, who married James McCoy; Polly, afterwards Mrs. Richard Young; Rebecca, who married Rev. Gordon; Thomas; George, a physician, and John, also a physician. By his second marriage Mr. Day had four children: James G., for many years a prominent jurist of Iowa; Matthew A., who served during the Civil war as a member of the 29th Iowa regiment, and died of measles while in the service; Joseph R., the subject of this sketch, and Ellen G., afterwards Mrs. Manley. All the children of both marriages, except the subject of this article, are now dead. Joseph R. Day lived in Jefferson county until he was eighteen years old, and in 1855 went to Union county, Ia., where he was a farmer until the outbreak of the Civil war. On Aug. 9, 1862, he enlisted at Council Bluffs, Ia., in Company H, 29th Iowa volunteer infantry, as a corporal, and was promoted to sergeant and served with distinction until the close of the war. He first went with his regiment to Columbus, Ky.; thence to Helena, Ark., where he joined the Red river expedition. Returning to Helena, he joined the Yazoo pass expedition under General Ross, in February, 1863, and participated in the battle of Pemberton, the siege of Vicksburg and the engagement at Helena, Ark., July 4, 1863. In August, 1863, he joined the Little Rock expedition and took part in the capture of that city in September of that year. He also fought valiantly in the battles of Elkin's ford, Camden, Mark's mills, Jenkins' ferry and others, and then, in April, 1864, returned to Little Rock, where he was engaged in garrison duty until the spring of 1865. He then went to New Orleans, thence to Mobile, and engaged in the siege and final assault and capture of Spanish Fort and Fort Blakely. Captain Day was honorably discharged from the service at New Orleans, Aug. 10, 1865, and immediately after the war engaged in the livery business at Brookfield, Mo., continuing at this occupation until January, 1872, when he located in Allegheny city, Pa., and was for the next twenty years a traveling salesman. In 1892 he moved to Homestead and started a livery stable, which he still maintains. In January, 1860, Mr. Day was married to Miss Martha J. Pyles, daughter of William Pyles, of Washington county. Of three children who grew to maturity, Frank I. is now deceased, and George M. and Ellen S. (Mrs. Charles Krugh) are living. Mr. Day was elected, in 1866, first lieutenant of a militia company in Missouri, where he served six years. He was for ten years captain of Company E, 14th regiment, N. G. P., and had charge of his company during the strike of 1892 at Homestead. He is the possessor of a handsome sword presented to him by that company. Captain Day is a member of O. U. A. M. post, No. 88, G. A. R., of Allegheny city, and of Camp No. 1, Union Veteran legion, of Pittsburg. In politics he is a republican.

CHARLES SUTTER, of McKee's Rocks, Pa., the popular and efficient postmaster, was born in Pittsburg, Pa., May 6, 1860, and is the youngest of seven children born to Peter and Philomena (Deckler) Sutter. Peter Sutter came to America from Germany in 1840, cast his first vote for William Henry Harrison, and, strange to relate, cast his last vote for Benjamin Harrison, this ballot being deposited only a short time prior to his death, at the advanced age of seventy-five years. Five of his children survive, viz.: Mrs. Adam Diehl; Mrs. Lewis Doumb, of Allegheny city; Jacob, of Springfield, Ill.; Lewis, a grocer of Beaver Falls, Pa., and Charles, our subject. Young Sutter obtained his early education in the public schools of Pittsburg, and on leaving his studies, secured a position in the grocery store of his brother-in-law, Adam Diehl, where he remained for fourteen years. He then began business for himself, owning several teams and being engaged in hauling and transferring for Booth & Flynn, the largest contractors of the city. Seven years later, he went to Coraopolis and opened a branch office for the Singer sewing machine company, and there continued until 1898, when he was transferred to McKee's Rocks by that concern. He remained in charge of their affairs at McKee's Rocks until 1901, when he was appointed to his present position of postmaster. He has made a splendid record in that important position, and has given general satisfaction to the people of that city. A beautiful new building was completed Nov. 1, 1903, and free delivery established for the city July 7, 1903, with seven carriers. The building was expressly fitted up for postoffice purposes. Mr. Sutter was married on May 7, 1893, to Mary, daughter of David Kelly, of Connellsville, Pa., and to them were born four children, Fred, Marie, Stella and Mabel. Mr. Sutter is a republican in politics, but prior to his present appointment neither held nor sought public office. By his efficiency and courtesy, he has so entrenched himself in the regard of the citizens of McKee's Rocks that it is safe to say that were the office an elective position, his tenure would be a lengthy one. Mr. Sutter is also a member of the Masons and the Presbyterian church.

PETER BERT, of the firm of McFetridge, Bert & Co., a leading mercantile firm of Hites, was born in Germany, March 22, 1836. His father, Adam Bert, a weaver by trade, died in 1864, while his mother, Annie M. (Glink) Bert, died in 1850. Both parents were natives of Germany. They had a family of five children, of whom only two survive. Peter Bert was reared and educated in Germany, confirmed there in the Reformed church, and at the age of nineteen came to Allegheny county, where he has ever since resided. He learned the shoemakers' trade when young, followed this vocation twenty-eight years, and also for some time kept a general store at Hoboken. The firm of McFetridge, Bert & Co. was formed in 1891, and has been most successful. In politics Mr. Bert is an ardent republican. He is an influential member of the Masonic fraternity, being a member of Zeredathah lodge, No. 448, F. and A. M.; Allegheny chapter, No. 217, R. A. M.;

Allegheny commandery, No. 35, Knights Templars, and of the Ancient and Accepted Scottish Rite, Gourgas Lodge of Perfection, Pittsburg. He is also a member of Etna lodge, No. 481, I. O. O. F.; Lincoln True Blue lodge, No. 37, Orangemen. He served in the Civil war as a member of Company F, artillery, enlisting in 1864 and serving until the close of the war, and is a member of Custer post, No. 38, G. A. R., of Etna. Mr. Bert was married, on April 10, 1859, to Miss Apolonia Lockhart, a native of Germany, and has had by this union eleven children, of whom the following seven are living: G. Henry, Elinor E., Albert, Frank, Edward, Annie Mary and Bertha. Mr. Bert and wife have thirteen grandchildren. G. Henry married Stella Thom, and has seven children: Mabel, Norman, Clarence, Harvey, Stella, George and Laverne; Albert married Margaret Whiteman, and has five children: Margaret, Maru, Helen, Jean and Agnes, and Frank, who married Sarah McFetridge, has one daughter, Ella Virginia.

GEORGE H. SCOTT, D. D. S., was born in Pittsburg, Dec. 2, 1857. His father, James Scott, a native of Brooklyn, N. Y., was a son of George and Jemima (Denyce) Scott, the mother being a native of Coney Island, while the father was of Irish birth. James Scott was married in Pittsburg to Annie Kelley, daughter of Abraham and Mary (Humphries) Kelley, both natives of Ireland, who came to Pennsylvania in an early day. Mr. Kelley was a soap and candle manufacturer. He and his wife both died in Pittsburg, and lie buried in Allegheny cemetery. James Scott died July 28, 1878, but his widow is still living, a resident of Pittsburg. Mr. and Mrs. James Scott were the parents of ten children, of whom nine are living. Dr. George H. Scott, the subject of this sketch, was reared and educated in Pittsburg, and graduated from the Pittsburg dental college in 1880. Since that time he has devoted himself to his profession, and has built up a most satisfactory practice both in Pittsburg and Verona. He has made his home in Verona since 1888, and lives in a beautiful residence on Front street. In Verona he has been actively identified with all movements for the betterment of the municipality, and occupies a prominent place in public activities. He was for two years burgess of Verona, and is now serving his third term in the council. Dr. Scott was married, in 1880, to Miss Jennie Shiddle, a native of Pittsburg, and had by this marriage one son, Bruce Y. His first wife dying in 1887, he married, in 1888, her sister, Mrs. McIlvanie. Dr. Scott is an active churchman. He was formerly a member of an Episcopal church in Pittsburg, and is now, with his wife, a member of the Episcopal church in Oakmont. He is a member of the Royal Arcanum and P. H. E. Dr. Scott is an accomplished musician, playing the violin and piano.

HERMAN W. GOODWIN, vice-principal of the union high schools for Turtle Creek, Wilmerding and East Pittsburg, was born in Venango county, Pa., Nov. 12, 1870, son of David W. and Lydia E. (Alcorn) Goodwin. David Goodwin was the son of Daniel D. and Polly (McIntosh) Goodwin, while his wife was the daughter of Samuel and Ann (Prather) Alcorn, early settlers of Venango county. Of the children of Mr. and Mrs. David Goodwin, John D. is superintendent of the Crawford county schools; Sarah A., wife of W. A. Bushnell, of Mount Zion, Ind.; Lura is the wife of C. R. Davison, of Sunville, Pa.; Herman W., the subject of this sketch; Edith is married to W. A. Culp, an oil operator, of Mount Zion, Ind., and Ralph D. is a teacher in Mount Zion, and also interested in oil. Prof. Herman W. Goodwin attended Sunville academy, and then taught school three years before completing his education at Allegheny college, of Meadville, Pa., from which he was graduated with the degree of A. B. Subsequent to this he was supervising principal of schools and principal of the high school at Brackettville, Tex., for three years before coming to Turtle Creek, in 1899. In 1900 he received the degree of A. M. from the Illinois Wesleyan university. The Turtle Creek high school has about eighty students in attendance. Professor Goodwin was married, July 19, 1898, to Miss Edith Reed, daughter of Thomas R. and Jennie (Robertson) Reed, of Indiana county, Pa. Mr. and Mrs. Goodwin have one son, David, born Oct. 1, 1902. Mr. Goodwin is a member of Las Moras lodge, No. 444, F. and A. M., of Brackettville, Tex. He owns a beautiful home on Highland avenue, Turtle Creek.

WILLIAM S. ALTER, merchant of Tarentum, was born in Armstrong county, Pa., May 13, 1847. His father was Jacob Alter, a native of Westmoreland county, who was a son of John Alter, and grandson of Jacob Alter, a pioneer of Westmoreland county, where he owned considerable land. Jacob Alter, father of the subject of this sketch, was a cooper by trade; also kept a general store in Freeport, and was justice of the peace. He was an abolitionist. He died in 1849. He had a brother, Dr. David Alter, of Freeport, who attained some prominence as a scientist and inventor, and was interested in telegraphy. He had the distinction of being the first man to make bromine. Jacob Alter married Prudence Stewart, a native of Armstrong county, and daughter of Isaac and Mary (Dunlap) Stewart. Isaac Stewart was a native of New Jersey, while his wife was born in Ireland, and came to America when twelve years old with her parents, Mr. and Mrs. James Dunlap. William S. Alter, whose name heads this article, was reared in Freeport, where he received a limited education, and when twelve years old went to work as driver on the canal. When very young he became captain of a canal boat, and after this spent several summers in transporting oil on the Allegheny river from Oil City to Pittsburg, and in the winters worked in a sawmill. He became a cleaner and inspector of railroad oil tanks, but was compelled by failing health to give up this work, being unable to do any hard labor for years. Mr. Alter then learned the tinners' trade with D. S. Wallace, of Freeport, followed this vocation five years, and for two years engaged in the hardware business in Freeport. Coming to Tarentum in 1883, he began his long and successful business career, at first as a member of the firm of Alter & Goldinger. Three years later he bought out his partner's interest, and has since that time run the business alone. He is now located in a fine store building, thirty-five by forty-eight feet in size, and three stories in height, which he built several years ago. In politics he is a republican, and at one time served a term as councilman. He has been in business in Tarentum for the past twenty years, with the exception of six years spent in farming. Mr. Alter married Mary E. Bole, of Freeport, and has had six children, viz.: Agnes J., Newton H., John (deceased), William T., Mary B. and Edwin

O. He and his wife are members of the Methodist Episcopal church. Mr. Alter has patented a number of inventions, which have proved successful. He invented a regenerative gas stove, an improvement on drawers for cabinets and other furniture, and an improved blind and curtain holder.

OTTO J. GROSS, of Coraopolis, Pa., a prominent merchant, was born at Mt. Oliver, Pa., Jan. 3, 1877. He is the fourth child of Peter F. and Barbara Marx Gross; the other children being William R., Amelia, Catharine (deceased), Anna, Emma, Bertha, Herman, Karl, Mabel and Hilda. His parents were born in Swarbruecken, Prussia, Germany, his father, on March 12, 1843, his mother, Nov. 11, 1852. His father came to America, arriving in New York, May 5, 1869; three days later he came to Pittsburg, Pa., where he was employed for a few months in the Garrison foundry. In the fall of 1869 he engaged in limestone quarrying, which he conducted successfully for several years. His mother came to this country with her parents in the spring of 1865, settling in Pittsburg. His parents were married Aug. 18, 1870, and resided in Mt. Oliver until the spring of 1884, when they went to Oakdale, Pa., and later to Federal, South Fayette township, Pa., where they still reside. After giving up the stone quarry, Mr. Gross' father became actively engaged in coal-mining, which he followed until 1896. Both his parents are members of the German Lutheran church. Otto Gross attended the public school at Oakdale, Pa.; later the old Centennial school at Federal, Pa., and when fifteen years of age began working in a general store at Hickman, Pa. He remained in that position for eight years, and then came to Coraopolis, where he engaged in the grocery business. He conducted that establishment for one year, and then admitted a partner, adding a line of chinaware and other specialties, and now the store of O. J. Gross & Co. carries the finest and largest stock of any concern of that nature in Coraopolis. He was married, in 1900, to Clarinda Annetta Kelso, of Sheridan, Pa., and they have one daughter, Marion Lovinia, born Feb. 10, 1902. Mr. Gross is a republican in his political belief, and is a member of the Methodist Episcopal church. Mr. Gross has been eminently successful in his business career, and is a splendid example of the German-American citizen, who is such an important factor in our political economy.

HENRY FOSTER HUTCHISON, of Cheswick, Pa., a well-known employe of the Allegheny coal company, was born on April 27, 1854, in Harmarville, Allegheny county, on the farm then owned by Henry D. Foster, and on which the Red Raven Splits factory now stands. He is the son of Peter and Anna (Wise) Hutchison, the former having been a farmer and oil-producer on Oil creek, in Venango county, and also in Clarion, Butler and McKean counties, having followed that vocation from 1864 to 1890. The elder Hutchison retired from the oil business, and was appointed postmaster of Springdale, filling that position until his death, in 1894, at the mature age of seventy-four years. He is survived by his widow, who now lives in Springdale, and is nearly eighty years of age. The paternal grandfather of Henry F. Hutchison was born in Scotland, near Edinburgh; came to America with his wife, and located near Rome, N. Y. His maternal grandparents, Christian and Barbara (Neff) Wise, came from Germany, settled at Harmarville, Pa., and there his grandfather followed weaving and farming until his death, in 1874. Henry F. Hutchison was educated in the elementary branches in the public schools of Harmarville, then attended the preparatory college at Leechburg until sixteen years of age, and was graduated from the commercial department of the Iron City college when in his eighteenth year. He was interested in the oil business with his father for about thirteen years, and conducted a store in Springdale. In 1887 he came to Cheswick and worked as a gardener until 1902, when he was placed in charge of the oil and lamps of the Allegheny coal company. He was married, in 1878, to Mary Elizabeth, daughter of Thomas and Catharine Pillow. Thomas Pillow was a farmer and the son of John Pillow, who was a native of Pennsylvania and a pioneer of East Deer township, having come to Allegheny county when it was a wilderness. John Pillow owned the farm on which the borough of Cheswick now stands, and was a prominent citizen of his time. Mr. and Mrs. Hutchison are members of the Methodist

Protestant church, but Mr. Hutchison was formerly a member and steward of the United Presbyterian church. He is a member of the Royal Arcanum, the Ancient Order of United Workmen, the Junior Order of American Mechanics and the democratic party. Mr. Hutchison was postmaster of Springdale, is now a member of the council of Cheswick, and is one of the substantial citizens of that community.

JOHN W. STEWART, for over twenty years engaged in the real estate and insurance business in McKeesport, was born in McKeesport, Pa., in 1834. His father was Hamilton Stewart, a native of McKeesport, born in 1799, farmer and also a carpenter. He died in 1880. The mother of the subject of this sketch was Nancy S. (Dinsmore) Stewart, who was born in Patton township, Allegheny county, in 1807, and died in 1878. John W. Stewart was educated in the public schools and at McKeesport academy, attending school until he reached the age of twenty-one. He was then for eleven years a farmer, and after that, until 1880, was engaged in carpentering, and as a contractor and builder In 1880 he opened a real estate and insurance office at No. 422 Walnut St., McKeesport, and has been successfully engaged in business there ever since. Mr. Stewart was married, in 1863, to Miss Elizabeth Gamble, of Armstrong county, and has had six children, of whom three are now living, M. Wilson, Dr. J. Boyd D. and Scott M. M. Wilson is now an attorney in Pittsburg, and Dr. J. Boyd D. is a practicing physician at Wilson Station, Allegheny county. Mrs. Stewart died in October, 1899. Mr. Stewart has been a trustee of the First Presbyterian church of McKeesport since 1871, and treasurer of the McKeesport hospital since 1898.

CHARLES UHLINGER, of the firm of C. Uhlinger & Co., real estate and insurance, was born in Switzerland in December, 1841, received a high school education there, and, in 1861, came to America, locating in New Jersey, where he spent a year on a farm. In 1862 he enlisted in Company H, 12th New Jersey volunteer infantry, served with distinction throughout the Civil war, and was discharged at its close in Washington, D. C. His war service over, he spent several years in the western States, employed in various capacities, and in 1873 came to Pittsburg, where he engaged in mercantile pursuits until 1877. In that year he came to Hites, where he has since been an honored resident. He was in business there for a time, and for twenty years held almost continuously the positions of justice of the peace and notary public. He entered the real estate and insurance business, in company with George H. McFetridge, under the firm name of C. Uhlinger & Co. Besides this business, he has several other financial interests, being a stockholder in the National bank of Tarentum and in the J. H. Baker manufacturing company of that place, and the owner of valuable real estate in Hites and Tarentum. He has always taken an active interest in public affairs, is an influential republican, and at one time held the position of township auditor. He is a member of Eli Hemphill post, No. 135, G. A. R., and belongs to the Methodist Episcopal church, in which he serves as a member of the official board. Mr. Uhlinger was married, in 1876, to Miss Kate Thumm, of Fort Wayne, Ind., and is the father of twins, Kate and Emma, and two younger children, Bertha and George.

OLIVER L. CRIBBS, grocer in Verona, was born in Clarion county, Pa., March 17, 1856. His father, John R. Cribbs, a blacksmith by trade, did the first blacksmithing at Redbank furnace, Clarion county, and afterwards went to Oil City, at the time of the boom, engaging in the real estate and wholesale and retail grocery business there. He amassed a considerable fortune in Oil City, and, in 1866, moved to Illinois, where he remained three years. Returning to Pennsylvania, he engaged in the grocery and lumber business, and continued in active business till 1894. O. L. Cribbs, the subject of this sketch, was reared in Pennsylvania, and received a common-school education. He was for a time interested in the oil-producing business, and was for four years in the employ of the Philadelphia gas company, but has spent most of his time in mercantile pursuits, being now a prominent grocer. Although reared a republican, Mr. Cribbs has voted the prohibition ticket for about sixteen years. He has served his borough one term as councilman and two terms as registering assessor. He is an influential member of the Methodist Episcopal church, in which he holds the position of steward and treasurer, has been for some time class leader in the church, and was for five years superintendent of the Free Methodist Sunday-school. Mr. Cribbs was married in September, 1876, to Miss Emma Dunsmore, and has three daughters, Bertha, Lola and Eva. Bertha and Eva are members of the Second United Presbyterian church, while Lola attends the Baptist church.

WILLIAM NICHOLAS, of Tarentum, for twenty years a trusted employe of the Pittsburg glass company, and for ten years foreman in the polishing rooms, was born in South Buffalo township, Armstrong county, April 4, 1854, and is a son of William and Eliza (Thomas) Nicholas, and grandson of John and Mary Jane Nicholas. John, who was a Prussian by birth, was related to the Nicholas family now on the throne of Prussia. He settled in Pittsburg in an early day, but afterwards returned to Prussia, where he died. Mrs. John Nicholas took as her second husband Rev. George Venebles, a very early settler of Pittsburg, who served in the Revolutionary war as chaplain. William Nicholas, Sr., father of the subject of this sketch, was a peddler by trade, in politics a whig and later a republican, and in religious belief an earnest Methodist. He was for thirty-five years a resident of Creighton, and the Methodist church of that place was organized in his home. He and his wife had eleven children, and of the family, seven sons and two daughters are living. One daughter, Letesia Ellen, died in 1886, and David John, a son, in 1864. He died on Jan. 11, 1890, while his wife died in 1896. She was a daughter of Thomas Thomas, a native of South Wales, who came to America in early life, settling at Pittsburg. He died at Brady's Bend, Armstrong county. William Nicholas, whose name heads this article, was reared and educated in Harrison township, and then began his life work as a glass worker. He has been successful in his line of work, and now enjoys the confidence of his employers and the good-will and esteem of his fellow-workmen. He now owns considerable property in Tarentum. In politics he is a republican. He is a member of A. O. U. W., Jr. A. O. U. M.

and the Tribe of Ben-Hur. In 1882 Mr. Nicholas married Miss Catherine Moss, and has by this union two children, Edna G. and David Moss, both of whom have been given the privilege of an education in the Creighton schools. Mrs. Nicholas, who was born in Allegheny city, July 16, 1856, is one of the two children born to David and Phillipina (Sneider) Moss, natives of Germany, who emigrated to America. He was, when a young man, a contractor in New Orleans, but spent his last years in Pittsburg, and died there Feb. 22, 1880. His widow is living, now a woman seventy-four years old. Mrs. Nicholas' paternal grandfather was Jacob Moss, a native of Germany, who spent his life there, and was a son of Mathias Moss, who was born in England, but died in Germany. Her maternal grandfather was William Sneider, a native of Germany, who died there at the age of fifty-six. He married Barbary Brown, a German woman, who lived to the unusual age of ninety-six. Mr. and Mrs. Nicholas are members of the Methodist Episcopal church.

W. A. SARGEANT, of Coraopolis, Pa., assistant manager of the Consolidated lamp and glass company, was born in Pittsburg, Pa., Feb. 3, 1868, son of Robert W. and Helen Octavia (Vera) Sargeant. His parents had three children, of whom he is the sole survivor. His father was a bricklayer by trade, an exceedingly active man, who died suddenly in 1896. His mother died when he was four years of age, and he was placed with relatives to board. He remained there until nine years of age, when he ran away to shift for himself, and went to Irwin, Pa., where he was practically lost to his relatives for a year, when he was accidentally seen by an acquaintance at the railroad station, and reported to his father, who took him to Pittsburg and placed him in school in that city. He remained in school until he was twelve years of age, when he began to learn the trade of decorating on glass with the firm of Challinor & Burgin, of Pittsburg, Pa., a concern that is now out of business. He was with them for eighteen months, then secured employment with the Phœnix glass company, of Phillipsburg, Pa., now known as the town of Monaca. He remained with that establishment for five years, in the capacity of decorator, and then went to Tarentum,

Pa., where he was employed as designer with the firm of Challinor & Taylor. Three years afterwards he again went with the Phœnix glass company, remained with them until 1890, and then removed to Anderson, Ind., where he was connected with the American glass company. Next he returned to the Phœnix glass company, and then to Fostoria, Ohio, with the Fostoria shade and lamp company. He left that company to take the management of the Chelsea pottery, of New Cumberland, W. Va., and from there again to the Phœnix glass company, and later was with the Libby glass company at the World's Fair at Chicago, where he received high honors. He went with the Fostoria shade and lamp company as manager of the decorating department, and when that company merged with another large plant and removed to Coraopolis under the name of the Consolidated lamp and glass company, Mr. Sargeant was made assistant general manager and designer of the plant. This is the largest plant of its kind in the United States, and Mr. Sargeant discharges the complex affairs of his position with rare skill and judgment. He was married, in 1892, to Ella Grace Jolley, of Monaca, Pa., and they have one child, Grandville LeMoyne. Mr. Sargeant is a republican in politics, a member of the Presbyterian church, and is a director in the Coraopolis realty company and in the Coraopolis savings and trust company. Mr. Sargeant has one of the prettiest homes in Coraopolis, and stands high in the esteem of all who know him. Mr. Sargeant's maternal grandfather was Col. Antoine François Joseph Vera, of French parents, who was born in Brussels, the capital of Belgium, on Dec. 9, 1795. He served in the army, as required by the laws of the country, and when nineteen years of age participated in the battle of Waterloo and witnessed Napoleon's sun set forever. In 1816 Colonel Vera sailed for New York, finally located in Beaver county, Pa., and was married, on July 14, 1822, to Eliza Couch, of Allegheny county, Pa., daughter of Joseph and Catherine Connor Couch. Their first home was at Beavertown, where he served one term as county commissioner, and in 1837 he had the brick made on the ground and erected a dwelling-house and brewery at Bridgewater. They were both members of the Methodist Episcopal church of Bridgewater until their deaths, he dying on June 4, 1858, at the age of fifty-six years, and she on Jan. 10, 1867, at the age of seventy-one years. Helen Octavia Vera, one of a pair of twins, was the tenth child of Colonel Vera, and was born at Bridgewater, Pa., on Aug. 10, 1843. She was educated at Beaver seminary, and married Robert W. Sargeant, Jan. 5, 1865, on his return from the army, where he had served in the 139th Pennsylvania volunteers, Allabach's brigade, third division, fifth corps, Army of the Potomac. They had two children, Annie E. and William A., the subject of this sketch.

MICHAEL C. O'DONOVAN, of McKee's Rocks, Pa., a prominent merchant and borough treasurer, was born at Walker's Mills, in Allegheny Co., Pa., Sept. 20, 1863, and is the son of Michael and Catherine (Collins) O'Donovan. His father came from County Cork, Ireland, and was engaged in industrial pursuits. He was the father of two children: T. C., agent of the Lake Erie railroad at Shoustown, Pa., and Michael C., the subject of this sketch. Mr. O'Donovan received his education in the common schools and at the Oakdale academy, in Allegheny county, and when fifteen years of age abandoned his studies to become a telegraph operator for the Pan Handle railroad. He was engaged for four years with that company, being located at different stations between Pittsburg and Noblestown, and later secured a similar position with the Lake Erie railroad at Boston, Pa. He was connected with that railroad for four years, part of the time as train dispatcher at McKee's Rocks. In 1888, he opened a small grocery store at McKee's Rocks, later added other lines of merchandise, and to-day has the largest mercantile establishment in that borough. He was married, in 1882, to Agnes, daughter of John and Mary Tracey, of Noblestown, Pa., and they have eight children, Mary Agnes, Katie, Nellie, Michael, Alice, Agnes, Margaret and Paul. Mr. O'Donovan affiliates with the democratic party, and was a member of the first council of the borough of McKee's Rocks, again held that office from 1895 to 1898, and at present is treasurer of the borough. Mr. O'Donovan has never sought office, but has consented to fill these positions solely because he regards public office as a public duty and one that good citizens should not shirk. He served as chairman of the sixth legislative district for his party in the last election, and conducted the campaign with skill and ability. He is a member of the St. Francis de Sales' Roman Catholic church, one of the church committee, and chairman of the St. Vincent de Paul society. His reputation among his business and political colleagues is very high, and when any public question enlists his interest it is regarded as sure of a successful consummation. His ability in the line of public service was first illustrated during his term as councilman, just after the borough was organized, when a traction company wanted the right of way on certain borough streets, but refused to come on the street in which he was interested. Despite the fact that the company declined to lay their tracks on that street and the further fact that the other five members of the council were opposed to the route as outlined by him, yet he created a condition which compelled the company to accept his plans and the other members of the council to agree with his ideas. Since that time his ability has been known and respected, and in many other ways has he demonstrated that when he undertakes a work he is going to succeed, if there is any possible way, and where no way exists, he proceeds to create one. In a contest where he represented his church, he succeeded in raising $8,542.50 in a very short time, and created a record that has never been equaled in that diocese by a layman.

JOSEPH K. FULTON, Sr., of Tarentum, Pa., a leading merchant and a prominent citizen, was born in Pittsburg, Pa., Jan. 12, 1837. He is a son of Rev. Andrew S. and Jane (Kerr) Fulton, the former a son of James Fulton, a native of Ireland, who came to the United States at an early date, first settled in Pittsburg, and, in 1837, engaged in the mercantile business at Tarentum, where he prospered until his death in February, 1850. His wife was Sarah Smith, a native of Ireland, and she died in Tarentum in 1842. They had a family of seven children, all of whom are now dead. Jane Kerr was the daughter of the Rev. Joseph R. Kerr (one of the first professors of the United Presbyterian theological seminary, of Pittsburg), and his wife, Agnes Reynolds Kerr. Rev. A. S. Fulton was educated in the University of Pittsburg and at the United Presbyterian theological seminary. He began his career as a minister at Union, Pa., later removing to Peoria, Ill., where, his health failing, he returned to Tarentum, where he died in 1845. They had only one child, the subject of this sketch. J. K. Fulton was reared in Tarentum, and when a boy began working in his grandfather's store; later was with his uncles, James B. and W. G. Fulton, who were in the mercantile business under the firm name of J. B. Fulton & Bro. At the death of J. B. Fulton, in 1884, the firm was continued by W. G. and J. K. Fulton, under the old firm name, until the death of W. G. Fulton, in 1895, when J. K. Fulton assumed entire charge of the business, which he now conducts under the name of J. K. Fulton, Sr. He was married, in 1873, to Julia B. Rynd, of Tarentum, Pa., and they have four children: Amelia; J. K. Fulton, Jr., member of the firm of Fulton & Inskeep, of Tarentum; A. J., clerk in the Tarentum savings and trust company, and William G.

JOHN JOSEPH VOGT, pastor of St. Joseph's church, Verona, was born in Dahm, Germany, Oct. 17, 1863, and is a son of Frank and Elizabeth (Goebel) Vogt, natives of Germany. Father Vogt has two brothers, also in the ministry—William, pastor of St. Joseph's church at Carnegie, and August A., assistant at South Side, Pittsburg, to Father Goebel, an uncle. The subject of this sketch was educated first in Germany, and then, coming to Pittsburg at the age of twelve, studied at the College of the Holy Ghost, graduating from that institution in 1883. After this he studied philosophy and theology at St. Mary's seminary, in Baltimore, Md. He spent six years as assistant to Father Goebel, in the West End, Pittsburg. After this he was located at St. Aloysius', in Reserve township, and later came to Verona, where, after only six months' service, he suffered a stroke of paralysis, caused by a stroke of lightning, and was obliged to give up his work and go to Europe for his health. After a summer on the continent, he so far recovered that he was able to take the chaplaincy at Cresson, Pa., and was later summoned by the urgent request of the people of Hollidaysburg, Pa., to become pastor of the St. Michael's congregation there. When the diocese of Altoona was formed, he was called to Pittsburg and sent to Verona to take charge of St. Joseph's church. Here, in the two years of his ministry, Father Vogt has endeared himself to all, and made a most enviable record as a pastor. In connection with the parish work is a flourishing school of some 150 pupils, which is managed by five school sisters of Notre Dame.

EMIL EDGAR MAURHOFF, civil engineer and notary public, of Tarentum, was born in Butler county, Pa., Jan. 28, 1848, and is a son of Emil and Johannah (Pollard) Maurhoff. Emil Maurhoff was born in Hanover, Germany, and his wife in Philadelphia. They were married in Butler county, and there spent the remainder of their lives. Mr. Maurhoff came from Germany to Baltimore in 1832, moved soon after to Butler county, and was a merchant in Saxonburg for many years. In early life he was a whig, for years the only man of his party in Saxonburg, and was afterwards a republican. In later life he was for twenty years justice of the peace, and also served eight years as postmaster. He was a surveyor; did much work in Butler county, and helped make the first map of the county. In his day he was one of the most prominent men of the community, and his name is still remembered with respect in that part of Pennsylvania in whose public life he played so important a part. He was one of the originators of Saxonia lodge of Odd Fellows at Saxonburg, and a charter member and organizer of Tarentum lodge, No. 587, I. O. O. F. He and his wife were members of the German Evangelical Protestant church. Mrs. Maurhoff was a daughter of John F. and Rosina Pollard, natives of Germany, who came to the United States in 1830, locating in Philadelphia. Afterwards they moved to North Carolina, then returned to Philadelphia, moving thence to Butler county, where they spent their last days. Emil E. Maurhoff, whose name begins this sketch, was reared and educated in Saxonburg, learned surveying from his father, and worked in his father's store. For the past twenty three years he has been a successful civil engineer, and has lived in Tarentum since 1892. He surveyed Brackenridge, laid out the borough of that name, and is now engineer of the sewer system and the grading of streets. Mr. Maurhoff is a stockholder in the J. H. Baker manufacturing company, and has had other financial connections, being at one time interested in the manufacture of brick in Butler county. He owns property in Tarentum and in Butler county. In politics he is a republican, was for three years county auditor of Butler county, and for seven years served as school director. He is a member of Saxonia lodge, No. 496, I. O. O. F., and of the Jr. O. U. A. M. On Sept. 6, 1870, he married Miss Matilda Koegler, a native of Butler county, and has had five children, of whom the third-born, Alice, is now deceased. The others are: C. H., F. W., Annie E. and Presley A. L. Mr. Maurhoff and wife are members of the English Lutheran church of Tarentum. In 1897 Mr. Maurhoff planned the church and superintended its erection.

J. CLYDE MILLER, a prominent insurance and real estate agent, of Homestead, was born in Mifflin township, Allegheny Co., Pa., March 7, 1870. He is a son of Jacob C. and Christina (Fulmer) Miller, and grandson of Jacob and Catherine (Bender) Miller, natives of Wurtemburg, Germany, who came to America in the thirties. After a short residence in Maryland, Mr. and Mrs. Jacob Miller, Sr., moved to Allegheny county, living there during the remainder of their lives. Jacob C. Miller, father of the subject of this sketch, was born in Allegheny county, April 8, 1841. He was for twelve years a miner, and, in 1879, located in Mifflin township, where he embarked extensively in the dairy business, in which he is still interested. He has seven children living: Emma, wife of John Wilds; J. Clyde, the subject of this sketch; Elizabeth, now Mrs. Albert Gordon; Ida, wife of Edward Ball, present burgess of West Homestead and assistant secretary of the Mercantile trust company, Pittsburg; Harry, teller of the First National bank of Homestead; John F., and Tena. J. Clyde Miller was educated in the public schools and at Curry institute, Pittsburg, and Dec. 1, 1892, began his business career as a dairyman at Homestead, but has, since 1900, devoted his attention to real estate and insurance. Mr. Miller married Miss Mamie McGreevy, daughter of John McGreevy, and ward of the late Dr. George Gladden, of Homestead, and has three children, Ruth, Clyde and George G. Mr. Miller is a member of the Presbyterian church. He served four years as captain of Company No. 1 of the Homestead fire department, and resigned because of business duties, but is still an active member of the company. He is captain of the Homestead troop, the only mounted organization in western Pennsylvania, and one of the finest in the State. Since attaining his majority, Mr. Miller has taken an active interest in politics, and is a stanch republican. He was elected councilman from the first ward, and during his three-year term cast more votes independent of party or faction than any other man who ever held the office of councilman in Homestead. Feb. 20, 1900, he was elected burgess of the borough of Homestead for a term of three years, also justice of the peace for five years, and has filled both positions most creditably. Outside of politics, Mr. Miller takes an active interest in public affairs, and favors every movement to advance the welfare of the community. He is prominent in charity work of various kinds, and takes great interest in athletic sports.

WILLIAM B. WHITE, of Springdale, Pa., senior member of the firm of White Bros., dealers in general merchandise, was born near Youngstown, Mahoning Co., Ohio, Dec. 22, 1858, son of John White, a prosperous farmer, and his wife, Eliza Dixon. His paternal grandparents were natives of Ireland and early settlers in America. Mr. White was educated in the public schools of Mahoning county, which he attended until seventeen years of age, and for the next four years devoted his attention to teaching in his native county. He took a commercial course at the normal school at Valparaiso, Ind., and was graduated from that well-known institution in 1887. He went to Iowa, where he clerked in a hotel for one year, afterwards to Denver and engaged in the real estate business for a short time. He secured a position with the Singer sewing machine company in their Denver office, and later went on the road for this company as special bookkeeper. He spent eight years with them, covering Nebraska, New Mexico, Mexico and Texas, and in 1897 returned to Ohio, engaging in the mercantile business with his brother at Paulton, near Apollo. For two years they prospered there, and, in 1900, removed their business to Springdale, Pa., and since have enjoyed a splendid patronage, being the only general mercantile establishment in that town. They also have in connection with their general store, a grain and feed store, and supply customers in Cheswick by wagon. Mr. White was married, in June, 1900, to Mary E., daughter of Joseph and Katharine Nealy, of Saltsburg, Pa., and they have two children, John L. and Louis. Mr. White is a member of the Odd Fellows, having joined in Shreveport, La., and of the democratic party. Robert F. White, the junior member of the firm, was born in Mahoning county, Ohio, Feb. 22, 1863, and attended the public schools of his native county until he was about twenty years of age. He entered the normal school of Valparaiso, Ind., and was graduated in a commercial course in the class of 1887. He taught school for the next eight years, and later engaged in the mercantile business with his brother at Paulton. He is also a member of the democratic party, but neither of them have sought office, preferring to devote their time and energies to the business in which they are succeeding so well.

JOHN T. MORGAN, of McKee's Rocks, Pa., tax collector of that borough, was born in Allegheny city, June 11, 1873, son of John and Mary Ann Morgan. His father was a ship-carpenter by trade, is now retired from business and is living quietly at McKee's Rocks, at the age of seventy-eight years. His parents had six children, five of whom are now living, their ancestors on both sides coming from Ireland. John T. Morgan secured his rudimentary education in the splendid schools of Allegheny city, and when fourteen years of age left his books and faced the world to work out his destiny. He was employed in various capacities, including that of cash boy in Joseph Horn's dry goods store, and when eighteen years of age went to work in Long & Co.'s iron works at McKee's Rocks. He continued with that concern until their failure, in 1890, and then secured employment with the National blank book company, of Pittsburg, with which establishment he remained for a year, and then became a clerk for the Pittsburg & Lake Erie railroad. He was with that system from 1891 to July 31, 1901, and the next day secured a position as stenographer with the Carnegie steel company, with whom he continued until 1903. In 1900 Mr. Morgan was elected tax collector of McKee's Rocks, and, in 1903, re-elected to that important office, receiving an overwhelming majority over his opponent. Mr. Morgan's political affiliations are with the republican party, and he is a member of the Alfaretta lodge, Knights of Pythias. Mr. Morgan is a well-known and highly respected citizen.

JOHN HARVEY DONNELL, M. D., of Natrona, Pa., a prominent physician, was born in Armstrong county, Pa., March 18, 1863, son of John and Catherine (John) Donnell. Dr. Donnell comes of a distinguished line of ancestry, his progenitors, three degrees removed, being Patrick and Peggie (Brice) Donnell, both natives of County Donegal, Ireland, who came to America and resided in Westmoreland county, Pa., until their deaths, at advanced ages. Their son, John, was reared and educated in Westmoreland county, and was one of the first citizens of Pennsylvania to engage in the manufacture of salt in Allegheny county. He died in 1873, at the age of seventy-four years, and is survived by a widow, aged ninety-four years. Prior to her marriage, she was Elizabeth Kennedy, and is a native of Westmoreland county. John Donnell, the second, son of John and Elizabeth (Kennedy) Donnell, and the father of Dr. John H. Donnell, was for forty years a successful merchant of Wattersonville, Pa., but is now retired from active business. For many years he was a democrat, and, under the banner of that party, sought legislative honors in 1876. He is now a republican, and has served as a justice of the peace for twenty years. He has been twice married; the first union resulting in one son, the subject of this sketch, and the second marriage in four children, three of whom are living. Dr. Donnell was reared in Allegheny county, and was educated at the Tarentum normal school, and for five years followed the occupation of a teacher. He was graduated from the medical department of the Western university in 1892; for one year was assistant physician to the Pennsylvania salt manufacturing company, of Natrona, and since has enjoyed a large business as a general practitioner. Dr. Donnell is prominent in medical circles, and holds membership in the Indiana County medical society and the Allegheny Valley medical association. He is a leading democrat, and has held several offices in Fawn township, having served as clerk, and later as auditor of that township, and has been an active member of the county democratic committee. He is closely identified with the Odd Fellows, and is a member of the Knights of the Mystic Chain. Dr. Donnell is also prominent in financial circles, is vice-president of the Home guarantee company, of New Kensington, Pa., and is a member of the board of directors of the National real estate company, of Washington, D. C. He was married, on March 24, 1893, to Mary C., daughter of E. D. and Catherine (Knepshield) Bigelow, both members of prominent Pennsylvania families. Dr. and Mrs. Donnell have the following three children: Mark B., Catherine G. and John Harvey. Dr. Donnell and his wife are members of the Methodist church of Natrona, and are prominent in the social affairs of the city.

THOMAS WARRELL BROCKMAN, a prominent funeral director, of Homestead, was born in East Finley township, Washington Co., Pa., Jan. 19, 1864. His parents, Nicholas Bearly and Sarah Elizabeth (Warrell) Brockman, were both natives of Washington county. Nicholas Bearly Brockman's father, also named Nicholas, was a native of Scotland, and for several years owned and operated a stage-line in Washington county. His wife was Susan (Bearly) Brockman. The maternal grandfather of Thomas W. Brockman was Thomas Warrell, a native of Ireland, who came with his parents to America about 1822 His wife, Phœbe Patterson, a native of Washington county, died in 1870. Thomas Warrell Brockman was reared on a farm in Washington county, and educated in the schools of that county and at Jefferson academy, graduating from the latter institution in 1883. After graduation he returned to the farm in Washington county, where he remained until 1890. From 1890 to 1895 he was engaged in the undertaking business at Prosperity, Washington county. On Oct. 1, 1895, Mr. Brockman moved to Homestead, where he has since been engaged in active business life. In October, 1898, he sold out his feed and builders' supplies business, which he had conducted for several years, and, March 1, 1899, purchased the undertaking business of J. H. Gillen. Mr. Brockman has since then devoted his time exclusively to the undertaking business, and has the leading undertaking establishment in Homestead Mr. Brockman was married, in October, 1884, to Martha E , daughter of John and Margaret (Hamilton) McMillen, of Prosperity, Pa. Mr. and Mrs. Brockman have four children, Sarah E., Margaret P., Lucille and Virginia R. Mr. Brockman and wife are members of the United

Presbyterian church. He is a member of Homestead lodge, No. 1049, I. O. O F., of which he is a past grand; of B. P. O. E., Gervais commandery, Knights of Malta, and several other fraternal orders. In politics he is a republican. He is now serving as school director from the fourth ward, Homestead.

HENRY BERG, capitalist, one of the wealthiest men in Verona, was born in Bavaria, Germany, Sept. 8, 1853, the only son of Henry and Anna M. (Bayer) Berg. The family left Germany on Feb. 14, 1866, and arrived at Pittsburg on March 11th of that year, with a total cash capital of nine dollars and fifty cents. The father, a blacksmith by trade, worked for two years for Peter Haberman & Co., at a place called Haberman's Run, and, coming to Penn township, Allegheny county, was employed as a blacksmith and coal miner by the Armstrong & Dixon coal company, until October, 1873, when he came to Verona and opened a hotel. The building burned on July 26, 1875, and he then built the house in which the subject of this sketch now lives. He started in business anew on April 1, 1876, and managed the business until his death, which occurred October 5th of that year, his widow and son keeping the hotel until May 1, 1888. On Aug. 1, 1893, Mr. Berg, the subject of this sketch, started for himself in the hotel business at Nos. 1117 and 1119 Liberty Ave., Pittsburg, managed the hotel until May 1, 1901, and then retired from active business life. He now owns valuable property in the third and seventeenth wards, Pittsburg, in Sharpsburg, Mount Oliver, Oakmont and Verona. He has been treasurer of the Suburban water company, of Allegheny county, Pa., since its organization in 1893; was one of the organizers and is now a director of the First National bank of Verona, and was an organizer and is at present a director of the German-American savings and trust company, at the corner of Sixth and Smithfield streets, third ward, Pittsburg, which was started Nov. 10, 1902. He is a republican in politics, and has served his borough eight years as councilman. Mr. Berg was married, Sept. 5, 1889, to Miss Cassea Anth. Mrs. Berg was born in the third ward, Pittsburg, Aug. 28, 1852, and died Dec. 2, 1893. Mr. Berg's mother, now seventy-two years old, makes her home with her son. Mr. Berg has traveled extensively in the United States, Mexico and Europe. He is a man of generous nature, gives freely to worthy charities, and is a man whose genial disposition has made him many friends. He is a member of the German Evangelical church of Pittsburg, a church among whose members have been numbered many of the most influential men of that city.

JOSEPH FRANK DONAGHY, of Coraopolis, Pa., a prominent contractor and capitalist, was born in Venango county, Pa., Sept. 26, 1866, son of George W. and Emaline (Mayo) Donaghy, his paternal ancestors having come from Ireland, and his maternal from Massachusetts. His parents had eleven children, ten of whom are now living, viz.: James M.; Nannie, wife of I. N. DeNoon; W. C.; J. F.; George M; Hiram M.; Emma; Jennie; Nettie, and John. His father was a contractor by occupation, and died in 1902 at the age of seventy-two years. His mother survives her husband, and is now in her fifty-eighth year. Joseph F. Donaghy received his educational training in the public schools of Butler, Pa., and in the schools of Pittsburg, where the family had removed when he was quite young. He left school in 1883, and for a short time was office boy for S. S. Marvin, the Pittsburg baker, and then began to learn the machinists' trade with the firm of Velte & McDonald, on Penn avenue, Pittsburg. He was with them for three and one-half years, and for the next eight years was connected with McGill & Co., on the same thoroughfare. He next became master mechanic of the Ellwood City tube works, where he remained for three years. While there he patented a machine for making tubes out of solid billets, which he sold to the National tube works, of McKeesport. He then took stock in the United States wire nail company, of Shoustown, Pa., became master mechanic of their plant for one year, and for two years was superintendent. He engaged in general contracting and building, and at present is engaged in erecting a large addition to the National brewery, of McKee's Rocks. He still acts as superintendent of the United States wire nail company in an executive capacity, and has just organized the Donaghy foundry and machine company, which is preparing to erect a large plant. He was married, in 1896, to Dora

S Colborn, of Ellwood city, and they have two children, Grace and Stanley. Mr. Donaghy is a republican in politics, and is a director of the Coraopolis realty company. He owns fine property in Coraopolis, and is one of the solid and substantial citizens of that borough.

BENJAMIN COE IRWIN, M. D., a prominent physician of Springdale, was born in Indiana county, Pa., July 20, 1863, and is a son of Rev. David Johnson Irwin, D. D., and Sarah H. (Coe) Irwin. Rev. David Irwin was born in Kittanning, Armstrong county, and was for many years one of the most prominent ministers of the Kittanning presbytery. He died, in 1899, at the age of sixty-five. His wife, Sarah H. (Coe) Irwin, was a daughter of Benjamin Coe, son of Benjamin Coe, a farmer and coal dealer in a very early day. His wife was Sarah (Hill) Coe. Rev. Irwin and wife reared a family of three sons and two daughters. Of these, Dr. B. C. Irwin is the subject of this sketch; Rev. J. P. Irwin has been for the past eight years foreign missionary to China; Rev. George B. Irwin is a minister of the Kittanning presbytery, having charge of the Presbyterian church of Cowansville, Armstrong county, and Margaret B. and Rozanna Irwin are teachers in the Tarentum schools. Dr. Benjamin Coe Irwin was reared on a farm and attended the Ederridge and Glade Run academies. He took a course of study in the medical department of the Western university, in Pittsburg, and graduated from that institution March 28, 1889. He spent ten years in the practice of his profession at New Alexandria, Westmoreland county, and has for the past four years been located at Springdale, where he has built up a lucrative practice. Dr. Irwin is a member of the Allegheny Valley medical society and the K. O. T. M., of Springdale, and is examiner for a number of insurance companies. In politics he is a republican; is at present a school directer, and takes great interest in educational affairs. Dr. Irwin was married, March 4, 1897, to Miss Elizabeth A. Douglas, of Greensburg, Pa., and has three children, David Johnson, Hattie Jane and James Harvey. The family are identified with the Presbyterian church, of which Dr. Irwin is a ruling elder.

JOHN BURKMAN, grocer at Ninth street and Washington avenue, Braddock, is a type of the many successful Scandinavians in Allegheny county. He was born in Sweden, May 1, 1860, son of John and Pernilla (Johnson) Burkman, and came to America upon reaching his majority, and settled in Braddock. For six years he worked in the Edgar Thompson mills, and then, with the savings which his hard work and rigid economy had accumulated, he opened a grocery in the building now occupied by L. H. Bishoff & Co. Five years later, in 1892, he bought the lots at Nos. 866 and 868 Washington Ave., and erected upon it a residence and a store building, where he now conducts a store which keeps on hand a large stock of groceries and a considerable line of merchandise as well. Mr. Burkman was married, July 31, 1884, to Lydia, daughter of Lawrence and Sophia Peterson, both emigrants from Sweden. Of the children of Mr. and Mrs. Burkman, three died in childhood, and John E. L., Charles, Gertrude, Paul and Elmer are living. The family are Lutherans. Mr. Burkman is a member of Braddock Field lodge, No. 529, I. O. O. F.; the Scandinavian Brotherhood, and the local Swedish society of Braddock.

JOHN RUDOLPH RICKENBAUGH, for twenty years in the employ of the Pittsburg plate glass company, and now foreman of the carpenter department of the company's works at Tarentum, was born in Allegheny county, Pa., May 20, 1852. He was reared and educated in Allegheny county, learned there the coopers' trade, and then became a carpenter. He now owns property in Tarentum, which he purchased with the savings of his labor. In politics he is a republican. In 1874 he married Miss Margaret M. Hodil, and has had six children, of whom Clara B., Matilda E., Brinton H. and Virginia M. are deceased. Those living are Laura E. and Calvin R. In religious belief Mr. and Mrs. Rickenbaugh are Presbyterians. Mr. Rickenbaugh comes of a family long prominent in Allegheny county. His parents, Jacob and Mary (Hettenfelder) Rickenbaugh, natives of Germany, came to Pittsburg in 1832, and died in O'Hara township, Allegheny county, the father in 1877 and the mother in 1884. They were the parents of five children, all living. Jacob Rickenbaugh was a teamster in Pittsburg in an early day, and owned the first four-horse team in that city. His later life was spent on a farm in East Deer township. He and his wife were members of the German Lutheran church. Mrs. John R. Rickenbaugh's parents were Samuel and Margaret (Grubbs) Hodil, and her paternal grandfather was a pioneer settler of Indiana township, where he spent his last days. He owned a large tract of land there. Samuel Hodil was born in Allegheny county, Sept. 19, 1805, and his wife was born Nov. 13, 1813. They were members of the Presbyterian church, and their nine children all adopted this faith. In politics Mr. Hodil was a republican. Mrs. Hodil was born in Germany, and her father was one of the early settlers of Indiana township.

CHARLES KITTERING BARNHART, of McKee's Rocks, a well-known contractor and justice of the peace, was born in Ligonier township, Westmoreland Co., Pa., July 16, 1864, and is the son of David and Sarah (Kittering) Barnhart. His father was a tanner in early life, later an employe of the Pennsylvania railroad, then proprietor of a grocery store, and now resides at McKee's Rocks, where he lives quietly retired from active life. His parents had four children, two of whom are now living, the other child being Benjamin J., a merchant of McKee's Rocks. The elder Barnhart is a stanch republican. Charles K. Barnhart obtained his education in the public schools of Ligonier and at Derry, Pa., and when fifteen years of age began to learn the trade of a plasterer with Jesse Cogan, of Westmoreland county. When twenty years of age, he went into that business for himself at Sheridan, Pa.; later removed to McKee's Rocks, where he is now located, and does the largest business in his line in the borough. He was married, in 1888, to Maria, daughter of William Richards, of Pittsburg, a roller in the steel mills for many years, and they have three children, two daughters and a son, their home life being an unusually happy one. Mr. Barnhart is a republican, served eight years in the borough council, being elected by the largest majority of any one, and was elected to his present position of justice of the peace on May 30, 1903. Mr. Barnhart is a prominent member of the B. P. O. Elks, and is very popular in the city where he makes his home.

THOMAS D. GARDNER, recognized as the leading real estate dealer of McKeesport, was born in that city May 10, 1857. His father, Fred J. Gardner, was a native of Manchester, England, while his mother was born in Dublin, Ireland. Mr. and Mrs. Gardner came to America early in the fifties, and after a short time spent in Pittsburg, took up their permanent residence in McKeesport, where Mr. Gardner conducted a bakery up to the time of his death, in 1865, after which the establishment was kept for several years by his widow. The children born to Mr. and Mrs. Fred J. Gardner were: Sadie, now Mrs. A. M. Kennedy; Carrie, married to Isaac Reager; Mary, who is the wife of Benjamin Shellenberger; Fred J., Jr., and Thomas D., the subject of this sketch. Thomas D. Gardner was reared and educated at McKeesport. When sixteen years old, he entered the employ of the National tube works as an office boy, and later worked for three years at the carpenter trade. After this he was for over three years a clerk in the Baltimore & Ohio railroad offices, and in July, 1880, became teller of the People's bank, where he was, in 1882, promoted to the position of assistant cashier. After ten years in the employ of this concern, Mr. Gardner became, in 1890, cashier of the National bank of McKeesport, where he remained until Jan. 1, 1896. Since then he has devoted his attention to real estate, being, up to Jan. 1, 1899, associated with Mr. Gilbert F. Myer, under the firm name of Gilbert F. Myer & Co. For the past four years he has been alone, with an office at No. 521 Walnut St., and has built up an extensive and profitable business. Mr. Gardner has been for eight years past a member of the school board, and was last year elected president of that body. He was a member of the first board of managers of the Y. M. C. A., which was organized about fifteen years ago, and is still actively interested in that organization. He is also a member of the board of trustees of the First Methodist Episcopal church of McKeesport, and has been for several years vice-president of the board of underwriters. For many years he has been secretary of the Youghiogheny lodge of Masons, and is a member of various other social organizations. Mr. Gardner was married, in June, 1881, to Miss Nellie Downs, daughter of Isaac N. and Jennie (Thompson) Downs, of West Newton, Pa., and has two children, Edmund R., a student at Bucknell college, and Harry C., attending high school. Mr. Gardner and family reside in the fifth ward, McKeesport. In politics he is a republican.

SAMUEL W. S. DINSMORE, M. D., of Sharpsburg, Pa., a prominent homœopathic physician, was born near Kittanning, Armstrong Co., Pa., Nov. 23, 1853, son of Robert and Mary (Reed) Dinsmore. His father was at one time a country merchant and followed droving in the eastern part of Pennsylvania until his health failed, and in 1835 came to North Buffalo township, Armstrong Co., Pa., purchased a farm and prospered at that vocation until his death, in 1853. Mr. Dinsmore was educated in the elementary branches in the public schools of Kittanning; when eleven years of age entered Reed's institute, in Clarion county; two years later he attended Bucknell university, where he remained but one year, owing to failure in health. He went to Hahnemann medical college, of Philadelphia, and was graduated from that well-known institution in 1876. Dr. Dinsmore began his professional career at Camden, N. J., and in 1877 came to Sharpsburg, and since then has been one of the leading physicians of that city. He had his offices at No. 210 North Main St., and enjoys a large and profitable practice. He was married, in 1878, to Emma, daughter of Lewis and Mary Jane Lewis, of Sharpsburg, her father having formerly been a member of the firm of Lewis, Bailey, Dalzell & Co., proprietors of the large iron works conducted by that firm in Sharpsburg. Dr. Dinsmore and his wife have one child, Marion H., a student. He and his family are members of the Baptist church, and he is a prominent Mason and past master of the local lodge. Dr. Dinsmore is president of the Allegheny county homœopathic medical society and is a member of the Pennsylvania State homœopathic society and the American institute of homœopathy. In politics he is a republican. Dr. Dinsmore was in the Vienna hospital six months, receiving a certificate of proficiency from that institution in the diseases of the nose and the throat.

EDWARD WELLS POWERS, coal operator, residing at No. 426 Beechwood Ave., Carnegie, was born in Trumbull county, Ohio, June 11, 1843, son of Franklin and Eliza (Moore) Powers, natives respectively of Youngstown, Ohio, and Washington county, Pa. Franklin Powers, a widely known stock dealer, died at the age of thirty-three in 1853. His wife, who is now in her eighty-third year, is a resident of Youngstown, Ohio. Mr. and Mrs. Franklin Powers had three other children besides the subject of this sketch: John W. enlisted early in 1863 in the 125th Ohio volunteer infantry, fought at Murfreesboro and Chickamauga, and died in hospital from wounds and exposure, after the last-named battle, in September, 1863; Frank M. is a jeweler in Youngstown, Ohio, and Clarence, who was born in 1850, died in his second year. E. W. Powers, the subject of this sketch, enlisted in 1862 in Company B, 84th Ohio volunteer infantry, and spent the first part of his service with his regiment on the upper Potomac, guarding fords and passes in the mountains. In the battle of Cynthiana, Ky., he received a wound in the arm and was taken prisoner. After being in the hands of the enemy three days, the prisoners were paroled, as the pursuit of the Federal forces was becoming too fierce for the rebels. Mr. Powers spent the remaining two months of his service at Johnston's island, guarding prisoners, and was honorably discharged in October, 1864. After the war he entered Allegheny college, at Meadville, Pa., but after one year left to engage in the hardware business at Sandy Lake, Pa. With this and other interests he was busy for nearly five years, when he opened a coal mine near Youngstown, Ohio; this, and work on another one that had previously been opened, in Austintown township, occupied his time for the next two years. During this time he was the founder and chief promoter of the Ohio powder works, situated in Liberty township. This company has achieved a prominent place in the growth of powder making in the country. In 1883 he moved to Carnegie (then Mansfield), and was the pioneer in developing the coal of the Thom's Run section of the Pittsburg district. He has been extensively interested in coal mines, and has owned several valuable mining properties, although he has never operated more than three at one time. In 1899 Mr. Powers sold out his coal interests to the Pittsburg coal company, and very soon after engaged in coal mining in Columbiana county, Ohio. On Aug. 11, 1880, Mr. Powers married Miss Mary G. Moore, daughter of Irwin and Genette (Clapp) Moore. Both parents are now deceased. Irwin Moore came to America from Ireland when he was nine years old, his parents emigrating from that country in the first quarter of the last century. The family is a very old and respected one. Edward Powers and Mary Moore were schoolmates of the late President McKinley at the old academy in Poland, Ohio. Of the children of Mr. and Mrs. Powers, Helen Du Boise died when three years old, and Edward W. when five. Frank Irwin Powers, the only living child, is a student at Rose polytechnic institute, Terre Haute, Ind.

W. J. DITHRICH, of Coraopolis, Pa., a prosperous wholesale liquor dealer, was born in Pittsburg, Pa., Feb. 1, 1863, and is the son of Michael and Mary (Ferguson) Dithrich, who had ten children, six of whom are now living, viz.: Edward C., postmaster of Coraopolis; Frank and Leonard, newspaper men in Pittsburg; Mary, widow of John Stevenson; Laura and W. J. His paternal ancestors came from Germany, and his maternal ones from Ireland. He received his early education in the splendid public schools of Pittsburg, and when eighteen years of age left school and engaged in the wholesale tobacco business. When he attained his majority he went into politics, securing a position in the office of Sheriff McCandless as a deputy sheriff, and later served in the same capacity under Sheriff McCleary. In 1895 he received the appointment of mercantile appraiser of Allegheny county, and served one year in that office, and subsequently was deputy coroner and chief clerk under Coroner McDowell, later occupying those positions under Coroner McGeary for a year. He resigned and established his present wholesale liquor business in Coraopolis.

He was married, in 1885, to Ellen, daughter of Michael Welsh, of Pittsburg, and they have four children, Anna, May, Heber and Edward. Mr. Dithrich is a republican in his political affiliations, and is highly esteemed in the home of his adoption.

JOSEPH J. WITTMANN, of Sharpsburg, Pa., a prosperous grocer, was born in Bavaria, Germany, May 2, 1859, and accompanied his parents, Joseph and Barbara (Schmidt) Wittmann, to America when he was two years of age. His father was connected with the rolling mill of Spang & Chalfant until 1888, when he retired from active life, and is now residing at Sharpsburg. His paternal grandfather, George Wittmann, was a farmer in the Fatherland, and lived to be seventy-eight years of age. Joseph was educated in St. Mary's parochial school, attending until he was twelve years of age, when he entered the rolling mill of Spang & Chalfant, starting at the lowest position, that of cutting sockets, at forty cents a day. Later he was with Heinz & Moble in the pickle business; for two years he was engaged in gardening; returned to the rolling mill of Spang & Chalfant as helper on the rolls, and later became a roller, and continued in that capacity for four years. In 1889 he embarked in the grocery business with his brother, three years later establishing his present business at No. 220 Eighth St., where he now enjoys a large share of the public patronage. He was married, in 1883, to Elizabeth, daughter of John F. and Katharine Prager, her father being a farmer of O'Hara township, and her mother having died in 1900, at the age of eighty years. They are the parents of ten children, the surviving ones of whom are: Mary, wife of Markus Ruess; Celia, clerking; Flora, Francis, Christina, Girard and Joseph, attending school; Dorothy and Rudolph, at home. He is a member of St. Mary's Catholic church, of which he has served as a trustee for fifteen years. He is a member of the Knights of St. George, the C. M. B. A. and the democratic party. He was a member of the board of health for several years, was vice-president of the federation of Catholic societies for the diocese of Pittsburg, and was a delegate to the national convention at St. Louis. He is also a member of the German State league.

EMIL FREDERICK AUGUST DITTMER, pastor of St. John's Evangelical Lutheran church, No. 519 Highland Ave., Carnegie, Pa., was born in Stettin, Germany, Aug. 3, 1851. His parents, Christian and Caroline (Stoevahs) Dittmer, came to America in 1855, to the Province of Ontario, Canada. Christian Dittmer had been interested in the grain business in Germany, and on coming to America he became a farmer, continuing at this until the outbreak of the Civil war, when he came over into the United States, and, enlisting at Detroit, fought three years as a member of the infantry. He had, previous to this time, served twelve years in the German army. After the war he returned to Canada and took up farming again. He died when about sixty-eight years old, in 1882, and his wife in 1899, at the age of seventy-nine. Both were members of the Lutheran church. Mrs. Dittmer was an ardent church-worker, a woman of kindly address, and was beloved by all who knew her. Of the eight children of Mr. and Mrs. Christian Dittmer, four died when young, and those remaining are: August, a farmer in Canada; Frank, a farmer on the old home farm; E. F. A., the subject of this sketch, and Matilda, now the wife of August Stief, a farmer in Canada. Rev. E. F. A. Dittmer attended the graded schools of Stratford, Ontario, and the high school there, and taught two years in Canada country schools. In 1874 he came to St. Louis and studied theology in the Concordia theological college, pursuing his studies later at Springfield, Ill., and then for a year at Capitol university, Columbus, Ohio. He was ordained to the ministry at Marysville, Ohio, May 24, 1880, and immediately started his life-work at Farley, Mo., where he remained until the fall of 1882. In October, 1882, he came to Mansfield, now Carnegie, where he has since remained, and endeared himself in the hearts of his congregation and all who know him. His church, small when Mr. Dittmer took charge of it, has grown in influence and numbers, and now has a congregation of 125 families, while the parochial school in connection, under charge of Prof. E. A. Mees, son of Dr. Mees, of Columbus, Ohio, is prosperous and growing steadily. The church is well housed and equipped for services. The Sunday-school has an attendance of about 135, and the young ladies' society of forty-five members is a valuable help to the pastor and a source of revenue for the church. Rev. Dittmer was married, Oct. 6, 1880, to Miss Mary Dietzsch, a native of Allegheny city, daughter of John M. and Regina (Barth) Dietzsch Of six children born to Mr. and Mrs. Dietzsch, Mrs. Dittmer and Mrs. Christina Kentzel, of Ross township, Allegheny county, are still living. Mrs. Dietzsch lives with her son-in-law, Rev. Dittmer. Of the two children born to Rev. Dittmer and wife, Estella died when three and a half years old, and Anna died at the age of eighteen months.

DOS TAYLOR, of Sharpsburg, Pa., manager of the glass works of H. J. Heinz, was born in Pittsburg, Pa., Feb. 14, 1859, son of David and Sophia (Scobell) Taylor. His father was a glass manufacturer until a few years prior to his death, when he retired from active life and resided at Aspinwall until his death, in 1902, at the age of seventy-one years. His mother died the same year, at the age of seventy years. His father was a son of Francis Taylor, a native of Ireland, who later lived in England, and came to America in 1830. Dos Taylor was educated in the public schools of Pittsburg and at the Western University of Pennsylvania, at Pittsburg, attending the last-named institution for four years. He learned glass-blowing and followed that business for five years; the next four years were spent in the glass-manufacturing business, and then he secured the position of superintendent of the Model glass works at Findlay, Ohio, making tableware; later he was with the Rochester tumbler works, of Rochester, Ohio, the Braddock glass company, and many others over the country, thus learning all branches of the glass-manufacturing business. In 1901 he was appointed to his present position of general manager of the H. J. Heinz glass factory, and since has ably managed the important affairs of that concern. He was married, in 1884, to Margaret R. (who is now deceased), daughter of William and Katharine (Dunlap) Jackson, of Tarentum, Pa., and to them was born one daughter, Katharine J., now attending college. He is a member of the Masons and of the republican party. Mr. Taylor is financially interested in a large glass furnace construction company of Pittsburg, the Tarentum National bank, the First National bank of

Birmingham, the Pittsburg clay pot company, the United States glass company, of Pittsburg, and in the lumber, oil and gas business in West Virginia and Pennsylvania. Mr. Taylor has visited every State in the Union and made several foreign trips.

ANDREW J. BOYLE was born in Cambria county, Pa., Feb. 12, 1846, son of Robert and Sarah (Sproul) Boyle. Robert Boyle was the son of John Boyle, who came to America from Ireland about 100 years ago, and his wife, Sarah (Sproul) Boyle, was a daughter of Samuel Sproul, a pioneer of Somerset county. After a brief education in the schools of his native county, Andrew J. Boyle went to work as water-carrier at the Johnstown blast furnaces in 1858, and three years later entered the finishing department of that plant. After this he worked at the rolls, and, in 1874, came to Braddock with Captain Jones, and assisted in building and equipping the roll mill at Braddock. At the new plant he was employed in various capacities, as catcher, rougher and roller, and when Mr. C. M Schwab became superintendent, about 1890, Mr. Boyle was promoted to the responsible position of night superintendent. This position is one requiring great executive ability, as the superintendent has charge of about 1,000 men, and Mr. Boyle has filled the position very creditably. Mr. Boyle was married, in May, 1868, to Jennie, daughter of Samuel and Barbara (Sell) Kuntz, early settlers in Somerset county. The children of this union are: Lulu May, wife of W. J. Bennett, clerk in the East Pittsburg bank; Ida Ann, wife of John Howat, superintendent in the tin works at Sharon; Emma, wife of Earl Hanna, a civil engineer at Donara; Minnie, wife of Walter Sidel, inspector for the Westinghouse company at East Pittsburg; Effie, wife of Howard Wilson, with the Cleveland wire company; Jennie, wife of John Thomas, roll turner for Jones & Laughlin; Birdie, at home; Edgar, in the locomotive department of the Edgar Thompson steel works, and Elmer, attending North Braddock school. Mr. Boyle is a member of Braddock Field lodge, No. 529, I. O. O. F.; Braddock lodge, A. O. U. W.; Banner council, No. 17, O. U. A. M., and the Woodmen of the World. In politics he is a republican. He and his family are members of the First Methodist Episcopal church of

Braddock. Mr. Boyle has recently completed and now occupies a beautiful new $8,000 home at the corner of Bell avenue and Rebecca street. Mr. Boyle served for several years as school director for the North Braddock district, and is recognized as one of the prominent and respected citizens of Braddock.

PETER J. OEFFNER, M. D., a prominent physician of Homestead, was born in Pittsburg, Pa., July 22, 1865. His parents, John F. and Margaret (Twentier) Oeffner, were natives of Germany, and came to America in 1848, locating at Pittsburg. Here the father was for a time employed in a planing mill, and later for twelve years conducted a newspaper route. During the Civil war he owned the steamboat "Greenback," which plied for two years on the Monongahela and Ohio rivers. The boat was sunk shortly after the close of the war while hauling a fleet of coal boats. Mr. Oeffner was killed in a railroad accident at Homestead in 1892. The children born to John F. and Margaret Oeffner were: Lawrence; Margaret, wife of William Farquhar; Anna, who married John Briggs; John; Mary, wife of Christian Ross; Lizzie, wife of George Ross; Emma, who married Harry Beck; Peter J., and William. Peter J. Oeffner was reared in Pittsburg, and received his education in the public schools and at Curry institute. After school days he learned the tinners' trade and followed this vocation for twelve years in Pittsburg and Homestead. In 1896 he began the study of medicine at the Georgia college of eclectic medicine, and graduated from that institution in 1899. While attending college he took a special course of study on the eye, ear and throat under J. Harvey Moore, M. D. Upon graduation, Dr. Oeffner located at Homestead, where he has since been actively engaged in attending to a steadily increasing practice. Since 1901 he has been surgeon for the Keystone car wheel works. He is also surgeon for the Harbison & Walker company, brick manufacturers, and the Pittsburg railway traction company. On Dec. 13, 1889, Dr. Oeffner married Miss Emma Evans, daughter of Joseph Evans, of Pittsburg, and a descendant of Sir Francis Drake, and has three children living, Abiram A., Ethel M. and Oliver. Dr. Oeffner is a member of the Eclectic medical association of Pennsylvania and the

Georgia eclectic medical association. He is also a member of Pittsburg council, No. 117, Jr. O. U. A. M.; Canton, Ohio, council, No. 41, U. C. T., and is medical examiner for the Protected Home Circle, Endowment rank of K. of P., Knights of Equity of the World and Bankers' life insurance company of New York. In politics he is a republican.

PETER HUTCHISON, deceased, of Springdale, Pa., a well-known citizen and postmaster during the latter years of his life, was born near Glasgow, Scotland, Oct 29, 1823, and, when ten years of age, accompanied his parents, James and Katharine (Crawford) Hutchison, to America. His mother's father was one of the leading lace-makers of Glasgow. His paternal grandfather had charge of extensive coal mines in Scotland, and was a prominent man in his community. His father engaged in farming after locating in Allegheny county, and had three children, of whom Peter was the youngest. He was educated in the public schools of Allegheny city, and from 1837 to 1846 he assisted his father on the farm. Then he took charge of the old farm, where Kountz Bros.' brick works now stand, and later removed to Springdale and engaged in the oil business. He was an oil producer, and worked in Venango, Butler, Armstrong and Clarion counties until 1891. He returned to Springdale, was appointed postmaster and served in that capacity until his death, Dec. 20, 1897, at the age of seventy-four years. Mr. Hutchison was married, in 1846, to Anna, daughter of Christian and Barbara (Neff) Wise, of Alsace-Lorraine, she being the second child of a family of five, and has resided in Springdale since 1877. Mr. and Mrs. Hutchison were the parents of nine children, five of whom are now living, namely: Mary, wife of H C. Patterson, of Aspinwall; Henry F., in the oil business and a resident of Cheswick; Sophia E , residing with her mother; Emma E., wife of Dr. S. H. Pettigrew, of Pittsburg, and John C., with the Brill car company, of Philadelphia. Mr. Hutchison was a member of the Methodist Protestant church and of the democratic party, and was a man that possessed the respect and esteem of all who knew him.

PERRY O. LAUGHNER, of Coraopolis, Pa., a leading dealer in hardware and oil-well supplies, was born at Six Points, Butler Co., Pa., Sept. 21, 1859, son of Samuel S. and Jane (Grant) Laughner. His parents had twelve children, ten of whom are now living: Mrs. Nancy Wise, James M., Mrs. Melissa McMullen, Mrs. Emma Gray, Elmer E., William E., John B., Nettie Pearl, Mrs. Gertrude McGugan and Perry O. His paternal ancestors came from Holland, and his maternal ones from Aberdeen, Scotland. His father was a carpenter in calling, was a great lover of wholesome fun, and quite proficient as a violinist. He was a republican, and a member of the German Reformed church. He died in 1884, survived by his wife, a woman of many excellent qualities, who died in 1887. Perry O. Laughner, when two years of age, accompanied his parents to Salem, Clarion county, and obtained his rudimentary education in the schools of that county. When seventeen years of age, he entered the State normal school, at Edinboro, and in the interim between school terms, taught in the county schools. Later he attended the Iron City college, at Pittsburg, and taught a winter term in his home school. He then went to the oil regions in McKean county, was there until 1882, and removed to Oil City, where for eight years he was an active member of the oil exchange. Subsequently, he went to Shannopin, where he opened a store with a stock of oil-well supplies, and one year later, in conjunction with his brother, opened stores of a similar character in Coraopolis and McDonald. The store in McDonald was sold in 1893, and the other stores were run up to 1899, when his partnership with his brother was dissolved, Mr. Laughner taking the store at Coraopolis and the one at Shannopin going to his brother. He was married, on May 30, 1882, to Emma C., daughter of William P. Findley, one of the pioneers of the Standard oil company, and they have three children living, Aymer V., Chalmers C. and Gladys Marie. Mr. Laughner is a republican in his political affiliations, attends the Methodist Episcopal church, and is closely identified with the Odd Fellows and the Masons. He is a man of many excellent qualities of heart and mind, and stands high in the esteem of the people of Coraopolis.

GEORGE B. HART, of Coraopolis, Pa., a prominent real estate dealer, was born in Allegheny city, March 16, 1860. He began his present occupation in the town in which he is now located, in 1890, and in this field of work he has been very successful throughout the State of Pennsylvania.

JOHN Q. A. IRVINE, of Etna, Pa., principal of the public schools and a prominent figure in educational work, was born near Callery Junction, Butler Co., Pa., and is the son of John and Angeline (Johnston) Irvine, his father having been a native of Butler county and by occupation a farmer. His great-grandfather was a native of Ireland, and came to Butler county in 1796. He was the first county surveyor of that county, and also a teacher in the public schools. The grandfather and father of Professor Irvine were teachers, and he has been engaged in educational work since 1878. Professor Irvine was educated in the primary branches in the public schools of his native county, later attended Westminster college and was graduated in a classical course from that famous seat of learning in 1875. He immediately began teaching, and after one year was made principal of the Jamestown academy. He taught in the public schools of Evans City for several years, and was principal of the Utica school in Venango county for one year. In 1881 he came to Etna as assistant principal of the schools. Four years later he became principal, and since then has served in that capacity with much ability. The schools of Etna are very thorough, with a high curriculum, and stand well among the educational institutions of the county. He is a member and trustee of the United Presbyterian church, member of the Heptasophs, the Junior Order of American Mechanics, the alumni of Westminster college, and of the republican party. He was married, in 1881, to

Alta E., daughter of William and Cornelia (Carroll) Duncan, of Butler county, and they have four children: Florence V., teacher in the public schools; Ralph Eugene, attending the Western University of Pennsylvania, at Pittsburg; Henrietta, student of the Pittsburg academy, and Helen, residing with her parents. Professor Irvine has been secretary of the Etna building and loan association for the past fifteen years, is closely identified with the progress of the community, and is one of Etna's leading citizens.

MAXIMILIAN BLUMENTHAL, of Sharpsburg, Pa., a leading dealer in clothing and men's furnishings, and a well-known athlete, was born in New York city, May 26, 1865. He is a son of Henry and Helen Blumenthal, his father having been a wholesale liquor dealer, who came to America from Prussia when a young man, located in New York city, and was engaged in the wholesale liquor business until his death. Mr. Blumenthal was educated in the public schools of New York city, and at sixteen years of age entered an athletic school, since which time he has devoted a great deal of attention to athletics. He has instructed many persons well known in the ring, and has had for pupils Frank Crig; Black Sam, champion wrestler of New York; Stephen Taylor, champion boxer of New York; Thomas Allen, of New York; Jimmie Murray; Herman Beck, the 158-pound champion of Pennsylvania; Frank Gollo, of Etna; Eddie McConnell, champion fancy bag-puncher of the world, and many others of the leading athletes of the United States. After graduating from school, he learned the graining trade in New York city, following that business for fourteen years, and in 1889 came to Sharpsburg and opened a clothing and men's furnishing store at No. 501 South Main St. He was manager of the Blumenthal baseball club, of Sharpsburg, which was well known in western Pennsylvania during the years 1892, 1893 and 1895. For two seasons he was on the road with an athletic show. He was married on May 1, 1887, to Rica, daughter of Herman and Bertha Schener, formerly of Germany, but later of Carnegie, Pa., where her father was in the clothing business. Mr. and Mrs. Blumenthal have had four children, two of whom are now living: Helen, attending the public schools and also receiving vocal and instrumental instruction in Pittsburg; Harry, a student of the public schools, also studying the violin and receiving instructions in athletics and bag-punching. Mr. Blumenthal is a member of the Odd Fellows, the Royal Arcanum, and is now conducting an athletic school in Sharpsburg.

ALFRED D. CONNER, one of Tarentum's foremost business men, was born in Armstrong county, Pa., in 1854. His father, John P. Conner, a native of Armstrong county, and a son of Matthew Conner, followed for many years the vocation of steamboat pilot, and was an influential member of the Baptist church. In political belief he was a republican. He died in 1877. Elizabeth (Roney) Conner, mother of the subject of this sketch, is still living at the age of seventy-six. Her parents were Thomas J. and Elizabeth (Elliott) Roney, residents of Butler county, where Mrs. Conner was born. Alfred D. Conner was educated at Reid institute, in Clarion county, began teaching school at the age of eighteen, and for ten years was a teacher in Armstrong and Allegheny counties. He then gave up educational work to enter upon a commercial career. He was for several years a clerk in Armstrong county, and, in 1887, went into business for himself in Tarentum, his store being located at the corner of Brackenridge alley and Bridge street. Mr. Conner has been most successful as a merchant, and has amassed a considerable fortune. He is now a stockholder in the Tarentum savings and trust company, and formerly had an interest in the First National bank. He owns considerable property in Tarentum, has a farm in Armstrong county, and is president of the Ford City ferry company. In politics he is an ardent republican, though never an aspirant to office. He is a member of Tarentum lodge, No. 587, I. O. O. F., and the Heptasophs, of Tarentum, and was a charter member of P. O. L. of A., of Tarentum. In 1880 Mr. Conner married Miss Sarah M. Green, of Armstrong county, and has had two children, Maud and Edwin C. Maud died in infancy. Edwin C. graduated from the Tarentum high school and from Duff's business college, of Pittsburg, and is now employed in the office of the Baker manufacturing company, of Tarentum.

CHARLES BIEHL, the leading clothing merchant in Tarentum, has been in business in that place continuously for the past twenty years. In 1902 he built a fine two-story brick store building 26 feet wide and 132 feet long, where he keeps an excellent assortment of men's and boys' clothing and does a prosperous and steadily increasing business. Mr. Biehl was born in Armstrong county, Pa., May 17, 1864, son of Louis Biehl, a native of Germany and an early settler of Armstrong county, where he spent his last days. He was reared and educated in Kittanning, Pa., and came to Tarentum in 1883. Besides his clothing business, Mr. Biehl is a stockholder in the People's National bank, the Fidelity glass company of Tarentum, and the Duster contracting company, of that place. In politics he is a republican, and was formerly a member of the council of Tarentum. He is a member of the Heptasophs and of Lodge No. 644, B. P. O. E. Mr. Biehl is liberal in his religious views, contributing generously to all denominations. He married Christiana Ellerman, of Tarentum, and has two children, Theodore and Clifford C.

JOHN G. WELLINGER, president of the Anchor brewing company, Tarentum, has held that position since the company was organized in 1896. Associated with him in the business are three sons: John C. Wellinger, treasurer of the company; Frederick Wellinger, secretary, and Charles H. Wellinger, superintendent of the bottling department. The company is now in a prosperous condition and is doing a flourishing business. John G. Wellinger was born in Germany, in 1838, educated in the schools of his native country, and came to Pittsburg in 1855. Shortly afterwards he located at Natrona, spent four years in the salt works there, a year in the oil works, and then went to Pittsburg, where he was engaged in various occupations until 1873. In that year he went into the ice business, admitted a partner in 1876, and the firm was then for ten years known as the Monongahela ice company. In 1886 it was merged with the Chautauqua ice company, and the name was changed to the Chautauqua Lake ice company, Mr. Wellinger continuing with the concern until 1896, when he began his career as a brewer. John G. Wellinger began life a poor boy, with no resources, and in early life met with many misfortunes. Over all of these, however, he has triumphed, and is now one of the well-to-do men in Tarentum. He is a stockholder in the J. H. Baker manufacturing company. In politics he has been a republican since he cast his first vote for Abraham Lincoln in 1860; was for two years township commissioner, and is a member of the council of Brackenridge borough, having been a member of the first council of the borough. He was also at one time member of the school board of what is now twenty-fourth ward, Pittsburg. He is a member of Germania lodge, No. 509, F. and A. M., of South Side, Pittsburg, and, since 1862, has been a member of Peter Fritz lodge, No. 486, I O. O. F. In 1860 Mr. Wellinger married Miss Margaret Langheinrich, a native of Germany, and is the father of ten children, viz.: Mary, Louisa, Margaret, John C., George H., Elizabeth, Frederick, Charles H., and William F. and Katie, the last two both now deceased.

MICHAEL HAMMER, a wealthy retired hotel keeper and proprietor of the Harrison house in Brackenridge borough, was born in Allegheny city, Feb. 7, 1850. His father, George Hammer, a native of Wittenburg, Germany, came to America about 1847, and was married in Allegheny city to Frances Ott, also a native of Germany. They had seven children, four of whom are living. George Hammer learned the stone-cutters' trade in Germany, followed it in Allegheny city and in Pittsburg, and died in Allegheny city, in 1867. In politics he was a democrat. Michael Hammer, whose name begins this article, was reared in Pittsburg, received some education there, and then worked for a number of years in the rolling mills in Pittsburg. In 1884 he came to Brackenridge borough, where, in company with Mr. John Felter, he engaged in the hotel business. In 1891 he bought out Mr. Felter's interest, managed the business for himself for two years, and, in 1893, retired from active life. He owns the Harrison house, two store buildings and a handsome residence in Tarentum, on East Sixth avenue, which he built in 1893. Mr. Hammer has, by his own thrift and native ability, won for himself a competence and spends a great portion of his time traveling for pleasure throughout the United States. He is a stockholder in the Fidelity glass company, the Tarentum glass company, J. H. Baker manufacturing company and the Tarentum National bank. In politics he is an independent. He is a member of B. P. O. Elks, of Tarentum. Mr. Hammer was married, in October, 1878, to Miss Margaret Heilman, of Cambria county, Pa.

JOHN KERR, deceased, for many years one of the best-known and most highly-respected citizens of O'Hara township, Allegheny Co., Pa., was born in St. Clair township of the same county, near Mount Lebanon United Presbyterian church, and was the oldest son of Samuel and Elizabeth (Stitt) Kerr. His father was one of the pioneer farmers of Allegheny county. John Kerr was educated by his parents, before the introduction of the common-school system in Allegheny county, and, after growing to manhood, entered the droving business and prospered in that vocation until 1842, when he purchased the farm known as "Solitude," in O'Hara, then Indiana, township. This farm is located one and one-half miles north of Sharpsburg, adjoining the Greenwood cemetery, on what is now known as the Sharpsburg and Kittanning county road. He remained on this farm until his death, which occurred on Jan. 24, 1891, after he had reached the advanced age of ninety-nine years, six months and twenty-four days. His widow still lives on the farm. On March 22, 1860, John Kerr was married to Matilda Ellen Neff, the youngest daughter of Peter and Jane (Ream) Neff, living near Dorseyville, Allegheny Co., Pa. Peter Neff was born in York county, Pa., and his wife was born in Cumberland county, Pa. In 1818 they purchased the farm near Dorseyville, where they lived the remainder of their lives, Peter Neff dying in his eighty-third year and his wife dying in her sixty-ninth year. Robert P. Kerr, a grand-nephew of John Kerr, and a great-grandson of Samuel and Elizabeth Kerr, was adopted by John Kerr and his wife soon after their marriage, and he has lived with them ever since 1863, though he owns a farm in West Deer township. He was married, in 1884, to Jennie M. Shaw, a niece of Mrs. John Kerr, and they have four children, viz.: Charles W., Helen M., Harriet N., and Florence J., all of school age and attending the public schools. Robert Kerr and his family are all members of the First United Presbyterian church of Etna. John Kerr was a United Presbyterian from his youth, except for a few years, when he was out of reach of a United Presbyterian church. In that time he attended a Presbyterian church, but about 1869 he united with the Etna church and remained a member of it until his death. In all his church work he had the moral and material support of his wife. Matilda (Neff) Kerr was brought up a Presbyterian, uniting with the church when she was seventeen years of age, and from that time to the present she has been a consistent member. After her marriage with John Kerr she was always associated with him in church work. She became a member of Etna church at the same time he did, and she still remains with that congregation, steadfast in the faith, and confident that beyond the grave she and her beloved husband will again be united.

JOHN JAY CRAWFORD, M. D., of Coraopolis, Pa., a distinguished physician and surgeon, was born in Mount Pleasant township, Washington Co., Pa., Jan. 22, 1860, son of Robert M. and Sarah Ann (Elder) Crawford. They were the parents of six children: W. O. Crawford, an attorney, of Pittsburg; Nancy M.; E. D. Crawford, a farmer, of Washington county; Cassie J. McNall; Robert O. Crawford, and Dr. J. J. His maternal ancestors were from eastern Pennsylvania, his grandfather having come from Easton, Pa., and his paternal ancestors from the north of Ireland. His paternal grandfather was a disciple of the old Covenanter faith, and Dr. Crawford's father, who died before his son was born, was one of the leading abolitionists. Dr. Crawford secured his elementary education in the public schools of Washington county, and when sixteen years of age entered the academy at Sewickley, Pa., where he was under Prof. James Dixon for two years. He spent two years at the Western university, of Pittsburg, and later entered Jefferson medical college, where he was graduated at the end of a three-year term. He matriculated at the Hahnemann homœopathic medical college, of Chicago, and was graduated with the highest honors in the class of 1884. Dr. Crawford began the practice of his profession at Imperial, Pa., in 1882, and for nineteen years was one of the leading physicians of that section, removing to Coraopolis, where he now enjoys a large and lucrative practice. Dr. Crawford was married, in 1886, to Atlanta S. Burns, of Imperial, Pa., and their home life is an ideal one. He is one of the leading physicians of western Pennsylvania, being president of the third board of examining surgeons of Pittsburg and otherwise identified with the best interests of his profession. His political affiliations are with the republican party, and he attends the Presbyterian church.

PAUL R. HOLLAND, cashier of the Turtle Creek First National bank, was born in Braddock, Pa., March 7, 1877, son of William A. and Ellen (Gordon) Holland. William A. Holland was born in Carroll county, Ohio, and has been for many years in the insurance business in Braddock. He is a son of William and Nancy (Thompson) Holland, of Starke county, Ohio, and grandson of Robert and Sarah Thompson, pioneer residents of Washington county, Pa. The mother of William Holland, the grandfather of the subject of this sketch, was of the Gettys family for whom Gettysburg was named. Ellen (Gordon) Holland, the mother of Paul R. Holland, is the daughter of John and Martha Gordon, who came from London. Paul R. Holland graduated from the Braddock high school in 1892, and spent the following four years in the real estate business in Braddock. When the Citizens' bank of Turtle Creek was organized, in 1896, he became bookkeeper and, in 1899, was made cashier of that institution. This position he held until April, 1902, when he opened a real estate and insurance office at No. 117 Penn Ave., where he had an extensive business in real estate, having represented several leading fire insurance companies. When the First National bank of Turtle Creek opened its doors for business in January, 1903, Mr. Holland was elected its cashier and one of the directors. The bank started with a capital of $50,000, and so popular has it become and so successful in every way, that the officers are contemplating the erection of a large and modern banking room on Penn avenue. Mr. Holland is a member of Turtle Creek castle, K. G. E. and Braddock lodge, No. 180, A. O. U. W. He is a member of the First Christian church of Braddock. Mr. Holland was married, Jan. 30, 1900, to Miss Sarah Jacobs, daughter of Calvin B. and Sarah Jacobs, of Hollidaysburg, Pa.

JOSEPH G. HOLZHEIMER, of Sharpsburg, Pa., a leading funeral director and liveryman, was born in the city where he now resides, Oct. 9, 1867, and is the son of Joseph and Regina (Winschell) Holzheimer. His father was a native of Baden, Germany, and, when nine years of age, accompanied his parents to America, settling in Pittsburg, where, later, he learned ornamental painting and followed that trade for some years. He started a chair factory in Pittsburg, which was subsequently destroyed by fire; then he engaged in the furniture business in Pittsburg, where he prospered until 1868, when he removed his furniture business to Sharpsburg, and there added an undertaking department. He continued in these lines until 1875, when the livery business was substituted for the furniture feature, and he successfully conducted both until his death, when he was succeeded by the subject of this sketch. Mr. Holzheimer was a pupil of the public schools of Sharpsburg until his fifteenth year, when he attended Duff's college and was graduated in a commercial course from that institution in 1883. On leaving school, he went into his father's business as assistant, and, in 1893, on the death of his father, assumed control of the business and organized a company composed of himself, H. W. Bock and John Holzheimer, under the firm name of Holzheimer & Bock, now one of the largest undertaking establishments of Allegheny county. His father was one of the oldest funeral directors of the county, and his business is one of the first established in Allegheny county. Mr. Holzheimer was happily married, on May 5, 1902, to Eva May, daughter of M. J. Connelly, an oil operator in West Virginia, but a resident of Allegheny city.

Mr. Holzheimer is a member of St. Mary's Catholic church, the Knights of Columbus, the Elks, the Y. M. I. and the democratic party. His father was a great worker for the democratic party, and served as president of the school board for ten years, and burgess and member of the council for several years. He is a director of the Mutual oil and gas company, of West Virginia, and is secretary of the Ben's Run oil company, operating in West Virginia, both of which concerns have their headquarters in Pittsburg. Mr. Holzheimer has devoted his leisure to travel, having made two trips to Europe, visiting most of the countries of importance, and has been to the West Indies and the Hawaiian islands.

DAVID S. BOYD, coal dealer and banker, of Turtle Creek, was born in Allegheny county, Nov. 1, 1865, son of E. W. and Sarah (Shaw) Boyd. E. W. Boyd was born in Westmoreland county, Pa., near Irwin station, Oct. 17, 1837, being a son of Thomas and Sarah (Wilson) Boyd. On Nov. 1, 1859, he married Sarah, daughter of David and Lydia (Stewart) Shaw, of Westmoreland county. Mrs. Boyd was born April 6, 1840. Mr. and Mrs. E. W. Boyd were the parents of the following children: Lydia (deceased), formerly Mrs. J. S. McIntosh; Sarah (also deceased), who married G. E. F. Gray, of Braddock; David Shaw, the subject of this article; Margaret, now Mrs. J. F. Lewis, of Braddock; James Kelso, a civil engineer in the Edgar Thompson works, and Martha G., at home. Mr. E. W. Boyd was reared on a farm in Westmoreland county, and removing to Allegheny county after his marriage, lived on a farm in Patton township until 1883, and then came to Turtle Creek, where he resided until his death, which occurred May 18, 1900. He was for many years a prominent farmer and coal dealer, and was widely and favorably known in the community. He organized the Citizens' bank of Turtle Creek, was its president up to the time of his death, and was a director of the Duquesne National bank. He took an active interest in public affairs and served for some years as school director. He was a member of the Order of Americus club, and, with his wife, belonged to the United Presbyterian church. David S. Boyd, whose name heads this sketch, was educated in the schools of Patton township and Pittsburg, and worked on his father's farm until 1884. He went into the gas works, later became engineer in the coal mines, and was from this position advanced to assistant superintendent, and, after his father's death, became superintendent. Mr. Boyd is one of the most progressive and respected citizens of Turtle Creek, has been for four years a member of the Turtle Creek council, and is a director of the Turtle Creek savings and trust company and the East Pittsburg building and loan association.

JOHN T. ANDERSON, of the firm of J. T. Anderson & Co., of Oakmont, was born in Allegheny city, Pa., Jan. 11, 1862. His father, Matthew Anderson, and his mother, Sarah (Robinson) Anderson, were both natives of Ireland. Matthew Anderson came to Allegheny city in 1844, and was for thirty years foreman for J. C. Patterson & Co., of Allegheny. He moved to Oakmont in 1871, and was for a time engaged as a contractor and builder, and, in 1881, established the firm of J. T. Anderson & Co. At his death, in 1887, his son took his interest in the firm and now owns the business. The plant was moved to Verona in 1889. The firm runs a planing mill, and makes a specialty of the manufacture of fine mantels. It has had a prosperous existence from the first, and is now a flourishing concern, employing forty-two men. J. T. Anderson, the subject of this sketch, was educated in the ward schools of Allegheny city, afterwards engaging in various lines of business. He was for six years foreman for L. Benz Bros., large contractors, in Pittsburg, before going into business for himself. Mr. Anderson was also the organizer of the J. W. Hodie company, builders, of Oakmont, and is now president and general manager of the concern. He has other extensive business interests, is director of the Interior lumber company, of Pittsburg, and the Hazelwood savings and trust company, of Hazelwood. He resides in Oakmont, is a prominent republican of that city, and has served three years on the Oakmont council, two years as president of that body and a year as chairman of the street committee. Mr. Anderson was married, in 1884, to Miss Annie Glover, of Pittsburg, daughter of Robert Glover, who was formerly connected with Thomas Coffin & Co., now the Dixon-Wood company. He was the first man to make glass house pots, and held the secret of their manufacture up to about the time of his death. Mr. and Mrs. Anderson have had six children, of whom all, except one, died in infancy—W. Presley, born May 11, 1892. Mr. Anderson and wife are members of the United Presbyterian church of Oakmont. He was for nine years a member of the board of trustees of the Ninth Presbyterian church of Pittsburg, and for five years president of the board.

THOMAS WARREN ROSENSTEEL, a well-known and universally popular pastor of Sharpsburg, was born near Loretto, Pa., Aug. 20, 1859. His preparatory studies were made at St. Francis college, Loretto, his classical course taken at Mt. St. Mary's, Emmetsburg, and philosophy and theology at the Grand seminary at Quebec, Canada, where, on June 13, 1886, he was ordained to the priesthood by his eminence, Cardinal Taschereau, archbishop of Quebec. On his return to his native diocese, Father Rosensteel was appointed assistant at St. John Gualberts, Johnstown, and after two successful years there, was transferred as assistant at St. Agnes City, where he remained fourteen months, and was then made first resident pastor at Ashville, Cambria county, attending at the same time to the missions at Frugality and Baker mines. Here Father Rosensteel encountered many difficulties, which he overcame one by one, building churches and pastoral residences at Ashville and Frugality, and improving wonderfully the conditions at Baker mines. After six years of hard work in this rough mountain district, he was appointed pastor of St. Matthews at Tyrone, where he built a handsome church. In the summer of 1900 he was chosen to fill a vacancy at St. Joseph's, Sharpsburg, caused by the death of Father Brady. The parochial school in connection with this church is now in process of building, and will be, when completed, one of the finest schools in the diocese of Pittsburg. This parish has for many years been struggling under financial difficulties, and now, since Father Rosensteel has taken charge, much of the old debt has been paid and many needed improvements made. Father Rosensteel is much beloved by all denominations. Father Rosensteel has one brother, also in the ministry, Rev. C. D. Rosensteel, of the Baltimore diocese.

WILLIAM H. PATTERSON, all his life a farmer in Patton township, was born in that township April 16, 1859, son of John and Margaret (Hughey) Patterson. John Patterson, in his day a well-known Allegheny county farmer, was born in 1830, and died Sept. 16, 1860. He had, besides the subject of this sketch, another son, Joseph, who died in infancy. William H. Patterson was educated in the common schools of Patton township, then settled down there, where he has since followed the vocation of a farmer. He has been married twice, the first time, in 1884, to Margaret Katz, and the second time to Jennie Norman. The present Mrs. Patterson, born Oct. 6, 1870, is a daughter of Samuel and Margaret Norman, of Allegheny county. Mr. and Mrs. Patterson have two children: Clarence Sylvester, born July 18, 1893, now attending school, and Gladys Marie, born Feb. 20, 1902. In political belief Mr. Patterson is a republican, although not actively interested in party matters. He and his wife are members of the Cross Roads Presbyterian church.

S. C. McCORMICK, of Coraopolis, Pa., a successful business man, was born in Jefferson county, Pa., on April 22, 1861, son of John L. and Nancy (McFarland) McCormick. His paternal ancestors were Scotch, and his maternal, Irish. His father was a lumberman during the greater part of his business career, an old-time democrat, and both of his parents were members of the Baptist church. He is the youngest of ten children, eight of whom are now living, and, exclusive of himself, are: R. M., J. E., W. W., F. I., Mrs. S. C. Snyder, Mrs. Maude Bell and Mrs. Emma Lewis. S. C. McCormick secured his early education in the schools of Clarion county, Pa., and when seventeen years of age left school and became engaged in the lumber business, which he followed till 1891, and for several years ran a large general store in Beaver county, Pa. Selling his stock in 1902, he came to Coraopolis and commenced the grocery business, where he has built one of the largest and best business blocks in the town, and has a well-stocked store that occupies the entire first floor of the structure. He is also a half owner of the Curry & McCormick company, which conducts a large livery and undertaking business. That firm have a very complete outfit, owning thirteen horses and other appurtenances, and have recently expended $9,000 in fitting up their place. Mr. McCormick was married, in 1881, to Mary Elizabeth Bruder, of Danville, Montour Co., Pa., and they have five children. His political affiliations are with the democratic party. Mr. McCormick is a highly successful business man, has made a great success of his commercial career, and owes not a little of his present prosperity to the aid and counsel of his wife, in whom he has an active coadjutor and assistant.

FRANK WOLFF, of Natrona, Pa., proprietor of the Washington hotel and a substantial citizen, was born in Allegheny city, Pa., Oct. 14, 1853, son of Frank and Mary (Seifert) Wolff, both natives of Germany, the former coming to Allegheny city in 1845, and the latter accompanying her parents to that city in 1848. Frank Wolff conducted an emigrant house, or hotel, in Pittsburg, and for many years in Allegheny city, and met with much success in that vocation, being possessed of a fine property at the time of his death. He and his wife were members of the Catholic church, and had seven children, five of whom are now living. His wife died in 1865, and later he was married to Louisa Mower, who bore him one child. The elder Wolff died in 1890, after a long and useful life extending through sixty-five years. Frank Wolff, the son, was reared and educated in Allegheny city, and in 1886 came to Natrona and purchased the property on which his hotel now stands. He erected the Washington hotel on this property, and since has conducted it with unusual success. Mr. Wolff is a prosperous business man, being a stockholder in the James H. Baker manufacturing company and owning property in Natrona and Allegheny city. He is a republican in politics, has been a delegate to several county conventions, and is an active member of that party. He is a member of U. R., Knights of Pythias, and Frankford lodge, No. 391, of

Natrona. He was married, in 1881, to Clara E., daughter of William and Catherine Bauer, of Butler county, Pa., and they have two children: Clara C., a graduate of the schools of Natrona and Grove City and of the Iron City college, and a bookkeeper for Bauman & Co., of Pittsburg, and Frank W., a graduate of the Natrona high school and a student of Grove City. Mr. Wolff is well and favorably known in Natrona, and is closely identified with the progress and development of the city.

SAMUEL B. SMITH, liveryman at Tarentum, was born in Allegheny city, Pa., Jan. 11, 1857. His father was R. P. Smith, and his grandfather, Mack Smith. Mack Smith was born in Vermont, moved to Connecticut and then to Pittsburg, where he became a teamster, his route lying between Pittsburg and Philadelphia. His wife, Frances (Perine) Smith, was a native of Connecticut. Both died in Allegheny city. R. P. Smith, father of the subject of this sketch, was a tinsmith by trade and a manufacturer, and delivered by wagons, selling his wares from house to house. Later he engaged in the hardware business. He was a prominent politician, at first a whig and afterwards one of the organizers of the republican party, and served his borough as councilman. He was a native of Connecticut, while his wife, Margaret (Daychair) Smith, was born in Ireland. They were members of the Presbyterian church. Mr. Smith was a member of the I. O. O. F. He died in Allegheny city in 1872, but his wife is still living, at the age of seventy-seven. The subject of this sketch is one of seven children, of whom three are living, Samuel B., Homer and Albert H. Samuel B. Smith was educated in the schools of Allegheny city, Springdale and Tarentum, and at the Iron City business college, in Pittsburg. He spent the first nineteen years of his life on a farm, and then, in 1876, came to Tarentum, where he has ever since successfully engaged in the livery business. He has dealt in horses for many years, and owns property in Tarentum. In politics Mr. Smith is a prominent republican, was for ten years assistant burgess of Tarentum, and is now a councilman. He was one of the organizers of the local fire department, and, for several years, its chief. He is a member of Tarentum lodge, No. 502, F. and

A. M. Mr. Smith was married, in 1887, to Miss Luella Hazlett, of Allegheny county, and has two children: Lillie Leverna, born April 10, 1888, and Fannie Luella, born May 28, 1890. He and his wife are members of the Methodist Episcopal church.

ANTON J. KATCHMAR, a prominent grocer and foreign exchange banker of Braddock, was born in the city of Leutschau (Löcse), Hungary, July 18, 1872, son of Anton and Anna Katchmar, who were of Slavic descent. He attended school until his twelfth year, and then learned the bakers' trade, at which he worked until 1889, when he came to America, landing in New York, Aug. 9, 1889. He immediately left for the coal regions, in Allegheny county, where he worked for a time, and then decided to try his fortunes in the great city of Pittsburg, of which he had heard. On reaching Pittsburg, Sept. 15, 1889, he found himself alone and friendless in the city, with only five cents in his pocket with which to buy food and lodging. Soon, however, he found some countrymen, who provided for his immediate wants, and one of them, Mr. Joseph Gallik, took the boy to his home in Allegheny city, and secured employment for him in the Heinz pickling works. Later Mr. Katchmar went back to his trade as a baker for a time, and then accepted a position as clerk in the wholesale liquor house of William Zoller, in Pittsburg. He next came to Braddock, where he worked for a while for the firm of Calahan & Vey, grocers, and spent three years in the employ of F. G. Bishoff & Co. March 26, 1898, Mr. Katchmar started in for himself in the grocery business on Third street. The next year he built a one-story storeroom at the corner of Hawkins avenue and Spring street, and, the business prospering, moved the frame building to No. 107 Hawkins avenue, where he still conducts a prosperous grocery. On the spot where the old building stood he erected a handsome three-story brick building, and, on Oct. 22, 1902, opened a foreign exchange banking and steamship ticket agency. Mr. Katchmar is well qualified to conduct such a business, being conversant with the Slavic Polish, Hungarian, Magyar, Croatian, German and English languages.

FREDERICK LUCIUS MUTH, M. D., a prominent young Wilmerding physician, was born in Mauch Chunk, Pa., Sept. 4, 1876, son of John and Jane E. (Mushlitz) Muth. He is descended on his father's side from German ancestors, while his mother traces her family to the old Pennsylvania Dutch. Dr. Muth received his professional education at the Hahnemann medical institute in Philadelphia, from which he was graduated in 1898. After graduation he practiced for a time in Huntington, Pa., and, in July, 1899, came to Wilmerding, where, in his comparatively short residence, he has built up an extensive practice. Dr. Muth is a member of I. O. O. F., Heptasophs and Knights of Pythias. His office is at No. 208 Westinghouse Ave., Wilmerding.

GEORGE P. WEAVER, grocer on Linden avenue, East Pittsburg, is a type of the self-made men who add so much to the commercial life of a city. He was born at Banksville, a suburb of Pittsburg, July 6, 1863, son of Abraham and Charlotte (Perry) Weaver. Abraham was the son of Benjamin and Martha Weaver, who lived in Tradega, Wales. Mrs. Weaver's parents were George and Charlotte Perry, old settlers of Banksville, who came to this country from England. George P. Weaver was married, Oct. 8, 1887, to Elizabeth A., daughter of John A. and Eliza (Harley) Richards, and granddaughter of Thomas and Elizabeth Richards and Joseph and Mary Ann Harley. The children born to Mr. and Mrs. Weaver are: Della H., born Nov. 6, 1888, now attending high school; John Abram, born Aug. 30, 1890; Mabel Irene, born Dec. 3, 1893, and Elizabeth Richards, born Feb. 23, 1897. Mr. Weaver was engaged for some time in railroad work in the capacity of engineer, in 1898 started a grocery near his present location in East Pittsburg, but finding the accommodations insufficient for his increasing trade, he erected, in 1900, the large store building which he now occupies. The upper part of this building he has fitted up for a comfortable residence. Mr. Weaver was early selected as a progressive citizen of his borough and one well fitted to serve in the council of East Pittsburg, and has been, since February, 1902, president of that body. Mr. Weaver has recently completed a fine row of flats on Beach street, and has opened a branch of his business at Wolftown, in North Braddock borough. His brother, William W. Weaver, erected, at the foot of Linden avenue, the fine, four-section brick building called the Weaver block, a handsome structure, which adds much to the architectural beauty of East Pittsburg.

WILLIAM ALBERT REED is pastor of the Beulah Presbyterian church, situated two miles east of Wilkinsburg, one of the oldest churches in Allegheny county. It was organized about 1784, and was called Beulah in 1804. James Milligan was one of the leading organizers and a charter member. Although the early history of the church is very scanty, it is known that Rev. Barr preached there about Sept. 24, 1787, and the first report of membership gives the church an enrollment of 124. There have been, in all, nine pastors, as follows: Rev. Barr, who was the first; Rev. James Graham, born in Cumberland county in 1776, and pastor from 1804 to his death, which occurred in 1845; Rev. T. M. Brown; Rev. Hastings; Rev. Hunter, who served from April, 1874, to April, 1877; Rev. Miller, 1878 to 1884; Rev. Ralston, D. D.; Rev. Hayes, 1894 to 1900, and the present pastor. The church has had a prosperous life, having a membership now of 125. The present officers are: Clerk of the session, N Montgomery, and J. L. McKeever, Matthew Taylor and Frederick A. Weber. The present pastor, William Albert Reed, was born in Clarion county, Pa., April 16, 1867, son of William L. and Elizabeth (Berlin) Reed. He was educated at the Clarion normal school, the Washington and Jefferson college, and the Western theological seminary at Allegheny city. He graduated from Washington and Jefferson college in 1897, and from the Western theological seminary in 1900, and was ordained to the ministry Oct. 16, 1900, as pastor of Beulah church. During his pastorate, Rev. Reed has proved himself an earnest and faithful worker, and has endeared himself in the hearts of his congregation. He was married, in 1898, to Viola, daughter of Robert and Mary Scofield, of Venango county. Mrs. Reed was born in Venango county, Nov. 21, 1872, and was educated at the California normal school. She assists her husband by serving as superintendent of the Beulah church Sunday-school. Rev. Reed and wife have one son, William Robert, born April 6, 1901.

GEORGE HENRY DUERR, a well-known merchant of Tarentum, was born in Sarversville, Butler Co., Pa., March 27, 1859, and was reared and educated there. His father, John Duerr, a German by birth, came to America in 1854, settling in Sarversville, where he died, April 24, 1900, at the age of seventy-three. He was a blacksmith by trade, but also a farmer, was a republican in politics, and at one time served a year as supervisor of Buffalo township, Butler county. He was a member of the German Evangelical church. His wife, Elizabeth (Miller) Duerr, mother of the subject of this article, was born in Winfield township, Butler county, and was a daughter of Henry Miller, a native of Germany who, with his wife, came to America in an early day, and was among the pioneer settlers of Butler county. There, too, they spent their last days. Mrs. Duerr is still living, now sixty-four years old. She is a member of the German Evangelical church. George H. Duerr, whose name heads this sketch, began his business career as a clerk in a store in Pittsburg, where he remained two years. Leaving Pittsburg in 1887, he came to Tarentum, locating at first on East Sixth avenue, and moving the following year to his present place of business. Here he built a store which he still owns, and now he has also two houses and lots in Tarentum. Mr. Duerr has been most successful as a merchant, and has, by industry and persistence, won for himself a competence. Besides his store, he manages a milk route which he has owned ever since coming to Tarentum, and which has also been the source of considerable revenue. He is a stockholder in the People's National bank. In politics he is a republican. On Feb. 9, 1887, Mr. Duerr married Miss Mary A. Smith, of Sarversville, Butler county, and has four children, Lewla, Lolla E., Lyman C. and Alice P. Mr. and Mrs. Duerr are members of the Methodist Episcopal church.

FRANK RANDOLF MASTERS, a prominent young dentist of Wilmerding, was born in Allegheny county, Pa., in 1872. His parents, John C. and Elizabeth (Kane) Masters, were born in Westmoreland county, where they still live on a farm, the father at the age of fifty-six. Frank R. Masters is the oldest of a family of seven children. The others are: Edwin G., Trusie B. (now Mrs. William Kisler), William, Roy, Jennie and Zella. Dr. Masters attended the common schools of Westmoreland county, where he received his early education, and then became a student in the Laird institute, and, in 1897, graduated from the Slippery Rock State normal school. In the fall of 1899 he entered the Pittsburg dental college, from which he graduated in 1902. In April, 1902, he began practicing dentistry in Wilmerding, and has been successful in his profession. Dr. Masters was married, Nov. 19, 1902, to Lottie E. Eakin, of Eakin's Corners, Venango Co., Pa. Dr. Masters is a member of the Methodist Episcopal church, to which his parents also belong. He is also a member of the Knights of the Golden Eagle, of Turtle Creek.

JOHN BENJAMIN JONES, Jr., justice of the peace at Homestead, was born in Pittsburg, Pa., Nov. 4, 1853. His father, John B. Jones, was born in Wales, while his mother, Mary Jane (Whittaker) Jones, was a native of Pittsburg. John B. Jones, Sr., came to America with his mother in 1831, when less than a year old, and was reared in Pittsburg. He became a coppersmith and glassworker, and was employed for many years by leading firms in Pittsburg, and afterwards moved to Homestead, where he was in the employ of Boyce, Higbee & Co. He died at the age of sixty-nine, Feb. 13, 1900. He reared a family of nine children, as follows: John B.; Mary E., widow of Richard Fawcett; Ralph E.; William C.; Alexander M.; Huldah M., wife of George B. Forster; Sherman C., superintendent of the open-hearth department, American wire and steel company, Pittsburg; Lyda E., wife of James S. Ross, and Margaret M., wife of Thomas J. Dulse. John B. Jones, Jr., the subject of this sketch, was educated in Pittsburg, and served his apprenticeship with McKee Bros., South Side, Pittsburg, as a glass-worker. He followed this trade thirty years, fifteen years of that time being spent in Homestead with Bryce, Higbee & Co. Since 1895 Mr. Jones has been successfully engaged in the real estate business in Homestead, and has been, since 1901, justice of the peace. He was at one time a councilman, and served two terms as school director. In politics he has always been an active republican. Mr. Jones was married, Jan. 1, 1879, to Henrietta, daughter of John and Annie Young. Mr. and Mrs. Jones have had ten children, of whom six are now living. They are: Howard S., Lila, Paul, Nellie, Willa and W. Harry. Mr. Jones is a member of the Heptasophs, of Homestead. In religion he is a Methodist.

WILLIAM L. BARNDOLLAR, of McKee's Rocks, Pa., a successful druggist, was born in Pittsburg, Pa., June 16, 1871, son of Samuel L. and Emma J. (Blood) Barndollar, his father being of German descent and his mother having descended from a prominent English family. Both parents are now living, and his father is well known as a tinsmith and as a man of exemplary character. William L. is the eldest of nine children, eight of whom are now living, and, besides himself, are: Charles B., a traveling salesman for a wholesale shoe house of Cincinnati, Ohio; Olive A., wife of L. S. Henry, a well-known employe of Joseph Horne & Co., of Pittsburg; Isabella D.; Gladys A., a stenographer, of Pittsburg; Hazel, a dressmaker; Goldie and Helen, school girls. Nettie A., the fourth child, died about fifteen years ago. William L. Barndollar obtained his early education in the public schools of Verona and Pittsburg, and when fourteen years of age began working with his father in the tin business. When eighteen years of age, he matriculated at the Pittsburg college of pharmacy, was graduated from that institution, licensed by the State board, and secured employment with William Dice, a prominent druggist of Allegheny city. Mr. Barndollar remained with that concern for six years, then worked with other drug houses until 1898, when he embarked in the drug business on his own account in Allegheny city. After a year he disposed of his stock, clerked for other parties for a year, and then started his present successful drug store in McKee's Rocks. He is a member of the Odd Fellows, the Order of Americus, the republican party, and was one of the organizers of the First Baptist church of McKee's Rocks, now being treasurer of that institution. He was married, on Jan. 12, 1898, to Elizabeth A., daughter of Joseph and Mary Walker, of Avon, Lorain Co., Ohio, and they have one child, Mildred L., aged four years.

G. E. FRANK GRAY, chief clerk for the Carnegie steel company, at the Edgar Thompson steel works, furnaces and foundries, Braddock, Pa., was born in North Versailles township, Allegheny Co., Pa., Sept. 3, 1856. He is a son of Richard H. Gray, a carpenter by trade, and Martha E. (Shaw) Gray. The subject of this article was educated in the public schools, and from January, 1873, to October, 1879, a passenger brakeman on the Pennsylvania railroad. He was for two years connected with the Dithridge chimney company, of Pittsburg, and, in 1881, entered the employ of Carnegie Bros. & Co. (limited), now Carnegie steel company, at the Edgar Thompson steel works, in the employ of which company he has risen to the responsible position of chief clerk. Besides this, he was for a year chief clerk of the Homestead steel works, and held a similar position at the Duquesne works seven years. In January, 1886, Mr. Gray married Sadie W., daughter of E. W. and Sarah Boyd, of Turtle Creek, and has one child, Martha S., born March 24, 1891, now attending school in Braddock. Mr. Gray is one of the respected citizens of Braddock, and takes a great interest in the welfare of the city. During his residence in Duquesne borough he was a member of the council for the term of two years, is a member of the board of health of Braddock, also a trustee and treasurer of the Carnegie free library. He is a member of the Independent Order of Heptasophs, and a member of the United Presbyterian church. Mr. Gray resides in Braddock in a handsome residence at No. 430 Second St.

SAMUEL PERRY MONTGOMERY, farmer, resides on a farm which has been in the possession of his family for over a century. The farm, originally of 207 acres, was received from the government by patent in March, 1786. Mr. Montgomery was born in Allegheny county, April 10, 1857, was educated at Pleasant Hill academy, and then learned the carpenters' trade. In 1878 he went to Kansas, and from there made an extended trip, in 1878-1879, throughout the western part of the United States. He has been for many years a resident of North Versailles township, Allegheny county, where he has held various township offices, among others those of assessor and truant officer. He is a member of the Masonic fraternity, Lodge No. 1067, of Wilmerding, I. O. O. F., Daughters of Rebecca, Jr. O. U. A. M. and Sons of Veterans. In politics he is a republican. He is a member of the United Presbyterian church. In February, 1882, Mr. Montgomery married Jennie E. Kline, daughter of George W. and Rebecca Kline, of Westmoreland county. Mr. and Mrs. Montgomery have seven children, viz.: David R., Rhoda B., Jennie E., Samuel George, Rebecca T., Alice C. and Howard John.

J. GEORGE WERTZ, of Sharpsburg, Pa., manager and treasurer of the Pittsburg hair felt company, was born in the city where he now resides, on July 5, 1855. He is a son of Gotlieb Wertz, who was a well-known butcher of Sharpsburg for a number of years, but is now retired from active business and resides on South Canal street, at the mature age of eighty-three years. Mr. Wertz attended the public schools of Sharpsburg until he was sixteen years of age, and for the next two years was a student of the Sharpsburg academy, where he completed his literary training. On leaving school, he embarked in the butcher business with his father and remained with him until 1874, when the elder Wertz retired from business and the concern was conducted by J. G. Wertz and his brother. They ran the meat market at No. 816 Main St. with much success until 1898, when Mr. Wertz organized a company and started a hair felt works in Sharpsburg, under the name of the Pittsburg hair felt company, with a capital stock of $50,000, and with himself as manager and treasurer. H. J. Bellman is the president and F. S. Young is the secretary of this company, and they do a large business, manufacturing hair felt for cold storage and refrigerator car insulation, pipe and boiler covering, and many other uses. Mr. Wertz is closely identified with the Masonic fraternity, having taken the Knight Templar degree, and is an active member of the republican party, having served as councilman for one term. He is an extensive traveler, having visited nearly all of the States, Canada, Europe and other places of interest. Mr. Wertz is a man of affairs and is a director of the Spear carbon company, of St. Mary's, Pa.; the Farmers' and Mechanics' bank of Sharpsburg; the Wachter glue company, of Baltimore, Md., and a number of other corporations.

JAMES CARSON has been a farmer nearly all his life, or until 1893, when he sold his farm to the Monongahela investment company. He was born in Allegheny county, Pa., on the farm on which he has lived, Oct. 19, 1838, being a son of William and Elizabeth Carson, respected old settlers. His father died in 1878, and his mother is still living, being in her ninetieth year. James Carson was educated at Pleasant Hill school, and then began his life-long vocation as a farmer. His ninety-three-acre farm has now been divided into building lots, and a greater part of the borough of East McKeesport has been built upon it. Mr. Carson was the first burgess of that borough, being appointed to that position for a one-year term. He has also served the public as school director, and enjoys the confidence and respect of the community in which he has long played an important part. He was married, in 1877, to Edith, daughter of William and Myrtilla (Carleton) McQuiston, of Saltsburg, Indiana county. Mrs. Carson is now dead. Of the children born of this union, Myrtilla is at home, and Paul Eugene is attending school at Muskingum, Ohio. Mr. Carson served in the Civil war as a member of Colonel Gallop's regiment, re-enlisting in 1864, and has a most creditable war-record. Enlisting in 1862, in the 123d regiment, Pennsylvania volunteer infantry, under Colonel Clarke, he served nine months, then enlisted in September, 1863, in the 204th infantry, and served until discharged, June 10, 1865.

JOHN W. HANNA, superintendent of the cemetery of North Braddock, was born March 2, 1860, in Hannastown, Allegheny Co., Pa., son of John and Margaret (Preachman) Hanna. He was educated in the common schools, and lived on his farm in Allegheny county until 1889. He held the position of road commissioner for seven years, and, in 1896, was elected to the office which he now holds. Mr. Hanna is prominent in religious and educational affairs, and a well-known and highly-respected citizen of Braddock. He is an active member of the Methodist Episcopal church, and superintendent of its Sunday-school. He is also a member of the North Braddock school board. Mr. Hanna is a member of the Knights of Malta and Jr. O. U. A. M.

ANTON HARTIG, who keeps the leading hotel in Brackenridge, the Harrison house, is a native of Saxony, born March 2, 1859. He is a son of August Hartig, a farmer by occupation, who now lives in a city in Germany retired from active life, while his mother, Cleonora (Muehler) Hartig, died in 1859. August Hartig had four children by his first marriage and six by a second wife. The man whose name begins this sketch was reared and educated in Saxony, came to America in 1880, and was engaged for some time in railroad work, at first on the Allegheny Valley railroad and afterwards in the shops in Allegheny city. After that he decided to enter upon a business career, and was for some fifteen years salesman and collector for the White sewing machine company. In 1896 and 1897 he was in the hotel business in Etna,

Allegheny county, and, in 1900, came to Brackenridge, then Harrison township, where he undertook the management of the Harrison house. This is the oldest hotel in Brackenridge and the most popular house in the place, and under Mr. Hartig's able management has drawn for itself a liberal patronage by the best class of travelers. In politics Mr. Hartig is a republican. In 1883 he married Miss Catherine Hellerman, daughter of Peter and Christina Hellerman. Mr. Hellerman, a native of Germany, emigrated with his family to Allegheny county, where he died, in 1889, at the age of eighty-two. His widow is living, now a woman eighty years old. Mr. and Mrs. Hartig are the parents of five children, Katie, Walter, Hilma, Rudolph and Clara. Hilma died in 1891, when three years old. Mr. Hartig and family are members of the German Protestant Evangelical church.

JOHN M. WITTMANN, of Sharpsburg, Pa., a prosperous grocer and a well-known citizen, was born in that city on Jan. 27, 1867. He is a son of Joseph and Barbara Wittmann, the former a mill worker for many years, and both now live with the subject of this sketch. John M. Wittmann attended St. Mary's parochial school, of Sharpsburg, until he was thirteen years of age, and for the next four years was a student of the public schools of that city. He went into the grocery business at Nos. 129 and 131 Alhnayer alley, and has since enjoyed a thriving business at that stand. He retains several clerks, operates a delivery wagon and makes deliveries to Hoboken, Aspinwall, Etna and Sharpsburg. He was married, in 1896, to Matilda, daughter of Michael and Mary (Geisenhoffer) Kruth, formerly of Germany, but now residents of Sharpsburg, and to them have been born three children, Edward, Herbert and Loretta. Mr. Wittmann is a member of St. Mary's Roman Catholic church, the C. M. B. A., the Knights of St. George, St. Aloysius literary society, of which he has been chairman for nine years, and of the democratic party, of which he was a member of the county committee for two terms. Mr. Wittmann has traveled extensively in this country and in Canada, is well read and thoroughly informed, and is a most successful business man.

ELMER M. EDWARDS, a prominent resident of Sharpsburg, was born near Portsmouth, Scioto Co., Ohio, April 26, 1866. He is a son of Wallace and Electa (Barnett) Edwards, of Scioto county. Mr. Edwards was educated at Xenia, Ohio, graduating from the schools there in 1881, and then worked for a time in Chicago and other places as an electrician and a telegraph operator. On April 1, 1902, he was elected for a one-year term as superintendent of the water-works at Sharpsburg. In politics he is a republican and an influential worker in local party contests. He is a member of the I. O. O. F., Sons of Veterans, Independent Order of Heptasophs and Modern Woodmen of America, and belongs to the Presbyterian church. Mr. Edwards was married, in 1890, to Caroline, daughter of W. H. and Mary A. Swaby, of Ohio. They have four children: Ethel, Wallace and Robert, in school, and one younger child, Paul. Mr. Edwards and family reside at No. 1724 Main St., Sharpsburg.

ALBERT LONABAUGH, butcher and proprietor of a meat market on West Railroad avenue, Oakmont, was born in West Deer township, Allegheny county, June 20, 1859, and is a son of Jacob and Sarah (Lawson) Lonabaugh, the father a native of Philadelphia, and from 1844 until his death in 1897, a resident of West Deer township, and the mother a native of Allegheny county. Jacob Lonabaugh was a butcher all his life, and taught his son that trade. He served in the Civil war from 1862 to the close as a member of Company B, 63d Pennsylvania volunteer infantry. Albert Lonabaugh, whose name heads this article, has received his education more from travel than from books, being a wide traveler, who has visited thirteen of the States of the Union. In 1882 he started a meat business in Oakmont, and has spent most of his time since then in business in Oakmont, where he owns considerable property. He spent a year, from 1883 to 1884, in Carleton, Thayer

Co., Neb., and, in 1894, went to Findlay, Ohio, where he remained three years, but has since that time been a resident of Oakmont, where he is engaged in the care of a flourishing business. As was his father before him, so Mr. Lonabaugh is a republican in politics, and has served six years in the council of Oakmont. He was married, in 1882, to Miss Mattie Weickel, of Ohio township, Allegheny county, daughter of Henry Weickel, who lived on his father's farm all his life and died at the age of eighty-four. Mr. and Mrs. Lonabaugh have had two children, Edna and Pauline, of whom Edna is now deceased. Mr. Lonabaugh has gained considerable reputation as a hunter, and has shot game in many parts of the United States.

ULYSSES GRANT WILLIAMS, president of the Turtle Creek savings and trust company, is one of the younger and more prominent business men of Turtle Creek. He was born in Braddock, Pa., July 11, 1865, son of Jacob and Sarah (Miller) Williams. Jacob Williams was the son of John and Elizabeth (Washabaugh) Williams, of Westmoreland county, and his wife was the daughter of John and Anna (Steiner) Miller, old settlers of the same county. Ulysses Grant Williams attended school in Braddock and Pittsburg, and pursued his studies in Duff's commercial college, graduating from that institution in 1882. After graduation he entered the employ of the Braddock National bank, where he remained for nine years. Mr. Williams was the leading spirit in the organization of the Citizens' bank, of Turtle Creek, in 1896, and when that organization gave way, July 1, 1902, to the Turtle Creek savings and trust company, he became president of the new bank. This institution was incorporated with a paid-in capital of $125,000, and has been steadily growing, so that it is now well established and holds the confidence of the citizens of the progressive community of Turtle Creek. Mr. Williams is a member of Valley lodge, No. 613, F. and A. M., of Turtle Creek; McKeesport chapter, No. 282, R. A. M.; Pittsburg commandery, No. 1, Knights Templars; Pennsylvania consistory, S. P. R. S., and Syria temple, A. A. O. T. M. S. He is a member of the First Christian church of Braddock.

WILLIAM W. HEZLEP, a well-known carpenter of Turtle Creek, was born in that city, Oct. 14, 1876. He is a son of Samuel and Eliza (Curry) Hezlep, the father born May 7, 1851, and died Jan. 27, 1883, and the mother died at Turtle Creek, June 28, 1894. Joseph B., father of Samuel Hezlep, a prominent merchant of Turtle Creek for forty-three years, died May 13, 1900. and his wife, Aug. 10, 1899. William W. Hezlep was reared in Turtle Creek, and educated in the public schools of that place, after which he became a carpenter, following that vocation up to the present time. Mr. Hezlep was married, in 1892, to Clara, daughter of John and Rosa Mensdorf, of Wilmerding, and to them were born two children, Joseph and Henry, both at home. Mr. Hezlep is a member of the United Presbyterian church of his native city.

ROBERT D. ELWOOD, president of the First National bank of Verona, was born in Apollo, Armstrong county, Pa., April 7, 1836, and was educated in public and private schools. He began business life as a clerk in a store, engaged for a time in the canal business, and, in 1861, enlisted as a soldier in the union army, in Company I, 78th Pennsylvania volunteer infantry. He served three years and four months, taking part in most of the engagements in which his regiment participated. Shortly after enlistment he was made second lieutenant, and afterwards was promoted to the position of captain. The war over, Captain Elwood engaged in mercantile pursuits in Apollo from 1865 to 1871, and, in 1872, went into the wholesale grain business in Pittsburg, in which he has since that time been successfully engaged. He was also for some years president of the Iron City milling company, of Pittsburg. He was one of the organizers of the First National bank of Verona, and has been its president from the first. He was also a director of the Second National bank of Pittsburg for a number of years. Captain Elwood has been for twenty-eight years a resident of Verona, and is one of the most prominent and influential citizens of that place. In politics he is a republican, and in religion a Presbyterian. He married Miss Mary H. Lewellyn, of Apollo, and has two children living, Thomas J. and Robert D., Jr. Captain Elwood is a Free Mason, a member of the Loyal Legion, Union Veteran legion, No. 1, of Pittsburg, and the G. A. R.

ABRAHAM OVERHOLT TINSTMAN, for a quarter of a century a resident of Turtle Creek, was born in East Huntington township, Westmoreland county, in 1834. He is of German descent, his maternal grandfather, Abraham Overholt, being one of the prominent early settlers of Westmoreland county. Abraham Overholt married Maria Stauffer, of Fayette county, and had a daughter, Anna, who was married, in 1830, to John Tinstman, father of the man whose name heads this article. Abraham Overholt Tinstman was the third of ten children. He was educated in the common schools of his native county, worked on a farm until he reached the age of twenty-five, when he became manager of the estate of his grandfather, Abraham Overholt, the estate embracing a mill, distillery and valuable lands, at Broad Ford, Fayette Co., Pa. In 1864 he became partner with his grandfather, and continued in this capacity until the death of the latter, which occurred in 1870. Mr. Tinstman has long been extensively interested in coal and coke. In 1868 he formed a partnership with Col. A. S. M. Morgan, of Pittsburg, under the name of Morgan & Co., and engaged in making coke near Broad Ford, Pa. In 1871 he formed a partnership with Messrs. Frick and Rist, under the name of Frick & Co., and continued with this concern in the manufacture of coke until 1880, when he established the firm of A. O. Tinstman & Co., in Pittsburg, being engaged in the same business for some years. Since 1885 he has dealt extensively in the purchase and sale of coal lands, his office being at No. 425 Fourth Ave., Pittsburg. In 1870 Mr. Tinstman was one of the organizers of the Mount Pleasant & Broad Ford railway company, and was president of the company until the road was purchased by the Baltimore & Ohio railroad company, six years later. Mr. Tinstman was married, July 1, 1875, to Harriet Cornelia, daughter of Gen.

C. P. and Sarah (Lippincot) Markle, of Westmoreland county, Pa., and has one son, Cyrus P., who has completed the civil engineering course at the Pennsylvania military college, at Chester, Pa. Mr. Tinstman and family have lived in Turtle Creek since the erection of their beautiful home there in 1879. The site of a pioneer cabin, long since gone to decay, and the home of a Mrs. Myers, who gave food and shelter to George Washington, are on the Tinstman grounds. During the Civil war, when General Morgan was making his famous raid through the State of Ohio, Mr. Tinstman raised a company in twenty-four hours at Broad Ford, Pa., and went to Salineville, where they arrived just in time to assist in Morgan's capture.

LOUIS M. STEPHENS, vice-president of the National bank of Tarentum, was born in Crawford county, Pa., June 3, 1819. When three years old he went to Mercer county with his parents, John and Hannah (Mattox) Stephens, remaining there until 1845, when he moved to Tarentum, his present home. He was the oldest of five sons and four daughters. Mr. Stephens received a limited education in a primitive backwoods schoolhouse, and learned the trade of a carpenter, at which he worked for many years. He was also a contractor and builder up to about the time of the Civil war, after which he engaged in the lumber business and was for some time a skiff builder. Mr. Stephens has been unusually successful in business, and has, entirely by his own efforts, amassed a considerable fortune, part of which is invested in property in Tarentum. He is also a stockholder and vice-president of the National bank of Tarentum. In politics he has been a life-long democrat. Mr. Stephens was married, in Allegheny city, to Isabel Gregg, and has had four children, of whom one is living, Lawrence, now in the oil business in Ohio. Mr. Stephens has been in his day a great hunter, has shot deer and other game, and is well versed in the habits of wild animals, of which he has made particular study. He is a man of limited schooling, but educated in the school of life, a close observer of human nature, and a man of excellent judgment.

EDWARD I. BALDWIN, of Coraopolis, a prosperous oil producer, was born in East Troy, N. Y., now Watervliet, on June 9, 1845, and is a son of John G. and Martha (Town) Baldwin. His father was a tailor, very quiet in his tastes, a man possessing a great fund of humor, and a disciple of Izaak Walton. He was a veteran of the Civil war, serving in the 15th New York infantry, and also in the 15th New York cavalry. Mr. John Baldwin was twice married, first to Martha Town, of Massachusetts, who bore him three children—E. I., A. R. and Annie E.—and the second time to Ruth Barnes, by whom he had two children, Jessie K. and Olin J. Besides our subject, the surviving children of Mr. Baldwin are: A. R., well known in banking and real estate, of Syracuse, N. Y.; Olin J., one of the leading contractors of Ithaca, N. Y.; Mrs. Jessie Barnes, a highly cultured woman, now principal of two schools at Auburn, and Mrs. Annie E. Barnes, of Massachusetts, who is deeply interested in temperance, missionary and religious work. Edward I. Baldwin was educated in the public schools of Fayetteville, N. Y., and when fourteen years of age began work on a farm, where he remained until the beginning of the Civil war. At eighteen years of age he enlisted in Company B, 15th New York cavalry, commanded by Col. R. M. Richardson, of Syracuse. The 15th was in the 3d cavalry corps commanded by the illustrious general, George A. Custer, who later met his fate at the famous massacre of the Little Big Horn, and served until mustered out in Louisville, Ky. At the close of the war, Mr. Baldwin went to the oil regions at Petroleum Center and Pithole, Pa., and engaged in teaming, hauling crude oil on Oil creek for two years. He then went to California, where he spent three years, being, as he says, "chief cook and bottle washer" on a wagon train, and a general rover on the plains. Returning to the oil regions in 1868, he engaged in the oil business at Pithole, in which he has been very successful financially, operating at one time nineteen wells in McKean, Butler and Allegheny counties. Mr. Baldwin was married, in 1870, to Lucy Norris, of Venango, Crawford county, and their union was blessed with ten children, six girls and four boys, seven of whom are living, the four sons being in the oil business. Mr. Baldwin is senior partner of the firm of

Baldwin & Son, in the general repair work, and agent for the Braden gas engine, the firm being known as the Star machine company, of Coraopolis. In 1877 he, his wife, three daughters and one son joined the Baptist church in Bradford, and are very prominent in the active duties of the same. Mr. Baldwin is a member of numerous fraternal organizations, among them being the F. and A. M., the I. O. O. F., John Melvin post, G. A. R., T. E. A., and others. He has taken prominent parts in the orders, represented a number of them in their respective grand lodges, and stands high in the opinions of his fellow members. He is a member of the board of health in his town, in politics is a republican, but is always willing to vote for the temperance man. His youngest son, Fred Custer Baldwin, served two years in the 47th regiment of the United States volunteers, and saw active service in the Philippine islands. Mr. Baldwin is a man who is well known and esteemed for his many sterling qualities, and possesses the friendship of all who know him.

WALTER NEWTON HUMPHREY, M. D., of Sharpsburg, Pa., a prominent general practitioner of medicine, was born at Portersville, Butler Co., Pa., June 7, 1870, son of William and Elizabeth (Riddle) Humphrey, both of whom are now living. His father is engaged in the mercantile business at Portersville, and is one of the leading men of that section of the county. Dr. Humphrey was educated in the public schools of his native city, graduated from the classical department of Grove City college in 1890, matriculated at Jefferson medical college the same year, and was graduated from that famous institution in 1893. He came to Sharpsburg, opened an office at No. 611 Main St., where he remained until 1900, when he removed to his present location, No. 1407 Middle St. He was married, in 1898, to Florence, daughter of James and Elmira (Gulick) Depue, both descendants of French Huguenots and residents of Belvidere, N. J., and to Dr. and Mrs. Humphrey has been born one child, William Depue Humphrey. Dr. Humphrey is a member of the Presbyterian church, the Heptasophs, the Allegheny county medical society and the Pennsylvania medical association, and in politics is a republican. An uncle of Dr. Humphrey, James Humphrey, was a member of the Pennsylvania State senate and an original forty-niner; another uncle was county commissioner in Butler county for two terms. Mrs. Humphrey had an uncle who was judge of the supreme court in the State of New Jersey for thirty-five years, and though a republican, was appointed to that honorable position by a democratic governor. Mrs. Humphrey's father was for many years a manufacturer of fertilizers, but has now retired from active life and is living quietly at Belvidere, N. J. Dr. Humphrey has made a decided success of his professional career, and is one of the leading physicians of that part of Allegheny county.

ISAAC MILLS.

RACHEL A. CLAY, one of the first settlers of Braddock, was born on the lot on which she now resides, Nov. 8, 1843. Her father, Isaac Mills, the first burgess of the borough, in 1829 purchased property on which was a log house, and, later, supplanted it with a better dwelling. The home in which Mrs. Clay now resides was built in 1848, but was remodeled in 1902, and is now a beautiful mansion surrounded by spacious grounds. Isaac Mills was a son of Stephen and Elizabeth (Osborne) Mills, natives of Morristown, N. J. He was born in New York city, Dec. 13, 1801, and came to Braddock with his parents in boyhood, where he spent the remainder of his life. He was very closely identified with all the growing interests of the city. He was extensively engaged in agricultural pursuits, his farm including over 300 acres, all now comprised in the borough of Braddock. He was a charter member of the First Christian church, built the first church, and always took an active part in church matters, contributing liberally whenever called upon. Of the ten children of Mr. and Mrs. Isaac Mills, Mary S. died when twenty-six years old; Eliza L. died in 1900 at the age of sixty-two; Isaac, who served three years in the 63d Pennsylvania volunteers, died in March, 1902, at the same age; Helena E. married C. C. Lobingier, and resides now at Fitzgerald, Ga.; Rachel A. is the subject of this article; Nancy Jane died April 14, 1870, at the age of twenty-four; Charles died in April, 1890, at the age of forty-three; Samuel S. was killed in August, 1864, when fifteen years old, by the accidental discharge of a pistol;

244 MEMOIRS OF ALLEGHENY COUNTY

James K. and Stephen D. are now prominent quarrymen and brickmakers of North Braddock. Mrs. Clay was a daughter of Isaac Mills and Elizabeth Betsy (Snodgrass) Mills, a daughter of Col. Samuel and Mary (McKinney) Snodgrass. She was born near Elizabeth, in Allegheny county, Jan. 14, 1813. Her ancestors were very early settlers in Pennsylvania. Rachel A. Clay, the subject of this sketch, graduated from Pleasant Hill seminary in 1862, and, after teaching for a time, was married, Dec. 5, 1876, to Henry Clay, city engineer of Elizabeth, N. J. Henry Clay was the son of John Clay, of New York city, and his mother was a descendant of Danvers Osborne, the first colonial governor of New Jersey. Henry Clay, husband of Rachel A. Clay, died one year after the birth of his only child, Elizabeth Mills Clay, who was born March 10, 1878. She was educated at the Bishop Bowman institute, of Pittsburg, from which she graduated in 1897, and was married, Feb. 2, 1898, to Louis Ashton Drexler, son of Joseph A. Drexler, a veteran of the Civil war. To Mr. and Mrs. Drexler have been born two children, Louis Ashton, Jr., born Oct. 2, 1899, and Henry Clay, born Aug. 7, 1901.

THE CARNEGIE FREE LIBRARY, at Braddock, Pa., which stands on Library street, just off of Main street, is a handsome structure built of granite and pressed brick, which was erected by Andrew Carnegie, the multi-millionaire steel magnate, at a cost of about $250,000. It is a building of three stories and a basement, and is 92 feet wide by 162 feet long. The library proper is on the second floor, where there is a spacious reading-room elegantly furnished and well lighted. The building was commenced in 1889 and was subsequently greatly enlarged, and was not completed until 1894. Mr. E. H. Anderson was superintendent from 1892 to 1895, when he was called to be superintendent of the Carnegie library at Pittsburg, Miss Helen Sperry taking his place at Braddock. She was succeeded by Mr. Walter Crane, who took charge Jan. 1, 1898, and continued as superintendent, until his untimely death, which occurred Oct. 18, 1902. It was Mr. Crane who made the library a workingman's library, and established branches at Wilkinsburg, Turtle Creek and Monongahela City. The library also has an important station at East Pittsburg, one at California, Pa., and one at Belle Vernon, Pa. It also furnishes a great abundance of reading-matter for the schools of Braddock and surrounding boroughs. At the close of business, Dec. 31, 1903, the library and its branches had on its shelves 34,101 volumes, and a total of 12,450 registered readers, not including some 5,000 pupils who were drawing books through the schools. The total number of books drawn for home use during the year 1902 was 202,238. The entire staff of the library and its branches consists of eleven persons. The Braddock building is also the home of the Carnegie club, and is equipped with baths, billiard tables, a swimming pool and bowling alley. Walter Crane was born in Scotland in 1856. When a young man, he worked several years in libraries in England, and, in the early eighties, he came to America, and, after a brief residence in Boston and Chicago, located at Joliet, Ill. At Joliet he had an opportunity to try his unique ideas about a workingman's library, and established there the first library of its kind in America. Here he remained nine years, and was then called to take charge of the library which Mr. Carnegie had built for the workingmen of Braddock. March 1, 1903, Mr. G. H. Lamb, who was at that time superintendent of the Braddock schools, accepted the position made vacant by Mr. Crane's death.

JACOB DIETERICH, of Etna, Pa., a prominent citizen and member of the council, was born in Hesse, Germany, Oct. 11, 1842, son of John C. and Elizabeth (Rock) Dieterich, his father having been a native of Germany and come to America in 1856, settled in Etna, and there his family have since resided. Mr. Dieterich attended the public schools of the Fatherland until thirteen years of age, when he came to America with his parents. He went into the nail mill of Spang & Co., remaining with this concern for fourteen years, working at different jobs, and then was employed in the mill of Bennett & Co. for two years. Subsequently he worked for Lewis, Bailey, Dalzell & Co., of Sharpsburg, until that firm sold out to Morehead Bros., when he went with the new firm as shearman of nail iron. Prior to this, in 1866-1868, he made mattresses under the firm name of Jacob Dieterich, and in 1888 retired from active business, and now resides at No. 251 Butler St., Etna. He was married, in 1868, to Henrietta, daughter of Jacob and Katharine Murlock, formerly of Würtemberg, Germany, and they have one child living, Anna, wife of Fred Molder, a successful farmer of Butler county. Mr. Dieterich is a member of the German Evangelical Lutheran church of Etna, and is closely identified with the republican party. He has served in his present position as a member of the council of Etna for twelve years, and is a prominent member of that body, being the chairman of several important committees and taking a leading part in their deliberations.

DANIEL A. SNYDER, of Sharpsburg, Pa., general superintendent of Morehead Bros. & Co.'s iron and nail works, of Sharpsburg, was born in Indiana, Indiana Co., Pa., Nov. 14, 1860, son of David and Mary Snyder, the former a native of Germany, who, when a boy, came to Mobile, Ala.; later removed to Indiana county, Pa, and there prospered as a farmer until his death. He was a member of the 55th Pennsylvania volunteers during the Civil war, and died in the hospital from the effects of wounds received in the fights around Petersburg, Va. His mother died in 1882. Daniel A. Snyder was educated in the public schools of his native county and at the Phillipsburg orphan school in Beaver county. When he was sixteen years of age he began to learn the trade of carpentering in Homer City, and for four years worked at his trade in Sharpsburg. He entered the mills of Morehead Bros. & Co. as a carpenter, serving in that capacity for seven or eight years; next was appointed millwright, which position he held until 1898, when he was appointed to his present position of general superintendent of the works. He was happily married, in 1883, to Lucy, daughter of E. P. and Susan (Fry) Hill, of Nineveh, Indiana Co., Pa., and to them has been born a daughter, Irene, a student of the schools of Sharpsburg. Mr. Snyder is a member of the Royal Arcanum, the Junior Order of American Mechanics, and of the republican party. In 1903 he was elected a member of the city council of Sharpsburg, and is a prominent member of that body, holding the chairmanship of several important committees.

JAMES H. PATTERSON, postmaster at Sharpsburg, was born in Elizabeth township, Allegheny Co., Pa., Dec. 11, 1859, son of John G. and Sarah (Bugh) Patterson, of Washington John G. Patterson was for many years pilot on the Monongahela river. Postmaster James H. Patterson was educated in the public schools, then entered the employ of the Tibby Bros. glass company, where he remained twenty-five years, holding for some years during that time the responsible position of manager of the works. He was appointed to his present position as postmaster, Feb. 8, 1901. During his administration he has proved himself a capable official, and has succeeded in having a much needed free delivery system established in Sharpsburg. Mr. Patterson is a prominent member of the Masonic fraternity, being a member of the Zeredathah lodge, No. 448. He is also a member of the Jr. O. U. A. M. and belongs to the Presbyterian church, in which he holds the position of trustee.

GEORGE I. HAUER, of Shoustown, Pa., station agent for the Pittsburg & Lake Erie railroad, was born at Lebanon, Pa., Dec. 17, 1868, son of Peter and Clarissa (Myers) Hauer. His father has been for years in the real estate and insurance business, and is now sixty-eight years of age. His ancestors on both sides came originally from Germany, and his parents had ten children, eight of whom are now living. George Hauer attended the public schools of his native town, and also Schell's business college, where he was graduated at the age of eighteen. He then entered the real estate business with his father, and subsequently was engaged as telegraph operator in Reading and Harrisburg for the Philadelphia & Reading railroad company. Later he went to Philadelphia as manager of the superintendent's office, and there remained for five years, when he again went into the real estate business with his father. He prospered there for four years, and then returned to the Philadelphia & Reading railroad as operator at Atlantic City, N. J., where he continued for three years. Later he became an operator for the Pittsburg & Lake Erie railroad, and, in 1902, was appointed to his present position of agent at Shoustown, Pa. He was married, in 1892, to Flora, daughter of James Clark, of McKee's Rocks, and they have four children, two sons and a like number of daughters. Mr. Hauer is independent in politics, and is a member of the Lutheran church, and also of the I. O. O. F.

JOSEPH GRIFFITH, cashier of the Clairton National bank, is a descendant of one of the oldest and most respectable families in the Monongahela valley. He was born at Cumberland, Allegheny Co., Md., in 1876, and is the son of William E. and Jane (Long) Griffith. His father has for many years been identified with the banking and newspaper interests of Maryland and Pennsylvania. He was born in Washington county, Pa., in January, 1842. At the beginning of the Civil war he enlisted as a private in an independent cavalry company that was afterward mustered into the United States service as Company B, of the 22d Pennsylvania cavalry, and was mustered out in May, 1865, with the rank of captain. He was a comrade-in-arms of President McKinley, and after the war was a near neighbor for several years in Stark county, Ohio. In 1872 he removed to Cumberland, Md., where for some time he was the editor of the Cumberland Daily News. Later he was for several years the national bank examiner for the State of Maryland, and, in 1884, was the Republican candidate for treasurer of State. He was the senior aide-de-camp on the staff of Governor Lowndes, with the rank of colonel, but he always felt far more pride in his title of captain, won upon the field of battle. He served as department commander of the Maryland Grand Army of the Republic, is a member of the Loyal Legion and the Knights Templars. He now lives in New York city, where he is the cashier for Fayerweather & Ladew, manufacturers of leather belting. Joseph Griffith was educated in the public schools of Cumberland, graduating from the high school in 1892. He then entered the office of J. B. Hawes, the leading architect of Cumberland, and remained there about a year, when he was offered, and accepted, a position in the office of the chief engineer of the West Virginia & Pittsburg railroad company. In 1894 he was appointed deputy State and county tax collector for Allegheny county, Md., but resigned two years later to accept the position of assistant cashier in the First National bank of Cumberland. While holding this position he also acted as assistant national bank examiner for Maryland. In April, 1902, he came to Clairton, Pa., to accept the position he now occupies. Besides being cashier of this bank, he is a director in the Meadow Mountain coal and coke company, and is a director and vice-president of the Potomac white sand company Though a young man of only twenty-seven years, Mr. Griffith's career has been most successful, and few men of his age are better known, or have a more enviable reputation in business circles. He is unmarried and is a member of the Presbyterian church, to which he is a liberal contributor.

HIRAM J. WHEELER, of Coraopolis, Pa., a prominent real estate dealer and oil producer, was born on Dec. 3, 1854, in Pomfret, Chautauqua Co., N. Y., son of Dwight and Josephine (Tarbox) Wheeler. His parents had eight children, seven of whom are now living and are: Ralph, Mrs. Eva Cranston, Hiram J., James B., Homer D., Mrs. Cora R. Bull and John W. Both of his parents were descended from Massachusetts families, and his father was a prosperous farmer. Mr. Wheeler was educated in the Pomfret schools up to his sixteenth year, and then matriculated at the State normal school at Fredonia, N. Y., from which he was graduated at the age of nineteen years. He engaged in the manufacture of cheese for two years, made an exhibition of fifty of his products at the Centennial exposition held at Philadelphia, and received a medal for the excellence of his display. In 1877 he went to the oil country, began operating in Bradford, Pa., and remained there for thirteen years. Afterward he came to Coraopolis, where he is engaged in the oil business and has extensive interests. He was married, in 1880, to Henrietta E. Culver, of Westfield, N. Y., and they have one child, Mildred R., a delightful young woman and one of the most accomplished musicians in the State. He is a director of the Ohio Valley trust company, the Coraopolis National bank and also of the Lake Carrier oil company, of Coraopolis. This latter company has a capital stock of $150,000, and is the largest in that part of the county. Mr. Wheeler also owns and operates a number of oil wells in Coraopolis. Mr. Wheeler is a republican by birth and by adoption, but has never held office except in the borough of Coraopolis, where he has just retired from the office of burgess after a three-year tenure. Previous to his first election as burgess, Mr. Wheeler served in the council of the borough, and at the last election was again chosen for that position, being the only republican elected. He and his wife are Unitarian in their religious belief, and are valued and respected members of the community in which they live.

GEORGE A. LASHELL, of Coraopolis, Pa., a prominent real estate dealer, with offices at No. 331 Fourth Ave., Pittsburg, Pa., was born in Newburgh, now Toronto, Jefferson Co., Ohio, April 27, 1845, son of Jacob and Sarah (Boley) Lashell. They had four children: Mary, who was drowned when ten years of age; George A.; John R., of Atlantic City, N. J., and Mrs. Leonora L. McKown, of West Bridgewater, Pa. His father was a farmer and river man, came from Huntingdon county, Pa., and later settled at what is now Lashell's Landing, Moon township, Allegheny Co., Pa. He was a prominent citizen, served as county commissioner for many years, and was widely known for his many generous acts. He has been dead a number of years, but is survived by his wife, who is yet in the best of health, though in her eightieth year. Mr. Lashell's paternal ancestors came from France, and his maternal from Germany, a splendid combination. Mr. Lashell attended the school of his native town, and later secured a splendid commercial education at the academy at Sewickley, and at the Iron City college, of Pittsburg. When twenty years of age, he left school to work on the farm, and also on the Ohio and Mississippi rivers, plying between Pittsburg and southern ports, with cargoes of lumber and produce. He was married, in 1868, to Margaret McElherren, of Robinson township, Allegheny county, and after his marriage went into the grain and feed business at Pittsburg. He prospered in that venture for about twelve years, then engaged in the real estate business, and has met with unusual success in that line of commercial endeavor. Mr. Lashell is vice-president of the Coraopolis savings and trust company, and owns a beautiful home and many other valuable pieces of real estate in Coraopolis. He was one of the organizers and general superintendent and treasurer of the Pittsburg, Neville Island & Coraopolis street railroad company, which was absorbed by the West End company, of Pittsburg He served as justice of the peace for five years, and is a member of the Odd Fellows, the Knights of Pythias, and the Maccabees. He is a democrat in politics.

SAMUEL McGREW BRINTON, one of the leading farmers of Patton township, Allegheny county, is a son of the late Stephen M. Brinton, and grandson of John Brinton. John Brinton, born in Chester county, married Sarah Mattock, a native of Westchester, Chester county, and a member of a prominent family of Chester county, on the Brandywine. John Brinton, a farmer by vocation, was an influential man in his day, held a number of township offices, and served in the War of 1812. He was a member of the Quaker church. Stephen Marshall Brinton died at Hot Springs, Ark., April 19, 1883. His wife was Mary (McGrew) Brinton. They had, besides the subject of this sketch, several other sons and daughters, viz.: Dr. W. M. Brinton, formerly a well-known physician of Sharpsburg, and a member of the Allegheny county medical association, who died Dec. 1, 1888; Marshall Homer, banker and statesman, of Ellsworth, Ia.; Mary E. (deceased), and Sarah B., wife of J. Howard Clark, a prominent Washington county farmer. Samuel M. Brinton, whose name heads this article, was born in Allegheny county, Pa., Aug. 23, 1848, and was educated in the public schools of Patton township, Millersville State normal school in Lancaster county, and at Duff's business college in Pittsburg, graduating from the latter institution in 1869. He has for many years been an important factor in the public activities of Patton township, where he has served as school director, auditor, assessor and in many other capacities. He is a member of the I. O. O. F. and F. and A. M., and belongs to the Pitcairn Presbyterian church. Mr. Brinton was married, Aug. 13, 1883, to Miss

Helen M. Collins, daughter of David and Mary Collins. David Collins was formerly county commissioner of Allegheny county. Of this union were born four children, Mary C., Jean G., Stephen Marshall and William M. Mrs. Brinton died March 2, 1895, and on June 9, 1897, Mr. Brinton married Cydonia Chadwick, a member of a prominent Westmoreland county family. One son has blessed this second union, Mark Homer, born in April, 1898. Mr. Brinton resides on the old Brinton homestead, where John Brinton located when he first came west of the mountains. His postoffice address is Pitcairn, Pa.

JOSEPH EDGAR EUWER, postmaster of Natrona, was born in Westmoreland county, Pa., Oct. 25, 1861, son of Robert and Matilda (Young) Euwer, also natives of Westmoreland county, and a grandson of Robert and Nancy Euwer. The first Robert Euwer was born in Ireland, and came to America in a very early day. He and his wife both died in Westmoreland county. The maternal grandparents of Joseph Edgar Euwer were Joseph and Margaret (Steel) Young, natives of Westmoreland county, and died there. Joseph Young, the grandfather, was a grandson of Captain Young, who fought in the Revolutionary war. Robert Euwer, father of the subject of this sketch, served three years in the Civil war as a member of Company C, 9th Pennsylvania reserves, and during the time fought with distinction in every battle in which his regiment took part. After the war he came to Natrona and followed various vocations until 1890, when he moved to Westmoreland county, where he resided up to the time of his death, which occurred Feb. 4, 1903. Joseph E. Euwer, whose name begins this article, was reared at Natrona. When a young man, he was for a short time brakeman on the Pennsylvania & Central railroad, between Columbia and Philadelphia, after which he was for two years engaged in mercantile pursuits in East Liberty. He received his appointment as postmaster at Natrona in 1897. In politics he is an ardent republican, and has always taken an active interest in the welfare of his party. On April 23, 1888, Mr. Euwer married Maggie C. Bush, a native of Westmoreland county, and has four children: Rankin Edgar, born May 30, 1889; Nora Grace, born

July 17, 1894; Robert McKinley, born July 21, 1896, and Edgar Lowell, born Oct. 17, 1900. Mr. Euwer and wife are members of the United Presbyterian church of Tarentum. Mrs. Euwer is a daughter of Eli Bush and wife, Jane (Iddings) Bush, who have been married fifty-four years (1903), and have had nine children, all of whom are living and all married. Mr. Bush and wife are members of the Presbyterian church of Poke Run, Pa. His parents were Jacob and Mary (Rimmel) Bush, both natives of Westmoreland county, Pa., but who died in Ohio. Mrs. Euwer is descended on her mother's side from William and Anna (Miller) Iddings, the former a native of Butler county, and the latter of Westmoreland county. William Iddings' father, also named William, was a soldier in the Revolutionary war. He was a second cousin of Gen. Anthony Wayne, known to fame as "Mad Anthony."

CASSIUS M. C. HARPER, of Boston, Pa., a prominent brick manufacturer, was born in Jefferson township, Allegheny Co., Pa., Oct. 24, 1857, son of Simon and Susannah (Ames) Harper, of Armstrong county, Pa., his father having been a prosperous merchant and postmaster of Boston for many years. Mr. Harper was educated in the common schools, attending the Belle View school, and on quitting his studies, commenced as a clerk in a store at Boston, which position he occupied for a number of years. He was also engaged in coal mining to some extent, and, in 1885, began the manufacturing of brick as a member of the firm of Kerr & Harper. This venture prospered, and about seven years since Mr. Harper purchased his partner's interest, and from that time has successfully conducted its affairs under his own name. Mr. Harper now has an extensive plant, employs twenty-five men, and has an annual output of 2,500,000 bricks, which are of the shale rock variety and made by the stiff mud process. This plant is in operation the entire year, and Mr. Harper also is a large shipper of sand in connection with the brick works. He was married, in 1877, to Kate L., daughter of Hugh and Elizabeth (Merrington) Thompson, of Allegheny county, and they have three children, viz.: Hugh G.; Elda R., wife of James Henderson, and Essie S. Mr. Harper is a leading Mason, being a member of both the commandery and the consistory, and is a prominent member of the Methodist Episcopal church of Boston, of which institution he is a member of the board of trustees. His political affiliations are with the republican party, and he is easily one of the leading citizens of that part of the county.

JOHN C. CROSS, of Cheswick, a well-known business man, was born in Clintonville, Venango county, March 21, 1856, son of W. C. and Mary Jane Cross. With his father, William Cross, he was engaged in the furnace business, jointly owning several furnaces in Venango county. W. C. Cross was for some time in the oil business on Oil creek, but being not altogether successful in that line, took up the mercantile calling until his death, in 1897. Jane Cross, grandmother to John C., was the founder of the famous Jane academy, from which Mr. Cross graduated at eighteen years of age. In 1876 he went with his father to the Bullion oil field, where they conducted a store for two years, removing then to Clintonville. Later he spent two and a half years at the oil fields, going into business for himself in 1881 as a contractor and driller, making many wells for the mills in Pittsburg and vicinity. Selling out, he went into the oil refining business, then entered the employ of the Chambers oil company, under William B. Hays, at Brush Creek; later went to the oil fields of Marietta, Ohio, where he leased considerable territory, being interested in six or eight wells, two of which were producers. In 1901 he moved to Cheswick and started a general store, which he still successfully conducts. He was married, in 1885, to Katherine M. Campbell, of New Castle, a daughter of Kirtland Campbell, foreman of a furnace in New Castle, Pa. He was somewhat of a genius in mechanics, erecting several furnaces in Sharon and Sharpsville, and is now employed by the National tube works, of McKeesport. Mr. Campbell and Mr. Cross were engaged in the oil business in Warren county, where they owned a lease with four wells. Mr. Campbell was the owner of the North Clarendon hotel, which was destroyed by fire in 1886. Mr. and Mrs. Cross are members of the Methodist church of Newport, Ohio. In politics Mr. Cross is a republican. His father was also of that belief.

WILLIAM M. STANTON, of Coraopolis, foreman of the Producers' and Refiners' oil company and a prominent citizen, was born in Warren county, May 28, 1859. He is the son of Hamilton R. and Sarah Jane (Wilson) Stanton, who were the parents of nine children, eight of whom are living. Hamilton R. was a Lincoln republican and prominent in his party while alive, and although himself incapacitated for military duty, seven of his brothers were volunteers in answer to Lincoln's call for men; in fact, Mr. Stanton's people and ancestors have taken to a military career during and since the war of 1776. Mr. Stanton possesses a most remarkable family tree, tracing his ancestors back to the Stantons of Longebridge and Warwick prior to 1460. From this branch descended Gen. Thomas Stanton, of Connecticut, the first known Stanton in America, who came over in the good ship "Bonaventura" in 1635. He filled many offices of trust, was appointed interpreter to the Indians by Governor Winthrop, and was also a signer of the first constitution of Connecticut, drawn up in 1639. Mr. Stanton has a correct history from Gen. Thos. Stanton's arrival in America down to the subject of this sketch. Mr. Stanton, after finishing school at the age of nineteen, worked as telegraph operator for the Pennsylvania railroad company at Warren for three years, then went into the oil field, operating for the Standard oil company as gauger of oil through Warren, McKean, Clarion and Venango counties for twelve years, and then came to Coraopolis, where he has since been connected with the Producers' and Refiners' company. Mr. Stanton has been twice married—first, in 1882, to Johanna Bromley, of Clearfield county, who died in 1899, leaving three daughters and two sons. The second time he was married to Ida Etoil Covert, daughter of Josiah Covert, a prominent pioneer of Butler county. Mr. Stanton has one daughter by this marriage. He has been prominently identified with the republican party, has served as a member and treasurer of the republican executive committee, was elected a member of the borough council, was later elected president of the council, was a member of the finance committee of the borough, was elected president and treasurer of the fire department, and otherwise served the borough in official capacity. Mr. Stanton was made a member of Canby lodge,

No. 520, F. and A. M., of St. Petersburg, Pa., in 1885, and is also a member of other fraternal organizations. Mr. Stanton owns his own handsome residence on the corner of Sixth avenue and Wood street, Coraopolis, has a substantial standing in the financial world, and enjoys the esteem and respect of the community.

GEORGE A. KOEHLER, of Cheswick, Pa., a prominent citizen and a well-known business man of Pittsburg, was born in Allegheny city, Pa., Oct. 30, 1853, son of Jacob and Mary (Winkleman) Koehler, the former having been a locksmith and later in the stove-fitting business with William Bissel on Pennsylvania avenue. Jacob Koehler was a native of Alsace-Lorraine, and came to America in 1848, located in Pittsburg, and there married Mary Winkleman, who was born and reared within three miles of him in the old country, but whom he had never met until both had come to the United States. They had a family of eleven children, nine of whom are now living. George A. was the fifth child, and was educated in the primary branches in the public schools, later attended the parochial and other colleges in Pittsburg until he reached his eighteenth year, when he began carrying the evening mail in Allegheny city. After six months he went into the scrap iron business at Nos. 6 and 8 Sawmill alley, continuing there until 1885, when he removed his business to Pittsburg, and under the firm name of Koehler & Co., transacted a large business at the corner of Columbia and Pike streets. In 1892 he formed a partnership with Myer Strang, under the firm name of Koehler & Strang, changing their location to No. 2830 Liberty Ave., where they do the largest business of their kind in Pittsburg, handling nearly a half a million dollars' worth of scrap iron annually. Mr. Koehler was married, in 1877, to Katharine Heiser, of Allegheny city, and they had two children: Rose Edna, attending college at St. Joseph's academy, Greenburg, Pa., and Anthony John George, a student of St. Mary's seminary. He was married the second time, on Feb. 18, 1903, to Mary, daughter of Casper and Louise (Wiegland) Gaertner, of Allegheny city, but formerly of Germany. He is a member of St. Mary's church of Allegheny city, and at present is a trustee of the church at Colfax, Pa. Mr.

Koehler is a member of the Benevolent and Protective Order of Elks, the Knights of Columbus and the Turners, of Allegheny city. In politics he is a democrat, and served on the common council of Allegheny city for six years, and at present is serving a second term as councilman of Cheswick borough. He is a member of C. M. B. A. and the C. B. L., of Allegheny city, and for twelve years was president of the Jacksonian club, of Allegheny city. Mr. Koehler has traveled extensively, having visited Nova Scotia, San Domingo, New Orleans, Port Huron, and has been in nearly every State of the Union. He began his present business on the borrowed capital of $17, which he secured from his brother, and now owns perhaps the finest property in Cheswick, and controls the largest scrap iron business in Pittsburg. He is a stockholder in the Central savings and trust company, and is a stockholder and director in the D. Lutz & Sons brewing company.

JOHN R. MONTGOMERY, a prominent business man, of Turtle Creek, was born in North Versailles township, Allegheny Co., Pa., July 17, 1863. He is a son of John M. and Elizabeth M. (Lewis) Montgomery. John M. Montgomery, in his day one of the best-known farmers in the community, served during the Civil war as a member of the 63d Pennsylvania volunteer infantry, was wounded during the war and died shortly after its close. The subject of this sketch is one of four children. The others are: Joseph M., a carpenter; Samuel P., a contractor, and Rebecca M., wife of Edward Taylor, who is a farmer. John R. Montgomery was reared and educated in North Versailles township. He was for about seven years a merchant in Turtle Creek, and is now in the contracting business. He is a man who has won the confidence and respect of the community, has served the public as township auditor and held several other offices. Mr. Montgomery was married, March 14, 1889, to Agnes C. Smith, who is a daughter of Jacob and Catherine Smith, and was born in Westmoreland county, March 18, 1871. Mr. and Mrs. Montgomery have two children, both attending school: Renard King, born Feb. 4, 1890, and Hertilla C., born Sept. 10, 1891. Mr. Montgomery is a member of the F. and A. M. and I. O. O. F.

GIDEON H. JAQUAY, justice of the peace of Rankin, was born in Carroll county, Ky., Feb. 12, 1853 He is the son of Anthony and Marietta (Hall) Jaquay. Anthony Jaquay was the first man to carry the art of daguerreotypy west of the Allegheny mountains. Gideon H. Jaquay, the subject of this sketch, was married, Dec. 31, 1872, to Emma J. Herr, of Pittsburg, Pa. To Mr. and Mrs. Jaquay have been born three children, of whom two are living. They are: Clara E., wife of Joseph Kelly, and Adda M., wife of Albert Roderns, both of Allegheny county. Mr. Jaquay came to Rankin with his family in 1889. He was elected to the office of justice of the peace in 1895, and fulfilled the duties of the position so creditably that he was re-elected in 1900. In religious belief he is a Presbyterian. He is a member of the Knights of Pythias, Ben-Hur, Woodmen of the World, Essenic Ancient Knights, the Knights of Malta and Knights of the Golden Eagle.

GEORGE L. McFARLAND, of Sharpsburg, Pa., a well-known dentist, was born in Rural Valley, Armstrong Co., Pa., Aug. 6, 1870, son of John and Martha J. (Steward) McFarland, the former being a prosperous farmer for many years, dying in 1892 at the mature age of seventy-six years. His paternal grandfather, William McFarland, served in the War of 1812, and died in Armstrong county at the advanced age of 106 years. His mother is now in her seventy-fourth year, and resides with her son at Sharpsburg. Mr. McFarland attended the public schools of Armstrong county until he was eighteen years of age, and for the next two years was a pupil of an academy near his home, teaching school in the winter. He matriculated at the Pennsylvania college of dentistry at Philadelphia, and two years later entered the Pittsburg college of dentistry at Pittsburg, and there was graduated in 1897, with the degree of doctor of dental surgery. In 1899 he located in Monessen, and there prospered as a dentist for three years; then came to

Sharpsburg, formed a partnership with R. D. Ambrose, with offices at No. 707 Main St., and since has practiced with much success. Dr. McFarland has a twin sister who is the wife of R. D. Ambrose. He is a member of the Presbyterian church of Sharpsburg, the Knights of Pythias at Monessen, the Elks at Monessen, and the Junior Order of American Mechanics at Rural Valley.

JAMES E. KARNS, retired, of Tarentum, was born in East Deer township, Allegheny Co., Pa., Sept. 5, 1828. His father, Charles W. Karns, son of James E. Karns, was a native of Westmoreland county, Pa. He was a river-man in his youth, afterwards became a weaver and then a potter. He came to Allegheny county in an early day and lived in that county until his death, which occurred in March, 1865, at Natrona. In politics he was a whig and then a republican. He was married, in 1827, to Miss Mary T. Cowan, a native of Allegheny county, daughter of Joseph Cowan, a pioneer settler of that county. Joseph Cowan married Mary Thompson, a Scotch lady, who came to America with her parents when seven years old. Mrs. Cowan died about 1835 at the advanced age of ninety-one. Charles W. Karns and wife were members of the United Presbyterian church. They had three sons and a daughter, as follows: James E., the subject of this sketch; Elizabeth T.; Joseph C., and Francis W., who lost his life while fighting for his country during the Civil war in 1862. James Karns was reared in Allegheny county, and at the age of seventeen began to learn the carpenters' trade in Pittsburg. On Jan. 29, 1852, he started for the gold fields of California, remaining there six years, working at his trade as a carpenter and as a miner. Returning to Allegheny county in 1858, he spent three years in the manufacture of lumber, was in the oil region two years, and spent two years in a planing mill at Springdale. Coming to Tarentum, he was for some years engaged as a contractor and builder, and did considerable work for the plate glass works at Creighton. He has been a resident of Tarentum since 1873, and has been retired from active life for about fifteen years. In politics he is now a republican, although formerly a prohibitionist, and has served in the council about fifteen years. Mr. Karns was married, in 1864, to

Miss Elizabeth A. Randolph, of Allegheny county. Six children were born of this union, viz.: Anna Margaret, Mary Agnes, Augusta E., Cornelia R., Charles W. (deceased) and Francis M. Mrs. Karns died July 12, 1880, and, on April 2, 1890, Mr. Karns married Miss Margaret English, daughter of John and Jane (McCrory) English, both natives of Ireland and early settlers of Tarentum. Mr. English died at the age of ninety, and his wife at eighty-six. Mr. Karns enlisted as a soldier in the Civil war, on Aug. 9, 1862, in Company I, 123d Pennsylvania volunteer infantry, and served nine months as first sergeant. He was in the rear guard at second Bull Run, fought five days at Chancellorsville, and took part in the battles of Antietam and Fredericksburg, being severely wounded at Fredericksburg. During his long residence in Tarentum, Mr. Karns has made many friends, and is regarded as one of the substantial and respected citizens of that place. He and his wife are members of the United Presbyterian church.

P. S. McMULLEN, of Glassport, Pa., a prominent architect and engineer, was born in Armstrong county, near Kittanning, Pa., May 3, 1861, son of George H. and Salome (King) McMullen, of Armstrong county, where his father was a successful contractor and builder. Young McMullen was educated in the common schools, and later took a course in civil engineering at Delmont academy, where he was graduated in 1883. Since that time Mr. McMullen has been engaged in architecture and engineering, being stationed at Apollo and Vandegrift, Pa., and in 1889 came to Glassport, where he has since followed his professions with much success. He was elected borough engineer of Glassport in March, 1901, and since has filled that position to the entire satisfaction of his constituents, but prior to this election had served the borough in that capacity. He was also borough engineer of Apollo for ten years, while living in that borough, and is one of the leading engineers of the county. He was happily married, in July, 1888, to Mattie A. Willard, of Apollo, Armstrong county, and they have had born to them the following children: Beatrice, Aug. 14, 1889; Ruth, Feb. 2, 1894, and Paul G., February, 1897. Mr. McMullen is prominent in financial circles as a director of the Glassport

National bank, and was one of the organizers of the Presbyterian church, of which he is a member and elder. His political associations and affiliations are with the republican party, and he is actively interested in its advancement and success.

DAVID D. DUNLAP, a well-known blacksmith and Civil war veteran, of Springdale, was born in Allegheny county, July 12, 1842. His father, John Dunlap, a native of County Antrim, Ireland, came to Allegheny county in 1838, and died there in 1870, while his mother, Margaret (Clark) Dunlap, died in 1883, at the age of eighty-eight. John Dunlap was a nurseryman and linen manufacturer in Ireland. He was a son of Hamilton and Ann Dunlap, who died in Ireland, the father at the extraordinary age of 104 and the mother at 101. Hamilton Dunlap was a linen inspector and a manufacturer in Ireland. Margaret (Clark) Dunlap, mother of the subject of this sketch, was a daughter of Samuel and Martha (London) Clark, natives of Ireland, who came to America in an early day, settled in East Deer township, Allegheny county, where they died. Samuel Clark was a farmer. David D. Dunlap, whose name heads this article, was reared and educated in Allegheny county, and has always made that county his home. He began to learn the blacksmiths' trade in 1856, and has successfully followed this vocation since that time, except when a soldier in the Civil war. He has lived, since 1870, in Springdale, where he owns two residences and a blacksmith shop. Mr. Dunlap enlisted, in 1861, in Company E, 63d Pennsylvania volunteer infantry, and was discharged Dec. 9, 1863, being incapacitated for further service by reason of a wound in the leg received from a kick by a mule, Aug. 18, 1863. He was then detailed to blacksmith duty. He fought with distinction at Pohick church, Yorktown, Williamsburg, Fair Oaks and Peach Orchard. Mr. Dunlap was married, in 1865, to Rebecca Anschultz, of Ohio, and had by this marriage three children, Louisa, Elizabeth and William J. Louisa and William J. are now deceased. On Oct. 20, 1874, he took as his second wife Julia Shoop, of Springdale, daughter of Michael and Julia (Bollinger) Shoop, old settlers of that place, both of whom are now dead. Two children blessed this marriage, Jennie W. and Jessie P. S. Jennie studied at a conservatory of music in Pittsburg, and also in Boston, and Rochester, N. Y., and is an accomplished musician, playing the pipe organ, mandolin and guitar, and has played as organist in several of the larger cities of the United States. She was married, July 13, 1899, to Thomas Loughman, a Pittsburg railroad man, and has one daughter, Margaret Aldah. Mr. Dunlap's other daughter, Jessie, was educated in Springdale, and is now employed in a glass factory. Mrs. Dunlap died Sept. 6, 1878. Mr. Dunlap has a brother, James W. Dunlap, who enlisted in 1861 in the 103d Pennsylvania regiment, fought in thirty-three battles in the Civil war, and was confined a year in Libby prison, Andersonville and Belle Isle. He now resides at Franklin, Pa., and is employed by the Sibly & Mille company, oil refiners. David D. Dunlap is an active and influential republican, and now holds the position of township clerk. He is a member of the G. A. R., Union Veteran legion, No. 1, of Pittsburg, and A. O. U. W.

TAYLOR McINTOSH MARTIN, son of John and Margaret (Sholes) Martin, was born April 29, 1871, and educated in the public schools of Wilkins township. He commenced farming in early life, and continued in this business until his numerous township offices became so important as to require all his time. In 1897 Mr. Martin was elected justice of the peace, and his faithful service won him a re-election in 1902. He served one term as school director, and declined a second nomination. He is now serving his second term as township assessor. In the sessions of the Allegheny county court for 1902-1903 he served as a member of the grand jury, and is actively identified with many branches of public activities. Mr. Martin was married in April, 1895, to Miss Adella Waddel, daughter of Thomas and Rachel Ann (Douds) Waddel, of Saltsburg, Indiana Co., Pa. His first child, John, died in infancy. The following children have since been born to Mr. and Mrs. Martin: Frank Cyphers, born June 23, 1896; Margaret, born March 8, 1898; Adella May, born May 28, 1900, and William H., born July 18, 1902. Mr. Martin is a member of the Presbyterian church. He is a member of Turtle Creek castle, No. 131, Knights of the Golden Eagle.

JOSEPH O. KIRKPATRICK, for over thirty years a resident of Turtle Creek, was born in Scotland, near Glasgow, Dec. 18, 1854, son of James and Sarah (Orr) Kirkpatrick. James Kirkpatrick, a farmer by vocation, came to America with his family in 1812, locating at Turtle Creek, where he spent the remainder of his life in the mining business. He died in 1896. Joseph O. Kirkpatrick was the eldest of seven children, was educated in Scotland, and since coming to America, in 1875, has followed the vocation of a miner, his home being in Turtle Creek. He is a member of the Presbyterian church of Turtle Creek. In politics he is a republican. In 1878 Mr. Kirkpatrick married Catharine Russell Faulds, daughter of Andrew and Ann (Hunter) Faulds, of Scotland. There were nine children born to this union, of whom seven are living: Anna H., wife of G. H. Bachmann; Sarah, living with her parents; James, at home; Mary Arrell, also at home; Andrew Alexander, attending school; Catharine Russell and Joseph Henry, aged, respectively, five and three.

PETER P. KUNTZ, of Natrona, Pa., general foreman of the water department of the Pennsylvania salt manufacturing company, was born in Wittenberg, Germany, July 2, 1842, son of Joseph and Mary Kuntz, both natives of Wittenberg, Germany, who came to Allegheny county in 1854, and resided there until their deaths. Joseph Kuntz was engaged in industrial lines, and for thirty years worked in the vineyard of Judge Brackenbridge. He and his wife were members of the Catholic church, and had seven children, four of whom are now living. Peter P. Kuntz remained in Germany until twelve years of age, attended the schools of the Fatherland, and, in America, was a student at the night schools of Natrona. He has been with the Pennsylvania salt manufacturing company during his entire business career, has held the position of foreman in the different departments for about forty-six years, and is now general foreman in the water department. He is a republican in politics, and he and his family are members of the Catholic church. He was married to Phlimone Held, a native of Butler county, and to them were born four living children, Joseph A., Ludwig T., Edward P. and Henry P. Mr. Kuntz is a man of high integrity and genuine worth, and his long connection with the Pennsylvania salt manufacturing company, in the important capacity of foreman, shows him to be a skilled workman and a reliable and trustworthy employe.

ROBERT BUTLER, of Port Vue, Pa., a successful grocery merchant, was born in Elizabeth township, Allegheny Co., Pa., March 17, 1863, and is a son of Peter and Ellen (Southern) Butler, his father having been a prosperous coal miner of that part of the county. Robert Butler was educated in the common schools of his native township, and on leaving school learned the butchers' trade, but never followed that occupation. He embarked in the coal business, which he continued for ten years, and about 1893 commenced the grocery business, which he has since followed with unvarying success. His store is now located on Seventh street, of Port Vue, and he enjoys a splendid trade, having some of the wealthiest and most influential men of the borough as his customers. He was married in Allegheny county, in 1890, to Mary L., daughter of John Adam and Mary (Bradshaw) Kaler, her mother a native of Westmoreland county and her father of Germany. Mr. Butler and his wife are the parents of two children, viz.: Della Ellen and Minnie May, both attending the schools of Port Vue. Mr. Butler has been prominently identified with the public affairs of the borough, and is now serving his second term as a member of its council, in which body he has made a fine record. He is a member of the Odd Fellows and the Junior Order of United American Mechanics, and also of the republican party. His religious affiliations are with the First Presbyterian church of Port Vue, of which he is a leading member and also a trustee.

FRIEDRICH W. SCHRANDT, justice of the peace, of Sharpsburg, was born in Bromberg, Germany, Oct. 1, 1847. His parents were Christian and Elizabeth Schrandt, Christian Schrandt being a farmer in Germany. F. W. Schrandt was educated in Germany, and came to the United States in 1875, locating in Clarion county, where he was employed for two years in the mines. In 1877 he went to Pittsburg, where, for some time, he engaged in the cigar business. In 1901 Mr. Schrandt was elected assessor, a position which he still holds, and was elected justice of the peace in Sharpsburg, in 1902, on the republican ticket. In connection with his work as justice of the peace, he does an extensive business in insurance, and handles mortgages and collections. He is conversant with seven languages, a valuable accomplishment in dealing with a varied foreign population. Mr. Schrandt married Elizabeth Wilbrecht, daughter of Gottlieb Wilbrecht, of Germany. Mrs. Schrandt is now deceased, but two children are living: Reinhold Frederick John and Hedwig Alwina, wife of John Reddinger, of Sharpsburg. Mr. Schrandt is a member of the German Lutheran church.

MATTHEW J. THOMPSON, of Buena Vista, Pa., a successful merchant and a prominent figure in municipal affairs, was born in Washington county, Ohio, Nov. 16, 1867, and was educated at the McKeesport academy and at Duff's business college, of Pittsburg. On leaving school, Mr. Thompson entered the mercantile business with his father, Harvey Thompson, a pioneer merchant of Buena Vista, and on the retirement of the latter, he, in partnership with his brother, Geo. W., assumed entire control of the large and prosperous mercantile establishment, which they have since conducted with marked success. Mr. Thompson was married, on Sept. 24, 1895, to Lida G. Culbert, now deceased, and to them was born a daughter, Lida C. Mr. Thompson was married the second time, on July 11, 1900, to Bessie A., daughter of Frank Russell, of Braddock, Pa., and they have two children, viz.: Susanna M. and Helen M. Mr. Thompson has been prominently identified with the public affairs of Buena Vista, and has served as a school director of the township and otherwise connected with the political economy of the community. He is a member of Youghiogheny lodge, No. 583, F. and A. M., McKeesport. His political affiliations are with the republican party, and, like all men of settled opinions, he is desirous of seeing his side in the ascendency, and accordingly lends his aid and influence to that consummation.

JOHN C. BOYLE, foreman for the Westinghouse air brake company, and president of the council of that borough, was born in County Donegal, Ireland, May 26, 1848, son of Peter and Grace (Strain) Boyle. The family came to America in 1850, locating in the sixth ward, Pittsburg, and Peter Boyle was for years toll clerk at the old Sixth street suspension bridge. J. C. Boyle was educated in the sixth ward schools, and learned the brass finishing trade, serving his apprenticeship with A. & J. Kenna, wash mounters, on Third avenue. He is now foreman of Department C., which is the brass finishing department, of the Westinghouse air brake company, a responsible position in which he has charge of about 250 men. Mr. Boyle has been long prominent in Wilmerding, where he moved, Feb. 18, 1890, and built the third residence in the place. He has served as president of the council for the past ten years. Mr. Boyle is a member of the C. M. B. A., Heptasophs, Y. M. I., Knights of Columbus and Veteran Employes of the W. A. B. Co., and belongs to the Young Men's republican tariff club, of Pittsburg. He was married, April 28, 1870, in Pittsburg, to Mary McFadden, now deceased. To them were born ten children, of whom six are living: Grace, Fannie, Kate, John C., Jr., Nellie and Kyron. John C., Jr., is now employed at the Westinghouse works, while Kyron works for the Pittsburg street railway company.

GEORGE W. THOMPSON, of Buena Vista, Pa., member of the well-known firm of Thompson Bros., general merchants of that village and one of the leading establishments of that part of the county, was born at Buena Vista, Allegheny Co., Pa., Nov. 8, 1879, son of Harvey Thompson, one of the pioneer merchants of that town. Mr. Thompson received his early education in the public schools of Buena Vista, and afterwards attended Grove City college in Mercer county, Pa. After leaving school, he formed a partnership with his brother, Matthew J., operating under the firm name of Thompson Bros., and purchased the business of their father on his retirement from active life, and since have conducted the same with great success. Mr. Thompson was married, in 1903, to Kathryn R., daughter of Dr. R. G. and Martha (Templeton) Ralston, of Cowansville, Pa., and their married life has been one of ideal felicity. Mr. Thompson is a member of the Masonic order, Youghiogheny lodge, No. 583, F. and A. M., McKeesport, and is one of the leading young men of Buena Vista.

THOMAS B. ADAMS, of Natrona, Pa., foreman of the copper extraction department of the Pennsylvania salt manufacturing company, was born in Allegheny county, Pa., Aug. 31, 1850, son of Alexander and Louisa (Bollinger) Adams. His father was a native of Westmoreland county, and was a salt boiler and foreman of salt works for years. He and his wife were members of the Baptist church, and had eight children, three of whom are now living. Thomas B. Adams was reared and educated in Natrona, where his parents located in 1854, and his entire business career has been in the employ of the Pennsylvania salt manufacturing company. He has long been a valued and trusted employe, and for the last sixteen years has been foreman of the copper extraction department of that company. Mr. Adams is financially interested in several business enterprises, and is a stockholder in the Pittsburg piano company, of Aspinwall, Pa. He is a republican in politics, and is a member of the Junior Order of American Mechanics. Mr. Adams was married, in 1870, to Barbara J. Bash, of Allegheny city, Pa., and to them were born eleven children, viz.: Alexander M., Mary J., Andy T. (deceased), David H., Michael G., Annie M., Kenneth R., Phœbe P., Joseph (deceased), and two who died in infancy. Mr. Adams is one of the solid and substantial citizens of Natrona, and possesses the esteem and good-will of the entire community.

EMIL C. STARKE, newsdealer in Tarentum and tax collector for that city, was born in Saxonburg, Butler Co., Pa., Jan. 29, 1870, being a son of Frederick Starke and a brother of Richard H. Starke, both of whom are mentioned elsewhere in this work. The subject of this sketch was reared and educated in Saxonburg, came to Tarentum when seventeen years old, learned the harness trade there, and engaged in business for several years with his brother, Richard H. Starke. The partnership was then dissolved, and Emil C. Starke has since been a newsdealer. In politics he is an ardent and influential republican, active in local party affairs. He was for two years delinquent tax collector for the borough of Tarentum, and in 1903 was elected tax collector for Tarentum. He is a member of Pollock lodge, No. 502, F. and A. M.; Tarentum lodge, No. 587, and Encampment No. 187, I. O. O. F.; Lodge No. 41, K. O. T. M., and Tarentum lodge, No. 644, B. P. O. Elks. In 1893 Mr. Starke married Miss Emma M. C. Ellerman, daughter of Henry Ellerman, deceased. Mr. Ellerman was for many years a prominent citizen of Tarentum. Mrs. Ellerman's mother, Lizzie (Goetz) Ellerman, was a daughter of J. M. Goetz, a pioneer resident of Tarentum. Mr. and Mrs. Starke are members of the Cumberland Presbyterian church. They have two children, Ernest F. and Mildred C.

CHRISTIAN ELLERMAN, now retired and for almost fifty years a resident of Tarentum, was born in Germany, Feb. 2, 1826. His parents, Frederick and Maria Ellerman, spent their lives in Germany, and both died when about eighty-three years old. The subject of this sketch was reared and educated in his native country, and was married there, in 1854, to Miss Mary Wilkett, also a native of Germany. In the same year, he and his wife came to Tarentum, where they have since lived, and are numbered among the respected and substantial residents of that borough. Mr. Ellerman was employed, until a few years ago, in the salt wells and coal mines, and by economy and good management acquired a considerable fortune, which is invested in Tarentum real estate. He now owns four houses and lots, and gave one place to his son. He and his family reside in one of the houses and the others are rented. Mr. and Mrs. Ellerman have reared a family of five children, all of whom are doing well. Their names are: Herman, Ella, Lizzie, Rosena and Annie. In politics Mr. Ellerman is a democrat. He and his wife are members of the Cumberland Presbyterian church of Tarentum.

WILLIAM C. TIBBY, secretary and general manager of the Tibby Bros. glass company at Sharpsburg, and president of the Sharpsburg council, was born in Pittsburg, Pa., April 24, 1866, son of William and Almira (Madden) Tibby. William Tibby, at one time councilman in Sharpsburg, was a glass-blower by trade. The glass works of the Tibby Bros. glass company were first started in the twelfth ward, and then, in 1866, moved to the old fifth ward. The company is now a flourishing concern, having a plant equipped with three furnaces, all in Sharpsburg, and employing about 250 men. William C. Tibby, whose name heads this article, was educated in the public schools and at the Western university, and started to learn the glass-blowers' trade in 1884.

He assumed the assistant managership of the Tibby company in 1889. Mr. Tibby has served as member of the council for the past nine years, and has been president of that body for three years. He is president of the Sharpsburg firemen's relief association of western Pennsylvania, member of Zaredathah lodge, No. 448, F. and A. M., and the Independent Order of Heptasophs and the I. O. O. F., No. 742. He belongs to the Sharpsburg Presbyterian church. Mr. Tibby was married, in 1890, to Mary E. Lewis, daughter of W. A. and Elizabeth (Smith) Lewis, formerly of Sharpsburg, but now of Pittsburg. Mrs. Tibby is now deceased.

JOHN LOEFFERT, of Millvale, Pa., president of the Standard box and lumber company, was born in Allegheny city, Pa., Aug. 5, 1868, son of George and Margaret (Grydel) Loeffert, his father having been a carpenter and is now a stockholder in the corporation of which his son is president. John Loeffert attended the public schools of Allegheny city until he was fourteen years of age, and later entered the Actual business college, of Pittsburg, where he was graduated in a commercial course in 1888. He engaged in the lumber business in Allegheny city with his father, under the firm name of George Loeffert & Son, and, in 1900, they removed to Millvale and reorganized and incorporated the business under the name of the Standard box and lumber company, with John Loeffert as president and manager, William Grusch as secretary, William A. Enrich as treasurer, and John Hoffman as superintendent. Mr. Loeffert was married, in 1889, to Ida A., daughter of Henry and Margaret (Beam) Lentz, and they have two children, Andrew J. and Margaret H., both students of the first ward school of Millvale. He is a member of the Masons, the republican party, and is one of the leading men of Millvale. Mr. Loeffert is a man of affairs in the business world, and besides his interests in Millvale, is president of the American building and loan association of Allegheny city.

MADISON B. LYNCH, the able treasurer of the Port Vue bridge company, was born at McKeesport, Pa., May 2, 1879, son of David H. and Melissa (Allen) Lynch, a sketch of the former also being included in this work. Mr. Lynch received his early educational training in the splendid and thorough schools of McKeesport, and since has supplemented that training by a wide experience in industrial, financial and political affairs. Mr. Lynch is the present toll-keeper of the Port Vue bridge company, and fills that important position with ability. He has been and is now prominently identified with the municipal affairs of Port Vue, having served two terms in his present position as member of the borough council, in which body he has made a fine record and has brought to bear upon borough matters the skill and ability with which his private affairs are directed. Mr. Lynch is a member of the Masonic fraternity, having taken his degrees in the Youghiogheny lodge, of McKeesport, and his political affiliations are with the republican party.

LEWIS FORSYTHE, late a resident of Coraopolis, was a native of Allegheny county, having been born at Peters Creek, Dec. 13, 1838. His education was obtained in the Lebanon school, Mifflin township, Allegheny county. For more than forty years he lived in Mifflin township, near Lebanon church (of which he was a trustee for one term), near his birthplace, where he was engaged in farming. In this business he amassed a competency, and in 1889 removed to Coraopolis. He was married, in 1877, to Miss Delilah A. Willock, and five children were born to them, three of whom are still living at Coraopolis. One son is attending Curry college, and the other is employed at the slating and tinning establishment of G. W. McBrier in Coraopolis. The daughter, Lucretia E., is engaged in teaching in the public schools. Mr. Forsythe's life was rather an uneventful one. He belonged to that class of whom the poet spoke as keeping the noiseless tenor of their way along the cool sequestered vale of life. Although interested in matters pertaining to the public weal, he never sought political preferment at the hands of his fellow-men, and the only office he ever held was that of supervisor of the roads of Moon township. In this position he discharged his duties with as much fidelity as though the office had been one fraught with importance and paying a high salary. At the time of his death, which occurred on June 1, 1902, he was a member of the First Presbyterian church of Coraopolis. His death was mourned by a large circle of church associates and neighbors, not as a man of great or public reputation, but as one of generous impulses and sterling worth.

JOHN BRENNAN, one of the earliest settlers of Braddock, was born on the Kyle Rue farm, near Kilkenny, Ireland, March 11, 1845. His grandfather, also named John Brennan, left the Kyle Rue farm to Thomas Brennan, the father of the subject of this sketch. Thomas Brennan came to this country in the sixties, and died at North Braddock in 1891 at the age of eighty-two. John Brennan, the subject of this article, received his education at the National school of the St. John's Roman Catholic church, and at the age of fourteen began clerking in a grocery, where he remained several years. In 1865 he came to America with his father, and, after residing a short time at East Dorset, Vt., they removed to Pittsburg, where the family resided on Washington street. Thence they went to Spring Hill (now Wilmerding), and they were the second family to locate in that place, and became communicants of the St. Thomas' Roman Catholic church of Braddock, which was their most convenient place of worship. At Spring Hill Mr. Brennan worked as a miner, and for thirteen years was a heater in the steel plant of Edgar Thompson & Co., now the Carnegie steel works. In 1889 he engaged in the grocery business, and by fair dealing and strict attention, he has been very successful. In the same year that he engaged in the grocery business he was elected a member of the council, and was three times re-elected without opposition. A short time after the beginning of his fourth term he was compelled to resign because of changing his residence.

His faithful services as councilman marked him as a man deserving further honors, and in February, 1901, he was chosen burgess of the borough by a large majority. Mr. Brennan was married, Aug. 15, 1874, to Alice, daughter of Charles and Hannah Sweeny, of Braddock. He and his wife live in a beautiful home at the corner of Fourth and Mills streets. They are members of the St. Thomas' Roman Catholic church of Braddock. In political belief Mr. Brennan has always been a democrat.

JOHN M. CLIFFORD, real estate and insurance agent at No. 721 Braddock Ave., and vice-president of the Citizens' bank of Braddock, was born in Ligonier, Westmoreland county, April 9, 1860. His father, Christopher Myers Clifford, was the son of Edward and Christiana (Myers) Clifford, whose parents were early settlers in Westmoreland county, and his mother, Susanna (McElroy) Clifford, was the daughter of John and Sarah McElroy, also early settlers in that region. John M. Clifford was educated in the schools of his native town, taught school for three terms, and then served for four and one-half years as freight and passenger clerk at Irwin, for the Pennsylvania railroad company. On July 1, 1887, he was transferred from Irwin to Braddock, and was appointed passenger and freight agent, and agent for the Adams express company in Braddock for eight and one-half years. In 1895 he opened a real estate and insurance business, in company with T. G. Aten, under the firm name of Aten & Clifford, and on Jan. 1, 1902, he bought out Mr. Aten's interest. Mr. Clifford's office is centrally located on Braddock avenue, next to the city hall, and is elegantly fitted up. Mr. Clifford was married, in 1883, to Cornelia F., daughter of Abner and Susan (Snodgrass) Cort, and granddaughter of Joseph Cort, an early settler near Irwin. Of the children of Mr. and Mrs. Clifford, John M., Jr., attended the Braddock and Edgewood schools, graduated from the high school and Duff's college in Pittsburg, and is now associated in business with his father, and is assistant cashier of the Citizens' bank of Braddock, Pa.; Frederick C. graduated from Duff's college with the class of 1903; Gertrude is a freshman in the Edgewood high school, and Alan G., George Edward and Marion are younger children attending the Edgewood schools. Mr. Clifford is a member of Orient lodge, No. 590, F. and A. M., of Wilkinsburg; Shiloh chapter, No. 257, R. A. M.; Tancred commandery, No. 48, Knights Templars, and of Mystic Shrine, Syria temple, of Pittsburg, Pa.; Pittsburg, No. 11, B. P. O. E.; Royal Arcanum, of Wilkinsburg, and Knights of Maccabees, of Wilkinsburg. He and his family are members of the Presbyterian church of Edgewood, Pa. In politics Mr. Clifford is a republican.

GEORGE W. FORSYTHE, a popular Natrona druggist, justice of the peace there, and one of the foremost citizens of that place, was born in Butler county, Pa., Jan. 9, 1859, and when a boy attended the common and select schools, and the academy at Sharpsburg, which was conducted by the Rev. Alexander Calvert. His education completed, he taught school four years, studied medicine for a time with Dr. F. V. Brooks, of Evans City, and after that took up pharmacy. In November, 1881, he began in Natrona a long and successful career as a druggist. In politics a republican, he has always taken a keen interest in the affairs of his party, has served as delegate to various district conventions, and, in 1900, was delegate to the national convention which nominated William McKinley for president and Theodore Roosevelt for vice-president. He was a leader in the Pittsburg delegation which urged Mr. Roosevelt's candidacy for the vice-presidency. Mr. Forsythe acted for fifteen years as tax assessor, was elected justice of the peace in 1897, and is now serving his second term in that office. He is clerk of the township commissioners of Harrison township. He was one of the organizers of the First National bank of Natrona and the Tarentum savings fund and loan association, and is one of the board of directors of the latter company. He is also a director and stockholder in the J. H. Baker manufacturing company and the Hamilton coal company. On Sept. 1, 1881, Mr. Forsythe married Miss Mary M. Liken, a native of Butler county, and has three children, O. Lloyd F., De Lorma D. and Carleton R. C. Mr. Forsythe is a great-grandson of Patrick Harvey, a native of Ireland who came to Westmoreland county in a very early day, and to Butler county as early as 1791, where he spent the remainder of his days. He served there, in those hardy pioneer times, as a member of Brady's famous band of scouts. He married Miss Jane Burns, a Scotch lady, and they reared a family of three sons and eight daughters. One of the sons, Patrick Harvey, Jr., had a daughter, Annie, a native of Butler county, who married William Forsythe, grandfather of the subject of this sketch. William Forsythe was born in Ireland, but emigrated to America and spent the latter part of his life in Butler county. Robert Forsythe, father of our subject, married Mary A. McCracken in 1863. She was born in Scotland in 1846, and with her parents came to America in 1849, settling on a farm near Freeport, Pa. He was a carpenter by trade, but in later life devoted his attention to farming. In politics he was a republican, and held various township offices. With his wife and family, he belonged to the United Presbyterian church. The man whose name heads this article is one of a family of seven children, six of whom are living, viz.: Samuel N., John E., Lewis N., Robert A., Annie M. (now deceased), and Viola N. Forsythe.

SAMUEL D. MILLER (deceased), of Aspinwall, Pa., for many years agent of the Aspinwall land company, was born in Moon township in September, 1825, and was the son of a farmer. He was educated in the public schools and at the Joseph Travella academy at Sewickley, and, when sixteen years of age, began to learn the carpentering trade with Bruce Tracy. He worked on some of the finest buildings in Sewickley, and was the first burgess of that place, and, in 1865, went to Oil City and engaged in the oil business for six years. He later constructed the waterworks at Oil City, Meadville and Olean, N. Y., and was superintendent of the building of the Allegheny city waterworks. In 1889 he organized the Aspinwall land company, and was the agent of this company until his death in August, 1902. Mr. Miller was also the builder of the Aspinwall waterworks, and was one of the most prominent citizens of that portion of the county. He was married, in 1847, to Mary A., daughter of John H. Little and of his wife, Margaret Clark Little, the former mentioned in history as a volunteer cook during the War of 1812. Samuel Miller and his wife were the parents of eleven children, six of whom are now living and are: Samuel D., Jr., manager of the V. Q. Hickman oil well supply company in Pittsburg; W. C., with a gas company in Ohio; H. G., manager of the Crawford gas company, of Granville, Ohio; W. F., foreman of the Standard oil company's shops in Oil City; Margaret L., wife of Samuel Chase, manager of an oil well supply company, and Ralph A., who succeeded his father as agent for the Aspinwall land company. He was prominently identified with the Presbyterian church of Aspinwall, having been one of its founders and for many years a trustee of that institution. Ralph A. Miller, who succeeded his father as agent for the Aspinwall land company, was educated in the public schools of Oil City, for ten years was a clerk with an oil well supply company, and, in 1898, came to Aspinwall as assistant to his father. On the death of his father, he was appointed agent of the Aspinwall land company, and since has filled that position with signal ability.

HARRY ATWATER, the foreman in the finishing department of the works of the American sheet steel company, was born in the city of McKeesport in 1861. At that time the population of McKeesport was but little over 2,000, but the educational facilities were equal to any in the country, and in the public schools of the city young Atwater acquired a good, practical education that has been of great assistance to him in later years. Upon leaving school he obtained employment in the W. Deweese-Wood mills, now operated by the American sheet steel company. His position in the works was a humble one at first, but his aptitude and determination enabled him to surmount all the obstacles as they arose, and promotion naturally followed. Step by step he was advanced until, for the last fifteen years, he has occupied the position of foreman in the finishing department. None envy him his success, for all know that it has been achieved through patient, intelligent efforts to further the interests of his employers, and that his promotion has come to him as a reward for meritorious service. Having risen from the ranks himself, he knows the capabilities of the men under him, the trials that they have to endure, and consequently there is very little friction in the finishing department under his guiding hands.

WILLIAM CROSSLAND, a prominent citizen of Port Vue, Pa., was born in Mifflin township, Allegheny Co., Pa., May 1, 1856. He is the son of English parents, his father coming to America about 1849, and his mother with her parents when she was a child of four years. Her parents settled in Allegheny county, near Pittsburg, about 1838. When Mr. Crossland was five years of age he accompanied his parents to England, and there remained for nine years, returning to America in 1870. The nine years spent in England were of little advantage to him, for at that time there was no compulsory education in that country and children were put to work at a tender age, he, when nine years of age, being placed in a flax mill as a half-timer, which meant he was to work half the day and attend school the other half, the manufacturer paying for the tuition. For two years he worked and attended school, when he was examined by an inspector in a cursory manner, declared to be of full age, and put to doing a man's work. About one year later, he quit the factory and began to work in the mines, and, with the exception of six months spent in a foundry, continued in that occupation during the rest of his stay in England. On his return to his native land, he continued to work in the mines, attending school when opportunity offered, usually about two months during the winter season. He finally succeeded in graduating from the commercial department of Adrian college, Michigan. From 1877 to 1886, Mr. Crossland was prominently identified with leading labor organizations, particularly with the Knights of Labor, which was a flourishing institution at that time. He represented District No. 9, which embraced the railroad and river miners, in the general assembly held at Cincinnati, Ohio, in September, 1883, and has had close associations with other organizations, fraternal and political. In 1892 he was a resident of Lincoln township, Allegheny county, when a part of the township was incorporated under the name of Port Vue borough, and he has since resided at that point and held various elective and appointive offices in that borough. When the first election was held in the borough he was chosen a justice of the peace, but owing to the shortness of the term did not take out a commission. At the organization of the first council in the newly created borough he was elected clerk and ably filled that position until March, 1901. In the meantime, he served on the school board as a director of the district for three years and as president of that body for one year. In fact, Mr. Crossland has been more or less directly connected with every movement of importance in the borough's history, and in February, 1903, was again elected justice of the peace, an office which he is now filling. In municipal affairs, Mr. Crossland is independent, voting for the man rather than the party, but in national matters he usually votes with the republicans, though for some time he was an ardent prohibitionist, and still believes that civilization would be more advanced if the manufacturing of alcoholic liquors was prohibited. Mr. Crossland was happily married, in 1883, to Margaret A. McCracken, and they have had born to them five children, two of whom now survive, viz.: Mabel E. and George H. Mr. Crossland's father is still living, but his mother died in December, 1902. He also has five brothers and two sisters residing in Allegheny county, Pa.

WILLIAM E. JOHNSTON, M. D., of Etna, Pa., a well-known physician and surgeon, was born in Cranberry township, Butler Co., Pa., Aug. 6, 1854, son of William and Sarah A. Johnston, the latter now residing with him. Dr. Johnston attended the public schools of Butler county and an academy near his home for several terms, during which period he taught in the winter months. He studied law for one year in Butler; with his brother engaged in the mercantile business at Hendersonville, Butler county, for three years; read medicine with Elder Crawford, of Butler county, for two years; entered the Starling medical college, of Columbus, and was graduated from that institution in 1882. He immediately began the practice of his profession at Etna, and since has been one of the leading physicians of that city, maintaining offices at No. 389 Butler St. He was married, in 1889, to Julia A., daughter of William and Ellen (Ramsey) Kennedy, of Etna, Pa., her father having come from Poland, Ohio, and her mother, a native of Wilmington, Lawrence Co., Pa., but now living in Sharpsburg. Dr. and Mrs. Johnston are the parents of four children: Leverne and Eleanor, attending school at Etna; Mary

Elizabeth and Helen Margaret, twins, at home. He and his family are members of the United Presbyterian church, and he is a Mason, past master of his lodge, an Elk and member of the democratic party. Dr. Johnston is closely identified with the Allegheny county, the Pennsylvania State and the American medical associations, and takes great interest in all matters that pertain to his profession and its advancement. The ancestors of Dr. Johnston were originally from Londonderry, Ireland, came to America prior to the Revolutionary war, and his grandfather, Benjamin Johnston, was a soldier of the new republic in the War of 1812. Dr. Johnston was examiner for the pension board, a delegate to the Kansas City convention of 1900, and is now burgess of Etna.

J. WILL MARTIN, of Elizabeth, Pa., a prominent furniture dealer and funeral director, was born at Elizabeth, Oct. 15, 1873, son of Thomas W. and Margaret E. (Penney) Martin, also of Elizabeth, where his father established the present furniture and undertaking business, in 1869, and continued the same with uniform success until his death, Nov. 6, 1893. His mother died on Dec. 30, 1886, leaving four children, viz.: Rev. Jesse P. and J. Will, twins; Thomas W., Jr., in the undertaking business with Thomas D. Turner, at Wilkinsburg, and John B., a valued employe of the Homestead National bank. J. Will Martin attended the public schools of Elizabeth until 1889 and was graduated at the Pittsburg academy in 1891, well equipped for the business of life. He then secured a position with John Murphy & Co., dealers in undertakers' supplies, and remained with that concern for two years, and, in 1894, assumed control of his father's undertaking business at Elizabeth, which he has successfully continued to the present time. He is also financially interested with his brother-in-law, Edward C. Finney, in the livery business at Clairton, Pa., where they enjoy a splendid patronage. Mr. Martin was married, on Oct. 9, 1895, to Ella D., daughter of Joseph and Arabella (McClure) Finney, of Lincoln township, and their home life is an ideal one. Mr. Martin and his wife are devout members of the United Presbyterian church of Elizabeth, to which they are liberal contributors, both financially and by personal efforts. Mr. Martin's father was an elder in the church for several years prior to his death. Jesse P., the twin brother of J. Will, is a United Presbyterian minister, having had charge of the congregation at Verona, Pa., but was compelled to give up active service on account of his health. Mr. J. Will Martin is a member of the Odd Fellows and the Heptasophs, and in politics is with the republican party.

GEORGE BAEHR, electrical engineer of the National tube company's plants at McKeesport, Pa., was born in Breslau, Germany, April 11, 1870. His primary education was obtained in the schools of Breslau, and at the age of twelve years he came with his parents to America, attending for the next three years the Greene street public school, at Newark, N. J. He then entered the service of the Edison electric company, and while thus employed attended evening school, first at the technical school, Newark, N. J., and later at Cooper institute. After completing this course, he was placed in charge of the dynamo room and instrument gallery of the Edison electric telegraph company, first district station, at Brooklyn, N. Y. At the end of one year he was made inspector of the company's isolated plants in the city of Brooklyn, and soon afterwards was made superintendent of the underground department. While in this position he invented and patented a quick-break electric switch, and then started into the business of manufacturing his new appliance, and also in making switchboards of a general character. He continued in this business for about three years, when he sold his interest and took charge of the repairs for the North Hudson electric railway company, of Jersey City, N. J. Three years later he entered the employ of the Crocker & Wheeler electric company, of Ampere, N. Y., where he had charge of outside construction, and continued with them until he accepted his present position at McKeesport with the National tube company, where he has been for five years. Besides the quick-break switch, which has proved a successful invention, and which is still in use, he has invented a number of other appliances, both before and after entering the employ of the National tube company. In connection with R. C. Crawford, the auditor of the company, he patented a double-run lap weld furnace, which is in successful operation in the pipe mill. He also patented a flexible coupling, a lever type controller for electric motors, an electric booster system, a 300-volt ceiling cut-out, a motor, and an arc lamp. His father, George L. Baehr, was a sculptor of note, one of the most noted of his works being the monument of Victory, at Breslau, commemorative of the Franco-Prussian war. He died at Breslau in 1896, his wife, Emilie, the mother of George Baehr, dying at the same place in the same year. George Baehr was married, in 1891, to Hannah Isabel, daughter of W. H. Smyth, of Jersey City, N. J. To them four children have been born: Grace Emilie, aged ten; William H., aged eight; George L., aged six, and Mary L., aged four. He is a member of Aliquippa lodge, No. 375, Free and Accepted Masons; the Royal Arcanum, and the American institute of electrical engineers, and is recognized as an authority upon all matters pertaining to electric power applications and lighting.

ALBERT G. SMITH, gardener on Neville island, son of Peter and Elizabeth Smith, was born on Neville island, Jan. 29, 1863, and received a common-school education. His father, Peter Smith, was born in Germany, and on coming to America, settled in Allegheny county. He was the father of five children: Henry, Elizabeth (deceased), Mary, George M. and Albert. Mr. Smith has in his possession the frame of an Emerson upright piano, a relic of the Johnstown flood. Peter Smith died on Neville island, May 5, 1876, in his seventy-second year, and his wife Oct. 31, 1894, in her seventy-first year. Albert G. Smith, subject of this sketch, was married, Feb. 14, 1885, to Miriam L. Cotton, and to them were born two children, Muriel V. and Albert M. Mr. Smith is a resident of Neville township, and has been connected with its government in an official capacity, having served as a member of the board of education and justice of the peace, which office he still holds. He and his family are members of the Presbyterian church, of which Mr. Smith is one of the trustees. Mr. Smith is an active man in his occupation, and a very prosperous gardener on the island. William Cotton, father of Mrs. A. G. Smith, was born in Mercer county, July 15, 1844; is of Irish extraction, and by occupation a farmer.

He was married, Oct. 18, 1865, to Sarah E. Fisher, and to them have been born seven children: Sherman A., Mary E., Miriam, Franklin, Nina, Florence and Albert. He was married a second time to Emma Searings, in June, 1898, and to them was born a daughter, Margrette. Mrs. Sarah E. Cotton was born June 19, 1845, in East Brook, Lawrence county, and died Nov. 25, 1892. Mr. Cotton was a soldier in the Civil war and took part in several important battles, the most noted being Gettysburg. He was with the army at General Lee's surrender, served under Gen. Phil Sheridan and was honorably discharged after serving almost two years. William Cotton, Sr., grandfather of Mrs. Smith, was born in Ireland, came to this country when but a lad and settled in Mercer county, where he was later employed as a mill roller. He was married to Matilda Cosgrove, and to them were born ten children, nine of whom are living, William, Jr., being the eldest. Mr. Cotton lived to be seventy, and Mrs. Cotton, seventy-seven, is now living in Oil City. Mrs. Sarah (Fisher) Cotton, mother of Mrs. A. G. Smith, was descended from Thomas G. Fisher and Mary (Burns) Fisher; the former descended from Thomas Fisher and Sarah (Johnston) Fisher, and the latter, Mary (Burns) Fisher, descended from Robert Burns and Eleanor (Bryan) Burns. Mary (Burns) Fisher, grandmother to Mrs. Smith, was a cousin of Scotland's greatest poet, Robert Burns. The genealogy of the family is very complete, and can easily be traced back many generations farther than has been done.

GEORGE H. COLE, a well-known resident of Neville township, Allegheny Co., Pa., was born in Allegheny city, Feb. 21, 1838, son of George W. and Dorcas W. Cole, his father having been born near Bangor, Me., and coming to Pittsburg in 1823, where he was an active and progressive business man. He conducted the first livery stable in Allegheny city, which was located at the corner of Federal and South Diamond streets. His political affiliations were with the whig party. He was married to Dorcas, daughter of Mr. Bragdon, who bore him five children, viz.: Augustus P., Caroline F., George H., Henrietta R. and Milton. George W. Cole died on his farm on Neville island in his seventy-eighth year, and his wife died in Allegheny city at a similar period of her career. George H. Cole accompanied his parents to Neville island when he was a child, and has been a resident of that island for more than sixty years. He was married to Anna M., daughter of Charles and Martha McMillin, and they have had ten children born to them, the living ones of whom are: Minnie, Nettie May, Sadie A., Harry E. and Elmer C. Mr. Cole has been a successful gardener for many years, and has been extensively engaged in that industry. He is one of the progressive and substantial citizens of that part of the county and has been connected with the township government in different official capacities.

WILLIAM PERRY BRADSHAW, who for the last twenty years has been a carpenter in the boat yards at Elizabeth, Pa., is a native of Jefferson township, Allegheny county. He is the son of William and Eliza (Dick) Bradshaw, and was born Feb. 24, 1849. William Bradshaw, the grandfather of William P., came to America in 1796, locating in Rostraver township, Westmoreland county, afterwards moving to Allegheny county, and locating at the mouth of Peters creek, in Jefferson township, where a branch of the family still resides. In August, 1903, the family held a reunion at Peters creek, at which were gathered 136 members, representing four generations, that being about one-half of the family now living. After receiving a common-school education, he engaged in agricultural pursuits until he took his present position. Mr. Bradshaw has been twice married. His first wife, whom he married in 1870, was Miss Mary B. Maple. She bore him two children, Jennie and William M. His second marriage was in 1900, to Elizabeth L. Norfolk, of Elizabeth. Politically, Mr. Bradshaw is a republican, and takes great interest in questions of a political nature. He served as school director for five years, has been assessor of Jefferson township, and is now a member of the school board of the borough of Elizabeth. In all these positions he discharged his duties with diligence and fidelity. He is a member of the Methodist Episcopal church, and carries the teachings of his church into his daily life. Believing in the old saying that "in union there is strength," he is also a member of the ship-carpenters' union, though he is not that kind of a union man that finds pleasure in stirring up trouble between the employer and the workmen, and the fact that he has held his position for twenty years, speaks well for his industry and his skill as a mechanic. Organized labor might be placed on a more substantial basis if more of its members were like him.

J. W. METTLER, general manager for the West Pittsburg oil refining company, a son of Jacob and Sarah Mettler, was born in East Brady, Clarion Co., Pa. His mother was the daughter of John and Sarah Kurtz, born in Ohio, near Mt. Carrick, Monroe county, while his father was born in Baden, Germany. Jacob Mettler came to America in 1847, settled in Pittsburg, where he followed his vocation of engineer for many years, and died in Fairview, Butler county, at the age of eighty-one. Sarah Mettler, his wife, died in the same house in her seventy-eighth year. To Jacob and Sarah Mettler were born twelve children, five of whom, besides our subject, are living: J. C. Mettler, of Butler county, foreman for the Forest oil company; J. N. Mettler, of Bradford, a liveryman; W. M. Mettler, of Baltimore, Md., in the insurance business; Mary Ihlenfeld, whose husband is in the merchant tailoring business, and Sarah Jeffrey, whose husband is in the employ of the West Pittsburg oil company. J. W. Mettler, the subject of this sketch, was educated in the common schools of East Brady, living on a farm until he was seventeen, and going out at that time to take his place in the world's great struggle for existence. He went first to Warren county, where he became an employe in the lumber business, but soon left this for a more adventurous life in the employ of the Mississippi logging company, on Lake Superior. At the age of twenty-two he returned to Pennsylvania and entered the oil refining business, in which he has been engaged continuously up to the present time. For three years he was with Levi Smith, of North Clarendon; for three more with the Valley oil company, of Oil City, a company which was run successfully under his management. Selling his interest in this company, he bought the Coraopolis refinery, meeting with a total loss by fire two years later. Mr. Mettler then started his fortunes anew, in Youngstown, Ohio, by entering the wholesale and retail oil business under the firm name of Schultz & Mettler, dealing extensively in horses at the same time. After selling out to the Standard oil company, the firm of Schultz & Mettler opened the Edinburg oil fields in the Mahoning valley, in Ohio. Mr. Mettler sold out a second time, to become superintendent and general manager of the Pittsburg oil refining company, and while in their employ sold the stock twice, realizing for the company, under his able management, great profits instead of their former heavy losses. About six months ago Mr. Mettler organized and built the West Pittsburg oil refinery, of Neville township, of which he is now director and general manager. He is one of the most able oil men of the company, and likewise a shrewd business man in other lines, commanding the confidence of his fellow-men. Mr. Mettler is a man of ability, and has the decision of mind necessary for a good business manager. He organized the Coraopolis savings and loan association, and is its president, director and executor. Interested as well in educational matters, he is a member of the board of education in Coraopolis, and not neglecting the spiritual call, is an active worker in the Methodist Episcopal church. Mr. Mettler was married, in 1884, to Mida Bangher, daughter of Solomon H. and Catharine Bangher, and to them have been born three children, all of whom are living: Anna May, Clara Belle and Clifford Lavagne.

HARRY E. HENDERSON, of Buena Vista, Pa., a well-known citizen and a prosperous farmer, was born on the old Henderson homestead near Buena Vista, Pa., Jan. 30, 1875, son of James P. and Cynthia M. (Fleming) Henderson, of Allegheny county. Young Henderson attended the Edinburgh State normal school for seven months, the Duquesne college, of Pittsburg, for two years, and also the schools of Slippery Rock, Pa., and received educational advantages that in every way qualified him for a successful career. On leaving school, Mr. Henderson devoted his attention to farming on the homestead farm, subsequently was on the clerical force of the Westinghouse air brake company at Wilmerding, and during the last year has again taken up farming on the old homestead. He was happily married, in 1895, to Nannie E., daughter of David and Fannie (Douglass) Rankin, and they have one child, Clyde Patterson, born April 29, 1898. He is closely allied to the republicans in political matters, and was elected on that ticket to the council of East McKeesport, in which body he made a fine record and stood well among his confrères. Mr. Henderson is a member of the Youghiogheny lodge of Masons, at McKeesport, and also of the United Presbyterian church. He now resides on the old homestead, and is one of the most popular citizens of that township.

PETER F. RHOADES, of Versailles, Pa., a prominent citizen and a popular passenger conductor in the service of the Baltimore & Ohio railroad, was born in Indiana county, Pa., July 25, 1852, son of Lewis and Matilda (Breniser) Rhoades, his father having been a prosperous farmer of Armstrong and Indiana counties, but resided the greater part of his career in the latter county. Mr. Rhoades was educated in the splendid schools of his native county, and when nineteen years of age began railroading, which vocation he has since successfully followed. He has served in all capacities in the transportation department of both the Pan Handle and the Baltimore & Ohio railroad companies, and for the past twenty-three years has been with the Baltimore & Ohio, seventeen years of that time in his present position of passenger conductor. He was married, in May, 1875, at Pittsburg, to Susan, daughter of Zachariah and Melvina (Wakefield) Taylor, of Indiana county, Pa., and they have four children, viz.: Erda N., wife of B. L. Holt, of McKeesport; Mabel B., Louis T. and Alice M. He has been closely connected with the municipal affairs of Versailles, having served as a member of the council for six years, and for four years was president of that body. He is prominently identified with the Masonic fraternity, being a Knight Templar and a thirty-second degree Mason, and also a member of the Mystic Shrine. He is also a leading member of the Order of Railroad Conductors, the republican party and of the Lutheran church. He has made his home in Versailles for the past sixteen years, and is one of the substantial and highly-respected citizens of that borough.

REV. JOHN SILL BLAYNEY, pastor of the Glenfield and Haysville Presbyterian churches, was born Aug. 31, 1874, on a farm in Ohio county, W. Va., about one mile from the Pennsylvania line. He received his common-school education at Rice school, about one mile from his home, and prepared for college at home, being tutored in languages by his pastor, William H. Lester, D. D., and in mathematics by his cousin, Nicholas E. Murray, a farmer of the neighborhood. Mr. Blayney, meanwhile, worked on his father's farm, becoming strong physically, and at seventeen years of age entered Washington and Jefferson college, becoming a member of the class of 1896. His religious education had not been neglected, having Christian parents of the highest character, and a home in which all united in worship and devotion to God. At the age of ten he united with the Presbyterian church of West Alexander, ceasing to be a member of it only when he was ordained to preach the gospel. Upon entering college, Mr. Blayney united with the college Y. M. C. A., assisted in carrying on a mission Sunday-school and had charge of a Sunday evening prayer-meeting service, under the direction of the college Y. M. C. A., at Laboratory, about two miles from Washington. He also joined the Philo and Union literary society in his first year in college, and took an active interest in all literary affairs of the society, winning second prize in original oration in the annual contest in 1896. Mr. Blayney took an active part in athletics as well, having charge of the graded athletics for one year. He still holds the record as champion mile runner, taking part in the inter-collegiate contest in Washington, in June, 1895—time, five minutes and four-fifths seconds. He graduated June 24, 1896, and having chosen the ministry as his profession, made the necessary preparations for entering some theological seminary in the fall, choosing the Western, at which he matriculated in September, 1896. During his seminary course, he was engaged in missionary and church work, being superintendent of the Westminster Presbyterian church Sabbath-school, of Allegheny, one year, and had charge of a mission in Old Third Presbyterian church, Pittsburg, two years under the Society of improvement of the poor. In January, 1899, Mr. Blayney began supplying the Presbyterian churches of Glenfield and Haysville, continuing until his graduation in May, 1899. Having received and accepted calls from these churches, he went at once to Glenfield, was ordained and installed there on May 25th by the Allegheny presbytery, at which time Dr. S. J. Glass presided and preached the sermon, Dr. J. C. Bruce charged the people, and Dr. William H. Lester, his first and only pastor, charged the pastor. He was installed in Haysville on May 26th, Dr. D. S. Kennedy presiding and preaching the sermon, Rev. R. S. Young charging the people, and Rev. H. M. Hosack charging the pastor. The people of Glenfield and Haysville were particularly fortunate in securing such a man as the Rev. J. S. Blayney as pastor. Under his charge the church was strengthened in every way, both through his untiring zeal in the cause and through the exemplary life he led in their midst. He resigned the pastorate here Nov. 15, 1903, to accept a call to the First Presbyterian church, at Wilcox, Pa., to begin work there Jan. 17, 1904. On June 28, 1899, Mr. Blayney was married to Margarite L. Boggs, of Harmony, Dr. J. C. Bruce, of Westminster church, officiating, and Rev. P. J. Slonaker, of Zelienople church, assisting. Margarite L. Boggs was born at Harmony, March 2, 1876, resided there until 1895, and in Allegheny until her marriage. Her father, Detmore P. Boggs, was born Jan. 15, 1844, near Evans City; married, in 1868, to Sarah Miller, of Harmony, who was born March 13, 1847. To them were born eleven children, nine of whom are living: three sons, bankers in Pittsburg; one son, pressman, of Pittsburg, and one son at home; one daughter, Olive M., married to Rev. H. T. Kerr, of Hutchinson, Kan.; another, Amy J., married to Rev. A. B. Allison, of Furrukabod, India; Margarite S., now Mrs. J. S. Blayney, and one daughter at home—making three Presbyterian sons-in-law in one family. The Rev. J S. Blayney and wife have three children: David Henry, born Aug. 19, 1900; Sarah Margarite, born Jan. 28, 1902, and Lois; born Nov. 9, 1903. Amanda (Sill) Blayney was the daughter of John Sill, who was born Nov. 10, 1809, in Allegheny county, three miles from McKeesport, where he died March 8, 1873, in his sixty-fifth year. His father was Col. Jesse Sill, who served in the War of 1812. John Sill married Margaret Mullen Mehaffy, Jan. 25, 1830, her parents being of Scotch descent. To John and Margaret Sill were born eleven children, of whom only three survive, one of these being Amanda, the mother of the subject of this sketch, who was born May 9, 1843. All her family were Presbyterians. David M. Blayney, father, was born April 4, 1835, in Ohio county, W. Va. In 1861 he enlisted in Company D, 12th regiment, West

Virginia volunteer infantry, serving as commissioned officer until discharged at the close of the war. Returning to Ohio county, he resumed his occupation as a farmer, and was married, in 1865, to Minerva Jane Griffith, of Beallsville, Monroe Co., Ohio, who died in 1869, leaving one son, Henry Griffith Blayney. David M. Blayney married Amanda M. Sill, Nov. 13, 1872, and from this union one son is living, John Sill Blayney. He removed from West Virginia in 1901 to West Alexander, his present home. He is of Scotch-Irish lineage, and all of the family are members of the Presbyterian church. Charles Blayney, father of David, was born in County Down, Ireland, in 1788, and is a descendant of Lord Blayney. He came to this country in 1791 and settled on a farm in Ohio county, W. Va. He served in the War of 1812, and after his return married Miss Potter, who had two sons, William and Vincent, and, in 1820, married Nancy Faris, to whom were born eleven children, two sons and three grandsons being ministers of the gospel. Charles died in 1860, aged seventy-two, and Nancy in 1880, aged eighty years.

WILLIAM L. DOUGLASS, of Boston, Pa., a well-known citizen and justice of the peace, was born in Elizabeth township, Allegheny Co., Pa., May 19, 1849, son of Col. William and Margaret (Howell) Douglass. Squire Douglass received his elementary education in the common schools, later attended the Elder's Ridge academy, and completed his classical training at the University of Chicago, from which institution he was graduated in 1871. Subsequently he was admitted to the bar of the supreme court of Illinois, and practiced that profession in Chicago for some time. He was married, in 1876, to Kate I., daughter of Andrew and Jane (Cornell) Werling, of Allegheny county, and they have one daughter, Jane W. In 1882 Mr. Douglass was appointed a justice of the peace by Gov. Henry M. Hoyt, a year later was elected to succeed himself, and since then has continued in that important position, the duties of which he has discharged to the entire satisfaction of his constituency. In 1864 Mr. Douglass enlisted in Battery E, 6th Pennsylvania heavy artillery, then being but fifteen years of age, and served until the close of that struggle. Squire

Douglass has lived in Boston the greater part of his mature life, and there assisted in the organization of the Boston bridge company, of which he is vice-president. He is also a handler of real estate and insurance, and has devoted considerable time to civil engineering, in which profession he is proficient. In 1895 he joined the Methodist Episcopal church and for a number of years has been a class leader, and is a director in the Bentleyville holiness association, which is the oldest camp in the State, and located in Washington county, near the National pike. Squire Douglass is also a member of the Grand Army of the Republic, the Masons, the Knights of Malta, the Knights of the Mystic Chain, and other orders, and is one of the leading men in that part of the county.

GEORGE W. PANCOAST, who for eight years has been a member of the council of Elizabeth, Pa., is a native of the borough in which he now lives. He is the son of William and Maria (Lytle) Pancoast, both of whom were old and honored residents of Elizabeth, where he was born Sept. 9, 1846. As a boy he attended the public schools of Elizabeth, receiving a good practical education, after which he went to work in a sawmill. He has never changed his occupation, and during the years that he has been engaged in the business he has assisted in the manufacture of millions of feet of lumber. There are few points about a saw-mill that he does not fully understand, and though other men may have selected occupations that seem more dignified, few have lived up to the possibilities of their calling better than he. Mr. Pancoast was married, in 1871, to Miss Angeline Speidel, of Elizabeth, and they have three children: William, Frank and Susie. The daughter is now the wife of Archibald Noble, of Homestead. In politics Mr. Pancoast is a republican, but he is a firm believer in good government, and was elected to the council, in 1895, upon the citizens' ticket. His work as a member of the council was approved by his constituents, as was shown by his re-election in 1898 and in 1901. During the eight years that he has been a member of the council, his every action and every vote have been in the interests of the general public, which he has so faithfully tried to serve.

WM. REYNOLDS LYON, M. D., was born in Indiana, Indiana Co., Pa., Sept. 6, 1869, the eldest of five children of Samuel and Sarah (Lowman) Lyon, the other children being Mary Argyl, George Mulholland, James Campbell and Alice Armstrong. His early education was received in private schools, and at the age of thirteen he entered the employ, in Chicago, Ill., of the western department of the Home insurance company of New York, of which his uncle, George M. Lyon, in association with Gen. Arthur C. Ducat, was manager. After thus spending three years, he entered Phillips' academy, Andover, Mass., where he remained four years, graduating in the class of 1890. The death of his father the following September interrupted his course of study, which he had expected to continue in Yale college, and left him with new responsibilities. He secured a position in the First National bank of Blairsville, Pa., which he occupied until beginning the study of medicine in Jefferson medical college, of Philadelphia, from which noted school he graduated in 1895 with honor. After spending a year in hospital and dispensary work, he located in Glenfield, Allegheny Co., Pa., where he continues in the successful practice of his profession. Dr. Lyon was married to Florence Mary Foote, of West Newton, Pa., daughter of Robert Todd and Catherine (Shields) Foote, June 30, 1898. During his residence in Glenfield, Dr. Lyon has been actively interested in the welfare of the community, and at present is a member of the borough council and fills the office of elder in the Presbyterian church. William R. Lyon's father was Samuel Lyon, who was born in Bedford, Pa., Feb. 19, 1835, the second son of William and Ruth (Reynolds) Lyon. He read law with his father and was admitted to the Bedford county bar in 1858. At the outbreak of the Civil war he recruited a volunteer company, and was commissioned first lieutenant of Company H, 107th regiment of the Pennsylvania volunteers, Nov. 21, 1861, and promoted to quartermaster July 19, 1862. He was present and engaged in a number of battles, among them being Chantilly, Cedar mountain, Bull Run, South mountain, Antietam and Gettysburg, serving throughout the war and afterwards re-enlisting for special service. He married Sarah Lowman, daughter of William and Mary (McLain) Lowman, of Indiana, Pa., in 1868, and afterwards made his home in Blairsville, in which place he died Sept. 13, 1890. During his residence in Blairsville, he engaged in the practice of law in Indiana and Westmoreland counties. William Lyon was the father of Samuel Lyon. He resided in Bedford, Pa., where he practiced law. He married Ruth Reynolds, daughter of William and Jane (Holliday) Reynolds, and a second marriage was to Catherine Mulholland, daughter of George Mulholland. Samuel Lyon, third son of William Lyon, was born Jan. 20, 1775. He was a merchant in Baltmore, Md. He married Hetty Broome, of Wilmington, Del., March, 1800. William Lyon, eldest son of John Lyon, preceded his father to the province of Pennsylvania, coming from Ireland in 1750. He was assistant surveyor to his uncle, John Armstrong, deputy surveyor and justice of the peace for Cumberland county. Together they laid out the town of Carlisle, by order of the proprietary, in 1751, and the seat of justice was then permanently established there. William Lyon then entered the provincial military service for the defense of the frontier against the French and Indians, and as first lieutenant of the Pennsylvania regiment, appointed Dec. 6, 1757, participated in Forbes' great expedition against Fort Duquesne in 1758. He resigned his commission in 1759, and in 1764 was appointed magistrate by Gov. John Penn. On the opening of the Revolution and the suppression of the provincial authority, he was appointed by the supreme executive council, a member of the committee of safety, Oct. 16, 1776; prothonotary for Cumberland county, March 12, 1777; clerk of Orphans' court, Feb. 9, 1779; register and recorder, Feb. 10, 1779. He held various court positions by reappointment until 1806. He was appointed by the supreme executive council to receive subscriptions for Cumberland county for a loan of $20,000,000, authorized by Congress, June 29, 1779. William Lyon was born in Ireland, March 17, 1729, and died in Carlisle, Feb. 7, 1809 He married, first, in 1756, Alice Armstrong, daughter of his uncle, John Armstrong, of Carlisle. Their son, James, married Jane Eyre. He married, secondly, in 1768, Ann Fleming, of Carlisle. John Lyon came with his family from

Emskillin, County Fermaugh, province of Ulster, Ireland, to the province of Pennsylvania, in the year 1763, and settled in Cumberland county, now Milford township, Juniata county, about two miles west of Mifflintown. The warrant for his tract of land (273 acres, 63 perches) is dated Sept. 18, 1766. In 1773 the proprietary granted to John Lyon et al. twenty acres of land for the use of the Presbyterian church of Tuscarora, where he is buried. He died in 1780. He married, in Ireland, Margaret Armstrong, sister of Col. John Armstrong, one of the prominent and patriotic Pennsylvanians of provincial times. He was one of General Washington's staff officers. The name Lyon has been prominent in the making of the commercial and political history of Allegheny county, and the men bearing the name are direct descendants of John Lyon.

Florence Mary Foote was born in Rostraver township, Westmoreland Co., Pa., Feb. 28, 1870, her parents being Robert Todd Foote, and Catherine (Shields) Foote. The home of her early childhood was the Foote farm, two miles from West Newton, one of the largest and at that time one of the best known farms in Westmoreland county. She was the fourth in a family of five children; her brothers and sisters dying in childhood, left her the last representative of an old and well-known family. After the death of her father, in 1876, she, with her mother, moved from the farm to West Newton, where she made her home until after her marriage. Her early education was in the West Newton public schools, from which she graduated with honors in 1885. Continuing her studies in the Blairsville ladies' seminary (now Blairsville college for women), she graduated in the class of 1890. Returning from Blairsville, the next two years were spent in the study of art and elocution, in both of which she became proficient. After a year spent in travel, she remained at home with her mother in West Newton, taking a prominent part in the social life of the community and in church work, she having been an active member of the First Presbyterian church of West Newton since her fifteenth year. On June 30, 1898, she was married to William Reynolds Lyon, M. D., the marriage ceremony being performed by Rev. John T. Meloy, D. D., who had been her pastor from her earliest youth. After an eastern trip, she returned with her husband to their home in Glenfield, Allegheny Co., Pa., where, as in her former home, she interested herself not only in the social life of the town, but as a member of the Presbyterian church was active in church and missionary work, so that in the five years of her wonderfully helpful, cheer-giving life in that place, she won unnumbered friends, and by her death, which occurred Sept. 11, 1903, the community lost one of its most valued and influential members. Robert Todd Foote, father of Florence Mary Foote, was the son of John Stiles and Margaret (Todd) Foote, of West Newton, Pa., and grandson of John and Lois (Mills) Foote, of Canton, Conn. He was a direct descendant of Nathaniel and Elizabeth (Denning) Foote, of England. Nathaniel Foote came to America in 1630, and was one of the first settlers of Wethersfield, Conn., and one of the founders of the colonies of Connecticut and New Haven. At the time of the settlement and founding of Hartford and Windsor, Conn., Nathaniel Foote was granted a ten-acre lot on the east side of Broad street, near the south end of the street. He also became owner of a tract of land of 400 acres, lying mostly in the Great Meadows. In 1644 he was appointed delegate to the general court, and filled many offices of trust in the community. He died in 1644, aged fifty-one years, and was buried in the ancient burying-ground in the rear of the meeting-house, where are gathered together the ashes of eleven generations of the Foote family. Many of the descendants of Nathaniel Foote have held positions of honor and trust under the colonial, national and State governments, and have given expression of their patriotism not only in the struggle for national independence and personal liberty, but in the establishing of churches, schools and colleges, most notably being interested in the founding and support of Yale college, of New Haven, Conn., and Harvard college, of Cambridge, Mass. They have been prominent as statesmen, officers and soldiers during Colonial, Revolutionary and Civil wars, and have won distinction not only in the preaching of the gospel of Christianity, but also in the practice of law and medicine, as well as in the field of letters. Catherine (Shields) Foote, mother of Florence M. Lyon, was born July 14, 1837. She was married to Robert Todd Foote, Dec. 20, 1860. Her father, Col. John R. Shields, of Elizabeth, Pa., was a son of George Shields, one of the earliest settlers of western Pennsylvania. Her mother, whose maiden name was Mary Fletcher, was born in Londonderry, Ireland. Mrs. Foote resides in Glenfield, Pa., with her son-in-law, Dr. William R. Lyon.

REV. JOHN K. MELHORN, A. M., was born Jan. 20, 1826, the sixth in a family of nine children. His parents, John Melhorn and Sarah, née Kaufroth, his wife, were of German ancestry and residents of Lancaster county, Pa. His father was a farmer, but was called from the peaceful plough and sickle by the War of 1812-14, he and his brother enlisting —the latter losing his life at the battle of Lundy's Lane, Canada; the former completing his service as captain of a company of volunteers. Some time after the war closed, in 1828, John Melhorn settled near Erie, Pa., where, amid the privations of the frontier, he reared his family, and as an honored citizen spent his days. Of sturdy stock, the beloved mother died at the advanced age of seventy-eight, and the venerable father in his eighty-sixth year. Their son, John K., was in his second year when the family came west. His boyhood was passed upon the shores of Lake Erie. In summer he worked on the farm; in the winter he faithfully used the brief terms of the public schools. Anxious, however, for an education, and desirous of becoming a minister, in the spring of 1844 John entered the Erie academy. He here continued his studies for four years, except when teaching a public school in the winters of 1846-47 and 1847-48. Washington college, Washington, Pa., was the alma mater of John K. Melhorn, A. B. He matriculated as a sophomore in the spring of 1848, and received his degree, September, 1850. Chosen as principal at once upon his graduation, for eighteen months he successfully conducted the academy at Circleville, Ohio. During this period he applied himself to theological studies also, and in their further prosecution, entered the Lutheran theological seminary, at Columbus, Ohio, in February, 1852. In June of the same year he was licensed to preach the gospel of the Son of God by the western district synod of Ohio, and, in 1854, at Jefferson, Ohio, was ordained to the office of the ministry by the English district synod of Ohio. His heart rejoiced. The aspiration of many years had been attained. Zealous for his holy vocation, immediately upon his licensure, at the close of June 1852, the Rev. John K. Melhorn accepted the call of Jacob's church, Fayette county, Pa., at a salary of $250 per annum, and began his pastorate, which continued for thirteen years. He preached every alternate Sunday also at Morris Cross Roads, where he organized a congregation and erected a church. For several years previous to 1861 he also served Zion and Bethel congregations, in Washington county, Pa., which he then gave up to take charge of four congregations in Preston county, W. Va. In this parish, at Crab Orchard, he built a church, and at Hazel Run organized a congregation. Reverend Melhorn's charges were far apart and his parishioners greatly scattered. Much of his time by day and by night was necessarily passed in the saddle, visiting the sick, attending funerals and weddings, and conducting church services frequently three and four times in the week. When ministering to the Jacob's church and affiliated fields, he traveled at least 65,000 miles on horseback, in these thirteen most laborious, yet very useful and fruitful years in the Master's service. In 1865 he took charge of the Freeport parish, Armstrong Co., Pa. Here he labored for six years, organizing the St. Mark's congregation, Springdale, Allegheny county, and St. Luke's, Saxonburg, Butler county; erecting a church for each of these congregations, and also one for St. Paul's, Sarversville, Butler Co., Pa. For eighteen years, from 1871, Reverend Melhorn was pastor of Grace Lutheran church, South Side, Pittsburg. While in this parish, on the alternate Sundays, for thirteen years, he served also St. John's, Homestead, Pa., which congregation he organized, and for which he built a church. For six years, from June, 1889, Reverend Melhorn had charge in Armstrong county, Pa., of St. John's, St. Matthew's, and Zion's or Fork's church; for Zion's he erected a new house of worship. In 1895, at the earnest request of the missionary president of the Pittsburg synod, the Allegheny mission came under his care. Here he cleared the church at Tarentum from debt, and erected a neat brick church for the congregation at Natrona. With the close of 1901, Reverend Melhorn retired from the regular pastoral work, but has been engaged almost continuously in pulpit duties for various parishes. At St. John's church, Homestead, Pa., where he is passing the evening of his days, on June 2, 1902, his brethren in the ministry held services to fitly commemorate the fiftieth anniversary of his work as a pastor. In this half century he preached 6,868 sermons, administered 950 baptisms, received 1,604 to full church membership, solemnized 468 marriages, officiated at 650 funerals, built 8 churches and organized 5 congregations. Reverend Melhorn has been honored by election to positions of trust and responsibility in the church. For three years he was president of the Pittsburg synod of the Evangelical

Lutheran church; for thirteen years he was missionary president of that body; for ten years he was a trustee of Thiel college, under the care of the same synod; for over thirty years he has been a member of the board of visitors to the Orphans' home and farm school, Zelienople, Pa. His upright figure, quick step and ringing voice yet indicate the vigorous constitution with which he is blessed. Careful in all his pulpit preparations, most faithful in his pastoral duties, of positive faith and strong conviction, Reverend Melhorn earnestly and fearlessly presents the divine message, and sends it home to the hearts and consciences of his hearers. He holds a high and honored place in the confidence and esteem of the churches and of his brethren in the sacred office. Reverend Melhorn and Miss Isabella C. Hill were joined in holy wedlock, July 2, 1852. Miss Hill was born in Washington county, Pa. Ten children blessed their home: Sarah Elizabeth, William Edwin, John Passavant, Eliza Estelle, May L. Zoe, Jennie Florence, Anna Bella, Minnie Etta, Charles Porterfield Krauth and Robert Samuel. At the residence of their daughter, Mrs. F. W. Hirt, at Erie, Pa., in July, 1902, Rev. and Mrs. Melhorn celebrated their golden wedding anniversary. Of Reverend Melhorn's fellow-students at the Erie academy, the Rev. A. H. Caughey, Hon. James Sill and Gen. D. B. McCreary shared the happy occasion. Eight children yet live, and children's children increase the joy and multiply the happiness of the long wedded years of the Rev. and Mrs. Melhorn.

WILLIAM WEIGLE was born in Fayette City, Pa., in 1852, son of John and Anna (Redlingshoefer) Weigle. When he was two years of age, the family moved to Brownsville, Pa., where he received his education. In 1874 he moved to Elizabeth, where he has since resided. Mr. Weigle was for several years employed by J. Walton & Co., and in 1884 he, with his brothers, leased the property in Elizabeth, which they have owned since 1892. In 1896 they began building marine ways, and organized a company called the Elizabeth marine ways company, under charter granted by the State of Pennsylvania. The company was organized with the following officers: President, W. W. O'Neal; secretary and treasurer, W. J. Kassidy; general manager, William Weigle; yard superintendents, John and Philip Weigle. The company builds all kinds of barges and steamboats to ply on western waters. Under the able management of Mr. Weigle, the company has steadily grown from a small concern employing thirty men to one requiring a working force of 250 men. The saw-mill in connection has a sawing capacity of 25,000 to 30,000 feet of lumber a day. In 1898 the business was sold to the Monongahela River consolidated coal and coke company, who have retained Mr. Weigle as manager. Mr. Weigle was married, in 1874, to Miss Anna Storer, daughter of Henry and Anna (Hutchinson) Storer. Mr. and Mrs. Weigle have had eight children, as follows: George J.; Blanche, now Mrs. Saul Walker, of Elizabeth; Helen, who married J. C. Warner, of Elizabeth; Lillian, Ward D., Sarah V., John William (deceased) and Lucile. Mr. Weigle is a Methodist in religious belief, and in politics a democrat. He is a member of the Monongahela lodge, No. 209, Independent Order of Odd Fellows, of Elizabeth, and McKeesport lodge, No. 136, B. P. O. Elks.

EVAN BEEDLE, who operates the leading general store at Jones' Station, Allegheny Co., Pa., is what might aptly be termed "a man of affairs." He is the son of Edward and Margaret (Humphrey) Beedle, and was born in Wales, in 1835. Coming to this country at the age of sixteen years, he worked in the coal mines about McKeesport, where the family settled, until 1867, when he located at Jones' Station and opened a general store. He still conducts this business, which has grown to be one of the leading mercantile establishments of the whole section, and in the meantime has owned and operated the Coal Bluff and Hillsdale mines, near Hillsdale, in Washington county and the Little Redstone mines in Fayette county, and carried on a general real estate and loan business. In 1900 he sold out his mining interests and since that time has devoted his time and attention to his mercantile and real estate operations. He is a director in the First National bank of West Elizabeth, and treasurer of the Monongahela Valley brewing company. He was married, in 1858, to Miss Sarah Ann Hodson, daughter of William and Charlotte Hodson, of Allegheny county.

To this union were born fifteen children, of whom the living are: William G., born April 10, 1859, now living in Union township, Washington Co., Pa.; Charlotte J., born Oct. 18, 1860, now Mrs. George Maurer, of Clairton; Sarah Ann, born Oct. 29, 1865, and now the wife of Roll Latta, of McKeesport; Stephen, born Oct. 18, 1869, now of Homestead, Pa.; John M., born Oct. 10, 1871, now living in Clairton; Margaret C., born Nov. 18, 1873, now the wife of E. P. Jones, of Jones' Station; Edward Watson, born Sept. 26, 1875, now living in Elizabeth; Henry R., born Sept. 23, 1879, and now living in Clairton; Evan C., born Sept. 22, 1884, still at home with his parents. Mr. Beedle is a republican in politics but has never been a candidate for public office, preferring to apply his talents to the upbuilding of his private undertakings. It must not be inferred from this that he is remiss in his duties as a citizen, for he takes a great interest in the election of good men to office and the proper conduct of public affairs.

ELMER A. SCHUETZ is senior member of the firm of the Herald printing company, publishers and editors of the Sharpsburg and Etna Herald, at Sharpsburg, Pa. The Herald was established in 1878, Mr. Schuetz becoming the proprietor in 1895, and since that time the paper has been greatly improved and its circulation has steadily increased. The company also does a large job printing business and has established a wide reputation for fine work. Elmer A. Schuetz was born in Etna, in 1869, and is a son of Michael and Magdaline (Miller) Schuetz. Michael Schuetz died in 1871, and Mrs. Schuetz supported herself and five children by conducting a millinery store. Of the children, Sophie R. died in 1886 and Sarah L. in 1895; Edward A. and Elmer A. conduct the Herald printing company, and Charley is a traveling salesman living at Aspinwall, Pa. Elmer A. Schuetz married Anna M., a daughter of John L. Rolshouse, who was for many years superintendent of the poor farm and ex-burgess of Sharpsburg. Mr. and Mrs. Schuetz have two children, Isabel Magdaline, past three years old, and Elmer Bernard, several months old, both very bright and interesting children. Mrs. Schuetz is a member of the Presbyterian church. Mr. Schuetz is a member of the Zeredatha lodge, Free and Accepted Masons, and in religion affiliates with the Baptist church. Edward A. Schuetz, junior member of the Herald printing company, is a brother of Elmer A., and entered the firm in 1903. Prior to this he was for fourteen years engaged in the manufacture of varnish. He was born in Etna in 1865 and has spent his life in the vicinity. He was married to Annie Olinda, a daughter of George W. Hahn, who was for many years purchasing agent of the H. J. Heinz company, of Pittsburg, and to them have been born two children, Edward A., now thirteen years of age, and Glen Hani, three years old. In religious belief Mr. Schuetz is a Baptist, and Mrs. Schuetz affiliates with the Presbyterians.

W. B. ALTER, of Hoboken, Pa., the leading merchant of that city, was born in Harrison township, Allegheny county, on Nov. 10, 1850, and is the son of S. R. and Hanna (Beale) Alter, the former being a well-known farmer of German descent. W. B. Alter was educated in the common schools of Allegheny county and for one term attended the Mount Union college. When sixteen years of age he left school and began his business career as an employe of a grocery house in Washington county. For three years he was manager of the store of J. S. Neale, and then engaged in the grocery business at California, Pa., where he met with much success until 1889, when he removed to Allegheny city. One year later he removed to a farm in Harrison township, where he prospered for a number of years, and in 1898 came to Hoboken and opened his present store. He is the leading merchant of Hoboken and enjoys a splendid patronage. He was married, in 1872, to Anna, daughter of Capt. William and Katharine McFall, and they had one daughter, Lillian, who is now the wife of H. R. Gardner, an office employe of the Consolidated glass company. He was married, the second time, to Mary J. McFall, of California, Pa. He is a member and steward of the Methodist church, superintendent of the Sunday-school and president of the local branch of the Epworth league. He is a member of the Odd Fellows, the Junior Order of United American Mechanics and of the republican party. Mr. Alter has been prominently connected with the public affairs of his community, having served three years as wharfmaster of California, auditor several terms, justice of the peace, being elected on the prohibition ticket, and was elected a school director of O'Hara township in 1903. Mr. Alter is one of the leading men of that community and possesses the esteem and respect of all who know him.

AMOS FRYER, who has for many years been a furniture dealer and undertaker of Bridgeville, Allegheny Co., Pa., was born in that county, May 11, 1847, and is a descendant of one of the oldest families in western Pennsylvania. The Fryers are of Scotch-Irish stock. The first of the family to come to America was Leonard Fryer, the grandfather of Amos, who came at a very early day from County Down, Ireland, and soon after his arrival in this country settled in Allegheny county. While serving in the army, he was wounded in a fight with the Indians near Cincinnati, Ohio. At the expiration of his term of enlistment, he walked from Cincinnati to Washington city to get his pay. Leonard Fryer married Ellen Porter, and they were the parents of thirteen children. The seventh son, Samuel, was the father of Amos Fryer, the subject of this sketch. He was born in 1803 and died in 1883. His wife's maiden name was Julia Abbott, whose family was among the Pennsylvania pioneers. Samuel and Julia Fryer were the parents of seven children, six of whom grew to maturity. Amos was educated in the common schools of Upper St. Clair township, after which he attended a business college in the city of Pittsburg, where he received a thorough commercial training. For generations the Fryers have been farmers, though Amos' father spent the last years of his life as a miller. Amos worked with his father on the farm until his twenty-seventh year, when he went into the undertaking business. For a time he conducted a lumber trade in connection, but about 1892 he sold out his lumber interests and put a stock of furniture in its place. Since then he has successfully carried on the business of furniture dealer and undertaker, in which he has built up a large patronage. Mr. Fryer is a member of Bridgeville lodge, No. 396, Independent Order of Odd Fellows, and of Chartiers Valley lodge, No. 840, Royal Arcanum. In politics he is a stalwart republican and is an active supporter of the principles of his party. For several terms he has served as school director, a position he holds at the present time. On Jan. 29, 1882, he was married to Miss Carrie J. Conrad, a daughter of Philip and Catherine Conrad. Her father was of German and her mother of Scotch-Irish descent. Mrs. Fryer was born in Armstrong county, Pa., Sept. 19, 1857. After attending the common and high schools of her native county, she was engaged for several years prior to her marriage as a teacher. To Amos and Carrie Fryer eight children have been born, six of whom are still living. They are Samuel Blake, Philip Blaine, Edna Catherine, Amos Ralph, Arthur Mealy and Elizabeth Irene. Margaret Dalzell and Harold Cook are deceased. Mr. and Mrs. Fryer are both members of the Presbyterian church.

JAMES E. KARNS, postmaster at Springdale, was born in Allegheny city, Dec. 28, 1827. He traces his ancestry back on his father's side to Francis Karns, who was born in Ireland and came to the United States in 1783. Francis Karns' wife was Margaret (Patten) Karns, also of Irish birth, who died in Butler, Pa., in 1818. A son of Francis Karns, James E. Karns, also of Irish birth, married Jean Wilson, a native of Ireland, and settled in Westmoreland county. Jean (Wilson) Karns was a daughter of Charles Wilson, who came to Westmoreland county before the Revolution. The father of the subject of this sketch was Francis Karns, a native of Butler county, born in 1798, a farmer by vocation, an active whig and republican, and a member of the State legislature in 1835 and 1837. He married Nancy Cowan, a native of Allegheny county, daughter of Joseph and Mary (Thompson) Cowan, the father a native of Franklin county, Pa., and the mother of Scotland. Joseph Thompson was a son of Alexander Thompson, a Scotchman by birth and an early settler in Franklin and Allegheny counties. Francis Karns and wife, the parents of the subject of this sketch, had one son, James E. Karns. Mr. Karns died in 1866 and his wife in 1871. They were members of the United Presbyterian church. James E. Karns, whose name heads this sketch, was educated in the common schools and by private tutor. For two years he was employed in the Apollo iron works, and has for the past eleven years been connected with the Karns manufacturing company, although now retired from active business life. The Karns manufacturing company, which was organized by Mr. Karns and his sons, manufactures all kinds of sheet iron and does a prosperous business. Mr. Karns is a prominent republican in politics, and has been postmaster at Springdale since the beginning of President McKinley's administration. During this time the postoffice has been made a third-class office. Mr. Karns was married, in 1852, to Miss Nancy Patterson, daughter of John and Mary (Oldfield) Patterson, early settlers of Allegheny county. The Pattersons are of an old family, the early members of which came to America prior to the Revolution, and Mrs. Karns is a descendant of John Brisbin, of Revolutionary war fame. Mr. and Mrs. Karns have had ten children, of whom six are living, as follows: John F., Isabel D., Elizabeth P., James H., Edward A. and Mott F. The deceased are: Mary W., George W., Nancy V. and William T. John F., Edward A. and James H. are members of the Karns manufacturing company. The firm employs about eight men. The Karns family are members of the United Presbyterian church.

WILLIAM KING, dealer in general merchandise at Buena Vista, Pa., is a native of County Tyrone, Ireland, where he was born in 1864. He is a son of George and Margaret (Ray) King, both of whom were natives of the north of Ireland. His father died in 1902. William was educated in the public schools in County Tyrone, and at the age of eighteen years he came to America, settling in Allegheny city. He found employment in the mines of West Newton and those along the Youghiogheny river, until 1889, when he became a stockholder in and manager of the Industrial co-operative association, which was organized for the purpose of dealing in merchandise of all sorts. The headquarters of the association were located at Buena Vista. In 1895 he purchased the interests of the other stockholders, and the stock, and continued the business under the name of the Industrial supply company. Since that time he has started a branch store at Connellsburg, Pa., and both the parent establishment and the branch are doing a good business. Mr. King was married, in 1886, to Miss Lizetta Kent, of Philadelphia, and to this union there have been born seven children: James William, in 1887; Frederick Hastings, in 1889; Clyde, in 1891; Elizabeth Margaret, in 1894; George Raymond, in 1896; Harold Lewellyn, in 1899, and Hazel Arabella, in 1901. He is an elder in the United Presbyterian church, and in politics is a republican, though he has never held a public office.

JAMES A. McDOWELL (deceased), of Tarentum, Pa., prominently connected for many years with the farming interests of Fawn township, was born on May 1, 1826, in Mifflin township, Allegheny Co., Pa., son of William and Hannah (Walker) McDowell, the former a native of Ireland and a son of Archibald and Jane McDowell. The mother was a native of Scotland, and the daughter of William and Mary Walker, natives of Scotland, who came to Mifflin township at an early day, and there lived and died. Archibald McDowell, the paternal grandfather of James A. McDowell, was born in Ireland, and was the son of John and Ann McDowell, who came to Mifflin township in 1810. James A. McDowell was reared on the farm, educated in the common schools, and when a young man began the life of a farmer in his native township. In 1859 he came to Fawn township, purchased seventy-five acres of land and farmed with much success until his death, on April 10, 1886. He was married, on Nov. 26, 1857, to Elizabeth, daughter of Robert and Ellen (Stewart) Jack, both natives of Ireland, who settled in Westmoreland county and there spent the rest of their lives. Mrs. McDowell died on Nov. 14, 1894, and was the mother of four children: William S., born Aug. 31, 1858, educated in the common schools, and is a successful farmer; Mary E., born in 1860, in Fawn township, and since the death of her mother has presided over the household affairs of her brothers; an infant, born Nov. 1, 1862; Robert W., born in Fawn township, June 3, 1864, educated in the common schools, and is a prosperous farmer. William S., Mary E. and Robert W. jointly own the old homestead, and are among the leading people of the vicinity.

W. F. RUSSELL, who conducts a livery and undertaking business in the town of Bridgeville, is a native of Washington county, Pa., where he was born May 5, 1866. For several generations the Russell family has been identified with the growth and progress of the Keystone State. About the middle of the eighteenth century Andrew Russell, a young Scotchman, married Isabel Mays, a native of Ireland, and, in 1758, the couple came to America, settling near Oxford, Chester Co., Pa. This Andrew Russell was the great-grandfather of the subject of this sketch. He was a blacksmith by trade, and followed that occupation all his life. Ten children—three sons and seven daughters—were born to him and his wife while living in Chester county. The sons were: Alexander, Robert and Andrew, Jr. The daughters were: Polly, Jane, Peggy, Hannah, Ibby, Lydia and Betsy. After the birth of their youngest child, they removed to Washington county, Pa., locating about four miles southeast of the town of Cannonsburg, where they lived until 1782, when they changed their residence to Chartiers township, in the same county, and there passed the remainder of their lives. He died on June 20, 1814, aged eighty-two years, his wife having previously died, May 5, 1802, at the age of seventy-three. Alexander, the oldest son of Andrew and Isabel Russell, was a musician, and during the war of the Revolution was a fife major in the American army. His death occurred on April 20, 1784, when he was but twenty-six years of age. Andrew Russell, Jr., the youngest son of the family and the grandfather of W. F., was born on Jan. 30, 1777. Contemporary with these early representatives of the Russell family were the McClellands, who also came from Scotland. Andrew Russell, Jr., married Ann McClelland, the daughter of James and Jane (Guthrie) McClelland, who were married in Scotland in 1776, and came to America the following year. Jane McClelland died on Feb. 15, 1824, aged seventy-five years. Her husband survived her for about five years, departing this life on May 1, 1829, in the eighty-second year of his age. Ann McClelland was born in 1781 and was married to Andrew Russell in 1801. Both lived to a good old age. He died on March 2, 1861, at the age of eighty-four, and she passed away on Feb. 17, 1868, in her eighty-seventh year.

Both were highly respected in the community where they lived. From 1832 until his death Andrew Russell was a ruling elder in the United Presbyterian church. Their children were thirteen in number, viz.: A daughter, who died in infancy; Andrew, who died at the age of five years; Jane, James, Isabel, Ann, Elizabeth, Andrew, Alexander, Robert H., John, Nancy and William M. William M. Russell, the youngest child of the family and father of W. F., was born in Washington county, Pa., in 1826. In his younger days he followed the occupation of a druggist, but the greater part of his life was spent as a tiller of the soil. In 1865 he was elected ruling elder of the Hickory United Presbyterian church, and served as such until he left the neighborhood. In 1855 he was married to Miss Margaret Jane, daughter of Joseph and Margaret (Wilson) Thompson. To this union ten children were born. Their names and the dates of their births are as follows: Joseph A., born Aug. 8, 1856, and died in infancy; Annie E., born April 19, 1858; Joseph T., born Sept. 19, 1859; Maggie W., born June 25, 1862; L. A., born June 15, 1863; Harriet J., born May 14, 1865; W. F., the subject of this sketch; James Nevin, born Nov. 23, 1869; Mary Belle, born Nov. 23, 1869, and Robert Lee, born Dec. 11, 1872. During his boyhood, W. F. lived the life common to boys on the farm. At the age of thirteen years he began the study of telegraphy and soon became a competent operator. After twenty years of active service in the employ of the Pennsylvania railroad company, he gave up the "sounder" and embarked in his present business. He has recently erected a commodious brick building, in which he has one of the best-appointed livery stables in Allegheny county. Ever since he became a voter, Mr. Russell has been a republican, and he takes an active interest in all matters touching the public welfare. He has served on the school board and as auditor of his township. Two years ago he was elected on the republican ticket to the office of justice of the peace for Bridgeville borough, and is now discharging the functions of that office to the entire satisfaction of the community. In church matters Mr. Russell has followed the example of his honored ancestors, and is a member of the United Presbyterian church. Three of his uncles were prominent in the ministry of that denomination. One was the pastor of the Fifty-third street church in New York city at the time of his death; another was for some time in charge of a large congregation in Boston, Mass., and the third occupied for ten years the pulpit of the Hickory church, in Washington county, Pa. For the past twelve years Mr. Russell has been one of the trustees of the Bridgeville Presbyterian church. In his church work and relations he has the full sympathy and support of his wife, to whom he was married on Nov. 3, 1885. She was Miss Jennie B. Galbraith, a daughter of Robert M. and Teresa Galbraith, of Burgettstown, Pa. Mrs. Russell was born at Cross Creek, Washington Co., Pa., Oct. 18, 1867. Mr. and Mrs. Russell are the parents of six children. The oldest son, Frank, is now seventeen years of age. He has taken a course in embalming and is now associated with his father in the undertaking business. Robert G., the second son, is fourteen years old and is the bookkeeper for his father. The other children are: Teresa, aged eleven; William, aged nine; Guy C., aged six, and Jennie Isabel, who is still in her first year. Mr. Russell is a member of Bridgeville lodge, No. 396, Independent Order of Odd Fellows, and holds the office of secretary of the lodge. In his fraternal relations he is highly respected, and he is generally regarded as a useful member of the community.

THOMAS W. BAIRD, of Port Vue, Pa., burgess of that borough and a valued employe of the National tube works, was born near Glasgow, Scotland, July 8, 1869, son of Alexander and Margaret (Waldie) Baird, natives of Scotland. His father is a successful blacksmith, and, in 1887, brought his family to America, landing in New York, and subsequently locating at McKeesport, where he has since prospered at his trade. Mr. Baird was educated in the public schools of Scotland and at the Grissley business college, of McKeesport, and in 1903 was graduated from the Scranton school of correspondence. Mr. Baird has held the important position of foreman of the National tube works for the past eight years, and prior to that served as shipping clerk in the works of that concern. He was married, on Sept. 5, 1897, to Catherine, daughter of John and Catherine Forrest, of Scotland, and they have two children, Catherine and Douglas O. Mr. Baird is the present burgess of Port Vue, having been elected for a three-year term on Feb. 17, 1903, and is making a fine record in that important position. Mr. Baird is a member of the Knights of Pythias and the Scottish clan, of McKeesport, and is a man who possesses the respect and esteem of all who know him.

JACOB G. VOGELEY, who died June 22, 1903, was one of Tarentum's representative and most progressive business men. He was born in Butler county, Sept. 24, 1853, and educated in the public schools and at Wetherspoon institute. At the age of twenty-one he went to California, where he spent seven years as a clerk, and returning to Pennsylvania, secured employment in the firm of Boggs & Buhl, in Allegheny. In 1883 he began his long and successful business career in Tarentum, where he soon proved to all that he was the embodiment of those qualities which go to make up a noble man. Mr. Vogeley was the son of George Vogeley, who was born in Germany, Nov. 11, 1824, and came to Pittsburg in 1836 with his parents, George and Mary (Mardof) Vogeley. They moved shortly to Butler, where they spent their last days, while the son, George Vogeley, father of Jacob G., remained in Pittsburg, where he learned the tobacco business. He worked in Pittsburg until 1846, was in business for a short time in Kittanning and Bridgewater, and from 1849 until his death, in 1896, was in the tobacco business in Butler. George Vogeley was married in Allegheny city to Mary E. Gass, who was born in Allegheny in 1831. She was a daughter of Jacob and Amelia Gass, pioneers of Allegheny county. Jacob Gass, Jr., was a native of Switzerland, emigrating to this country in 1812, where he became a farmer and a carpet and coverlet weaver. His farm embraced the present site of the P. & Ft. W. R. R. depot in Allegheny. George and Mary E. (Gass) Vogeley were the parents of nine children, of whom six are living, two having died in infancy, and one, a son, while a resident of Butler. Mr. Vogeley was a republican, and for a number of years director of the poor in Butler. He and his wife were members of the Presbyterian church. Mr. Jacob G. Vogeley, subject of this sketch, was a man of wide experience in various lines of business. He was a stockholder in the Fidelity glass company, the Tarentum glass company, the J. H. Baker manufacturing company, the National bank of Tarentum, and the Tarentum savings and trust company, being a director in the last-named company. Mr. Vogeley was a republican in politics, and although not an aspirant for office, had served nine years as school director. He was a member of Pollock lodge, No. 502, F. and A. M.; Tarentum lodge, No. 587, I. O. O. F.; the Royal Arcanum and Heptasophs. Mr. Vogeley was married, in 1882, to Annie C. Wohllet, of Tarentum, a native of Philadelphia, and to them were born three children: Charles G., born June 16, 1883; Lillian P., born Aug. 28, 1885, and Edna L., born Dec. 4, 1890. In religious belief the family is Presbyterian.

SAMUEL P. WOODSIDE, a resident of Ben Avon, son of Hugh and Mary (Paisley) Woodside, was born in Allegheny city, Sept. 16, 1860, and educated in the public schools of Allegheny city and Newell's institute, Pittsburg. He began his business career in 1878 in the car record office of the Pennsylvania railroad company, under Charles L. Cole, of Pittsburg. In April, 1880, he entered the service of the general agent of the Erie railroad, holding this position till Feb. 1, 1884, when for a short time he acted as claim clerk for the Pittsburg & Western railroad. On June 1, 1884, he was appointed agent for the Globe fast freight line, of Pittsburg, and on Feb. 1, 1885, became auditor for the same line in Buffalo, N. Y. Then for a few months Mr. Woodside took up the real estate business with James W. Drape & Co., of Pittsburg, returning to the railroad in September, 1885, as contracting freight agent of the Erie railroad. For a year after that he held the same office for the B. & O. railroad, returning again to the Erie railroad as general agent, where he remained until August, 1902. He is now traffic manager of the Pittsburg coal company. Mr. Woodside was married, Sept. 16, 1885, to Elizabeth W. Walker, and to them have been born four children: S. P., Jr., Isabelle V., Mary E., and Anna N. The Woodside family is of Scotch-Irish descent, the paternal side leaving Scotland for Ireland about 1610 and settling at the Stroan, County Antrim. The father landed in Philadelphia in 1845, and moved to Pittsburg in the early fifties. Hugh Woodside, father of the subject of this sketch, was born in County Antrim, Ireland, in 1826. His parents were Robert and Elizabeth (Nevin) Woodside. Hugh was their fifth child, and left the parental roof for America in company with his brother, now Rev. John S. Woodside, of India. He married Mary Jane Paisley, a native of Pittsburg, and the fruit of this marriage was five sons and one daughter. His wife died March 19, 1886, and two of his sons are also deceased, leaving three sons, Samuel, Nevin and Hugh, and one daughter, Anna, now Mrs. Harwood, still living. Mr. Woodside was a singularly pure-minded, industrious and honorable man. He was a member of the Presbyterian church and active in its work. He was connected with different industries and held positions of importance and trust. Mary Jane Woodside, mother of the subject of this sketch, was the daughter of Samuel and Mary (Graham) Paisley, born June 16, 1834, and died March 19, 1886. She was also a Presbyterian in her religious belief.

J. H. METZLER, of Tarentum, Pa., a prosperous sheet steel roller, was born in Armstrong county, Pa., Sept. 5, 1863, son of Samuel and Elizabeth Metzler, the father a native of Tennessee, and the mother born in the Keystone State. They were married in Armstrong county, Pa., removed south and later returned north, the father now living in Westmoreland county, the mother having died in 1898. His father served throughout the Civil war and in later life has been a farmer and boatman. J. H. Metzler, the youngest of seven children, was reared on a farm and educated in the common schools and the high school of Leechburg. He was actively engaged in the oil business from 1882 to 1892, visiting all the leading oil fields of the United States, traveling in sixteen states in all. He then began to learn the trade of steel rolling at Harrisburg, Pa., and later went to Apollo, Pa., starting at the very bottom, and is now a skilled and experienced steel roller. He was employed at Apollo, Leechburg, Vandergrift, Cummings and other places, and in 1901 came to Tarentum, where he is now in the employ of the Allegheny steel and iron company. He is an active republican in political matters and served as constable in Vandergrift, and as tax collector in Armstrong county. He is closely identified with a number of the leading fraternal orders, holding membership in the Masons, the Knights of Pythias and the Royal Arcanum. He was married, on Jan. 17, 1893, to Dora May, daughter of Philip and Katurah (Baker) Young, all natives of Blair county, Pa., where Mrs. Metzler's parents now reside. Mr. Young is prominently identified with the public affairs of his community, and has served for nine years as steward of the Blair county almshouse. A brother of Mrs. Metzler, Hays B. Young, served in the artillery during the Spanish-American war and was also in the regular army for one year. Mr. and Mrs. Metzler are members of Trinity Evangelical Lutheran church and have one son, Randolph M.

CONRAD HUTH, of Natrona, Pa., proprietor of the River Avenue hotel and a well-known and prosperous citizen, was born in Germany, Feb. 2, 1850, son of Andrew and Margaret (Rommel) Huth, both natives of Germany, who came to America in 1874, settled in Allegheny city, and resided there until their deaths in 1877 and 1895, respectively. The elder Huth was a prominent contractor in the Fatherland, but on coming to Allegheny city, retired from active business and lived quietly until his death. They had a family of six children, four of whom are now living. Conrad Huth was reared and educated in his native country and in 1869 came to Massillon, Ohio, where he worked in a brewery for a short time. In 1870 he came to Pittsburg, where he worked at the coopers' trade for twelve years, and with the exception of two and one-half years spent at Freeport, has since resided in Allegheny county. He worked at his trade for different concerns, in 1883 engaged in business on his own account, and in 1897 purchased the hotel which he now conducts and which is known as the River Avenue hotel. Mr. Huth is a man of affairs, being a stockholder in the James H. Baker manufacturing company, of Harrison township, and a stockholder and director in the First National bank of Natrona. Mr. Huth came to America with nothing but a large stock of ability, integrity and energy, has found that these commodities are valuable assets in the western hemisphere, and to-day he is prosperous and well established. He was married, on July 21, 1878, to Bertha Fuhrman, a native of Germany, who came to America with her parents, Frank and Anna Fuhrman, and has since resided in Pennsylvania. They have eight children, viz.: Agnes, Mary, Annie, Conrad, John, Rosa, Katie and Loretta. Mr. Huth and his wife are members of the Catholic church, and are prominent in the social affairs of Natrona.

JOHN SHIELDS, of Emblem, Pa., a valued employe of the Osceola coal company and a well-known citizen of that place, was born in Scotland, April 14, 1846, and is the son of Thomas and Margaret (Walker) Shields, natives of Scotland, who came to America in 1848, when their son was but a small child. Mr. Shields was educated in the public schools of Allegheny county, and then devoted his attention to coal-mining until 1877, when he went with the Osceola coal company, and has since held an important position with that concern. Mr. Shields is prominent in the republican party, and for four years served as auditor of Elizabeth township, in which capacity he made a fine record and fully justified the confidence of his neighbors and friends who placed him in that responsible office.

JOHN D. ROBB, one of the leading citizens of North Fayette township, is a native of Allegheny county, where he was born on May 19, 1839. His parents were Joseph and Sarah (Rosenberry) Robb, the former of whom was born in Allegheny county, in 1809, and the latter in Washington county, July 4, 1816. They were married on June 13, 1837, and had two children, the subject of this sketch and a daughter, Elizabeth, who was born on June 16, 1838, and died on the 18th of the following August. Joseph Robb met with an untimely death by being caught under a large log as it was rolling down hill. After the death of his father, John went with his mother to Washington county, where they lived for six years and then returned to Allegheny county. Mr. Robb has continued a resident of the county since that time, living on the farm where he was born, and which he inherited from his father. His first education was received in the common schools of North Fayette township, after which he attended, for several terms, the Wilkinsburg academy in the city of Pittsburg. The republican majority in Pennsylvania has become proverbial in the political annals of the country. Mr. Robb is one of those who can always be relied on to sustain that majority, as he has been a consistent member of the party ever since he attained the age of a voter. Mr. Robb has been twice married. His first wife was Miss Eliza McMurry, who was born on Aug. 7, 1838, and became Mrs. Robb on March 19, 1863. She bore her husband six children, viz.: Harry, born Jan. 10, 1864; Sarah Addie, July 25, 1865; William McMurry, March 3, 1867, and died March 9, 1873; Margaret, June 27, 1868; Elizabeth, March 8, 1870, and Joseph Wilson, Aug. 3, 1875, who lived but nine days. Eliza Robb passed to her final rest on Dec. 18, 1880, and on March 23, 1898, Mr. Robb married his second wife, Mrs. Sarah Young (née Hopper), a daughter of Robert and Abigail (Hickman) Hopper. She was born on Sept. 19, 1847, and was married to her first husband, William H. Young, on Feb. 2, 1882. He died on Sept. 4, 1893. Mr. and Mrs. Robb are both members of the Oakdale Presbyterian church, the present pastor of which is Rev. James Majunkin. Margaret Robb, the fourth child of John and Eliza Robb, was married, Oct. 2, 1895, to James G. Hopper, and died Nov. 29, 1903.

REV. JOHN HICKEY, rector of St. Thomas' congregation at Braddock, was born in Kilkenny, Ireland, on Nov 11, 1834. When he was twelve years of age, he came with his parents to the United States, and it was in this country principally that he has been educated. At the age of fourteen, he entered St. Michael seminary, but on account of too close application to study, his health became impaired to such an extent that he was obliged to return to the residence of his maternal uncle, Rev. Joseph Cody, at Sugar Creek, Armstrong county, where he remained three years. Under the advice of the Rt. Rev. Michael O'Conner, then bishop of the Pittsburg diocese, he took up the study of Latin and German in St. Vincent's college, and prepared for Mount St. Mary's college, at Emmitsburg, Md., from which he received his A. M. in 1855. After a three years' course in theology, he was ordained to the priesthood by Bishop O'Conner, in St. Paul's cathedral, Pittsburg, in 1858, and in the fall of the same year was recalled by his alma mater as professor of belles lettres, a position which he filled with much distinction for one year. In 1860 Father Hickey succeeded Doctor O'Conner as assistant professor in St. Michael's diocesan seminary, two years later took temporary charge of a church at Freeport, and the following year became rector of the cathedral at Pittsburg. While in this charge he finished building the cathedral, erected the present episcopal residence, established the parishes of St. Malachy, St. Agnes and St. James, and founded an orphan asylum with accommodations for 600 children. Father Hickey remained at the cathedral for fourteen years, filling the offices of rector, vicar-general and several times administrator of the diocese during the absence of the bishop. In the summer of 1879 he went abroad, visiting Rome and other parts of Europe for three years, and on his return was appointed to his present position. In 1883 he built a schoolhouse large enough for 1,000 children, and has done many other things for the spreading of the gospel and the higher education of the people. Father Hickey has been offered positions of greater remuneration and with larger congregations, but through the love he bears the people and the love they bear him, both Catholic and Protestant, he refuses, and still serves the parishoners of Braddock. During the labor troubles at the Edgar Thompson steel works, he took such an interest in the welfare of the working classes as to endear himself to all.

RALEIGH RUSSELL HUGGINS, M. D., of Sharpsburg, Pa., a well-known physician, was born in Marietta, Ohio, Oct. 1, 1870, and is the son of Jason and Margaret (Hart) Huggins, both of whom are still living. His father was for many years a dealer in lumber, but has now retired and lives with his son at Sharpsburg. Dr. Huggins was educated at the Marietta academy and college, and when eighteen years of age entered the Miami medical college at Cincinnati, Ohio, and was graduated from that institution in 1891. The same year he came to Sharpsburg and began the practice of his profession, with his office at the corner of Thirteenth and Main streets. One year later he removed to his present office at No. 1314 Middle St., and also has an office in the Smith block in Pittsburg. He is a member of Grace M. E. church of Sharpsburg, the Heptasophs, and is a thirty-second degree Mason. He is also a member of the Allegheny Valley medical society, the Allegheny County medical society, the State medical association, the Pittsburg academy of medicine, and the American medical association. He is a member of the republican party, but has persistently refused all offers of political preferment. Dr. Huggins is justly regarded as an able and skilled physician and possesses the confidence of the entire community.

THOMAS W. BARKER, of Tarentum, Pa., prominently identified with the agricultural interests of Fawn township, was born in Allegheny county, Pa., Jan. 31, 1852, son of Thomas and Dorothy (Poritt) Barker, both natives of England. Thomas Barker, Sr., came to America with his parents, Thomas and Anna (Lincoln) Barker, first settled in Ashtabula county, Ohio, and later located in Elizabeth, Pa., where the elder Thomas died in 1848, at the age of seventy-eight years. His wife resided on a farm in Fawn township, now owned by the subject of this sketch, until her death in 1855, aged eighty-three years. They reared a family of seven children, all of whom are now dead. Their son, Thomas, engaged in farming with his brother, William, in 1853, they jointly owning seventy-six acres of land, and continued to farm until his death, Feb. 21, 1889. He was the father of two children: Mary, the wife of Robert Dawson, and Thomas W., the subject of this sketch. Thomas W. Barker was reared on a farm, educated in the common schools, and has followed farming all his business life, now owning fifty-three acres of the old homestead. He is a general farmer, and has met with much success in that vocation. He is prominently identified with the democratic party, and while he has served several terms as supervisor, he has never sought office. Mr. Barker was married, on March 9, 1880, to Isabel Moore, a native of Butler county and a daughter of James E. and Susan (Ashbaugh) Moore, the former a native of Pittsburg, and the latter of Armstrong county. Mr. and Mrs. Barker are the parents of four children: Margaret E., a milliner, of Pittsburg; Harry M., John K. and Walter O. Mr. Barker is a prosperous and successful farmer, a good citizen, and enjoys the respect and confidence of his neighbors.

WILLIAM H. CLAY, of Boston, Pa., a well-known citizen and a prosperous farmer, was born in Jefferson county, Pa., Oct. 5, 1867, son of Thornton and Mary J. (Pancoast) Clay, his father having been a native of Columbiana county, Ohio, and a member of the borough council and of the school board of Elizabeth, where he died in 1903. Mr. Clay was educated in the schools of Elizabeth, and has devoted his entire business career to farming, first residing on his farm in Lincoln township, and for the past thirteen years on his present place in Elizabeth township. He was married, on Feb. 17, 1892, to Elizabeth J., daughter of Robert and Sarah (Lewis) Kees, of Lincoln township, and they have had four children, three of whom are now living, viz.: Henry, Clyde and Samuel; Mary J. having died when four years of age. Mr. Clay is one of the most prominent men of the township, has served for four years on the school board, of which he is now secretary, and is a member of the republican county executive committee. Mr. Clay is also a member of the Methodist Episcopal church, and takes an active interest in its great work for the betterment and elevation of the human family.

ARISTIDE J. SCHMIDT, of Natrona, Pa., a successful farmer, was born in France, May 17, 1837, son of Xavier and Frances (Tellier) Schmidt, both natives and life residents of France. His father was a farmer in early life, later became a glass-blower, and lived to the age of seventy-nine years. He was the father of twelve children, two of whom are now living. Mr. Schmidt was reared and educated in his native country, there learned the glass-blowers' trade, and when a young man, went to England, where he followed the occupation of a glass-blower for twelve years. In 1866 he came to America and spent thirteen years in the various cities of the United States, engaged in working at his trade. In 1883 he came to Allegheny county, purchased a farm of eighty-four acres in Harrison township, and since has farmed in that location. He was married, on March 11, 1860, to Augustine Epertherner, born in France in 1843, and the daughter of Louis and Augustine (Bregy) Epertherner, both natives of "La Belle France." The Epertherners removed to England, where Mr. Epertherner died in 1868, and Mrs. Epertherner came to Allegheny county in 1882, and there resided until her death in 1900. Mr. Schmidt, his wife and family are members of the Catholic church. Mr. and Mrs. Schmidt are the parents of eleven children, viz.: Augustine, Louisa M., Henrietta L., Josephine P., Aristide H. and Xavier A. (twins), Adele, Emile J., Estelle M., Louis E. and Oscar P. Mr. Schmidt is a prosperous and successful farmer, has reared a large family of fine children, and is a progressive and substantial citizen.

HARRY C. SCOTT, of Glenfield, Pa., a well-known and highly respected citizen, was born in Washington county, Pa., June 16, 1864, son of John and Mary Scott. Mr. Scott was educated in the public schools of Monongahela city, and at an early age began working at the newspaper business, in which line he later secured an agency for the Leader, Chronicle, Telegraph and Times. He prospered in that venture and about 1882 obtained employment as a compositor on the Pittsburg Leader, with which journal he remained for seven years; then for fifteen years was in the employ of a railroad known as the Star Union line, and since that time has been employed in his present responsible position with the prominent real estate firm of Black & Baird. Mr. Scott was married, on Aug. 14, 1887, to Charlotte E., daughter of Charles B. and Anna McCullough, and they have had five children, viz.: Leon F. (deceased), born March 10, 1891; Anna L., born Nov. 1, 1888; Paul P., born May 28, 1893; Thomas G., born May 28, 1896, and Martha P., born Sept. 28, 1900. Mrs. Scott is a most estimable woman and is highly educated, having received both a common and high school course of instruction, and, being of a literary turn, has constantly reviewed her work, and by so doing has kept abreast of the modern and advanced ideas. Mr. Scott is a prominent member of the Presbyterian church of Glenfield, having served in his present position as elder for several years, and takes an active interest in all church affairs. He has been a member of the board of education for the past ten years and also served as clerk of the borough of Glenfield. He is closely identified with the Royal Arcanum and the Heptasophs, and is one of the leading men of Glenfield.

DR. DANIEL G. ROWLEY, a prominent physician of the town of Culmerville, Allegheny county, was born in the county, May 18, 1858, and has practiced medicine for a number of years in Culmerville. His grandfather, Daniel Rowley, was born in Vermont, in 1780, of Revolutionary stock. Upon arriving at the years of manhood, he came to Lockport, Westmoreland Co., Pa., but ten years later removed to the State of Indiana, locating near Indianapolis, and died there in 1840. His wife was a Miss Cheeney, who was born in Vermont in 1785, and died at Freeport, Pa., in 1865. They had seven daughters and one son. One of the daughters, Mrs. Taylor, is still living at the age of eighty, at McKee's Rocks, Pa. The son, Myron H. Rowley, was born in Vermont, Oct. 13, 1805. He removed with his parents to Lockport, and later to Indiana. While living in the latter State he began the study of medicine, and in 1829 graduated from the medical college at Cincinnati, Ohio. After receiving his degree, he located at Millerstown, in Fawn township, Allegheny county, where he practiced medicine for sixty-three years, or until his death, which occurred on July 1, 1897. He was positive in his religious and political views, being a member of the Methodist Episcopal church and the republican party. Dr. Myron Rowley was twice married, the first wife in Indiana when he was but twenty years of age. She bore him two children: William, born in 1826, and died near Norfolk, Va., in 1864, while serving in the army; and Mary, born in 1828, and died in Butler county, Pa., in 1890. His first wife died in 1852, in Allegheny county, and about three years after her death he married his second wife, Margaretta Smith. To this union there were born four children, three daughters and one son, all of whom are still living. The daughters are Paulina A., Sarah B. and Laura J. The son is Dr. Daniel G. Rowley, the subject of this sketch. After acquiring a good education, Dr. Rowley read medicine with his father, and ever since finishing his medical education has practiced his profession in Allegheny county. On Sept. 27, 1893, he was married to Miss Clara A., a daughter of James E. and Nancy (Porter) Hazlett. Her father was born July 18, 1837, and was married to Nancy Porter in 1859. They were the parents of six children, the names and dates of birth of which were: William P., July 29, 1860; Clara A., now Mrs. Rowley, Nov. 8, 1862; George, April 2, 1865; Harry, Dec. 23, 1868; Mary, July 28, 1872, and Eliott, Dec. 10, 1874. Four of these children are still living. Harry died on Nov. 2, 1881, and Eliott on Oct. 28, 1898. Both of Mrs. Rowley's parents are members of the United Presbyterian church. Dr. Rowley and his wife have one son, Myron E., who was born on April 13, 1899. Both are members of the United Presbyterian church, among the members of which they have a large number of friends. Their circle of friends is not limited, however, to the members of their church. To many a home Dr. Rowley has brought comfort and cheer by the exercise of his healing art, and to these homes he is always a welcome visitor, where a chair by the fireside and a plate at the table always await him and his companion.

WILLIAM H. CROUCH, of Port Vue, Pa., a prosperous business man and for many years a well-known justice of the peace, was born in Washington county, Pa., Jan. 9, 1854, son of George and Mary Anne (Sickles) Crouch, his father having been a prominent citizen and manager of the Penney coal company, of near McKeesport. Young Crouch received his education in the common schools, but owing to the stringency of the times was early put to work in the mines, but later in life attended Duff's business college, of Pittsburg, where he was graduated in a commercial course. Mr. Crouch worked at coal-mining at various times for about twenty-five years, and in 1887 purchased a farm in Allegheny county, where he resided for four years. Later he removed to the Edmunson farm in Port Vue borough, and for twelve years has successfully followed dairying and gardening on that place. He was married, on July 3, 1878, to Nannie, daughter of John and Sarah (Mackey)

Smock, of Westmoreland county, and they have five children, viz.: Rena; Sarah, wife of Charles Smith, of Port Vue; Charles, Clyde and Inez. Mr. Crouch was elected a justice of the peace of Port Vue borough and served continuously for ten years, during which time he made a fine record in that difficult position. He has also served as a school director and a member of the council of Port Vue, and for one year was president of the latter body. He is a stanch republican and for several years has served that party as county committeeman. He is a member of the Odd Fellows, the Ancient Order of United Workmen, the Junior Order of United American Mechanics and the Masons, of which latter order he is a Knight Templar and Shriner. Mr. Crouch is also treasurer and manager of the hay, grain and feed department of the contracting firm of D. B. Ault company, on Fourth avenue, McKeesport, and has been connected with that concern for the past two years.

MAURICE McCARTHY, of Elizabeth, Pa., pastor of St. Michael's Roman Catholic church, was born in County Kerry, Ireland, March 21, 1866, son of William and Annie (Costello) McCarthy. Father McCarthy was educated in his native country, attending the national schools of his own county, St. Michael's at Listowel, the University of Dublin and the All Hallows college of Dublin. He was ordained to the priesthood, June 21, 1891, by Bishop Donnelly, of Dublin, and his first appointment was as assistant pastor of St. Mary's church, of New Castle, Pa., he having come to America in September, 1891. He continued at New Castle until Jan. 6, 1896, when he took charge of St. Michael's church of Elizabeth, and since has filled that pulpit with ardor and ability. This church has a membership of about 100 families, is one of the oldest in the diocese, and on Sept. 29, 1892, celebrated its golden jubilee with solemn and appropriate ceremonies, which were attended by all the priests of the diocese. James G. Blaine, "the plumed knight," was once a member of its congregation, and the remains of his sister are now interred in the churchyard. Father McCarthy is also in charge of a new church that is being erected at Clairton, Pa., ground for which was broken on May 20, 1903, and it is expected that the church and parochial school will cost $50,000.

R. H. BAXTER, of Glassport, Pa., manager and treasurer of the Glassport lumber company, was born in Westmoreland county, Pa., Nov. 5, 1868, and is the son of William A. and Harriett M. Baxter. Mr. Baxter was educated in the primary branches in the public schools of Burrell township, and completed his literary training at Parnassus college. On leaving school, Mr. Baxter began to learn the carpenters' trade at Apollo, Pa., to which town his family had removed in 1888. He then went to Homestead for a two-year stay, and later located in Pittsburg, where he made a special study of the building business, while continuing to work at his trade. In 1894 he returned to Apollo; later removed to Vandergrift, where he was engaged in contracting for one year, and then became superintendent of construction for the Vandergrift lumber company, continuing in that capacity until 1900, when he came to Glassport, Pa., as manager and treasurer of the Glassport lumber company, and is also in charge of the Clairton lumber company. Mr. Baxter was married, in 1891, to Mae M. McElroy, and they have one daughter, Helen. Mr. Baxter is a member of the republican party, and is prominently identified with the business and social affairs of the city in which he resides.

THOMAS R. FAWCETT, a brick manufacturer of McKeesport, was born in Birmingham, Allegheny county, Dec. 1, 1835. He obtained a good, practical education in the common schools, and at the age of nineteen went to work on a farm. During the Civil war he served as a private in the 204th regiment, Pennsylvania volunteers, and the 5th Pennsylvania artillery, participating in a number of engagements and receiving an honorable discharge at the close of the war. After peace was restored, he was for twelve years the watchman in the Oliver Bros. wire works at Pittsburg. Since that time he has been engaged in his present occupation. In 1862 he was married to Catherine, daughter of Aaron and Sarah Brindel, of Allegheny county. To this marriage there were born the following children: Christopher L., who is employed by his father in the brick business; Margaret (deceased); William D., a dentist in McKeesport; Elizabeth, wife of George Bonhouse, of Mount Washington; Mary, at home; Thomas Albert and Clarence B. (twins), Harry G. and Walter. Mr. Fawcett is a member of the First Methodist Episcopal church of McKeesport, and Col. John W. Patterson post, No. 151, South Side, Grand Army of the Republic. It is a fact worthy of note that the Fawcett heirs now own the identical spot where General Braddock encamped the night before his historic and fatal defeat.

JOHN C. LITTLE was born in County Tyrone, Ireland, July 29, 1857. His parents, Joseph and Mary A. Little, came to America when John was a boy, and located in Pittsburg, Pa. John attended the third ward public schools of Pittsburg, and at an early age circumstances prompted him to become a wage-earner. While still a lad, he obtained employment in the steel works of Hussey, Howe & Co., in Pittsburg. His first work was on the small train of rolls at the eight-inch mill, and in time he became competent in that line of work. After several years of service at the rolls, he accepted a position in the crucible department of the same firm. Several years' service in this department gave him considerable knowledge of the process of making crucible steel, and when the late Mr. C. Y. Wheeler, who had been manager of the works, purchased a small steel plant at Demmler, Pa., afterwards known as the Sterling steel company, young Little, being ambitious and thinking to enhance his personal opportunities, secured employment with the new concern, which afterwards became world-famous as manufacturer of the Wheeler-Sterling projectile. Mr. Wheeler was the inventor of this projectile, which proved effective in piercing the hardest and toughest of armor plate, eventually destroying Cervera's fleet off Santiago harbor in the Spanish-American war. After several years with this establishment, Mr. Little gave up mill work and accepted a position with Barnes Bros.' Troy laundry, in Pittsburg. This firm sent him to McKeesport, Pa., to look after their interests in that city.

After continuing in the employ of Barnes Bros. for upward of two years, Mr. Little's natural business acumen led him to believe that McKeesport was a good field for the laundry business, and there being no local plant in McKeesport, he formed the Enterprise laundry company, becoming at once vice-president and general manager. After conducting the business for a short time as a firm, Mr. Little purchased the interests of his partners in the company and changed the name to the Enterprise laundry. The name was original with Mr. Little, and was and is quite appropriate, for his entire business career has been one of enterprise. A few years ago Mr. Little acquired the property at Nos. 631 and 633 Fifth Ave., McKeesport, which runs through from Fifth avenue to Jerome street, erecting on the Fifth-avenue frontage a handsome three-story building, and a three-story laundry building on Jerome street. From its very inception the business has steadily increased, until it extends to every town and hamlet in the Monongahela valley. His promptness and thorough business methods have given him a name and reputation which few men attain in the business world, and to this is attributed a great measure of his success. Mr. Little has not only been progressive in the laundry business, but is an enterprising and public-spirited citizen, always in the forefront of anything pertaining to the welfare or progress of the city he calls home. He is of a philanthropic and charitable disposition, but dislikes ostentation, preferring to conceal his charities from the outside world. In addition to the laundry business, Mr. Little is a stockholder and director in the Virginia consolidated copper company, which is located in Page county, Va.; a stockholder in the Commercial trust company, of McKeesport; the People's ice, light and cold storage company, of McKeesport; in the Pacific steel company; the Producer mining and smelting company, of Arizona, and is interested in several smaller enterprises. In politics Mr. Little is a republican, and takes a lively interest in all local and county contests. He is also active in lodge affairs, being a charter member and past exalted ruler of McKeesport lodge, No. 136, B. P. O. Elks; a member of the Tribe of Ben-Hur; also of the K. of A. O. E., of the Independent Order of Foresters, and Independent Order of Heptasophs. He is a member of St. Stephen's Episcopal church of McKeesport. In 1890 Miss Tillie Segrand, of Piqua, Ohio, became Mrs. Little, and two daughters, A. Eleanor and Matilda I., have come to bless the union. Mr. Little is domestic in his tastes, and enjoys his home life. In his relations with men he is courteous and affable, and all his business transactions are conducted with the strictest integrity. Wherever known, he is trusted and respected, and with his high ideals in business life, it is but a natural sequence that his success has been remarkable and lasting.

MEREDITH C. STITT, at present a well-known and popular mechanic of Tarentum, is a sample of that fine line of American citizenship to whose sturdy industry and indomitable pluck the republic owes much of its solidity and prosperity. He is a son of William J. Stitt, a lifelong resident and one of the substantial farmers of Armstrong county, Pa. Starting life as a carpenter, he eventually changed his occupation to farm work, and was thus engaged when the opening guns of the Civil war stirred the blood of all patriotic men, and none more so than those living in the old Keystone State. Mr. Stitt promptly enlisted in one of the regiments of his native State and served creditably throughout the great struggle with no more serious injury than a wound in the hand. Shortly after returning home he was married to Theresa, daughter of William and Elizabeth (Linhart) Shipman, both of whom died in Armstrong county after a long and honored residence. After their wedding, Mr. and Mrs. William J. Stitt took up their abode on a farm and became popular citizens of their neighborhood as well as useful members of the Lutheran church. The birth of their son, Meredith C. Stitt, who is the principal subject of this sketch, occurred on the home farm in Armstrong county, Jan. 28, 1874. His childhood and early boyhood were spent at home, and such book education as he received was obtained in the nearby district school before entering his sixteenth year. When fifteen years old, a position was obtained for him with the iron and steel company located at Apollo, in his native county, and there he began learning the trade which he has steadily followed ever since. When the mill was started at Vandergrift, he went to that place and took part in the first work done by this establishment. He remained there, in different capacities, until July 15, 1901, when he took up his residence at Tarentum, which has ever since been his place of abode. Immediately after his arrival, he obtained employment with the Allegheny steel and iron company, which he retains at present, in the department devoted to sheet steel rolling. Mr. Stitt, after the hard work and severe trials incident to his chosen calling, has achieved substantial success and enjoys high standing both with his employers and fellow workmen. That he is also favorably regarded in social and fraternal circles is manifest from the fact of his holding membership in the following named societies: Pollock lodge, No. 502, F. and A. M.; Vandergrift lodge, No. 1116, I. O. O. F.; Prosperity lodge, No. 437, K. of P.; Tarentum lodge, No. 644, B. P. O. E. April 27, 1893, Mr. Stitt married Miss Julia D., daughter of Alexander Henry, a brick-layer of Armstrong county, now deceased. Merle C., the only child of this union, was born Nov. 25, 1894. Mr. Stitt's political affiliations, like those of his father, have always been with the democratic party. He and his wife are members of Trinity Evangelical church, at Tarentum.

JOHN P. ONCKEN, an esteemed mechanic of Natrona, is a contribution to Pennsylvania from that famous Fatherland whence have come so large and valuable a portion of the republic's citizenship. Herman Oncken, of Germany, after marrying Wilhelmina W. Ukena, remained in his native land until 1883, when he removed with his family to Pennsylvania and located in Allegheny county. He remained at Natrona until the death of his wife, which occurred Jan. 25, 1898, but some years subsequent to that sad event, returned to Germany, where he has since resided. Of the four living children, Mrs. Charles Huffman, Frank W. and John P. reside at Natrona, while Mrs. Charles Barr is a resident of Vandergrift. John P. Oncken, first-born of the above enumerated children, was born in Germany, Dec. 1, 1872, and consequently was in his eleventh year when the emigration of his parents brought them to the Keystone State. He attended school in his native land for several years, and after reaching Pennsylvania resumed his studies in the public schools of Natrona. He began the serious business of life at the age of sixteen, his first engagement being with the Fidelity and the Fiscus glass works, where he took primary lessons in the metal trades. Later he secured a position in the sheet mill at Apollo, and after remaining there a short time, went to Vandergrift, where he became one of the first workmen in the mill at that place. In 1901 he located at Natrona and soon secured employment as a sheet steel heater in the works of the Allegheny steel and iron company. Mr. Oncken has made his own way in the world, having no other assistance than his steady industry, skill and reliability in whatever positions he was selected to fill. He has become a property holder and one of the substantial citizens of Natrona, highly respected by his employers and others. He has long been prominent in fraternal work and was the organizer of the Knights of the Golden Eagle at Vandergrift Heights, which, beginning with fifty-one charter members, has increased steadily until at the present time the lodge boasts a membership of 150. In addition to his activity with this fraternity, Mr. Oncken holds membership in Mineral Point lodge, No. 615, Independent Order of Odd Fellows, and Armstrong lodge, No. 412, Knights of Pythias. In politics he has always been an adherent of republican principles and takes an intelligent interest in public affairs. On April 11, 1899, Mr. Oncken was united in marriage with Miss Linnie M. Foster, of Armstrong county, Pa., and they are both members of Trinity Lutheran church at Natrona.

JOHN KAPTEINA, of Springdale, Pa., foreman of the Heidekamp mirror company, was born in Prussia, April 16, 1852, son of Charles and Eva Kapteina, the former a prosperous farmer of the Fatherland. Mr. Kapteina was educated in the public schools of his native country, and when thirteen years of age became an assistant to his father on the farm, where he remained until nineteen years of age. He went into the army for two and a half years, then into the glass works at Satke, Germany, and for nine years followed that business there. In October, 1882, he came to Creighton, Allegheny county, and for eighteen years was foreman for the Pittsburg plate glass company at that place. In 1900 he removed to Springdale, and since has occupied the position of foreman of the Heidekamp mirror company at that town. He was married, in 1879, to Jennie Baranowsky, of Germany, and they have seven children: Otto, in the glass works at Springdale; Martha, a dressmaker in Springdale; Laura, a bookkeeper for the glass works;

Elfred, attending school in Springdale; John, Edward and Irene, at school. He is a member of the Lutheran church of Tarentum, the Royal Arcanum, the Heptasophs, and of the republican party. Mr. Kapteina is a prosperous and substantial citizen, and is well known and liked in that part of the county.

WILLIAM BEW, an old resident of Allegheny county, has been active for many years in the political and business life of his community. His father, Thomas Bew, was of English parentage, but emigrated to Pennsylvania in 1855, when a young man. Locating in Allegheny city, he followed the occupation of shoemaking until death closed his earthly career. He married Margaret, daughter of Isaac Kuhn, an early settler of Allegheny county, by whom he had seven children, five still living. Thomas Bew was a man of exemplary life, a member of the Episcopal church and a democrat in his political affiliations. His widow is at present a resident of Mansfield, Ohio, where, at the age of seventy-four years, she still takes an interest in the affairs of the Methodist Episcopal church, of which she has long been an honored member. William Bew, one of the five surviving children of Thomas and Margaret Bew, was born in Allegheny city, Pa., March 16, 1861, and spent his early life in the confines of his native city. His first venture in business was an effort to master the intricacies of the drug trade, but not finding that to his liking, he soon sought occupation in other pursuits. After two and one-half years behind the counter, he engaged in coal-mining and continued in that line for about seventeen years. In 1901 he secured a situation with the Allegheny steel and iron company and at present fills a position as sheet steel heater in the establishment. Mr. Bew has spent his entire life in Allegheny county, and since the twentieth year of his age has resided in Harrison township. He is a property owner in Brackenridge borough and for many years has been prominent in local affairs. He was elected to the council at the time the borough was organized and at present is president of that body. As one of the leaders and popular members of the Republican party, with which he has affiliated since early manhood, Mr. Bew was elected a member of its executive committee for Allegheny county and has served in that capacity for four years. His interest in fraternal matters has been chiefly confined to the Royal Arcanum, in which honorable order he has long held membership. On Sept. 8, 1881, Mr. Bew was married to Miss Hannah Bonner, a native of Westmoreland county, whose birth occurred March 16, 1862, at Lucesco. She is a daughter of Patrick and Anna (Dugan) Bonner. Her father emigrated from Ireland about 1840, coming to Pennsylvania, and her mother came over about five years later and had been in this country but a few years when she became the wife of Patrick Bonner. Shortly after this marriage, they settled in the Allegheny valley, where they remained until their death. The mother died there Nov. 21, 1892, and the father passed away Sept. 8, 1895, after becoming the parents of seven children, of whom five are still living. Mr. and Mrs. William Bew have three children: William C., born Aug. 31, 1882; Florence M., born Feb. 24, 1884, and Elizabeth I., born Aug. 13, 1886.

PETER HEILE, of Rural Ridge, Pa., a prosperous farmer, was born in Germany, Nov. 17, 1834, son of George and Margaret Heile, both natives and life residents of the Fatherland. Peter Heile was reared in Germany, educated in that country in the rudimentary branches, and in 1851 came to Allegheny county and attended school at Harmarville, Pa. He resided at East Liberty for one year, at Harmarville for eleven years, and then came to Indiana township and located on the farm of seventy-one acres which he now owns. He cleared the place, made all improvements and there has prospered as a farmer since 1864. He is a republican in politics and has served as school director for one term. He was married, in 1856, to Elizabeth, daughter of James and Margaret Griswell, natives of Ireland, who, on coming to America, located at Pittsburg and subsequently removed to Harmarville. Mr. and Mrs. Heile are members of the Methodist church. They are the parents of the following four children: James, who was educated in Tarentum and at Curry's university of Pittsburg, for ten years was engaged in teaching and for the last five years has held a responsible position with the Real Estate and Trust company of Pittsburg; Nellie, educated in the Pittsburg academy and is a successful teacher; William B., a farmer, and Lizzie, who was educated at the Pittsburg academy and followed the profession of a teacher until she became the wife of John Campbell, of Pittsburg. Mr. Heile is a prosperous and successful farmer and is a fine example of the German-American citizen, a true and worthy element in our social economy.

JAMES B. HAMILTON, of Tarentum, is one of the army of industrious mechanics whose combined labors have made western Pennsylvania the most important iron center in the world. Though of English nativity, he has spent most of his life on American soil, and is thoroughly imbued with devotion to the institutions of this country. His parents, Alexander and Elizabeth Hamilton, natives of Scotland, emigrated to the United States in 1878, and located at Oil City, Pa. Later they spent some time at McKeesport, and at present reside in Scott Haven, the father having retired from business. James B. Hamilton, one of their four children, was born at Bidlington, England, July 7, 1877, and was consequently an infant in arms when his parents came to Pennsylvania. He received his education at Scott Haven and Volant college, and in 1898 began work in the steel mill at Vandergrift. In 1901, when the mill was started at Tarentum by the Allegheny steel and iron company, he came to that place, and is now employed in that establishment as a roller. In 1902 Mr. Hamilton married Miss Nellie, daughter of George A. and Catharine (Kistler) Hunger, of Vandergrift, Westmoreland Co., Pa. Matthew Hunger, grandfather of Mrs. Hamilton, a native of Hamburg, Germany, came to Oil City when a young man, and is now a resident of Kittanning, Pa. Captain Kistler, maternal grandfather of Mrs. Hamilton, was a boatman on the Allegheny river, and resides at Leechburg. Mrs. Hamilton's father has long been active as a republican in politics, having been justice of the peace six years and is now serving his second term as burgess in Vandergrift. He is also extensively known as a business man, being a dealer in lumber and builders' supplies. He is prominent in Masonic circles, has been an Odd Fellow for twenty-five years, and is a member of the Royal Arcanum. He and his wife are members of the Lutheran church, to which Mr. and Mrs. Hamilton also belong. Mr. Hamilton affiliates with the republican party, and is a member of Kiskiminetas lodge, No. 617, F. and A. M., of Vandergrift.

ADAM DAUM, a prosperous and well-to-do citizen of Brackenridge, is of German nativity, but has long been a resident of Pennsylvania. His parents, John and Elizabeth (Peter) Daum, were born in Germany in 1809, and emigrated to the United States in 1854, arriving at Baltimore October 26th of that year. In 1862 they removed to Allegheny, Pa., where the father died, Oct. 8, 1881, his wife surviving until May 29, 1896. Their children, consisting of five sons and two daughters, are thus recorded in the family records: George, born Oct. 30, 1832, died Jan. 23, 1858; Louis R., born Jan. 6, 1834; John, born Nov. 18, 1835, died March 5, 1902; Elizabeth, born Nov. 12, 1839; Adam, subject of sketch, date of birth given below; Eliza, born March 9, 1844, and Ernest C., born March 22, 1848. Adam Daum, fifth of the children above mentioned, was born in Germany, Dec. 9, 1841, and hence was in his thirteenth year when the family arrived in Baltimore. He attended school in his native country, and completed his education while residing in Baltimore and Allegheny city. His father being a cooper, he learned that trade under him, and followed this occupation from 1857 until 1884. In the latter year he began work in a glass factory in Brackenridge borough, conducted by the firm of Schallnor & Taylor, and this has been his line of employment ever since. At the present time he is employed in the establishment of the Tarentum glass company, at Brackenridge. Mr. Daum came to Brackenridge borough in 1876, and has continued his residence there since that time. He owns a comfortable home on Henry street, erected by himself in 1890, and, altogether, has met with a fair share of prosperity in his ventures, all his possessions being the result of his own industry and saving. He has borne his share in the social and political activities of his home place, and enjoys general esteem among his neighbors and fellow-citizens. He was one of the first councilmen of Brackenridge, and still holds that official position. Mr. Daum served as a

Union soldier during the Civil war, first in Company C, Knapp's battery, and afterwards in Company I, 78th Pennsylvania regiment. He was made an Odd Fellow in 1865, and at present is a member of Robert Blume lodge, No. 414, of that order, at Allegheny city. Since 1870 he has also been a member of Humboldt lodge, No. 39, of the Ancient Order of United Workmen. On Aug. 29, 1866, Mr. Daum was married to Miss Mary Ruth, of Allegheny city, and has three children: Edward L., died at the age of twenty-five years. Ernest C., a presser in the Tarentum glass works, married Mary Brennan, and has five children: Edward, Agis, Marie, Ernest C. and William Francis. Henry, the third son, is a mold-maker in the Tarentum glass factory. He married Georgetta Thompson, and they have had four children: Edith (deceased), Ruth, Mabel and Adam. Mr. and Mrs. Adam Daum are members of the German E. P. church at Tarentum.

HARVEY THOMPSON, of Buena Vista, Pa., a prominent citizen and for many years a leading merchant, now retired, was born in Jefferson county, Ohio, Sept. 18, 1838, son of Matthew and Anne (Hunt) Thompson. His father was a native of Fayette county, Pa., and for a long time was identified with agricultural pursuits in Jefferson county, Ohio, and his mother a native of Glens Falls, N. Y. Harvey Thompson was educated in the common schools of his native State and began his business life on his father's farm in Jefferson county, of the Buckeye State. In 1862 he came to Pennsylvania, and, in 1873, located in Buena Vista, where for thirty years he was successfully engaged in the general mercantile business. He was happily married, in 1861, to Anna, daughter of James and Deborah McWilliams, of Washington county, Ohio, and they have the following children: Nancy R., wife of T. M. Bell (deceased), of Buena Vista; Mary Irene, wife of William Mickleberry, of Bozeman, Mont.; Mollie E., wife of G. L. Kent, of Bozeman, Mont.; Jennie C. Lay, of Buena Vista, Pa.; Maggie S., wife of Andrew K. Culbert; George W. and Matthew J., prominent merchants of Buena Vista; Hanna and Bessie, living at home. Mr. Thompson is a member of the United Presbyterian church.

BENNETT P. GREENE, one of the well-known employes of the steel mill at Tarentum, comes of New York ancestry long resident in Pennsylvania. His paternal grandfather was David Greene, who married a Miss Moon, and one of the offspring of this union was a son whom they christened Joseph W. The latter married Julia F. Prindle, who, as well as himself, was a native of Thurman, N. Y. Bennett Prindle, father of Julia, was born in Connecticut, but while still young, removed with his parents to New York, where he grew to manhood. There he married Phœbe Downs, a native of that State. At an early day he left the Empire State and went to Jefferson county, Pa., settled at Brockwayville, and there spent the remainder of his life. Joseph W. Greene was a boy only fifteen years old when the fever of western emigration seized him, as a result of which he walked from New York to Brockwayville, with which place all his subsequent life was identified. In politics he was identified first with the whig, and later with the republican party, and he rose to be a man of influence and consequence in his community. This is proven by the fact that he was county commissioner at one time, and held the office of justice of the peace for thirty-five years. His regular trade, however, was that of a painter, and the traditions of the county are to the effect that he did a great deal of excellent work during his long and busy life. By his marriage with Julia Prindle, there were eleven children, of whom seven survive. The father passed away in 1887, but his widow, now of venerable age, still resides at Brockwayville. Both were members of the Methodist Episcopal church, and the edifice devoted to the worship of that denomination at Brockwayville was built by Mr. Greene some years before his death. Both Joseph W. Greene and his father-in-law, Bennett Prindle, were soldiers in the War of 1812. Bennett Prindle Greene, one of the surviving sons, was born July 8, 1867, at the family homestead in Brockwayville. After his graduation from the city high school, to whose teachers he was indebted for a good common-school education, he learned the painters' trade under the competent care of his father. Until 1898 he followed the business of contracting, and while so engaged at Vandergrift, in the year above mentioned, decided to engage in the metal industry. With this end in view he obtained employment in the steel mill at Vandergrift and remained there until 1901, when he came to Tarentum, since which time he has been working as a sheet steel roller. While a resident of Brockwayville, Mr. Greene achieved considerable prominence in politics as a republican, acting as judge and inspector of elections and being elected auditor. When only twenty-one years old he was made a member of the Knights of Pythias lodge at Brockwayville, and belongs to the lodge of the same knightly order at Tarentum. In 1885 Mr. Greene was married to Jennie, daughter of Thomas and Agnes (Smith) McMillian, both natives of Scotland, the former born in 1828, and the latter ten years later. They emigrated to the United States in 1862, and located in Bradford county, Pa., where the wife died in 1873, and the husband, who was a coal-miner, in 1891. They were members of the Catholic church, and had nine children, of whom four are living. Mr. and Mrs. Greene have five children: Lewis W., Florence A., Pearl, Bennett P., Jr., and Nellie. Clarence W. Greene, a brother of the subject of this sketch, served as a soldier during the Spanish-American war, and was honorably discharged on account of disability.

HARRY E. BRUNER, of Tarentum, Pa., a prosperous sheet steel heater, was born in Armstrong county, Pa., Dec. 15, 1866, son of Andrew J. and Catharine (Crawford) Bruner, both born in Armstrong county, Pa., where they now reside. His father is a successful farmer, a republican in his political affiliations, has held a number of township offices, and he and his wife are members of the Baptist church. Harry Bruner was reared on the parental farm, attended the common schools and in 1887 was graduated from the Iron City business college. He began his business career as an employe of a plate glass concern in Armstrong county, later worked in the same line at Tarentum and then learned the trade of sheet steel heating at Leechburg, Pa. He was employed as a sheet steel heater in McKeesport until 1901, when he came to Tarentum and is now in the employ of the Allegheny iron and steel company. Mr. Bruner is a prosperous and substantial citizen and owns a handsome residence on Third avenue. He was married, in 1889, to Bertha, daughter of Charles and Mary (Hugle) Garlick, the former a native of England and the latter of Toronto, Canada. They came to Pittsburg in the sixties, removed to Tarentum in 1875, where Mr. Garlick died in 1886 and his wife three years later. Charles Garlick was a successful merchant, a republican in politics and was the father of seven children, four of whom are now living. Mr. Bruner is a republican in his political convictions, is a member of the Heptasophs, the Knights of the Golden Eagle and the Patriotic Sons of America, and he and his wife are members of the Baptist church.

JOHN H. MILLHEIM, of Hites, Pa., a prosperous farmer, was born in Springdale, Pa., Feb. 22, 1863, and is a son of Jacob and Elizabeth (Couch) Millheim, the former a native of Switzerland, the latter of Springdale, Pa., and the daughter of Henry and Elizabeth (Albertson) Couch. Jacob Millheim came to the United States when sixteen years of age, located in Allegheny county, and was variously employed as a farm laborer and as a boatman on the canal and also on the Allegheny river. He purchased a farm in Indiana township, and prospered as a farmer until his death in 1897. His widow now lives on the farm and is the mother of nine children, seven of whom are still living. John H. Millheim was reared on the farm, received his educational training in the common schools of Springdale and West Deer township, and has devoted his entire business career to agricultural pursuits. In 1890 he purchased a fine farm a short distance from Hites, and raises fruits and truck and also makes a specialty of breeding fine stock, several of his animals having taken prizes at fairs. He is a republican in politics, but has never aspired to public office. He was married, on Jan. 22, 1884, to Katie F., daughter of Warner and Esther (McCready) Simon, the former a native of Hesse Cassel, Germany, who came to the United States when eighteen years of age, and located at Squirrel Hill, now a part of Pittsburg. Later he removed to Westmoreland county, and finally to the farm which Mr. Millheim now owns. Mr. and Mrs. Millheim are the parents of nine children, Bertha E., Harmar E., Esther J., John W., Edwin F., Mabel M. (deceased), Roy W., Earl A. and Hazel.

ROBERT BEATTY, at present an esteemed resident of Tarentum, has spent a useful life and achieved success in the honorable occupation of an engineer. His parents, William and Mary (English) Beatty, were both born in Scotland, but emigrated at an early age to Pittsburg, Pa., where they reared a family of children, all of whom became honored citizens and are still living in various parts of the country. The father served in the Mexican war, and soon after that event was killed in California. His wife died in Armstrong county in 1862. James, the youngest of their three sons, is a merchant in Boone county, Ia.; Samuel is a retired oil producer of Venango county, Pa.; Robert is the subject of this sketch, and Ellen, the only daughter, is the wife of Mr. Shrader, a wealthy farmer of Armstrong county. Robert Beatty was born in Pittsburg, Sept. 3, 1843; attended the city schools until his ninth year, and then began work in the Phillips glass house. Three years later he began studying engineering, in time became expert in that line, and has devoted most of his adult life to different branches of that business. His professional career, however, was interrupted in early manhood by the Civil war, in which he served with great credit to himself and benefit to his country. On April 27, 1861, he enlisted in Company G, 11th Pennsylvania reserve corps, with which he served until Jan. 13, 1864. On August 22d of that year he joined Company H, 18th regiment, Pennsylvania cavalry, with which he remained until June 8, 1865. He took part in eighteen battles and many skirmishes, including Bull Run, South mountain, Antietam, Seven Days' fight, Fredericksburg, Gettysburg, Wilderness, Spottsylvania, North Anna river, Bethesda church, and the cavalry engagement at Waynesboro. During the seven days' fighting around Richmond he was in the bloody battles at Malvern Hill, Gainesville, Charles City, Cross Roads and other engagements of minor importance. After returning home, Mr. Beatty resumed work in his chosen profession, being employed on railroads and in rolling mills at Pittsburg. In 1885 he entered the electric light business, and a year later had charge of the Sharpsburg waterworks. In 1894 he came to Tarentum, and put the traction company in operation, and in 1902 went to St. Louis with the Pittsburg reduction company as chief engineer. He remained in the Missouri metropolis until May 15, 1903, when he returned to Tarentum to take charge of the electric lighting plant of that place as superintendent, which position he has since retained. He is a natural mechanic, of superior ability, and enjoys high standing with those whom he has served in various positions of trust and responsibility. He has adhered to republican principles throughout life, and refers with pride to the fact that he cast his first vote for Abraham Lincoln, when that immortal martyr was making his race for re-election in 1864. He is a member of Custer post, No. 38, Grand Army of the Republic, at Etna, Pa., and, like other members of the Beatty family, has always been an adherent of the Presbyterian church. In August, 1865, Mr. Beatty was married to Miss Lucy McHenry, of Westmoreland county, Pa., and has seven children: Charles M., an engineer and electrician; Robert R., an engineer and machinist; Lillian, Bertha, Mary E., Grace and Hortense. The family reside in a handsome home on the banks of the Allegheny river, which represents part of Mr. Beatty's accumulations as the result of an industrious and useful life.

J. CLYDE McPHERSON, who has not reached his twenty-fourth birthday, enjoys the distinction of being the youngest sheet steel roller in the mills at Tarentum. He is a son of Alpheus and Frances (Orcutt) McPherson, both natives of Jefferson county, Pa., and residents of Leechburg since May 4, 1896. The former is employed as a shearman in the Leechburg steel mill by the American sheet steel company. He affiliates with the republicans, and for thirty-three years has been a member of the Independent Order of Odd Fellows. His father, Jackson McPherson, a native of Rehrersburg, Pa., came to Jefferson county at an early day, married a Miss McCutcheon, and died there in January, 1899. He served as a soldier in the Civil war. The maternal grandparents of our subject were James and Vina (Flick) Orcutt, the former of Maine, and the latter a native of Jefferson county, now residents of Knoxville, Ia. J. Clyde McPherson, one of the seven children of his parents, of whom six are living, was born in Jefferson county, Pa., Oct. 30, 1880. He was reared and educated at Corsica, in his native county, and in May, 1896, began work in the steel mill at Leechburg. In 1901 he came to Tarentum to accept a position with the Allegheny steel and iron company, and is the youngest sheet steel roller in their employment. On May 23, 1899, he married Miss Lillian, daughter of Robert and Elizabeth (Keenan) Crawford, of Leechburg. Mrs. McPherson's grandparents were Robert and Lillas (Nutman) Crawford, natives of Scotland, who emigrated to Pennsylvania, where the former died at Grove City, and the latter in Sharon. Their son, Robert, was a boy of eight years when his parents came to the United States, and his wife, whom he married in Pennsylvania, died in 1892. At present he is a mine foreman at Youngstown, Ohio, where he holds membership in the Knights of Pythias order, and exercises his voting franchise in favor of republican principles. Of his eight children, seven are still living. Mr. and Mrs. McPherson have two children, Margaret and Francis E.

DAVID K. CARNEY, a well-known iron-worker of Tarentum, has an honorable genealogy extending on both sides through many generations of Pennsylvanians. Patrick Carney, his paternal great-grandfather, served as a soldier in the Revolutionary war. By his marriage with Mary Russell, he left a son named John Carney, who married Mary Vensel. By this last-mentioned marriage there were several children, among them Philip Carney, born Aug. 1, 1814, and he was married, Dec. 29, 1843, to Lucinda Jane Fiscus, whose birth occurred June 28, 1827. The grandparents of the latter were Abraham and Catherine (Aukerman) Fiscus, of Westmoreland county, Pa. Their son, Philip Fiscus, born July 15, 1799, died April 5, 1855. He married Nancy Smith, whose birth occurred March 29, 1798, and her death July 3, 1860, her father being Archibald Smith, of Scotland, and her mother, Mary Anderson, of Ireland. Philip and Lucinda Jane (Fiscus) Carney, above mentioned, have long been residents of Armstrong county, where, at the venerable ages of eighty-nine and seventy-six years, respectively, they enjoy the esteem of a wide circle of friends. During his long and useful life, Philip Carney has been engaged in farming, and achieved high rank as a progressive agriculturist.

He has always voted the democratic ticket, and has held nearly every official position in his township. He and his wife have long been consistent and esteemed members of the Presbyterian church. This honored couple have had twelve children, of whom ten are living, and among the number is David K Carney, whose birth occurred in Armstrong county, Pa., Nov. 22, 1870. He was reared on his father's farm and given the benefit of good school attention until the completion of his twentieth year, when he decided to enter upon the serious business of life. Securing employment in the steel mill at Apollo, he remained there several years, then went to Vandergrift and continued in the same line until 1901, when he came to Tarentum at the establishment of the mill at that place. Since then he has been in the employment of the Allegheny steel and iron company as a sheet steel roller. He is of a quiet and unobtrusive disposition, independent in politics, and popular with his fellow-laborers and general acquaintances. On July 3, 1894, Mr. Carney was united in marriage with Miss Maggie B. Sincley, of Westmoreland county, and they have two children, Chester F. and Mildred L.

HENRY L. MARSHALL, though still quite a young man, has been engaged as an iron-worker for a number of years, and during that time has established himself as a good citizen and a reliable employe. The Marshalls have long been identified with the industries of the Keystone State, and James Marshall, grandfather of our subject, was a pioneer of Indiana county at an early day. He left a son named William H., who became a farmer in Indiana county and cultivated the soil until his death in December, 1902. He married Margaret Hill, also a native of Indiana county, who still survives and resides on the old homestead. Of their eleven children, nine are still living, and Henry L. Marshall, one of the younger sons, was born in Indiana county, Nov. 16, 1878. While growing up on the farm and taking part as a boy in the routine work of the farm, he attended the common schools during the winter sessions, and thus obtained a fair elementary education. When eighteen years old he obtained a position in the steel mill at Scottdale, Pa., which he retained for several years, but also worked a while subsequently at Vandergrift. In 1901 he located at Tarentum and secured employment with the Allegheny iron and steel company as a sheet steel heater. He has risen steadily from humble beginnings, by dint of hard work and close attention to business, until he is regarded as one of the most efficient of the many mechanics in the busy industries of Allegheny county. In politics Mr. Marshall gives his allegiance to the republican party, and his fraternal connections are with the Knights of Pythias and the Benevolent and Protective Order of Elks, at Tarentum. In November, 1902, Mr. Marshall was united in marriage with Miss Mary, daughter of W. H. Harbinson, a worthy young lady of Brackenridge borough, Pa. The young couple are members of the Cumberland Presbyterian church, and enjoy popularity in the circle of society to which they belong.

THOMAS FERGUSON, well known in Allegheny county, though a native Pennsylvanian, is of Irish parentage. John Ferguson, born in Ireland, April 25, 1807, married Mary Duff, born May 12, 1810, and in 1833 the couple left their native land for the United States. They lived awhile in Pittsburg, but later located on a farm of fifty acres in Perrysville, which, however, was subsequently sold, and in 1851 Mr. Ferguson came to West Deer township, where he bought and settled on a farm of 100 acres. Afterwards he purchased a farm of 103 acres in Butler county, which is at present occupied by his son, John. He was successful in his operations and achieved prominence as a general farmer and stock-raiser. He died at his Butler county home, June 28, 1890, aged eighty-three years, and his wife passed away, Jan. 31, 1899, nearly completing her eighty-ninth year. Of their six children, four are living. Thomas Ferguson, one of the latter, was born in West Deer township, Allegheny Co., Pa., June 4, 1851. He grew up on the home place, which he inherited at his father's death, and has devoted his entire adult life to general farming, owning 100 acres of land, and is regarded as one of the most expert farmers in his section. April 25, 1876, Mr. Ferguson married Sarah, daughter of Rev. John B. and Rebecca (Harrell) Miller, of West Deer township, both now deceased. Mr. and Mrs. Ferguson have six children:

Mary, Maggie, Rebecca, Sadie, Thomas B. and Clarence M. Mary, now the wife of William J. Clendenning, a farmer of West Deer township, has three children, Ethel, Francis and Hazel. Maggie, the second daughter, now the wife of George Camming, has one child, Howard. Rebecca, the third daughter, is now the wife of Ira Sefton, of Butler county. Sadie, wife of George Fisher, has one child, Olive Ruth. Mr. Ferguson is a republican, and has been road commissioner about fifteen years. He and his wife are members of West Deer United Presbyterian church.

DAVID SCOTT, as a breeder of fine stock of various kinds and for successful achievements as a business man, is one of the best known farmers of West Deer township. He is a son of John and Sarah (Dain) Scott, both natives of Ireland, who emigrated about 1822 and settled in Allegheny county, where he purchased 250 acres of land. He cultivated this land with industry and judgment, and had greatly increased its value before the final summons came that terminated his earthly career. First a whig, he afterwards became a democrat, and the religion of himself and wife was that taught by the Episcopal church. He died March 11, 1875, aged eighty-three years, after long surviving his faithful spouse, who passed away in 1866 at the age of seventy-two years. When this worthy couple reached America, they had seven children, which number was increased by nine after their arrival, but the only survivors are Mrs. Sarah Carlisle and the subject of this sketch. David Scott, his father's only male representative, was born in West Deer township, Allegheny Co., Pa., Jan. 11, 1839. After attending the country schools in his neighborhood, he took a course in the Pittsburg commercial college, and afterwards worked for some time in a business house of that city. Afterwards, however, he returned to the farm and made agriculture the principal business of his life. He owns seventy-five acres of the old homestead place, where for many years he has carried on general farming, making a specialty of pure-bred Berkshire swine and Jersey cattle. He is a democrat in politics, has acted as school director for six years, and is now completing a twenty-year service as justice of the peace. In May, 1861, Mr. Scott was married to Miss

Elizabeth Caldwell, of Allegheny county, by whom he has had ten children: Addie, Margaret (deceased), Sarah J., John, Cornelia, William Etta, Robert G., Wilson C., Dane and Maude (deceased). In August, 1861, at the breaking out of the Civil war, Mr. Scott's brother, William, organized a company of infantry, in which he held the rank of captain, but, owing to its failure to obtain a full quota of enlisted men, his company was combined with another and merged into Company B, 61st regiment, Pennsylvania volunteer infantry, of which William was made lieutenant. The first action in which the regiment participated was the battle of Fair Oaks, fought in June, 1862. Lieutenant Scott passed safely through the battle, but afterwards, while searching for missing comrades, was picked off by a sharpshooter's bullet and died on the field. The high regard in which this gallant Pennsylvania patriot was held is indicated by the fact that the William Scott post, in West Deer township, is named in his honor.

ROBERT E. ABER, a prosperous farmer and stock-raiser of Gibsonia, is a representative of the industrious class who have done so much for the development of Allegheny county. His grandfather was William S. Aber, who married a Miss Elliott, and became an early settler of Plum township, where he lived until the time of his death. His son, Allen, who grew up on his father's place in Plum township, eventually also became a farmer, and followed that occupation during all the days of his adult life. He married Mary A. Ross, whose parents were of Scottish extraction and became early settlers of Westmoreland county, Pa. Allen Aber died Feb. 15, 1886, and his wife passed away March 23, 1889. Both were members of the United Presbyterian church, and Mr. Aber was an adherent of republican principles. Of their eight children, only three are now living. Robert E. Aber, one of the three survivors last mentioned, was born in Allegheny county, Pa., June 19, 1851. He grew up on his father's farm in West Deer township, attended the common schools, and meantime mastered the details essential to success in agriculture. In due time he became a land owner on his own account, and obtained rank as one of the successful cultivators of his country. He has 150 acres of land, which he cultivates by up-to-date methods, and makes a specialty of hay. Mr. Aber is a republican in politics, and is in all respects a substantial and reliable citizen. On June 19, 1883, he married Miss Maggie, daughter of Robert and Mary (Henderson) Wilson, of Harmer township, Allegheny county, now deceased. Mr. and Mrs. Aber have six children: Mary, Tillie and Dillie (twins), Robert M., Sarah and William. The family are connected with the United Presbyterian church.

ALBERT EINSPORN, the genial "mine host" of the Hotel Kepler, is widely and favorably known to the traveling public and all others who enjoy good living. His parents were Gottlieb and Mary (Berborenz) Einsporn, who emigrated from Germany in 1886 and located in Allegheny county, at Creighton. The father died at Ford City, in February, 1901, but his widow still survives. He was a plate-glass worker and was employed by Capt. G. B. Ford, at Ford City. He and his wife were members of the Lutheran church. They had six sons and one daughter, all of whom are living. Albert Einsporn was born in Germany, May 20, 1866, and was approaching his majority when his parents reached the American shore. He had been educated before leaving Germany, where he studied chemistry, and after reaching Allegheny county, turned his attention to decorating, which occupation he pursued in the glass factory at Tarentum for several years after his arrival. He was employed by Chandler & Taylor, and remained with that firm until their establishment was destroyed by fire in 1891. After that disaster, Mr. Einsporn engaged in the hotel business as an employe of Henry Stamm, and remained with him eight years. He was also manager of the Ford City hotel, owned by the Pittsburg plate glass company. On May 26, 1903, he returned to Tarentum and purchased the Hotel Kepler, in Brackenridge borough, and has since been proprietor of the same. He is a republican in politics and has fraternal connections with Etna lodge of Odd Fellows, the German Beneficial Union of Pittsburg, and Fraternal Order of Eagles, New Kensington, Pa. In November, 1890, Mr. Einsporn was married to Miss Louisa, daughter of Joseph and Barbara (Benner) Nickolaus, who, when three years old, was brought by her parents from Germany to Louisville, Ky. Mr. Nickolaus was one of the first men employed by Captain Ford in the Louisville glass works. Mr. and Mrs. Einsporn have four children: Albert, Mary, Christine and Helen. Mr. Einsporn's family affiliates with the Roman Catholic church, but he is a member of the Evangelical German Protestant church, in connection with which he has held official positions.

FRANK SEFTON, junior member of the well-known firm of Myers & Sefton, is of Irish descent, but his ancestors have been connected with Pennsylvania's progress for more than a hundred years. Henry Sefton, founder of the family, came from Ireland to Butler county as far back as 1790, there married Jane Quinn and spent his life in assisting the other pioneers to build up what is now the great Keystone State. He left a son named John, who married Isabel Bryson, a native of Ireland, and died in 1888, aged eighty-seven years, his wife surviving him until 1899 and passing away at the age of eighty-eight. They had three sons and one daughter, and among the former was John B. Sefton, who was born in Butler county, April 9, 1836. On April 14, 1859, he married Martha, daughter of James and Rosanna (McKee) Ferguson, who came from Ireland in 1853 to Butler county, where the former died in 1864 and his wife in 1859. John B. Sefton was reared on his father's farm, and after growing up learned the carpenters' trade and has followed that occupation throughout life. He has always been a republican in politics and held the official positions of auditor and school director in Butler county. He and his wife are members of the United Presbyterian church. They had ten children, of whom eight are living. Frank Sefton, one of the family last mentioned, was born in Butler county, Pa., July 7, 1863. After the usual routine education on the farm and in the district schools, he learned the carpenters' trade under his father's capable instruction, and his whole life since then has been devoted to that occupation. In 1882 he came to Tarentum and, with the exception of three years, has been engaged since that time as a contractor and builder in partnership with W. H. Myers. The firm of Myers & Sefton has done a large amount of business during its existence of over eighteen years and has been very successful from a financial point of view. They enjoy high standing as business men and are stockholders both in the People's National bank and the Tarentum savings and trust company. Mr. Sefton is a republican in politics and has served one term in the council. He is a member of the Keystone band and takes an active interest in the social and industrial progress of his community. On Jan. 20, 1891, Mr. Sefton was united in marriage with Miss Minnie, daughter of James E. Karns. Their four children are named William Randolph, Helen Isabel, James Karns and Francis Liggett. Mr. Sefton owns a residence on East Muth avenue, in Tarentum, in which the family make their home, and he and his wife are members of the Presbyterian church.

SAMUEL MULLET, of Hites, Pa., a successful farmer, was born in Indiana township, Allegheny county, July 6, 1850, and is the son of Samuel and Margaret (Staufford) Mullet, both natives of Germany. His father came to America when he was sixteen years of age, and, with the exception of three years spent in California, resided in Allegheny county, a successful and prosperous farmer. He and his wife were members of the German Lutheran church, and the parents of six children, two of whom are now living. By a previous marriage he had three children, and one of them survives his parents. Samuel Mullet, Jr., was reared in East Deer township, and there received such educational advantages as were afforded by the common schools. He spent four years in Tarentum, being employed for two years by a glass concern, and for a similar period by the house of Grafton & Bennett. Later he purchased a farm of thirty-five acres, on which there was an oil well, and has since followed trucking and fruit farming with much success. Mr. Mullet caught the western fever and spent two years in Colorado, and there was variously employed. He was married to Maggie G., daughter of Adam Walter, of Indiana township, and she died on June 10, 1901, leaving four children: Walter J., Morrison H., Russell E. and Sarah Jane. On Nov. 11, 1903, Mr. Mullet was married the second time, espousing Maggie, daughter of James and Jane (McPhillmey) Hutchison, of Indiana township.

Mr. Mullet is a republican in politics and is closely identified with the Methodist church. He is well and favorably known in the community in which he resides and possesses the esteem and respect of his neighbors.

JAMES E. HAZLETT, of West Deer township, is probably better known among horse dealers than any other farmer of his section, as he is an excellent judge of these animals and has dealt extensively in them throughout his life. His tastes and success in stock-raising may also be regarded as an inheritance, as he comes of a long line of successful tillers of the soil. As far back as the last quarter of the eighteenth century, the pioneer settlement of Allegheny county was increased by the arrival from Ireland of William Hazlett. He located in West Deer township, married a Miss Lesley, became a farmer and did his full share in developing the resources of his adopted community. George Hazlett, son of the above-mentioned couple, was born May 26, 1800, and in later life became one of the successful agriculturists of his native county. He owned a large tract of land in West Deer township, but spent twenty-one years in Harrison township, returning to his old homestead in 1851. On Jan. 27, 1829, he was married to Eliza Karns, whose birth occurred in what is now Harrison township, Allegheny county, Jan. 25, 1802. Her father, James E. Karns, is mentioned in a sketch which appears elsewhere in this work. George Hazlett died Nov. 7, 1871, at his home in West Deer township, his wife's death occurring Aug. 4, 1870. In politics, he was connected throughout life with the whig or republican party, and held the offices of collector and assessor for a number of years. He and his wife were members of the United Presbyterian church. Of their six children, consisting equally of sons and daughters, only the three sons survive. James E. Hazlett, one of these surviving sons, was born July 18, 1837, in what is now Brackenridge borough, Pa. He was brought up in the usual way of country boys but from an early age manifested a natural aptitude for farming, especially the branch devoted to live-stock breeding. His home is in West Deer township, where he owns 149 acres of land, much of which is devoted to the cultivation of hay. In partnership with his brother, John, he also owns 125 acres in Indiana township, and altogether is quite an extensive, as well as unusually successful, farmer and breeder. He is an excellent judge of horses and during the winter has charge of many fine animals sent to him by their owners in Pittsburg. Mr. Hazlett is a republican and has served as assessor for three terms. On Oct. 27, 1859, Mr. Hazlett married Miss Nancy A., daughter of William and Catherine A. (Boyd) Porter. Mrs. Hazlett was born in West Deer township, June 4, 1840. Her grandfather, Robert Porter, was a pioneer of that section and for many years served as justice of the peace. Mr. and Mrs. Hazlett have had six children: William Porter, Clara Augusta, George Wilson, Harry Leland (deceased), Anna Mary and Clarence Elliott (deceased). The parents are members of the United Presbyterian church of Deer Creek, Pa.

ROBERT MARTIN GIBSON, the veteran merchant of Richland township, possesses a name which has been made familiar over a wide section of southwestern Pennsylvania by reason of the business connections and public activities of those who have borne it. These activities, confined principally to Allegheny county, extend over a period of nearly a century, but it has been the gentleman above named and his father who have done the most to familiarize as well as popularize the family name. The emigrant ancestors, when still young, emigrated from Ireland about 1806 and located in Allegheny county, where they spent the remainder of their days. They left a son, Thomas Gibson, who married Rachael, daughter of Jacob Dixon, a man deserving of more than a passing notice. He was one of the first settlers of Allegheny county, having gone there during the last half of the eighteenth century and located in Pine township, where he bought and cultivated a farm. He served under Washington during the Revolutionary war and was the only man in Allegheny county who drew a pension as the reward for such service. After the war, he returned to his old home, where he lived many years in the quietude of farm life and died at a ripe old age in full enjoyment of the esteem always accorded a life well spent. Thomas and Rachael Gibson left a son named Charles, who was destined to make an honorable name for himself and leave his impress on the community in which he resided. He settled in Richland township in 1840, and from that time until his death, fifty-four years later, was a prominent figure in the political, social and industrial life of that part of Allegheny county. He was a farmer, miller, carpenter and general man of affairs, there seldom being a local enterprise set in motion without his active aid and generous support. He was president of the Perrysville plank road, president of the Allegheny and Butler plank road, and president of the Pittsburg & Western railroad. In connection with his equally enterprising son, who is the subject of this sketch, he had much to do with getting the last-mentioned road built and was one of the originators of the enterprise, as well as an original stockholder. In his capacity as a carpenter, he built the Second Cross Roads Presbyterian church and paid more than half of the expenses connected with this undertaking. For many years he was not only an active member but a trustee of the church, held the position of school director and other minor offices, including that of postmaster for several years at Gibsonia, a town which was named in his honor. On Feb. 15, 1841, he married Elizabeth Logne, a native of York county, Pa., by whom he had three sons and three daughters, of whom four are living. This worthy couple lived to advanced ages, the wife dying April 14, 1885, and her husband July 25, 1894. Robert Martin Gibson, one of the four surviving children above mentioned, was born on the parental farm in Richland township, Allegheny Co., Pa., May 11, 1845. He was educated in the local schools and Jefferson college and was trained in the business of farming and milling under his father's tutelage. Though his father at one time owned 1,700 acres of land, and though he also is an extensive land owner and farmed considerably in his earlier years, his tastes and inclinations led him to seek commercial pursuits. Being much interested in the progress of the Pittsburg & Western railroad, he took charge of the office of that corporation at Sharpsburg, and remained there eighteen months. His first venture as a merchant was at Gibsonia, afterwards at Bakerstown, where he remained three years, but subsequently he established himself in Gibsonia and has been a merchant of that place for over twenty-two years. He was formerly a democrat and took quite an active interest in his party's affairs, but of late years has been inclined to independence in politics. At one time he was nominated as democratic candidate for the legislature, and, though Richland township is largely republican, he carried it by a handsome majority. He has held the office of school director and is at present the postmaster at Gibsonia. On Feb. 22, 1881, Mr. Gibson married Miss Anna M., daughter of John and Nancy Owens, early settlers of Pine township, where both died. By this union there were two children: Elizabeth L. and Nancy O. By a former marriage there were also two children: Charlie C. and Margaret (deceased). He and his wife were brought up as Presbyterians, but are now connected with the Christian and Missionary Alliance association. He was trustee of the Cross Roads Presbyterian church for many years and one of the promoters of the Bakerstown parsonage, serving on the building committee and being one of the largest contributors to the building fund. He supports a missionary in the foreign field and his two daughters support four orphan children in the United Brethren Fullers missionary school in India. Mr. Gibson is president of the Allegheny and Butler plank road, and promoter of free rural mail delivery, having charge of four routes with prospect for a fifth in northern Allegheny county.

WILLIAM H. HECKERT, popular merchant and postmaster at Bakerstown, has long been one of the progressive citizens of that community. He is a son of Joseph Heckert, who came with his parents to Butler county from his birthplace in eastern Pennsylvania when eight years old, and grew up as a farmer. He married Susannah Kilgore, spent his life in agricultural pursuits, and died in 1884 at the age of sixty-five years, his wife passing away in 1867. Their eldest daughter died in infancy but the other seven children, consisting of five sons and two daughters are living. The parents were members of the Presbyterian church. William H. Heckert, one of the five sons above mentioned, was born on his father's farm in Butler county, Pa., Oct. 12, 1858, and received his education in the schools of the vicinity and at Witherspoon institute. For some time after growing up, he was engaged in farming and the oil business, but in 1890 came to Bakerstown, where, a year or two afterwards, he began merchandising. For a year and a half he was in partnership with Leonard Steiner, after which Robert Steiner was added to the firm, but a year subsequently a dissolution took place, and since then Mr.

Heckert has been alone. He deals in hardware, flour, salt, feed, farming implements and other commodities, and has been successful in his business operations. He is a stockholder in the Bakerstown cemetery association, and treasurer of that organization. He has served six years on the school board of Bakerstown, and is a member of the Junior Order of United American Mechanics. His political affiliations are with the republican party, and he has for three years past held the position of postmaster at Bakerstown. On Feb. 16, 1889, Mr. Heckert was united in marriage with Miss Amelia Steiner, of Butler county, Pa. They have six children: William Paul, Robert Leonard, Charles Watson, Joseph Kilgore, John Steiner and Frank Bly. Mr. and Mrs. Heckert are members of the Presbyterian church.

HENRY HARDT, a well-known and prosperous farmer of Richland township, is a representative of a nationality which has done much for the development of southwestern Pennsylvania, and, in fact, of every State in the American union. His parents, John and Dolly (Tischert) Hardt, emigrated from Germany in 1865, remained two years in Pittsburg, and in 1867 located in Hampton township. In 1880 the family removed to Richland township, where the father died in 1884, and his wife in 1887. They were exemplary members of the Lutheran church, and in every way worthy as neighbors and citizens. Henry Hardt, their son, was born in Germany, March 4, 1849, and was educated in the schools of his native country before coming to America with his parents. He has spent his whole life in the townships of Richland and Hampton, engaged in farm work, and has earned the reputation of being one of the most clever and industrious of the citizens of that section. By hard work and economy he has acquired ownership of 123 acres of land, which he devotes to general farming. He is a republican in politics, and has held the office of supervisor. In 1874 Mr. Hardt married Miss Anna, daughter of George and Margaret (Beck) Haverline, both natives of Germany, the latter now deceased, and the former living at the age of eighty years. By this marriage there were two children: John H., the eldest, who holds the office of supervisor, married

Katie Mier, and has two children, Annie and Lena. Louisa, Mr. Hardt's only daughter by his first marriage, is now the wife of Henry Critzer. The first wife dying in 1882, Mr. Hardt next married Mary Kimmer, by whom he has three children, Henry H., Charles and Otto. The family are members of the Lutheran church.

HENRY MONNIER, a well-known and successful fine stock breeder of West Deer township, is of Pennsylvania nativity, but of Swiss parentage. Charles Henry Monnier, who was born in Switzerland in 1802, emigrated to Allegheny county when about twenty-one years old. Three years after his arrival, or, to speak more accurately, in 1825, Frederick and Harriet Vorp also became residents of Allegheny county as immigrants from Switzerland. Along with them came a daughter named Harriet, who was about eight years old on arriving, having been born in the Alpine republic in 1817. When this young lady grew to womanhood, she became the bride of Charles Henry Monnier, her fellow countryman, and to this union was due the Monnier family of Allegheny county. The Vorps subsequently removed to Kenton, Ohio, where the parents died, and although they had four children, the only survivor is Amih Vorp, a cooper by trade, who still resides at Kenton. Charles Henry and Harriet (Vorp) Monnier had six children, of whom four are living. The father, who was a farmer by occupation, died Feb. 2, 1887, and his wife, Jan. 15, 1903. Their son, Henry Monnier, subject of this sketch, was born on his father's farm in West Deer township, Allegheny Co., Pa., May 6, 1841. His rearing and education differed in no particular from that usual with boys in that part of Pennsylvania, but the result of it all was to fit him for the business in which he has succeeded so well. He owns 107½ acres of land, which he devotes to general farming, but his specialty is the breeding of Jersey cattle and Chester white hogs. On April 23, 1868, Mr. Monnier was married to Miss Eliza, daughter of Isaac and Mary (Reinhart) Crawford, of Allegheny county, to which they came as settlers early in the nineteenth century. Mr. and Mrs. Monnier have had ten children: William Henry (deceased), Albert J., Sarah A., Charles E., Frank E.,

Clara B., Ida A., Ella M., Leonard C., and a deceased infant unnamed. As the name would indicate, the Monnier family is of French extraction.

CHARLES THOMAS DATT, a well-known stock breeder of Richland township, is one of that extensive German colony who have done so much for the development of Allegheny county in every department of trade and commerce and so greatly enriched the citizenship of the State. George and Catharine E. (Feil) Datt emigrated from Germany to the United States in 1848 and first located at Pittsburg, but in the same year settled on the farm in Richland township now owned by their son. They cultivated their land well and industriously, lived quiet and blameless lives, and were consistent members of the Evangelical association. The father died in 1885 and his wife passed away in 1902, the former aged seventy-two and the latter eighty-eight years. Only five of their nine children are now living and among the number is the subject of this sketch. Charles Thomas Datt was born in Richland township, Allegheny Co., Pa., on the farm where he now resides and which was an inheritance from his honored father. This place consists of 100 acres and is devoted by Mr. Datt to general farming, though of late years he has paid much attention to fine stock and dairy cows. He breeds the famous Shorthorn cattle and Berkshire hogs, and in fact keeps the best of everything he handles. Proximity to a great city causes a lively demand for milk, and finding this profitable, Mr. Datt has entered extensively into the production and sale of this indispensable article of diet. He is a good manager, industrious and painstaking, and these qualities have enabled him to prosper in his undertakings. In 1890 Mr. Datt married Miss Katie, daughter of George Fisher, a minister of Allegheny county, who died in February, 1900. Mr. and Mrs. Datt have had six children: George William, Catharine Elizabeth, Charles Henry, Blanche, Mary Ellen (deceased) and Harriet Emma. The family are members of the United Evangelical church. Mr. Datt's maternal grandparents were Thomas and Elizabeth Feil, natives of Germany, who lived and died in their native land.

WILLIAM P. CUNNINGHAM, a well-known West Deer township farmer, is descended from Irish ancestors, who became identified with the State of Pennsylvania in the early years of the nineteenth century. It was in 1810 that Abraham and Nancy (Glasgow) Cunningham left their native soil in Ireland and crossed the ocean in search of a new home in the western wilderness. They located first in Butler county, Pa., but later removed to Allegheny county, and bought the 200 acres of land which is now in the possession of his grandsons. The father died about 1861, and his wife in 1865. They left a son named Hugh Cunningham, who became a farmer and rose to be a useful man in his community. He married Eliza, daughter of James and Margaret (Murray) McNeal, early settlers of Butler county, where both ended their lives. Eliza Cunningham died in 1862, after becoming the mother of seven children: Abraham, James, Robert, Samuel, William, Margaret and Sarah. All these are dead except the first mentioned. By a second marriage, with Jane Park, Hugh Cunningham had two children, William P. and Hannah Ellen (deceased). The parents of Jane Cunningham were William and Hannah (Raunals) Park, of Butler county, Pa. They were members of the United Presbyterian church at Glade Run, Pa., and had eight children, of whom five are living. Hugh Cunningham died in 1891. William P. Cunningham, only son by his father's second marriage, was born in West Deer township, Allegheny Co., Pa., on the farm he now owns, April 13, 1867. After growing up in the usual way, he eventually inherited 100 acres of the old homestead place, which he has since devoted to general farming. On July 4, 1900, he was married to Miss Jennie M., daughter of Robert J. and Margaret (McMillen) Conley. The former is now living in Adams township, Butler county, and his father, John Conley, is also living at the age of eighty-three years. He was an early settler of Allegheny county. Mr. and Mrs. William Cunningham have an only daughter, Estella Ellen, who was born July 29, 1902. The parents are members of the Deer Creek United Presbyterian church. Abraham Cunningham, only living child of Hugh Cunningham by his first marriage, and the eldest of the family, was born on the farm he now owns in West Deer township, March 11, 1846. He has sixty acres of the old homestead, which he devotes to general farming. He is a republican in politics, a member of the school board, and was register and assessor at one time. On Nov. 5, 1868, he married Miss Kate, daughter of Robert and Katie (Scott) Harbison, of Butler county. The former was a son of James and Mary (Brown) Harbison, natives of Ireland and early settlers of Butler county, where they ended their days. Robert Harbison was a farmer, and he and his wife were members of the Deer Creek United Presbyterian church. They had six daughters and two sons, of whom five daughters and one son are living. Mr. Harbison died Jan. 7, 1896, but his widow survives. Mr. and Mrs. Abraham Cunningham have had six children. The first, an infant, died unnamed; Robert W. (deceased), Lida L., Lloyd H., Dean H. and Mollie C. Lloyd H., the fourth child, first married Kate Austin, who died in 1900, leaving one child, Samuel, who is living with his grandfather. His second wife was Lillie Mahl, of Bakerstown, who has one child, an infant unnamed. Mollie C., youngest daughter of our subject, married James Sterling, of Bakerstown, and has one child, Alice A. Mr. and Mrs. Abraham Cunningham are members of the West Deer United Presbyterian church.

ANDREW JACKMAN (deceased) was a descendant of one of the oldest and most highly respected families in Allegheny county. He was born on the old Jackman homestead, in Avalon, Pa., in the year 1810, his parents being William and Mary Jackman, whose names are yet familiar to many of the old settlers. The public schools of that period were far inferior to those of the present day, yet in those early schools Andrew Jackman acquired a good, practical education —one that enabled him to successfully conduct the ordinary business affairs of a farmer, which was his occupation throughout his entire life. In his early manhood he led to the altar Miss Mary Anne Taylor, and for several years after his marriage he continued to reside near the town of Bellevue, in Allegheny county. He then removed to the State of Ohio, bought a large farm there, upon which he lived for twelve years, at the end of which time he returned to the same farm he had left in Allegheny county, Pa., and which has belonged to some member of the

Jackman family for more than a century. Andrew and Mary Jackman were the parents of five children, viz.: William H., John T., Elizabeth, Mary (now deceased) and Matilda. During his life Andrew Jackman was a consistent Christian. He was an active member of the Methodist Episcopal church, and carried the principles of his church into his dealings with his fellow-men. For many years he was one of the trustees of the Bellevue Methodist Episcopal church, and also held other offices in the church. He died in 1898, in the eighty-eighth year of his age, loved and honored by the entire community. His widow, Mrs. Mary A. Jackman, who still survives him, is one of the oldest and most universally respected women in Allegheny county.

WILLIAM JACKMAN, oldest resident in Bellevue, son of William and Mary Jackman, was born in Ohio township, Feb. 21, 1824, where the borough of Avalon has since been built. His educational advantages were very limited, necessarily so, as at that time there had been nothing but subscription schools, the present system of free schools not having been established until some time later. The ancestry of the family dates back to County Cavan, Ireland. William Jackman, grandfather of the subject of this sketch, landed with his family in America in 1787. He was the father of eight children, among them the father of our subject, also William Jackman. The grandfather came from Baltimore by wagon and settled in Washington county, near Brownsville, where he purchased a farm of forty acres, upon which he lived until his death. William Jackman, the second, came to Allegheny county in company with his brother and sister, Barnard and Margaret, in 1805, and located in Ohio township, where he purchased a large farm. The land at that time was heavily timbered and he began to clear this land, building a log cabin for a shelter, and later on a two-story house from hewn timber. The Indians at that time were very numerous in his neighborhood and hostile as well. William Jackman was married to Mary Howden, and to them were born a large family of children, five of whom are still living. He died in 1849, at the age of seventy-two, and his wife died also in her seventy-second year, both being buried in Mt. Lebanon cemetery, in Bellevue. William Jackman, the third, spent his early life on his father's farm, and at his death managed it for himself. In 1878 he opened a grocery store in what was then known as West Bellevue, which he conducted successfully for twelve years. After retiring from mercantile life, he directed his attention to his property and real estate. Mr. Jackman was married, in 1856, to Elizabeth Reel, and to them have been born five children, four of whom are living: Alma, Ella, Elizabeth (deceased), Mary and William. His family are members of the Methodist Episcopal church of Bellevue. Mr. Jackman is now in his seventy-ninth year and is in excellent health. He has been for many years one of the substantial farmers and straightforward business men of Allegheny county.

JACOB E. BAME, of Aspinwall, manager of the tailoring department of Strasburg & Joseph, was born in Whitestown, Butler Co., Pa., Oct. 18, 1864, son of George L. and Katharine (Ziegler) Bame, his father being a prosperous farmer of that county. Mr. Bame was educated in the public schools of Harmony, Butler Co., Pa., and also attended a select college until he was twenty years of age. He learned the tailoring business with Seidel Bros., of Sharpsburg, Pa., and remained with them for twelve years, when he formed a partnership with one of the Seidels, and for two years they conducted a tailoring business in Allegheny city. On the dissolution of this firm he began the tailoring business at Aspinwall, and conducted it with much success until 1902, when he disposed of his business and became manager of the tailoring department of Strasburg & Joseph. He was married, in June, 1900, to May, daughter of Aaron and Clara (Emmel) Blasdell, and they have two children. Ruby and Emmett. Aaron Blasdell, the father of Mrs. Bame, was a soldier in the Civil war, and died shortly after its close from the effects of injuries and exposure. Mr. Bame is a member and steward of the Methodist church of Aspinwall, and is a member of the Junior Order of American Mechanics and the Maccabees. He is also a member of the republican party, and is well and favorably known in that part of Allegheny county.

WILLIAM S. MARSHALL, of West Deer township, has claim upon the local historian of Allegheny county as a successful farmer, a breeder of high-grade cattle, a veteran of the Civil war, and an all-around good citizen in all that that term implies. Himself a native of Ireland, he comes of ancestors noted for their robust physiques, capacity for hard work, steadiness of purpose and remarkable longevity. His grandfather, Robert, was not far from ninety when he died, his grandmother reached the phenomenal age of 103 years, his father was ninety-seven when he died, and his mother, at her death, had completed the eighty-sixth year of her age. Samuel and Martha (Swan) Marshall, parents of our subject, came from Ireland to Pittsburg in 1848, and shortly afterwards located in West Deer township, on 200 acres of land. His death occurred on this farm, Dec. 28, 1871, and his wife passed away July 7, 1878. Of their nine children, seven grew to maturity, but only three are now living: Mrs. Parks, of Butler county; Moses Marshall, of Kansas, and William S. Marshall, the subject of this sketch. The latter was born in Ireland, Feb. 29, 1832, and was consequently about sixteen years old when his parents reached Pennsylvania. He assisted his father on the Allegheny county farm, became expert as he grew up in all the requirements of agriculture in that section, and laid the foundations of his future success on an enduring basis of industry, economy and strict attention to business. At the present time he owns ninety-seven acres of land, and has acquired reputation as a breeder of registered Holstein cattle. In August, 1864, he enlisted in Company A, 6th Pennsylvania heavy artillery, and served eleven months with this command with such soldierly fidelity as to give him creditable standing with his veteran comrades. As a result he now holds the position as commander of William Scott post, Grand Army of the Republic, of which he has long been a member. His political affiliations have always been with the republican party. In 1856 Mr. Marshall was married to Mary, daughter of John and Mary (Duff) Ferguson, who are mentioned elsewhere in this work in the sketch of Thomas Ferguson. By this marriage there were seven daughters and one son, who, with their respective families, are mentioned specifically, as follows: Thomas Marshall, born

June 14, 1857, and married, Feb. 11, 1891, to Sarah, daughter of Henry and Eliza (Crawford) Monnier, of West Deer township. They have four children: William J., Samuel F., Mary J. and Selden H. Rebecca, wife of Samuel J. McIntyre, who has nine children: Mary A., Maggie, George, Thomas, Lillie, Iva L., Martha, Emma and Clara I.; Mary A., eldest child in the above list, wife of John Bardonar, has one son, John M. Martha J., wife of William Scott, has one child, Leon V. Mary, wife of William H. Dawson, of West Deer township, has seven children: Flora, Cora, Laura, Ralph, Samuel, Alberta P. and William Scott. Nancy I., wife of Selden W. Goodrich, had five children: Meral (deceased), Vera, Sarah A., William M. and Harold E. Lillian (deceased). Clara E., wife of Daniel Smith, has three children: J. Ronald, Lawrence and Leona; by a previous marriage to George Ritman, she had one daughter, Georgia E. Emma E., wife of Samuel Swab, has no children. The mother of the above-mentioned children died Dec. 20, 1875, and in November, 1880, Mr. Marshall married Miss Margaret Hare. The entire family are members of the United Presbyterian church, and few families have more friends or are more highly respected by those who know them intimately.

HENRY L. BLIND, a resident of Ross township, son of Conrad and Elizabeth Blind, was born in Allegheny city, Jan. 5, 1873, and educated in the common schools of Ross township. His boyhood days were spent on the farm, under the instruction of Mother Nature, his time being employed for the most part in gardening, and later in the cultivation of flowers. Two years ago the firm of H. L. Blind & Bros. was organized, with H. L. Blind, the subject of this sketch, as manager. The business has been constantly increasing, until the firm now ranks among the largest in the production of cut flowers. Their sales are principally to the wholesale dealers, yet they do a large shipping trade also. The secondary part of their business consists in the growing and sale of potted plants. This firm, although new, has one of the best records, in their increase of sales, among the different firms of the county. The demand for their stock cannot be supplied.

THE QUAILL FAMILY.

Among the pioneer families of western Pennsylvania few have become better known or achieved a greater distinction than the Quaill family. Robert Quaill, the founder of the family in America, was a native of County Cavan, Ireland. In 1770 Mary Roberts was born in the same county, there grew to womanhood, and, on Oct. 11, 1792, she and Robert Quaill were united in marriage. A few years later, owing to political disturbances, they bade farewell to their beloved Erin, and in December, 1798, landed in America. They first settled in Washington county, Pa., but in 1809 removed to Ross township, Allegheny county, where they lived until 1816, when they settled on what has since become known, far and near, as the "Quaill farm," adjoining the present

GEORGE QUAILL.    ELIZABETH (REEL) QUAILL.    DAVID REEL QUAILL.

borough of Bellevue. Robert was a fine scholar, well educated in the higher branches, and was one of the first teachers in the county of Allegheny. He spent the latter years of his life as a tutor to the sons of wealthy planters in the south, where he contracted the fever and died in the winter of 1822. His wife, Mary (Roberts) Quaill, died on the farm in Ross township, in March, 1854. The children of this couple were six in number, viz.: John, Eliza, George, Mary, Anna and Robert. Eliza became Mrs. Thompson, and Mary married a man named Eakin. Anna died at the age of eight years. Robert was taken prisoner during the Mexican war, and was shot by order of General Santa Anna. George Quaill, son of Robert and Mary Quaill, was born March 6, 1799, while his parents were living near the town of California, Washington Co., Pa. Under the training of his father he received a good education, and was regarded as one of the best informed men of his day, being especially noted for his wonderful memory. He was keenly interested in all political questions of that early day, and was one of the first three whigs to organize that party in Ross township. Afterwards he was assessor of that township when it included Allegheny city, Sharpsburg, and a large part of the county lying north of the river. He also held other local offices, all of which he filled with credit to himself and to the entire satisfaction of his neighbors who honored him with the election. He was the first singing teacher in that part of the country, and for many years he led in the singing (then called clerking) in the Highlands Presbyterian church, and later for the Fleming chapel, a Methodist Episcopal church. He was generous, almost to a fault, and none were ever turned away hungry from his door or appealed to him in vain for aid in time of distress. May 19, 1825, George Quaill was married to Elizabeth Reel, the youngest daughter of Casper Reel, who was the first white settler in Ross township. (See sketch of David Reel, Jr.) The marriage ceremony was performed by Rev. Thomas Patterson, the first pastor of Highlands Presbyterian church, and the wedding took place in "Reel Hall," the house in which Elizabeth Reel was born on Nov. 8, 1803. Nine children were born to this marriage, as follows: Robert, who met his death by drowning at New Orleans in 1858; David Reel, who married Sarah J. Shafer, a member of another old Allegheny family; Elizabeth, who became the wife of John McClelland, a captain in the Civil war; Mary Eleanor, who became Mrs. Matthew Woods; George Ferris, married Hannah Kidd; William Roberts, a veteran of the Civil war; Nancy Jane; Isabélla Amanda, who became the wife of Rev. James M. Swan, also a veteran of the Civil war; and Joseph McCune, who now resides with his family on the old "Quaill farm," in Ross township. George and Elizabeth Quaill lived to celebrate their golden wedding, May 19, 1875, in the same house where they began housekeeping fifty years before. It is worthy of note that two persons who were present at the marriage of this couple, in 1825, were also present at the golden wedding. They were Mrs. Mary (Quaill) Eakin, of Beaver, Pa., a sister of George Quaill, and William Jackman, of Bellevue, Pa. Both George Quaill and his wife lived to a ripe old age. He died Dec. 16, 1880, loved and honored by all who knew him. She passed away on Nov. 20, 1891. It has been said of her that she never grew old, but that she retained her faculties to the last. She died at the residence of her daughter.

In all generations the Quaills have been noted for their public spirit and patriotism. In every war in which the United States has played a part the family has been represented. They have also taken a great interest and an active part in the settlement of political questions. George Quaill, Sr., after the death of the whig party became an ardent republican, and continued with that party to the day of his death. Capt. John McClelland, who married Elizabeth Quaill, commanded Company E, 63d Pennsylvania volunteer infantry, during the Civil war. Rev. James M. Swan, who married another sister, Isabella A. Quaill, was an orderly sergeant in Company F, 30th regiment, Ohio volunteer infantry, and William Roberts Quaill served through the war in the 123d Pennsylvania infantry, commanded by Colonel Clark. Mention has been made of Robert Quaill, Jr., who was shot while a prisoner in the hands of the enemy during the Mexican war. Casper Reel, the father of Elizabeth (Reel) Quaill, took part in the American Revolution and some of the minor Indian wars. When war was declared against Spain, in the spring of 1898, Theodore Thomas Quaill, a son of George Ferris and Hannah (Kidd) Quaill, grandson of George and Elizabeth (Reel) Quaill, and great-grandson of Casper Reel, was one of the first to enlist in the regiment organized at Canton, Ohio, and afterwards known as "McKinley's Own." There must be something pleasant for the present generation in the thought that their ancestors were among those who went fearlessly into the trackless forest and changed a wilderness into a "country of homes." The mere contemplation of the deeds of valor of these ancestors is the best lesson in patriotism, and it is certainly a source of great gratification to know that their swords were drawn in defense of the homes they had labored so assiduously to build up, and the principles that our forefathers inculcated in the Declaration of Independence. Not all of the Quaills were warriors, however. Most of the family led the quiet, uneventful lives of farmers. But they were made of that fiber that impels men to forsake the plow for the rifle, and the peaceful fireside for the tented field, whenever any invasion of their rights is threatened. To conquer the forces of nature, to make two blades of grass grow where but one grew before, to actively assist in the maintenance of pure political institutions, are acts as worthy of praise and emulation as the victories won by the sword, and are doubtless what were meant by him who said: "Peace hath her victories, no less renowned than war."

DAVID H. CUNNINGHAM (deceased) was born on the old homestead in Baldwin township, Allegheny county, March 10, 1817. His father was George Cunningham, a native of Scotland, who came to America in 1802 with his wife, Jane Moore, and two children. He took up 218 acres of land, an estate which is still in the possession of the family. George Cunningham was the father of twelve children, of whom the subject of this sketch was the last survivor, his death occurring July 19, 1902. Mr. and Mrs. Cunningham were members of the Lebanon Presbyterian church. Politically, he, like his son, was an ardent republican. His son, David, was first a whig, a supporter of William Henry Harrison, then a republican, casting his last vote for William McKinley. He never lost a vote from his first one till the year 1900. David H. Cunningham came to Ross township in 1835, learned the blacksmith trade with his brother, William, and followed it successfully for thirty-four years, after which he turned his attention to agriculture and at the time of his death was one of the leading farmers of his township. He was married first to Martha Hiland, daughter of Robert and Sarah (Dixon) Hiland, the father coming here in 1798, the mother a daughter of William and Jane Dixon. Robert Hiland was a justice of the peace for many years, and otherwise officially connected with the county. He was an elder in the Presbyterian church at the time of his death. To Mr. and Mrs. Cunningham were born five children: Alfred, William, Robert, Sarah and Joseph. He was married the second time to Mary Givan, daughter of William Givan, having no children by this second marriage. In religious belief, Mr. Cunningham was a Presbyterian.

PETER IVORY (deceased), son of Peter and Catharine (Rogers) Ivory, was born in Pittsburg, Feb. 19, 1819. In the fall of 1819 he removed with his parents to Ross township, where his boyhood days were spent on his father's farm, and where he received his education in the district schools. Growing to manhood, he became a stock dealer for a number of years, and at the opening of the Civil war was appointed an official of the commissary department, which position he held during the war. Politically, he was a strong advocate of the Jeffersonian democracy. Mr. Ivory was a man who had the confidence of the public, having held all the different offices in his own township, and served as justice of the peace for twenty-five years. He was postmaster at the time of his death, and was succeeded by his son, T. Conway, who still holds that position. Mr. Ivory was one of the organizers of the Allegheny & Perrysville plank road company, of which he was president and secretary for more than thirty years. He was the first president of the Pine Creek & Wexford road, and at the time of his death, his son, T. Conway, succeeded him in that office. In religious belief he was a devoted member of the Roman Catholic church. On June 5, 1863, Mr. Ivory was married to Joanna Conway, of Conway, Beaver county, who belonged to one of the pioneer families of that county. She is a sister of the late Capt. J. J. Conway, who went into the war with the rank of lieutenant and was promoted to the rank of captain, winning this honor by his important service in the second battle of Bull Run. He was severely wounded in the battle of Fredericksburg, but after recovering resumed his service, and continued until the close of the war. Mrs. Ivory is also a sister of the well-known John Conway, of Rochester, Pa., who has a large private bank, and is well known in business circles throughout the State. To Mr. and Mrs. Peter Ivory were born five children: Peter Ivory, Jr., a graduate of the Union business college, now manager of the Park & Falls street railroad; T. Conway, a popular business man of Allegheny county; Minnie; Mrs. Catharine (Ivory) Grant, of West View, and Eleanor M., wife of Dr. A. M. McCabe, of Allegheny. Peter Ivory, the father of the subject of this sketch, was born in the county of West Meath, Ireland, and came to America in 1817, settling first in Pittsburg. Removing two years later to Ross township, he purchased a large farm, on which he lived until his death, Nov. 10, 1849. He, like his son, was a democrat and a member of the Catholic church. He was the father of two children, Peter and Mrs. Mary (Ivory) Good, who died April 21, 1901. At the time of the death of Peter Ivory, Jr., May 20, 1896, he was the owner of a tract of 400 acres of land adjoining the city of Allegheny, the estate being still in the possession of the family. Mr. Ivory was noted for his charity and good works; his kindness of heart was known to many, no one in trouble appealing to him in vain. He was a man of sterling integrity, honest and upright in all his dealings; in fact, the highest tribute that could be paid to a man's honesty was to say he was as honest as "Squire Ivory."

S. A. BRINEY, one of the trusted foremen in the Tarentum steel works, has devoted his whole life to the iron business and has mastered all the details of this useful industry. He is a son of David and Sarah E. (Jack) Briney, the former of Armstrong county and the latter a native of Iowa. The father has been an iron-worker all his life, but is now retired. He and his wife are members of the Lutheran church. They have two sons and three daughters living and two sons dead. S. A. Briney, one of the two living sons, was born in Armstrong county, Pa., Aug. 18, 1879, and received but limited schooling during his youth. At the early age of eleven years he began work in the steel mill at Apollo, and at various periods subsequently was engaged in the same line in New York, Wheeling, W. Va., Leechburg, Ford City and Vandergrift, Pa. In 1901 he came to Tarentum and engaged with the Allegheny steel and iron company, in which establishment he now holds the position of foreman of the pickling department. He is progressive in his views, votes the republican ticket as a matter of conviction, and is regarded as a competent and reliable mechanic. On Oct. 15, 1902, Mr. Briney was united in matrimony with Miss Marie M., daughter of the late Herman Bockle, of Brackenridge. Mrs. Briney is a member of the Cumberland Presbyterian church and both she and her husband have many friends in the community where they reside.

PHILIP FAULK, a resident of Ross township, son of David and Elizabeth (Glass) Faulk, was born in the district of Elsis, county of Waslon, France, May 15, 1821, and was given a good, practical education in his native country. His boyhood days were spent on a farm, but as he became a man, the farm limits were too narrow for him, and at the age of nineteen he sailed for America in the "Albany." His voyage was long, and would have been tedious, had it not been for his three associates, Charley and Louis Hammel and Jacob Gyre. After sixty-two days on the sea, he landed safely in New York, went by water from New York to Philadelphia, and after staying there a few days, continued the journey on foot over the mountains to Pittsburg, where he arrived in December, 1840, being eleven days on the road. The time of year was such as to insure much bad weather; often did he find the snow four feet deep. Mr. Faulk arrived at Pittsburg between Christmas and New Year's, and after spending a few days in visiting his relatives, and being anxious to learn the English language, he began to inquire among the English people for employment, which he found with Judge William Boggs, of Pittsburg. At the time of the great fire in 1845, he helped draw the fire engine from Allegheny to Pittsburg. In the same year he began business in partnership with his brother, Michael, as a truck gardener. They were located on Locust street, fronting the river in Manchester, near what is known as Sampson's landing. About three years later he removed to Ross township, where he purchased a farm of twenty acres, on which stands an old pioneer log cabin, one room and an attic making up the whole house. This old cabin is still preserved by Mr. Faulk, and is one of the oldest marks of pioneer history in the county, having been built over 100 years. Mr. Faulk was married, in 1847, to Agnes Craig, daughter of William Craig. She was born in Wigtonshire, Scotland, April 5, 1830, and died Jan. 6, 1900. Mr. and Mrs. Faulk were married in Manchester, Rev. Wm. Gordon officiating. In 1849 they moved from Manchester to the farm on which Mr. Faulk still resides. To this marriage were born eleven children: Robert, David, Maggie J., Agnes, William J., Louis P., Ellen C., Walter, Lizzie, Oscar A. and Albert C., Robert, the eldest, being a soldier in the Civil war. Mr. Faulk is one of the respected citizens of this township, and by his energy and industry has worked himself up among the best farmers of his township. He and his three sons, Walter, Oscar and Albert, have formed a partnership under the firm name of P. Faulk & Sons, florists, fruit and berry growers, and make a specialty of fruit. Mr. Faulk is one of the oldest producers of berries in the county, having started in as early as 1847. Mr. Faulk is now in his eighty-third year, and is still in excellent health.

LEWIS OLIVER CAMERON, a resident of Bellevue, son of James and Rachel Cameron, was born June 14, 1818, in Shippensburg, Cumberland county. His father, James Cameron, was the son of Calvin Cameron, who came from Scotland, near Lochaber, with his two brothers, James and John, and settled in Lancaster county in 1763. Lewis Oliver Cameron was educated in the schools afforded by the times, in the days when the old log schoolhouse was prominent. He lived on his father's farm until he was fourteen years of age, and then began looking out for himself, his first job being that of deck hand on the Pennsylvania canal. From this he drove a boat, later owned a boat himself, becoming known as Captain Cameron, and followed this business for two years. Having previously learned the trade of the times, he went to Pittsburg in 1845, and represented the Pennock & Mitchell company for five years, as manufacturer for their wares. In this he was very successful from a financial standpoint, and began manufacturing stoves, tin cups and sheet iron, on Liberty street, opposite Seventh street. He suffered on account of panic, but through good management cleared some money, enabling him to enter the oil business, in which he was engaged for several years. Later he became interested in real estate, and still follows that vocation. Mr. Cameron is one of the oldest oil men in the county, and the first man to refine it. While under contract for the Pennock & Mitchell company, he had spent much extra time in trying to improve the old lard and fat lamps, and after much experimenting succeeded in producing the clear oil from the black, thick product of the earth. Mr. Cameron has a long and successful career to look back upon, and that he was a man of a versatile character is shown by the different patents bearing his name. One, "the little heater," is widely known; painters know the value of Cameron's mixed gloss paints, and the patent combination globe street lantern is a wonderful improvement in the lighting of a city. Mr. Cameron's record as a soldier is one of the best, and among his greatest treasures one may find two letters from "Headquarters at Richmond," dated April 4 and 7, 1865, which thank him for the good work he did during those days of bloodshed. He was very prominently connected with the occupying of Richmond, the first flag waved in that city after the war being at his request. Mr. Cameron was in hearty sympathy with the last war, and was greatly pleased over Cuba's freedom and the inauguration of President Palma. Mr. Cameron is a very active man for his age, and although he has passed three score and ten, few young men can outwalk him.

FRED SCHWITTER, proprietor of Schwitter's sweet cream dairy, in Ross township, was born in Canton Glarus, Switzerland, in 1847. On attaining his majority, he came to America, landed at New York, and without food, money or friends, made his way to Allegheny county. In his native land, Mr. Schwitter was a silk dyer, but in this country he found it difficult to get employment at his trade, so he turned his hand at whatever he could find to do. With true Swiss pluck, he worked at various occupations until 1871, when, having saved a few dollars, he started in the dairy business on a small scale, prospering from the first. After ten years he was able to purchase a farm of his own, and, in 1881, bought the old Morrow homestead, five miles from Allegheny city. This farm contains seventy-five acres, and since it came into his possession, has become one of the finest in the county. During the thirty years that he has been a purveyor of milk and cream to the people of Allegheny city, he has never allowed the quality of his goods to depreciate, and his dairy is known all over the county for the purity of its products. Mr. Schwitter has recently purchased a fine home in his native city, the property of the first millionaire of Glarus. He has leased his property in Ross township, known as the Highland farm, for a term of five years, and will make his residence for a time in his new home in Switzerland. Mr. Schwitter is a very public-spirited citizen, and though he loves his native land, as all his countrymen do, yet he is deeply interested in all that conduces to the welfare of his adopted country, and has been prominently identified with the public works of the county. His name was among the organizers of the Perrysville & Bellevue land company, and he was instrumental in getting the street railway extended to his home. Mr. Schwitter is a republican in politics, but does not take an active part in party affairs. He is a member of the Catholic church.

JOHN H. POWER (deceased) was born in Pendleton county, Ky., Oct. 5, 1822. His father was Hiram Power, born in Montgomery county, Ky., Jan. 27, 1796, and died in Cincinnati, Ohio, in 1832. He was a carpenter and farmer, and had several brothers who were Methodist ministers. The paternal grandfather was also named Hiram, and was a pioneer settler of Kentucky, of Irish descent. The mother of the subject of this sketch was Hester (Parker) Power, born in Westmoreland county, Pa., Nov. 7, 1803. After the death of the first husband, Hiram Power, she married Rev. Isaac Smith. Reverend Smith died May 17, 1869, and his wife on Feb. 3, 1889. John H. Power was reared in Kentucky until his fifteenth year, receiving a common-school education. He then removed to Norwalk, Ohio, and from there went to Salem, Ohio, where he was for a time a clerk for his uncle, J. H. Power. He also learned the blacksmith trade, and followed this vocation a number of years. He was for sixteen years employed on the Lake Shore railroad, being located at Norwalk, and then came, in 1869, to Pittsburg, and became manager of A. French & Co.'s spring works, remaining with this firm until January, 1873. On Feb. 6, 1873, he became foreman for the Allegheny Valley railroad, and in 1876 went to Verona, but after the borough was divided, he was a resident of Oakmont, where he retired from active life in 1901, and where he died May 20, 1903. Mr. Power was always actively connected with the Methodist Episcopal church. In politics he was a republican, and served as burgess of Verona in 1881 and 1882. He was a member of Verona lodge, No. 548, F. and A. M. Mr.

Power was married, Nov. 22, 1844, to Miss Roxanna M. Haskell, of Huron county, Ohio, and had by this marriage four children. The first two, Helen Evaline and Ellen Adaline, were twins. Helen Evaline is now deceased, as are two later children, Charles Beard and Mary, but a number of grandchildren and great-grandchildren are living. Mrs. Power died Aug. 6, 1890, in Oakmont, at the age of sixty-four. Helen Evaline married Thompson Smith, of Fairfield, Ohio, and had two children, John A. and Lillie B. John A. is married and has two children, and Lillie B., now Mrs. Clarence D. Taylor, has one son, Edmond George. Ellen Adaline Power, the only living child of this family, is now the wife of John F. Weirs, and has three children, Charles, Courtland and Jennie.

WILEY G. REEL, of the firm of Louden, Reel & Call, is a resident of Bellevue, Pa., and is one of the promising young business men of the county of Allegheny. He is the son of William V. and Elizabeth (Spence) Reel and was born on Aug. 1, 1868. Until he was nineteen years of age he worked on a farm and attended the township and Bellevue public schools, in which he acquired a good education. When he arrived at the age of nineteen, he went into the shops of Thomas Carlin & Sons, of Allegheny city, to learn the trade of a machinist. After working at this business for a time, he went into the oil field located on the David Reel farm, in Ross township, Allegheny Co., Pa., where he remained until 1898. That year he was sent by some Boston capitalists to Cape Breton island, and after his return to Allegheny in the fall, he began operations as an oil well driller in Armstrong county, Pa. The following year he formed a partnership with W. A. Louden, under the firm name of Louden & Reel, to carry on the business of drilling oil and gas wells throughout the Pennsylvania field. In the fall of 1902 the firm name was changed to Louden, Reel & Call, and its operations were extended to Allegheny, Washington and Armstrong counties in Pennsylvania, and to Tyler county in West Virginia. Mr. Reel is also a stockholder in, and, after the death of R. M. Hays, July 6, 1903, was president of the Lustre oil company, which operates in Ohio and Indiana: and a stockholder and manager of the Bellevue and Homestead oil and gas company. He is also interested in the Reel combination gas and steam engine company, of Pittsburg, Pa. He is a thirty-second degree Mason, holding membership in the following different Masonic organizations: Bellevue lodge, No. 530; Allegheny chapter, No. 217; Allegheny commandery, No. 35, Knights Templars; Pittsburg consistory, and Syria Temple, Nobles of the Mystic Shrine. He is also a member of Col. T. M. Bayne lodge, No. 1098, Independent Order of Odd Fellows; West Bellevue council, No. 240, Junior Order of United American Mechanics, located at Avalon, Pa., and of the Bellevue Methodist Episcopal church. Politically he is a republican, and, although he takes an interest in public questions, he never "talks politics" at the expense of his business. Few men at the age of thirty-five have accomplished more in a business way, and none have brighter prospects for the future. In September, 1903, he was elected director and manager of the Ilo oil company, and on September 15th of the same year, was sent to Fairmount, Ind., to take charge of their territory in that State.

HARRY L. RIBLET, sheet steel roller in the employ of the Allegheny steel and iron company, of Brackenridge borough, was born in Mercer county, Pa., March 15, 1867, son of James H. and Catharine (Stivenson) Riblet, the father a native of Mercer county, and the mother of Armstrong county, Pa. James H. Riblet, born May 23, 1841, by vocation a farmer, is now retired from active life, and lives with his wife, who was born May 2, 1849, in Scottdale. In politics he is a republican. In religion he and his wife are Presbyterians. They are the parents of four children, all living, who are: Harry L.; Blanche, wife of Charles Kistler, of Canton; Rose, wife of Harry Beale, of Tarentum, Pa., and Mabel, wife of Frank Renouf, of Port Vue, Pa. James H. Riblet's father was John Riblet, who was born in Hagerstown, Md., came to Mercer county in an early day, and died there at the age of seventy, while his wife was a daughter of William Stivenson, a native of Armstrong county, whose father was one of the first settlers of that county. Harry L. Riblet was reared and educated in Mercer county, and has worked in steel works since he was fourteen years old. He formerly worked for some years at Apollo, Pa., and in 1901 came to Tarentum. He has proved himself a capable and faithful workman, and has been roller for the past eleven years. He is a stockholder in the Tarentum savings and loan company, and owns, besides a comfortable residence on Third avenue, Tarentum, considerable other property. In politics he is a republican. Mr. Riblet was married, in 1891, to Miss Nellie Wilmot, of Apollo, and has had six children, viz.: Mildred, Pauline (deceased), Olivette, Blanche, John and Jeanette. Mrs. Riblet is a member of the Presbyterian church.

WILLIAM H. HEATH, of Greenock, Pa., a successful lumber dealer and contractor, was born at Greenock, Elizabeth township, Allegheny Co., Pa., Aug. 29, 1866, son of O. M. and Sarah (Speckman) Heath, his father having been one of the oldest and most respected residents of that township. The elder Heath enlisted in the 155th regiment of Pennsylvania infantry, which was a zouave organization, and served throughout the Civil war with fidelity and courage. William H. Heath was reared and educated in Allegheny county and on leaving school devoted his attention to carpentering at Greenock, where all of his business career has been devoted to that occupation. In 1895 he began the lumber and contracting business and since has followed the same with much success, in which lines his practical knowledge of carpentering stands him in good stead. He was married, in 1888, to Jennie, daughter of Capt. W. B. and Mahala (Morton) Harrison, of McKeesport, and they have three children, viz.: Earl S., Pearl U. and Ross D., the two eldest attending the local schools. Mr. Heath has been identified with public affairs in a prominent manner and served as auditor and clerk of the township for four years. He is closely and prominently connected with the republican party, has served as committeeman and otherwise taken an active and intelligent interest in its advancement and success. Mr. Heath is also a member of the Knights of the Mystic Chain, and is widely known as a man of sterling character and splendid business ability.

SAMUEL HAMILTON, A. M., Ph. D., superintendent of the schools of Allegheny county, was born in Washington county, Pa., June 30, 1856. He is the son of Samuel and Mary (Patterson) Hamilton. His father was born of Scotch-Irish stock in Washington county, Pa., Aug. 13, 1807, and was a man of fine literary tastes, who traveled extensively in Europe. While there he married Mary, daughter of Kairns Patterson, of Donegal, Ireland, and after his return settled on a farm in Washington county. To them were born eight children, of whom Samuel, the subject of this sketch, is the fourth son. Near the close of the rebellion, the father, too old to be drafted, raised a company and went to the front. After the close of the war he bought a small farm in Plum township, where he died in 1867, leaving a wife and seven children. The family were Presbyterians, the father being an elder in that church. After the death of his father, Samuel worked for the farmers of the neighborhood in summer and attended the district school in winter. Naturally of studious habits, he prepared himself for the work of teaching, and at the age of seventeen, took charge of the school in which he had been a pupil. While teaching, he pursued his studies under a tutor and attended the academy during vacation. He afterward completed a course in Laird institute, where he worked as a teacher while pushing his studies as a pupil. He was also a student for a time in the Oakdale academy. In 1878 he took charge of the schools of Chartiers borough, now known as Carnegie, Pa., where he remained for three years, and then accepted a similar position in Braddock, and while engaged in this work he read law with James McF. Carpenter, of Pittsburg. In September, 1886, before completing his law studies, he was appointed superintendent of the schools of Allegheny county, was elected the next year and has since been re-elected five times. During his incumbency as superintendent of schools, the county has grown from 576 schools to almost 1,500, and the number of high schools from one to twenty-six. His service in that office has been appreciated in the most substantial way by an increase in salary from $2,000, when first appointed, to $5,000, the amount now received. This is the highest salary ever paid to a county superintendent in the United States. In 1888 he organized the Allegheny county school directors' association; he aided in forming similar organizations in other counties, and the movement thus inaugurated resulted in the formation of a State directors' association in 1896. Superintendent Hamilton served as president of the Pennsylvania State teachers' association in 1893-94. He completed the work and in 1900 received the degree of Ph. D. from the Grove City college. As early as 1883 he interested Andrew Carnegie in school libraries, and received from him $500 for the public school library at Braddock. This is said to be Mr. Carnegie's first gift to the cause to which he has since given many millions. Mr. Hamilton has in all these busy years kept in touch with the business world. He helped to organize a building and loan association in Braddock and served as one of its managers. He was for many years a director in the Masonic hall association, and a member of the board of managers of the Carnegie library. In 1897 he helped organize the State bank of Braddock, of which he is a director. He represented his ward in the city council for six years and served as its president for three. Mr. Hamilton has also taken a prominent part in the religious and fraternal affairs in the community. He is a Presbyterian and for twenty years has been a teacher in the Bible class in the Sabbath-school. When the Calvary Presbyterian church of Braddock was organized, he was one of the moving spirits and he is now an elder in that church. In fraternal circles he has been exceedingly active. He is a member of Braddock's Field lodge, No. 510; Shiloh chapter, No. 257; Gorgas lodge of Perfection, and Pittsburg chapter, Rose Croix. He is a past officer in Pennsylvania council, Princes of Jerusalem; Tancred commandery, No. 48, K. T.; a member of Pennsylvania consistory, S. P. R. S., and in 1902 was crowned as an honorary member of the supreme council of the thirty-third and last degree of the northern Masonic jurisdiction of the United States. On June 2, 1886, he married Minnie M., only child of John and Sarah E. McCune, of Braddock, and to them was born one son, Paul Holland Hamilton. His wife died May 9, 1887, and he was again married, on June 1, 1898, to Mary R., daughter of John and Mary Kennedy, of New Brighton, Pa. To them was born one daughter, Elizabeth Hamilton. On Jan. 15, 1902, while boarding a train at Braddock, Mr. Hamilton met with an accident which necessitated the amputation of both of his limbs, one at the ankle and the other below the knee. His vigor was marvelous and his recovery rapid. In twenty days he was back from the hospital, and on June 1st was again at work with the aid of artificial limbs. While he was confined to the hospital and his home 276 teachers sent flowers, many of them twice, and some three and four times. Others sent fruit, house plants and books and more than 500 children sent flowers or fruit; and from dozens of other friends came flowers by mail and by express. Mr. Hamilton was again elected to the office of county superintendent in June, 1903.

WILLIAM H. REEL, who for many years was active in the business and political life of Allegheny county, died on Sunday, May 26, 1901, at his home, No. 202 Delp St., Avalon, Pa., after an illness of two weeks. He was a descendant of one of the pioneer families; his grandfather, also named William, is said to have been the first white man to settle in what is now Ross township. His parents were Conrad and Rosanna Reel, his father being the first postmaster in Ross township. At that time the borough of Allegheny had not been organized and the people there were compelled to go to this postoffice for their mail. He was also one of the early collectors of internal revenue, when the district extended to the city of Erie. William H. Reel was born and reared in Ross township. He received his education in the common schools of that township and Allegheny city. In his early life he was associated with his father and brothers in the first woolen mill in this part of the country. (See sketch of Charles C. Reel.) In political matters he was always an active and enthusiastic democrat, and in 1875 was appointed as a clerk in the office of the auditor-general, at Harrisburg, where he served one term of four years, at the expiration of which he returned to Allegheny city. For more than twenty years he was connected with the Western penitentiary of Pennsylvania, during which time he had charge of the dye houses. He was one of the charter members of the Randall club, which was named in honor of Samuel J. Randall, who represented a Pennsylvania district in congress for a number of years. Mr. Reel was a devout Catholic, and throughout his life was interested in the charitable work of his church. He had a pew in St. Peter's church and another at St. Xavier's. For many years he was a director of St. Paul's orphan asylum, and while on the board did much to advance the interests and extend the influence of the institution.

He was one of the incorporators of St. Mary's cemetery, of Pittsburg. Solemn requiem mass was celebrated over the remains in St. Xavier's church on Wednesday, May 29, 1901. The honorary pall bearers were Hon. B. McKenna, Michael Ward, Edward Friel, Martin Gannon and four of the employes of the penitentiary, viz.: Messrs. Stewart, Hill, Johnson and Griffith. The active pall bearers were eight of Mr. Reel's nephews. There is something inspiring in the life of a good man that stimulates those who knew him to higher efforts and nobler aims. Such a life was that of William H. Reel. Industrious and energetic in all the common affairs of life, actuated by pure, moral motives, honest and upright in all his dealings with his fellow-men, filled with sympathy for the unfortunate, and dispensing charity with a lavish hand, his good deeds will live long after he has passed to his eternal rest.

GEORGE T. ATKINS, of Elizabeth, Pa., a successful tailor and burgess of that borough, was born in Monongahela, Pa., Aug. 20, 1866, son of William H. and Susan (Hillman) Atkins, of Monongahela, Pa. He was educated in the thorough schools of that city, and then devoted his attention to the tailors' trade. After serving his apprenticeship at that trade, he, in 1893, engaged in business at Zelienople, Butler Co., Pa., and one year later removed to Elizabeth, where he has since prospered in the tailoring business. Mr. Atkins was married, in 1889, to Flora J., daughter of Andrew and Mary Jane (Orr) Woods, of Pittsburg, and they have two children, viz.: Mary J. and George T., Jr., both attending the local schools. Mr. Atkins is well known and exceedingly popular in Elizabeth, and in February, 1903, was elected burgess of that borough on the republican ticket, and was the only republican elected in that contest, a fact that attests his personal popularity in Elizabeth. Mr. Atkins is closely identified with the Knights of the Maccabees and the Junior Order of United American Mechanics, of which order he is also a member of the uniform rank. He is a prominent and influential member of the Methodist Episcopal church and an active worker in its ranks, being recording steward.

CHARLES J. HIEBER, a resident of Perrysville, son of John and Margaret (Emerick) Hieber, was born in Beaver county, Jan. 17, 1863, and was educated in the common schools. His boyhood days were spent on a farm, and in early manhood, at the age of twenty-two, he left the farm to become a blacksmith. After two years at this, he became a contractor for building oil derricks, at which he worked for three years, then becoming engaged at his present occupation in the general merchandise business, under the name of Hieber & Brant, one of the most enterprising firms of the county. On July 6, 1903, Mr. Hieber purchased the interest of Mr. Brant, and under the new regime it will doubtless retain its former high standard. He came to this county at the age of sixteen, having also lived for a time in Butler county. Mr. Hieber was married, Nov. 26, 1902, to Della M. Deimling, daughter of George V. Deimling, of Perrysville. Mr. Hieber is a member of the Masonic fraternity, Bellevue lodge, No. 530, and of R. Biddle Roberts lodge, No. 530, I. O. O. F., of Allegheny city. He is connected in an official way in the government of his township, having served nine years as its auditor, and is also a notary public. Mr. Hieber is a stockholder in the McKee's Rocks trust company, also a stockholder in the Frank H. Hieber wagon manufacturing company, of McKee's Rocks. He is also a very prominent man in church circles, being a German Lutheran. In politics he is a republican. The family is of German descent, John Hieber, father of the subject of this sketch, being born in Leutenbach, Würtemburg, Germany, June 23, 1838. He was married, Sept. 29, 1859, to Margaret Emerick, daughter of Henry Emerick, and to them were born thirteen children: Frank H., of McKee's Rocks, general manager of the Frank H. Hieber wagon manufacturing company; Sarah M., wife of Adolph D. Beuerman, grocer of Allegheny city (both deceased); Charles J. and George W., of Perrysville, blacksmiths; David L., of Allegheny city, grocer; Elizabeth M. Stubble, of Allegheny city; Bertha C. Blind, wife of H. L. Blind, florist of West View; Albert D., assistant foreman of Hieber manufacturing company; Hannah D., wife of William H. Brant, of the firm of Hieber & Brant; Amelia A. Kind, wife of E. A. Kind, of Allegheny city; John H. (deceased); Wilson S., clerk for the firm of

Hieber & Brant, and Amanda M., of Perrysville. George V. Deimling, father of the wife of the subject of this sketch, was born Nov. 23, 1845, in Allegheny city. He lived there until the breaking out of the Civil war, enlisted then as a volunteer in Company G, 74th regiment, infantry department. He was in the front in several important battles—Cross Keys, Freeman's Ford, White Sulphur Springs, second Bull Run and Gettysburg; was taken prisoner at the latter place and put in Libby prison for three months. He escaped from prison and returned to the service again, going then to South Carolina, where he was honorably discharged in October, 1864. Mr. Deimling was the proprietor of the West View hotel for ten years. John Hieber, the father of Charles J., came to this country at the age of sixteen. He first settled at Etna, then drifted to Beaver county, at the age of twenty-one was married and now resides in Perrysville. Mrs. Margaret (Emerick) Hieber was born in Beaver county, Oct. 28, 1839, and is of German descent, her grandfather having been a native of Zweibrücken, Germany, and the owner of a ship, which made regular trips between his native city and Delaware. Mrs. Hieber's grandfather settled in Delaware at a very early day, and her father was a native of that state, but both died in Pennsylvania.

JOHN I. SHANKS, son of William A. Shanks, was born in Neville township, Nov. 19, 1858, and educated in the public schools of that place. For more than thirty years he was a gardener on the island, where he owned a small farm at one time. About two years ago he sold his farm, since which time he has been living a retired life. Mr. Shanks was married to Hattie W. Gibson, of Neville island, and to them were born three children: Leland R., Paul D. and Wayne C. Mrs. Shanks died March 19, 1897. Mr. Shanks is one of Neville township's prominent men, and is a man of first-class business qualities. He is one of the directors in the Coraopolis National bank and one of its charter members. He is also a director in the Ohio Valley trust company, of Coraopolis; a stockholder in the Bellevue realty company, of Bellevue, and a stockholder in the North American savings bank, of Pittsburg, Pa.

F. B. MINER, M. D., a physician in Perrysville, son of Ansel and Emma (Bartlett) Miner, was born in Trumbull county, Ohio, Jan. 28, 1865. He received his education in the grades and high school in Warren, Ohio, and matriculated at Allegheny college, graduating in 1889 with the degree of A. B., and receiving A. M. a short time later. In the fall of 1889 he entered the University of Michigan, in the medical department, taking the first two years of the course in this school and completing it in the Long Island college hospital of Brooklyn, N. Y. In 1892 he began practicing his profession in Warren, Ohio, remaining in that field four years. In 1893 Dr. Miner was elected county coroner, serving in that office two years. In 1896 he located in Gardner, N. D., where he practiced for over four years, returning in 1900 to Allegheny county, where he has a very large practice in Perrysville and vicinity. The family, on the father's side, dates back to the old Connecticut stock, and on the mother's to English ancestry. He was married to Winnifred Wilkinson, in 1892, and to them have been born one son, Alfred W. Mrs. Miner was the daughter of Rev. T. H. Wilkinson, associate editor of the Pittsburg Christian Advocate. Mrs. Miner died Feb. 13, 1903.

FRED. C. HINKEL, a resident of Ross township, son of Charles and Maria Hinkel, was born in South Side, Pittsburg, Oct. 19, 1872, and educated in the public schools of that city. His whole life has been spent in agricultural pursuits—first in gardening, at which he was very prosperous, and recently as a florist. Mr. Hinkel is the manager of the large farm known as the Hinkel farm, an estate well adapted to agriculture. He is among the largest growers in the Allegheny market, his trade being, for the most part, in the country, and does business both wholesale and retail, the former being much the larger. The principal products of this farm are lettuce, rhubarb and cucumbers, and so great is the demand for the Hinkel farm products, that a yield of thrice the size could readily be disposed of. Mr. Hinkel was married, in July, 1898, to Lillie Heid, and to this union have been born two children, William and Maria. Mr. Hinkel has served on many important committees of public interest, and has in every way acted the part of the unprejudiced, conscientious citizen. He is a young man of prominence in the county, and a man who has won the admiration and applause of all who know him. The family is German Lutheran in religious affiliation, belonging to the church of that denomination in Perrysville. Mr. Hinkel is a member of the society of American florists and oriental horticulturists.

E. J. PUGH, of Natrona, Pa., a well-known farmer, was born in Clinton township, Butler Co., Pa., Oct. 13, 1835, son of Peter and Elizabeth (Brasey) Pugh, natives of Butler county and Ohio, respectively. His father was a successful farmer, a republican in political matters, and the father of twelve children, four of whom are now living. E. J. Pugh was reared on a farm and attended the common schools, the greater part of his educational training being secured through his own efforts. He has followed coal-mining, farming and various other occupations, and by thrift and economy has accumulated a competency, and now owns thirty-three acres of land, under which lies a fine grade of coal. He also owns property in Harrison township. He has also been engaged in the mercantile business for a great many years, and here, as elsewhere, has met with much success. Mr. Pugh is a republican in politics, and he and his wife are members of the Methodist church. He was married, in 1854, to Kezia J. Fox, of Butler county, Pa., and while they have had no children of their own, they have raised five, two of whom they adopted, viz.: Lillie B. and S. B. Lillie B. became the wife of William Bryan, of Brackenridge borough, and has two children, William and Sylvia May. S. B. is a mere youth, and still resides with his adopted parents. Mr. Pugh is a successful and prosperous business man, and possesses the respect and good-will of all of his neighbors.

JOHN WILKINS, foreman of the marine ways at Elizabeth, Pa., is a son of William and Eliza (Smith) Wilkins, and was born in Washington county, Pa., March 2, 1869, his parents both being natives of that county. He was educated in the schools of West Brownsville, and after leaving school learned the trade of ship-carpenter. For the last eight years he has held his present position, the duties of which he has discharged with signal ability and to the entire satisfaction of his employers. He was married, in 1890, to Miss Mary Crawford, of Fayette county, and to them have been born four children, named Helen, Rinard, Ruth and John. Mr. Wilkins has always taken a lively interest in all matters pertaining to municipal affairs. He served the people of the borough of Elizabeth for three years in the council, and for one year was president of that body. He was elected on the citizens' ticket, although politically he is a republican. He is a member of the Royal Arcanum, which is the only order of a social or fraternal character to claim his membership. As a mechanic he is master of his trade, and as a citizen he is honored and respected in the community where he lives.

JAMES WALKER, a representative farmer of North Fayette township, was born in Allegheny county in 1844. He is a son of James and Mary (McGregor) Walker, both of whom were natives of Allegheny county, where the father followed the vocation of a farmer. James Walker, Sr., was born in 1813 and died in 1895, having attained the age of eighty-two years. His wife died in 1850. Mr. Walker was married a second time, to Julia Ann Robinson, who survives him at the age of eighty-four. James Walker, Jr., in his boyhood and youth lived the customary life of a farmer's son. The summers were passed in aiding his father to plant and harvest the crops, and in the winter seasons he attended the common schools of North Fayette township, where he acquired a thorough knowledge of the common branches. Mr. Walker lived with his grandfather McGregor until the latter's death in 1865, when he went to Pittsburg, and later worked three years in a mill at Uniontown, returning to his present home in 1877. Mr. Walker has always affiliated with the democratic party, though he has never been an active participant in political affairs, nor has ever aspired to public office. He married late in life, being united to Miss Ella A. Reed, on May 26, 1897. She was born in 1859. Both husband and wife are members of the United Presbyterian church and consistently practice the precepts of their religion in their daily lives.

CHARLES C. ELWARNER, wreck-master on the Pan Handle railroad, residing at the corner of Sixth and Dick streets, Carnegie, was born in Dresden, Ohio, Sept. 12, 1850. His parents, Christopher and Lizzie (Morningstar) Elwarner, are both dead. Mr. Elwarner is one of two children. An older brother, John, died when young. Christopher Elwarner was a prominent butcher all his active life. Charles C. Elwarner, the subject of this sketch, was educated in the public schools at Dresden and Coshocton, Ohio, and when a boy assisted his father. His first occupation in his long service with the Pan Handle railroad was as special officer, located at Coshocton, for putting up telegraph lines, and after about a year of this work, he was employed for a time as a brakeman, and then spent several years in the shops at Dennison, Ohio. After this he became assistant wreck-master at Dennison, and in 1887 came to Carnegie, where he has been employed as wreck-master for over seventeen years. He has been very successful in his life, is known as a master workman, and is deservedly popular among his craft. Mr. Elwarner has been twice married. He took as his first wife Miss Mary Carey, of Coshocton, Ohio, and had by this marriage three children: John P., for the past four years an engineer, living at home; Ella, residing at home, and Mary, now the wife of Mark Murphy, a brass-fitter, of Cleveland, Ohio. His wife having died in February, 1887, Mr. Elwarner was married, Nov. 13, 1889, to Miss Mary Gandley, of Pittsburg, Pa., a daughter of William and Mary (Jordan) Gandley.

The father was a foreman of car shops in England, and died there, and in 1868 Mrs. Gandley came to America, locating in South Side, Pittsburg. Mrs. Elwarner is the youngest of the children. The others are: Bridget, wife of Patrick Jordan, a resident of Pittsburg; Thomas, a bottle-blower, residing in Monongahela City, and John, also a bottle-blower, living in Pittsburg. Four children have been born of this second marriage: Eugene V., Vronicha, Charles C., Jr., and William W. Mrs. Elwarner is a member of St. Luke's Roman Catholic church. Mr. Elwarner is one of the "Pan Handle trio," the other two members being E. M. Meyers and John McGrogan, of Carnegie. He is also a member of the following fraternal orders: Centennial lodge, No. 544, F. and A. M.; Cyrus chapter, No. 280, R. A. M.; Mansfield castle, No. 476, K. G. E.; Mansfield temple, No. 103, L. G. E.; Mansfield Valley council, No. 840, Royal Arcanum; Carnegie lodge, No. 831, B. P. O. Elks, and of the volunteer relief department of the P. C. C. & St. L. railway company. He is one of the most highly respected citizens of Carnegie, a man of most attractive personality, and enjoys the esteem and good-will of the community.

A. M. YOCHUM, A. M., a resident of Perrysville, pastor of St. Theresa's church, a son of Peter Yochum, was born in Pittsburg, Feb. 11, 1858. His boyhood days were spent in Pittsburg, and in that city he received his elementary education. After choosing his life-work, he took his classical training in St. Vincent's college, and his philosophical and theological courses at St. Vincent's seminary, one of the oldest schools in the state. He entered school in 1887 and finished in 1895, being ordained to the priesthood May 10, 1895. His first pastoral charge was assistant rector of Holy Name, Troy Hill, Allegheny city. He remained in this place for more than four years, becoming attached to his church, both for its possibilities and on account of Father Mollinger's chapel, famous for the large collections of relics and vessels preserved there. Father Yochum was promoted to his present charge in June, 1899. His father, Peter Yochum, came to this country in 1854, and was one of Pittsburg's prominent business men. He was born Feb. 11, 1821, and died Nov. 16, 1893.

PHILIP WEIGLE was born at West Brownsville, Washington Co., Pa., Feb. 10, 1860, son of John and Anna (Redlingshoefer) Weigle. Mr. and Mrs. John Weigle had the following children: William, George, John, Philip, Michael, George B. McC., William Duncan, Elizabeth (now Mrs. Jenkins), Frank and Charles C. (deceased), Margaret (now Mrs. Balsimer), and Charles R. Philip Weigle came to Elizabeth in 1881, where he has since resided. In 1884 the firm of Weigle Bros. was organized for the manufacture of coal-boats and barges, Philip Weigle being one of the organizers of the concern. The other brothers who composed the firm were William, George, John and Michael. The concern was sold in 1898 to the Monongahela River consolidated coal and coke company and Mr. Weigle is now an employe of that firm. In political belief he is a democrat.

CHARLES R. WEIGLE, bookkeeper for the Monongahela consolidated coal and coke company, of Elizabeth, was born in Brownsville, Washington Co., Pa , in 1874. His parents were John and Anna D. Weigle. C. R. Weigle came with his parents to Elizabeth in 1881, where he attended the public schools. Later he attended Duquesne college, from which he graduated in 1894. Soon after graduation he became associated with Weigle Bros. & Co., docks, the firm doing a general docking and repairing business. Mr. Weigle was secretary and treasurer of the company for about five years, and then the business was sold out to the Monongahela consolidated coal and coke company. Since that time he has been associated with the latter firm, and has held the position of bookkeeper since 1900. Mr. Weigle was married, in 1901, to Miss Sarah Hall, daughter of Elijah and Sarah Hall, of Elizabeth, and he has one child, Herman H., born Jan. 27, 1903. Mr. Weigle is a democrat in political belief. He has served three years as councilman.

JAMES L. JOHNSTON, for fifteen years a prominent and respected citizen of Wilkinsburg, was born in Pittsburg, Allegheny county, Oct. 22, 1832, son of George R. and Sarah Ann (Little) Johnston, the father, George R. Johnston, a farmer and engineer. The man whose name heads this article was the second of a family of eight children. He was educated at Wilkinsburg and at the East Liberty academy, studying under Professor Smith, was for many years a successful farmer, and also operated coal mines, selling to Dixon, Stewart & Co., large coal operators in Allegheny county. He has lived in Wilkinsburg since 1888. Mr. Johnston is a member of the famous Beulah Presbyterian church. He was married, in 1861, to Rachel G. Graham, a daughter of Rev. James Graham, one of the early pastors of Beulah church. Rev. Graham was born in 1776, and was from 1804 to 1845 minister of Beulah church. He was a man universally loved and respected for his earnestness and kindly Christian spirit.

WILLIAM E. YATES, saddler at No. 9 Fourth Ave., Carnegie, was born in Mount Sidney, Augusta Co., Va., May 1, 1834. His parents were Maj. John and Ann Yates. The major was a harness-maker in Mount Sidney for many years. He was a strong Union man and violently opposed to secession, did everything in his power to keep his State from going out of the Union, and when he saw that his efforts were vain, he tried to weaken the confederacy in every way in his power. A company had been organized in Mount Sidney about 1855, and on April 17, 1861, the company was called out by the confederate authorities and taken to Harper's Ferry, but not being full, was disbanded, and returned home to recruit and reorganize. Two of the major's sons were members of the company. As soon as the major heard of the company and what it proposed to do, he made a speech, urging the boys to disperse, and so influential a man was he, and so efficacious were his arguments, that he prevented the company from reorganizing. This and other acts made Major Yates so unpopular among his seceding neighbors that his life was in constant danger during the war. He was taken prisoner and carried to Richmond, where he was in jail about eight months in all. The major so contrived that none of his four sons were impressed into the southern army. Two of the boys he succeeded in getting north, and the other two he kept concealed for almost two years, so that they might not be forced to fight against their country. The major was a generous man, and cherished no hard feeling against those with whom he could not agree. On the occasion of General Custer's visit to the valley, Major Yates asked that he treat the rebels and Union men alike, and spare the property of the poor, and this was done. When the war was over, Major Yates was appointed postmaster. Some eight months after the war he lost his sight, and his daughter served as his assistant. He was postmaster continuously until his death, which occurred Dec. 15, 1881. His wife died in 1871, at the age of seventy-one years. Major Yates and wife had eight children: Tommie, the eldest, who died in infancy; James, a farmer near Arbor Hill, Va., who died at the age of sixty-eight; William E., the subject of this sketch; Charles W. (deceased); Andrew Mc., who succeeded his father as postmaster; Sallie, who was for a time postmistress; Ella (deceased) and Mattie. William E. Yates was educated in the common schools of Virginia, and learned his father's trade, as a saddler. He started in business for himself in West Philadelphia, where he worked on Market street for a year, and then went to Pittsburg, where he worked in the arsenal. Later he followed his trade in Burgettstown, Pa., for fifteen years, and then, in 1880, came to what is now Carnegie, Pa., where he has since resided. He held the position of postmaster during Cleveland's first administration, and filled the office most creditably. On Nov. 28, 1867, Mr. Yates married Miss Anna M. Rankin, adopted daughter of Matthew Rankin, and daughter of Collins Kimball. Of the five children born to Mr. and Mrs. Yates, only two are living: John O., who married Miss Mary Schulte, and has one child, Ruth; and William R., who is in business in Carnegie. Mrs. Yates died April 11, 1898, at the age of fifty-eight. Mr. Yates is a member of the Presbyterian church. He is a Mason and an Odd Fellow, and a member of the A. O. U. W., and is prominent in all three organizations. Mr. Yates is the proprietor of a medicine called "Yates' Nervine," which is said to be a harmless and efficacious cure for St. Vitus' dance and all other nervous disorders.

CALVIN BECK, one of the popular employes in the steel and iron industry at Tarentum, is a son of Daniel and Mary (Stiveson) Beck, and all are natives of Armstrong county, Pa. The father, who was a farmer by occupation, died some years ago at the age of eighty-four, but his widow survives in her seventy-fourth year. They reared a family of twelve children, nine of whom are still living. Calvin Beck was born in Armstrong county, Pa., Sept. 6, 1868. He was brought up on the farm, attended school somewhat irregularly during his boyhood and at an early age started out to make his own living. His first venture was in the steel mill at Apollo, but later he was engaged in the same line at Scottdale, Leechburg and Vandergrift. In 1901 he came to Tarentum, and since then has been employed with the Allegheny steel and iron company as a sheet steel roller. He is a republican in his political convictions and holds membership in the Knights of Pythias fraternity. In 1892 Mr. Beck was married to Miss Katie Jack, by whom he has two children, Willavem and Ruth. Mr. Beck is a member of the Lutheran church, while his wife is connected with the United Protestant denomination.

DANIEL HUEY, of Tarentum, Pa., a well-known farmer, was born on the old homestead of his parents, March 1, 1845, son of Joseph and Jane E. (Hunter) Huey, both natives of Pennsylvania, who settled in Fawn township in 1835. They resided there until the death of Joseph Huey. Mrs. Huey removed to Tarentum, where she now lives at an advanced age. Joseph Huey was a prosperous farmer, and he and his wife were members of the Presbyterian church. Daniel Huey was reared on the farm, attended the common schools, and has devoted his business life to the occupation of farming. He owns fifty acres of land and has met with much success as a general farmer. He is a democrat in politics, as was his father before him, and the elder Huey was a judge of electious, assessor and a school director. Daniel Huey was married, in 1869, to Margaret J., daughter of Jacob and Martha (Byerly) Burtner, natives of Allegheny and Armstrong counties respectively. Mr. and Mrs. Huey are the parents of four children: Myrtle M., wife of Elmer Pringle, and is the mother of three children, Richard M., Alta P. and Glen; Joseph Henry, who for the last three years has resided in California; Letha A., wife of Alfred Woodrow, and Bertha A., the last two twins. Mr. Huey is a successful farmer and substantial citizen, and is highly esteemed by his neighbors.

J. BAILEY SULLIVAN, M. D., was born in Ireland, April 13, 1851, son of M. C. and Margaret (Bailey) Sullivan, both of whom lived and died in Ireland. Dr. Sullivan came to New York when sixteen years old, attended school in that city, and afterwards taught in Manhattan college. In 1874 he came to Pittsburg and immediately engaged in teaching. In 1888 he graduated from Pulte medical college, in Cincinnati, Ohio, and has been successfully engaged in practicing medicine in Pittsburg since that time. For the past ten years Dr. Sullivan's family resided at their beautiful suburban home at Verona, which was recently disposed of. They are at present living in their East End residence in Pittsburg. Besides a practicing physician, Dr. Sullivan is also an able educator, having for several years been principal of the Ralston school, the Riverside school and the Duquesne school, all of Pittsburg. He was married, in 1880, to Miss Elizabeth Speaker, whose parents were natives of Germany, and came to Pittsburg in 1848. Dr. Sullivan and wife have nine children living: Clare, Margretta, Adeline, Herbert, Regina, Clement, Winifred, Austin and Ambrose. The family are Catholics in religious belief. Dr. Sullivan owns property in Oklahoma, adjacent to the city of Lawton, where he intends to establish his future home.

WILLIAM H. CUNNINGHAM, a successful McKeesport real estate man, was born in Allegheny city, Pa., Aug. 2, 1872. He came to McKeesport with his parents in 1882, and attended the public schools there, afterwards taking a commercial course at the Gressly business college, and then entered the employ of the

National tube company, where he remained nine years, filling various responsible positions. In 1894 Mr. Cunningham became connected with the firm of E. H. Leizure & Co., in the real estate business, and three years later started in the business for himself, in company with R. W. Junker, at the corner of Sixth avenue and Walnut street. This partnership continued until September, 1902, and since that time Mr. Cunningham has been in the real estate business alone, being located at No. 519 Market St. Mr. Cunningham and his wife and daughter, Mary E., reside in the third ward, McKeesport. Mrs. Cunningham was formerly Miss Sarah Wallace, and is a daughter of Lewis and Emma Wallace, of McKeesport. Mr. Cunningham is a member of the Cumberland Presbyterian church. Politically, he is a republican.

HUGH SIMONS, of Hoboken, Pa., a well-known river contractor, was born in Pittsburg, Pa., Sept. 16, 1845, son of William and Mary (Ireland) Simons, his father being a contractor on the river. Hugh Simons attended the public schools of his native city, and when sixteen years of age began with his father on the river, where he continued until he attained his majority. Then, his father having purchased a farm in Westmoreland county, they removed to this farm and there remained until 1878, when he returned to Pittsburg and entered the employ of O. Scaife in iron-roofing work. He continued in that capacity for one year and then returned to Westmoreland county, where he was engaged in farming for the next seven years. He then removed to Hoboken and was in the employ of the Allegheny county workhouse until 1893, when the state prohibited the making of barrels by penal institutions, and as that was his business, he was forced to retire. He then engaged in contracting on the river and has prospered in that occupation to the present time. He was married, in 1867, to Mary L., daughter of Henry F. and Margaret Bergman, both natives of Germany. Mr. and Mrs. Simons have eight children, viz.: Frank W., an undertaker, of Allegheny city; Hattie Blanche, wife of Samuel M. Kier, a steel melter, of Aspinwall; Clyde A., auditor of the American mirror plate company, of Pittsburg; Margaret, wife of Frank F. Morrison, a farmer, of Westmoreland county; Algy Warren, a carpenter, of Montrose; Della M.; Allen N., learning the undertaking business with his brother Frank in Allegheny city; Dallas Alton, attending the public schools. Mr. Simons is a member of the Methodist church of Hoboken, the Junior Order of United American Mechanics, the river improvement association and of the republican party. He has served several times on the election board, and in 1903 was elected a justice of the peace for the term of five years.

WILLIAM ROSS HARRISON, of Harmarville, Pa., a prosperous farmer, was born in the old Ross mansion in O'Hara township, Allegheny Co., Pa., June 28, 1849, son of Sampson and Jane (Nixon) Harrison. His father was a gardener while at Ross farm, and in 1851 removed to Harmar township, purchased a farm about two miles north of Cheswick, and there followed agricultural pursuits until his death, in 1886, at the age of eighty-one years. His mother died of cancer, in 1855, at the age of forty-five years. William R. Harrison was educated in the common schools of Harmar township, attending the Henderson school until he reached his twentieth year. He then began to assist his father on the farm, later assumed charge of the farm and has successfully conducted the same to the present time. Mr. Harrison was married, in 1882, to Eleanor, daughter of Peter and Padaline (Bell) Quinette, of Indiana township, and they have two children: Harry, with his father on the farm, and Frederick, attending the public schools of Harmar township. Mr. Harrison is a member of the Methodist church, the Ancient Order of United Workmen and the republican party. He has served as school director and auditor, and has traveled extensively over the western and central states.

WILLIAM F. WILSON, a well-known McKeesport architect, has had a long experience in the practice of his profession both in McKeesport and Pittsburg. He learned to be an architect with Henry Moeser, was associated in business with him for twelve years in Pittsburg, and then was for two years in partnership with Charles Schuster. He has for several years been located in McKeesport, with offices in the Oppenheimer building, at the corner of Fifth avenue and Market street, where he has been most successful. Mr. Wilson was born in Greenock, Allegheny Co., Pa., in 1859, son of Robert N. and Mary Wilson, and received his education mainly in the public schools, studying also a year and a half under a private tutor. He is a republican in politics. He is a member of McKeesport lodge, No. 136, B. P. O. Elks. Mr. Wilson resides in Versailles borough.

ELLWOOD W. ELLISON, the well-known railroad engineer of Versailles, Pa., was born in Muscatine county, Ia., Nov. 23, 1860. He is a son of J. G. and Mary (Armstrong) Ellison. His father is one of the old and prominent citizens of Allegheny city. E. W. Ellison was educated in the public schools of Allegheny county and graduated from Carier academy in 1877. Since 1880 he has been in the employ of the Baltimore & Ohio railroad company, working his way up to the position of an engineer, which he holds at the present time. He was married, in 1890, to Miss Florence D. McClure, a daughter of W. A. and Mary (Douglas) McClure, of Elizabeth township. They have four children: William Alexander, Mary C., Asia Forest and James G. The firm hand and clear vision required in the locomotive engineer have a tendency to develop the stronger qualities in one's nature. It has been so in the case of Mr. Ellison. He is self-reliant and positive without being overbearing, and his judgment is usually correct. He takes an active interest in municipal matters, and it is not surprising that he was elected to the council of Versailles on the citizens' ticket in 1901. His term has not yet expired, and his record in the council has demonstrated the wisdom of the people in choosing him for their representative. Mr. Ellison is a member of the Woodmen of the World and of the Brotherhood of Locomotive Engineers, in both of which organizations he has a high standing.

MILTON LOEB, a promising young attorney of McKeesport, is a son of the late Ferdinand and Miriam Loeb, and was born in Philadelphia, Pa., in 1874. When seven years old, he moved with his parents to Sunbury, Northumberland county, where he attended school until he reached the age of seventeen, and then completed his education at Bucknell college. Upon leaving college, he studied law a year in the office of Judge F. Carroll Bruster, in Philadelphia, and then, being called home by the death of his father, read law in Sunbury, in the office of Senator S. P. Wilverton. He was admitted to the bar, practiced successfully for several years in Sunbury, and then came to McKeesport, where he has since been engaged in the practice of his profession, his office being in the Patterson building. While a resident of Sunbury, Mr. Loeb took an active interest in politics, was chairman of the republican committee, and for a number of years solicitor of the school board. He belongs to the Knights of Pythias and B. P. O. Elks, being a prominent member of the last-named society, in which he has creditably filled several important offices.

WILLIAM OLIVER CAMPBELL, of Sharpsburg, Pa., a successful farmer of O'Hara township, was born in that township, Feb. 2, 1861, son of James C. and Isabelle (Marshall) Campbell, of O'Hara township, Allegheny Co., Pa. His father was a well-known farmer and was a son of Thomas Campbell, who was a native of County Down, Ireland, and came to America when a young man and here married Mary, daughter of James Crawford, of Allegheny city, Pa., who owned all the land now owned by the Campbell brothers and the adjoining farm owned by Mr. Crawford. William O. Campbell was educated at the Robinson school, of O'Hara township, which he attended until fifteen years of age. He then began to assist his father on the farm and continued in that capacity until his twenty-fourth year, when his father retired from active life. For the next six years the farm was run by the sons of James C. Campbell, and then it was divided between them, W. O. Campbell securing the eastern half. This part of the original farm consists of forty-seven and one-half acres and is situated on the Mill road, two and one-half miles from Sharpsburg, in O'Hara township, Allegheny Co., Pa. Mr. Campbell was married, on March 28, 1899, to Mary, daughter of Hugh and Susan (Price) Pollock, formerly of Pittsburg, but then residing in Indiana township. Hugh Pollock was a native of County Down, Ireland, and when a mere infant accompanied his parents, James and Nancy

(McCord) Pollock, to America, and there he married Susan Price, a native of Germantown, a suburb of Philadelphia. Mr. and Mrs. Campbell have one daughter, Helen Lenore, residing with her parents. Mr. Campbell is a member of the Presbyterian church, the Junior Order of United American Mechanics and of the republican party. He is well and favorably known in that part of the county and is a man of genuine worth.

ROBERT H. COOK, who conducts a flour and feed exchange in the town of Bridgeville, in Upper St. Clair township, is one of the representative citizens of Allegheny county, Pa. He is of Scotch-Irish descent, and is the son of Moses C. and Lavina Cook, both of whom were natives of Washington county, Pa. His mother died when he was less than two years of age, and his father died in 1903, in his eighty-sixth year. John Cook, the paternal grandfather of Robert, was born in Chambersburg, Franklin Co., Pa. His wife, Robert's grandmother, at the age of twenty-seven, was thrown from a horse against a ragged fence, receiving fatal injuries. Robert H. Cook was born in Allegheny county, Oct. 23, 1867. As a boy, he worked upon his father's farm, attending the common schools during the fall and winter months. Later he attended the high school for two years, thus acquiring a good education. In 1898 he was married to Miss Elizabeth Nichols, a daughter of Joel Nichols. Joel Nichols was a printer by trade. Both he and his wife were members of the Society of Friends. Mrs. Cook was born in Belmont county, Ohio, in 1866. She is a well-educated woman, having taken the common-school course and graduated from the high school at St. Clairsville, Ohio. Mr. and Mrs. Cook are both members of the Presbyterian church. They have no children. Mr. Cook takes a great interest in political affairs. He has always affiliated with the democratic party, but in 1902 he was one of the seven councilmen elected on the citizens' ticket to represent the Bridgeville borough. As a member of the council he has demonstrated that he is fully capable of grasping public questions, and has labored assiduously for the promotion of the public welfare.

JOHN S. McGINLEY, superintendent at Springdale for the Philadelphia gas company, was born in Harmarville, Allegheny county, Nov. 10, 1850. His parents, John and Catherine (Gallagher) McGinley, both natives of Ireland, came to Brooklyn, N. Y., in 1830, to Allegheny county about 1845, and from there moved to Freeport, Armstrong county, where Mr. McGinley died in July, 1885, and his wife in October of the same year. They were the parents of four sons and two daughters, of whom two sons and two daughters are living. They were members of the Catholic church. Mrs. McGinley's parents were David and Nancy (Sterritt) Gallagher, early settlers in Freeport, who died there. John S. McGinley, the subject of this sketch, was reared and educated at Freeport, and there spent several years with the Standard oil company, and was for a time employed by McGinnis, Smith & Co., steam and gas-fitters. In July, 1888, he came to Springdale and assumed charge of the office of the Philadelphia gas company, and has been thus engaged ever since. Mr. McGinley is an independent in politics, and a Catholic in religion. He is a member of the Independent Order of Heptasophs, of Tarentum, Pa. He was married, in 1873, to Miss Mary F. Braiden, of Pittsburg, and has two children, Lyda and Kate. Mr. McGinley has been successful in his business career, and has made many friends in Springdale.

REV. EUGENE VOLKAY, pastor of the Greek Catholic church at Monessen, Pa., was born in the year 1864, at Szmerckova, Ung county, Hungary. His parents were Anthony and Anna (Koflanovics) Volkay. His father was a priest of Ujszemere, Hungary, and died in 1874, the wife dying in 1878. Eugene Volkay received his elementary education in the schools of Ungvar. Being the son of a priest, he had the privilege of obtaining board in the house of the priest's wife during his attendance at the grammar school, from which he graduated in 1883, and then he spent four years in the theological seminary. In both the grammar school and the theological seminary he was awarded the highest distinction for diligence and approved work. During his course in theology he belonged to what was called the "Literary Club," and in the priests' sons' boarding school he was chosen as provisor, or *informatur*. After finishing his theological course he was married to Anna, the daughter of the Very Rev. Andrew Nehrebeczky. His marriage occurred on March 8, 1888, and on November 25th of the same year he was ordained as a priest in Hungary. His first service was at Gezseny as an assistant priest, and later he filled the position of temporary priest at Klokocso, Ung county, Hungary. On March 25, 1890, he landed in the United States and went to Hazleton, Pa., where he remained until 1892, when he went back to Europe and brought his wife to this country. For some time he resided at Hazleton, where he organized the Greek Catholic congregation, and then removed to Brooklyn, N. Y., where he stayed for four years, organizing a parish there and building a church and parish house. His next move was to New York city, where he bought property on East Sixth street on which to build a church. For two years he worked hard and unceasingly to organize a congregation and erect a church, but for lack of co-operation his efforts in this direction did not meet with any measure of success. At the end of these two years he went back to Hazleton, Pa., and remained there about eighteen months. A severe illness of his wife compelled him to give up his charge at Hazleton, and after a short stay in Philadelphia, he went to Scranton, Pa., upon the advice of his physician, and continued there until August, 1901. For about a year he was then in charge of a church at Bridgeport, after which he came to Monessen to perfect the organization of the parish, which at that time was only temporary. His efforts at Monessen have been crowned with success, and the church there has flourished under his ministration. Father Volkay has organized congregations at New Britain, Conn.; Salem, Mass.; Syracuse and Auburn, N. Y.; Trenton, Perth Amboy and Bayonne City, N. J., and Phœnixville and Reading, Pa. He has also taken a considerable part in the organization of different societies, principally the Greek Catholic union. Of this society he was one of the founders, and he was the first priest to bring his family from Hungary to the United States.

LLOYD F. THOMPSON, for twelve years station agent for the Allegheny Valley railroad at Verona, was born in Armstrong county, Pa., June 15, 1868. His father, Jacob N. Thompson, son of Robert and Mary (Nolf) Thompson, was for the greater part of his life a merchant at Mahoning, Armstrong county, a republican in politics, school director, and a member of the I. O. O. F. He was a veteran of the Civil war. He was a native of Clarion county, but spent most of his life in Armstrong county, and died there.

His wife, Mary (Myers) Thompson, mother of the subject of this sketch, was the daughter of Samuel and Mary (Rhodes) Myers, pioneers of Armstrong county, where they spent their last days. Mrs. Thompson died in 1897. Jacob N. and Mary (Myers) Thompson had six children, of whom only two survive. Lloyd F. Thompson, subject of this sketch, was reared and educated at Mahoning, and engaged in business there for a short time with his father. In 1888 he began his career as a railroad man as telegraph operator at Verona for the Allegheny Valley railroad, and was after a few years made station agent, in which capacity he has pleased his employers and made himself justly popular with the traveling public. He is a republican in politics, and has served his borough several terms as school director and clerk of the council. He is a member of the Royal Arcanum. Mr. Thompson was married, in 1890, to Miss Gertrude B. Wiggins, of Mahoning, and has had five children, viz.: May (deceased), Edgar B., Lloyd Earl, Howard D. and Gertrude. Mr. and Mrs. Thompson are members of the Second United Presbyterian church of Verona.

DANIEL BOWMAN, a prominent farmer of Scott township, Allegheny Co., Pa., was born in that county, March 15, 1848. He is a son of Max and Catharine Bowman, both of whom were natives of Germany. They came to America about the year 1846, in an old-fashioned sailing vessel, and settled at Pittsburg, Pa., where they passed the remainder of their lives. Catharine Bowman died about five years after coming to this country, but her husband lived until 1897, when he too passed away. Max Bowman was a stone-mason by trade, and for many years plied his trade in Pittsburg and the adjacent towns. The death of Catharine Bowman left Daniel an orphan at a tender age, and he grew to manhood without knowing the blessings of a mother's care, living with different families, wherever he could find a home. The last family with whom he lived during his boyhood was that of Simon Coutch, where he lived ten years. From the time he was able to earn anything, Daniel worked by the month at whatever he could find to do, his first wages being three dollars a month. Under these circumstances his opportunity to secure an education was very limited indeed. Yet he managed to obtain a fair knowledge of the common branches, to which he has added, by self-study and culture, until he is a well-informed man. In February, 1864, at the age of sixteen, he enlisted as a recruit in the 87th Pennsylvania volunteer infantry, and served as a private until July 15, 1865, when he was honorably discharged from the service with the mustering out of his regiment. After the war he continued to work by the month until his marriage to Miss Christina Frick, which occurred on April 2, 1872. She was a daughter of Peter and Christina Frick, and was born in Allegheny county about the year 1847. Like her husband, she had lived a somewhat strenuous life during her girlhood, and is a fitting helpmate for her frugal and industrious husband. For three years after his marriage, Mr. Bowman followed the occupation of a farmer. Since then he has been continuously in the positions of supervisor and tax collector of Scott township. Politically, he is a republican, and has always stood ready to work for the success of his party. He has twice been elected justice of the peace, each time for a term of five years, and is now serving his second term. Before his first election to this office he served two years by appointment. Mr. Bowman is generally recognized as one of the substantial citizens of the township. He is a member of Thomas Espy post, No. 153, Grand Army of the Republic, and enjoys nothing more than a social meeting with his old comrades, with whom he bore arms in defense of his country, when he was scarcely out of his boyhood. Mr. and Mrs. Bowman have one son, Charles, who was born in February, 1874, and who still lives at home with his parents.

CALEB LEE, Jr., was born in Pittsburg, Pa., Nov. 18, 1837, a son of Caleb and Margaret (Skelton) Lee, the father a native of Dutchess county, N. Y., and the mother a native of Pittsburg, and daughter of Dr. John P. Skelton, a Pittsburg pioneer, who resided there many years, and spent his last days near Hulton, Pa. Caleb Lee, Sr., was a tailor by trade, at one time the leading tailor of Pittsburg, and for many years alderman of that city. He and his wife have had fifteen children, of whom four are living. Caleb, Sr., was born in 1800 and died in 1878, while his wife, who was born in 1805, died in 1883. Caleb Lee, Jr., the subject of this sketch, was educated in Pittsburg, and learned the tailors' trade, working at it with his father for eight years. In 1858 he moved on a farm near Hulton, resided there until 1879, and has since made his home in Hulton and Oakmont. He and his wife now live in

Oakmont, where, away from the cares of life, they spend their time in secluded ease. On Aug. 26, 1852, Mr. Lee was married to Miss Mary Knox, of Allegheny county, Pa., daughter of Robert and Isabella (Legett) Knox, has two children, a number of grandchildren, and one great-grandchild. Robert K., the oldest, born in 1853, is a farmer. He married Elizabeth McKelvy, of Plum township, and has two children. Of these, Robert, now a resident of Kensington, Pa., married Ellen Farren, and has one child, Ellen; and Caleb, born in 1879, is a clerk in Pittsburg. He was for three years with the National tube company, and is now in the employ of the Allegheny Valley railroad company. Mr. Lee's other child, Jennie, born in 1858, is the wife of Harry Paul, and has four children: Alice, Mary, Susan and Harry J. Mr. and Mrs. Lee celebrated the fiftieth anniversary of their wedding, Aug. 26, 1902. Mr. Lee is a republican in politics, though never politically ambitious. His wife is a member of the Presbyterian church.

CORNELIUS O'SHEA, of Port Perry, Pa., a successful and prosperous hotelkeeper, was born at Cork, Ireland, July 22, 1845, son of Cornelius and Mary (Hyde) O'Shea, his father having been a conductor on the Great Southern & Western railroad from Cork to Dublin, and died in 1872. The elder O'Shea was the father of seven children, the subject of this sketch being third in order of birth. Cornelius O'Shea came to America when seventeen years of age, landing in New York city, May 10, 1862, and subsequently secured employment at the Baldwin locomotive works, of Philadelphia, but remained there only a few weeks. He then enlisted in the marine corps for a term of two years, and at the expiration of his service was discharged and went to Johnstown, Cambria Co., Pa., and secured a position with the mills of that place, where he learned the melting trade. He was married, on May 13, 1875, to Annie, daughter of Squire and Mary Fitzpatrick, of Johnstown, Pa., and they have had seven children, viz.: Mary, wife of Harry Rose, of Allegheny city; Annie, wife of M. P. Leyden, of Glenwood; Margaret, Elizabeth, Nellie, and two others (deceased). On July 10, 1875, he accompanied Captain Jones to Braddock and remained in his employ until July 22, 1884, when he went with the firm of Jones & Laughlin, of Pittsburg, and continued with that concern for seven years. He also served on the Pittsburg police force for a term of two years, and in 1896 began the hotel business at Port Perry, where he has since prospered in that line. He is prominently identified with the public affairs of that section of the county and is a township commissioner of North Versailles township, having been one of the first five commissioners of that township. An interesting part of Mr. O'Shea's history, and one of which he is justly proud, is that he melted the first pound of iron ever melted in the great Edgar Thompson steel works, Braddock.

JOSEPH HEIDENKAMP, of the Heidenkamp mirror company, of Springdale, is a self-made man, who has by sheer pluck and ability risen from a humble position to the head of a large and prosperous manufacturing concern. He was born in Germany, Dec. 13, 1863, and educated in the schools of his native country. When twenty years old, he came to Creighton, Allegheny county, with less than five dollars in his pocket, and for ten years worked for the Pittsburg plate glass company. He then began in a small way as a manufacturer of French mirror glass, employing only one man and a boy, his plant being located in Tarentum and known as the Tarentum mirror and glass works. This continued until 1900, and grew to a large concern, employing about forty men, and having a capacity of $20,000 worth of mirror and art glass a month. In May, 1900, Mr. Heidenkamp came to Springdale, purchased forty-five acres of land and built a large plant, the concern having a capital of $300,000. Mr. Heidenkamp owns two-thirds of the capital stock. The plant had at first a capacity of 60,000 square feet of polished plate glass and mirrors per month, but on account of the high quality of the goods produced, and the consequent increased demand for them, it was found necessary to more than double the capacity of the factory, so that now the company turns out yearly 2,000,000 square feet of plate glass and mirrors. The plant is equipped with four furnaces, twenty-four pots to each furnace, and now employs over 300 men. The company owns forty-two houses, which are rented to the employes. Mr. Heidenkamp is a republican in politics and a Catholic in religion. He organized the Catholic church at Springdale, and built for the congregation a building in which to hold services until a regular church building had been erected. Mr. Heidenkamp was married, in 1884, to Miss Louise Baldus, of Allegheny county, a native of

Germany, and has a family of six children, viz.: Annie L., now employed in her father's office, educated at St. Aloysius' college; Theresa, educated at the same place; Mary, Elizabeth, Joseph and Louise.

SAMUEL JONAS HORNER, a contracting plasterer and member of the Wilkinsburg council from the first ward, was born in Armagh, Indiana Co., Pa., Sept. 29, 1870. His ancestors were among the early settlers of western Pennsylvania. His great-grandfather was born in Adams county about the middle of the eighteenth century, the exact date not being known. In 1780 he crossed the mountains in company with his brother and attempted to settle where Johnstown now stands, but they were driven away by the Indians. They settled near Somerset, where the great-grandfather married Hannah Besecker, a native of Germany, who came to America in her infancy. They settled near Johnstown, where they raised a family of six girls and two boys, the next to the youngest, Jonas A. Horner, being the grandfather of the subject of this sketch. In 1835 he was married to Miss Mary Penrod, of Berlin, Pa. Her father was drowned in the Conemaugh river, at the Packsaddle, when she was a babe. Franklin Horner, the father of our subject, was born Sept. 20, 1836. On July 24, 1861, he enlisted in Company H, 12th regiment, Pennsylvania volunteer cavalry, for a term of three years. During the war he participated in the following engagements: Dranesville, Va.; Mechanicsville, Va.; Gaines' Mill, Va.; Gainesville, Va.; the second Bull Run; South mountain, Md.; Antietam, Md.; Fredericksburg, Va.; Gettysburg, Pa.; Mine Run, Va.; Bristol Station, Va.; the Wilderness, Va.; Spottsylvania Court House, Va., and Bethesda church, Va. He was promoted to the rank of first sergeant in August, 1861, and at Gaines' Mill, in June, 1862, he was captured and held prisoner until the following August, when he was exchanged. While a prisoner he was commissioned second lieutenant, and was mustered out with that rank on June 11, 1864, at Harrisburg, Pa. Franklin Horner and Sallie Alice Killin were married at Armagh, Pa., July 1, 1869. They had a family of three boys and one girl. Samuel J. Horner was educated in the public schools of the city of Pittsburg, to which place his parents removed, and in 1889 he started in to learn the plasterers' trade. In 1894 he went into business for himself as a contractor of plastering. Since Nov. 14, 1887, he has been a member of the Junior Order of United American Mechanics, and on May 1, 1891, he became a member of the Patriotic Order of the Sons of America. He is also a charter member of Charles Freeman lodge, No. 1036, Independent Order of Odd Fellows, and of Valetta commandery, No. 129, Ancient and Illustrious Order of the Knights of Malta. In politics he is a republican, and as such was elected to the council in the borough of Wilkinsburg in February, 1903. He is unmarried and resides with his parents in the first ward.

BARKLEY J. KLINGENSMITH, a prominent railroad man of Verona, was born in Armstrong county, Pa., May 4, 1860. His parents, Peter and Sarah (Schuster) Klingensmith, were natives of Westmoreland county, but moved to Armstrong county, where the father died, Nov. 6, 1893, and the mother, Feb. 22, 1889. The grandfather of the subject of this sketch was Peter Klingensmith, a pioneer settler of Westmoreland county. He and his wife both died in Armstrong county. They had six sons and four daughters, only one of whom survives. Peter Klingensmith, first referred to, was a farmer, and later a business man at White Rock, Pa. He was a prominent democrat, and served his township as school director and overseer of the poor for fourteen years. He and his wife were Lutherans. Of six sons and four daughters born to them, three sons and three daughters are living. B. J. Klingensmith, whose name heads this article, having received a common-school education, began railroading, and has been in the employ of the Allegheny Valley railroad about twenty years, eight years as conductor. He is a well-known citizen of Verona, owning a home there, besides several other residences. He is a democrat in politics, although not politically ambitious. He is a member of the Royal Arcanum. Mr. Klingensmith was married, June 18, 1885, to Miss Annie M. Pickels, a native of Armstrong county, and a daughter of Jonathan and Nancy A. (Snyder) Pickels, early settlers of Armstrong county, both now deceased. Jonathan Pickels was a son of Jonathan Pickels, a native of England and a pioneer in Armstrong county. Mrs. Klingensmith's maternal grandparents were Joseph and Mary (King) Snyder, natives of Westmoreland county. Mr. Snyder died at Logansport, Pa., but his wife is still living, at the advanced age of eighty-seven. Mr.

and Mrs. Klingensmith have had three children, of whom Barkley D. is dead, and the other two are Portia L. and J. Gordon. The family attend the Methodist church.

WILLIAM M. BRINKER, a prominent real estate dealer of Wilkinsburg, is a native of Clarion county, where he was born in 1843. His education was acquired mainly in the common schools and at Rimersburg academy. In 1877 he came to Allegheny county, and for about twenty years was engaged in the wholesale grocery business on Liberty avenue, in the city of Pittsburg, and at Wilkinsburg. After retiring from the grocery business he became interested in real estate operations, and soon came to be recognized as one of the leading real estate men. He was the originator of apartment buildings in Allegheny county, and is the owner of the largest apartment building there. It was built about five years ago, is five stories high, has ten stores and fifty-five suites of apartments, and accommodates about 160 tenants. In his real estate business he acts as broker in the sale and rental of property, but in the work of building and selling he invests his own capital and acts solely for himself. In 1892 he built fifty-three houses. He now owns several valuable pieces of property, among them Bessica plan of lots, in East Wilkinsburg, and is the heaviest taxpayer in the Wilkinsburg borough. Mr. Brinker was married, in 1873, to Miss Mary Scott, of Clearfield county, and they have four children—one son and three daughters. Two of the daughters are married, the eldest being the wife of H. U. Hart, a civil engineer in the employ of the Westinghouse company, in Havre, France, and the second daughter, the wife of H. W. Kellar, a teller in the Keystone bank, of Pittsburg. During the Civil war Mr. Brinker served three years as a member of Company C, 78th Pennsylvania volunteer infantry. As an evidence of his public spirit, he was the originator of the Wilkinsburg electric light and water companies, and was the first president of the latter. He is a member of the Masonic fraternity and of the Presbyterian church. Politically, he is a democrat, but he never held a public office of any kind.

WILLIAM McCLINTON (deceased) was in his lifetime one of the best-known and most highly-respected farmers of Moon township, Allegheny county. He was a son of Nathaniel and Mary (Hare) McClinton, the father's family being natives of Ireland, coming from County Antrim in about the year 1817. The paternal grandparents were Nathaniel and Nancy (Sevis) McClinton, who settled on a farm where the Dixmont hospital now stands, residing there about seven years. In 1826 they removed to Moon township, and that farm has passed from one generation to another, being now in the possession of some of the descendants. William McClinton's father and mother were among the thirteen original organizers of the Sharon Presbyterian church, of which Dr. Jennings was the first pastor, and in which he preached for fifty years. The children born to Nathaniel and Mary McClinton were ten in number: John, Robert, Nathaniel, Mary, Nancy, Jane, William, Martha, Alexander and Samuel H. Of these children, John, Robert, Nancy and William are deceased; Nathaniel is living in Kansas, and the others live in Allegheny county. Mary is the wife of Joseph Parker; Nancy, wife of Bradberry Morgan; Jane, wife of Joseph Chapman; Martha, wife of William McElhaney; John married Mary Jane Miller; Robert married Louise Bowman; Nathaniel married, first, Matilda Pickring, and second, Mary Davis, who is still living; Alexander married Susan Campbell, and Samuel H. married Jane Bartley. Mary (Hare) McClinton died on Nov. 12, 1852, and her husband on July 6, 1876. William McClinton, the seventh child of the family and the subject of this sketch, was born in Moon township on June 19, 1834, upon the farm on which he passed his life and where he died on Nov. 10, 1902. In his boyhood days he received his education in the common schools, after which he took up the life of a farmer. In this work, to which he devoted his best energies, he was excelled by few. He was interested in the political affairs of the country, but he was more interested in his stock and crops, and mixed but little in the turmoil of political strife. At the age of thirty-nine he was married to Mary Ellen, daughter of James and Mary (Stoncipher) McCormick, and to them were born three children: Albert Nathaniel, Mary Eva and Maud Janette. All are members of the

Presbyterian church, and are held in high esteem by the people of the neighborhood in which their ancestors have been honored and respected for three-quarters of a century. The McCormicks were among the first settlers of Moon township. Benjamin and Anne (Brown) McCormick, Scotch-Irish Presbyterians, came to this country at an early day, settling first in Maryland, where Hugh McCormick, the grandfather of Mrs. McClinton, was born. The family soon removed to Moon township, where Hugh married Margaret Nichle, reared a family of four sons and one daughter, and died in 1852 at the age of eighty-six. The children were: Benjamin, John, Mary, wife of Joseph Scott, Hugh (all now deceased), and James, the father of Mrs. McClinton. James McCormick was born on Feb. 13, 1813, on the old homestead, a part of which is now his home. On March 24, 1842, he was married to Mary, daughter of John and Rachel (Schaffer) Stoncipher, and to this union ten children were born: Margaret, wife of Henry Knopf (deceased); Rachel A., wife of Nathaniel Mulholland; Mary E., wife of William McClinton (deceased); Eliza J., wife of John Wilson; John, who married Anna Knopf; Joseph Scott, who married Anna Hallie Ramsey; Emma M. (deceased); Kate L. M., wife of Joseph A. McCurdy; James I. (deceased), and Elmer. James McCormick cast his first vote for president in 1836, and since that time has been a whig and a republican. His wife died on July 29, 1886, aged sixty-four years. During her life she was a member of the Presbyterian church, which she and her husband joined in early life, and he still continues firm in that faith.

ORLANDO METCALF, treasurer of the Verona tool works, was born in Pittsburg, on the corner of Cliff and Fulton streets, July 31, 1840, and is a son of Orlando and Mary M. (Knap) Metcalf, both natives of New York, the father, of Metcalf Hill, Cooperstown, and the mother, of New Berlin. His paternal grandfather was a soldier in the Revolution, and lost his hearing while in the service. Orlando Metcalf, Sr., father of the subject of this sketch, came to Pittsburg in 1828, and died there in 1850, and his wife in 1876. He attended Union college, New York; graduated from that institution, then studied law, and practiced first in Canton, Ohio, and afterwards in Pittsburg. He was for about twenty years a partner of Andrew W. Loomis. The subject of this sketch is one of seven children, of whom three are living. Orlando Metcalf, whose name heads this article, was educated in Pittsburg, and from 1858 to 1873 had charge of the financial end of the Old Fort Pitt foundry. He then organized, in company with J. W. Paul, the firm of Metcalf, Paul & Co., now the Verona tool works. He spent fourteen years in Colorado, still retaining his interest in the company, and on returning to Verona, in 1892, became its treasurer, in which capacity he has since continued. Mr. Metcalf is a republican in national politics, but votes in local elections independently. He was married, in November, 1863, to Agnes McElroy, daughter of James M. McElroy, a Pittsburg merchant, and has had seven children. They are: Mary, Agnes, Edith, Orlando, Elizabeth, Lois (deceased) and Emma E Mr. Metcalf and family were formerly attendants at the old Trinity church of Pittsburg, and are now identified with St. Thomas' church in Oakmont.

JOHN SCOTT, who owns and conducts one of the finest farms in North Fayette township, was born in County Down, Ireland, in the year 1827. His parents were Moses and Elizabeth (Martin) Scott. Moses Scott was a farmer and a fine example of that Irish peasantry of whom so much has been said in poetry and song. He died in 1847 at the age of fifty-five years. About three years after the death of his father, John Scott was married to Miss Isabella McKibben, a daughter of Robert McKibben. Two weeks after the wedding he set sail for America and reached Pittsburg, Pa., on a Saturday night with only ten cents in his pocket. Some men would have become discouraged under such circumstances, but not so with John Scott. With true Irish pluck he went to work on the following Monday morning at seventy-five cents a day, out of which he had to pay his living expenses. After renting farms for twenty years, he saved enough money to purchase the one he now owns, paying $7,000 for it. Since then he has expended more than $2,000 in the erection of buildings. Since coming to America, Mr. Scott has faithfully and intelligently discharged the duties of his adopted citizenship. Ever since he has been naturalized he has affiliated with the republican party, but he has never taken an active part in party work. Mr. Scott is an influential member of the Montour Presbyterian church. For a number of years he has been a member of the board of trustees and also of the board of sessions. To

John and Isabella Scott were born four children: Maria Elizabeth, Sarah Jane, Robert John and Margaret Ann. Isabella Scott died on May 14, 1863, in her twenty-ninth year. About two years later Mr. Scott married again, his second wife being Miss Nancy McCrigger, daughter of James McCrigger, a well-known citizen of Allegheny county. The second Mrs. Scott died in May, 1893, at the age of seventy-two. Since that time Mr. Scott has lived a widower, enjoying the happy reflections consequent upon a well-spent life, and the fruits of his early industry and frugality. In his old age he is surrounded by a circle of friends, all of whom respect him as a law-abiding Christian gentleman, and love him because of his genial disposition and his warm Irish heart.

JOHN W. HEMPHILL, merchant tailor and president of the First National bank of Tarentum, was born in Roxbury, Pa., Dec. 2, 1840. His parents, John and Anna (Longsdorff) Hemphill, were both natives of Pennsylvania, the father being a son of Joseph Hemphill, who was an Irishman by birth and a soldier in the Revolution, and the mother, a daughter of a German who fought in the same war. John Hemphill, father of the subject of this sketch, was left an orphan early in life. He was a tailor by trade, locating in Allegheny county in 1846, and was a prominent tailor in Tarentum up to the time of his death, which occurred in 1859. He and his wife were members of the Methodist Episcopal church. They had eleven children, of whom four are living. John Hemphill was a democrat in politics, was at one time assessor, and held various minor offices. J. W. Hemphill, whose name heads this sketch, was reared and educated in Tarentum, and learned from his father the trade of a tailor, at which he has been very successful. He now owns considerable property in Tarentum, and is one of the most influential citizens of that place. He has various large financial interests; was one of the organizers of the First National bank of Tarentum in 1890, and has since been its president; is president of the Tarentum water company; director of the Tarentum glass company and the Baker manufacturing company, and a stockholder in the Allegheny plate glass company and the Allegheny steel and iron company. He is also vice-president of the Allegheny river improvement association. Mr. Hemphill served three years in the Civil war as a member of Company A, United States zouaves, John P. Glass, captain. The regiment afterwards joined General Sickles' brigade of New York, and was known as the 74th New York regiment, volunteer infantry. Mr.

Hemphill served with his regiment in the campaigns under McClellan, Pope, Hooker, Meade and Grant, and was wounded in the second battle of Bull Run. Mr. Hemphill was married, Aug. 11, 1864, to Miss Nancy Staley, daughter of James M. Staley, an Allegheny county pioneer, formerly engaged in the oil and salt business, and in his time one of the most prominent men of Tarentum. Mr. and Mrs. Hemphill have had five children. Of these, Elva N. was educated in Tarentum high school, and is now at home; John S., a graduate of Tarentum high school, and a tailor by trade, engaged in business at Monessen, Pa., and died in December, 1902; James is with the Carnegie steel company, at Duquesne, Pa.; Orland is employed in Alton, Ill., in one of the largest glass manufacturing establishments in the United States, and Harry H. is with his father, a member of the firm of J. W. Hemphill & Son. Mr. Hemphill is a republican in politics, and has served his borough as burgess, councilman and school director. He takes a great interest in the welfare of Tarentum, and is always identified with every movement for its advancement. He is a member and past master of Pollock lodge, No. 502, F. and A. M., and belongs to the G. A. R. He and his family are members of the Methodist Episcopal church.

JOHN HULTZ, one of the best-known farmers in Scott township, Allegheny Co., Pa., is descended from one of the first settlers in western Pennsylvania. Several years before the beginning of the troubles that culminated in the Revolutionary war, Zudock Hultz came to this country. Some time afterwards he entered and received a patent to the land which is now owned and occupied by his great-grandson, who is the subject of this sketch. When Zudock Hultz first settled in Allegheny county, the Indians were very troublesome. In one of their forays into the white settlements, several of his children were murdered by the Indians, but with the courage of a martyr he stuck to his homestead, making it possible for his posterity to enjoy in peace that which cost him so dearly. Henry Hultz, a son of Zudock and grandfather of John, was born in Allegheny county, and was old enough to bear arms in the American army in the war of the Revolution. John

Hultz is the son of Elson and Matilda (Alison) Hultz, and was born in Allegheny county, Aug. 6, 1851. Both his parents were natives of the county, the Alisons being among the early settlers. John received his education in the common schools, began life as a farmer, and has followed that vocation ever since. He is considered one of the progressive men of the township, his farm being cultivated according to the most approved methods. He takes an active interest in political matters, is a consistent republican, but never aspired to public office. In 1880 he was married to Miss Mary McMillen, daughter of Wilson and Phebe (Sharlow) McMillen. Her father was born in Allegheny county, of Irish parentage, and her mother was a native of Germany. Mrs. Hultz was born in Allegheny county, April 14, 1851, and was educated in the common schools of the county. Of the children born to John and Mary Hultz, three are living, viz.: Roy, Mary E. and Frank V. Both Mr. and Mrs. Hultz are members of the United Presbyterian church.

DAVID MURPHY CONWAY, proprietor of a general store at Creighton, and postmaster at that place, was born in Rialto, Ohio, Sept. 13, 1870. He spent his early boyhood in Ohio and Illinois, came to Elkhorn, Allegheny county, when nine years old, and at fourteen moved to Tarentum, where for thirteen years he was employed in the glass works, with the exception of two years spent with a theatrical company as cornetist with the great soloist, Emil Keneke. In 1899 he bought a half interest in a store in Creighton, purchased the other half in 1901, and has been most successfully engaged in business for himself since that time. He has, besides this, other important financial interests, being a stockholder and director in the Tarentum savings and loan company, stockholder in the Tarentum savings and trust company, and secretary and treasurer of the Enterprise coal company. Although an ardent democrat in politics, he was elected unanimously in 1898 as councilman from the third ward, Tarentum, a ward in which there are 300 republicans and only forty-four democrats. He served in the council four years, acting as president of that body. Mr. Conway is a member of the Royal Arcanum, Protected Home Circle, Catholic Mutual Benefit Association, and the Knights of Columbus, and, with his wife, belongs to St. Peter's Roman Catholic church of Tarentum. He was married, in April, 1896, to Miss Anna McGinley, of Culmerville, Pa., and has four children: Stella M., Margaret, Thomas F. and Julia H. Mr. Conway's parents were Thomas (now deceased) and Alice (Murphy) Conway. Thomas Conway was born in Dublin, Ireland, in 1842, was reared in India, and served as drummer boy in the British army. Coming to the United States in 1861, he served with distinction during the Civil war, taking part, among others, in the engagements at Fredericksburg and Chancellorsville. After the war he located at Rialto, Ohio, worked there for several years as a paper-maker, came to Elkhorn, Pa., in 1879, and died there, Feb. 21, 1881. He was one of the most influential members of the Ancient Order of Hibernians, and was instrumental in establishing many branches of the order in western Ohio and Illinois. He was a great traveler, and during his life journeyed over most of Asia and visited many places in the United States. In political belief he was a democrat. Alice (Murphy) Conway, mother of the subject of this sketch, was born in Waterford, Ireland, in 1849; came to the United States when young, and married Mr. Conway in Hamilton, Ohio. She is the mother of five children—three daughters and two sons—all of whom are living. Mr. Conway resides at Tarentum, Pa.

N. K. SULLIVAN, an old and well-known resident of Versailles township, was born in Somerset county, Pa., May 24, 1840. His parents were Philip and Rebecca (King) Sullivan. Philip Sullivan was a tanner by trade and for many years followed that occupation in Somerset county. Mr. Sullivan was the second in a family of ten children and was educated in the common schools. When Fort Sumter was fired on at the beginning of the Civil war, he was one of the first to respond to President Lincoln's call for troops to preserve the Union. On April 18, 1861, a few weeks before he reached his majority, he enlisted as a private in Company K, 18th Ohio volunteer infantry, under Captain Henderson, Colonel Bigbee commanding the regiment. At the expiration of four months he was discharged from the service and returned to Pennsylvania. On Sept. 4, 1861, he enlisted in Company D, 54th Pennsylvania infantry, Col. Jacob M. Campbell's regiment, and served until New Year's day, 1865, when he was mustered out at Harrisburg, Pa. The 54th was in some of the hottest battles of the war, among them being Cedar Creek, Winchester, Fisher's Hill, Lynchburg, Salem, Harper's Ferry and Berryville. In all these engagements Mr. Sullivan was on the firing-line and rendered valiant service for his country. He was mustered out as orderly sergeant of his company. After being discharged he went to Pittsburg, and in February, 1865, he entered the service of the Pennsylvania railroad company as a conductor. After five years with this company he changed to the Baltimore & Ohio, on whose lines he was a conductor for nineteen years. On May 29, 1866, he was married to Miss Mary A. Quinn, of Pittsburg, and to this union there were born the following children: Roseltha S., wife of H. C. Christy; Rebecca, wife of William Duncan; Mary, wife of Joseph Kennedy; Emma, wife of George Fisher, of McKeesport; Laura, who is at home, and a son. Mr. Sullivan is a republican, and takes a keen interest in all matters bearing on the political situation. After his arduous military service and twenty-four years of duty as a railroad conductor, he has retired from the active affairs of life, though since leaving the train service, he has been engaged in several occupations with varying success.

WILLIAM L. LOUCKS, station agent at Tarentum for the Pennsylvania railroad company, was born at Mount Pleasant, Westmoreland Co., Pa., March 9, 1844. His father, J. M. Loucks, was a farmer, a democrat in politics, and held several minor public offices. He was a Free Mason. He was born in Westmoreland county, and died there in 1863. His wife, Mary A. (Pool) Loucks, died in Allegheny county in 1900, at the age of seventy-four. They had six children, of whom four are living. William L. Loucks, the subject of this sketch, was reared on a farm, and attended school at Greensburg, Westmoreland county. After graduating from high school, he began his successful career as a railroad man, in 1863, as a brakeman for the Pennsylvania railroad company. A year later he became assistant agent for the company at Brinton, remained there three years, and then spent four months in the Derry yards. He has been located at Tarentum since 1868, and now has charge of the depot and manages the freight department as well. He has complete charge of the company's business at Tarentum, doing everything except operating. He was an operator for sixteen years. Mr. Loucks has been a resident of Tarentum for thirty-five years, and owns considerable property in the borough. He is a democrat in politics, and has served six years in the council and nine years as school director. He is a member of

Tarentum lodge, No. 587, I. O. O. F., and Encampment No. 187. Mr. Loucks was married, in 1869, to Miss Mary M. Marks, of Port Perry, Pa., and has two children, Albert and Howard. Mr. and Mrs. Loucks are members of the Methodist Episcopal church of Tarentum.

CHARLES J. SINN, a prominent farmer and dairyman of Port Vue township, Allegheny Co., Pa., was born in Allegheny county, July 6, 1872, son of Ludwick and Mary (Sheal) Sinn, both natives of Germany and the parents of eight children, of which Charles J. was second in order of birth. He received his educational training in the public schools of his native county and at the German schools of McKeesport, and has devoted his business career to farming and running a dairy. He has been very successful in his business affairs, has a fine farm and all necessary accessories, and is regarded as one of the solid and reliable men of that part of the county. In his political affiliations and convictions Mr. Sinn is a republican, and has served as a school director and as assessor of Port Vue township. He is a member of the Junior Order of United American Mechanics and the Woodmen of the World, with both of which orders he is prominently identified in their works for the physical and moral betterment of humanity.

JOHN D. ELWELL, wagon-maker at Tarentum, was born in New Jersey, Sept. 30, 1831. His father, John Elwell, was born in New Jersey in 1797, and died in that State in 1845. He was a farmer, a whig in politics, and in religious belief a Methodist. His wife, Martha (Stanton) Elwell, was also born in 1797 and died at the age of fifty. She was a daughter of George Stanton, whose father fought in the Revolutionary war. Mr. and Mrs. John Elwell had four sons and one daughter, of whom two sons are living: John D., the subject of this sketch, and George, also a resident of Allegheny county. John D. Elwell was reared on a farm and educated in the common schools. He learned the trade of wagon-maker when a boy, and has followed it all his life, working first in Salem county, N. J. On Sept. 12, 1856, he came to Pittsburg, and, in 1858, moved to Tarentum, where he has since resided, and now owns considerable property. Mr. Elwell is a democrat in political belief, and has served in the council of Tarentum. He was married, in April, 1860, to Miss Anne E. Duphorn, a native of Tarentum. Mrs. Elwell died March 8, 1899. They had six children, viz.: Sarah, John, Mattie, Marie, William and Pearl. All but John are living. Mr. Elwell is a member of the Methodist Episcopal church, as was his wife. Mrs. Elwell was a daughter of George and Sarah (Lookabaugh) Duphorn, who came in an early day from Maryland, and settled first in Westmoreland county, and later in Allegheny county. Mr. Duphorn was a cooper by trade, but for the last thirty years of his life devoted his attention to his duties as justice of the peace. He was a soldier in the War of 1812, and two sons, George and Samuel, fought in the Civil war. Mr. Elwell was also a soldier in the Civil war, where he served his time as a member of Company F, 123d Pennsylvania volunteer infantry, and took part in a number of engagements in the war. He served under Colonel Clark, first under Capt. John Boyd, and then under Capt. Michael Baird.

EDWARD ABBOTT, a well-known farmer of Scott township, Allegheny Co., Pa., was born in that county in 1856. He is a son of Christian and Magdalena (Schmeltz) Abbott. (See sketch of John Wise.) Christian Abbott came with his parents to America at a time when transportation facilities were very meager. Several families would band themselves together, get a six-horse team and cross the mountains into western Pennsylvania. It was in this way that he came to Allegheny county. He died June 22, 1897. Edward Abbott was educated in the common schools, and upon reaching his majority became a farmer, which occupation he has followed to the present time. He has a fine farm of eighty acres, well improved, with a good two-story frame residence and substantial out-buildings. In 1881 he was married to Miss Lizzie Jacobs, daughter of George and Catharine Jacobs, both natives of Germany. Mrs. Abbott was born in Allegheny county, Oct. 4, 1857, and, like her husband, was educated in the common schools. Mr. and Mrs. Abbott are the parents of the following children, all of whom are living: Christian, Katie, Albert, Edward, Rosa,

Howard, Helena, Emma, Clarence and Clara. Formerly Mr. Abbott was a democrat in politics, but of late years he has been identified with the republican party. Although he takes a lively interest in all questions relating to public affairs, he does not take an active part in political work. Both he and his wife are members of the German Lutheran church, and both are highly respected by their neighbors.

GEORGE T. OWENS, a well-known real estate and insurance man and justice of the peace, of Tarentum, was born in Washington, D. C., Nov. 2, 1848, was reared in West Virginia and Pennsylvania, and educated in the public schools. He learned the machinists' and carpenters' trades, and was for many years a contracting carpenter. He has lived in Tarentum sixteen years. Mr. Owens engaged in the insurance and real estate business in 1896. In February that same year he was elected justice of the peace. His term extends until 1907. He is a republican in politics, has always taken an active interest in local party affairs, and has filled a large place in the public life of Tarentum. He has served the public six years as member of the council, was two years president of that body, and served one term on the school board. He is a member of Tarentum lodge, No. 587, I. O. O. F., and also of the Heptasophs and B. P. O. Elks. He was married, May 14, 1872, to Miss Julia A. Bartholic, of Tarentum, and has had two sons and four daughters. Of these, the oldest, Lydia M., is now deceased. The others are: William H., Sarah B., George R., Corinna and Edna Pearl. The family are members of the Methodist Episcopal church. George T. Owens comes of a family which was of Welsh extraction, and is a descendant of Thomas Owens. His father, John H. Owens, a native of Baltimore, a blacksmith by trade, was born Feb. 2, 1824; came to Natrona in 1867, and died in 1886. He was a democrat in political belief, and, with his wife, was a Methodist in religion. Mr. and Mrs. John H. Owens had seven children, of whom five are living. Mrs. Owens, who was born April 24, 1824, is still living. She was, before her marriage, Sarah Gillott; is a native of England, having been born near Liverpool, and was a daughter of Joseph and Sarah (Middleton) Gillott. She came to America at an early age with her parents, the family locating at Tarentum in 1832, where Mr. and Mrs. Gillott both died. They were Baptists in religious belief. Joseph Gillott was a marble-worker by trade.

HARRY R. MARTIN, of Harmarville, Pa., manager of the Harmarville supply store, was born in Allegheny city, Allegheny Co., Pa., Sept. 10, 1862, son of John and Sarah (Potts) Martin. His father was a brick-molder and died soon after our subject was born; consequently young Martin was reared by Mr. and Mrs. Robert Kyle, of Butler county, and in that county he was educated, attending the public schools during the winter term until he was twenty-one years of age. Then he helped Mr. Kyle on the farm until 1894, when he entered Duff's college, of Pittsburg, Pa., and was graduated in a commercial course in 1895. He was a traveling salesman for a number of years for Pittsburg firms, later became a clerk in a store in Washington, Pa., and left this position to become a traveling salesman for the Lewiston monumental company, of Lewiston, Me. He remained with this firm until May, 1902, when he was appointed manager of the Harmarville supply store, of Harmarville, Pa., and has since ably filled that important position. He was happily married, in 1896, to Elizabeth Scott Steward, daughter of William and Katharine (Graham) Steward, of Allegheny city. They have two children: Mary Isabelle Kyle and Robert William Kyle. Mr. Martin is a member of the Central United Presbyterian church, and is closely identified with the republican party. Mr. Martin was thrown on his own resources at an early age, and the success he has achieved has been by his own efforts. He is well known in Harmarville, and is one of the substantial citizens of that city.

JAMES A. MELLON, retired, of Springdale, was born in Springdale township, Allegheny Co., Pa., July 19, 1830. His father was Joseph Mellon, who came to Allegheny county in 1822, and was a native of Westmoreland county. He was a fisherman, and afterwards a farmer, owning considerable property. Joseph Mellon's wife, Mary (Halsted) Mellon, was a daughter of Josiah Halsted, a pioneer settler, who located where Springdale now is, and cleared a large tract of land. Mr. and Mrs. Joseph Mellon were members of the United Presbyterian church. The mother died in May, 1889, and the father in January, 1900. James A. Mellon, whose name heads this sketch, was reared a fisherman, and followed this vocation until 1854. He also, in company with two brothers, Jonah and Samuel, ran a market boat on the canal until 1865. He has now retired from active life, having amassed a considerable fortune, part of which is invested in Springdale real estate. In politics, as was his father, he is an ardent democrat, and has served his borough as school director. Mr. Mellon was married, in 1855, to Miss Rebecca J. Lemon, who was born in Springdale in 1836, daughter of John and Elizabeth (Hunter) Lemon, early pioneers. Mr. Mellon's mother is still living, now ninety years old. Mr. and Mrs. Mellon have two children, Joseph and Alice. Joseph is connected with the Philadelphia gas company, while Alice is now the wife of James Wensel, and lives in Springdale. Mr. and Mrs. Mellon are members of the United Presbyterian church.

OLIVER C. CAMP, cashier of the National Bank of Tarentum, and prominently connected with various other business enterprises, was born in Armstrong county, Pa., March 16, 1848. His father, Henry Camp, was a son of Jacob Camp, a native of Greensburg, Westmoreland county, but for many years a resident of Armstrong county, where he lived on a farm and died at seventy-five. He married Caroline Reamer, a native of Westmoreland county, at Greensburg, and they came to Armstrong county on horseback. They had nine children, of whom four survive: Henry, the father of the subject of this sketch; Levi O., a resident of Galesburg, Ill.; Mary A., of Armstrong county, and Lydia, who married John Davis, lives in Iowa and has five children. Henry Camp was for many years a contractor and builder of Allegheny city, but is now retired from active life and lives on Squirrel Hill, Pittsburg. He was born in Greensburg, Westmoreland Co., Pa., June 20, 1819. He married Jessie McIntyre, a native of Stranraer, Scotland, born Jan. 30, 1817, who came to Allegheny county in 1835 with her parents, William and Jeane (Nish) McIntyre. Mr. and Mrs. McIntyre afterwards settled on a 250-acre farm in Armstrong county, where they died, he at the age of seventy-five and she at ninety-eight. They had a family of nine children, of whom two are living: Mrs. Henry Camp and Charles, who is a prominent citizen of Armstrong county. Mr. and Mrs Henry Camp had six children, all of whom are living except Isabella and Richard H. Their names are: Oliver C., Isabella, W. H., Aggie D., Richard H. and James M. Mr. Camp is in politics a democrat. His wife was for forty years a member of the United Presbyterian church of Allegheny city. Oliver C.

Camp, whose name heads this sketch, was reared and educated in Allegheny city. He went to work at an early age as a messenger boy and from that became an expert telegraph operator, and followed this vocation until 1878. At that time he came to Tarentum and engaged in mercantile pursuits for several years. When the National bank of Tarentum was organized, in 1890, he became the principal stockholder and its cashier. Besides this he is engaged in various other lines of business. He was one of the organizers and the first treasurer of the Tarentum glass company; was one of the organizers and is now secretary and assistant treasurer of the James H. Baker manufacturing company; is secretary and treasurer of the Hamilton coal-mining company and director in the bank of that company; is director and treasurer of the Allegheny Valley brick company; was treasurer of the first Allegheny River improvement association and is a member of the executive committee of the new association, and is treasurer of a number of minor concerns in Tarentum. He is also treasurer of the borough of Tarentum. Mr. Camp is a member of the Improved Order of Heptasophs and the Bankers' association of Pittsburg. He was married, in 1887, to Josephine M. Galbraith, daughter of Dr. Thomas Galbraith (deceased). Dr. Galbraith was one of the oldest doctors in Tarentum at the time of his death, and was the oldest member of the United Presbyterian church. He went to California in 1849. He was a most successful physician and a prominent citizen of Tarentum, where he served as burgess and school director. Dr. Galbraith married Margaret Gilford, and had ten daughters and one son, of whom all are living except one daughter. Mr. and Mrs. Camp are members of the United Presbyterian church. They had two sons, Oliver C., born Dec. 18, 1890, and James G., born Aug. 25, 1892.

JOHN S. COE, a retired farmer and a resident of Tarentum since 1891, was born in Allegheny county, Pa., July 27, 1827. His grandfather, Benjamin Coe, was a pioneer settler of Allegheny county in the days when the Indians laid claim to the territory, and fought for his country in the Revolution. Benjamin Coe's son, also named Benjamin, father of the subject of this sketch, was a farmer and tanner, a prominent man in his time. He married Nancy Shields, a native of Armstrong county, where her parents, Joseph and Rebecca (Craig) Shields, were early settlers. Benjamin Coe was in politics at first a whig and later a republican. He died Nov. 6, 1873, and his wife Jan. 3, 1864. They were the parents of nine children, of whom three are living. John S. Coe, whose name heads this sketch, was reared on a farm and educated in the common schools, and was for many years a successful farmer. He now lives a retired life in Tarentum, where he owns property. He is a stockholder in the Fidelity glass company and the Tarentum glass company. He has been in politics a lifelong republican, and was formerly school director of Fawn township, Allegheny county. Mr. Coe was married, March 24, 1853, to Miss Hannah J. Boyd, who was born in Allegheny county in 1832. Mrs. Coe's parents were James and Sarah Boyd, the father a native of Ligonier, Pa., and both early residents of Allegheny county. Mr. Boyd died, at the age of eighty-six, Jan. 15, 1888, and his wife at seventy-eight, Oct. 11, 1875. They had twelve children, of whom four are living. Mr. and Mrs. Coe have no children of their own, but adopted two. Of these, Sarah died Nov. 3, 1899, at the age of twenty-two. Mr. and Mrs. Coe have been for a half century members of the Presbyterian church, of which Mr. Coe has been elder for over forty years.

JOSEPH M. McMAHON, superintendent of the molding department of the Tarentum glass company, was born in South Side, Pittsburg, June 20, 1853, and is a son of Robert and Ellen (Hurrell) McMahon, the father a native of Ireland, and the mother of Pittsburg. Robert McMahon came to Kittanning, Pa., about 1836, with his father, John McMahon, his mother having died in Ireland. John McMahon died in Kittanning. Robert McMahon, a machinist by trade, spent his life in Pittsburg, and died there in February, 1901, when seventy-three years old. His wife died in 1889, at the age of fifty-nine. They had seven children, of whom five are living. Robert McMahon was a democrat in politics, although a man of liberal views; was a Baptist in religion, and was one of the first members of Monongahela lodge, F. and A. M., of South Side, Pittsburg. He was at one time boiler inspector of Allegheny county under Governor Pattison. Mrs. Ellen (Hurrell) McMahon, mother of the subject of this sketch, was a daughter of Thomas and Ellen (Pounds) Hurrell. Thomas Hurrell, a native of England, was one of the early settlers of Pittsburg, and one of the first brick-makers of the city. He died in Pittsburg about 1830. His wife was born in Butler county about 1794, and died in South Side, Pittsburg, in 1870. Joseph M. McMahon, whose name heads this article, was reared in Pittsburg, educated in the public schools, and at fourteen went to work packing spikes for Gilworth,

Porter & Co. A few months later he began to learn the trade of a glass-mold maker in the glass works of Kirchner & Parker, in Pittsburg. Later he worked at his trade for King, Son & Co. and other houses until 1883, when his ability and faithfulness won him the position of superintendent of the mold shops for Richards & Hartley. In 1884 the firm moved to Harrison township, now Brackenridge borough, where they continued in business until absorbed by the United States glass company in 1890. Two years later Mr. McMahon left the works and engaged in the real estate business in Pittsburg. Then, in 1893, the Tarentum glass company was formed, and he was made superintendent of the molding department, a position which he has since held. He is also a stockholder in the company. Mr. McMahon resides in Brackenridge borough, where he owns considerable property, and had the distinction of serving as chairman of the committee which had charge of the organization of the borough. In politics he is a republican. He has been for twenty-four years a member of Orion council, Royal Arcanum, of South Side, Pittsburg, and of the Heptasophs of Tarentum. In 1894 he was married to Miss Elizabeth Jones, of Pittsburg, and has three children: John H., David L. and Howard C. Mr. and Mrs. McMahon are regular attendants upon the services of the United Presbyterian church of Tarentum.

GEORGE WASHINGTON CRYTZER, for many years the leading contracting carpenter in Brackenridge, was born in Armstrong county, Pa., Feb. 15, 1837, and is a son of Michael and Rachel (Heitman) Crytzer. Mrs. Crytzer, a native of Armstrong county, was the daughter of Solomon Heitman, a native of Pennsylvania, who died, when fifty-six years old, in Armstrong county. Her mother, whose maiden name was Yount, lived to the advanced age of eighty-seven, and died in Armstrong county. Michael Crytzer, father of the subject of this sketch, was a carpenter by trade, in politics a republican, and, with his wife, belonged to the Lutheran church. He and his wife both died in 1859, he at the age of fifty-four, and she at fifty-two. They were the parents of eleven children, five of whom are living. George W. Crytzer, whose name begins this article, was reared and educated in Armstrong county, and began learning the carpenters' trade when only fourteen years old. So proficient did he become at his trade, that before he reached manhood he began contracting and was a contractor in Armstrong county until 1884. In that year he came to Harrison township, now Brackenridge borough, where he has since engaged in the contracting business with most flattering success. Mr. Crytzer now owns considerable property in Brackenridge borough. He is a democrat in politics. He is a member of the I. O. O. F. and the Mystic Chain. In 1862 he married Miss Margaret Neal, of Armstrong county, and had by this union eleven children, viz.: Ella, Frank (deceased), Elizabeth B., William, Harry E., Charles (deceased), John (deceased), Florence, George, Howard, and Emma (deceased). Mrs. Crytzer died in June, 1881. Mr. Crytzer had two brothers who served in the Civil war. Benjamin F. was killed in a skirmish, and John A. H., who served throughout the war, now lives in Armstrong county. Another brother, Harry, resides in Harmarville, Pa., where he is manager of Kuntz Bros.' brick-yard.

WILLIAM McALPIN, one of Tarentum's old and respected citizens, now retired from active life, was born in Ireland, Sept. 6, 1817, being one of the eight children born to Hugh and Margaret (McCullough) McAlpin, natives of Ireland, who spent their lives there. He was reared in Ireland, and married there to Miss Eliza Stewart, by whom he had one daughter, now married to William F. Goodwin, a hardware merchant in Tarentum. Mr. and Mrs. Goodwin have three children. Mr. McAlpin came to America with his wife in 1840, and was for eleven years foreman of the dyeing department of a cotton factory at Frankfort, Pa. In 1852 he moved to Allegheny city, where he was employed in a similar capacity until the outbreak of the Civil war, when he embarked in the grocery business. He continued in this business until 1871, when he moved to Tarentum, where he has since resided, retired from active life. He owns valuable property in Tarentum and Allegheny city, acquired by the savings of a long and successful career. Mr. McAlpin was in early life a whig, but has been a republican since the founding of that party, and while never politically ambitious, has always been an active worker in the interests of his party. He is an ancient Odd Fellow, having joined Willy lodge, No. 14, Frankfort, Pa., in 1845, and was the father of the lodge of the I. O. O. F. in Baltimore, Md. On July 3, 1875, Mr. McAlpin's first wife died, and, on Oct. 2, 1878, he married Miss Mary A. McDowell, a native of Washington county, though reared in Allegheny county, and a daughter of James and Elizabeth (Dunlap) McDowell, natives of Ireland, who came to America in 1833, and died in Tarentum. Mr. McDowell was a farmer by vocation, and a democrat in political belief. By his second marriage,

Mr. McAlpin has one son, James McAlpin, born Sept. 29, 1880. James McAlpin was reared in Tarentum, and graduated from the high school there. After that he was for three years assistant postmaster, for a short time a clerk, and is now bookkeeper in the National bank of Tarentum.

WILLIAM CONWELL, glass-worker, has worked at his trade in most of the glass houses in the United States. For the past fifteen years he has been employed by the Tarentum glass company, and has, during these years, won for himself the confidence of his employers and the good-will and esteem of his fellow-workmen. Mr. Conwell was born in Pittsburg, Pa., March 26, 1859, being a son of Stephen D. Conwell, mentioned elsewhere in this book. He was reared and educated in Pittsburg. Mr. Conwell is a republican in politics, and while always actively interested in the welfare of his party, he has never aspired to hold office. He is married, and, with his wife and family, resides in a fine residence on Brackenridge avenue, Tarentum, which he owns, as well as other property in Brackenridge borough. Mrs. Conwell was formerly Miss Mary Casey, of Pittsburg. Mr. and Mrs. Conwell were married in 1892, and have three children: Frank, Ella M. and George D. The family attend the Catholic church, of which Mrs. Conwell and the children are members.

GEORGE ARCHIE McWILLIAMS, florist and gardener, was born in Harrison township, Allegheny Co., Pa., Oct. 2, 1858; was reared on a farm, attended the public schools, and graduated from the Natrona high school. He engaged for a number of years in the dairy business, and, in 1896, began to devote his attention to the raising of flowers and to general gardening, on the valuable place which he now owns and which is situated near Brackenridge, a business in which he has been most successfully engaged since that time. He is an ardent republican in politics, keenly interested in the welfare of his party, has served as assessor, and is now township auditor. He is a member of Pollock lodge, No. 502, F. and A. M.; Natrona lodge, No. 644, I. O. O. F., and the B. P. O. Elks of Tarentum. He is a member of the Presbyterian church. Mr. McWilliams is one of a family of eleven children, three of whom, besides himself, are living, viz.: DeWitt Clinton, of Oregon; Mrs. Alice Otterman, of Natrona, and Morgan B., of Natrona. The parents of these children were John N. and Elizabeth (Rodenbaugh) McWilliams, both residents of Northumberland county, who came to Allegheny county in 1836, and settled in what is now Harrison township. There the father died, Nov. 12, 1883, and the mother, Oct. 2, 1900. John McWilliams was a veterinary surgeon, well known throughout the county, and owned a farm near Natrona. He was a democrat in politics, a local political leader, and held various township offices. In religion he and his wife were Presbyterians.

CHARLES C. PFORDT, proprietor of a large department store at Natrona, is a son of the late Charles and Christina (Heckel) Pfordt, and a grandson of Andrew Heckel, a native of France and a pioneer settler of Beaver county. Andrew Heckel was a teacher by profession, and also helped build the Erie canal. He married Henrietta Whitman, and both died in Butler county, near Zelienople. Charles Pfordt, Sr., father of the Charles Pfordt whose name heads this sketch, came to Allegheny city from his native country, France, in 1858, and spent the remainder of his life in Allegheny county, with the exception of a year during the Civil war. On April 17, 1861, he enlisted in Company G, 139th Pennsylvania volunteer infantry, and, when his time was up, enlisted as first sergeant in the 123d Pennsylvania volunteer infantry, and served nine months longer. During his enlistment, he took part in all the battles in which his regiment participated, fighting at Fredericksburg, Chancellorsville and South mountain. He was a butcher by vocation, a republican in politics, and, with his wife, belonged to the Lutheran church. He was at one time school director in Reserve township, Allegheny county. He was a Free Mason, being a member of Jefferson lodge, of Allegheny city, and belonged to the I. O. O. F., Knights of Pythias and the Improved Order of Red Men. The last ten years of his life were spent in Pittsburg, where he died in 1898. Charles C. Pfordt, the subject of this sketch, was one of a family of eight children, seven of whom are living. He was born in Allegheny county, Dec. 29, 1864; attended the Pittsburg schools, and for five years studied music under Prof. M. P. Leisser. In 1887 he graduated from Duff's business college, and went then to Beaver county, where for six years he was manager of the Park fire clay company, of Rochester. In 1894 he came to Natrona, where he has since engaged most successfully in mercantile pursuits, and owns there a large department store. He also owns other property in Natrona, and is extensively interested in natural oil. Politically, he is a republican, and takes a lively interest in the welfare of his party. He was at one time a member of the Young Men's tariff club, of Pittsburg, and is now an influential member of the county committee. He served several years in the county treasurer's office under Thomas G. McClune. Mr. Pfordt is an enthusiastic Mason, being a member of Rochester lodge, No. 229, F. and A. M.; Eureka chapter, No. 167, R. A. M., of Rochester, and Pittsburg commandery, No. 1, Knights Templars. On Aug. 1, 1889, he married Miss Nancy Eslip, a native of Natrona, daughter of Frederick Eslip, who was born in Saxony, and Margaret (Potts) Eslip, a native of Allegheny county, who was a daughter of William and Nancy (Harvey) Potts, pioneer settlers of Allegheny county, where they spent their last days. Mr. and Mrs. Pfordt have had five children: Fred, Eleanor, Margaret, Nancy and Laura. The first-born, Fred, died when five years old. Mr. Pfordt and wife are members of the Methodist Episcopal church of Natrona.

PAUL RUDERT, of the firm of Rudert & Senn, jewelers and opticians, Tarentum, has been in the jewelry business since 1875. In that year he engaged in business in Hookstown, Beaver county, continuing there until 1886, when he moved to Tarentum, where he has been most successful. His partner, Mr. Senn, began to work for him in 1893, and was admitted to partnership in 1903. Paul Rudert is a native of Germany, born Feb. 16, 1857, son of Oscar Rudert, a native of Germany, who came to America in 1868, and settled with his family in Allegheny city. Here he engaged in business twelve years, and then bought a farm in East Deer township, on which he spent the rest of his life, and died in 1899 at the age of seventy-three. Mrs. Rudert is living, now sixty-six years old. Mr. Rudert was a republican in politics, and belonged to the Lutheran church, of which his widow is a member. He acquired considerable property, and was well-to-do at the time of his death. Paul Rudert, whose name heads this article, was one of a family of three sons and one daughter, of which the daughter is now deceased. He was educated in Germany and Allegheny city. Mr. Rudert has been most successful in his business career, and owns, besides his store building, a handsome residence in Tarentum. He is one of the most prosperous and progressive citizens of Tarentum. He is a stockholder in the Tarentum savings and trust company and the Rutherford paper company. He is an independent in politics, and has never been politically ambitious. Mr. Rudert is a member of the Knights of Pythias and Royal Arcanum of Tarentum. In 1882 he married Miss Mary Werner, of Allegheny city, and had by this marriage three children: Amelia J., Estella R. and Flora H. His first wife died in 1889, and, in 1892, he married Miss Rose Senn, daughter of Peter and Susan (Schneider) Senn, the father a native of Switzerland, and the mother of France. Mr. and Mrs. Senn came to Allegheny county in 1863, and now reside at Allegheny, Pa. They are the parents of nine children, all of whom are living. Mr. Senn, a veteran of the Civil war, is now retired from active life. In politics he is a republican. Mr. Rudert has by his second wife one daughter, Edna. The family are Lutherans. Joseph Senn, junior member of the firm of Rudert & Senn, and one of the promising young business men of Tarentum, was born in Pittsburg in 1879, and received his education there. He is an independent in politics and is a member of the Mystic Chain.

HENRY ZIMMERMANN, manufacturer of high-grade tobies, and wholesale dealer in fine cigars and tobaccos, of Tarentum, was born in Canton Glarus, Switzerland, Dec. 18, 1848, and is a son of David and Magdalina (Knobel) Zimmermann, both of whom were born in Switzerland, and spent their lives in the home country. Besides the subject of this sketch, they had another son, David, also now a resident of Allegheny county. Henry Zimmermann was reared and educated in Switzerland, and there learned the shoemakers' trade, to which he devoted thirty-five years of his life. Coming to America at eighteen, he located in Pittsburg, where for some years he worked for W. E. Schmetz. Mr. Zimmermann has since coming to America spent all but four years in Allegheny county. In 1876 he went to Tarentum, worked at his trade there until 1889, when he went to the State of Washington. Returning after a short stay, he worked in Tarentum until 1898 as a shoemaker, and then engaged in his present business, in which he has met with flattering success. He is a republican in politics. He is a member of Allegheny lodge, No. 223, F. and A. M., and of Tarentum lodge, No. 587, I. O. O. F. In 1873 Mr. Zimmermann married Miss Rosina Heer, a native of Switzerland, and has had three children: Minnie (deceased), C. H. and Ella B. C. H. Zimmermann was born Nov. 8, 1878, was educated in Tarentum, learned the tobacco business, and now has charge of his father's factory. Henry Zimmermann and family are regular attendants upon the services of the German Evangelical Protestant church.

GEORGE SCHWARZ, a prominent butcher of Tarentum, was born Aug. 3, 1853, in Germany, where his parents, Christian and Caroline (Mackey) Schwarz, lived and died. Mr. Schwarz has had an eventful career. He was reared and educated in Germany, and lived there until 1885. He then came to America, spent a year in Cincinnati, and then worked for a time in a factory in McKeesport. After this he returned to Germany, and was for ten years a sailor on the high seas. He came to Tarentum in 1898 and embarked in the meat business, having learned the butchers' trade thoroughly before coming to America. He has been very successful, and now owns, besides his butcher shop, some property in Tarentum. In politics he is a republican. Mr. Schwarz's first wife was Miss Minnie Bloom, of Germany. He had by this union two sons, Henry and Karl. In 1896 he married Miss Philipena Wenner, of Hoboken, N. J.

HERBERT L. WARNER, furniture dealer and undertaker of Tarentum, was born in Harrison township, Allegheny Co., Pa., April 20, 1876. His father, James F. Warner, a native of Armstrong county, Pa., settled in Allegheny county about 1860, and now resides in Harrison township. He served four years in the Civil war. He is a republican in politics. The mother of the subject of this sketch, Isabel (Hesselgesser) Warner, was born in Butler county. Mr. and Mrs. Warner have four children, all living. Herbert L. Warner, whose name heads this article, was reared and educated in Harrison township, and was a clerk for J. C. Stewart for nine years before going into business for himself. He engaged in the undertaking and livery business in 1901, and in February, 1902, started in the furniture business also, the firm name being Parke & Warner. Mr. Warner is one of the most successful young business men of Tarentum, and owes his success entirely to his own efforts. His place of business is a well-equipped two-story building, 22 feet wide and 150 feet deep. He is a republican in politics. He is a member of the K. O. T. M. and P. O. S. of A. Mr. Warner was married, Feb. 27, 1902, to Miss Wilma Parke, of Harrison township, and has one daughter, Agnes Jean, born Feb. 20, 1903. Mrs. Warner is a daughter of John S. and Minnie (Dunlop) Parke, of Tarentum. Mr. Parke has been in various lines of business and owns a farm in Harrison township. He is a republican in politics, and is a member of the I. O. O. F. Mr. Warner and wife are members of the United Presbyterian church of Tarentum.

CHARLES MOORE, of Freeport, Pa., a prosperous farmer, was born in Ireland, March 1, 1820, and is the son of Charles and Susanah (Might) Moore, both natives and life-residents of Ireland, but of Scotch descent. They were the parents of twelve children, all of whom are dead except the subject of this sketch. He remained in Ireland until he was fourteen years of age, and then came to Pittsburg, Pa., and, with the exception of five and one-half years spent in California, has resided in Allegheny county. Mr. Moore has devoted his attention to farming, in which he has been successful, and now owns 140 acres of land in Harrison township, where he has lived since 1859. He was originally a whig, but on the formation of the republican party, became identified with that organization, and has since been an active member. He was married, on Dec. 24, 1857, to Isabella McIntosh, a native of Ohio, but descended from Scottish Highland ancestry, and she died on July 28, 1894. They have had six children, viz.: George (deceased), Charles C., Andrew, Susanah, Jennie and Isabella. Mr. Moore is well and favorably known in the community in which he has spent so many years of his life, and possesses the friendship and respect of all his neighbors.

GEORGE BURTNER, of Tarentum, Pa., a well-known and prosperous farmer, was born in what is now Harrison township, on Jan. 5, 1835, son of George and Maria (Rowley) Burtner. His father was a son of Philip Burtner, a native of the eastern part of Pennsylvania, who came to Pittsburg in the latter part of the eighteenth century, and later located at what is now Tarentum. His son, George, the father of the subject of this sketch, was born in 1802, and married Maria, daughter of Daniel and Polly (Cheney) Rowley, who settled in Harrison township about 1818. George and Maria Burtner were the parents of four children, all of whom are now living. He was a prosperous farmer, owned seventy-eight acres of land, served as one of the school commissioners, and was a leading republican. He died in 1879, aged seventy-eight years, and his wife died in 1897, aged ninety years. George Burtner, the son, was reared on a farm, educated in the common schools, and for twelve years worked in a saw-mill, but farming has been his principal occupation. He owns thirty-five and one-half acres of land, and is quite successful as a general farmer. He is a republican in political matters, has been a school director for the past seven years, and has also been a member of the election board. He was married, in 1863, to Mary A. Swartzlander, of Armstrong county, Pa., and they have four children: George A., Henry G., Margaret C. and William F. Mr. Burtner is a member of the Odd Fellows, and he and his wife are identified with the Methodist church. He enlisted in August, 1864, in the Union army, and served in the artillery branch of the service until the close of the war. The ancestors of Maria Rowley, his mother, were prominent in the colonial history of the country, having served in the patriot army during the struggle for independence, and the next generation played an important part in the War of 1812.

J. O. SHAFFER, a well-known iron-worker of Tarentum, has considerable property, and, what is still better, a high character for integrity as a citizen and efficiency as a mechanic, as the result of a business career extending over thirteen years. His great-grandfather was a pioneer of Armstrong county, and his grandparents were Isaac and Elizabeth (Schall) Shaffer, both of whom reached an advanced age, and died in the same year (1895), the former eighty-six and the latter eighty-five years old. John P. Shaffer, son of the last-mentioned couple, has spent his life as a farmer in his native county of Armstrong, where he still resides in the enjoyment of the respect and influence of his neighbors. He has been quite active in local politics as a democrat, and is also influential in educational affairs, being for some time a school director, and at present a supervisor. He is also a prominent member of the Independent Order of Odd Fellows, and connected with the Lutheran church. In early manhood he married Salina, daughter of Isaac and Hester (King) Fitzgerald, the former of Scotland, and the latter a native of Germany, who emigrated to Armstrong county many years ago and spent the remainder of their lives within its boundaries. By this union there were nine children, of whom only seven are now living. One of the latter is J. O. Shaffer, whose birth occurred in Armstrong county, Pa., June 25, 1874. He grew up on his father's farm, and for educational purposes had the benefit of attendance in the excellent schools of Kittanning. His ambition was to become a skilled iron-worker, and with this end in view, he became an apprentice, in 1890, in the steel mill at Apollo. After remaining in that establishment several years, he went to Vandergrift and put in time at the mill in that place until his removal to Tarentum in 1901. Soon after his arrival he resumed work with the Allegheny steel and iron company as a sheet steel roller, in which capacity he had been employed for several years previously. He was one of the pioneer workers in the steel mill at Vandergrift, and quite active in the fraternal and official life of that industrial center. He held office as member of the council at Vandergrift Heights for two years, being elected as a republican, and resigned a three-year term as school director, to which he had been chosen by the people. Mr. Shaffer's fraternal connections are with the Odd Fellows lodge, No. 1116, and the Knights of Pythias, at Vandergrift, and the Royal Arcanum, the Elks, and the Woodmen of the World, at Tarentum, being a charter member of the last-mentioned order. On July 25, 1896, Mr. Shaffer was married to Miss Gertrude R., daughter of David M. and Mary (Bostworth) Croyle, the former a native of Armstrong county, and the latter of England. Mrs. Shaffer is one of their eight children, of whom seven are still living. Her father, who is a carpenter and bridge-builder by trade, still resides in Armstrong county, but her mother died in 1883. Mr. and Mrs. Shaffer have four children: Chester Boyd, Verna Claire, Rubie Pearl and Mary Croyle. The family reside in a comfortable home on Walnut street, which, together with a farm that he owns in Armstrong county, constitutes the substantial reward for years of industry and economy on the part of the head of the household. The parents are members of the Baptist church at Tarentum, and enjoy general esteem both as neighbors and citizens.

ELMER J. BASH, at present with the steel and iron mill at Tarentum, comes of an old and honored Pennsylvania family, which, on the paternal side, trace their ancestry to one of the emigrants who came over in the "Mayflower." Eventually, the descendants of the old Puritan voyagers became settlers of western Pennsylvania, and the name has long been a familiar one in Westmoreland and Armstrong counties. Henry Bash, a native of Westmoreland county, married Rachael Collins during the early part of the nineteenth century, but later they removed to Armstrong county, where both ended their earthly pilgrimage in honored old age. Among their children was a son named Michael, who married Miss Sarah, daughter of Joseph and Elizabeth (Gumbert) Grim, also natives of Armstrong county. Michael enlisted in the Federal army at the outbreak of the Civil war, and had the harrowing experience of being cooped up in Libby prison for six months, besides at one time being wounded during one of the numerous engagements in which his command participated. In 1865 he removed with his family to Tarentum, but after a residence of three years at that place, returned to Armstrong county, where he and his wife have since made their home. For some years he worked in the iron industry, but at present is a traveling salesman for the Standard oil company. His children consisted of six sons and one daughter, and of these five are still living. Elmer J. Bash, one of the six sons above mentioned, was born July 4, 1867, while his parents resided at Tarentum, Pa., but was taken to Armstrong county in the year following his birth, and spent his childhood at Apollo. When fourteen years old, he began work in the steel mill near his father's home, and remained with the company owning this plant until 1899. In July, 1901, he removed to Tarentum, secured a position with the Allegheny steel and iron company, and at the present time is working as a sheet steel heater in that establishment. Mr. Bash is independent in politics, and his fraternal connections are with Lodge No. 587, I. O. O. F.; Encampment No. 287, the K. O. T. M. and the Royal Arcanum. In 1888 Mr. Bash was united in marriage with Miss Ella Britton, of Armstrong county, and they have five children: Ethel M., Cleveland, Gladys, Hazel and Alice. Mr. and Mrs. Bash are members of Trinity Reformed church at Apollo.

DAVID WOLF, of Tarentum, Pa., a successful farmer, was born in Harrison township, Nov. 18, 1845, son of Samuel and Mary J. (Haney) Wolf, both natives of Armstrong county, who came to Allegheny county in 1838 and settled in Fawn township. The father was a successful farmer, owned eighty-seven acres of land and other property, and spent the declining years of his life in Tarentum. He was closely identified with the republican party, served as supervisor and a school director, and he and his wife were members of the Methodist church. They had a family of thirteen children, seven of whom are now living. David Wolf was reared on the farm, attended the common schools, and for thirty-three years was engaged in the oil business. He now resides on his farm of fifty acres in Fawn township, and is three miles from Freeport and six miles from Tarentum. He makes a specialty of raising fruits and berries, and is extensively engaged in trucking. Mr. Wolf is a leading republican, and has been supervisor, auditor and a member of the election board. He was married, in 1864, to Belle Courter, a native of Harrison township, and they have had five children: Laura, John, Nealy, Aggie (deceased) and an infant. Mr. Wolf and his wife are members of the Methodist church, and are prominent in the religious and social circles of their community.

CHRIST STARK, of Tarentum, Pa., a substantial farmer, was born in Indiana township, Allegheny county, Oct. 14, 1849, son of Christ and Mary (Fetherkile) Stark, both natives of Germany. They came to Pittsburg in the early days, later resided in Indiana township for twelve years, and then removed to West Deer township. He was a successful farmer, a republican in politics, and was the father of nine children, seven of whom survive their parents. Christ Stark, the son, was reared on a farm, educated in the common schools, and resided in Indiana and West Deer townships until 1889, when he began general farming on the farm of fifty acres which he now owns. He was married, on Jan. 22, 1880, to Polly, daughter of John and Ruth (Hamilton) Christy, both well-known residents of that section of Pennsylvania. The paternal grandparents of Mrs. Stark were James and Polly (North) Christy, both natives of Pennsylvania and prominent in the affairs of Westmoreland county. Mr. and Mrs. Stark are the parents of four children: Charles Clifford, Clarence Edward, William John Christian and Mary Pearl. Mr. Stark is an ardent republican, and is closely identified with that party. He and his family attend the Bull Creek Presbyterian church, of which Mrs. Stark and the children are members. Mr. Stark has been quite successful as a farmer, has accumulated a competency, and is one of the leading men of his community.

SAMUEL D. CLARK, of Hites, Pa., a prosperous and well-known farmer, was born on the farm in East Deer township which has been in the Clark family since 1834, on Jan. 4, 1860, and is the son of David and Jane (Hamilton) Clark, both natives of Ireland. David Clark came to America in 1831, and one year later his parents, Samuel and Mary (Louden) Clark, followed him to the United States. In 1834 they settled on the farm which their grandson now owns, and there they resided until their deaths in 1848 and 1861, respectively. They were members of the United Presbyterian church, and had a family of nine children. The maternal grandparents of Samuel D. Clark were John and Rebecca (Rankin) Hamilton, both natives and life-residents of Ireland. David Clark, the father of Samuel D., devoted the greater part of his life to farming, was a democrat in politics, and a member of the United Presbyterian church. Samuel D. Clark was reared on the farm, educated in the common schools, and all of his business career has been devoted to tilling the soil. He now owns fifty-eight acres of the original homestead settled by his grandfather in

1834. This homestead consisted of 274 acres, and the Clarks have lived on this farm longer than any other family in East Deer township has resided on their present farm. Mr. Clark has been a lifelong republican, taking active part in the politics of his township. He is now serving his second term as inspector of elections, and in 1901 was appointed to fill an unexpired term as supervisor. Mr. Clark has two sisters living: Margaret E. R., wife of Peter McCorkle, of East Deer township, and Mary J., who keeps house for her brother. Samuel D. Clark is one of the best known citizens of East Deer township, and is a solid and substantial farmer.

WILLIAM WOLFERD, at present one of the trusted and esteemed employes of the Allegheny steel and iron company, comes of good Pennsylvania stock, on the side of both father and mother. William and Susanna Wolferd, his paternal grandparents, were early settlers of Westmoreland county, where they spent their lives of usefulness and ended their days. The grandparents of Mr. Wolferd on his mother's side were early settlers of Allegheny county, with whose affairs they were identified until death ended their earthly careers. The parents of William Wolferd are Christopher and Ellen (Painter) Wolferd, natives of Westmoreland county, of which they are still respected residents. The father is a carpenter by trade, but at present is retired from active business. He reared a family of thirteen children, of whom nine are still living. His son, William Wolferd, was born in Westmoreland county, March 4, 1861, and spent his youth in work on the farm and attendance at the common schools of the neighborhood. When eighteen years old, he began working in a steel mill and continued in this employment at the same place for fifteen years. At the end of that time he spent a year at Vandergrift, and in 1901 came to Tarentum, since which time he has been engaged with the Allegheny steel and iron company as a smelter. He is an expert in his line of business, and has always been regarded by his employers as one of their best and most reliable hands in the duties entrusted to him. In 1880 Mr. Wolferd married Miss Nora Hill, of Leechburg, Pa., which union resulted in the birth of nine children: Bert, Grace, May, Florence, Fern, Claire, Horner, Vera, and Violette (deceased). The family are connected with the Trinity Lutheran church at Tarentum, and Mr. Wolferd's political associations, like those of his father, have always been with the democratic party.

FRANCIS B. BLACK, of Harmarville, Pa., a well-known farmer, was born in Harmar township, Nov. 30, 1825, and is the son of James and Elizabeth (Batty) Black. The father of James Black was Robert Black, a native of Ireland, who settled in South Carolina on coming to the United States, and subsequently located in Allegheny county, where he owned 500 acres of land. His wife was Sarah Aiken, a native of Ireland, who died in Indiana township in 1863, her husband having died in 1853. James Black, the father of Francis B. Black, was a prosperous farmer, a whig, and later a republican, and died in 1889. He and his wife were members of the Covenanter church, later of the United Presbyterian church, and finally of the Methodist church. Francis B. Black was reared on his father's farm, attended the common schools, and has devoted his entire business life to agricultural pursuits. He now owns a farm of thirty-five acres, and has been very successful in his vocation. He is prominently identified with the republican party, and is now serving as inspector of elections. He was married, in 1854, to Mrs. Mary (Martin) McMurdy, daughter of one of the pioneer settlers of Allegheny county, and they had the following children: James (deceased), Francis, Robert, Agnes, Jeanette, Susie and Elizabeth. Mr. Black and his wife are members of the Methodist Episcopal church, and are identified with the charitable and religious works of their community.

CRAIG M. SOBER, of Tarentum, Pa., a well-known sheet steel roller, was born in Westmoreland county, Pa., April 5, 1874, son of Andrew and Frances (Hill) Sober, his father and mother both natives of the Keystone State. They were married in Armstrong county; there his mother died on April 27, 1889, and his father is now one of the leading citizens and a highly successful farmer of Allegheny township, Westmoreland county. He is a leading republican, and has held a number of township offices. He is the father of eight children, all of whom are now living except the oldest one. Craig M. Sober was reared on the farm, attended the schools of his neighborhood, and began his business career in the steel mills of Leechburg, Pa. There he learned sheet steel rolling, was employed in that city for several years, worked for over five years in Pittsburg, then at Vandergrift, Pa., until 1901, when he came to Tarentum, and is now employed as a sheet steel roller by the Allegheny steel and iron company. Mr. Sober has acquired a competency by his industry and frugality, and owns property in Vandergrift, Tarentum and other places. He is an ardent and active republican, and is a prominent member of the Odd Fellows and the Knights of Pythias. He was married, on Feb. 22, 1900, to Anna, daughter of David and Lavina (France) Miller, of Armstrong county. Mr. Miller was a prominent farmer, a democrat in his political affiliations, and died in May, 1902. Mr. Sober and his wife are members of Trinity Lutheran church, and are the parents of two children: Clifford Hill and Arthur France.

W. HARVEY MYERS, senior member of the popular contracting and building firm of Myers & Sefton, is descended from Pennsylvania pioneers on the side of both father and mother. His grandfather, John Myers, who married a Miss Boyd, settled in Armstrong county at an early day, and died there in 1883, at the advanced age of eighty-two. His son, Elijah Myers, was reared on the farm and learned the carpenters' trade, which constituted the occupation of his subsequent life. In 1864 he enlisted in the 14th regiment, Pennsylvania cavalry, and served with that command until the close of the war, being wounded in the right arm while fighting on the skirmish line. He married Lavina, daughter of Henry and Catherine (Klingensmith) Shearer, the latter a native of Allegheny county, and the former an early settler of Armstrong county, where he died in 1898, at the age of seventy-six years. He was a member of the 14th Pennsylvania cavalry from 1864 until the close of the war. Elijah Myers, who still resides in Armstrong county, has always been a student, and by self-education has made himself a well-informed man. He and his wife are members of the Methodist Episcopal church. Of their ten children, four sons and five daughters are living. W. Harvey Myers, one of the four surviving sons, was born in Armstrong county, Pa., March 25, 1862. He grew up after the usual manner of country boys and learned the carpenters' trade under the painstaking care of his father, beginning work in that line when sixteen years old. In 1883 he came to Tarentum, and three years later formed a partnership with Frank Sefton to carry on the business of contracting and building. Since the formation of this company, they have been the leading contractors and builders at Tarentum, and have achieved marked success, both financially and professionally. The firm owns stock in the People's National bank and the Tarentum savings and trust company, Mr. Myers being a director in the last-mentioned institution. His political affiliations are with the republican party, and for six years he served as a member of the Tarentum council. June 1, 1885, Mr. Myers was married to

Miss Isabel, daughter of J. B. Sefton, who is elsewhere mentioned in this work. They have seven children: Charles Bryson, Esta Lavina, Martha Alta, Mary McCall, Alice Myrtle, Etta Ruth and Lillie Edie. Mr. and Mrs. Myers are members of the Methodist Episcopal church.

BENJAMIN W. HUGHES, of West Deer township, may without flattery be described as a model farmer, a useful citizen, and a man who comes as near enjoying life as is possible to mortals in this somewhat vexatious world. The common term "well fixed" applies with peculiar propriety to Mr. Hughes, as he owns a valuable farm, which he takes delight in cultivating, has an elegant home residence, and a lot of fine stock of various kinds. It is possible he gets much of his sanguine temperament and happy disposition from a transfusion of warm Irish blood. His grandparents, Johnson and Martha (Wallace) Hughes, came from Ireland to Pennsylvania in 1818, and located first in East End, Pittsburg. In 1849 they settled in West Deer township, on the farm now owned by their grandson, and here ended their earthly career, the former in 1872, the latter in 1858. James, son of these Irish immigrants, married Hannah, daughter of John and Jane (Denney) Crawford, the former a native of Butler county, the latter of Allegheny county, and both residents of Pine township, where they died. James Hughes became a prosperous farmer, owned 218 acres of land, and was quite well-to-do at the time of his death in 1896, ten years after his wife, who departed this life in 1886. Of their four children, two died in infancy and John on Jan. 17, 1903, leaving Benjamin W. Hughes as the only survivor. He was born in West Deer township, Allegheny Co., Pa., April 8, 1858, and at his father's death inherited the home farm with all its equipments. He took up the work in earnest, enlarged and improved the facilities, and branched out vigorously as an up-to-date and progressive agriculturist. While pursuing general farming and stock-raising, he pays especial attention to breeding Poland-China hogs. He has a beautiful home, enjoys life to its full extent, takes delight in the many bounties bestowed by nature on dwellers in the country, and is interested in everything calculated to benefit his county. He affiliates with the democratic party, and has served as supervisor and on the election board. Mr. Hughes has never married, but makes amends for this fault, if it be one, by furnishing his friends an excellent example of the model bachelor.

JOHN A. DICK, at present one of the trusted employes of the glass company at Tarentum, has been engaged in this line of work from early boyhood. His father, Franklin B. Dick, a native of Pittsburg, has been a glass-presser during the whole of his working life, and at present is a resident of Brackenridge. In early manhood he married Hannah, daughter of John Ward, an old-time settler of Pittsburg, who, during his earlier years, was engaged in river work. He enlisted in the Union army during the Civil war, served creditably through that great struggle and died in 1870. His wife, Martha, survived him many years and died in Brackenridge in 1893, aged seventy-four years. Mrs. Hannah Dick died in 1900, aged forty-nine years, after becoming the mother of seven children, of whom six are living. Among the latter is John A. Dick, subject of this sketch, whose birth occurred in Pittsburg, Pa., Nov. 5, 1869. Such education as he obtained was received in the Pittsburg school, which he attended irregularly until his thirteenth year, when he entered a glass factory, and from that time up to the present has continued in that occupation. In 1884 he removed to Brackenridge borough, and at present is engaged as a presser in the establishment of the Tarentum glass company. In politics Mr. Dick is a republican, and his only fraternal connections are with the Modern Woodmen of America, in which order he has held membership for some years. In 1889 Mr. Dick was united in marriage with Miss Alice Jordan, of Allegheny county, by whom he has four children: Wilbur, Nellie, Hazel and Mildred. Mrs. Dick is a member of the Methodist Episcopal church.

WILLIAM L. HUNTER, one of the well-known employes of the iron mill at Tarentum, is descended from early settlers of Pennsylvania. His paternal grandfather, Robert Hunter, was born in Pennsylvania, Oct. 27, 1782; came at an early day to Indiana county and married Mary Lawrence, a native of New Jersey, who came with her parents in childhood to that section. Robert Hunter served in the War of 1812 and his father was a soldier in the war of the Revolution. Robert L. Hunter, son of the former, was born in Indiana county, went to Illinois about 1866, and was there married to Martha McGinnis, a native of New Castle, Pa. His first wife having died in 1870, he was married, in 1874, to Mary J. Warner, who, as his widow, now resides at Tarentum. He was a shoemaker by trade, and a member of the Methodist Episcopal church. William L. Hunter, the only child by his father's first marriage above mentioned, was born at Aledo, Mercer Co., Ill.,

Oct. 5, 1868. He was consequently five years old when his father returned to Pennsylvania, and he received his education in this State. In 1887 he secured employment in the steel mill at Leechburg, and worked at different places until 1901, when he came to Tarentum with the Allegheny steel and iron company, with which he is now engaged as a sheet steel heater. His political affiliations are with the republican party, and he is a member of the American insurance union. On Nov. 21, 1895, Mr. Hunter was united in marriage with Miss Gertrude M. Bladen, of Leechburg, Pa., by whom he has three children: Robert W., Eleanor and Martha. Mr. and Mrs. Hunter are members of the Methodist Episcopal church at Tarentum.

THOMAS A. McGINNISS, the well-known brick-mason in the iron and steel works at Tarentum, is of Irish parentage, but English birth. His parents, George and Rachael (Smith) McGinniss, natives of Ireland, spent some time in England before their emigration to the United States in 1867. They located first at Elizabeth, N. J., but went from there to Nanticoke, Luzerne Co., Pa., where the father died in 1897. His wife survived him about one year, and died at Yonkers, N. Y., in 1898. He was an engineer by profession and a workman of superior ability. He left six children, and among this number was Thomas A. McGinniss, the subject of this sketch, whose birth occurred in England in June, 1866. He was scarcely a year old when his parents arrived in America, and his early training and education were received during the family's residence at Elizabeth. He learned the bricklayers' trade and worked at this occupation in the east for fifteen years. In 1901 he came to Tarentum and began work on the plant erected by the Allegheny steel and iron company, being the first man on the grounds to start the work. He has done all the excavating and brick-work for the company's furnace, and for some time has been superintendent of the brick department. Mr. McGinniss is an adherent of the republican party, and in 1902 he was elected to the Brackenridge borough council for a term of three years. He is a member of Tent No. 57, K. O. T. M., at Sharpsburg, Pa. In 1885 Mr. McGinniss was united in marriage with Miss Catherine J. Carey, of Nanticoke, Pa., and they have seven children: Margaret, Thomas, James, Mary, Ethel, William and Anna. Mr. and Mrs. McGinniss are members of St. Joseph's Catholic church at Natrona, Pa.

WILLIAM S. REESE, of Natrona, Pa., superintendent of the smelting department of the Pennsylvania salt manufacturing company, was born in England, Sept. 1, 1843, son of Thomas and Mary (Johns) Reese, natives of England. His mother died in England in 1845, and the same year he accompanied his father to Baltimore and called that city home, though they lived in many different places, as became necessary in his father's trade of coppersmelter. Mr. Reese was educated in the different cities to which his father's occupation called them, and when he grew to manhood, he, following in the footsteps of his father, learned the copper-smelting trade. He has traveled extensively in this country, Europe and Mexico, while following that occupation, and, in 1889, came to Natrona to superintend the building of the smelting department of the Pennsylvania salt manufacturing company, and has since been superintendent of that department. He is a member of the Odd Fellows, and has been a Knight of Pythias since 1868. He was married, in 1869, to Elizabeth Hughes, of Baltimore, Md., to whom were born two children, Leonard D. T. and Beulah B. Mr. Reese enlisted in the artillery branch of the Union army in 1864, and saw distinguished service to the close of the war. He is well and favorably known in Natrona, and is one of the most valued employes of the Pennsylvania salt manufacturing company.

WILLIAM DICK, a prosperous and prominent citizen of Tarentum, has long been identified with the growth of the town in his capacity as a contractor and builder. His grandfather, David Dick, came from Ireland during the first half of the nineteenth century, located in Allegheny county, Pa., and there spent the remainder of his life. He married Letitia, daughter of James and Mary (Canahan) Bartley, all natives of Allegheny county, but long since passed away. Among their children was James Dick, who married Nancy Leslie, and after growing up learned the trade of a brick-maker, which occupation he pursued for some time in his native county of Allegheny. About 1873 he located at Tarentum, and died there Jan. 1, 1896, surviving his wife ten years, as she departed from this life in 1886. He held the office of school director for several years, and was liberal in his religious views, while his wife was a consistent member of the Reformed Presbyterian church. They had nine children, of whom seven are living, and among these is William Dick, whose birth occurred in Allegheny county, Pa., Sept. 5, 1850. After growing up at his home in West Deer township, he learned the trade of brick-laying, and by steady application to this occupation, was soon on the high-road to success. In 1885 he located at Tarentum, and for eighteen years has devoted his time to the business of contracting and building. He has achieved commendable success, and now owns property in Tarentum, besides being a stockholder and director in the People's National bank at that place. He served as a republican member of the council for one term, and is connected with the Order of Heptasophs. On July 8, 1875, Mr. Dick was united in marriage with Miss Eleanor, daughter of the late Elias Anderson, of West Deer township, Allegheny county. Their only son, James W. Dick, was well educated at Tarentum and at the Grove City college, learned the brick-layers' trade, and is a young man of promise. Mr. and Mrs. Dick are members of the Reformed Presbyterian church at Tarentum.

WILLIAM McCULLOUGH is a well-to-do and much-esteemed farmer of West Deer township, where he owns twenty acres of land and is comfortably situated. His parents, Andrew and Isabella McCullough, were natives of Ireland, who emigrated to this country in 1838 and located in Butler county, Pa. Soon afterwards they changed their residence to Allegheny county, where the father engaged in agricultural operations until he eventually owned a good farm in West Deer township. A whig and republican in politics, he worked industriously, wronged no man, and lived a blameless life until in April, 1880, he was called to render his final account in the world beyond the grave. On Sept. 5, 1883, or about three years later, his good wife bade farewell to earthly cares, and joined her husband in the sleep that knows no waking. They had six sons and two daughters, and all but two of the children are still living. William McCullough was born in November, 1850, during the brief residence of his parents in Butler county, Pa. He was brought up on the farm and learned all the details of the business, while also acquiring those habits of industry and economy essential to success in cultivating the soil. Mr. McCullough has always been a hard-working man, and enjoys cordial esteem among his neighbors. As previously remarked, he owns a neat little farm in West Deer township, which he manages with skill and good judgment. He is a democrat in politics, and has held the office of constable, besides serving on the board of elections. Like his father and mother before him, Mr. McCullough is a member of the Presbyterian church, and he is guided by the best religious precepts in the treatment of his fellow-men.

ADAM VOGEL, of Tarentum, Pa., well known as a successful farmer, was born in Germany, Feb. 13, 1855, son of Frederick and Caroline (Weaver) Vogel, natives and life-residents of the Fatherland. Frederick Vogel was a prosperous stone-mason, and was the father of three children, two of whom are now living. Adam Vogel was reared in Germany, and educated in the thorough schools of that country. He came to the United States in 1881, settled in Allegheny county, and for twelve years was employed in the caustic shop of the Pennsylvania salt manufacturing company. In 1894 he purchased a farm of 130 acres in Fawn township, and since has prospered as a general farmer. He was married, in May, 1870, to Catharine, daughter of Jacob and Elizabeth (Weaver) Scherrer, both natives of Germany, where they passed their entire lives. Mr. and Mrs. Vogel are the parents of seven children, namely: Caroline (deceased), Annie E., Adam (deceased), Willie, Rosa, Frederick (deceased) and Adam. Mr. Vogel is closely identified with the republican party, and is an active worker for its advancement and success. He and his family are members of the German Lutheran church, and they are prominent in the social and religious circles of Tarentum. Mr. Vogel, by the exercise of industry, economy and thrift, has accumulated a competency, and is recognized as one of the solid and substantial citizens of the city in which he resides.

HENRY E. LEE, of Tarentum, Pa., a successful farmer and a well-known citizen, was born in Pittsburg, Pa., June 18, 1847, son of James and Charlotte (Barker) Lee, the former a native of New Jersey, and a son of John and Jane (Davidson) Lee, natives of Scotland, who settled in New Jersey in 1811, subsequently removed to Pittsburg, and there lived and died. James Lee was reared and educated in Pittsburg, learned the trade of a glass-blower, and, in 1851, settled in Fawn township, where he resided until his death, which occurred while in Allegheny city in 1889. He was a republican in politics, a school director for several terms, and also assessor. He and his wife were members of the Baptist church, and were the parents of eleven children, four of whom are now living. Mrs. Lee was the daughter of Thomas and Anna (Lincoln) Barker, and was a poetess of considerable ability, having written a number of poems which are highly prized by her family. Henry E. Lee was reared on a farm, educated in the common schools, and has been quite successful as a general farmer. He is prominently identified with the republican party, has been a school director for twelve years, assessor several terms, and for seven years tax collector of Fawn township. He is a member of Freeport lodge, No. 444, Knights of Pythias, and he and his family are members of the Methodist church. He was married, in 1873, to Ida M. Beale, a native of Freeport, and a daughter of Thomas Beale, prominently identified with the steamboat traffic of the early days. They have four children: Laura J., formerly a well-known teacher of music, and now the wife of John Bricker, of Buffalo township, Butler county; Olive C., Howard J. and Jessie A. Mr. Lee always takes an active interest in politics, and is a leader in all movements for the advancement and betterment of his community.

JOSEPH C. DUNN, a retired business man, politician, and at present assessor of Tarentum, was born in Fawn township, Allegheny Co., Pa., Oct. 19, 1837. His father, Robert Dunn, was born in Ireland, came to America in early manhood and located in Tarentum, where he died in 1859. He was a lawyer and physician, but gave most of his time to medicine, practicing successfully in Tarentum for many years. His wife, Margaret (Coe) Dunn, mother of the subject of this sketch, was born in Allegheny county, daughter of Daniel Coe, an early settler, whose brother, Benjamin Coe, is mentioned elsewhere in this book. Mrs. Dunn died Nov. 19, 1880. Mr. and Mrs. Robert Dunn were members of the United Presbyterian church. They had three sons, who are all now living. The subject of this sketch was reared and educated in Tarentum, where he afterwards engaged in business for many years. He was at first a clerk, and then formed a partnership with George M. Morrison, which lasted until the latter's death. After this Mr. Dunn ran the business alone until 1883, when he retired. He now owns considerable property in Tarentum. He is an ardent republican, is active in politics, and had served several terms as councilman before he obtained the position of assessor, which he has held for some years. He is an Ancient Odd Fellow. Mr. Dunn was married, Nov. 23, 1865, to Miss Mary A. Neel, a native of Louisville, Ky. Her parents, James C. and Jane Neel, spent their last days in Allegheny county. Mr. Dunn enlisted, in 1861, in Company C, 9th Pennsylvania reserves, and served in the Union army about two years, fighting with distinction before Richmond, at the second battle of Bull Run, and in a number of other engagements. Mr. Dunn and wife are members of the Presbyterian church.

JOHN HARDT, a worthy farmer of Richland township, who is well and favorably known in the community where he lives, is a son of the gentleman of the same name who is mentioned in another part of this work. Mr. Hardt was born in Germany, July 6, 1853, and first attended school in his native country, and later in Allegheny county, Pa., after coming to the United States. He was reared on a farm, and throughout his life has been engaged in agricultural pursuits. He now owns 115 acres of land, devoted to general farming, which is kept in a good state of cultivation. Though not an office-seeker, and preferring to attend strictly to his own business, Mr. Hardt is in accord with the general policies of the republican party and always votes that ticket. In 1882 Mr. Hardt was united in marriage with Miss Maggie, daughter of George Haverline, who receives mention elsewhere in this work. Mr. and Mrs. Hardt have had six children: George (deceased), Annie M., Emma B., Dora T., Walter D. and Henry E. (deceased). The parents are members of the Lutheran church.

JOHN A. HUGHES, fruit-grower and general farmer of West Deer township, is one of the many thrifty agriculturists whose labors have done so much for the development and enrichment of Allegheny county. He is a grandson of Jonathan Hughes, who is mentioned in another part of this work. His father, Alexander Hughes, was born in East End, Pittsburg, Dec. 15, 1827, and after growing up, became owner of the farm in West Deer township at present owned by his son. He held the office of school director several years, and was one of the originators of the Presbyterian church at Bakerstown, and for about twenty years was one of the elders. He married Anna, daughter of William and Mary (Henry) Wilson, natives of County Monaghan, Ireland, who settled in Butler county, Pa., in 1850. The father spent his life on a farm in Middlesex township, now owned by his son, James Wilson. He died June 7, 1857, and his widow passed away Dec. 15, 1896, at the home of the grandson, aged ninety-three years. Her daughter, Anna J., was born in Ireland in 1842, and was eight years old when her parents reached Pennsylvania. Alexander and Anna J. (Wilson) Hughes had five children: James Wilson (deceased), unnamed infant (deceased), Anna Mary, Lida Martha and John A. Anna Mary, the third child, is the wife of Charles Fortenbacher, an employe of Feich Bros., No. 414 Wood St., Pittsburg. Lida Martha is the wife of Robert Whiteside, a farmer of Butler county.

The father died May 21, 1902. John A. Hughes, the youngest of his children, was born in West Deer township, Allegheny Co., Pa., July 22, 1881. At the death of his father he inherited the old homestead of 120 acres, which he devotes to general farming, paying especial attention to the raising of fruits and potatoes. He is a popular young man in his neighborhood, and looked on as a rising agriculturist of promise. On Oct. 8, 1902, he was married to Miss Anna M. Stewart, of Oakland, East End, Pittsburg. Mr. Hughes affiliates with the democratic party, and he and his wife are members of the Presbyterian church at Bakerstown.

J. A. CROFT, for many years engaged in the milling business at Bakerstown, was formerly equally well known as a farmer, and is still the owner of considerable land in western Pennsylvania. His grandparents, Joseph and Mary (Humphrey) Croft, were natives of England, who came to Pennsylvania and subsequently settled on a farm where Allegheny city now stands. Both spent the remainder of their lives in Allegheny county, where they eventually died. Their son, Lewis Croft, after reaching manhood's estate, acquired a farm in Butler county, and achieved success in agricultural pursuits. He held the office of school director for fifteen years, and for thirty years was a steward of the Methodist Episcopal church, of which himself and wife have been almost lifelong members. At the present time this worthy couple, now well advanced in years, are living in retirement in Butler county with Mrs. M. E. Jack, one of their daughters. All of their three children, consisting of two daughters and one son, are still living. J. A. Croft, the only son in the family above described, was born on his father's farm in Butler county, Pa., Oct. 22, 1850. After growing up he followed farming many years, but eventually learned the milling trade, and has spent the latter part of his life in that business. He built the mill at Bakerstown, with which he is now connected, and also purchased and conducted the Fayette City mill until its destruction by fire in 1902. Mr. D. Logan is his partner in the Bakerstown mill, which has a capacity of sixty barrels, and the firm has met success in their operations. Mr. Croft owns a farm of 122 acres in Butler county, and one of ninety-two acres in Crawford county, Pa. He has never aspired to public office, but has held the positions of school director and inspector of elections. His fraternal connections are with the Saxonburg lodge, No. 496, of the Odd Fellows; the Encampment at the same place, the K. O. T. M. and Grange. In

1875 Mr. Croft married Miss Mary A. Henry, of Butler county, who died Dec. 23, 1891, after becoming the mother of six children. Three of these died in infancy. A daughter named Blanche, in her seventh year, and two sons survive. Joseph Marion, the eldest of these, is a railroad engineer, and Albert Chester, the younger brother, is in the office of the Pittsburg & Lake Erie railroad company. Both are young men of promise.

F. F. HALLAM, city engineer of McKeesport, was born in Washington, Pa., in 1861, and lived there until he reached the age of sixteen, attending the public schools. He then entered Washington and Jefferson college, where he completed his education, studying at that institution until he reached his senior year. Upon leaving school, he spent four years in construction work for the Pennsylvania railroad company; then was employed for a time by the Milwaukee Northern, and after that by the Duluth, South Shore & Atlantic, with headquarters at Marquette, Mich. In 1889 he became superintendent of construction at Johnstown, Pa.; spent two years at that work, and then was employed for two years as locating engineer for the Adirondack & St. Lawrence company. Coming to McKeesport in 1893, he opened an office as civil engineer, was for several years engaged in attending to private business, and then, in 1897, was elected city engineer, in which capacity he has since been employed, and proved himself a capable and energetic official. Mr. Hallam is a republican in politics. He is a member of McKeesport lodge, No. 136, B. P. O. Elks.

L. O. BARR, widely known throughout the Allegheny valley as a contractor and man of affairs, comes of a long line of mechanical ancestry. The family was founded in Pennsylvania by Samuel Barr, who came from Ireland many generations ago and took up his residence in Indiana county, where he spent the remainder of his days. His son, James Barr, who was a shoemaker by trade, married Mary Long and reared a family, but he and his wife have long since joined the great majority. Their son, James, after growing up in his native county of Indiana, Pa., became a carpenter and millwright, met with success, and rose to be a prominent man in his community. His political affiliations have always been with the republican party, and he is a member of the Order of Odd Fellows. He married Miss Margaret, daughter of John and Susan (Ashbaugh) Hill, the former a carpenter by trade, and both long residents of Armstrong county, where they ended their days.

Mr. and Mrs. James Barr now reside at Freeport, Pa. Of their twelve children, eight are living, and L. O. Barr, the subject of this sketch, is the seventh son. His birth occurred in Indiana county, Pa., March 31, 1868, and when nine years old he was apprenticed to learn the trade of carriage-painting. After he acquired the details of this business, he also learned house-painting, and of late years has been engaged in the last-mentioned occupation in connection with paper-hanging. Aug. 4, 1890, he came to Tarentum and opened up as a contractor, since which time his business increased by degrees until it extends over a wide section of the surrounding communities, and necessitates the employment of from fifteen to twenty men. Mr. Barr is independent in politics, with republican leanings, and has fraternal connection with Natrona lodge, No. 743, I. O. O. F.; A. O. K. of M. C., No. 39, of Tarentum, and the P. O. S. of A., of Tarentum. On May 20, 1891, Mr. Barr married Miss Lottie, daughter of Henry Bergman, an early settler of Brackenridge borough. The latter was a native of Germany, and there married Elizabeth Gliezengcamp before emigrating to Pennsylvania, where they still reside. Mr. and Mrs. Barr have had four children: Nora, William (deceased), Beulah and Clara (deceased). The parents are members of the Cumberland Presbyterian church at Tarentum.

CONGAL ALLOYSIUS McDERMOTT, pastor of St. Peter's Roman Catholic church, McKeesport, was born in County Donegal, Ireland, in 1854, and came to America with his parents, in infancy. The family settled first in Schuylkill county, Pa., where Father McDermott attended the public schools until 1864. He then attended public school at Hazleton, Pa., until 1867, and after that went to St. Charles' college, in Maryland. Completing his studies there in 1872, he spent three years at St. Mary's academy, in Baltimore, finishing the course there in 1875, and then studied a year at St. Michael's seminary, in McKeesport. He was ordained to the priesthood, Dec. 5, 1876, and became assistant at Freeport, Pa. After a short time in Freeport, he went to Collinsville, and from there to St. John's church, South Side, Pittsburg. His health failing, Father McDermott next spent a year at St. Augustine's church, in Cambria county, and then returned to Pittsburg and became assistant at St. Patrick's church. A short time after this, in 1880, he was given his first independent charge, the control of the Catholic church and missions at Brownsville, Pa. Here he remained thirteen months, and then took charge of a new parish at

Uniontown, Pa. Leaving Uniontown in 1885, he was sent to Collinsville, where, through his efforts, a church and school were built. He remained there until 1890, and was then, until 1895, rector of St. Paul's cathedral, in Pittsburg. His health again failing, Father McDermott came to McKeesport, where, as pastor of St. Peter's church, he has endeared himself to his parishioners and proved himself a faithful and competent priest.

WILLIAM HARDY, chief of the McKeesport fire department, was born in McKeesport in 1863, and received a limited education there. He went into the rolling mills at an early age and worked for a number of years in the mills, first at McKeesport, and afterwards at Wheeling. Returning to McKeesport in 1889, he went into the fire department as a regular fireman, and subsequently rose to be captain. He then spent two years as city water inspector, and became chief of the fire department in August, 1901. He has made an excellent record as head of the fire department. In 1902 the fire loss was less in McKeesport than it had been in years. There were 192 alarms turned in, but the total damage from fire amounted to only $1,300, covered by $9,000 insurance. The total amount of fire insurance in McKeesport is $242,000. Chief Hardy is a member of McKeesport lodge, No. 136, B. P. O. Elks, and of the Knights of Pythias.

GEORGE J. F. FALKENSTEIN, paymaster for the W. Deweese-Wood company, of McKeesport, and a prominent politician of that place, was born in Chambersburg, Franklin Co., Pa., Aug. 14, 1863. When a year old, he moved with his parents to Baltimore, Md., and attended the Zion school there until he reached the age of seventeen. Then, while still living with his parents, he worked for a year and a half in the Baltimore post-office. Coming to McKeesport in 1883, Mr. Falkenstein entered the employ of the W. Deweese-Wood company as bill clerk, and rose from this position to become pay-roll clerk and finally paymaster, the place which he now holds. He is a republican in politics and prominent in local party affairs. He has served in the select council of McKeesport since 1895, and has been for the past four years president of that body. His political career has been fair and honest, untainted by any hint of corrupt methods. He was defeated in February, 1900, as republican candidate for mayor, but in 1903 he met with no opposition at the primaries, and in the succeeding election he was elected by a plurality of 261 votes. He was a charter member of the local lodge of the B. P. O. Elks, which was started in 1889, is secretary of that organization and past exalted ruler. He has been a member of the grand lodge of the order since 1890, has acted on various important committees, and was district deputy one term. During this time he organized seven lodges, a record equaled by only one other deputy. He is a member of the auditing committee of the grand lodge. Mr. Falkenstein was a member of the committee which had charge of the erection of the McKeesport library, and is now one of the directors thereof. He is a member of the German Evangelical church.

FRANK M. EVERETT, city treasurer of McKeesport, was born in West Newton, Pa., in 1864, but came to McKeesport with his parents in 1866, and has since resided there. He was educated in the public schools and at McKeesport academy, leaving the academy at fourteen to accept a position in a tube works. After this he was for ten years puddler for the W. Deweese-Wood company. Mr. Everett's long career in the public service began in 1892, when he was appointed delinquent tax collector for the fifth ward. In December, 1893, upon the death of his father, who was city treasurer, Mr. Everett was appointed to fill the unexpired term, was elected to the office in the following election, and has held the position ever since. In politics he is a republican. Mr. Everett was married, Dec. 6, 1900, to Miss Sarah Seddon, daughter of Mr. and Mrs. Walter Seddon, of McKeesport, and has one son, Frank M., Jr. The family reside in the fifth ward, McKeesport.

R. L. BLACK, who for many years has been farming in a quiet and modest way in West Deer township, owns and resides upon the farm which was settled nearly a century ago by his grandparents. The latter came from Ireland in the earlier years of the nineteenth century, located on the above-mentioned land in Allegheny county, and farmed it until the close of their lives. The estate was then inherited by their son, Benjamin, who married Rachael Love, a daughter of West Deer township pioneers, and he spent his whole life in the cultivation of his ancestral acres. He was a republican in politics, a member, with his wife, of the United Presbyterian church, and both led blameless and uneventful lives in the quiet of the countryside until called to render their last account for deeds done in the flesh. Of their six children, only two are living, one of these being R. L. Black, the subject of this sketch. His birth occurred at the old homestead in West Deer township, Allegheny Co., Pa., Feb. 6, 1853, and he grew up on the farm without incident or accident worthy of special mention. From early childhood he was trained to farm work, and when in due time he was called on to assume the management, he was well qualified for the duties. He owns and successfully cultivates eighty-eight acres of land, paying special attention to hay and potatoes, for which products his land is well adapted and for which a ready market is found in the nearby metropolis of Pittsburg. Mr. Black affiliates with the republican party, and has held the offices of register and assessor. On Oct. 16, 1891, he was united in marriage with Miss Maria, daughter of Robert and Margaret (Gibson) Swaney, early settlers of Allegheny county, the former now deceased. Mr. and Mrs. Black have four children: Edward Chester, Wilda Margaret, Mary Olive and Lida Laura.

CLYDE F. YOUNG, assistant accountant at the National tube works, McKeesport, was born in Turtle Creek, Pa., in 1876, son of Rev. A. I. Young, a prominent Pennsylvania minister. He was educated first in the public schools, graduating from the high school, and then attended Monmouth college, at Monmouth, Ill., from which he was graduated with the degree of A. B. Upon leaving college, he entered the employ of the National tube company, going at first into the shipping department, and in the service of this company rose to his present responsible position as assistant to the chief accountant. Mr. Young is a republican in political belief and takes an active interest in local party affairs. He resides in McKeesport, in the sixth ward, and is a member of the First Presbyterian church of that city.

WALTER S. ABBOTT, editor and proprietor of the McKeesport Daily Times, was born in McKeesport, Pa., March 12, 1853, and attended school there until he reached the age of sixteen. He then gave up his studies and learned the printing trade, at which he was engaged for about five years. At twenty-one he entered the employ of R. G. Dun & Co., and remained with this concern fourteen years, filling all the positions in the Pittsburg office, and, in 1885, taking charge of the company's office at Wheeling, West Va. On July 1, 1887, he purchased the McKeesport Times, and has since devoted his attention to the management of a paper which is daily becoming more popular. While in the employ of R. G. Dun & Co., Mr. Abbott was also engaged in newspaper work, so that he undertook the management of the Times well equipped by past journalistic experience. The Times is the pioneer McKeesport newspaper, its first issue having been in August, 1871. At the time Mr. Abbott took charge of it, it was a small, four-page sheet, but under his management it has been increased to a paper of eight and ten pages, with adequate telegraph and local service, and now has a daily circulation of about 5,000. Mr. Abbott is a charter member and past master of Youghiogheny lodge, No. 583, F. and A. M., and a member of McKeesport chapter, No. 283, Royal Arch Masons. He is also a member of Pittsburg commandery, No. 1, Knights Templars.

JAMES MORRISON, who holds the responsible position of superintendent of the works of the Fidelity glass company at Brackenridge, was born in Philadelphia, Jan. 8, 1867, son of Henry and Anna (Grimes) Morrison, natives of the north of Ireland, who emigrated to America and were married in Philadelphia. Later, in 1872, they moved to Pittsburg, where Mrs. Morrison died in 1876. Mr. Morrison is now a well-known baker in Pittsburg, and owns a bakery there. He is a democrat in political belief, and in religion a Methodist. Mrs. Morrison was a member of the Methodist church. They had, besides the subject of this sketch, a daughter, Martha, who died in Pittsburg, in 1892. James Morrison was reared in Pittsburg, attended school there in the eighth, eleventh and thirteenth wards, and then learned the trade of a glass-blower. He first worked for eleven years for J. T. & A. Hamilton, Twenty-sixth and Railroad streets, Pittsburg, and while a resident of Pittsburg, served three years on the O'Hara school board. In 1892 Mr. Morrison moved to Anderson, Madison Co., Ind., where he worked for several years at his trade, and was then made superintendent of the American flint bottle company at Summitville. He held that position two years, and then came, in 1901, to Brackenridge to accept his present position with the Fidelity glass company. In politics he is a democrat, is actively interested in the welfare of his party, and while a resident of Anderson, in 1898, represented Madison county in the State legislature. He is a member of the B. P. O. Elks, of Tarentum. Mr. Morrison was married, in 1887, to Miss Catherine Hannan, of Pittsburg, and is the father of three children: Adda B., James A. and Lewis. The Morrison family are regular attendants upon the services of the Methodist Episcopal church.

HERBERT S. VAN KIRK, M. D., a prominent young McKeesport physician, was born in McKeesport in 1876, being a son of T. R. Van Kirk. He attended the public schools, Penn military academy and Lehigh university, and later entered the medical department of the University of Pennsylvania, from which he was graduated in 1899. After graduation he practiced a short time in Philadelphia, and then came to McKeesport, where he has since devoted his attention to a steadily increasing practice. He is also a member of the staff of the McKeesport city hospital. Dr. Van Kirk's office is at No. 1021 Walnut St. In political belief, the doctor is a republican.

J. E. O'BRIEN, local agent for the Cudahy packing company at McKeesport, was born in Keokuk, Ia., in 1875, son of John and Mary O'Brien. He attended the public schools and also took a business course, and then spent two years as clerk for the Chicago, Burlington & Quincy railroad company. After this he entered the employ of the Cudahy packing company, serving first in various capacities at Keokuk for four years, and then for a time as manager of the Clinton branch. From this position he was advanced to the management of the company's office at Lincoln, Neb., where he remained a year, and then, in 1899, was transferred to McKeesport. As agent for the Cudahy company, he has met with unusual success, and has made many friends. Mr. O'Brien was married, in 1899, to Miss Louise Krone, of Lincoln, Neb., and has two children: Mary L. and John K. The family reside in the fifth ward, McKeesport. Mr. O'Brien is an ardent republican in political belief. He is a member of St. Peter's Roman Catholic church.

CONARD G. KRIGBAUM, flour and feed dealer of McKeesport, was born at Marietta, Ohio, in 1868, son of the late Capt. C. G. and Katherine Krigbaum, and educated in the public schools and at an academy. While attending school he worked in a flour-mill and learned the milling business. Later he went into railroad work, being employed at first by the C. W. & B. railroad company and learning with this company to be a telegraph operator. He was for a year station agent at Harmar, Ohio, for a time after that brakeman for the T. & O. C. railroad company, and when only eighteen years old was made conductor. He held this position a year, was for eight months conductor for the Big Four railroad company, and then gave up railroading to enter a flour-mill at

Newark, Ohio. After five months' service he was sent to McKeesport to represent Londenslager & Co. in the flour and feed business. In 1897 he bought out his employers, and has since been successfully engaged in the flour and feed business for himself, being located at the corner of Sinclair and Jerome streets. Mr. Krigbaum is an enthusiastic member of the Masonic fraternity, being a member of Youghiogheny lodge, No. 583; McKeesport chapter, No. 282; Ascalon commandery, No. 59, and Syria temple, of Pittsburg. He is a member of the Masonic country club of Pittsburg. He is also a member of Titus lodge, No. 207, Knights of Pythias, and Ariel commandery, No. 145. In politics he is a republican. He belongs to the First Baptist church. Mr. Krigbaum was married, in August, 1890, to Miss Eleanor Anderson, daughter of Thomas B. and Amanda Anderson, of Newark, Ohio, and has one daughter, Katherine, now about nine years old. Mr. Krigbaum's home is in the sixth ward, McKeesport, Pa.

CHARLES D. KOEHLER, foreman for the McKeesport machine company, was born in Hollidaysburg, Pa., Oct. 12, 1863, son of Charles D. and Ruth Koehler. He attended the public schools until he reached the age of sixteen, then spent two years on a farm, and then, coming to McKeesport, was for seven years molder for the National tube company. In 1886 he became foreman for the McKeesport machine company, and has filled that responsible position most creditably since then. Mr. Koehler was married, Nov. 27, 1883, to Miss Effie Hayse, daughter of Charles Hayse, of Duquesne, Pa. He is a member of Lodge No. 121, Independent Order of Heptasophs; Lodge No. 116, Knights of Malta, and the Woodmen of the World. He is a republican in politics, and a Presbyterian in religious belief. Mr. Koehler and wife reside in the sixth ward, McKeesport.

HARRY ETHERIDGE, superintendent of the Allegheny county light company at Pittsburg, was born in Maisemore, Gloucestershire, England, in 1865, son of the late Henry and Elizabeth Etheridge, and was educated in the English schools, specializing in scientific studies. His first employment was with an India rubber and gutta-percha company at Silvertown, Essex, near London, where he remained seven years as foreman. Coming to the United States in 1887, he spent two years as electrician for the Allegheny county light company, then four years with the Writing telegraph company, and after that came to McKeesport. Here he was general superintendent of the Monongahela light and power company, whose territory embraces the southwestern part of Allegheny county. Mr. Etheridge is endowed with an excellent scientific training, which accounts for his success. He resides in the fourth ward in McKeesport, and takes an active part in its political affairs from a republican standpoint. He is a prominent Mason, being a member and past master of McKeesport lodge, No. 375; a member of Pittsburg commandery, No. 1, Knights Templars; high priest of McKeesport chapter, No. 282; a member of Pennsylvania consistory, of Syria temple, and Mount Maria council, No. 1. His religious affiliations are with the Episcopal church.

H. W. GRAY, accountant, was born in McKeesport, being a son of the late G. W. and Martha Gray. G. W. Gray, in his time a prominent river man, was widely known as "Captain Wash" Gray. He was a native of Mifflin township, Allegheny county, and died in 1879. H. W. Gray, whose name heads this sketch, was born in 1858, educated in the public schools, and spent five years on the river with his father. He entered the employ of the National tube company, going into the rolling mills as weighmaster. After this he was employed for a time in the axle department, spent a year with the National tubular axle company, of York, Pa., and on returning to McKeesport, went into the Monongahela furnace and steel department of the National tube company. Here he has since been employed as expert accountant, having entire charge of the office force. Mr. Gray married, in 1888, Miss Mary J. Lewis, daughter of Thomas E. and Rachael Lewis, and has two children: Rachael and Jack. Mr. Lewis is a republican in politics and a Presbyterian in religious belief. His home is in McKeesport, in the fifth ward.

DANIEL BRINEY SPENCER, of Natrona, Pa., a leading undertaker and liveryman, was born in Armstrong county, Pa., Jan. 22, 1863. He is a son of Chambers and Elizabeth (Briney) Spencer, the former a son of Flavel Spencer, and a grandson of William Spencer, a native of Germany and a pioneer of Armstrong county, and the latter a daughter of Daniel Briney, and a granddaughter of Michael Briney and his wife, Elizabeth. The wife of Flavel Spencer was Elizabeth, daughter of Jacob Wattenbaugh, a native of Germany and a pioneer of Armstrong county, who had the distinction of capturing the last hostile Indians in that county. Chambers Spencer was for many years a farmer of prominence, but has now retired from active life, and is residing at Parnassus, Westmoreland county. He is a democrat in politics, a member of the Presbyterian church, and the father of ten children. Daniel B. Spencer was reared on a farm, educated in the common schools, and followed farming until 1893, when he came to Natrona and engaged in the livery business. He prospered in that venture, and, in 1901, added embalming and undertaking to his business, and is also engaged in the sale of flour, feed, hay and straw. Mr. Spencer is an independent in politics, and formerly was a justice of the peace of Indiana county. He is a member of the Knights of the Maccabees, and prominently identified with that order. Mr. Spencer was married, on Oct. 10, 1887, to Sophie Ashbaugh, of Westmoreland county, Pa., and to them were born two children, Delnora and Alta May, the latter of whom died in infancy. Mrs. Spencer and her daughter are members of the Presbyterian church, and are identified with the religious and social affairs of that body.

YOST BROS., foundrymen, began their foundry business at Hites in 1900, and have been most successful. Prior to this they followed threshing two years, and were for eight years in the sawmill business. The father of George H. and William F. Yost, who compose the firm of Yost Bros., was Conrad Yost, a native of Germany, while their mother, Kate (Unger) Yost, was born in Columbus, Ohio. They were married in Allegheny county, where Conrad Yost came when a young man, and reared a family of four sons and three daughters, all of whom are living. Both parents were members of the German Evangelical church. The father was for the greater portion of his life employed in salt works, but spent his last days on a farm in East Deer township. He died in 1894, and his wife in 1892. George H. Yost, the senior member of the firm of Yost Bros., was born on a farm in East Deer township, Allegheny Co., Pa., April 12, 1869; educated in the common schools, and learned the molders' trade at Creighton, Pa. In politics he is a republican. William F. Yost was born June 3, 1872; was educated in the public schools, and learned the molders' trade before going into business with his brother. He is also a republican. He is married and has three children: Garnett, Carl W. and William G. Mrs. Yost was formerly Miss Mary Wilson, of East Deer township. William F. Yost is a member of the Orangemen of Hites. Besides their foundry at Hites, the Yost Bros. own a valuable farm of sixty-five acres in East Deer township.

JOHN N. BOCK, of Natrona, Pa., a prosperous blacksmith, was born in Germany, July 16, 1863, son of Conrad and Liza (Boman) Bock, both life-residents of the Fatherland. His father was a blacksmith, and reared a family of six children, all of whom remained in Germany except the subject of this sketch. He was reared and educated in his native land, and there learned the blacksmith trade under his brother. In 1891 he came to Natrona, and, after working two years at his trade for other people, opened a blacksmith shop on his own account in 1893. This business has prospered, and Mr. Bock, by his thrift and energy, has accumulated a competency, and has fine holdings of property in Natrona. He is a republican in politics, and is a member of the German beneficial society. He was happily married in Natrona to Mary, daughter of Peter Smith, a pioneer of Allegheny county, Pa., and to them have been born three children, Freda, Carl and George. Mr. Bock's family are members of the German Lutheran church, and are prominent in religious and social circles. In deciding to become a blacksmith, Mr. Bock was following in the footsteps of his father and older brothers, and his success in his chosen calling naturally suggests that his talents in that line are more or less inherited. He is a thorough workman, a master of his trade, and one of Natrona's substantial citizens.

WILLIAM J. CLINTON, of Natrona, Pa., foreman of the acid works of the Pennsylvania salt manufacturing company, was born in Westmoreland county, Pa., Feb. 11, 1865, and is a son of John and Mary (Ross) Clinton, the former a native of Ireland, the latter of Pennsylvania and a daughter of Robert Ross, a pioneer of Allegheny county, and later a resident of Tarentum. John Clinton came from Ireland to Pittsburg, subsequently removed to Hites, and there was well known as a coal-miner and also as an extensive dealer in live-stock. He was a member of the Catholic church, the father of ten children, five of whom are living, and is survived by his widow, who is now seventy-eight years of age and resides at Natrona. William J. Clinton was reared and educated at Hites, and when twelve years of age began to work in the coal mines. Later he learned the trade of lead-burning, followed that occupation for eighteen years, and has been an employe of the Pennsylvania salt manufacturing company for twenty-one years. In 1901 he was appointed foreman of the acid works of that company, and is now filling that position. Mr. Clinton is an ardent republican, and is a school director of Natrona. He is a member of Natrona lodge, No. 743, of the Odd Fellows, and an active worker for the society. He was married, in 1887, to Mary M. Stellar, of Natrona, and they have had four children: Clyde Harrison, Edith May, Walter, and Garnett (deceased). Mr. Clinton and his wife are members of the Methodist church, and are prominent in religious and social affairs.

FRANK WOLFE, of Natrona, Pa., a well-known employe of the James H. Baker manufacturing company, was born in Allegheny county, July 5, 1864, son of John and Mary (Miller) Wolfe, both natives of Illinois and early settlers of Allegheny county. His father was a republican in politics, and a prosperous coal-miner, who died May 18, 1891. He and his wife were members of the Methodist church, and were the parents of six children, five of whom are now living. Frank Wolfe was reared and educated in Harrison township, the most of his business career being spent in the employ of the Pennsylvania salt manufacturing company, but now holding a responsible position with the James H. Baker manufacturing company. Mr. Wolfe is a man of energy and ability, has accumulated some money, and owns property in Natrona. He is a republican in political matters, and he and his wife are members of the German Lutheran church of Natrona. He was married, on Jan. 1, 1885, to Mary E. Bergman, a native and resident of Natrona, and a daughter of Henry and Louisa (Glesencamp) Bergman, both natives of Germany, who came to America in 1865, and now reside in Harrison township. Mr. and Mrs. Wolfe are the parents of five children, four of whom are living and are as follows: Harry B., Frank L., Lawrence E. and Leonard J.

GEORGE R. JOHNSTON, of Natrona, Pa., a prosperous and successful farmer, was born on Jan. 9, 1863, on the old homestead in Harrison township, Allegheny county, son of George and Sarah (McKee) Johnston, the former a native of Ireland, and the latter born in Allegheny county, Pa. She was a daughter of James and Mary (Wise) McKee, early settlers and long residents of Allegheny county. George Johnston came to America in 1842, located in Canada, and two years later removed to Pittsburg, Pa., and subsequently went to Etna, Pa., where he resided until 1852, when he went to California. He was successful in the west, and in 1857 came to Harrison township, purchased 156 acres of land, and there resided until his death in 1887. He was a member of the Episcopal church, and the father of the following nine children: Mary J., born Jan. 10, 1851, and died Oct. 21, 1853; Lizzie, born April 17,

1853; Joseph C., born Aug. 23, 1857; Phœbe, born July 29, 1859, and died Dec. 21, 1863; Mary A., born Dec. 27, 1861, and died March 25, 1862; George R., born Jan. 9, 1863; Emma, born Aug. 6, 1865; Maggie, born Oct. 25, 1867, and died Aug. 6, 1868; Robert, born Sept. 25, 1869, and died Feb. 15, 1872. Mr. Johnston, the father, was a leading democrat, and closely identified with the Odd Fellows. George R. Johnston was reared on the farm, attended the common schools, and has been a practical farmer all of his business career. He still owns the greater part of the old homestead, and devotes his attention to general farming and trucking. He is prominently identified with the democratic party. He is a member of the Methodist church. Mr. Johnston was married, in 1896, to Ruth M. Brown, of Westmoreland county, and they have three children, Doratha, Joseph B. and George.

DAVID H. LYNCH, of McKeesport, Pa., a prominent citizen, was born in Westmoreland county, Pa., in 1840, and is the son of the late John Lynch and his wife, Margaret. Mr. Lynch received his elementary training in the district schools, and was graduated at Duff's college, of Pittsburg, in 1860. In 1863 he enlisted in Company M, 4th Pennsylvania cavalry, and served until September, 1865, taking part in many engagements and seeing the various phases of life incident to a military career. After the war he returned to Allegheny county, clerked in a general store for two years, and then went to Louisville, where he was in the coal business for two years. He was one of the principal men in the formation of the firm of Lysle, Bailey & Co., general merchants, of Camden, Pa., but three years later disposed of his interests in that concern and became a member of the firm of Walton, Lynch & Co., carrying a very extensive line of general merchandise. Three years later Mr. Lynch built a boat, the "Samuel Miller," of which he was captain for a number of years, engaged in towing coal between the cities of Pittsburg and Louisville. He was also interested in coal-mining at Webster, Pa., up to 1878, and was shipping coal to the southern markets for several years. Captain Lynch is now vice-president of the Thomas Moore distilling company, of McKeesport, and has occupied that position since the business was incorporated. He was married, in 1861, to Melissa Allen (now deceased), and has four grown children: Jessie, Grace Dale (deceased), Edwin Stanton and Madison B. Captain Lynch is a republican in his political affiliations, and is a highly-esteemed citizen of McKeesport.

D. P. McCUNE, of McKeesport, Pa., a prosperous contractor and builder, was born in Elizabeth township, Allegheny Co., Pa., in 1846, being a son of John B. and Mary W. McCune. He was educated in the rudimentary branches in the district schools of his native township, and later attended the Curry institute, of Pittsburg. On completing his education, he began as a contractor in Pittsburg, and five years later became superintendent of construction for the Robert H. Powell furnace company, in Bradford county. He went to Dunbar, Fayette county, and supervised the building of the furnace in that city, being in that line for eight years. In 1891 Mr. McCune came to McKeesport and began his present business of contracting and building, having offices at No. 520 Locust St., doing a large and profitable business. He was married, in 1872, to Louise J. Colbert, of Boston, Pa., to whom have been born five children: William H., Arthur C., Emma B., D. Pollock and Jessie W. Mr. McCune is a prominent republican, resides in the second ward, and has served five years as a member of the council of McKeesport, having four years yet to serve. He is a leading member of that body, being on the printing, poor, auditing and other committees, and takes a prominent part in its proceedings. He is a Mason of the chapter degree, and enjoys the respect and esteem of all who know him.

PETER C. PATTERSON, a capable young engineer in the employ of the National tube company, comes of that sturdy stock from which so many successful men in the world's history and progress have been developed, his father and mother, Peter and Mary R. Patterson, both being natives of Scotland. He was born in Brooklyn, N. Y., May 31, 1869, but when he was about three years old his parents removed to McKeesport, Pa., where he attended the ward and high schools, and later spent some time as a student in the Western University of Pennsylvania. While attending school, and when only about twelve years of age, he apprenticed himself, during vacations, to the National tube company, in the machine shops at McKeesport, and after finishing his education he was employed for a year in the shops. Though there is a popular belief that corporations have no souls, it has never been truly said of them that they fail to recognize and reward special ability when it is developed among their employes. The truth of this is fully illustrated in the case of Mr. Patterson. As fast as he has demonstrated his ability to assume new responsibilities, promotions have come to him at the hands of the National tube company. From the machine shop he was transferred to the draughting department, and after some time there he was made foreman of the shops in which he had served his apprenticeship. Next he was made constructing engineer, then superintendent of the lap mill, and for the last three years the National tube company has claimed his services in the capacity of mechanical engineer, with headquarters in the city of Pittsburg, Pa. While engaged in these various positions his inventive genius brought forth new ideas in machinery for the manufacture of tubing, and a number of his patents are now used in the works. Mr. Patterson is a member of the American society of mechanical engineers, the Engineers' society of western Pennsylvania, the Iron and Steel institute of Great Britain, and has served on the board of water commissioners of the city of McKeesport, Pa., where his practical knowledge of water-works plants proved a valuable acquisition to the board.

CHARLES A. MEYERS, superintendent of the annealing and finishing department of the American tin plate works at McKeesport, was born in Darmstadt, Germany, in 1841, and is a son of the late John P. Meyers, who was an engineer in the German army. Charles A. Meyers was educated in the military schools of his native country, then came to America in 1860, and served throughout the Civil war. Enlisting in Company B, 14th New York cavalry, he served for a time as sergeant, was later appointed lieutenant, and finally rose to the position of provost-marshal of the 19th army corps, which position he held until discharged in 1865. After the war he located at New Orleans, where for several years he took a prominent part in politics, and in 1869 went to Cincinnati to become foreman for the Cincinnati coffin company. Upon leaving this concern he accepted a position as foreman of the National casket works at Allegheny, Pa., and remained there thirteen years. His connection with the American tin plate works in McKeesport dates from 1894. Here he has filled various responsible positions, and now has charge of the annealing and finishing department. Mr. Meyers was married, in 1864, to Miss Mary McColly, of New Orleans. They have had six children, of whom the first-born, Elizabeth, is now deceased. The others are: Mary, Charles, John, William and James. Mr. Meyers is a member of the Masonic fraternity and the Presbyterian church. In politics he is a republican. His home is in the eighth ward, McKeesport.

HENRY STAMM, for almost twenty years a well-known hotel keeper in Brackenridge borough, was born in Switzerland, July 26, 1859. His parents, Martin and Dorothea (Pletsche) Stamm, spent their lives in Switzerland, where Mr. Stamm was a farmer. They were the parents of six children, five of whom are living. Henry Stamm and two sisters emigrated to the United States, Mr. Stamm coming in 1879, and his sisters some time afterwards. Mr. Stamm located in Sharpsburg, worked on a farm there for a time, was for several years employed in an oil refinery, and for a year kept a hotel in Sharpsburg. In 1884 he moved to Harrison township, now Brackenridge borough, buying the hotel property where he is now located, and on which he has since made various improvements. Mr. Stamm came to America a poor boy, but has by thrift and industry won for himself financial independence and the respect and good-will of the community. He was one of the organizers of, and is now a stockholder in, the Fidelity glass company and the Tarentum glass company. In politics a republican, he has served a term as assessor of Harrison township. He is a member of Etna lodge, No. 861, I. O. O. F., of Etna. On Aug. 12, 1884, he married Miss Barbara Lehman, of Germany, and is the father of seven children: Mary B., Annie P., Lucy, Emma, Ida, Emelia and Henry S. Mr. Stamm and family are members of the German Evangelical Protestant church.

JOHN N. KEPPEL, a successful baker of Brackenridge borough, was born in Germany, April 15, 1863, and is a son of Christopher and Margaret (Stoeher) Keppel, natives of Germany, who spent their lives there. He is one of a family of ten children —nine sons and one daughter—of whom all are living except two sons. Four of his brothers are now in the United States. Mr. Keppel was reared and educated in Germany, learned the baker trade there, and when seventeen years old embarked for America. He worked at his trade for about four years in Pittsburg and two years in Tarentum, and, in 1885, came to Harrison township, now Brackenridge borough, where he engaged in business for himself. His bakery there has been most successful, and Mr. Keppel now owns the property where he lives, and also two brick houses and lots. In 1885 he married Miss Caroline Cook, of Harrison township, by whom he has had five children, viz.: Matilda, Annie, Amelia, Clara and John C. (deceased). Mr. Keppel is a republican, and has the distinction of having served in the first council of Brackenridge. He is a member of Tarentum lodge, No. 587,

I. O. O. F., and, with his wife, belongs to the Rebecca lodge of that order, at Tarentum. He is also a member of the German Beneficial Union; of Tarentum tent, No. 4, K. O. T. M., and belongs to the German Lutheran church of Natrona, of which his wife is also a member.

THOMAS R. REA, priest at Glassport, was born in County Cork, Ireland, in 1871, son of Patrick and Mary Rea. He was educated first in the Irish schools, where he studied the classics, and specialized in Latin, beginning his ecclesiastical studies at All Hallows' academy, Dublin, in 1889. After a year at the academy, he came to America and studied first a year with the Franciscan fathers at Allegany, N. Y., and then, until 1894, at St. Vincent's college, in Westmoreland county. In 1894 he was ordained by Bishop Phelan, and became assistant to Father Nolan, at St. Peter's parish, McKeesport. After that he was assistant to Father McDermott, and on Jan. 4, 1900, was sent as pastor to St. Augustine, Cambria county, where he remained a year and a half, and then, in 1901, undertook his present charge. The Glassport parish is a comparatively new one, but Father Rea has now a congregation of 100 families, which is housed in a comfortable church, and the people have also recently erected a home at a cost of $6,000. In 1898 there were only three Catholic families in Glassport. During his short stay, Father Rea has proved himself a faithful and competent priest, and has won many to his faith.

GEORGE B. HERWICK, real estate and insurance agent of McKeesport and a prominent republican of that city, was born in Fayette county, Pa., in 1862, and attended the public schools there until he reached the age of fifteen. He worked three years for his father in a saw-mill in Fayette county, and when twenty years old came to McKeesport, where he was employed for five years in the National tube works, taking at the same time a business course in a night school. In 1888 he was given his first public office—that of city clerk of McKeesport—served one three-year term in this capacity, and in 1891 was elected to the position of city controller. Here his efficient services won him, in 1894, re-election for another three-year term. In 1897 he embarked in the real estate and insurance business, in which he has been successfully engaged since that time. He was located first at No. 911 Walnut St., and has been since 1900 at No. 418, on the same street. Mr. Herwick has been a member of the board of water commissioners of

McKeesport for two years. He is a member of McKeesport lodge, No. 583, F. and A. M.; Jr. O. U. A. M., and the Knights of Malta. He belongs to the Methodist church. Mr. Herwick was married, in 1890, to Miss Alice Gould, daughter of Daniel Gould, of McKeesport, and has four children—three daughters and one son. The family reside in the sixth ward, McKeesport.

WILLIAM KAUFMAN HERWIG, superintendent of the Boston iron and steel company and water commissioner of McKeesport, was born in Dravosburg, Pa., in 1859, son of George J. Herwig, and educated in the public schools of McKeesport. He went into the mills at an early age, and has won his present responsible position by his own unaided efforts. For three years he was weighmaster in the National rolling mills, puddler two years, heater one year, shipping and receiving clerk two years, foreman seven years, and for ten years assistant superintendent. He obtained his present position about a year ago. In political belief Mr. Herwig is a republican, active in local party affairs, and is at present water commissioner of McKeesport. He is a member of McKeesport lodge, No. 378, F. and A. M., and of the Pittsburg commandery of that order, and also belongs to the McKeesport lodge, No. 136, B. P. O. E.; Knights of the Golden Eagle, No. 334, and the Royal Arcanum. In religious belief he is a Presbyterian. Mr. Herwig was married, in 1899, to Clara V. Stein, daughter of John and Catherine Stein, of Cumberland, Md.

JOHN F. NICOL, superintendent of the Pittsburg coal and coke company, at Otto, Pa., was born in McKeesport, Pa., in 1857, son of William and Katherine Nicol. He was educated in the public schools of McKeesport and at Duff's business college, Pittsburg, and then was for three years and seven months machinist for the National tube company. After this, in the employ of the same company and other concerns, he went into the gas fields as an operator; spent some time putting in gas lines, reducing stations and pumping stations, and has the distinction of having put in the first gas pumps in the state of Texas. From 1892 to 1896 he had charge of the McKeesport paper department, and got the department into good condition before he left it. He entered the employ of the Pittsburg coal and coke company in 1896. Mr. Nicol is recognized as an expert in his line of work, and spends a great deal of his time doing special work in various places for large concerns. In 1899 he married Miss Lilly Hampson, daughter of Richard and Mary Hampson, of McKeesport. Mr. Nicol is a prominent and influential member of the Masonic fraternity, being a member of McKeesport lodge, No. 583; Shiloh chapter, No. 257; Tancred commandery, No. 28, Knights Templars, and Syria temple, Mystic Shrine. In politics he is a republican and served several years on the county committee. Mr. Nicol resides in Glassport borough. He is a Presbyterian in religious belief.

J. LEWIS HAMMITT, a leading McKeesport grocer and president of the McKeesport school board, was born in that city in 1862, being a son of J. K. and Rebecca Hammitt. He attended the McKeesport schools, and at fourteen went to work for his father, who was a grocer. Later he succeeded to the management of the store, bought his father's interest in 1896, and has been in business for himself since then. The grocery was moved in 1880 to a location on Fourth street, was again moved three years later to the corner of Fifth and Center streets, where it has since been located. Mr. Hammitt is a prominent republican of the sixth ward, was elected to the school board in 1893, was re-elected in 1901, and is now its president. He is an enthusiastic Mason, being a member of McKeesport lodge, No. 375; Duquesne chapter, No. 193, and Pittsburg commandery, No. 1, Knights Templars. He is an influential member of the First Baptist church, in which he holds the office of trustee. Mr. Hammitt was married, in 1891, to Miss Clare C. Hodgkinson, of New Brighton, and has one son, J. Lewis, Jr.

JEREMIAH A. BEATTIE, superintendent of the McKeesport & Connellsville railroad at McKeesport, was born in Pittsburg in 1856, being a son of Thomas W. and Mary Beattie. After a limited education in the public schools, he spent a year as errand boy for T. & J. T. McCance, merchant tailors, of Pittsburg, and was for four years employed in the Crescent tube works, rising in this time from a common laborer, through the different departments, to the position of welder. Leaving the tube works in his seventeenth year, Mr. Beattie spent three years with his father in the study of pig iron, its different dispositions, grading, etc., and at the expiration of that period was qualified to accept a position as foreman for the Sligo iron works, South Side, Pittsburg. He remained with this concern two years, and then, the original Homestead steel works being under construction, he became general labor foreman, William Clark being general manager of the works.

When the works were completed, Mr. Beattie became superintendent of transportation and labor, and remained with the concern until October, 1886. At that time he accepted the position of superintendent of the McKeesport connecting railway and of the works of the National tube company. Mr. Beattie has been superintendent for the National tube company (transportation department) for seventeen years, and has proved himself at all times a capable and efficient official. He is a member of the Heptasophs and Loyal Legion, belongs to the republican party, and is a member of St. Peter's church. He was married, in 1885, to Miss Elizabeth McNamara, daughter of P. and Mary McNamara, and has three children: Thomas C., Genevieve and Charles Taylor. Mr. Beattie's home is in the seventh ward, McKeesport.

CHARLES P. FIEDLER, clerk of the McKeesport board of education, was born in Pittsburg, Pa., in 1866, and is the son of Jacob and Sophia Fiedler, both of whom are old residents of Allegheny county. Until he was about fourteen years of age, he attended the Pittsburg public schools. His parents then removed to McKeesport, where he finished his education so far as the public schools were concerned, though he afterwards took a course in the Iron City college. Mr. Fiedler began his business career by carrying papers, having a route for a Pittsburg man for one year. He then went to work for the National rolling mill company, his first job being that of loading iron on the cars. From there he was transferred to the furnaces, then to the weigh office, and finally to recorder, where he remained until Feb. 2, 1903, when he was elected clerk of the board of education, succeeding W. J. Roseborough. In 1898 he was married to Miss Rebecca Smith, of McKeesport, and they have three children: James, Sarah and Mabel. He resides in the third ward of the city of McKeesport. Mr. Fiedler is a member of the Junior Order of United American Mechanics, and is an enthusiastic republican. Whatever promotions may have come to him in business, or honors that may have been conferred upon him in the way of holding office, are due to his own energy and sterling integrity. Whether selling papers, loading iron or weighing the product of the rolling mills, he was always careful and conscientious, thus winning the confidence of his employers, and in his present position his work is marked by the same features, insuring him the respect and esteem of his fellow-citizens who elected him. As he is still a young man, it is more than probable that further honors await him.

HEZEKIAH C. GRIFFIN, burgess of the borough of Glassport and roller for the National tube company, was born in Brownsville, Fayette Co., Pa., Sept. 14, 1855, being a son of Peter and Marie Griffin. He was educated in the public schools of Brownsville, and then spent six years in the iron-works of J. R. Jackson & Co. Leaving Brownsville, he spent eleven months in the employ of J. R. Jackson, in Pittsburg, working as a roller. When Mr. Jackson came to McKeesport to act as general manager of the Wharton mill, Mr. Griffin came with him and spent five years as roller in that mill. Since then he has been roller for the National tube company. He resides in Glassport, where he is serving his second term as burgess and is recognized as one of the leading citizens of the borough. Before becoming burgess he served three years in the council. In politics he is a republican. Mr. Griffin was married, in 1876, to Miss Mary E. Gummert, daughter of John and Martha E. Gummert, of Brownsville. They have three children: Edna, wife of C. N. Hartman; Harry C. and Vita G. Mr. Griffin is a member of the Odd Fellows and belongs to the encampment at Brownsville, also the Order of Americus and of McKeesport lodge, No. 136, B. P. O. Elks.

JAMES L. PENNEY, for over forty years a practicing physician in McKeesport, was born in Library, Allegheny Co., Pa., in 1838. He received his early education in the McKeesport schools and at Carmichael's college. After this he studied medicine three years in the office of his father, who was a leading physician in his day, and then finished his medical preparation at Western Reserve university, at Cleveland, Ohio. Returning to McKeesport, Dr. Penney began to practice in the spring of 1859, and two years later, April 22, 1861, he was commissioned surgeon in the Union army in the Civil war. After two years of service he was called home by the fatal illness of his father, and upon the death of the latter succeeded to his practice. Dr. Penney has been successfully engaged in the practice of his profession in McKeesport ever since. He married Sarah Allen, daughter of the late David Allen, and has one son and one daughter. Dr. Penney traces his ancestry to a great-grandfather who was a Revolutionary patriot and fought in the battle of Lexington, and who, after the Revolution, became one of the pioneers of Allegheny county, locating there in 1786. The doctor is a member of the Sons of the Revolution and of Philanthropy lodge, No. 225, F. and A. M., at Greensburg. In religious belief he is a Baptist.

FRANK W. PRATT, of McKeesport, Pa., a well-known barber and member of the common council, was born in Youngstown, Ohio, in 1873, and is a son of the late John Pratt and his wife, Arah. Mr. Pratt was educated in the public schools of his native town, and began to learn the trade of a barber in that city. Seven years later, in 1890, he came to McKeesport and worked with Fred Held for a short time. Later he was with Joseph Yester, then went to Pittsburg for a few months, and subsequently to East Liverpool, Ohio, where he worked at his trade for eighteen months. He returned to McKeesport, purchased his present shop at No. 1003 Walnut St., and there has met with much success. He was happily married to Isabelle, daughter of John and Rebecca Giles, and to them have been born four children: Rebecca (deceased), Anna S., Arah M. and Frank W., Jr. (deceased). Mr. Pratt is a stanch republican in his political affiliations, was appointed on the city republican committee, and was re-elected at the expiration of his term. He was elected to the common council in 1901 from the third ward, receiving the largest vote ever given a candidate in that ward, and was again elected in 1902. He is a prominent member of the common council, serving on the police and auditing committees, and taking a leading part in the deliberations of that body. He is a member of the First Methodist church and the Woodmen of the World, and is well known and liked in the city where he resides.

JAMES N. WAMPLER, a son of John and Ellen Wampler, of McKeesport, and a prominent merchant and councilman of that city, was born in McKeesport, Oct. 5, 1867. He received a fair education in the public schools, and then worked four years for Shelley Bros. After this he was for three years manager for the McKeesport Daily News, and worked the same length of time in a similar capacity for the McKeesport Times. After this he was engaged for a time in managing routes for a Pittsburg paper, and then was for three years yard foreman for Neel & Wampler, in the lumber business. He then started, at No. 505 Fifth Ave., McKeesport, a news stand and confectionery store, which he has since successfully conducted. Mr. Wampler is a democrat in politics, and although a resident of a ward which is strongly republican, he has for eight years represented the fourth ward in the common council of McKeesport. His record in the council has been a most creditable one. He has served one year as president of that body, and two years as chairman of the finance committee, and has, during his long service, never missed a council or committee meeting. Mr. Wampler married Miss Effie M. Urll, of McKeesport, daughter of G. T. Urll, and has five children, viz.: John W., Allen James, Robert James, Olive May and Anna.

SAMUEL MILLIKEN, city treasurer of McKeesport, was born in that city, Feb. 17, 1869, son of James W. and Frances (Wampler) Milliken, and was educated in the McKeesport public schools. Entering the W. Deweese-Wood works at an early age, he was promoted from place to place to the position of roller, and then, about four years ago, was appointed bond clerk in the office of the county controller. He has also, after seven years' study of law at home, passed the preliminary examination for admission to the Allegheny county bar. In the spring of 1903 Mr. Milliken was elected city treasurer of McKeesport, having received the nomination for that office from the republican party in the preceding January. He has long been prominent in local party affairs, having served on the republican city executive committee and also on the county committee. Mr. Milliken married Florence Izgood, daughter of Henry and Mary Izgood, of McKeesport, and has four children. He is a member of the American Mechanics, Knights of Malta, Foresters, Knights of Pythias, Woodmen of the World and B. P. O. Elks.

EMIL F. HOLINGER, superintendent of the seamless department, National tube company, of McKeesport, was born in Sweden in 1862, and was a son of Oscar and Augusta Holinger, both now deceased. When a boy he attended the public schools in Sweden, took a thorough college course, and then spent a seven-year apprenticeship at Motola, Sweden, working in the machine shop, engine-erecting shop, boiler-erecting shop, and finally in the shipyard. Thus excellently equipped by education and practical training, Mr. Holinger began his career, and was for a year and a half superintendent in Sweden before coming to the United States. Stopping first at Brooklyn, he was for four years employed as draughtsman and foreman for the United States projectile company, and in 1896 came to McKeesport, where his first labor was to plan and superintend the construction of a new mill for the National tube company. Since then he has been superintendent of the seamless department, a position of trust and responsibility, in which he has served in a most satisfactory manner. In politics Mr. Holinger is a republican. He is a member of McKeesport lodge, No. 375, F. and A. M.; McKeesport chapter, No. 282, and Pittsburg consistory, and belongs to the Swedish Lutheran church. Mr. Holinger was married, in 1891, to Miss Hilma Anderson, of Sweden, and is the father of three children: Sigred, Emil and Gertrude. He and his family reside in McKeesport, in the seventh ward.

H. H. SPROAT, yardmaster at McKeesport for the Pittsburg & Lake Erie railroad company, began his service with this company in Pittsburg as freight receiver. He was afterwards promoted to billing officer, came to McKeesport in 1896, and was for two years yard clerk. He filled the position of night yardmaster for three years, and in 1901 was given his present responsible position as yardmaster. Mr. Sproat was born at West Newton, Pa., in 1876, a son of N. B. and Alice Sproat; moved later to Connellsville, and was educated there, attending the ward schools and later the high school. He was for six years in the shoe business in Connellsville, and later entered the employ of the Pittsburg & Lake Erie railroad company, as explained above. In political belief Mr. Sproat is a republican, and in religion a Methodist. He resides in McKeesport, in the first ward.

F. S. BRUSH, of McKeesport, Pa., foreman of the Monongahela furnace, steel department, in the National tube company, was born in Youngstown, Ohio, in 1866, son of H. and Mary J. Brush. Mr. Brush was educated in the public schools of the "lower town" of his native city, and on leaving school secured employment with the manufacturing firm of Cartwright, McCurdy & Co. He remained with that concern for three years, worked on the farm for a year, and subsequently went to Homestead, Pa., where for two years he was in the employ of the William Clark company. The next nine years were spent in Wheeling, W. Va., with the Riverside iron company, and in 1893 Mr. Brush came to McKeesport as blower for the Monongahela furnace of the National tube company. After a service of two years as blower, he was appointed to his present position of foreman, and has since ably filled that station. Mr. Brush was happily married, in 1888, to Laura C. Marble, of McMechen, W. Va., and they have had three children: Frank E. (deceased), Chester E. and Herbert H. Mr. Brush is a member of the Masons, the republican party and the First Presbyterian church He is well known in McKeesport and is very popular with all classes.

WILLIAM LEHMER CURRY, assistant manager of the McKeesport tin plate works, was born in Pittsburg, Pa., in 1875, son of Henry M. and Harriet G. Curry. After the customary preliminary education in the public schools, he took a course in electrical engineering at the Massachusetts institute of technology, and graduated from that excellent institution in 1899, obtaining the degree of B. S. He then spent three years in the engineering department of the Carnegie steel company's works at Duquesne, and entered upon the duties of assistant superintendent of the McKeesport tin plate works in November, 1902. In his short service in this capacity, Mr. Curry has shown himself to be a man of ability, and his excellent preparation for the place has made him a valuable employe in this new concern. Mr. Curry is a republican in politics. He resides in the East End, Pittsburg.

WILLIAM LEWIS FAWCETT, No. 507 Locust St., McKeesport, is a son of C. C. and Sarah E. Fawcett, of McKeesport, and was born in Braddock, Pa., July 20, 1869. He attended the public schools until 1886, and then took a commercial course at Curry's institute, Pittsburg. Having completed his business education, he was employed first by McCrady Bros., dealers in builders' supplies, and then for six years by the Braddock gas and electric light company. After this he spent six years in the employ of the National tube company, and in July, 1902, went into the real estate business, in which he has since been successfully engaged. He now represents a plan known as "The Fawcett Plan of Lots," in McKeesport, and has other real estate interests. Mr. Fawcett married Miss Blanche Thomas, daughter of the late J. W. Thomas, of McKeesport, and has one daughter, Louise. He is a republican in politics. Mr. Fawcett and family reside in the eighth ward, McKeesport.

E. W. BOOTS, civil engineer, has been a resident of McKeesport since 1892. He was born in New Brighton, Pa., in 1870; attended the public schools there, and finished his education in Geneva college, at Beaver Falls, Pa. He began his long service with the Pittsburg & Lake Erie railroad company in 1888. In that year he secured a position as chainman in the civil engineer corps, was rapidly promoted from this position to roadman, leveler, transit-man, and in 1890 was made resident engineer and stationed at various points along the company's route. In 1892 he was given the responsible position of assistant engineer, and has since been employed in that capacity, being located at McKeesport. In 1892 Mr. Boots married Miss Mattie Moore, of New Brighton, Pa., and now lives with his family in the seventh ward, McKeesport. Mr. and Mrs. Boots have two children: Edward C., aged nine, and Frances E., a child of four. Mr. Boots is an enthusiastic member of the Masonic fraternity, being a member of Lodge No. 259, F. and A. M.; McKeesport chapter, No. 282, R. A. M., and Pennsylvania consistory of Pittsburg. He also belongs to various other organizations, being a member of Lodge No. 190, Knights of Maccabees of the World; Lodge No. 6, Loyal Benefit Association, and Council No. 1041, Royal Arcanum. In politics he is a republican. He is a member of the First Methodist Episcopal church of McKeesport.

DR. E. W. DEAN, No. 428 Library St., Braddock, Pa., was born in Northwood, Ohio, Dec. 2, 1849. His father, Henry Dean, was an emigrant from the north of Ireland, and his mother, Helen (Armour) Dean, was of old South Carolina stock. Henry Dean was a merchant and located in St. Louis, where our subject received his early education in a private school. Later, in 1862, he moved with his family to Pittsburg, where the son attended the Wilkinsburg schools for a time, and then entered the Thiel college, of Greenville, from which he graduated in 1870 with the degree of A. B. He then attended the Hahnemann medical college, in Philadelphia, and received his diploma in 1875. After practicing medicine a year in East Liberty, Pa., Dr. Dean moved to Braddock, where he has since resided and built up an extensive practice. In 1886-87, 1887-88 and 1888-89 he took four-month terms at the New York post-graduate school in the specialties of the eye, ear, nose and throat, and in 1893-94 spent fourteen months in Europe, nine months of which were spent in the Moorfield and Westminster ophthalmic hospitals, in London, and the rest of the time at specialty work at Grey's Inn hospital and in the hospitals of Berlin and Vienna. Dr. Dean was married, Oct. 8, 1876, to Helen D., daughter of James and Sarah A. (Rowan) Anderson, pioneer settlers of Pittsburg. The children born of this marriage are: Cecile H., assistant principal of the North Braddock high school; Howard E., class of 1904, medical department of the University of Pennsylvania; Charles L., class of 1905, Massachusetts institute of technology, at Boston; Netta, a student of North Braddock high school, class of 1903, and Harvey A., class of 1904, Edgewood high school. Dr. Dean, wife and three children are members of the United Presbyterian church. In political belief the doctor is a republican, and served for several years in the Braddock council. He is a member of the Allegheny county homœopathic society, the State society and the American institute of homœopathy. He is a member of Braddock Field lodge, No. 510, F. and A. M.; Shiloh chapter, No. 257, R. A. M., and Tancred commandery, No. 48, Knights Templars, of Pittsburg.

JOHN LUCKERT, merchant, has been successfully engaged in the bakery business in McKeesport for over fifteen years. Mr. Luckert was born in Pittsburg in 1862, son of Henry and Caroline Luckert, and came to McKeesport in 1864 with his mother, his father being in the Civil war at the time. He was educated in the public schools and went to work for the National tube company, being employed in various capacities, the last few years as assistant foreman in the welding department. In 1887 he bought a bakery on Fifth avenue, in the Hartman block; ran the business in this location for five years, and then removed to his present location at Nos. 510 and 512 Locust St. He is a member of the Order of Americus and Tribe of Ben-Hur. He was married, almost twenty years ago, to Sarah E. Marks, daughter of John Marks, of McKeesport, and has three children: Clifford, Elsie and John. Mr. Luckert and family reside in McKeesport, in the eighth ward. In politics he is a republican.

JOHN F. LEWIS was born in Toronto, Canada, Aug. 22, 1862, son of William H. and Annie (Lloyd) Lewis. William H. Lewis was a Welshman by birth, and by profession a master in the iron trade. He died in Braddock in 1898. Of the children of Mr. and Mrs. William H. Lewis, besides the subject of this article, Mary, who married Samuel Dowdle, of Allegheny, died in 1876; Annie married Joseph Wills, of Braddock, and died about 1880; Edwin is connected with the armor plate mills at Homestead; Annita is at home; Sherman is with the Westinghouse air brake company at Wilmerding; Charles is employed at the armor plate machine shop; William died when three years old, and Harry is a machinist in the Edgar Thompson plant. John F. Lewis left the grammar school to go to work when thirteen years old, but continued in school for part of the time for three years afterwards. He was variously employed for some years in the machine department, engineering and draughting rooms, until his superior ability had marked him as a leader and he was promoted to the responsible position of master-mechanic on the Edgar Thompson furnaces in 1897. In this position he had charge of about 300 men, and on June 1, 1903, he was made assistant general superintendent of the plant. Mr. Lewis was married, in April, 1890, to Margaret, daughter of Eli and Sarah (Shaw) Boyd, who were old residents of the Turtle Creek neighborhood. Of the children born of this union, William died when three years old, and Catharine, David and Margaret, aged respectively about ten, eight and four years, are at home. Mr. Lewis, although a comparatively young man, has had twenty-nine years' experience with the steel company and has made a host of friends. About five years ago he built a fine home on Kirkpatrick avenue, above the smoke and dirt of the busy city. He and his wife are members of the Braddock United Presbyterian church.

STEPHEN D. MILLS, son of Isaac Mills, one of the earliest and most prominent settlers of Braddock, is in business in Braddock with his brother, James K. Mills. The firm does a large business in brick and stone, and manufacture about 3,000,000 shale brick every year. Mr. Mills was born in Allegheny county, Pa., May 23, 1855, and received his education in the Braddock schools and at West Middletown, Pa. He is married and has five children living. His wife, Barbara M. McLary, daughter of James and Elizabeth (Sutch) McLary, was born May 9, 1856. Of the children of Mr. and Mrs. Mills now living, William W. is a graduate of the medical department of the University of Pennsylvania; Bessie is a graduate of Braddock high school; Mabel R. is attending Braddock high school; Stephen R. is also in school, and Eliza L. is a child four years old. Mr. Mills and family live in a beautiful residence at No. 512 Camp Ave., Braddock.

JULIUS K. FISHER, jeweler at No. 734 Braddock Ave., Braddock, was born in Bavaria, Germany, Feb. 2, 1854, son of Jacob and Rosa (Kuehn) Fisher. He received a common-school education in Germany, and when thirteen years old came to America and made a tour as a pack peddler. Later he secured a position in a Philadelphia jewelry house, where he learned the watchmakers' trade, and after a time moved to Braddock and opened a jewelry store. March 3, 1878, he was married at Wilmington, Del., to Sarah, daughter of Simon and Henrietta (Abrams) Nogler. The children of J. K. Fisher and wife are: Addie, wife of S. Speyer, who is a member of the firm of J. K. Fisher & Co.; Mulford K., a student in the Jefferson medical college, of Philadelphia, in the class of 1905, and Julius K., Jr., who is a partner with his father in the jewelry business. Mr. Fisher, the subject of this article, served two terms as assistant burgess of Braddock borough, and has ever been considered a thrifty, honest and progressive business man. He and his family are members of the Reformed Hebrew congregation, Rodef Sholem temple, Pittsburg. Mr. Fisher is a member of the State Capital lodge, No. 560, I. O. O. F., of Harrisburg, and holds the office of district deputy for Allegheny county in the Royal Arcanum. He is a member of the Maccabees. He holds the office of vice-president of District G, Woodmen of the World, comprising New York, Pennsylvania, Ohio and New Jersey, and is a past officer of the Tribe of Ben-Hur.

J. BUCHER AYRES, superintendent of the National rolling mill at McKeesport, was born in Philadelphia in 1856, and received his education there. He studied along scientific lines, filling responsible positions in various mills throughout the state, and later came to McKeesport, where he entered the employ of the National tube company. During his long service with this company, Mr. Ayres has made a careful study of the condition of his employes, and has done much for their social and moral betterment. He is an earnest advocate of temperance. Mr. Ayres is an active member of the Presbyterian church of McKeesport, of which he is an elder; has been superintendent of its Sunday-school and filled various other honorary positions in the church. He was married, in 1887, to Miss Cleonie Ayres, and has one daughter, Alice Lyon. Mr. Ayres is a member of the local lodge, No. 136, B. P. O. Elks, and of the Independent Order of Heptasophs.

JAMES K. MILLS was born in Braddock, May 23, 1853, of old pioneer stock. His father, Isaac Mills, son of Stephen and Elizabeth (Osborne) Mills, was born Dec. 13, 1801, in what is now New York city, came with his parents to Allegheny county when a young man, and lived on what is now the city farm, but was then called the Troy tract. Isaac Mills bought 260 acres of what is now Braddock and North Braddock, and was foremost in the advancement of Braddock Field, where he started a factory and was the leading spirit to push the incorporation of the borough. When this was accomplished, in 1867, he was chosen as the first burgess and re-elected in the following spring. Elizabeth Mills, mother of the subject of this sketch, was the daughter of Samuel and Mary (McKinney) Snodgrass, and granddaughter of Matthew McKinney, an early pioneer. James K. Mills, in company with his brother, Stephen Mills, is a prominent quarryman and brick-maker of North Braddock. He was educated in the public schools and at Bethany college, West Virginia. He served as postmaster of Braddock from 1876 to 1882, and was borough treasurer in 1878. Mr. Mills was married, June 23, 1887, to Lillie W., daughter of Theobald B. and Henrietta (Brothers) Heims, of Tyrone, Pa., and granddaughter of Thomas and Anna (Bishop) Heims, who were from Adams county and of German descent. Mr. and Mrs. Mills have one son, Theo. Heims, born May 31, 1890, now a pupil in the Braddock schools.

B. L. COURSIN, alderman from the third ward, McKeesport, was born in the eleventh ward, McKeesport, in 1860, son of B. P. and Sarah P. Coursin. He was educated first at an academy at Mansfield, Ohio; then in a private school in McKeesport, and finally at the Iron City business college, Pittsburg. Mr. Coursin has had a long and interesting career in the public service. He was first for three years employed in the internal revenue service under the late Thomas W. Davis, and has also served as tobacco inspector of the twenty-third district. He was successfully engaged in the ice business from 1887 to 1896, and was then appointed alderman from the third ward, a position which he has since held, having the distinction of being the first committing alderman given power under Mayor R. J. Black. Mr. Coursin was married, in 1883, to Miss Martha A. Cook, of McKeesport, daughter of Capt. Eli A. Cook, who died in 1896. Mr. and Mrs. Coursin have one daughter, Sarah H. Mr. Coursin is a member of R. O. L. and the Independent Order of Heptasophs.

GEORGE A. CROSBY, a prominent citizen of North Braddock, was born in Johnstown, Pa., Feb. 15, 1858. His father, James Crosby, was a son of James, Sr., and Catherine (Wallace) Crosby, who came to Westmoreland county about the middle of the past century. Nancy (Horner) Crosby, the mother of George A. Crosby, was a daughter of Jacob Horner, who founded the Sandy Vale cemetery at Johnstown, and a granddaughter of Jacob Horner, Sr., who came to that section in the eighteenth century. Mr. G. A. Crosby was educated in Johnstown, Pa., in the common and high schools, and located in Braddock, March 13, 1876, taking a position at the Edgar Thompson steel works. He is at present pension clerk in the general office. Mr. Crosby was married, June 2, 1881, to Annie, daughter of Isaac and Annie Mary (Maxwell) McCauley, pioneer settlers near Turtle Creek. Mr. and Mrs. Crosby have two children: Annie Louise, born April 1, 1882, is the wife of W. R. Brown, clerk in Mellon & Co.'s bank of Pittsburg, and Clyde Imbrie, born Aug. 18, 1884, is taking a course in mechanical draughting at the Edgar Thompson steel works. Mr. Crosby is a member of Valetta commandery, No. 129, Knights of Malta; secretary of Braddock circle, No. 83, Protected Home Circle, and a member of Arias court, No. 4, Tribe of Ben-Hur. He is secretary of the North Braddock school board and was for several years treasurer and director of the Carnegie co-operative association. His home is a sightly place at No. 203 Kirkpatrick Ave., North Braddock.

JAMES W. STAHL, local manager at McKeesport for Nelson, Morris & Co., has had a successful career in the meat business. Born in Kenosha, Wis., in 1877, son of M. P. Stahl, he received his education in the district school at Pleasant Prairie and at the Catholic schools and the high school in Kenosha, and then began his public life with his father, who was in the meat and grocery business in Kenosha. He became a traveling salesman for Cudahy Bros., in Milwaukee; then entered the service of Nelson, Morris & Co., being employed at first at the stock-yards in Chicago, and later as city salesman in that city. In June, 1902, he came to McKeesport to take charge of the company's interest there. The district of which he is manager includes, besides McKeesport, several other cities and embraces a territory seventy-five miles square. Mr. Stahl is a republican in politics. He is a member of St. Peter's Roman Catholic church.

GEORGE H. LAMB, superintendent of the Braddock public schools, was born in Mercer county, Pa., Jan. 21, 1859. His father, John B. Lamb, was a farmer in Mercer county, and of English descent, while the ancestors of his mother, Prudence (Egbert) Lamb, were American patriots who fought in the Revolution. George H. Lamb was educated in the common schools and attended Allegheny college, Meadville, Pa., where he graduated in 1885 with the degree of A. B., and later received the degree of A. M. from the same institution. Professor Lamb then spent two years as principal of the McElwain institute at New Lebanon, five years as principal of the public schools in Mercer, and was for eight years principal of the grammar department in the public schools at Youngstown, Ohio. Since September, 1900, he has been superintendent of the Braddock schools, and under his administration the schools have been much improved in curriculum, method and general efficiency. Braddock borough now has fifty-eight teachers and supervisors, with a total enrollment of 2,250 pupils. The high school had an enrollment of 108 in the session of 1902-03 and a graduating class of seventeen. Professor Lamb was married, July 28, 1885, to Effie, daughter of Abner and Leonora (Clark) Viets, both of old pioneer families that located in the western reserve about 100 years ago. Mr. and Mrs. Lamb have two children: Harold H., born March 31, 1889, and Mary, born April 22, 1893. Professor Lamb is a republican in national politics. In religion he and his wife are members of the Methodist Episcopal church. Mr. Lamb is a member of Sandy Lake lodge, No. 573, I. O. O. F.

EDWARD BARD, chief of the North Braddock police force, was born in Allegheny county, July 30, 1866. He is a son of George and Nancy Bard, prominent old settlers of Allegheny county. Mr. Bard was educated in the public schools of Braddock. In 1897 he became a member of the police force of North Braddock, where his ability and careful attention to duty won him promotion to chief of the force, the position which he now holds. In this capacity he has served his city with distinction and his prospects for the future are promising. Mr. Bard is a member of Braddock Field lodge, No. 529, I. O. O. F.

LOWERY H. BISHOFF, a prominent produce and commission merchant, was born at Albrightsville, W. Va., May 1, 1865. His father, William H. Bishoff, had a general store at Confluence, Somerset county, and his mother, Drucilla (Bumgartner) Bishoff, was the daughter of Michael Bumgartner, who came to America from Germany early in the last century. Five children were born to Mr. and Mrs. William H. Bishoff, besides Lowery H., the subject of this sketch. They are: T. E. L., who is in the milk business in Rankin; Charles S., a photographer in Missouri; Lettie, wife of Harry Beechman, a Rankin merchant; Fogel G., in business in Rankin, and Maude, who is at home. Lowery H. Bishoff was educated in the Braddock high school, and then opened a produce and commission house at Ninth and Washington streets. The business has steadily grown since that time, and now commands an extensive trade. Mr. Bishoff resides in Rankin, where he occupies a beautiful brick residence at Kenmawr and Third streets. He served as councilman of Rankin, 1894-97; school director, 1898-1901, and burgess, 1900-03. Rankin, which had but two houses in 1883, is now a busy manufacturing city of 6,000 inhabitants. Mr. Bishoff was married, July 21, 1888, to Fannie, daughter of J. A. and Victoria Van Tassel, of New York city. The children born of this union are: Eugene, born November, 1889; Edna, born Feb. 1, 1893, and Frank, born Nov. 15, 1898. Mr. Bishoff is a member of St. John's lodge, No. 219, F. and A. M.; Pennsylvania consistory, and Syria temple of the Mystic Shrine, all of Pittsburg. In political belief he is a republican.

CHARLES F. BOAX, of McKeesport, Pa., foreman for the National tube company, was born in Chicago, Ill., in 1875, and is the son of the late James J. Boax and his wife, Margaret. Mr. Boax accompanied his parents to McKeesport when he was quite young, and was educated in the graded and high schools of that city. On leaving school he commenced to learn the machinists' trade with the National tube company, and while serving his apprenticeship took a course at the Scranton school of mechanics. He then worked in the United States shops at Baltimore, Washington and Pittsburg, and later returned to the National tube company as foreman of the threading department. Subsequently he was given his present position of foreman of the lap-weld department, and has made a splendid record in that important station. Mr. Boax is a member of the republican party and the Presbyterian church, and is a man who commands the respect of all with whom he comes in contact.

GEORGE THOENLEY STREET, pastor of the First Baptist church of Braddock, was born in Lancashire, England, May 4, 1851. His parents, Joshua and Mary (Thoenley) Street, came to America in 1867, and located in Philadelphia. George T. Street was educated at Bucknell university, at Lewisburg, Union Co., Pa., and at Crozer theological seminary, at Chester, Pa., and was ordained to preach at the Danville Baptist church shortly after leaving college. He moved to Caro, Mich., in 1883, and to Union City, Pa., in 1886, and from there went to take charge of Mt. Washington church, South Side, Pittsburg, in 1888, where he remained ten years. Since February, 1898, he has been pastor of the First Baptist church of Braddock, and during this time the church has been greatly strengthened under his able administration. The church was organized in 1881 with about twenty-five charter members, and for about a year worship was held in the first ward schoolhouse. A frame church was then erected, which was torn down in 1902 to give place to the handsome brick building which is now used. This new church was erected at a cost of $20,000, and is one of the finest buildings of its kind in the city. Mr. Street was married, May 4, 1882, to Elizabeth A., daughter of Jacob and Melinda (Kendall) Dawson. From this union were born three children. Florence M. is assistant librarian at the Braddock Carnegie free library; Reginald Dawson is attending Braddock high school, class of 1905, and George Thoenley, Jr., entered the high school in the fall of 1903.

L. LEWIS TODD, borough secretary of Braddock, was born at Shaner Station, Westmoreland Co., Pa., Oct. 14, 1873. His parents, Peter S. and Margaret J. (Wiley) Todd, were also natives of Westmoreland. L. Lewis Todd was educated in private schools, and also attended the Braddock high school, from which he graduated in 1889. After several years' subsequent study with a private tutor, he was elected principal of the Braddock high school, where he taught eight years, from 1893 to 1901, and was then chosen by the council to fill the position which he now holds. This position, in a city of the size and importance of Braddock, is a responsible one, and Mr. Todd has filled it in a manner worthy of praise. Mr. Todd was married, Aug. 9, 1895, to Ada B., daughter of William H. and Jennie (Dalzell) Conert, of Allegheny city, and he and his wife are prominent in social circles. Mr. Todd is a member of Edgar Thompson council, No. 512, Royal Arcanum.

ALPHA K. KLINE, pastor of the St. Luke's Reformed church of Braddock, was born at Boquet, Westmoreland Co., Pa., Sept. 27, 1847, son of John and Elizabeth (Knoffenberger) Kline. He attended the select schools and Westmoreland institute at Mt. Pleasant, Pa., and later went to the Franklin and Marshall college, from which he graduated in 1872. He next pursued his studies in the theological seminary at Lancaster, Pa., and, graduating in 1876, was ordained to preach in May, 1876. His first charge was at South Bend and Plum Creek, from 1876 to 1883. In 1883 he became pastor of a church at Woodstock, Va. Mr. Kline has also served as principal of the Delmont and Harrison city academy, and principal of Harrison city public schools. In pursuance of his religious duties he has held many positions of honor, including the office of president of the Missionary Alliance of Pittsburg and vicinity. He was also instrumental in securing the establishment of missions at Homestead, Pitcairn, Duquesne and Homerville, and has always taken an active interest in religious and educational affairs. The church of which he is now pastor has flourished under his administration and has a membership of about 150. Mr. Kline was married, May 23, 1877, to Sarah, daughter of William and Susan Johnson, of Franklin county. In 1890 Rev. Kline and wife, in company with Dr. W. K. Kline, of Greensburg, made an extensive European trip. They visited England, all the countries of the southern part of Europe, Egypt and the Holy Land.

J. KNOX MILLIGAN was born Dec. 30, 1866, in Northwood, Logan Co., Ohio, son of Alexander and Mary (Brisbin) Milligan, of Westmoreland county, Pa. He received his education in the common schools and at Geneva college, of Northwood, Ohio. In 1884 he came to Rankin and went into the roofing business. He has continued in this line ever since, and has built up an extensive and prosperous business. Mr. Milligan was married, Oct. 30, 1890, to Maggie B., daughter of Samuel and Elizabeth Boyd, of Leechburg, Pa. Mr. and Mrs. Milligan have one child, Sara Belle, born April 2, 1892, now attending the Rankin schools. Mr. Milligan has been since 1900 president of the Rankin school board. He is a member of the United Presbyterian church of Braddock and is also a member of the board of trustees. He occupies a prominent position in Rankin, and is recognized as a progressive business man.

ALLEN KIRKPATRICK, for fifty years in the wholesale grocery business at No. 903 Liberty Ave., Pittsburg, was born near Belfast, Ireland, in 1827, son of Dr. Joseph Kirkpatrick, and came to America when ten years old, in company with his brothers. In 1852 he established in Pittsburg the wholesale grocery business which still bears his name. Mr. Kirkpatrick married Rebecca, daughter of George H. and Margaret (Taughinbaugh) Bell, and now resides in an historic home in North Braddock. This house was built in 1804 by a Mr. Wallace, one of the first settlers of North Braddock, just east of where the Pennsylvania railroad station now stands. In 1840 the place was purchased by George H. Bell, who was of German descent, although born near Gettysburg in 1802. He and his wife, Margaret (Taughinbaugh) Bell, occupied the house for many years and made a number of improvements upon it. Upon the death of Mr. Bell, in 1861, his wife inherited the property and when Mrs. Bell died, the following year, it fell to her daughter, Rebecca, who had previous to this time married Allen Kirkpatrick, the subject of this sketch. The house and grounds have been greatly improved at various times and the place is now one of the most beautiful and interesting homes in North Braddock. Of the children of Mr. and Mrs. Kirkpatrick, Margaret Bell married Alexander M. Scott, who is now managing partner in the firm of Allen Kirkpatrick & Co.; Robert, a twin brother, died in 1888 at the age of twenty-seven; Mary E. is the wife of David F. Collingwood, treasurer of Allegheny county; Anna and Georgia died in infancy, and Allen, Jr., who was educated in the public schools and the Kiskiminetas school, has been since his twentieth year an efficient assistant in his father's business.

JULIUS MEDVETZKY, of McKeesport, Pa., rector of St. Nicholas' Greek Catholic church, was born in Hungary on Dec. 3, 1865, being a son of Andrew and Emma Medvetzky. He was educated in all branches in his native country, came to the United States in 1899, and had charge of St. John's Greek Catholic church at Lansford, Pa., for two years. Later he came to his present charge, and now has in course of construction a new church, which is to be a splendid building to cost $35,000 and a fitting temple for the holy purpose for which it is erected. The Rev. Mr. Medvetzky was married, in 1889, to Margaritte Baluggansczky, and to them have been born four children—three sons and a daughter. He is well equipped by nature and training for the great work that he has undertaken, and his career has been marked by that character of success that comes only to those who put their entire heart in their daily task, and whose constant aim is that the labors of to-day shall excel those of yesterday.

WILLIAM J. ROSEBOROUGH, secretary of the McKeesport board of education, was born in Altoona, Pa., in 1865, son of Samuel and Sarah Roseborough. He received a good education, completing the course of study in the schools of his native city, and worked for his father, who was a carpenter, until 1886. Coming then to McKeesport, he was for five years employed in the National tube works, and was then elected to the city fire department, in which he served in all the positions, being chief of the department five years. He was elected member of the school board in 1900, and was by that body elected to the position of secretary, an office which he has since held. Mr. Roseborough was president of the Western Pennsylvania firemen's association in 1900 and 1901, and is at present secretary of the executive committee of that organization. He is a member of Lodge No. 109, Junior Order of United American Mechanics, and Lodge No. 116, Knights of Malta, and belongs to the St. John's Lutheran church. Mr. Roseborough was married, in 1891, to Miss Clara C. Jackson, daughter of John Jackson, of McKeesport, and has three children: Sarah Leona, Elsa May and Charles Edward.

DAVID WILLIAM AULD, a popular McKeesport real estate man, was born in Effingham, Ill., in September, 1869. In 1901 he went into the real estate business in the office of T. D. Gardner, where he is employed in various capacities, having, as his special charge, the renting department. He was married, in 1897, to Miss Jane Miller, of McKeesport, and has two children: Eliza A. and Sarah Miller. He resides with his family in the seventh ward, McKeesport. Mr. Auld moved to Pennsylvania with his parents, J. P. and Eliza Auld, when he was seven years old, and attended school in Versailles township, and later in McKeesport. He spent two years in the National rolling mills, where he learned the blacksmiths' trade, and after that was employed for three years as a machinist in the Westinghouse plant at Wilmerding. He spent six months in the employ of W. E. Osborne & Co., wholesale produce merchants, and after that engaged in the milk business in McKeesport a year before embarking in his present business. Mr. Auld is a member of Youghiogheny lodge, No. 583, F. and A. M., and of Lodge No. 338, B. P. O. Elks. In politics he is an ardent republican.

NEIL McGINLEY was born June 2, 1857, in Cambria county, Pa., son of Charles and Ellen (Ward) McGinley, who came to America from Ireland in 1845. He received his education at Johnstown, Pa., and when twenty years old came to Braddock and learned the heaters' trade, following this occupation for fifteen years. In 1893 he started a hotel at No. 1005 Braddock Ave., and after a year sold out his business and moved to McDonald, Pa., where he opened another hotel and remained three years. Mr. McGinley then sold out his hotel business and engaged for a year in the wholesale liquor trade at Cumberland, Md. He then purchased in Braddock the hotel interest of Isaac Lloyd, at Nos. 1000 to

1004 Braddock Ave., where he is still in business. Mr. McGinley conducts here one of the finest hotels in Braddock. The hotel is modernly equipped, with office, dining-room and bar on the first floor, forty rooms, one parlor and other appointments of the latest and most improved nature. Mr. McGinley was elected to the Braddock council in 1889, where he served three years as representative from the first ward, to the entire satisfaction of his constituents. On Feb. 5, 1884, he was married to Jennie, daughter of Michael and Bridget (Hennessy) Croty, of Wilkinsburg, former residents of Titusville, Crawford county. Of the children of Mr. and Mrs. McGinley, Cornelia took a course in the Braddock schools and is now attending the Iron City business college, and Charles, Howard and Marcella, younger children, are at home. Mr. McGinley is a member of Pittsburg lodge, No. 11, B. P. O. Elks. He and his wife are members of St. Thomas' Roman Catholic church.

ALBERT KAZINCZY, priest of St. Michael's Roman Catholic parish of Braddock, was born in Hungary, Aug. 24, 1871, son of Emanuel and Teresa (Ossikowsky) Kazinczy. His paternal grandfather was a noted nobleman and prominent linguist of Hungary, while his maternal grandfather was a prominent Polish nobleman who fled to Hungary during a political revolution. Father Kazinczy received his early education in Europe, and after coming to this country, took a final course in theology at St. Vincent's seminary, at Latrobe, Pa. He was ordained to the ministry at Scranton, Pa., Oct. 14, 1894, and shortly afterwards organized a church at Pittston, Luzerne Co., Pa. He also had charge of the Slavic congregation of the Holy Ghost parish at Olyphant for a year prior to coming to Braddock, in July, 1896. St. Michael's congregation purchased in 1889, for $11,000, the property formerly held by the Protestant Christian church, at the corner of Braddock avenue and Frazier street. Since then a twenty-foot brick front has been added and many other improvements have been made, so that the property is now valued at $30,000 and is entirely free from debt. The congregation consists of between 250 and 300 families. Attached to the church is a parochial school with an attendance of 200, which is conducted by five Sisters of St. Vincent de Paul, who have recently come from Europe. Father Kazinczy is well educated and well posted in religious matters, and being able to speak fluently five different languages, he is equipped to deal with the conflicting foreign elements of a manufacturing city like Braddock.

DAVID B. LITTLE, a prominent citizen and member of the common council of Swissvale, was born in Pittsburg, July 19, 1862, and is the son of William and Mary Little, both now deceased. He received his education in the common schools and high school of Pittsburg and then entered the employ of the Gillespie tool company, where he remained four years. He later was employed for four years by Hubbard & Co., and then began working for the Union switch and signal company, of Swissvale. He now holds the position of purchasing agent for the company, which is the largest of its kind in the United States, employing between 1,300 and 1,500 men. Mr. Little was married, March 22, 1893, to Miss Alice Jamison, daughter of John A. Jamison, of Swissvale. In 1899 he was elected the first burgess of the borough of Swissvale. Besides this honor, Mr. Little has also served as treasurer of the township of Braddock, to which position he was elected in 1893. He is a member of Crescent lodge, F. and A. M., of Pittsburg, and is recognized as one of the prominent and progressive citizens of his borough.

WALTER HARDWICK, foreman of the lap-weld and threading department of the National tube works, has been in the employ of that company ever since he was ten years of age. He was born in the tenth ward of the city of McKeesport, Pa., in 1876, and after three and one-half years in the common schools, he entered the draughting room of the tube works. During the three years he was in this department he attended the Y. M. C. A. night school, acquiring a fair English education. He entered the machine shops of the works as an apprentice and remained there eight years, becoming a competent machinist. In 1896 he went west, working at his trade in different cities until he reached San Francisco, but in the fall of the same year he returned to McKeesport. For a time he worked in the galvanizing department of the National tube company, at Versailles, as a machinist, and in 1899 was promoted to his present position, first as night foreman and later in charge of the department during the daytime. To completely qualify himself for the duties of the position, he took a mechanical course in the American correspondence schools, which has enabled him to master all difficulties as they have presented themselves. His father, Robert Hardwick, was a native of Lancashire, England. He came to America about the year 1857, and for a number of years was a river pilot. He married Laura Curran, the daughter of a Pittsburg grocer, left the river and became a foreman in the coupling department of the great tube works. He is still living, enjoying with his wife the fruits of a life of industry and frugality. Walter Hardwick is unmarried. He has one brother, Howard, who is a machinist in the tube works, and three sisters, Grace, Phœbe and Lillian. He is a member of the Episcopal church and the Y. M. C. A. and in politics claims the distinction of being independent. His energy and application to business have met their reward in his advancement to his present position and offer an example to other young men to learn the great lesson of self-denial.

ANTHONY W. GLOVER, a member of the school board of the town of Rankin, was born at Uniontown, Fayette Co., Pa., Oct. 29, 1877, and is a son of Theophilus and Lida M. (Suck) Glover. He was educated in the public schools of Uniontown, Pa. After leaving school he learned the carpenters' trade, which he has since followed. Mr. Glover came to Braddock in 1890 while still in his teens. In 1899 he was married to Miss Mary Robinson, daughter of William and Mary Robinson, of Johnstown, Pa. To this marriage there have been born three children: Clyde (deceased), Goldsberry and Marian. In 1901 Mr. Glover was elected a member of the Rankin school board for a term of two years, and in 1902 for a three-year term to the council. He is a member of the Knights of Pythias, the Knights of the Golden Eagle and the Knights of Malta. In all these orders, as well as in the social life of Rankin, he has a high standing, due to his genial disposition and his progressive ideas. His home is at No. 110 Fourth St.

CHARLES FELL, who holds the important position of superintendent of the lap-weld department of the National tube company's works at McKeesport, has risen to this place in a comparatively short time, purely by his own ability. He began to learn the blacksmiths' trade at an early age, going, after a year in another shop, into the coupling forge department of the National tube company, where he remained six years and finished learning the trade of a machine blacksmith. He was for two years assistant foreman, and for three years foreman of the coupling forge department, and later foreman of the lap-weld furnace. After that he was made night superintendent of the lap-weld department, and then given his present position as day superintendent, a place in which he has under him 1,600 men. Mr. Fell was born in Chartiers valley in 1866, being a son of the late Daniel Fell; came to McKeesport when nine years old, and was educated in the public schools of the first ward. In politics he is a republican and in religious belief a Methodist. He resides in the fifth ward. Mr. Fell was married, in 1888, to Miss Nettie Hill, of Alverton, Westmoreland county, and has three children: Bessie I., George W. and Charles E.

GEORGE H. McGEARY, a prominent physician of Braddock, was born in Westmoreland county, Pa., May 5, 1863. His father, John E. McGeary, was the son of James McGeary, who was of Irish descent, while his mother, Sarah J. (McLaughlin) McGeary, was the daughter of George and Margaret (Nelson) McLaughlin. The McLaughlin family came from Ireland, while the Nelsons were Scotch. Dr. McGeary attended Pine Run academy at Markle, Westmoreland Co., Pa., and then taught school for six years. In April, 1885, he commenced the study of medicine in the office of Dr. E. W. Dean, of Braddock, took the full course of the New York homœopathic medical college and graduated in April, 1888. After graduation, he practiced medicine for five years in Homestead, Pa., and then moved to Braddock, where he has since resided and built up a lucrative practice, with offices at No. 428 Library St. The doctor is surgeon for the Carnegie steel company and the McClintoc & Marshall construction company. He is physician for the Court Pride of the Union, No. 18, F. of A., and a member of Edgar Thompson council, Royal Arcanum. Dr. McGeary was married, in June, 1895, to Estella, daughter of Christian and Louise (Downs) Shively, of South Side, Pittsburg. He has one son, John Elliott, Jr., born Aug. 15, 1898.

JOHN MARTIN, dairyman, was born in Penn township, Allegheny county, in February, 1849. His parents, John and Jane (Potts) Martin, were both natives of Ireland. After a commonschool education in Penn township, Mr. Martin engaged in the blacksmith trade, then in coal-mining, at which he was employed until 1885, when he commenced farming on the James Lenhart place. In February, 1888, he bought the fifty-six acres in Wilkins township on which he now resides. Here he keeps fifty cows and has built up an extensive dairy business. An electric car line will soon be built between Turtle Creek and Wilmerding, passing Mr. Martin's farm. Mr. Martin was married, May 24, 1870, to Margaret, daughter of William and Susan (Hershey) Sholes. William

Sholes was the son of George and Margaret Sholes, while his wife was the daughter of Christopher and Nancy (Stoner) Hershey. The children of John and Margaret Martin are: Mary Stoner, wife of James Small, who resides on an adjoining farm; Taylor McIntosh, noted in another place in this work; John Lenard, at home; Charles Randolph, a railroad fireman; Sussanah, who is married to Ralph Reed, of Braddock; Norman Clark, a railroad fireman; Francis Z., Olive, Jessie and Lida Margaret, at home. One child, James Roy, died in infancy. Mr. Martin had three brothers, Hugh, Thomas and William, who served in the Union army during the Civil war. He is one of the commissioners of Wilkins township and a prominent man in his community. In religious belief he and his family are Presbyterians.

FRANK KOLA, son of L. J. and Sadie Kola, is one of the most promising young business men of Elizabeth. He was born in Cleveland, Ohio, in 1880, and received his early education in the public schools of that city. Later he attended the Spencerian business college, from which he graduated in 1897. After six months spent in the employ of the Noble refining company, he obtained a position with the National safe and lock company, of Cleveland, as assistant cashier and bookkeeper. On Oct. 1, 1902, he became secretary of the newly organized Clark safe and vault company, of Elizabeth, but left the employ of that firm Sept. 1, 1903, and took a position with the Clairton steel company. Mr. Kola is an independent in politics.

LOUIS HABER, the senior member of the well-known clothing firm of Haber Bros., at the corner of Fifth and Market streets, McKeesport, Pa., is a native of the town where he is now engaged in business. He was born Jan. 17, 1870. After attending the common and high schools of his native town, he took a course in Duff's commercial college, at Pittsburg, and at the age of sixteen he entered the hat store of J. N. Dersam, at McKeesport, as a salesman. After four years with Mr. Dersam, he went to work in the clothing store of his brother-in-law, L. Koch, where the firm of Haber Bros. is now located. Upon the death of Mr. Koch, Louis Haber bought the business and on Jan. 1, 1893, formed a partnership with a Mr. Loeb. The business was continued under the firm name of Haber & Loeb until Dec. 1, 1896. Edward Haber was taken into the firm July 1, 1899, and the name changed to Haber Bros. His father, Joseph Haber, died April 15, 1883, while his mother, Bertha Haber, is still living. Louis Haber is a member of several secret and benevolent orders: of Youghiogheny lodge, No. 583, Free and Accepted Masons; lodge No. 136, B. P. O. Elks; treasurer of No. 590, Order of Heptasophs; a member of the beneficiary order of Ben-Hur, and the Junior Order of United American Mechanics. Still on the morning side of life's meridian, he has by a strict attention to business, aided by his early training, built up one of the substantial concerns of the city of McKeesport. The clothing house of Haber Bros. is on the high-road to prosperity and the energy and intelligence of the senior partner has played no small part in establishing its reputation.

GEORGE N. PFAUB, of Etna, Pa., a prosperous merchant and borough treasurer, was born in Pittsburg, Pa., March 30, 1865, son of John L. and Mary (Toerge) Pfaub. His father was a native of Bavaria, Germany, and came to America with his parents when three years of age, subsequently learning the coopering trade. His mother came to America when eleven years of age, settled in New York, and later removed to Pittsburg. Mr. Pfaub was educated in the public schools of Pittsburg, and at twelve years of age began work in a cooper shop, where he remained for four years; he went into the rolling mill of Morehead Bros., at Sharpsburg, and worked on the muck rolls for two years; then secured a position with Spang & Chalfant's mill, where for five years he was employed in different positions. In 1888 he started a grocery store in Etna, in partnership with John Metzger, three years later purchasing the interest of his partner, conducting it for two years longer. He removed to his present location at No. 354 Butler St., and in 1901 opened a feed, grain and hay store near his grocery. He has prospered in all these lines, and does a large and profitable business. He was married, in 1893, to Laura W., daughter of Capt. John D. Hieber, former marriage license clerk in the Allegheny county court-house, and of his wife, Katharine (Bealer) Hieber. Mr. and Mrs. Pfaub have two children: Emma K., attending the public schools, and Helen E., not of school age. He is a member and elder in the German Evangelical church of Etna, and a member of the Royal Arcanum and of the republican party. He has served in his present position as member of the school board for the past three years, was member of the board of health for one year, and in 1903 was elected borough treasurer. Two of his uncles, George and Fred Toerge, are among the leading teachers of music of Pittsburg, and are widely known as musicians of rare ability.

HOWARD HENRY WESTWOOD, pastor of the First Methodist Episcopal church of Swissvale, was born in Baltimore, Md., Jan. 20, 1846, and has lived a varied and useful life. His parents were John H. and Cassandra Westwood, of Baltimore. Rev. Mr. Westwood was educated at Home City college, in Baltimore, and ordained to preach in 1878, his first charge being in West Virginia, where he remained seven years. He was transferred to the East Ohio conference, where he remained for sixteen years, and then assigned to the pastorate of the Methodist church in Swissvale, in October, 1902. This church was organized in Dalzell hall, May 8, 1893, with twenty-seven members, under the direction of Rev. J. F. Murray, and has since increased its membership to ninety-four. The church building was erected in 1893, and dedicated on October 8th of that year, with G. B. Gray as pastor. Rev. H. H. Westwood was married, in 1873, to Miss Ida E. Cowman, of Harrison, W. Va., and to them have been born two children, Wilbur S. and Grace A., both at home. His first wife died Aug. 29, 1881, and on Nov. 14, 1882, Mr. Westwood married Miss Annie G. Sewell, of Baltimore. During the Civil war Rev. Mr. Westwood enlisted as a private in Company E, 9th Maryland volunteers, and served with distinction for about a year and a half. He is a member of the F. and A. M. and the Knights of Maccabees.

ALBERT J. GIVINS, M. D., of Millvale, Pa., a prominent physician and surgeon, was born in Pittsburg, Pa., Feb. 15, 1859. He is a son of Samuel D. and Emile M. Givins, his father having been a roller in the Graff, Bennett & Co. mill, but now resides with his son at Millvale and conducts a store in Shaler township, near Millvale. Dr. Givins attended the public schools of Shaler township until thirteen years of age, became a pupil of Duff's commercial college and was graduated from that institution in 1876. He kept books for H. W. Moore for one year, and later matriculated at the Cleveland medical college, now the Western Reserve university, and was graduated with the degree of doctor of medicine in 1881. He entered the marine hospital service, and nine months later began the practice of his profession at Hites, remaining there for three years. In 1884 he located on Grant avenue, Millvale, subsequently removed to his present location at No. 223 North Ave., and enjoys a splendid practice, being the oldest physician, with one exception, in the city. He was married, in 1882, to Margaret Dixon, to whom were born four children, two of whom are living: Edna A., died Sept. 10, 1892; Emile, died Sept. 9,

1903; Katharine, a twin of Emile, and Bessie, the two attending school at Millvale. Dr. Givins is a member of the Methodist church, the Masons, the Royal Arcanum, the Maccabees, the Ancient Order of United Workmen, the Protective Home Circle and the alumni of the Western Reserve university. He has always been an ardent student of all matters pertaining to his profession, received the second degree in his final examinations at his college, and attended a post-graduate course at Rush medical college, Chicago, in 1901, where he received instruction in the latest advancement of the profession and enjoyed the advantage of personal contact with some of the brightest medical minds of the day.

WILLIAM L. HUNTER, a prominent physician and president of the First National bank of Turtle Creek, has been one of the leading practitioners of Turtle Creek for the past thirty-five years. He was born in Westmoreland county, Feb. 8, 1844. His father was James Hunter, son of Samuel Hunter, an old settler of Westmoreland county, while his mother, Annice (Lightcap) Hunter, was the daughter of Solomon Lightcap, also an early settler. Dr. Hunter attended the Elder's Ridge academy, in Indiana county, and then went to the Jefferson medical college, at Philadelphia, from which he graduated in 1868, and immediately began to practice medicine in Turtle Creek. Dr. Hunter owns considerable property in Turtle Creek, and has recently erected several valuable business blocks. He purchased a piece of property from Captain McMasters, at the corner of Pennsylvania avenue and Railroad street, and in 1902 erected on the lot a handsome, double-front frame building. He has also erected, on the lot opposite his residence on Pennsylvania avenue, a four-story brick building, suitable for business, office and lodge use, the property valuation being $50,000. When the First National bank was incorporated, in December, 1902, with a capital of $50,000, Dr. Hunter became a stockholder and was elected president of the bank. He was appointed postmaster of Turtle Creek by President Garfield, and has held this position continuously since that time, except during President Cleveland's administrations. The doctor was married, Nov. 23, 1870, to Rachel, daughter of John and Leonora (Markle) McMasters. John McMasters was the son of John and Rachel (Hughey) McMasters, and a grandson of John Hughey, who fought in the war of the Revolution. Leonora McMasters, the mother of Mrs. Hunter, was the daughter of David and Maria (Cowan) Markle, early settlers in Westmoreland county. Maria Cowan's father, Capt. William Cowan, held a commission in the Revolutionary army. Dr. Hunter and wife have two children: Leonora, a graduate of Pennsylvania college for women, Pittsburg, now married to J. Grant Anderson, of North Highland avenue, Pittsburg, and Annice Gail, who graduated at Mrs. Long's school, in Philadelphia, now married to Francis Fleming Slick, of Johnstown, Pa.

HERMAN A. BRASSERT was born in London, Jan. 24, 1875, of German parentage. His parents, Charles A. and Mary (Stein) Brassert, returned to Germany when he was but a small child, and Mr. Brassert was educated in Berlin, where he took a thorough course in metallurgy and chemistry. He came to America on a prospecting tour in 1897, and secured a position with the Carnegie steel company, where his ability was quickly recognized, and he was made superintendent over the eleven furnaces of the Edgar Thompson steel works. This plant is the largest of its kind in the United States, and probably has a greater output than any other in the world, giving employment to about 1,500 men. Mr. Brassert was married, Feb. 10, 1902, to Maury, daughter of W. W. and Mary F. Childs, of Brooklyn, N. Y., and resides with his wife in a beautiful home at the corner of Jones and Kirkpatrick avenues, North Braddock.

EZEKIEL GORDON, Jr., of River View, Pa., a well-known contractor on the river, was born on July 23, 1859, in Fairview, now called Montrose, O'Hara township, Allegheny Co., Pa., son of Capt. Ezekiel and Isabella (Hulings) Gordon. Young Gordon attended the common schools of O'Hara township, of Kiskiminetas township, of Armstrong county, and of Harmarville, and when seventeen years of age left school and began to assist his father, who was a steamboat contractor. When he attained his majority, he secured a position as a steel melter with the Crescent steel company, of Pittsburg, Pa., and continued with this company until 1891, when he removed to Whitehall, Allegheny county, and engaged in the hotel business. He prospered there until 1898, when he bought the hotel in Montrose formerly owned by his father, and conducted the same very successfully until January, 1903, when he disposed of it, and since has been contracting on the river with his steamboat, the "Charles Turner." He was married, on July 20, 1886, to Jane, daughter of James S. and Eleanor (Marshall) Powers, of Turtle Creek, Pa., the former having served as justice of the peace for twenty years. His father, Ezekiel Gordon, was for three years in the employment of the government as steamboat captain, the battle of Monmouth was fought on his great-grandfather's farm, and his mother's grandfather, Samuel Hulings, was among the pioneer settlers of Allegheny county. Samuel Hulings and his wife experienced many phases of the hardships which confront the pioneer, and they had numerous fights with the Indians while preparing the way for the high state of civilization which Allegheny county now enjoys. Mr. Gordon is one of the leading men of that part of Allegheny county, and is well and favorably known.

CHARLES A. PHILLIPS, of Sharpsburg, Pa., dealer in lumber and a member of the firm of Vaught, Phillips & Co., operating a planing-mill, was born in Etna, Allegheny Co., Pa., March 31, 1870, and attended the public schools of his native town until fourteen years of age, when he became cashier for Somers Bros. & Co., commission merchants on Liberty street, Pittsburg. He remained in that position for three years, then became bookkeeper for Egli, Vaught & Co., of Sharpsburg, continuing in that capacity for four years, when the firm was reorganized and became Vaught, Phillips & Co., dealers in rough and worked lumber and also operating a planing-mill. This is a prosperous and progressive firm, and they enjoy a splendid local patronage. Mr. Phillips is prominently identified with the Masonic order, having taken the thirty-second degree, and is a member of the Heptasophs, the Royal Arcanum and of the republican party. He has served as borough treasurer of Etna for the past five years and has made a splendid record in that fiduciary capacity. Mr. Phillips is a safe and conservative business man and possesses the confidence and esteem of the community.

EDWARD J. PFEIFER, of Millvale, Pa., member of the firm of Pfeifer & Grall, undertakers and embalmers, was born in Shaler township, Allegheny Co., Pa., Aug. 22, 1878, in an old stone house which is said to be one of the oldest buildings in Allegheny county, there being no record of when it was built. The history of this house has been traced back over 100 years, when it was owned by a half-breed Indian, named Gilbreath, and has gone by the appellation "Old Evergreen," until it was torn down in 1901. He is the son of Peter and Elizabeth (Sautters) Pfeifer, the former having been a cooper up to a few years prior to his death, when he removed to the farm above mentioned and there passed the rest of his days, dying in 1881. His mother is still residing in Shaler township. Mr. Pfeifer was educated in the public schools of Shaler township, and when fourteen years of age began to earn his living by doing odd jobs. In 1894 he secured a position with A. L. King, the funeral director of Millvale, and remained with Mr. King until 1902, when he and his present partner, Mr. Philip Grall, purchased the business of Mr. King, and since then the firm of Pfeifer & Grall have enjoyed a splendid patronage in their undertaking and livery business. Mr. Pfeifer is a member of the German Lutheran church, the Knights of Pythias, the German Beneficial Union and of the Maccabees. In politics he is a republican. Mr. Pfeifer's mother is a native of Germany, his father was born in Allegheny county, and Edward J. is the youngest of a family of five children. Mr. Pfeifer has made rapid strides in the commercial world and is a young man of sound business judgment.

THOMAS McMASTERS LARIMER, the leading real estate dealer in Turtle Creek, is a native of that place, born April 24, 1876. He is a son of John McMasters and Mary E. (Markel) Larimer, and comes of one of the oldest and most prominent families of the Turtle Creek valley. John McMasters Larimer (now deceased) was for over twenty years a well-known grocer of Turtle Creek. Mr. Larimer attended the public schools of Turtle Creek, and then took a supplementary course of study at an academy in Pittsburg. Thus prepared by education as well as by natural business ability, he embarked for himself in 1898 in the real estate business in Turtle Creek, and has already met with encouraging success.

JOHN JACOB BECK, of Sharpsburg, Pa., one of the leading butchers of that city, was born in Manchester, now a part of Allegheny city, Pa., Oct. 9, 1864, son of John Jacob and Katharine Beck, the former having been a carpenter and contractor of Allegheny county until his death, in 1880, at the age of fifty-four years. He was one of the builders of Isabella blast furnace, of Etna, and during the latter years of his life was assistant superintendent of that concern. Mr. Beck attended the public schools of Sharpsburg until he was thirteen years of age and for two years was a pupil of a German school in Sharpsburg. He learned butchering with Wertz Bros., and for nine years was an employe of that firm. He became a partner in the new firm of Wertz & Beck, which continued until 1899, when Mr. Wertz withdrew from that business, and Mr. Beck has since conducted the business on his own account, his present market being located at No. 1740 Main St., Sharpsburg. Mr. Beck was happily married, in 1887, to Miss L. M. Wertz, daughter of Gotlieb Wertz, the pioneer butcher of Sharpsburg, and they have two children, Alverta Elizabeth and John Howard, students of the public schools of Sharpsburg. He is a member of the Methodist church, the Royal Arcanum and the Odd Fellows. His political affiliations are with the republican party, and he is an active and ardent worker for its success and advancement. He has served as a member of the council of Sharpsburg for three years, and has taken a prominent part in the deliberations of that body. Mr. Beck is a stockholder and director of the Glenshaw glass factory, of Glenshaw, Pa., and is a business man of recognized ability and sound commercial standing.

LAWRENCE A. BROOKS, one of Wilmerding's prominent business men, was born in Allegheny county, Pa., Jan. 14, 1864, son of J. M. and Anna A. (Keogh) Brooks. J. M. Brooks was a butcher by vocation, and his son, L. A. Brooks, after an education in the McKeesport schools, learned the business, and father and son were in business together in McKeesport for twenty years. In 1893 L. A. Brooks came to Wilmerding, where he has since been engaged in the meat business on Station street. Mr. Brooks has long been active in local public affairs, has served as member of the school board, and was for three years councilman. His home is in East McKeesport. Mr. Brooks was married, in 1887, to Emma Brown, daughter of J. M. and Margaret Brown, of Westmoreland county, and has seven children—six boys and one girl—viz.: Francis, May, Harry, Paul, Lester, Allen and Lawrence. Francis, the eldest boy, is at present messenger for the Pennsylvania railroad company, but expects soon to go into business with his father. Mr. Brooks is a member of the Knights of Pythias.

SAMUEL M. MYERS was born in Lancaster county, Pa., June 16, 1873, son of Christian W. and Rebecca E. (Martin) Myers. Christian Myers was the son of Col. Samuel B. Myers, a veteran of the Civil war, who served on the confederate side as commander of the 7th Virginia cavalry. Rebecca E. (Martin) Myers was the daughter of David Martin, who married a Miss Erb. Both Mr. and Mrs. Martin were of German descent, and in religious belief held to the Dunkard faith. Samuel M. Myers attended the Harrisburg high school, and then went to Franklin and Marshall college, of Lancaster county, where he graduated in 1896. For several years he read law in the office of Hon. Robert Snodgrass, of Harrisburg, and in June, 1900, was admitted to practice in the courts of Dauphin county. He has since come to Pittsburg and been admitted to practice in Allegheny county. Mr. Myers has formed a partnership with M. J. Hosack, under the firm name of Hosack & Myers, with offices at No. 1103 Park building. He has recently purchased a home in Wilmerding, and been made solicitor for the borough and for the Wilmerding National bank. Upon the organization of the First National bank of Turtle Creek, Dec. 1, 1902, he was made director and solicitor for that institution. The firm of which Mr. Myers is a member were elected solicitors of Wilkins township, in March, 1903. Mr. Myers is a member of the Odd Fellows and Masons of Wilmerding. He was married, July 25, 1896, to Gertrude, daughter of Amos and Teresa (Hague) Mellinger, both of early families of Lancaster county. Mr. and Mrs. Myers have one son, Christian, born in Harrisburg, July 1, 1897.

WILLIAM A. CRAFT, a successful farmer of Patton township, Allegheny Co., Pa., was born at Towanda, Bradford Co., Pa., June 2, 1854, son of George W. and Catherine (Moon) Craft, his father at that time being a blacksmith of Bradford county, later served in the Civil war for three years and nine months and in 1878 removed to near Rugby, Pierce Co., N. D., where he is now prospering at the blacksmith trade. William A. Craft was educated in the common schools of St. Mary's, Elk Co., Pa., and in 1875 located in Allegheny county, Pa., where he followed the occupation of mining for a number of years. Mr. Craft was happily married, in 1879, to Rebecca N., daughter of George and Eleanor Lang, of Allegheny county, and they have had six children born to them, viz.: George, Charles F., Catherine, Edward, Nellie and Stella, of whom the eldest daughter, Catherine, is the wife of William Kuhns, of Pitcairn. Mr. Craft is now residing on the original Lang farm, in Patton township, and is a prominent citizen of that community, having been appointed justice of the peace in 1892, and since has held that important position. He has also served as auditor for two years, constable for four years and in his political convictions and associations is a democrat. He is a member of the Odd Fellows and the Knights of the Mystic Chain, and is one of the leading men of that part of Allegheny county.

PARKS ARNOLD AMBROSE, of Sharpsburg, Pa., a prominent practitioner of dentistry, was born in Kittanning, Armstrong county, Aug. 15, 1865, son of Frank and Rebecca (Dougherty) Ambrose. His father was for many years a leading farmer of Armstrong county, but has now retired from active life. He is a son of Benjamin Ambrose, who was a native of Armstrong county and descended from Irish ancestry. Dr. Ambrose attended the public schools of his native county until his seventeenth year, went to the Worthington academy for three terms, and attended Grove college for one year. While attending the two last-named institutions he devoted his spare time to teaching in the public schools of Armstrong county. On leaving college he secured a position with the Allegheny railroad at River View, and studied bookkeeping while occupying this place. In 1896 he matriculated at the Pittsburg dental college and was graduated in 1899, receiving the degree of doctor of dental surgery. He immediately began the practice of his profession at Sharpsburg, maintaining offices at No. 707 Main St. until 1902, when he removed to his present location at No. 241 North Main St. He is the fifth child of a family of eight, most of the family residing in Armstrong county. One brother is a dentist of Pittsburg and Sharpsburg. Dr. Ambrose is a member of the Royal Arcanum and the republican party, and is generally recognized as a most successful and competent dentist.

NORMAN R. GRAHAM, M. D., of Sharpsburg, Pa., a well-known physician and surgeon, was born in Sharpsburg, Pa., Jan. 19, 1866, son of Robert T. and Permelia (Buffington) Graham, both deceased. His father was a dealer in lumber in Etna, and was a son of Joseph and Nancy (Thompson) Graham, of Irish descent. He was educated in the public schools of Denver, Col., where he remained until 1873, when he returned to Pittsburg and began the study of medicine, reading for one year under Dr. George T. McCord, a leading physician of that city. He entered the Jefferson medical college, Philadelphia, was graduated in the class of 1887, and has since practiced with much success at Sharpsburg, maintaining offices at No. 114 North Main St. He was married, in 1887, to Lavina B., daughter of Patrick and Nancy (Brickell) Kinnihan, of Bakerstown, Allegheny Co., Pa., and two children have been born to them, one of whom is now living— Edwin A., a student of the public schools of Sharpsburg. Dr. Graham is a prominent member of the leading fraternal organization, the Masons, and has taken the thirty-second degree in that ancient order. He has been surgeon for the West Pennsylvania railroad for the last twelve years, and is examining surgeon for the United States pension board at Allegheny city, Pa. He is a member of the Allegheny county, the Pennsylvania state and the American medical associations, and keeps thoroughly abreast of the progress of his profession.

GEORGE WILLIAM RIETHMILLER, of Sharpsburg, Pa., dealer in groceries and feed, was born in that city, July 14, 1868, son of Conrad and Elizabeth (Zimmerman) Riethmiller. His father was a native of Germany, came to America in 1848, settling at Pittsburg, and later became a grocery merchant at Sharpsburg in 1876. His mother was a native of Saxony, Germany, and came to America with her parents in 1845, settling at Pittsburg. Mr. Riethmiller attended the public schools of Sharpsburg until he was twelve years of age, and then worked in the grocery business with his father. He continued with his father for twelve years and then went into the grocery business on his own account at No. 405 South Main St., still occupying that stand. He operates a number of wagons and makes deliveries in Sharpsburg, Aspinwall, Etna and as far west as Pittsburg. He was married, in 1892, to Minnie, daughter of Adam and Elizabeth (Wilhelme) Wagener, of O'Hara township, but formerly of Pittsburg, and they have one child, La Verne, attending the public schools of Sharpsburg. He is a member of the German Evangelical Lutheran church, of the Royal Arcanum and the republican party, but has refused all offers of political preferment. He is one of the substantial business men of Sharpsburg and is well and favorably known in that city.

THOMAS JAMES LOVE was born Oct. 9, 1844, in Lancashire, near Manchester, England. He is the son of Thomas and Mary (Carter) Love, who had a family of eleven children, of which the subject of this sketch was the fifth child. Mr. Love received his education in England, and was for some years in the coal business in that country. He came to the United States in 1869, landed in New York city, and located in Westmoreland county in that year, going into the coal business there. He was married, in 1868, in England, to Helen, daughter of William and Alice Hayes, a prominent family of Manchester, England. Mrs. Love was born April 20, 1849. Having had no children of their own, they have reared two boys, Joseph and William. Mr. Love located in Turtle Creek about 1881, where he is still interested in the coal business. He went into the hotel business in North Versailles township in 1898, and still conducts that venture in a first-class manner. Mr. Love is county committeeman in this county, having filled many township offices at Turtle Creek. He has been a member of the Knights of Pythias in Turtle Creek for thirty-one years. The other members of Mr. Love's family in this community are: Betsey, wife of the late Adam Crumpton, of Turtle Creek; Tamer, wife of Edward Kinsey, also of Turtle Creek, and Mary, wife of Joshua Fellows, of the same place. A brother, Peter, was killed in a railroad accident in 1892. In all of the relations of life, Mr. Love is faithful and true to every obligation. As a citizen, as a business man, as a neighbor and a friend, he is respected by all, and enjoys the cordial good-will of every one who knows him.

HENRY M. KERR, of Boston, Pa., a prominent citizen and well-known business man, was born in Armstrong county, Pa., Sept. 24, 1833, son of Robert and Mary A. (Myers) Kerr, his father having been a successful carpenter and the builder of the first canal boat used on the Pennsylvania canal. Henry M. Kerr was one of a family of fifteen children, was educated in the common schools of Armstrong county and after leaving school was engaged in working on the river, boating and rafting logs from the headwaters of the Monongahela river to New Orleans, and also from the headwaters of the Mississippi to the Crescent city, the country at that time being very wild and inhabited by savage Indians. In 1861 he enlisted in the Union army for service in the Civil war as a member of Company E, 4th Pennsylvania cavalry, later was promoted to a sergeantcy and served in that capacity until mustered out at Light House Point, Va., Aug. 16, 1864. They saw arduous service in that great conflict and participated in some of the most hotly-contested battles of the war. Their first commanding officer was Colonel Childs, who was killed. He was succeeded by Colonel Cavode, who was also killed; then there were a number of others in command, and at the close of the war their colonel was S. M. B. Young, now one of the highest officers of the United States army. Mr. Kerr met with numerous personal adventures which would require too much space to narrate here, and in all of the various phases of a military career that he experienced, bore himself in a manner that was a credit to himself and to the command of which he was a member. Mr. Kerr was married, in 1865, to Mary A., daughter of Jonathan and Annie (Titus) Bolton, of Allegheny county, and they had five children, four of whom are living, viz.: Georgianna; Leota, wife of Harvey Heath; John B., killed in a railroad accident in 1902; William C., and Robert C. Mr. Kerr has been connected with the Boston bridge company for the past five years, and is a member of the Grand Army of the Republic, the Junior Order of United American Mechanics, the Odd Fellows, the Masons, the Methodist Episcopal church and the republican party. Mr. Kerr is one of the solid and substantial citizens of Boston and is widely and favorably known in that community, where he has passed so many years of his life.

JOHN C. McCLURE, of Port Vue, Pa., a prominent citizen and successful farmer, was born in Lincoln township, Allegheny county, Pa., July 6, 1868, son of Andrew and Jane (Edmunson) McClure, his father being a prosperous farmer of Allegheny county. Young McClure was educated in the common schools of his native township and at the McKeesport business college, and since that time has devoted his attention to farming and selling coal from his place in Lincoln township. He has been very successful in his business affairs, has accumulated a competency and is one of the substantial citizens of the borough. He was happily married, in 1903, to Margaret Kunkelman, of Dravosburg, and their home life is an ideal one. Mr. McClure has been prominently identified with the public affairs of the borough, having served as a member of the council for five years, and in 1900 was elected burgess of Port Vue for a term of three years, on the republican ticket. He is a member of the Junior Order of United American Mechanics and of the First Presbyterian church of Port Vue, and is one of the leading men of that place.

M. W. CHAMBERS, assistant engineer in the Westinghouse works in East Pittsburg, and for nine years a respected resident of Turtle Creek, was born in Lancashire, England, Jan. 14, 1858, son of Miles and Mary (Malton) Chambers. Miles Chambers was a supervisor and architect in Liverpool. M. W. Chambers was educated in the public schools, learned the carpenters' trade, and in 1880 came to America, locating in Pittsburg. He was employed for about a year by the Pittsburg & Lake Erie railroad company, and then for several years by William Sterling, on Seventh avenue. In 1887 he entered the employ of the Westinghouse company, where by ability and faithful attention to duty he has won promotion to his present responsible and lucrative position. Mr. Chambers was married in England, Dec. 23, 1878, to Agnes

Hayton, daughter of Thompson and Martha (Wiseman) Hayton. The Hayton family is a prominent one in the town of Wygan, England. The children born of this union are: Thomas, foreman in the employ of the American steel and wire company; Agnes, at home and Adelia, wife of W. L. Jones, auditor for the Pittsburg coal company. Mr. Chambers is a republican in politics, but does not vote according to party lines when the better candidate is a member of a rival party. He is a member of the F. and A. M.

JOHN I. RANKIN, superintendent of production and stores for the Westinghouse air brake company, was born in Pittsburg, Feb. 9, 1867. The Westinghouse plant at Wilmerding is the largest of its kind in the world, employing over 3,000 hands. The subject of this sketch is a son of James I. and Catherine B. (Warmcastle) Rankin, of Pittsburg. James I. Rankin was a blacksmith by trade, while the Warmcastles were farmers in the territory which is now East End, Pittsburg. John I. Rankin was educated in the public schools, from which he graduated in 1880, and then was employed for many years by the Pennsylvania railroad company. In 1890 he was appointed agent of the company at Wilmerding, held that position until Jan. 1, 1898, when he entered the employ of the Electrical manufacturing company, of East Pittsburg. On Jan. 1, 1900, he left the service of this company to become storekeeper for the Westinghouse company, and on Aug. 1, 1902, was promoted to his present responsible position. Mr. Rankin has served several years as councilman in Wilmerding, is president of the board of trustees of the Y. M. C. A., and a member of the United Presbyterian church, of which he has been treasurer since 1895. Politically, he is a republican. Mr. Rankin was married, on New Year's day, 1901, to Miss Mary Ada, daughter of the late Ezra B. and Mary A. (Binsley) Westfall, of Williamsport, Pa. Mr. Westfall was for many years a prominent division superintendent for the Pennsylvania railroad company. Mr. and Mrs. Rankin have two children: Lillian M. and Carl S.

JOSEPH C. CAROTHERS, a well-known Turtle Creek farmer, was born in Allegheny county, Jan. 5, 1859. He received his education in the common schools, at Turtle Creek academy, Wilkinsburg academy, and Washington and Jefferson college, and has spent almost all his life on the farm in Patton township on which he now resides. The place is known as the old Carothers homestead. He is a member of the school board of Patton township, and of the First Presbyterian church of Turtle Creek, in which he has served as trustee. In politics he is a republican. Mr. Carothers is a grandson of Charles Carothers, who was born in County Down, Ireland, about 1769, and died in 1848. He came to America and was married in Allegheny county to Margaret McDade. They had four sons and two daughters, of whom Robert, the father of the subject of this sketch, was the first-born. Robert Carothers was born in 1790, and died in 1863. He married Sarah, daughter of David and Jane Show, of Versailles township, Allegheny county, and had nine children, of whom Joseph C. was the eighth. Robert Carothers, a farmer by vocation, was a colonel of militia; served in the state legislature at Harrisburg, was also a county commissioner, and was appointed for life to the position of justice of the peace. He and his father, Charles Carothers, were elders in the Beulah church, and later in the Cross Roads church. Dr. Charles Carothers, brother of Robert, and uncle of the subject of this article, was for many years a practicing physician in Wilkinsburg. He also was an elder in the Beulah church.

ABRAM H. S. BLACK, borough clerk of Sharpsburg, was born in New Berlin, Union county, Pa., Feb. 7, 1865, and is a son of Abram and Elizabeth (Franz) Black, natives of Lebanon county. Mr. Black was educated in the schools of Oil City and at the German institute, Randolph, N. Y. He has been borough clerk of Sharpsburg for the past three years, and was formerly township auditor for one year. He is a republican in politics and active in local party affairs. Before he obtained his present position he was for four years engaged in the undertaking business in Sharpsburg. Mr. Black is a prominent member of the Masonic fraternity, is a Knight Templar, and also belongs to the Sons of Veterans and the Independent Order of Heptasophs. He is a member of the Methodist Episcopal church. He was married, in 1891, to Emily Bean, daughter of Reuben and Mary Bean, respected residents of Akron, Ohio. Mr. Black's home is at No. 216 Thirteenth St., Sharpsburg.

DILLA A. LANE was born in Geneva, Ashtabula Co., Ohio, in 1859, son of James and Manda (Troop) Lane. Mr. Lane was educated in Geneva, and when a young man was employed in railroad work as a brakeman. Later he was promoted to the position of conductor and it was while working at this that he suffered an accident which changed his future life. He resigned his position, was for three years engaged in the hotel business and then went into the manufacture of toothpicks by means of a machine of his own invention, which machine is still in use. Mr. Lane next invented a machine for making skewers, and was engaged in the manufacture of that article for two years, when his apparatus was destroyed by fire. Mr. Lane rebuilt the machinery and sold out to M. C. Geider, of Marietta, Ohio, guaranteeing the machine to cut 125,000 skewers per day. In 1888 he returned to his old home in Geneva and the next year entered the employ of the National safe and lock company, of Cleveland, Ohio, where he remained until Oct. 1, 1902. He then became superintendent of the Clark safe and vault company, at Elizabeth, which was recently organized and is already doing a prosperous business, with its main offices at Pittsburg. The plant is an up-to-date concern with a constantly increasing capacity and expects to employ about 250 men. Mr. Lane married Miss Nellie Belknap, of Geneva, Ohio, and has three children: Lena, now Mrs. Otto Vagts, of Elizabeth; Chester and Cora. In national politics he is a republican.

HERMAN SHULTZ, of Springdale, Pa., foreman of the polishing department of the Heidenkamp mirror company, was born near Berlin, Germany, May 26, 1878, son of Frank and Katharine Shultz, both natives of Germany. His father was connected with the glass-works of Germany, and in 1886 removed his family to America, where he died. Herman attended the public schools of Germany until he was eight years old, and after coming to the United States and settling at Tarentum, he attended the schools of Harrison township. When he was twelve years of age his father died, and as the support of the family devolved on him, the rest of his education was secured at night school. He was employed in the bottle-works at Tarentum for about eighteen months, went into the plate glass works at Tarentum and there remained until 1901. He occupied nearly all positions in the works during this time, and in 1901 he was appointed foreman in the polishing department at Springdale and has thirty-two men under him in that department. He has two brothers and two sisters: Paul, foreman in the glass-works; Frank, attending school; Pauline, wife of Fabian Gross, an employe of the glass-works at Springdale, and Melia, at home. Mr. Shultz is a member of the Catholic church and a trustee of same, member of the Knights of St. John Sacred Hearts, and is a republican in politics. Mr. Shultz's father was a soldier in the German army for three years and made a splendid record in that capacity.

AUGUST BELSMEYER, foreman in the clothing department of the firm of Jones & Laughlin, Pittsburg, Pa., was born in Columbus, Ind., in 1863. He received his education in the public schools of his native city and in 1881, in connection with an uncle, established the firm of Greenwood & Belsmeyer, merchant tailors, at Wilson, N. C. Later he was in the merchant tailoring business at Raleigh, N. C., and still later he was the head of the firm of A. Belsmeyer & Co., merchant tailors, at Durham, N. C. In 1889 he entered the employ of William Smith & Son, Washington, Pa., as foreman and cutter in their merchant tailoring department. Five years later he engaged with Mr. E. Gray, general manager for the Jones & Laughlin Co., with whom he is still associated. Mr. Belsmeyer was one of the incorporators of the St. Clair savings and trust company and is now one of the directors. In political matters he is a consistent republican and at the last municipal election was chosen to represent Knoxville borough in the council. In the social life of Knoxville he is well known, being a member of several fraternal societies. He was married, in 1886, to Miss Susan E. Hudson, a daughter of Edward T. Hudson, of Richmond, Va. To this marriage there have been born four children: Mary, Dorothea, Bernard and Louis. Mr. Belsmeyer's business career shows what a boy of pluck and determination can do. Starting in boyhood without special advantages, he has worked his way up to his present responsible position by his own efforts.

JAMES SHANER, of Aspinwall, Pa., a well-known citizen and prominently identified with the oil business of that section, was born in Butler, Pa., Nov. 23, 1855, son of James A. and Susan (Shirley) Shaner, his father having been long connected with the shoemaking industry of that town. Mr. Shaner attended the public schools until thirteen years of age, when he left his studies to engage in the oil business, which he has followed since that time. He began in the oil well supply business at Parker's Landing, Armstrong Co., Pa., removed to Millerstown in 1878 and there remained until 1882. For some time he was employed at Richmond, N. Y., and in 1884 became connected with the Jarecki manufacturing company, stationed at Butler, Pa., until 1890, when he was transferred by the company to Washington, Pa. He remained there until 1895 and was again sent to Butler as local manager, remaining until 1898. For the next two years he served this company in West Virginia, came to Pittsburg as their representative in 1900, and since has continued to represent them in western Pennsylvania, though he has resided in Aspinwall since 1895. He was married, in 1882, to Ella M., daughter of Capt. James and Fannie B. Hazlett, and to them have been born three children, viz.: Fannie; Shirley S., with the Standard oil company, and Raymond D. Mr. Shaner is a prominent member of the First United Presbyterian church of Aspinwall. He is one of the leading secret order men of that city and is a member of the Odd Fellows, the Masons, of which order he has taken the thirty-second degree; the Maccabees, the Elks, the Knights of Honor, the Royal Arcanum, and Junior Order of United American Mechanics. He comes of a long line of stanch republicans and is considered the leading member of that party in Aspinwall. He served three years as councilman of Oakdale, Pa., and was elected a member of council the first year of his residence in Aspinwall. He has also been elected justice of the peace on several occasions but has declined to serve.

ADAM LANG, of Coulter, Pa., a prominent citizen and a successful coal-miner, was born in Allegheny county, Pa., June 26, 1850, son of Henry and Katharine Lang, both Hessians by birth. Mr. Lang has devoted his entire business career to coal-mining, of which vocation he has made a decided success and has accumulated a competency. He was married, on July 3, 1877, in Allegheny county, to Abbie, daughter of Horace and Elizabeth Gibbons, of Coulter, Allegheny county, Pa., and they have the following children: James, William and Katharine. Mr. Lang is prominently identified with a number of the leading fraternal orders and holds membership in the Benevolent and Protective Order of Elks, and the Independent Order of Odd Fellows. He is one of the leading citizens of that portion of the county and is well and favorably known throughout that community.

JOHN THADDEUS AUSTEN, of Aspinwall, Pa., a prominent citizen, was born March 26, 1864, in Bakerstown, Allegheny county, son of Charles and Anna (Jones) Austen, the former a leading carpenter of that town. He was educated in the public schools, and at the age of fifteen years began to learn the carpenters' trade under his father. After four years spent at this trade he engaged with E. Myrick, of Sharpsburg, in the hardware business and for seven years followed that vocation. For the next eighteen months he was employed in a pipe mill at Pittsburg and then entered the hardware store of S. J. Saint, of Sharpsburg, where he remained for seven years. He engaged in the feed business under the firm name of Austen Bros., at Etna, and conducted this business for four years. In 1899 he opened a grocery store in Aspinwall and met with much success in this venture, selling his interest in the business in March, 1903. Since then he has resided in Aspinwall and is one of the leading citizens of that city. He was married, on Jan. 27, 1887, to Hattie E. Robinson, and to them have been born six children, five of whom are now living, viz.: Clarence, Irene, Ruby, Willard and Elizabeth. Mr. Austen is a member of the Sharpsburg Baptist church, the Junior Order of United American Mechanics, the Royal Arcanum, and is a republican in politics. The great-grandfather of Mr. Austen was Charles Austen, a distinguished soldier of England, holding the position of captain in the guards and also serving as a lieutenant in the royal navy. He came to America in a sail-boat in 1820, and was the head of this branch of the Austen family in the United States.

JOSEPH REINHART, of Coulter, Pa., a prosperous and successful butcher, was born in South Versailles township, Allegheny county, Pa., April 8, 1860, son of Florean and Monica (Miller) Reinhart, his father having died in 1875. Mr. Reinhart was educated in the public schools of his native township and on leaving school learned the butchers' trade, at which he has worked all the years of his business career, and since 1884 has been in business at his present stand in Coulter, Pa., where he has prospered and enjoyed a large and paying business. Mr. Reinhart was married, in 1885, to Mary A., daughter of James and Mary (Driscoll) McLaughlin, of South Versailles township, and they have five children, viz.: Frank, Stella, Celia, James and Harry, all residing with their parents. He is a member of the Roman Catholic church and a widely-known and highly-respected citizen. Mr. Reinhart also operates a large dairy on his farm of 200 acres in South Versailles township, and has a splendid standing in the commercial and financial world.

HENRY EDWARD KELLY, of Cheswick, Pa., superintendent of the Cheswick manufacturing company, was born in Forest county, Pa., on Aug. 7, 1876, son of Archibald B. and Frances A. (May) Kelly. His father is cashier of the Forest County National bank and is prominently identified with the lumber business of that section. Young Kelly attended the Kiskiminetas Springs school for four years, and later the Western university, of Pittsburg, graduating in the electrical engineering course in 1898. He then accepted a position with the Pressed Steel car company and was with them for two years. In 1900 he became treasurer of the Pittsburg electric lamp company, remaining two years, when he accepted the position of superintendent of the Cheswick manufacturing company, of Cheswick, Pa., of which he is also treasurer. They manufacture agricultural steel and hollow ware, and have a large and prosperous business. This company was chartered in 1893 with a capital stock of $50,000. Mr. Kelly is a Presbyterian, and in politics a republican, all of his ancestors having been closely identified with that party. John May, a progenitor of the mother of Mr. Kelly, was one of the Puritans who came to America in 1640. Mr. Kelly is a progressive and capable business man and has achieved unusual success in his commercial career.

REV. CLEMENT KROGMANN, pastor of St. Wendoline's church, Carrick, Pa., was born Oct. 23, 1858, in Lohne, Oldenburg, Germany, and is the son of Joseph and Elizabeth (Tombrael) Krogmann. His elementary education was acquired by eight years' attendance in the parochial schools of his native town, and four years in the high school in the same place. Afterwards he entered the gymnasium of Vechta, where he remained until he completed the entire course of study. On March 25, 1884, he landed in the United States, and went directly to Carthagena, Mercer Co., Ohio, where he studied philosophy for one year. He then went to Latrobe, Pa., and took a three-year course in theology in St. Vincent's college. On March 21, 1888, he was ordained to the priesthood by the Right Rev. R. Phelan, at Latrobe, and entered upon his duties. Father Krogmann said his first mass in St. Mary's church, at Pine Creek, Allegheny Co., Pa., and his first administration was in St. Joseph's church, at Pittsburg, where he stayed four and a half years. After leaving St. Joseph's, he was one year in charge of St. Alphonsus' church, at Wexford, Pa.; one year at St. Aloysius' church, in Reserve township, Allegheny county; three and a half years at Verona as pastor of St. Joseph's church, and on Aug. 15, 1891, he entered upon his present charge. During the twelve years of his service at St. Wendoline's he has seen his work blessed with success. The congregation has steadily increased in numbers under his charge, and he is beloved by all his parishioners.

ANDREW COLEMAN, liveryman and hauling contractor, has been a resident of Clairton since 1900 only, but he is one of the best-known men in the city. He is a son of John and Mary Jane (Ramsey) Coleman, and was born in the town of Camden, Pa., in 1872. His father was born in 1846, and died in 1900. His mother is still living. Andrew was educated in the public schools of Camden, after which he worked in the mines there until 1900, when he came to Clairton and engaged in the contract hauling business. Prompt attention to business and reasonable prices for his work brought him plenty to do, and from the first his business has prospered. Within the last year he has added a livery department to his business, and he is now the leader in that line in Clairton. He was married, in 1894, to Miss Alice Lewis. They have three children: Margaret, born in 1896; John, born in 1897, and Joseph, born in 1899. Mr. Coleman is a member of Coal Valley council, No. 98, Junior Order of United American Mechanics, and in many ways is a model citizen. Although he is interested in public affairs, he does not neglect his business to take an active part in political contests, finding more pleasure in his family circle than in the primaries, and more profit in attending to his growing business than in the political arena.

HOWARD G. DOUGAN, one of the leading plumbers and gas-fitters of Clairton, Pa., was born in the city of Buffalo, N. Y., April 29, 1872. His father was Thomas Dougan, a native of New York city, but now deceased, and the maiden name of his mother was Mary Jane Summerville. She is a native of County Armagh, Ireland, and is still living. H. G. Dougan received his education in the public schools of Buffalo. Upon leaving school he worked about two years as a messenger boy for the Western Union telegraph company. He then went into a lithographing establishment as an apprentice, but only remained at the business about a year, when he decided to learn the plumbers' trade. He therefore entered the employment of Early & Stygail, of Buffalo, and served his apprenticeship, learning the plumbing business in all its details. He worked at his trade as a journeyman until 1899, when he became the manager of the Smith Bros. plumbing business, at Ridgeway, Pa. About a year later he accepted a position as manager for the Charleroi plumbing company, and removed to Clairton. On Nov. 17, 1902, he opened a shop of his own and does a general plumbing and gas-fitting business. During his long career as a journeyman he learned that only skilled labor should be trusted to do plumbing, and consequently only that kind of labor finds a place in his establishment. All his work is done under his personal supervision, which insures satisfaction to his patrons. He is a member of the Pittsburg branch of the National plumbers' association. In 1900 he was married to Miss Marie Secheien, of Wilcox, Elk Co., Pa. They have one little daughter, Marie, born April 8, 1901. Mr. Dougan is a member of the Presbyterian church, and an evidence of his popularity may be seen in the fact that in June, 1903, he was elected tax collector for the borough of Clairton.

JOHN W. RANKIN, of Boston, Pa., a successful farmer and a prominent citizen, was born in Elizabeth township, Allegheny Co., Pa., June 30, 1862, son of Samuel C. and Rebecca (Williamson) Rankin, his father having been a prosperous farmer of Elizabeth township until his death in 1895, at the age of sixty-five years. John W. Rankin was educated in the public schools of his native county, and since leaving school has devoted his entire attention to farming, of which vocation he has made an unqualified success and has a splendid place in Elizabeth township. Mr. Rankin is an ardent and active republican, and has occupied a prominent place in the public affairs of the township, having been elected to his present position on the school board in 1902, and also having served for two years as tax collector of the township.

ANDREW F. PEAIRS, a prominent dairy and stock farmer of Elizabeth township, is a descendant of one of the oldest families in western Pennsylvania. One of his ancestors entered a homestead in the year 1778, in what is now Elizabeth township, Allegheny Co., Pa., and it has been in possession of the Peairs family ever since, and is now the residence of the subject of this sketch. Mr. Peairs was born upon this farm, Feb. 2, 1850. His parents were Joseph and Margaret (Fife) Peairs. His father died in 1897. Andrew F. Peairs was educated in the Elizabeth public schools, and has spent his entire life upon the homestead where he was born and where he is now engaged in conducting one of the finest dairy and stock farms in this section of the country. He makes a specialty of Guernsey cattle, and a glance at some of his herds shows that he thoroughly understands the business of breeding and rearing cattle. Mr. Peairs disposes of the surplus of his herds, amounting to about twelve head a year, for breeding purposes and for which he receives very fancy prices. He is unmarried, and is an independent in politics.

ROBERT J. SHIELDS, M. D., of Industry, Pa., a prominent physician and surgeon, was born in Washington county, Pa., April 28, 1854, son of James and Amanda C. Shields, both of Irish descent, who resided the greater part of their lives in Washington county, where his father, a successful miner, died in 1868. Dr. Shields accompanied his parents to Allegheny county when a mere infant, and was educated in the common schools of that county and at the West Pennsylvania university, where he was graduated in medicine in 1888, with the degree of doctor of medicine. The same year Dr. Shields initiated his professional career at Industry, and has since been one of the leading physicians of that part of the county. His practice is a large and lucrative one and is among the best families of that community. He was married, in 1890, to Mary, daughter of James and Anna (Brown) Black, of Coultersville, Pa., and their married life has been a halcyon one. Dr. Shields is a member of the Odd Fellows and the Foresters, and is one of the most substantial and highly respected citizens of that section.

U. GRANT JOHNSTIN, of McKeesport, Pa., a prominent cement-work contractor, was born in Lancaster county, Pa., April 5, 1865, son of E. H. and Mary (Miller) Johnstin, of Lancaster county, Pa. Young Johnstin was educated in the common schools of Somerset county, Pa., and on leaving school, devoted his attention to plastering, which business he followed with much success in Somerset, Westmoreland and Allegheny counties. In 1885 Mr. Johnstin located at McKeesport, and there continued the plastering business until 1901, when he turned his attention to cement work and now makes a specialty of concrete sidewalks, walls and other structures of that nature. He was happily married, on Feb. 6, 1889, to Mary K., daughter of Robert and Mary Francis, of Connellsville, Pa., and they have five children, viz.: Louis, Grace, Carrie, Mildred and Harry, the three eldest attending the splendid schools of McKeesport. Mr. Johnstin is a stanch republican and was elected a member of the common council in 1900, and since that time has served continuously in that body, where he has made a fine record and is regarded as one of its leading and most influential members. Mr. Johnstin is prominently identified with a number of the leading fraternal orders and holds membership in the Elks, the Junior Order of United American Mechanics, the Modern Woodmen of America, the Royal Arcanum, the Maccabees and the Woodmen of the World.

JOHN M. FOSS, a well-known florist of Etna, was born in Christiania, Norway, in 1865, and educated in his native country. There he learned the florists' trade, and followed this vocation for seven years. In 1885 he decided to try his fortunes in America and located in Allegheny county. He now has a greenhouse in Etna, where he does a thriving business. Mr. Foss married Miss Bertha Cook, of Sharpsburg, and has three children. He and his family reside in Etna. Mr. Foss is a member of the German Lutheran church.

AUGUST J. NEEDLING, real estate agent and justice of the peace at Millvale, was born in Pittsburg, Pa., in 1870. His father, Joseph Needling, was a contractor and builder, and was killed in an accident in the rolling mills at Millvale in 1876. Margaret, the mother of A. J. Needling, was the daughter of August Joseph Heil. She died in Millvale in 1882. Mr. and Mrs. Joseph Needling had four children, as follows: August J., the subject of this sketch; Elizabeth, now married to James Barbin, an insurance agent in Pittsburg; Mary, now a sister and music teacher in a convent, and Joseph (deceased). August J. Needling married Miss Minnie Trapp, daughter of John and Mary (Wirth) Trapp. Mr. and Mrs. Trapp had five other children born to them. They were: Mary, John, Annie, Joseph and Lawrence. Mr. and Mrs. Needling have one child, Vronie, now five years old. Mr. Needling is a prominent and enterprising young business man of Millvale, and at his office on Grand avenue he carries on an extensive and profitable business in real estate, besides holding the position of justice of the peace.

CHRIST L. BICKEL, of Sharpsburg, Pa., a prosperous farmer, was born in Prussia, Sept. 6, 1841, son of John Godfried and Anna Susanna (Wegand) Bickel. His father was a farmer, stonemason and a dealer in wool and hides. Young Bickel attended the public schools of the Fatherland until he was eleven years of age, when he accompanied his parents to America and they settled on Pine creek, in Indiana township, now O'Hara, and there he resumed his interrupted studies. He later began to assist his father on the farm, where he remained until he was twenty-four years of age, when he removed to Allegheny city and there secured employment as a teamster for Allen McClintock. He continued in that capacity for upwards of three years, and then removed to O'Hara township, engaged in farming, and has prospered in that vocation up to the present time. In 1899 he added a greenhouse to his other possessions, and now conducts this in connection with his farm. He was married, in 1865, to Elizabeth, daughter of Henry Herman and Anna K. Vonsende, of Allegheny city. The parents of Mrs. Bickel were formerly of Germany, but were married after coming to the United States, and had seven children, of whom Mrs. Bickel was the eldest. Mr. and Mrs. Bickel are the parents of eleven children, seven of whom are now living and are: Charles L., an employe of the brick-works; John Henry, in a foundry of Pittsburg; Anna Margaret, wife of John Wagner (deceased); William A., with his father on the farm; George D., Mary C., and Elizabeth, now in Pittsburg learning sewing. Mr. Bickel is a leading member of the German Lutheran church of Etna, Pa., and was a member of sessions for six years. He is a member of the Odd Fellows. the Rebeccas and of the democratic party, and is one of the substantial citizens of that community. Henry Vonsende, the father of Mrs. Bickel, was killed in the battle of Antietam while serving the country of his adoption, and a brother of Mrs. Bickel served in the Pennsylvania volunteers during the Civil war.

ERNEST L. ERHARD, M. D., of Glassport, Pa., a prominent physician and surgeon, was born at New Millport, Clearfield Co., Pa., June 30, 1870, son of Philip and Mary (Schoening) Erhard, of Clearfield county, Pa., where his father was a successful carpenter and builder. Dr. Erhard was graduated from the public schools of his native county and later attended the State normal school at Lock Haven, where he was graduated in 1885. Subsequently he matriculated at West Pennsylvania medical institute of Pittsburg, and was graduated from that sterling institution March 26, 1895, with the degree of doctor of medicine. Dr. Erhard initiated his professional career at Indiana, Pa., in 1895, where he practiced with much success until 1900, when he removed to his present location at Glassport and since has enjoyed a high standing among the leading physicians of that part of the county. He was married, in 1897, to Laura, daughter of George and Agnes Patchin, of Clearfield county, Pa., and their wedded life has been a happy one. He is a prominent member of the Odd Fellows, the Masons, the Heptasophs and the Modern Woodmen of America. He has a large and lucrative practice among the best families of Glassport and was recently elected surgeon of the mills located at that borough.

BERNARD J. HYNES, of Coulter, Pa., pastor of St. Patrick's Catholic church of Alpsville, Pa., was born at Skerries, County Dublin, Ireland, Aug. 1, 1866, son of William and Mary Hynes, of Ireland. Father Hynes was educated in the classical courses at St. Charles' college in Howard county, Md., and at Seton Hall college in New Jersey, graduating from the latter institution in 1887. He then studied theology at Mt. St. Mary's college, Maryland, and there was ordained by Bishop Watterson, on June 25, 1891. His first charge was at the Sacred Heart church of the East End, Pittsburg, where he remained until 1895, when he went on a Protestant mission for a short while, and later was at St. Paul's orphan asylum of Pittsburg and also assistant at St. Mary's church of that city. In 1897 he went to Leisenring, Fayette Co., Pa., where he was in charge of St. Vincent's church of that place until he came to his present church at Alpsville, Pa., in May, 1903. This church has a membership of forty-five families and is in every way a highly successful organization. Father Hynes, like the great majority of Catholic priests, is a man of the highest educational attainments and is in every way qualified for the arduous duties of his sacred calling.

OLIVER EVANS, a prominent citizen and successful farmer of Versailles township, Allegheny county, Pa., was born at McKeesport, Pa., June 3, 1853, son of Oliver and Mary (Sampson) Evans, his father being a prosperous farmer and dairyman of Allegheny county. Oliver Evans, subject of this sketch, received his educational training at the McKeesport public schools and the Millersville normal school, and has devoted his entire business career to farming and kindred pursuits. He has been quite successful in his business life and now conducts a large dairy in connection with his farm in Versailles township. He was happily married, in 1873, to Fannie, daughter of Eli and Katherine (Arthur) Cook, of McKeesport, Pa., and they have five children, viz.: Oliver, Jr., farming in Westmoreland county, Pa.; Katie, attending school at McKeesport; Rebecca S., Allen and Mary A. Mr. Evans is easily one of the most prominent men in that part of Allegheny county and his services have been in demand by his neighbors and friends to fill public positions of responsibility and trust. He has been a school director for the past fifteen years, is now president of the board, and for four years served as supervisor of the township, in which several positions his splendid records fully justify the good opinions of those who placed him in those offices.

GEORGE W. LOGAN, a genial and popular B. & O. conductor, is a native of Allegheny county, where he was born Oct. 8, 1869. He is a son of James and Jennie (Hayne) Logan. His father was a prominent contractor and builder. G. W. Logan was educated in the schools of McKeesport, and after leaving school he entered the employ of the Baltimore & Ohio railroad company. Step by step he has been advanced, until he now has charge of a train as conductor, and has a high standing in the opinions of his superiors. He was married, in 1901, to Miss Nellie, a daughter of William and Mary Hackett, of Allegheny county. They have one little daughter named Mary. Mr. Logan is a member of the Brotherhood of Railroad Trainmen, and in politics is a zealous republican. He was elected in 1898 on the republican ticket to the council of Versailles borough for a term of five years.

DAVID G. LENHART, of Greenock, Pa., the popular and efficient storekeeper of the Osceola coal company, was born in Harrison City, Westmoreland Co., Pa., June 15, 1853, son of Peter and Margaret (Gongnan) Lenhart, of Westmoreland county, where his father was a successful farmer until his death in 1889. Mr. Lenhart was educated in the common schools of his native county and on leaving school devoted his attention to the grocery and the butcher business, at which he prospered for many years. In 1889 he came to Allegheny county, located at Greenock, and for the past fourteen years has occupied his present responsible position of storekeeper for the Osceola coal company. He was married, in 1884, to Jennie Taylor, of Westmoreland county, and they have three children, viz.: Cora, Elrod and Eva, of whom Cora, the eldest, is a graduate of the McKeesport college and is an accomplished young woman. Mr. Lenhart is a man of ability and integrity and is widely and favorably known in that section of the county.

EDWARD C. FINNEY, a funeral director of Clairton, Pa., is a son of Joseph N. and Arabella (McClure) Finney, both of whom are natives of Allegheny county. Joseph Finney was born in Elizabeth township, and Arabella McClure in Lincoln township, where the two families are among the oldest settlers. Edward C. Finney was educated in the public schools of Reynoldton and Elizabeth, Pa. After leaving school he entered the employ of J. W. Martin, of Elizabeth, in the furniture and undertaking business, and while connected with Mr. Martin he took a complete course in the art of embalming. He remained in the establishment of Mr. Martin until May, 1903, when he became associated with J. Will Martin, under the firm name of Finney & Martin, and they located at Clairton in the capacity of funeral directors and liverymen. Mr. Finney was born in 1878, and is therefore only about twenty-five years of age. But what he lacks in experience, when compared with some of the older funeral directors, is more than offset by the high degree of technical knowledge of his profession which he brings into his business, and the energy and ambition of youth. He is an honored member of the Knights of the Maccabees, belonging to Tent No. 371, of Elizabeth, Pa., and is affiliated with the United Presbyterian church of Boston, Pa. In both church and lodge affairs he takes an active interest, and in these connections as well as in business matters he is entitled to the distinction of being one of the progressive men of Allegheny county.

CHARLES K. HOFFMEYER, a florist of Scott township, Allegheny county, Pa., is one of the leading citizens of his township. His father, Leopold Hoffmeyer, was born in Germany, in 1809. In 1832 Catharina Tritschler was born in the same neighborhood, and in 1849 she became the wife of Leopold Hoffmeyer. To this marriage eight children were born, Charles being the oldest son and second child of the family. He was born on April 1, 1853. The other children are: Leopoldina, born in 1852 and now the wife of Charles Reichart, of Glasgow, Scotland; Theresa, born in 1854; Josephina, born in 1855; Emil Henry, born in 1856, now in Nebraska; Anna, born in 1857; Amelia, born in 1858, and Frieda, born in 1860. Leopold Hoffmeyer was a copper hame-smith by trade, and Charles, after acquiring a high-school education, learned the trade with his father and worked at it until he came to this country. Under the laws of the German empire, every young man capable of bearing arms is required to serve two years in the army. Charles began this service but was discharged at the expiration of thirteen months on account of the death of his father. That was in 1874; his mother had died in 1864. About four years after the death of his father, and after the younger children of the family had reached an age that no longer required the elder brother's care, Charles came to America, in December, 1877. Not finding employment at his trade, he determined to learn the florists' trade, and after four years' work went into business for himself as a florist. Beginning on a small scale he has gradually extended his plant until he now has more than 28,000 square feet of glass in his floral greenhouses. Most of this is supported in iron frames and the whole building is heated and ventilated by the most modern appliances. He has studied carefully the literature of floriculture, and the success that has come to him is the result of patient industry and the intelligent direction of his efforts. Mr. Hoffmeyer keeps himself well informed on the topics of the times. In politics he affiliates with the republican party but has never felt that he had the time to become an active worker in political affairs. In 1888 he was married to Miss Julia Dorothy Weiss, a native of Allegheny county, where she was born in 1855. Her father, John Weiss, came from Germany about the middle of the last century and settled at Pittsburg. For many years he followed the trade of blacksmithing, but the last years of his life were spent on a farm in Scott township, where Mrs. Hoffmeyer received her education in the common schools. Mr. and Mrs. Hoffmeyer are both members of the United Presbyterian church. They have no children of their own, but about three years since they adopted a little girl, Jennie, at that time about four years of age; also in September, 1903, adopted a boy four years old with the name Carl.

FREDERICK FINK, who owns and operates a fruit and garden farm of fifty-seven acres in Scott township, Allegheny county, Pa., is one of the most prosperous and progressive men in his section of the country. He was born in Germany, Jan. 25, 1851, and came with his parents, Ernest and Catharine (Detter) Fink, to America when he was but three years old. Ernest Fink was born in 1805, and his wife in 1815. Both were natives of Germany. Upon coming to this country they settled at Pittsburg, where his father was employed as a laborer for three years. At the end of that time they removed to Scott township, where Ernest Fink followed the occupation of a fruit-grower and gardener until his death, which occurred in July, 1888. His wife departed this life the succeeding May. Frederick Fink lived with his father until he attained his majority, attending the common schools of the township, where he obtained a good elementary education. His farm is one of the best in the township and is kept in first-class condition by the industry and good management of the owner. In 1874 Mr. Fink was married to Miss Elizabeth Handenshield, who was born in Allegheny county on Dec. 10, 1854. Her father, Jacob Handenshield, was a native of Germany, and her mother, whose maiden name was Mary Daugherty, was born in America, but was of Irish extraction. To Frederick and Elizabeth Fink were born eleven children. They are: Edward, Harrison, Frederick, Charles, George, Myrtle, Elmer, Arthur, Emma, Viola and Chester. Mr. Fink votes the republican ticket as a general thing, but takes no active part in political work. He is a member of no religious denomination, though his wife belongs to the United Presbyterian church. He is a man of good moral habits and his neighbors speak of him as an exemplary citizen.

WILLIAM E. WISE, a lifelong resident of Allegheny county, Pa., and for many years a farmer of Scott township, was born on Oct. 23, 1863. He is a son of John and Margaret (Schmidt) Wise. (See sketch of John Wise.) As a boy, William attended the neighborhood schools and afterwards took a two-year course in the school attached to the Smithfield Street German Evangelical church, in the city of Pittsburg. To the education thus acquired he has added by reading and he is one of the well-informed men of his township. Ever since he was a child he has resided upon the farm he now owns and which, by his skill and industry, he has brought to a high state of cultivation. Like several of his neighbors, Mr. Wise is engaged in raising small fruits and vegetables for the city markets. The buildings upon his farm are among the best in the vicinity and his orchard is always in the very best condition. On the last day of April, 1890, he was married to Miss Dora, the daughter of Henry and Wilhelmina (Spreen) Mohlman. Both her parents are natives of Germany. Her father came to this country when he was about twenty years of age and her mother a year or so later. They were married in Allegheny county, where their daughter, now Mrs. Wise, was born March 13, 1865. She was educated in the common schools of Green Tree borough and the German Evangelical school of Pittsburg—the same school attended by her husband. Both of her parents are still living. The father, though seventy years of age, still follows his vocation of wagon-maker, and the mother, now sixty-six, is still hale and hearty. William and Dora Wise have two children: Julia Amelia, born July 13, 1891, and William E., born Feb. 25, 1899. Mr. Wise is a member of the German Evangelical church and his wife belongs to the United Presbyterian. In politics he is a republican, but thinks more of the comforts of his family circle and the management of his farm than he does of the conflicts of the political arena.

SAMUEL P. McCAFFREY, superintendent of the Bridgeville district for the Pittsburg coal company, was born in the town of Lindsay, Ontario, Sept. 30, 1861. His parents, Peter and Catherine McCaffrey, were natives of Ireland. They came to this country in their youth and were married in New York city. A few years after their marriage they removed to Canada, locating in the town of Lindsay, where Mr. McCaffrey was for several years chief of police. During the Civil war, he left his family in Canada and came back to the United States, where he found employment as a steamboat engineer on the Mississippi river. In 1865 he brought his family to the United States and the remaining years of his life were passed in the vicinity of Pittsburg. Both parents lived to a good old age. Catherine McCaffrey died at Mansfield, now Carnegie, Pa., July 5, 1901. Her husband survived her about a year and passed to his reward on July 17, 1902, aged seventy-six years. At the age of eleven, Samuel P. McCaffrey began work in a coal mine and he has followed that occupation all his life. By the conscientious performance of the work assigned him, he has risen step by step from a breaker-boy to his present position. In 1894 he became foreman for A. J. Shulte, in the Bridgeville mine. This was the first opportunity that had ever been given him to show what he could do toward the management of a mine. When the Bridgeville mining company was organized, in February, 1896, and took charge of the Shulte mine, the new owners were so well pleased with Mr. McCaffrey's work that he was continued as foreman. In November, 1899, the mine passed to the control of the Pittsburg coal company. Since that time, with the exception of about sixteen months, Mr. McCaffrey has been in the employ of that company. On Sept. 8, 1902, he was made superintendent of the Bridgeville district, a position he has held continuously ever since. Mr. McCaffrey received a common-school education only, but, being thrown on his own resources at a comparatively early age, he has developed the habit of thinking for himself. As a natural consequence of his independent thought, he is independent in his political views, voting for the man he considers the best fitted for the office, regardless of party lines. In 1902 he was elected councilman for the Bridgeville borough, on the citizens' ticket, and he has discharged the duties of the position with rare ability and a strict regard for the interests of his constituents. In 1881 he was married to Miss Margaret Riley, a daughter of Philip and Margaret Riley. Mrs. McCaffrey is a native of England, where she was born on Aug. 11, 1862. She came with her parents to America when she was about five years of age and was educated in the common schools of Allegheny county. Her father died in November, 1895, at the age of seventy, and her mother is still living, being now sixty-seven years old. Mr. and Mrs. McCaffrey are the parents of seven children, viz.: William, Alice, Annie, John, Edward, Charles and Bernardine. He is a member of Bridgeville council, Knights of the Maccabees, and of Branch No. 60, Catholic Mutual Benefit Association. He and his wife are both members of the Roman Catholic church. He has a comfortable home in Bridgeville, worth at least $5,000, the fruits of his industry and frugality.

JOHN SCHMITT, one of the leading farmers of Scott township, Allegheny Co., Pa., is of German lineage, his parents, George A. and Magdaline (Brush) Schmitt, both being natives of Bavaria, where the father was born in 1801, and the mother about five years later. In 1835 George A. Schmitt and his wife said good-bye to the Fatherland and sought a home in America. They settled at Pittsburg, Pa., where for many years he was a workman in the Scio iron works. John Schmitt, the subject of this sketch, was born in Allegheny county in 1838. His education was obtained in the Pittsburg public schools. When he was twelve years of age he started in to learn the glass-blowers' trade and followed that occupation for more than thirty years. In 1891 he gave up glass-blowing and moved upon the farm which he had bought some time before. Since then he has been engaged in farming and market gardening. On Sept. 27, 1862, he was married to Miss Mary C. Henkel, daughter of Martin and Rosanna (Gab) Henkel. Mrs. Schmitt was born in Allegheny city, Pa., on Sept. 18, 1844. Her parents were both natives of Germany, the father being born about 1814 and the mother about 1817. He died in 1891, and she followed him in 1895. He was a cabinet-maker by trade, and was regarded a fine workman in his day. Mr. and Mrs. Schmitt are the parents of seven children, as follows: John, Rosa, Magdaline, Celia, George A., Mary and Frank. Five of the children are still living, John and Mary being deceased. Mr. Schmitt is a man of modest demeanor. Whether at the glass furnace or on his farm, he has always faithfully discharged his duties as he understood them. The same is true at the ballot-box. He has never been a partisan, but takes an independent view of the political situation, and votes for the best man, regardless of party affiliations.

WILLIAM LEVEN GRANGER, of Duquesne, Pa., borough clerk and dealer in real estate, was born at Baltimore, Md., Aug. 31, 1865, son of Leven and Martha (Joyner) Granger, both natives of Maryland. His paternal grandfather, Leven Granger, a native of Wales and a sea captain by profession, settled on the eastern shore of Maryland and there passed the rest of his days. His maternal grandfather, William B. Joyner, was a native of Maryland and a prominent citizen of Baltimore, where he lived and died. Leven Granger, father of the subject, was also a sea captain and made his home at Baltimore, where he died in 1870, at the age of sixty years. William L. Granger was reared in Baltimore, educated in the public schools of that city, and began life as a sailor. He followed that occupation for two and a half years, was a bookkeeper in Baltimore for four years, then for ten years was a traveling salesman, in 1899 located at Duquesne and engaged in the real estate business, which he has since successfully followed and is now a member of the well-known firm of E. P. Faidley & Co. Mr. Granger was married, on Sept. 12, 1899, to Gertrude B., daughter of E. P. Faidley, of Duquesne, and they have one daughter, Martha J. Mr. Granger is a member of the Masons, the Maccabees and the Royal Arcanum, and is now serving his second term as borough clerk of Duquesne. His political affiliations are with the republican party, in which he is a leading and active member and a zealous worker for party superiority.

JOHN ROBERT KERRUISH, of Homestead, Pa., a prosperous plumber and gas-fitter, was born in Toledo, Ohio, Oct. 6, 1877, son of John T. and Josephine (Robinson) Kerruish, natives of the Isle of Man and Pennsylvania, respectively. His father came to the United States in 1870 and located at Toledo, Ohio, where he embarked in contracting and building and was actively and successfully engaged in that business for twenty-nine years in that city. In 1899 he came to Homestead, and there continued building and contracting until his death, Dec. 26, 1901. He left a family of five children, viz.: Alice A., John R., Ralph J., Helen M. and Bessie M. John R. Kerruish was reared in Toledo, educated in the public schools of that city and Milan, Ohio, and served four years' apprenticeship at the plumbers' trade in Toledo. Later he worked as a journeyman for six years and in 1901 located at Homestead, where he embarked in the plumbing business under the firm name of Gibson & Kerruish. This firm prospered in their business venture and on March 4, 1903, Mr. Kerruish purchased his partner's interest and has since conducted the business under his own name. He was married, on Oct. 23, 1901, to Bertha I., daughter of Henry and Louise (Krumm) Henning, of Toledo, Ohio, and their home life is a very happy one. Mr. Kerruish's political affiliations are with the republican party and he is generally regarded as a safe and conservative business man and a progressive and substantial citizen.

CHARLES DUWELL, of Duquesne, Pa., pastor of St. Joseph's German Catholic church, was born in Allegheny city, Nov. 30, 1870, son of Joseph and Mary (Sauer) Duwell, natives of Germany and Allegheny county, respectively. Father Duwell was reared in his native city and educated at St. Vincent's college, at Latrobe, where he was graduated in May, 1894, and there ordained to the priesthood on May 28, 1894, by Bishop Phelan. He was then appointed assistant pastor of St. Joseph's church at Mount Oliver, later transferred to St. Joseph's church at Allegheny city and in 1898 sent to St. Mary's church at Altoona. In 1899 Father Duwell was placed in charge of St. Joseph's church at Duquesne and since has ably filled that pulpit. This church was established in 1897 with a membership of forty families, the first services being held in the public schoolhouse by Rev. Joseph Ehrhard, who was succeeded by Rev. Joseph Linder, and he in turn by the present incumbent, who assumed control on Aug. 13, 1899. The membership under the present pastor has been largely increased, necessitating the building of a new church edifice, which is now in course of construction and will be of brick, with a seating capacity of 600, and will cost when completed $22,000. The church was organized in 1897 by Peter Stinner, Sr., Peter Zewe, Sr., and Melchior Wolff, all of whom are now living, and the parish school was initiated by Father Linder in 1898, with an attendance of ninety-five pupils.

FRANCIS ALEXANDER TAYLOR, of Whitaker, Mifflin township, Allegheny Co., Pa., a prominent and progressive citizen, was born in Nova Scotia, Nov. 4, 1872, son of Francis R. and Georgiana (Johnston) Taylor, natives of Nova Scotia and of English and Scotch descent. His parents removed to Allegheny county in 1877, and to Mifflin township in 1890, but prior to locating in Mifflin township, his father had followed mining in several places. The elder Taylor served as supervisor of Mifflin township and held other positions of honor and prominence, and now resides at Whitaker, the father of thirteen children, twelve of whom grew to maturity, viz.: Anna, wife of John Orris; William H., Francis A., Thomas J.; Phœbe M., wife of George Orris; Samuel H., George A. (deceased), Sadie J., Agnes A., Violet E , Charles and Christiana. Francis A. Taylor was reared in Allegheny county from five years of age, educated in the public schools and at the age of twelve years began work in the mines. He was connected with the mines for a number of years, and in 1900 secured employment as a steel-worker with the Carnegie steel company, with whom he remained two years, when he went with the Jones & Laughlin company and since has continued with that concern. He was married, on Oct. 8, 1891, to Christiana B., daughter of James and Jeanette (Drumble) Strang, of Mifflin township, and they have four children, viz.: Janet, Francis R., James A. and George A. Mr. Taylor is a member of the Odd Fellows and of the Whitaker fire department, and in his political affiliations and convictions is a republican. In 1902 Mr. Taylor was appointed one of the school directors of Mifflin township and in February, 1903, was elected to succeed himself in that position for a full term of three years.

HENRY CLAY KOOSER, of Duquesne, Pa., the pioneer flour and feed merchant of that borough, was born in Springfield township, Fayette Co., Pa., Oct. 6, 1857, son of Elijah and Julia (Peters) Kooser, natives of Fayette and Adams counties, Pa., respectively. His paternal grandfather, Peter Kooser, a native of Somerset county, Pa., was a fuller by trade and spent his entire career in Somerset and Fayette counties, in the latter of which he died in 1866, at the age of seventy-two years. His wife was Rebecca Moore, a woman of many fine traits of character. His maternal grandfather was Henry Peters, a native of Adams county, Pa., who was a blacksmith by trade and married a Miss Potruff. He had a long and useful career and died in his native county at the age of eighty-one years. The father of the subject was a miller by trade and for many years was engaged in business with his brother, John A., under the firm name of Kooser Bros., at Mill Run, Pa. He died in March, 1879, at the age of seventy-eight years, and was the father of the following children: Ann, wife of George W. Henderson; Elizabeth, wife of A. B. Kern; Henry C., Jacob, John F. and Daniel R. (twins), and Frank L. and Edward E. (twins). Henry C. Kooser was reared in Fayette county, educated in the public schools and learned the millers' trade with Kooser Bros., at Mill Run, which occupation he followed for fifteen years. In 1892 he located at Duquesne, established his present business and since has continued the same with much success. He was married, on Oct. 3, 1891, to Kate P., widow of Robert Nicholson and daughter of David and Jane (Garvin) Lupton, of Pittsburg, and their married life has been a happy one. He is a prominent member of the Masons, the Knights of Pythias and the Royal Arcanum, and is affiliated with the republican party. Mr. Kooser is a member of one of the old colonial families of America, his great-grandfather having served in the patriot army during the Revolutionary war and occupied a prominent place in the early history of the republic.

ANDREW FRANCIS McCLURE, a prominent farmer of Mifflin township, was born on the farm where he now lives, Aug. 28, 1860, and is a son of Alexander McKim and Sarah (Cox) McClure. His father was a native of Mifflin township. For many years he followed farming, but later was engaged in lumbering at Big Run, where he died, in 1896, at the age of seventy-three years. His mother was a native of England. His grandfather, Andrew McClure, was a prominent farmer of Mifflin township, and his great-grandfather, whose name was also Andrew, was one of the early settlers of Allegheny county, where he held the office of associate judge and represented the county in the legislature several terms. His maternal grandfather, William Cox, was a native of England. He came to America in the early part of the nineteenth century and located in Allegheny county. For many years he operated a salt works opposite Homestead. During the latter years of his life he was one of the most prominent and wealthy farmers of Mifflin township. Alexander McClure, the father of our subject, was the father of ten children, all of whom grew to maturity. They were: Hannah J., wife of James Patterson; Josephine, wife of Edward Seifert; Susan M.; William A.; Catherine L., wife of James Barell; Andrew F.; Emma L., wife of William Tyson; John; Nora D., wife of S. E. Thomas, and Sarah B., wife of Harvey Stuckslager. Of these children, Susan and William are now dead. Andrew F. McClure was reared upon the old homestead, where he has always lived as a tiller of the soil. On Dec. 19, 1882, he was married to Susannah, daughter of William and Mary (Johns) Charles, natives of Wales. To this union there have been born seven children: Sarah B., Alexander McK., William C., John A., Margaret M., Andrew F., Jr., and Charles H. Mr. McClure believes in the truth of the old adage that "a rolling stone gathers no moss," and has spent his entire life on the farm where he was born. He has prospered there and successfully reared a family of children. He is regarded as one of the most progressive men in the township, and is now serving his second term as school director. He is a republican in his political views, and it is no exaggeration to say that he is one of the leading men of his township. He is a member of the Methodist Episcopal church; Magdala lodge, No. 991, Independent Order of Odd Fellows; Plutarch lodge, Knights of Pythias, of Dravosburg, and Lodge No. 650, B. P. O. Elks, of Homestead. His standing in all these organizations, as well as in the community where he lives, is of the highest order, as he is a man of many friends and few enemies.

LAWRENCE SCHOPP, a steel melter in the Homestead steel works, was born at Braddock, Pa., Dec. 26, 1855, and is a son of Frank and Lena (Ackerman) Schopp, both natives of Germany. His maternal grandfather, Nicholas Ackerman, came to America in 1845 and passed the rest of his life in Mifflin township. Five years later Frank Schopp, father of Lawrence, came from Germany and located in the same neighborhood. For about ten years he was employed in the mines, but upon the breaking out of the Civil war he enlisted in Company A, 191st Maryland volunteer infantry. At the second battle of Bull Run he was wounded in the thigh and was honorably discharged from the service on account of his disability. He died eleven days after reaching his home in Pennsylvania, leaving two children: Christina, now the wife of Lewis Geyer, and Lawrence. Lawrence Schopp was thus left an orphan when he was about seven years old. During his boyhood he attended the public schools and then learned the barbers' trade in Pittsburg. For about two years he worked as a journeyman barber and then went into business for himself in the city of Homestead. For the last twenty years he has been in the employ of the Homestead steel works. He owns a cozy home at Whitaker, where he has lived, man and boy, for forty years. On Nov. 20, 1882, he was married to Amelia, daughter of Charles and Amelia (Barthol) Schulz, of Braddock, Pa. They have four children: Herbert, Hilda, Frederick and Clarence. Mr. Schopp is regarded as one of the enterprising and up-to-date men of Whitaker. In politics he is a republican and takes a keen interest in all political questions, upon which he keeps himself well informed. He is a charter member of Whitaker tent, No. 425, Knights of the Maccabees, and has a high standing in the order.

JOHN CHRISTOPHER WHEATLEY, a steel worker in the great Homestead steel works, was born in Jefferson township, Allegheny county, Jan. 13, 1869. His parents, Christopher and Margaret (Chaters) Wheatley, were both natives of County Durham, England. They came to America in 1853, and settled at Mahanoy City, Schuylkill Co., Pa., where for about ten years Mr. Wheatley was engaged as a contracting miner. For the last forty years he has been a resident of Allegheny county. The greater part of that time he followed the business of mine contractor, though he is now living a retired life in Mifflin township. He reared a family of eight children: Jane A., wife of William Dobbins; George, Thomas; Mary E., wife of Samuel Danks; Margaret A., wife of James Foster; Elizabeth, wife of John Hamilton; Sarah, wife of Jacob E. Hicks, and John C. For seven years after leaving school, John C. Wheatley followed the hazardous occupation of a coal miner, beginning when he was but fourteen years of age. Ever since 1890 he has been employed in the Homestead steel works. He was married, Aug. 9, 1891, to Miss Agnes Dean, a daughter of Anthony and Martha (Linsey) Dean, of Mifflin township. They have two children: Sarah and Marguerite. Mr. Wheatley is a member of the Episcopal church, and of Whitaker tent, No. 425, Knights of the Maccabees. He affiliates with the republican party and takes an interest in political matters, but has never held nor been a candidate for public office.

JOHN STEIN, of Duquesne, Pa., a prosperous painter and leader of Stein's orchestra, was born in Mifflin township, Allegheny Co., Pa., about 1866, and is a son of Nicholas and Mary Stein, natives of Germany, who came to the United States about 1853 and for many years resided in Mifflin township, where his mother now lives at the advanced age of seventy-three years. His father, who died in 1878, was a miner by trade and had eight children, viz.: Peter, Jacob; Kate, wife of Peter Abells; Lizzie, wife of John Taylor; Nicholas, George; Mary, wife of John Schultz, and John. John Stein was reared in Mifflin township, educated in the common schools, and began to earn his own living in the mines at a tender age. When eighteen years old, young Stein began the carpenters' trade, but not liking that work after a trial of two years, turned his attention to painting and for the past fifteen years has prospered at that vocation. Mr. Stein possesses a natural talent for music, which he has cultivated and improved by careful and persistent study, and is now one of the best-known musicians of that section of the county. He has made a specialty of music for the past twenty years, and his services are in great demand at the various musical entertainments of that vicinity. He is a member of St. Agnes' Catholic church of Thompson's Run and of the Painters' union, and in his political opinions and associations he is independent, voting for the man rather than blindly following a party leader.

MELCHIOR WOLF, Sr., president of the Monongahela Valley brewing company, of Clairton, Pa., has been a resident of the town of Duquesne since 1887. He is a son of Joseph and Walburga (Berker) Wolf, and was born in Würtemburg, Germany, April 18, 1844. In the schools of the Fatherland he secured a good education, after which he learned the bakers' trade. He worked at this trade for nearly three years, but in 1865 he came to America and located at Pittsburg, where his brother, Anton, had come ten years before. During the Civil war Anton had been a member of the 1st Pittsburg volunteer cavalry, serving four years and being honorably discharged as the regimental color-bearer. Melchior Wolf found employment in a Pittsburg bakery and remained there about a year, when he went to Cincinnati, Ohio, and worked in a bakery in that city for about two and a half years. He then returned to Pittsburg, formed a partnership with his brother, and started an ale brewery in West Elizabeth. They sold out in a short time to John Werner, and Melchior started a bakery of his own. He soon added a stock of general merchandise and continued in this business until 1887, when he removed to Duquesne. There he again engaged in conducting a bakery and general store until 1900, when he retired from the business. He was one of the promoters of the Monongahela brewing company, which was established in 1901 and in which he is a large stockholder. He was elected president of the company when it first began business and has continued in that office to the present time. His long experience in business eminently qualified him for the place, and the affairs of the company have been satisfactorily conducted under his management. He was married, in 1869, to Johanna Stromeyer, of Pittsburg. She bore him two children; Melchior F. and Jacob. After the death of his first wife he married Mrs. Maggie (Rommel) Evans, a daughter of William and Mary Rommel, of Germany, by whom he has seven children, viz.: Maggie, wife of John McGee; Joseph, John, Mary, William, George and Anton, the last named being deceased. Mr. Wolf and his wife are both members of St. Joseph's Catholic church of Duquesne, of which he was one of the founders, when it was established in 1897, and he has done a great deal toward developing and strengthening it. Politically, he is a democrat, and takes a great interest in political matters, particularly those affecting local interests. He served eight years in the council of West Elizabeth, and two years in the council since coming to Duquesne. As a councilman in both towns he always favored such policies as had a tendency to promote the general welfare, and with rare judgment he always selected the right side of every proposition.

SAMUEL TAYLOR, a resident of Kilbuck township, and a descendant of a pioneer family of Allegheny county, was born at the old homestead, Jan. 29, 1843. The home farm of 100 acres was left by the father to his son and the son has lived upon this estate all his life and kept it in an improved condition. Mr. Taylor was educated in the schools of his own township. He was married, on Sept. 13, 1870, to Agnes M. Oakley, daughter of A. G. and Mary A. (Wolfe) Oakley, and to them have been born ten children: Ebert (deceased), Clifford T., Jessie A., William (deceased), Ada B., Samuel G., Albert E., John S. R., Ralph W. and Malcolm S. Mr. Taylor has the confidence of the people of his community, having held different offices of trust in the township in which he lives. His father, James Taylor, was the son of John Taylor and Agnes (Carnahan) Taylor, to whom were born seven children: James, John, David, Sarah, Jane, Alexandria and Wilson C. His first wife dying, he was married the second time to Polly Means. James Taylor was born April 14, 1803, at the original Taylor homestead located in what is now Avalon borough. He was married, on Aug. 26, 1826, to Martha Parks, and to them were born ten children, three of whom are living. Those deceased are: James, John, George W., John E., David C., William C. and one daughter who died in infancy. Those living are Ross, Joseph and Samuel, the latter being the subject of this sketch. James Taylor began his married life as a farmer on Davis island, Allegheny county, in 1827. His principal productions were melons, and on this island he prospered until the flood of 1832 swept away all that his past efforts had accumulated, excepting one horse and two cows. Endeavoring to get out of reach of a similar disaster, he decided to move to Ohio township, where he purchased a farm of 106 acres and lived there until 1870, when he again moved to Avalon. He built a new house on a part of the original homestead and lived there until his death, in 1872; his wife died in 1876. John Taylor, grandfather of Samuel Taylor, was born in Ireland, and came to America in 1789. He died in 1843 and his wife in 1860, both being buried in the Presbyterian cemetery in Perrysville. John Taylor, in company with James Courtney, Wesley Dickson and Casper Reel, left Ireland in 1788 to locate in the new world. With no particular place in view, but thinking to obtain more land by going farther into the continent and thinking also to avoid any entanglements by buying direct from the Indians, they traveled overland until they struck the headwaters of the Monongahela river. Here they spent one month burning and digging out canoes to continue down the river. But during this preparation they were surrounded by the hostile Indians with a view to plunder. Two weeks later they succeeded in outwitting the savages and paddled down the stream. They continued their journey down to Pittsburg, the different members of the pioneer party dropping out when they found a site that pleased them. At length John Taylor was left alone on the pioneer expedition, and one night, while lying in the bottom of the canoe, he heard the noise of rushing waters, which proved upon investigation to be that his boat was grounded, so he decided to spend the night there. In the morning he looked over the most beautiful scene he had beheld on the long river journey. The soil was fertile and the vegetation had the appearance of being easily cleared—and thus was founded the Taylor place in Avalon. He decided to stop for a while to see how the land would please him, and on exploring the surrounding country, blundered into a well-kept corn patch, in which some Indian squaws were digging. Upon seeing him, they ran screaming into the wigwams, and the braves soon appeared in the open, whereupon Taylor hastened to assure them that he meant no harm. He found not a little difficulty in convincing them, however, for they could not conceive how his mission could be one of peace, after meeting with so many who were not so inclined. The Indians conducted him to their chief, and, after much bartering, he was granted Indian title to his land. After he had worked a short time, another tribe came and laid claim to his land, but Taylor refused to give it up even after threats and attempts to torture. He broke up their assault with a few rifle bullets and thus convinced them of his sturdy pioneer spirit. His title again came into dispute, when it was said to interfere with William Penn's grant, so rather than relinquish the land he had cleared, he paid for it a second time, getting a government title.

HERMAN P. BRANDT, a resident of Perrysville, son of Peter and Margaret (Schnabel) Brandt, was born in Allegheny county, Nov. 16, 1877. He was educated in the common schools of his own township and later entered the Pennsylvania College of Embalming, from which he graduated with honors. He then became engaged with the well-known firm of Ley & Geiselhart, and on Feb. 10, 1902, Mr. Brandt opened an office for himself in Perrysville, being the youngest undertaker in business for himself in Allegheny county. His youth seems not to have stood in the way of his success, for in point of business he is among the first of his calling, his business entering into and covering more territory than that of any other undertaker in the county. Although living out of the city, he has every convenience in the way of telephone or telegraph service, and, in fact, anything incident to his work. His increasing business demands a large livery hire and an assistant, the latter, Mr. Ambrose Smith, like Mr. Brandt, being one of the hustling young men of the county. Mr. Brandt has had experience far beyond his years and bids fair to be one of our foremost men in the future. He is connected with several of the fraternal organizations, being a member of the Masonic order, Bellevue lodge, also a member of the I. O. O. F., of Allegheny city. He is also an active member of the Lutheran church of Franklin township. Peter Brandt, father of the subject of this sketch, is a son of Philip Brandt, one of the living pioneers of Allegheny county. Peter Brandt is the father of five children: Mrs. Amelia Miller, of Sewickley; Herman P., Walter C., Emma C., a student in the Indiana state normal and connected with the undertaking establishment of Herman Brandt, and Russel L. (deceased). The Brandt family is one of the prominent families of Allegheny county.

SYLVESTER E. RHOADES, a prominent and enterprising farmer of Mifflin township, and a life-long resident of Allegheny county, is the only child of John K. and Margaret (McClure) Rhoades. The Rhoades family is one of the old Pennsylvania families. Frederick Rhoades, the grandfather of Sylvester, was a native of Lancaster county and was a son of Casper Rhoades, one of the pioneers of that county. After the death of Casper Rhoades, his widow removed to Allegheny county and there Frederick was reared to manhood, spent his life as a farmer and died, in 1868, in his sixty-third year. John K. Rhoades, Sylvester's father, was a native of Mifflin township. He also was a farmer, and died, in 1893, at the age of sixty-five. With the exception of three years in Westmoreland county, his entire life was passed in the township where he was born. His wife's father, Andrew McClure, was one of the old settlers of Mifflin township. Sylvester E. Rhoades was born July 10, 1853. He was reared and educated in Mifflin township. He owns a fine farm of 160 acres, upon which he has lived since 1866. He was married, in 1877, to Miss Maria B., a daughter of John and Jane (Moore) Wilock, also residents of Mifflin township, and they have three children living. They are: John K., Jeannette M. and Margaret B. Mr. Rhoades is a republican in politics and a member of the Presbyterian church.

FERDINAND CHARLES ECKERT, of McKee's Rocks, Pa., manager for the prominent lumber firm of John Davis & Co., was born in Allegheny city, Pa., April 4, 1860, son of J. H. and Charlotta (Kroener) Eckert. They were the parents of ten children, eight of whom are now living, viz.: Albert H., Emma, Henry, William G., Ernest F., Theodore W., Ferdinand C., and Charles R., who is a prominent attorney of Butler county and recently a candidate for congress on the democratic ticket. The father came from Baden, Germany, and settled in Allegheny county, where for many years he was a successful butcher, and now, at the age of seventy-five years, resides in Monaca, Beaver county, retired from active business. He is a democrat of long standing and for many years has been a member of the First German Evangelical Protestant church of Pittsburg. The mother came from Darmstadt, Germany, was married to Mr. Eckert in Allegheny city, and is now sixty-seven years of age. Ferdinand C. Eckert obtained his early education in the common schools of Beaver county, and when eighteen years of age began to learn the butchers' trade. He served an apprenticeship of seven years, and then entered that business on his own account at McKee's Rocks. He prospered in that venture for four years, then obtained employment as a carpenter with the Pennsylvania & Lake Erie railroad company. After four years Mr. Eckert returned to his father's farm in Beaver county and remained there until 1902, when he secured his present position as manager of the well-known lumber firm of John Davis & Co., of McKee's Rocks. This firm conducts a large lumber business, including a planing mill, and stands high on the commercial and financial lists. Mr. Eckert was married, in 1884, to Mary Steinmiller, of Allegheny city, and they have five children: Emma, Nora, Stella, Charles and John. He is a member of the democratic party, the Maennerchor singing society, the

Heptasophs, the Society of the Mystic Chain and the Masons. He is a man of strict integrity, also very companionable, and possesses the esteem and friendship of all who know him.

DR. FRANCIS J. MADDEN, a promising young physician of Duquesne, was born in the city of Cleveland, Ohio, May 31, 1870. He is a son of Cornelius S. and Ellen (McGarrity) Madden, both natives of Canada, but of Irish parentage. While Francis was still in his childhood, his parents removed to Wilkinsburg, Allegheny Co., Pa., and his primary education was acquired in the public schools of that place. His parents still reside there. In 1892 he entered the medical department of the Western university of Pennsylvania, at Pittsburg, and was graduated in 1895. He at once began the practice of his profession at Wilkinsburg. Two years later he removed to Blairsville, Pa., where he remained until the spring of 1900, when he located at Duquesne, Pa. Since that time he has built up a good practice there, and is popular, not only with his patients, but with the entire community. On April 15, 1896, he was married to Miss Justina M. Whalen, a daughter of Patrick and Justina (Heilman) Whalen, of Wilkinsburg, and they have one son, Paul. Dr. Madden is a member of the Allegheny County medical society. He is also a member of Duquesne camp, No. 80, Woodmen of the World, of which he is the medical examiner, and council commander of Monongahela council, No. 265, Foresters of America, of which he is the court physician. He is a member of and regular attendant at the Holy Name Catholic church of Duquesne and is secretary of the church. In politics he is a democrat, but devotes far more of his time and attention to his domestic affairs and to his patients than he does to the conflicts of the political arena.

GUSTAV A. BOSS, of McKee's Rocks, Pa., a prominent jeweler, was born in Allegheny city, Pa., Nov. 30, 1865, son of Casper and Carrie (Sauer) Boss. His parents had five children, three of whom are now living. They are: Albert, Peter J. and Gustav A., the subject of this sketch. Both of his parents came from Germany, his father having been born in Marburg, was a tanner by trade, and soon after coming to America enlisted in defense of the Union. He was located at St. Louis at that time, but enlisted in Company H, 27th Illinois volunteers, and served three years and three months with that regiment, receiving an honorable discharge at the expiration of his service. He was a man of robust physique and genial personality, and was very popular with all who knew him. Both of his grandfathers were tanners in the Fatherland and his father worked at that trade in this country prior to his army service. Gustav A. Boss obtained his education in the splendid schools of Allegheny city, and when fifteen years of age began to learn the jewelers' trade with his brother, Albert, at Carnegie, Pa. He remained there for three years and then secured employment with the firm of George W. Biggs & Co., of Pittsburg, with whom he continued for eight years. He then came to McKee's Rocks, opened his present jewelry store, and has since met with much success in that venture. He is regarded as a splendid business man, conducts a thoroughly modern establishment and owns valuable property in McKee's Rocks and Pittsburg. He was married, in 1888, to Philippina, daughter of Jacob Morganstern, of Carnegie, Pa., and they have five children: Carrie, Clara, Blanche, Eva and Florence. Mr. Boss is a republican in politics, is a member of the English Lutheran church and of the Royal Arcanum.

ROBERT FRANKLIN CONKLE, M. D., of Coraopolis, Pa., a distinguished physician and surgeon, was born in Hookstown, Beaver Co., Pa., Nov. 28, 1848, son of Henry and Catherine (Metts) Conkle. His parents had eight children, six of whom are now living: Anna Mary, Mrs. Mattie Bronson, Harriet Stewart (who resides in South Dakota), Samuel M., John S., and Robert F., the subject of this sketch, who is the eldest child. His father was a successful farmer, a very genial man, and a member of the democratic party and the Presbyterian church. His paternal ancestors came from Germany. Dr. Conkle received his rudimentary educational training in the public schools of Hookstown and at the Presbyterian academy at New Wilmington, and his medical education at the Western Reserve college, of Cleveland, Ohio, from which noted institution he was graduated in 1871. He immediately entered on the practice of his profession at Summitville, Columbiana Co., Ohio, where he remained for five and one-half years, and in 1877 came to Coraopolis, and since has stood high among the leading physicians of that community. He was married, in 1873, to Sarah Stevenson, of Frankfort Springs, Pa., and they had one child, Mary Emma, a most estimable young woman, who was drowned in 1901 while on a pleasure excursion to North East, Pa. Dr. Conkle is the oldest physician in point of practice in Coraopolis, enjoys a very large business, and is known far and near for his many deeds of charity and benevolence in connection with his professional duties. He is interested in a sanitarium for the care and cure of inebriates, and has accomplished much good among this unfortunate class. His political affiliations are with the democratic party, and he is a member of the Presbyterian church.

WILLIAM A. CRUSAN, of Coraopolis, Pa., a prosperous grocer, was born in Braddock, Pa., May 30, 1873, son of William A. and Malinda (Scott) Crusan, his father having been a foundryman, an expert workman and a good citizen. He died in 1890, and his wife is now living at the age of sixty-two years. She is a member of the Disciples' church, a woman of splendid character, who gave her son the best of Christian surroundings. William Crusan received his educational training in the public schools of Verona, to which town his family had removed when he was quite young, and when fifteen years of age secured a position with Wallace & McAffee, of Pittsburg, which firm is now merged with the Consolidated lamp and glass company. He was employed in the packing room of these companies for fourteen years, and in 1902 began his present grocery business at Coraopolis. Mr. Crusan conducts an exceedingly well-appointed store, and is a man of exemplary character and unusual business ability. He was married, on Aug. 2, 1903, to Atlanta Houghtelin, and their home life is a happy one. Mr. Crusan is a strong advocate of temperance and votes the prohibition ticket. He is a deacon and trustee of the First Baptist church, and also superintendent of the Sunday-school.

GEORGE A. DICK, a popular butcher of Hites, has been successfully engaged in business there for the past twenty-eight years. He was born in East Deer township, Allegheny Co., Pa., Nov. 13, 1852, received a common-school education in the public schools, and began his apprenticeship to the butcher business at the age of fifteen. Mr. Dick's parents, Adam and Mary (Neuwander) Dick, were married, in 1845, and both are living. They celebrated their golden wedding anniversary in 1895, and on that occasion ninety-five relatives were present. Mr. and Mrs. Dick are members of the German Evangelical Protestant church. Adam Dick was born in Switzerland, came to Allegheny city when seventeen years old, in 1834, and followed the vocation of a shoemaker for many years. He has for the past twenty-five years, however, lived a retired life at the home of his son, George. His wife, a daughter of Nicholas and Barbara Neuwander, came to Allegheny city with her parents in 1843, when eight years old. Nicholas Neuwander was a farmer and dairyman, and owned a milk route in Allegheny city. He and his wife spent their last days in New Castle, Lawrence county. George A. Dick, whose name heads this sketch, is one of a family of seven children, five of whom are living. In politics he is a republican, has served on the school board for the past twenty-one years, and occupies a prominent place in the community. With his family, he is a member of the German Evangelical Protestant church of Tarentum. On May 23, 1878, Mr. Dick married Miss Josephine Shoppene, of Indiana township, Allegheny county, and is the father of two sons. The elder son, William G., born March 17, 1883, attended the Iron City business college in Pittsburg, from which he was graduated in 1897, and is now bookkeeper for the J. H. Baker manufacturing company. He is a member of Pollock lodge, No. 502, F. and A. M., and of Tarentum lodge, No. 587, I. O. O. F. The second son, Andrew R., was born March 23, 1887, and is now employed by Yost Bros. as a molder.

JOHN WISE, a prominent fruit grower and market gardener of Scott township, Allegheny Co., Pa., was born in Germany, Sept. 6, 1845. His father was John Wise, a native of Würtemburg, Germany, where he was born, Sept. 26, 1815. His mother's maiden name was Margaret Schmidt. She was born in Würtemburg, April 12, 1820. When John Wise, Sr., was about thirty-five years old he came to America. He walked all the way from Philadelphia to Pittsburg, where he found employment at his trade, that of a blacksmith. Three years later his family joined him in Pittsburg. In 1858 he gave up blacksmithing, bought a farm in Scott township, and passed the remainder of his life as a gardener and fruit grower. This business he carried on successfully until his death, which occurred on Feb. 25, 1889. His wife died on May 4, 1892, both having lived long and useful lives. John Wise, Jr., the subject of this sketch, attended school in his native land for about two and a half years, and after coming to America, finished his education in the Pittsburg public schools. Ever since arriving at the years of manhood, he has followed the business of growing small fruits and vegetables for the Pittsburg market. Scott township is noted for its fruit and garden farms, but few of them are better kept or more productive than that of John Wise, who devotes his entire time to his work and to the study of how to secure better results. Politically, he is a republican, but he never takes an active part in political contests. In 1874 he was married to Miss Amelia Abbott, the daughter of Christian and Magdalena (Schmeltz) Abbott. Her father was born in Saxony, and her mother in Hesse Darmstadt, the former coming to this country when he was nine years old, and the latter when she was nineteen. They were married in Allegheny county, and Mrs. Wise was born there, Sept. 22, 1854. John Wise and his wife have had seven children, as follows: Catherine L., born Aug. 14, 1875; Carrie M., born Aug. 11, 1877; Elmer E., born Aug. 4, 1879; Anna C., born June 16, 1882; Emma J., born Oct. 25, 1885; John C., born March 5, 1887, and Nellie A., born Feb. 27, 1890. Of these children, all are living except Elmer and John. Mr. Wise and family belong to the United Presbyterian church at Carnegie.

JOHN HENRY MURRAY, of Coraopolis, Pa., superintendent of the Duquesne steel foundry company of Kendall station, Pa., was born in Dundee, Scotland, Oct. 16, 1868. He is a son of Morton and Isabelle Murray, both long since deceased, his father's business being that of a cattle-drover. Of the three children born to them, all are now living. When six years of age Mr. Murray, in company with his brother and sister, left their parents and the old home in Scotland, and came to Los Angeles, Cal., where they were reared by an aunt. His brother Thomas and his sister Josephine have remained in that city, where his brother is now a prosperous handler of hardware, and his sister is the wife of Thomas Hatton, a well-known grocer. Mr. Murray attended the public schools of Los Angeles until thirteen years of age, and then went to New Jersey to work in the iron mills. He was in the mills of that state for six years, learned his trade, and in 1887 went to Pittsburg, where he secured employment with the Pittsburg steel casting company. He was with that concern for five years, for thirteen months with the Corbin steel company and later went with the Duquesne steel foundry company. The first two years of his connection with that corporation was in the capacity of master mechanic, and since then he has ably filled his present position of superintendent. Mr. Murray was married, in 1891, to Sarah, daughter of James and Catherine Ellis, of Allegheny city, and has one daughter, Catherine. He is a republican in his political convictions and his religious affiliations are with the Presbyterian church. Mr. Murray is a member of the Masons and a number of other fraternal orders and is in hearty sympathy with these societies in their work for the betterment of the human race.

HARRY W. FERREE, of Coraopolis, Pa., foreman of the carpenter shop of the Pittsburg & Lake Erie railroad at McKee's Rocks, was born in old Middletown, now Coraopolis, the postoffice address then being Vance Fort, Pa., and was the fourth child of Jacob and Nancy (Phillips) Ferree. His father was a successful farmer, and the Ferree family is one of the oldest and most highly respected ones in Coraopolis. The Ferrees are of French-Huguenot extraction and originally settled in Lancaster county. Jacob Ferree, the head of the family in America, was twice married, first in France, by which union he had three sons, one of whom was a colonel in the War of 1812. The Ferrees were among the pioneers of Coraopolis, and in 1800 purchased 330 acres of land where the borough now stands. Harry Ferree attended the public schools of his native town until nineteen years of age, when he began to learn the carpenters' trade and since has followed that vocation with much success. In 1883 he secured a position with the Pittsburg & Lake Erie railroad, and at present is general foreman of the car construction shops of that system at McKee's Rocks. This is a position of importance and Mr. Ferree has made a splendid record there. He was married, on April 29, 1886, to Nettie Nesbitt, of Moon township, Allegheny county, and they have one son, Eclare. Mr. Ferree is a republican in politics and his religious faith is that of the Presbyterian church.

JOHN M. RYAN, of McKee's Rocks, Pa., superintendent and stockholder of the Fort Pitt malleable gray iron company, was born in Torrington, Conn., Aug. 16, 1859, son of John and Mary (Lalley) Ryan. His father was a bricklayer and had two children, of whom John M. is the only survivor. Mr. Ryan attended the public schools until fourteen years of age, then began to learn core-making and later devoted his attention to the molders' trade in the plant of Turner & Seymour, of Torrington. He remained with that concern for four years, when he went to Naugatuck, Conn., with the Tuttle & Whitman malleable iron company. He continued with them for two years, then with the Sessions firm, of Bristol, Conn.; next with the Wisconsin malleable iron company, of Milwaukee; later with the Chicago malleable iron company, then with the Cleveland malleable iron company, and in 1887 came to Pittsburg to work for the McConway-Torley company, with whom he remained for fourteen years. In 1901 he was one of the organizers and a subscriber to the stock of the Fort Pitt malleable gray iron company and since has occupied the responsible position of superintendent of that concern. This is a company which employs 225 men, of whom eighty per cent. are skilled workmen, and their products are of high class and value. Mr. Ryan was married, in 1886, to Mary E., daughter of James Leo, of Cleveland, Ohio, and they have two daughters. Mr. Ryan is a democrat in his political affiliations and is a member of the Roman Catholic church and of the C. M. B. A. He is regarded by his business associates as a man of exceptional executive ability and his management of the complex interests of the large business that he supervises has been of such a nature as to elicit encomiums from many high sources.

Made in the USA
Coppell, TX
23 June 2020